THE COMPLETE ENCYCLOPEDIA OF
HORSE RACING

First published in 2001 by
Carlton Books Limited
20 Mortimer Street
London W1T 3JW

Second edition published in 2006

10 9 8 7 6 5 4 3 2 1

A CIP catalogue record for this book is available from the British Library

ISBN 10: 1 84442 127 9
ISBN 13: 978 1 84442 127 5

The publishers would like to thank the following people and organizations for their assistance in compiling some of the information and statistics contained here: Adam Boyle, James Crispe, Mme Dominique Gabel-Litny of France-Galop, The Irish Turf Club, Harold Nass, Weatherby's Ltd.

THE COMPLETE ENCYCLOPEDIA OF
HORSE RACING

THE ILLUSTRATED GUIDE TO THE WORLD
OF THE THOROUGHBRED

BILL MOONEY & GEORGE ENNOR

CARLTON
BOOKS

Contents

INTRODUCTION

As was the case with the first edition, it is impossible to satisfy everyone completely with the second edition of *The Complete Encyclopedia of Horse Racing.* The sport has been established for many generations on six of the world's seven continents. To include every individual, equine and human, who has made a major contribution to racing would be far beyond the scope of any single volume, and probably beyond practicality in even a multi-volume set.

Racing may be the most universal of all the major sports. It annually manifests itself at its very best in the Gold Cup at Ascot, the Prix de l'Arc de Triomphe at Longchamp, the Melbourne Cup at Flemington, the Japan Cup at Tokyo Race Course and the Kentucky Derby at Churchill Downs – and at numerous other venues, as well. All of these events have themselves, on many occasions, received full treatment in books. Our encyclopedia is intended for those who wish to experience a taster of them all, and who also want to delve into the past and present of racing, and to learn about those who have helped forge – and continue to forge – the sport's history and heritage.

Who is the greatest racehorse of all time? Might it be Ribot, Carbine, Man o' War or Secretariat? Who is the greatest jockey? Perhaps Lester Piggott, or Eddie Arcaro or Lanfranco Dettori? And what is the greatest jump race – the Grand National or the Cheltenham Gold Cup? Our encyclopedia is not designed to settle these debates, but to provide information to aid their continuance. Details are also provided of records, scandals, controversies, racecourses and racing practices in various countries.

There is a touch of sadness involved with the publication of the second edition of "The Complete Encyclopedia of Horse Racing". George Ennor, who did such a splendid job co-authoring the first edition, passed away during the winter of 2006. The signature of George's efforts remains a vital component of the book. Much of the initial work he did remains intact. It is a humbling honour to follow in George's footsteps.

Since the publication of the encyclopedia's first edition, other transitions have occurred as well. Racing figures of global standing such as Sheikh Maktoum Bin Rashid Al-Maktoum, Bill Shoemaker, Dick Hern and Jack Ingram have passed on. Jerry Bailey, who many believe is the greatest American jockey since Arcaro, has retired. Australia has seen the emergence of a racing star of legendary proportions in Makybe Diva, who won three consecutive Melbourne Cups. The French jockey Olivier Peslier has achieved greatness, and the Hong Kong Cup has matured into one of the world's most prominent racing events.

Heartfelt thanks are due to Carlton Books, and its editorial manager for sports books, Martin Corteel, for producing this second edition. It is sincerely hoped that readers will consider the effort worthwhile.

Bill Mooney
Lexington, Kentucky
September, 2006

Page 3: **Grandstand finish:** Crowds love a spectacle, such as this win by Makybe Diva in the 2005 Melbourne Cup.
Page 4: **Turn for home:** The field for the 2006 Derby show how important it is to get good position for the run-in.
Page 5 top: **Cigar:** With career earnings of $9,999,815, Cigar (Jerry Bailey up) set a new world record.
Page 5 left: **Morroco:** Not all the interested parties around the parade ring are human or equine.
Above: **Unique challenge:** The Grand National's fences are unlike any other and, although soft, require expert jumping.
Pages 8–9: **They're off!:** Starting stalls ensure that all horses get an equal chance of a fast break.

EXPLAINING THE TERMS

Horse racing has a language all of its own. The terms to describe a horse follow, as does an easy guide to working out weights and measures described in the book.

Descriptions

The horses' descriptions are as follows:

NASHWAN
◊ ch c
◊ Foaled: 1986, by Blushing Groom out of Height of Fashion (Bustino)

First line: horse's name. Names are copyright in each jurisdiction during a horse's lifetime, but a few may not be repeated because of exceptional success, i.e. no owner again will be able to call a racehorse Arkle.

Second line: first letter/s describe colouring: b = bay; bl = black; br = brown; ch = chestnut; db = dark bay; gr = grey; p = piebald; r = roan. Second letter/s: c = colt ; f = filly ; g = gelding; m = mare; st = stallion.

Bay is a shade of brown; grey is anything from light black to white; chestnut (sometimes chesnut) is auburn or orange; piebald is patches of two colours; roan = patches of many different colours. A colt is complete younger male horse; a filly is a female horse four years and under; a gelding is any male horse unable to breed; a mare is a female horse five years or older; a stallion is a male horse who normally stands at stud after retiring.

Third line: The breeding line gives the year of foaling or birth (all horses in the Northern Hemisphere age one year on 1 January – whether born on 2 January or 30 December – in the Southern Hemisphere the "birthday" is on 1 July); by = sire (stallion or father); out of = dam (mare or mother); (Dam's sire = maternal grandfather).

Therefore: Nashwan was a chestnut colt, foaled in 1986; his sire was Blushing Groom; his dam was Height Of Fashion; her sire was Bustino.

French classics

The five French classic races are as follows:

French race	British/Irish equivalent
Poule d'Essai des Poulains	2,000 Guineas
Poule d'Essai des Pouliches	1,000 Guineas
Prix du Jockey Club	Derby
Prix de Diane	Oaks
*Prix Royal-Oak	St. Leger

*The Prix Royal-Oak and the Irish St. Leger have been open-age races – for three-year-olds and upwards – since 1979 and 1983, respectively, and they are no longer considered classics.

Weights

The weights horses have to carry – jockey plus any penalties – are measured in stones and pounds (st and lb, in the British Isles), pounds (US) or kilogrammes (kg – Europe and Australia). The following are common weights (1kg = 2.2lb (pounds); 14lb = 1st).

Pounds	St lb	Kg
14	1st 0lb	6.35
84	6st 0lb	38
91	6st 7lb	41.25
98	7st 0lb	44.25
100	7st 2lb	45.25
105	7st 7lb	47.5
112	8st 0lb	50.75
120	8st 8lb	54.5
126	9st 0lb	57
130	9st 4lb	59
135	9st 9lb	61.25
140	10st 0lb	63.25
147	10st 7lb	66.25
154	11st 0lb	69.25
161	11st 7lb	73.25
168	12st 0lb	76
175	12st 7lb	79.5

Distances

Race distances are measured differently around the world. Here are the most common distances and their equivalents (1 metre = 1.09 yards; 220yds =1 furlong; 8 furlongs = 1 mile). Lengths beaten are measured now in time between horses not distance. One length is 0.2 seconds (flat), 0.25 (jump).

Yards	Furlongs	Miles	Metres
110	$1/2$	$1/16$	100
220	1 (1f)	$1/8$	200
440	2 (2f)	$1/4$	400
660	3 (3f)	$3/8$	600
880	4 (4f)	$1/2$	800
1100	5 (5f)	$5/8$	1000
1320	6 (6f)	$3/4$	1200
1540	7 (7f)	$7/8$	1400
1760	8 (1m)	1	1600
1980	9 (1m 1f)	$1^1/8$	1800
2200	10 (1m 2f)	$1^1/4$	2000
2420	11 (1m 3f)	$1^3/8$	2200
2640	12 (1m 4f)	$1^1/2$	2400
2860	13 (1m 5f)	$1^5/8$	2600
3080	14 (1m 6f)	$1^3/4$	2800
3300	15 (1m 7f)	$1^7/8$	3000
3520	16 (2m)	2	3200

CHAPTER 1

THE EARLY HISTORY OF RACING

There is no record of the first horse race, but it is safe to say that it predates Christianity by centuries as opposed to decades. In classical mythology Pegasus was a winged horse – and there isn't a gambler alive who doesn't wish that his selection was so uniquely blessed when placing his bet. Equestrian racing took place in the Ancient Olympic Games which began in 776 BC.

BRITISH RACING HISTORY

THE ROMAN EMPEROR Septimus Severus staged races at York, probably on the Knavesmire where the racecourse has stood since 1709 and where – as its name suggests – villains used to be executed. It is likely that other Roman garrison towns staged similar events to entertain the troops and the imperial administrators, few of whom will have thought much of being sent to the frozen wastes of Britannia from the warmth and sybaritic luxury of Rome. The Romans' occupation ended in 410 AD.

Another place where this may well have happened is Chester. Inevitably no form book from those days has survived, but there is reference to racing on the Roodeye, as the Chester track is known, in the early 1500s. There was also early racing at Carlisle, where the Carlisle Bell was first presented in 1559 by Lady Dacre with the accreditation, "the sweftes horse this bel to tak, for mi lade Daker sake." The Carlisle Bell is still run today, as a one-mile handicap, for a prize of £25,000 – in 2005 it was won by the six-year-old gelding Hartshead, ridden by Fergal Lynch.

The Sport of Kings

Rather surprisingly, Henry VIII – a keen hunter until he was physically unable to ride – took no interest in racing, but his daughter Queen Elizabeth I is recorded as having been racing on Salisbury Plain in the 1580s. She witnessed a race for the Golden Bell which was valued at the considerable sum for the times of £50.

King James VI of Scotland – King James I of England – was so impressed by the country when following a coursing match near Newmarket that he arranged for the court to be moved from London to East Anglia. During his reign the rules were drawn up for the Kiplingcotes Derby, which

appears to have been the first attempt to put down in writing how the sport should be conducted, and there is a record of a match race (many early events were matches) taking place at Newmarket shortly before James died in 1625.

His son, Charles I, was another keen racing man and the first grandstand at Newmarket was erected during his troubled reign. Under Charles II, racing became a major part of court entertainment from the 1660s. The Newmarket Town Plate, though not a race administered by the Jockey Club, remains a link with those days. The King rode the first winner of The Newmarket Plate in 1671, and it is still run on the July Course over 3³/4 miles on the second Sunday in October.

The discovery of a salt spring in the early 17th century saw Epsom become a fashionable spa town and Charles II was there in 1661. There were also races around Doncaster and Leicester.

Three great sires

The first of the three horses which played a vital part in the evolution of the modern racehorse was the Byerley Turk, almost certainly of Arab blood, who was spotted by Captain Robert Byerley in 1684 when he was fighting against the Turks at the siege of Buda in what is now Hungary (Budapest). He later rode the horse as his charger at the battle of the Boyne in 1690 and it is reported that it was only because of the horse's speed that Byerley avoided capture by the troops fighting for the deposed James II.

The other two horses who were responsible for the evolution of the thoroughbred racehorse came in the early 18th century and both were from the Middle East. The first was the Darley Arabian, who was bought in Aleppo in 1704 for Mr James Darley by his son. He was the ancestor of Eclipse. The other, the Godolphin Arabian, came some 25 years later and appears to have been a present to King Louis XIV of France from the Emperor of Morocco. In due course the Godolphin Arabian was bought by Mr Edward Coke before becoming the property of Lord Godolphin. The three horses were named after their owners once they had reached the British Isles.

The first race of the Royal Meeting at Ascot commemorates Queen Anne, who played a vital part in the inception of racing there. Her Majesty was driving from Windsor Castle when it occurred to her that the Royal Heath was the ideal spot for a race meeting and, after the building of a grandstand and setting up post and rails to make a course, Ascot's first race, for the Queen's Plate, was held on 13 August 1711, attracting five runners. She was an enthusiastic horsewoman, and her horses were looked after by Tregonwell Frampton, the forerunner of a modern-day trainer, who filled that role for three Kings as well as Anne until he died in 1727. Also in 1727, there was the first publication of an annual record of races that had been staged. The sport was becoming so popular that politicians decided that they should intervene with a ruling that no race should be worth less than £50.

National organization did not arrive until late in the 18th Century when the Jockey Club started to provide overall control of the sport. The exact moment the Club appointed itself to administer racing is not known, but the publication of a Sporting Kalendar in 1752, produced by John Pond – an auctioneer at Covent Garden in London and at Newmarket – referred to a race to be run at Newmarket for horses the property of the noblemen and gentlemen of the Jockey Club at the Star and Garter in Pall Mall (London). It seems that the club acquired its authority more or less by default. Because its members were among the most important and influential in the country, what they said was widely accepted and the authority to run racing almost devolved on them.

Newmarket had become the most important location for racing, not least by virtue of its royal patronage, so it was inevitable that the new club would need to operate from there and the members obtained a plot of land where the current Jockey Club is located. It was not long before the Club decided to introduce rules; in 1758 they decided that jockeys who rode in races at Newmarket should weigh in afterwards, to confirm that the horses have carried the burdens that had been decreed for them.

Away from racing's administration, the horse population was beginning to develop. In 1764, Eclipse – by Marske and bred by the Duke of Cumberland – was born. The Duke died when Eclipse was a yearling and he was bought by William Wildman, who had a stud at Mickleham in Surrey, for 75gns. Eclipse won his first race as a five-year-old in 1769. He was soon acquired by Dennis O'Kelly, for whom the horse won 17 times. He scared off possible rivals to such effect that seven of wins were walkovers, and when he went to stud in 1771 he sired the winners of 862 races worth £158,047 – by comparison, the first Derby in 1780 had a first prize of £1,065.

When races were first held they were for horses of four and more and invariably over long distances; Flying Childers – the greatest son of the Darley Arabian – recorded his final win in a race of six miles, but events for younger horses over shorter distances were gradually introduced. There was one for three-year-olds at Bedale in North Yorkshire in 1731 and the first contest for two-year-olds was staged at Newmarket in 1769. Around this time Richard Tattersall began his

Box clever: Lord George Bentinck used a horse box in 1836.

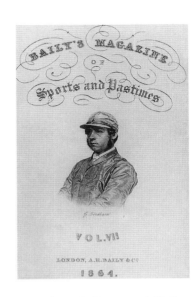

Second best: George Fordham was probably the most accomplished of Fred Archer's rivals in the late 19th century.

bloodstock sales at Hyde Park Corner in London and they were conducted there, and then at Knightsbridge Green – a short distance down the road – until the end of World War II, at which point the sales site was moved to Newmarket.

In 1770 the Jockey Club issued its first set of orders, though these applied only to races run at Newmarket because it could not as yet exercise national authority. Gradually, it became apparent that the Club's ability and experience in handling disputes and other matters at Newmarket made it well qualified to do so all over the country.

In 1773 James Weatherby, whose descendants own the firm which produces all official racing documentation under the authority of the Jockey Club and the British Horseracing Board, produced the first edition of the Racing Calendar. This weekly publication remains the means of official racing news despatched to the sport's participants.

The Classics

The first running of the St. Leger at Doncaster came in 1776. It the oldest and longest of the five British classic races. Devised by Colonel Anthony St. Leger, after whom it is named, the race was run over two miles, for three-year-olds only, at Cantley Common and attracted a field of six, none of whom was named at the time. Two-year-olds continued to be allowed to race without names until 1946, though older horses had to be identified by name from 1913. The emergence of Epsom as a racecourse of importance followed soon after the running of the first St. Leger, with the Oaks being staged for the first time in 1779 and the Derby the following year.

The first bookmakers appeared on racecourses towards the end of the 18th century, coinciding with the first important handicap race in which horses were given weight in accordance with their apparent ability, so that in theory every runner had an equal chance. There were 19 runners for a two-mile race at Ascot in 1791 with total prize money of 2,950gns and any bookmakers on the Royal Heath would have been rubbing their hands at the 20–1 success of the Prince Regent's Baronet, ridden by Sam Chifney.

Later in 1791, Chifney and the Prince Regent (later George IV) were involved in the Escape affair at Newmarket. The stewards felt that Chifney had prevented the Prince's horse from winning on one day, but backed Escape when he won on the next. They told the Prince that if Chifney continued to ride his horses no gentleman would start against him. The Prince stood by his jockey and gave up racing.

The Jockey Club deserves good marks for its attempt at vigilance, but events in the next century were to show that there were still plenty of villains about. In 1821, the Jockey Club Stewards warned off a person for the first time, though the victim of their decision was rather lower down the social order than a jockey. A tout called William Taylor, who no doubt worked for bookmakers, was told to stay off Newmarket Heath because he had watched a trial through a telescope. It typified the Club's determination to keep everything as secret as they could but, in fairness to them, only a few years earlier another tout, Daniel Dawson, had been hanged for poisoning racehorses on the Heath.

Steeplechasing was very much the poor relation of the flat and much slower in its development. Though the first recorded race over obstacles took place in Ireland in 1752 when two riders went from one church to another – hence the name "steeplechasing" – it was some 40 years before an equivalent event took place in England, and the first race over a course with specially produced obstacles was held at Bedford in 1811. The first recorded races at Liverpool took place in 1829, and those at Cheltenham two years later, with the Grand National first being held in 1837.

Contestants in those and other races had to walk to the courses in the early part of the 19th century. The first sign of a change came with the use of a trailer to transport a horse in 1816. The use of a similar vehicle cost bookmakers a fortune in 1836 when Elis won the St. Leger. The layers were certain that the colt could not run. Elis was owned by Lord George Bentinck, who was the second of three Jockey Club Stewards who were effectively the Club's prime figureheads. The first – in the late 1700s – had been Sir Charles Bunbury, who lost a coin toss with Lord Derby over the naming of the Epsom classic. The third was Admiral John Rous, whose era spanned the mid-19th century.

In 1837, the Jockey Club said that if racecourses and their patrons wanted the Club to act as arbitrators in disputes at their courses, they would be obliged to stage their meetings in accordance with the Club's rules. Admiral John Rous was elected a Steward of the Jockey Club in 1838 and filled a variety of roles before becoming in effect the sport's supremo. In 1850 he produced his weight-for-age scale, which laid down what should be the weight differences between horses of different ages over each distance at each stage of the year. Rous's calculations are still in effect today with only very minor alterations.

Fred Archer – superstar jockey

For all the wishes of the Jockey Club to keep the potential racegoing public as ill-informed as possible, the steadily increasing newspaper coverage of racing rather thwarted that idea and the second half of the 19th century produced the sport's first folk hero. This was the jockey Fred Archer, whose adulation was on a level with that achieved by the greats of the 20th century. Archer shot himself in a fit of depression at the age of only 29, the gloom having been brought on first by the death in childbirth of his wife the previous year, and then by his constant battle with the scales which left him very prone to any form of infection. At the time of his suicide Fred Archer had ridden 2,748 winners from 8,084 rides (a strike rate of better than one in three), he had been champion jockey in 13 of the 17 seasons that he had held a licence – only George Fordham of his contemporaries could really compete with him – and he had 21 classic victories to his credit.

Inevitably Archer rode many of the best horses of his era, one of them being Iroquois, who became the first American winner of the Derby when he was successful in 1881. Iroquois was not only owned and bred by Pierre Lorillard but he was trained by Jacob Pincus who came over from the U.S. to Newmarket. Pincus provoked the mirth of the locals when he used timing in conjunction with working his horses, rather as Tod Sloan was ridiculed when he introduced his revolutionary riding style in 1890s. The locals duly learned.

Archer also rode Ormonde to the 1886 Derby and St. Leger to complete the horse's Triple Crown in his last year. But maybe the outstanding moment of Archer's remarkable career was when he won the 1880 Derby on Bend Or, he was riding effectively with only one arm having been savaged by a horse less than a month before. Bend Or won by only half a head from Robert The Devil.

Ormonde was trained by John Porter, whose tally of seven Derby winners was equalled only by Robert Robson, who was the first of his profession to achieve what might be called star status; until the 20th century, no trainers, or training grooms as they were often described, were recorded for winning horses. Porter trained three other Triple Crown winners: Common, Flying Fox and the filly La Flèche. He also trained for the Prince of Wales (later Edward VII), who later persuaded the Jockey Club to allow Porter to open Newbury racecourse.

In many ways racing was conducted on an ad hoc basis until the 20th century. Jockeys were not licensed until 1879, though, surprisingly, the draw for starting positions was introduced two years before that. Trainers were not licensed until 1905, though the starting gate (not stalls) came into use in 1897 and a film was made of the Derby two years earlier. And the fixture list was such a shambles that it was possible to claim the existence, and bet on, a totally imaginary meeting.

The Great Contest: E.H. Hunt's painting depicts Fred Archer on Bend Or beating Robert The Devil in 1881's Epsom Gold Cup.

EARLY HISTORY OF U.S. RACING

EARLY RECORDS ARE SPOTTY, but most historians believe that organized racing in the United States of America was first staged during the early to mid-17th century in the southern colonies, with the fastest horses in one community competing against those of another. Plantation owners, particularly, developed a fondness for the sport.

Laws were subsequently passed by various settlements prohibiting racing down public streets. Measures were also enacted prohibiting common labourers from staging races. The sport, so stated the edicts, was an endeavour reserved for "gentlemen".

But racing also sparked northern interest. The first formal racetrack was laid out in 1665 at the behest of Colonel Richard Nicolls, the governor of New York. Two miles in length, it was situated on Long Island's Hempstead Plain near Elmont, which is the home of the present-day Belmont Park. Nicolls named it Newmarket, after the famous English course. Nothing remains of America's Newmarket today.

Sometime around 1730, the English stallion, Bulle Rock, was imported into Virginia. Bulle Rock was by the Darley Arabian out of a daughter of the Byerly Turk, which thus made him a son and grandson of two of the three foundation sires of the thoroughbred breed.

Thus commenced an infusion of pedigreed stock that greatly enhanced racing interest. It's estimated that by the time of the American Revolution, more than 100 stallions and some 70 mares had been brought to the colonies from England. During the 17th century's final two decades, four winners of the Epsom Derby were shipped to America's shores. Among these was Diomed, who had won the inaugural running of the race in 1780.

Charleston, South Carolina, is generally credited with the formation of the first local jockey club in 1732. The Maryland Jockey Club was founded in Annapolis in 1743. Records show that the three-mile Annapolis Subscription Plate was won on 4 May of that year by Dr. George Steuart's horse, Dungannon. The race trophy, a silver bowl 4½ inches in height and 7½ inches in diameter, propped upon a 4-inch diameter base, remains today in the possession of Baltimore's Museum of Art.

The Sport of Presidents

George Washington, who later became first president of the United States, often attended

Executive action: Andrew Jackson was one of several early U.S. presidents who actively participated in the Sport of Kings.

Maryland Jockey Club races from 1771–73, and may actually have owned some of the horses who raced. From 1775–81, racing at Annapolis was suspended upon recommendation of the Continental Congress, while the revolt against England was being conducted.

Racing resumed in Maryland in 1782, at the end of the revolutionary war. Within a decade, organized race meets were also being conducted by George Washington's brother, Charles Washington, in the streets of a small community in what is now West Virginia's eastern panhandle. And so it was that the Charles Town Races came into existence, in the municipality of Charles Town, both of which bear Charles Washington's name.

One of the first events to gain national notice was the match between American Eclipse, representing the Northern states, and Sir Henry, representing the Southern interests. This took place at Union on May 27, 1823. The contest involved a trio of heats; Sir Henry won the first; American Eclipse swept the final two.

Match races, often involving multiple heats

Up in smoke: The Metairie Course in New Orleans, Louisiana, was a nationally prominent site of mid-19th century thoroughbred racing.

(the best two out of three, or three out of five) were popular endeavours throughout the 19th century. The *American Racing Manual* lists 99 such contests taking place between 1822–99. Undoubtedly, many more were not officially recorded. American Eclipse, Fashion, Norfolk, Maid of Honor, Nannie McNairy, Finesse, Thad Stevens, and Domino all scored multiple match triumphs. Heat racing fell out of favour as the 19th century progressed, but match events continued in the 20th century, and are still occasionally carded, although rarely for top-ranked horses.

It is believed that the 1806 duel between Andrew Jackson and Charles Dickinson stemmed from the results of a horse race. Truxon, owned by Jackson et al, had defeated Ploughboy, who campaigned for Dickinson and a partner, by 60 yards in a heavy rainstorm at Nashville, Tennessee. The match had been

postponed once, amidst charges of subterfuge and other mischief, and the outcome further enraged the already volatile tempers.

The two men finally had it out with pistols at 24 paces. Dickinson fired first. He either missed or gave Jackson a slight foot wound – accounts disagree. After expressing surprise at his own poor aim, Dickinson toed the mark like a gentleman, allowing Jackson to shoot him through the intestines. Dickinson died the following day. Jackson went on to serve two terms as U.S. President.

The Birth of Kentucky Racing

Kentucky's temperate climate, rich soil, and gently rolling landscape made it an excellent locale for horse farms, particularly in the central portion of the state. Thoroughbred breeding operations and racetracks were established there accordingly, and it remains the focal point of the

industry today. The Phoenix Stakes, named for the Phoenix Hotel in Lexington, was first run at that town's Kentucky Association track in 1831.

Discontinued and revived several times, the Phoenix Stakes is now the Phoenix Breeders' Cup. Run at Keeneland in October of each year, it is recognized as the oldest stakes event still in existence in America.

By 1830, racing had become the favourite sporting activity in New Orleans, Louisiana. The Metairie Course, founded on Metairie Ridge in Jefferson Parish in 1838, became arguably the great focal point of the sport in the South. In 1851, the already fashionable track was purchased by a group headed by the transplanted New York promoter, Richard Ten Broeck.

Under Ten Broeck's control, Metairie grew even more prominent. New barns were erected, the grandstand was enlarged, parlours and retiring rooms were constructed for female patrons. And the racing product reached a status second to none, highlighted by the match triumphs of Lexington over Sallie Waters in 1853, and Lexington over Lecomte in 1855. The Metairie property survived the Civil War, but was subsequently razed and turned into a cemetery, which is what it remains today. The cemetery's main road is set exactly where the racing surface once was.

On 25 September 1852, racing commenced at a 400-acre sight adjacent to the intersection of Bayou and Gentilly Roads in New Orleans. Also named the Union Course, it conducted standardbred racing that year, and hosted its inaugural thoroughbred meet beginning on 1 April 1853. Financial problems caused the track to shut down in 1857. Two years later, it reopened as the Creole Course, which was converted into the Mechanics and Agricultural Fair Grounds during the American Civil War period of 1861–65.

Following Metairie's demise, the Mechanics and Agricultural properties were renovated and expanded by the Louisiana Jockey Club, and formally reopened as the Fair Grounds track on April 13, 1872. Today, Fair Grounds is one of the most successful tracks in all of North America, with a heritage that predates Saratoga's by more than a decade.

Racing at Saratoga commenced on August 3, 1863. The meet's founding father, John "Old Smoke" Morrissey, was an Irish immigrant who five years earlier had been crowned heavyweight boxing champion of North America. Morrissey was well connected politically. He owned and operated saloons and a gambling house. He was twice charged with shooting waiters, and committing assault with intent to kill on three occasions. None of these resulted in a conviction. In his later years, Morrissey served two terms in the U.S. Congress.

Morrissey's partners in the original Saratoga track were John Hunter, Leonard Jerome, and William R. Travers. The following year, the partners built a new track across the street, which has evolved into the present-day Saratoga. Travers was named president of the Saratoga Association, and its most prominent event, the Travers Stakes, was named after him and first run in 1864. The initial winner was named Kentucky.

Most of the South's racing stock was decimated during the Civil War. Southern soldiers rode many of their thoroughbreds into battle. Others were confiscated by the invading Northern armies as they swept below the Mason-Dixon Line. These, and other circumstances, effected a relocation of many of racing's center stages. States such as New York, New Jersey,

Maryland, Ohio, Illinois and Kentucky saw their prominence within the sport grow. At the same time, racing in most of the traditional South, save for Louisiana and Tennessee, declined.

Lexington

Somewhat ironically, the Civil War's advent coincided with the emergence of Lexington as the most prominent stallion to stand on America's shores to date. He was foaled on 17 March 1850, at Dr. Elisha Warfield's farm, The Meadows, near Lexington, Kentucky. Lexington's sire, Boston, died several months before his famous offspring was born, but was posthumously recognized as America's leading stallion from 1851–53. Lexington himself topped the sire list for 14 consecutive years, from 1861–74, and posthumously in 1876 and 1878.

His colour turning blood bay as he grew older, Lexington initially raced for Dr. Wakefield, then was sold for $2,500 to Richard Ten Broeck and a trio of partners. The colt's name was initially Darley; Ten Broeck changed it to Lexington. He was sent to stud after trouncing Lecomte in New Orleans, and was subsequently sold to Robert A. Alexander, proprietor of Woodburn Farm in central Kentucky, for $15,000.

Lexington's progeny included Alice Ward, Arizona, Asteroid, Bayflower, Duke of Magenta, Harry Bassett, Hira, Idlewild, Kentucky, Kingfisher, Monarchist, Norfolk, Preakness, Tom Ochiltree, Salina, Sultana, Thunder, Tom Bowling and Uncas, all of whom wrote their own chapters in American racing lore. For much of his career at stud, Alexander used him as a "closed stallion", denying his access to outside mares.

Indeed, there are only two instances when Lexington left Woodburn. The first took place in 1859 when he was exhibited at the Great St. Louis Fair. The second came in 1865, when he was sent to Illinois to prevent seizure by Confederate raiders. His eyesight having failed, Lexington was known in his later years as "The Blind Hero of Woodburn". He died on 1 July 1875, and his skeleton is preserved by the Smithsonian Institute in Washington DC.

Prior to the Civil War, many of the great thoroughbreds in the South were tended to by black men in bondage. This created a heritage that they, as freemen, carried into the post-War era. Ansel Williamson, born a slave circa 1806 in Virginia, is credited with training the first Kentucky Derby winner, Aristides. That same year, he sent Calvin out to win the Belmont Stakes. Both colts were homebreds representing Henry Price McGrath, whose McGrathiana Stud was one of the leading Kentucky farms of the era. Horses conditioned by Williamson also won four

runnings of the Jersey Derby, and two renewals of the Travers Stakes at Saratoga. He died in June 1881, in Lexington.

The 19th century's most heralded black jockey, Isaac Burns Murphy, was born on David Tanner's Pleasant Green Hill Farm in Fayette County, Kentucky, in 1860. Murphy rode in his first race at age 14. He won the 1884 Kentucky Derby aboard Buchanan, and subsequently became the first jockey to score in back-to-back runnings of that race, with Riley and Kingman, in 1890 and 1891, respectively.

Dubbed "the Coloured Archer", in favourable comparison to the great English rider of the period, Fred Archer, Murphy claimed an overall career record of 628 victories from 1,412 mounts, which works out as a win ratio of 44.5%. Research by some historians indicates that his success rate was more along the lines of 32%, which would still be rather extraordinary. Murphy died of pneumonia on 12 February 1896. A forgotten figure for decades, he is now the beneficiary of a rebirth of interest, which reaches an annual peak at Kentucky Derby time.

Out West, racing dates back to at least 1838, when the Houston Jockey Club was formed. Within two years, at least four racing organizations operated in the Houston area. In 1855, a match race was conducted in Dallas between a local thoroughbred, Steel Dust, and a Tennessee invader, Shiloh. The event generated a great deal of anticipation, but Steel Dust was so unruly before the start of the race (newspaper reports stated he fell forward and did several somersaults) that he had to be scratched, and Shiloh won in a walkover.

In 1869, the first Dallas Jockey Club was formed. On 2 November 1887, a mare named Kittie Pease set a U.S. record at Dallas, winning a pair of five-furlong heats in indentical clockings of exactly one minute. The inaugural Texas Derby was run in 1890. Raced over a distance of 1½ miles, it featured a $2,500-added purse and was won by a colt named Guido, who made 31 starts that year at tracks ranging from Sacramento, California, to Nashville, Tennessee, and won 22 of them. Guido is one of many heroes in a region where racing's historical records are sparse.

Canadian racing

North of the border, Canadian racing grew as the century wore on. Written accounts of race meets in the Niagara region dates back to 1797. Courses were built in various locales in the Toronto area during the 1830s. In 1857, an attorney, William C. Keele, constructed the Carleton track in the city's western parameters. Three years later, Carleton hosted the inaugural running of the Queen's

Plate, named after Queen Victoria. A field of eight went postward. Conditions called for three one-mile heats, a purse of 50 guineas, and a subscriber's fee, payable to the Toronto Turf Club, of $8. A colt named Bob Marshall won the first heat. But the five-year-old gelding, Don Juan, swept the final two, thus becoming the victor.

In the ensuing four decades, the Queen's Plate grew into the prize most coveted by Canadian owners and breeders. From 1877–81, it was won three times by horses owned by John White, who was a member of the Canadian Parliament from Milton. In 1891, Joseph E. Seagram, the Canadian whiskey magnate, won the Queen's Plate with his homebred gelding, Victorious. Horses campaigning for Seagram family members were victorious in the race 20 times over the next 45 years.

The Queen's Plate was staged at several different tracks until, in 1883, it was provided a more permanent home at the old Woodbine course. The newer Woodbine opened in 1956, and immediately became the Queen's Plate's new host site. Although its distance and conditions have changed since its inception 140 years ago, the race has maintained an uninterrupted history of consecutive runnings.

Many links to 19th-century racing have vanished. But not all. Hawthorne racecourse, built on 119 acres in Cicero Township, Illinois, near Chicago, began its inaugural meet on 20 May 1891. Its founder was Edward Corrigan, whose "house horse", Brookwood, won the opening day feature, the Chicago Derby. Hawthorne is one of six North American tracks built during the 19th century that remain in operation – the others are Fair Grounds, Saratoga, Pimlico Race Course, Churchill Downs, and the Maryland State Fair in Timonium. Hawthorne's grandstand has twice burned down and twice been rebuilt. Today, it retains little of the flavour of eras bygone.

The original Aqueduct opened in Queens, New York, in 1894. It was situated on 23 acres, had a six-furlong (^{3}/4-mile) oval and seating for 2,000. Considered an "outlaw track", Aqueduct did not receive sanctioning from The Jockey Club until the fall of the following year. Since then, Aqueduct's facilities have been rebuilt, torn down, and constructed anew from the ground up. The present venue, which covers 192 acres, has a 1^1/8-mile main oval, and can seat 17,000, hosts 6^1/2 months of live racing per annum.

Toward the end of the 19th century, equine heroes continued to come forth. Kingston, who raced from 1886–94, retired with 89 career triumphs, a mark that will assuredly stand as the American record for all time. His stablemate, Domino, raced from 1893–95 and accumulated what were then record career earnings of $193,550. Both campaigned for James R. and Foxhall Keene. Domino subsequently became one of America's most influential sires. His name, in the words of turf scribe Paula Welch, "peppers the distant recesses of pedigrees of virtually every thoroughbred alive today."

Imp, an Ohio-bred filly, raced from 1896–1901, accumulating 62 career victories. Imp's travels took her from her home state to Kentucky, Illinois, Indiana, the District of Columbia, and New York, a formidable itinerary in those days. Illustrious, too, were the exploits of Ben Brush, who won 25 of 40 career starts between 1895–97. Included were victories in the 1896 Kentucky and Latonia Derbys, and in 18 other stakes as well.

There was also Henry Of Navarre, a New Jersey-bred, who won the 1894 Belmont and Travers Stakes, and registered an overall career record of 29 victories from 42 starts. And then there was the great Salvator, who on 28 August 1890, set a world record for a mile over a straight course at New Jersey's Monmouth Park, 1:35^1/2. Racing against time while aided by prompters, Salvator set the Monmouth patrons to such a frenzy with his effort that they almost tried to carry him off the course on their shoulders.

Records set during the 19th century haven't been uniformly voided. Salvator's still stands. Of course, no eight-furlong straightaway currently exists in America where a horse could challenge it. The prevailing American record for four miles against time, 7:11, was registered by a four-year-old filly named Lucretia Borgia on 20 May 1897. The official statistics keeper of that era, *Goodwin's Turf Guide*, said Lucretia Borgia's feat took place at a meet in San Francisco, California. *The American Racing Manual* maintains it took place on the other side of the bay in Oakland. Regardless, Lucretia Borgia's standard has withstood challenge for well over 100 years. The fact that it has been many decades since anyone has put a horse through a four-mile gallop, in a race, against time, or otherwise, is undoubtedly a factor.

Perhaps the most far-reaching development at the end of the 19th century was the creation of the publication, *Daily Racing Form*. The inaugural issue was published in Chicago in November 1894. Since then, the *Form* has had an uninterrupted run, providing racing participants and patrons with past performances of horses, race charts, breeding information, and news and statistics from tracks throughout North America on a daily basis.

The value of the information continuum that the *Form* has provided far outdistances that of any other North American periodical. While the paper is now based in New York, it continues to cover all major and most minor race meets. The bulk of its archives have recently been donated to the Keeneland Association in Lexington. Keeneland is constructing a new 15,000 square-foot library, in which the material will be housed, available for both professional and public use.

Colored Archer: Isaac Burns Murphy, America's "Colored Archer", rode magnificently and died young, as did his English contemporary.

HISTORY OF AUSTRALIAN RACING

RACING HAS BEEN FIRMLY ENTRENCHED as a part of Australia's way of life since the earliest days of the 19th century. This interest and involvement is best exemplified by the Melbourne Cup at Flemington which, since being first run in 1861, has become famous as "the race that stops the nation".

When the major carnivals are being held in Melbourne in the spring – and Sydney in the autumn – the excitement of racing, with its myriad of silks and colours and spine-tingling finishes, has the Australian people captivated. So have the exploits of champions such as Carbine, Phar Lap, Tulloch and more recently Kingston Town, while Bart Cummings, who has prepared more feature-race winners than any other Australian trainer, has been acknowledged as a national icon. This has ensured racing of an important place in the annals of the nation's history, despite a decline in attendances and increasing competition from other forms of entertainment.

There was, in fact, an exceptional period of growth and investment in the business of racing and breeding thoroughbred horses towards the latter part of the 20th century. This resulted in racing – with a capital investment of some Aus$1.6billion annually – becoming fully appreciated as one of Australia's most important industries as the new century dawned.

New South Wales

The industry has also become a substantial contributor to government finances, which has virtually ensured its successful future. It is, though, a long way from the arrival of the first fleet into a horseless country in 1788 with just four mares, a stallion and three yearlings aboard. Match races were soon being held along the roads of the new colony but a three-day fixture held in Sydney's Hyde Park in October 1810 is considered to be the first official race meeting held in Australia.

Further meetings were conducted on the Hyde Park course in August 1811, 1812 and 1813. The chief organisers of those fixtures, which received government approval, were the officers of the 73rd Regiment. When the regiment was transferred to Ceylon in March 1814, racing lapsed until autumn 1819, when another three-day fixture was arranged. Further meetings were held, on an irregular basis, until 1825, when a Turf Club was formed in Sydney with the colony's Governor, Sir Thomas

Brisbane, as patron.

The following year the Turf Club established a course at Parramatta and from that time onwards racing and breeding – even though every horse in Australia is from imported origin – began to flourish. In 1828 the Australian Racing and Jockey Club was formed and records indicate that the Hawkesbury Race Club, the nation's oldest existing racing club, was operating by 1832. The Australian Jockey Club, which is the nation's senior racing body, was conceived in April 1842 and began holding meetings at a course at Homebush in September of that year.

In 1860, the AJC transferred to its present site at Randwick where a course had been designed under the direction of the club's chairman the Honourable E. Deas Thomson. The AJC Derby was first run in 1861 and soon afterwards feature events including the Doncaster Handicap, Sydney Cup, Champagne Stakes, Epsom Handicap, Metropolitan Stakes and AJC Sires Produce Stakes were introduced.

Tasmania

By that time racing was also being were held in other outposts. Only 10 years after Tasmania was established as a penal colony in 1804, a race meeting was held near Hobart and, in 1826, the first Tasmanian Turf Club was created.

Western Australia

Racing began at Fremantle in October of 1833 – only four years after a settlement was established on the Swan River – and in 1838 the Western Australian Stud Club was formed. A meeting was run on the site of the present Ascot racecourse in 1848 and in 1852 the Western Australian Turf Club was constituted. However, the Perth Cup was not introduced until 1879 and two other principal events – the Western Australian Derby and Railway Stakes – had their baptism in 1887.

Victoria

The inaugural race meetings in Victoria were staged in March 1838 and racing began on the present site of Flemington racecourse in March 1840. The Victoria Jockey Club instituted the Victoria Derby in 1855 and two years later the Victoria St. Leger came into being.

Displaying considerable foresight, the Jockey Club also introduced the Melbourne Cup in 1861, which was run over two miles until altered to the metric equivalent in 1972. Over the years

the race has come to be recognised as the world's greatest handicap and now has a respected place on the international stage. The event attracted a crowd of 118,877 in 1926 when Spearfelt was triumphant and that remained the record attendance until 2000 when 121,015 witnessed Brew defeating 21 rivals.

There were said to be only 4,000 on hand for the inaugural running of the Cup, which was won by the William Tell five-year-old Archer trained by Etienne de Mestre. Archer, who was walked around 800km from Nowra on the south coast of New South Wales for his assignments at Flemington, was successful again the following year. Only Rain Lover (1968–69) and Think Big (1974–75) have since been able to win the Cup in consecutive years, while Peter Pan is the only other dual winner with victories in 1932 and 1934.

Conflict between the Jockey Club and the Victoria Turf Club led directly to the formation of the present controlling body, the Victoria Racing Club, in March 1864. Another principal body – the Victoria Amateur Turf Club – was constituted in October of 1875 and, four years later, the VATC initiated the Caulfield Cup, as a handicap over 1½ miles (2400 metres).

Since its instigation, the Caulfield Cup has been deemed an ideal race for stayers being aimed at the Melbourne Cup and over the years Poseidon, The Trump, Rivette, Rising Fast, Even Stevens, Galilee, Gurner's Lane, Let's Elope, Doriemus and Might And Power have managed to complete the double.

South Australia

Surveyor-General Colonel Light was a prime instigator of racing in South Australia, which held its first meeting in Adelaide on 1 and 2 January 1838. On being established in January 1856 the South Australian Jockey Club instituted the South Australian Derby in 1860 and the Adelaide Cup four years later.

Queensland

Although Queensland was settled in 1824 there is no indication of racing behind conducted in the state until July 1843, when a three-day meeting featured the Brisbane Town Plate. The Queensland Turf Club came into existence in August of 1863 and in 1871 the QTC took over the Queensland Derby, which had been presented in the previous three years by the Gayndah Jockey Club.

CHAPTER 2

RACING AROUND THE WORLD

Horse racing is as much about a sunny Sunday in Souissi (Morocco) as it is about the pomp and circumstance of the Derby or Prix de l'Arc de Triomphe. Racing fans will endure almost any weather and conditions to watch — and bet on — horses.

IN BRITAIN, horse racing is known as "the Sport of Kings", and reigning monarchs have won classic races. In France, racing is chic, with most of the top tracks being situated in and around Paris. Italy's two biggest courses are close to her most glamorous cities — Rome and Milan.

However, the U.S. racing industry's heartland is in agrarian Kentucky, the Bluegrass State. Ireland and New Zealand, countries with relatively small populations covering large areas, boast racing industries which enjoy far greater success than their demographics suggest. Then there is the Czech Republic, home to a genuinely outstanding racing experience, the four-mile Velka Pardubicka.

Almost all of Asia is horse mad. Hong Kong – one of the world's most populous regions – boasts two courses, one shoe-horned into a tiny area surrounded by skyscrapers, the other built on land reclaimed from the sea using soil from the top of a mountain. Japan's premier meeting attracts crowds in excess of 150,000. Middle Eastern Sheikhs have brought untold wealth to the sport worldwide.

Racing is truly a global sport and this chapter celebrates the worldwide appeal of the horse, whether scooting around a dusty pampas track in Argentina or parading in front of sovereigns, lords and ladies at Royal Ascot.

Mixing work and pleasure: Dwarfed by Hong Kong's skyscrapers, Happy Valley is the ultimate urban racecourse.

GREAT BRITAIN

THE GENERAL PATTERN OF RACING in Britain – England, Scotland and Wales – changed very slowly in the 20th century, and has not undergone significant alteration in the early years of the 21st century, either. Until the mid-1980s, the autocratic Jockey Club, the sport's overseers since the 1750s, was still the dominant force, enforcing rules that now seem very harsh. If, for example, a villain nobbled a horse to ensure the animal ran badly, the trainer forfeited his licence, without appeal, even if palpably he had done nothing wrong. Such sentences were invariably sine die, and many people who were warned off never came back.

At the turn of the 21st century, however, there were more race meetings in Britain than ever before, despite 59 courses having closed down in the preceding 100 years – coincidentally,

the same number of courses that were operational in 2001. Some were of minimal significance. Blackpool lasted only four years, and Bournemouth barely three, but major courses that have disappeared in this time include well-established venues such as Hurst Park, Manchester (the 1941 St. Leger venue), Gatwick (now an airport, but the site of wartime Nationals from 1915 to 1917) and Birmingham.

Flat racing continues to be offered at about three dozen of Great Britain's courses, half of which offer no other form of racing. Flat events remain the domain of powerful owner/breeders from foreign lands, such as the Maktoum family and the HH Aga Khan, who have established equine empires within Great Britain's boundaries. But horses purchased at auction continue to have considerable impacts. The major

Royal Meeting: A £200-million redevelopment of Ascot Racecourse was completed in June 2006.

sales have become increasingly more significant, and yearlings sell for large sums – a colt by Kingmambo was auctioned at Tattersalls in October, 2005, for $2.3 million. Much of the increase in the monies that exchange hands at the top level of the breeding world can be attributed to sires such as Sadler's Wells, who has 14 times led England and Ireland's combined general sire list, and has been France's champion sire on many occasions as well.

Sadler's Wells anchors the powerful Coolmore Stud operation, whose outstanding success is linked to the descendants of the great Northern Dancer. This first came to light in Europe with the 1970 Triple Crown success of

Nijinsky II and Vincent O'Brien, for whom the colt was the third of O'Brien's six Derby winners. O'Brien's career achievements with both his flat horses and his jumpers will be difficult to equal, although Aiden O'Brien (same surname, but no relation) could challenge him. Epsom Derby winners are now deemed so valuable at stud that owners almost invariably retire them at the end of their three-year-old campaigns.

British administrators were very slow to institute many racing practices. Starting gates with stall doors became the norm in the United States in the 1930s, but it was not until 1965 that the Jockey Club first sanctioned them in Britain and they did not come into universal use until much later. Stalls are not used for National Hunt races, nor for a very few longer flat races.

It took until 1966, following a landmark ruling by the High Court, for the Jockey Club to allow women to participate on level terms with men as trainers – Florence Nagle instituting the proceedings – and the Jockey Club was ridiculed in the judgment. The Jockey Club was subsequently less obstinate about riding, although again it took concerted action. Permission for women to ride came for amateur races only in 1971, against professionals on the flat in 1975 and over jumps the following year. Women jockeys still form only a tiny minority of riders, and they rarely compete in top races.

For many years, racing during the winter invariably fell foul of the weather. This led to repeated calls for some form of underground heating so that frozen tracks could thaw, but this was never more than an idea because of logistics and expense. Instead, two forms of non-turf surface, Equitrack and Fibresand – similar to those on which racing is held in North America – were introduced, and were heralded as "all-weather surfaces". Lingfield Park staged the first such meeting on 30 October, 1989. Southwell did the same eight days later, and Wolverhampton joined the all-weather circuit in early 1990. They attracted plenty of runners, although prize money and the standard of racing were very low.

Lingfield and Southwell had some all-weather hurdle racing, too, but an unacceptably high equine fatality rate and poor quality of competition led to discontinuations in early 1994. All-weather racing also proved not to be totally impervious to harsh weather, and both lost meetings because of frozen tracks. Attempts were made to stage races of high purse values to attract better quality fields, but the results constituted little more than betting-shop fodder. On a more positive note, Wolverhampton installed floodlights, and its summer Saturday night race programmes became very popular.

Being self-elected and answerable to nobody, the Jockey Club had long been regarded as out of touch with the real world, and by the 1990s it was felt that if overtures to the government to return more betting-tax revenue to racing were to succeed at all, racing's administration had to be seen to be more democratic. This led to the establishment of the British Horseracing Board (BHB) under the aegis of the Jockey Club's simultaneous Senior Steward, Lord Hartington. The BHB came into existence in the summer of 1993, although not until Lord Hartington made strenuous efforts to persuade some of the Jockey Club's members in favour of new authority.

Today, the Jockey Club still retains charge of disciplinary matters and licensing, with the BHB dealing with all other aspects, including fixtures and race planning. This has produced greater flexibility, and major races that have been abandoned can now be re-staged at short notice elsewhere. But the new board hasn't produced much reaction from the government.

Arguably, the biggest change to the overall picture of contemporary British racing – on the flat at least – is the huge, present-day impact of owners and breeders from the Middle East. In 2005, the HH Aga Khan's homebred, Azamour, was champion older male in England and Ireland, his victories including the King George VI and Queen Elizabeth Diamond Stakes and the Prince of Wales Stakes. Eswarah, owned and bred by Sheikh Hamdan bin Rashid al-Maktoum, won the Oaks – it was the 11th time a filly representing a member of the Maktoum family had accounted for the event in a 21-year period.

But the prominent British owner/breeder has not vanished from the landscape. Cheveley Park Stud on the outskirts of Newmarket, owned and operated since 1975 by David and Patricia Thompson, sent out Nannina to win the Fillies' Mile in 2005, and also sent out Peeress to win the Chariot Stakes. Both winners were homebreds.

The Middle Eastern owner/breeders haven't taken much interest in jumping, although Sheikh Mohammed bin Rashid al-Maktoum's Kribensis and Royal Gait won the Champion Hurdle in 1990 and 1992, respectively. Prince Khalid Abdullah also won major hurdle races with Sanmartino. About two dozen British courses are for jumping events exclusively, and another dozen and a half intermingle jumping events with those on the flat. By the end of the 20th century, J.P. McManus had become a huge presence in the jumping world, winning the Champion Hurdle in three consecutive years from 1998–2000 with Istabraq. The daring deeds of Best Mate, who won three consecutive runnings of the Cheltenham Gold Cup between 2002–2004 for owner Jim Lewis, made him a folk hero among the jumping set, a status he will long retain in the memories of those who saw him compete.

Another aspect of change in British racing is the number of horses under a trainer's care. When Sir Noel Murless retired in 1976, he had a string of 60 horses. At the same time, John Dunlap was a rarity in having 100 in his yard. Now, strings as large or larger than that are usual among the top trainers. Some even have as many as 200 horses under their care. This does little to persuade the UK's politicians that racing is dying because of lack of finances.

Rural charm: Cartmel in Cumbria has strong local support.

IRELAND

Real sand: Laytown's annual meeting on the beach is unique and dependent on the tide being a long way out.

THERE ARE 27 COURSES in Ireland of which two, Down Royal and Downpatrick, are in Ulster and all bar three are used for flat racing and jumping. The exceptions are the Curragh (home to all the Irish classics), Laytown (where racing takes place on the beach) and Kilbeggan (the only exclusively jumping course). Racing in Ireland is run by the Turf Club (for flat racing) and the Irish National Hunt Committee (jumping). There has been no amalgamation between the bodies as has happened in Britain.

Inevitably there are far fewer meetings through the year but one notable feature of racing in Ireland, however, is the duration of some of the Festivals. Galway, for example runs for seven days in July and August, Tralee (August/September) lasts for six and Listowel also has a six-day session in September. In contrast there is racing at the same track in Great Britain on five days in a row only at Ascot in June and at Goodwood in July/August; the principal reason for this is that because the meetings in Ireland are for both flat and jumping, there is the scope to stage enough races to fill so large a schedule. Racing is also staged in Ireland on just about every Sunday of the year, and many of the country's major events, like the Irish Derby, the Gold Cup and the Champion Hurdle, are staged on the sabbath, though the Irish Grand National remains rooted to Easter Monday.

It is very noticeable, on a pro rata basis, how many small stables there are in Ireland compared with Britain. Although there are a number of big, powerful strings, like those currently of Aidan O'Brien, Dermot Weld, John Oxx and Jim Bolger on the flat, and Noel Meade over jumps, there are many stables with single-figure contingents. This is partly because in Ireland trainers can have a permit, which is effectively a restricted licence, for flat racing as well as for jumping; in Britain a permit is available only for jumpers. Although opportunities in Ireland are restricted due to the fact that there are fewer races, the country's racing still attracts major owners from overseas. For example, John Oxx, who trained the 2000 Derby and Prix de l'Arc de Triomphe winner, Sinndar, also won the 2003 Irish Derby with Alamshar. Both colts campaigned for their breeder, the HH Aga Khan. Alamshar also accounted for the King George VI and Queen Elizabeth Diamond Stakes that season, and was Ireland's champion three-year-old. In 2004, the Oxx/Aga Khan team duo won the Irish Champion Stakes with Azamour, who was also recognised as Ireland's three-year-old champion colt; and in 2005, they won the Irish Oaks with Shawanda. And in 2005, Godolphin's Dubawi accounted for the Irish 2000 Guineas, and was divisional champion as well.

One major advantage which the racing and breeding worlds in Ireland have over their counterparts in Great Britain relates to the question of taxation. Stud owners get very generous concessions from the government in Ireland, where the off-course betting tax was halved to five percent in the summer of 2000. Stallion owners are increasingly inclined to stand their horses in Ireland and some of the leading stallion station operators in Britain have found the costs unsustainable. As some of the most popular stallions in Ireland cover more than 200 mares in a season it is easy to see what vast income can be derived from such an operation.

The attraction of the tax arrangements in Ireland results in many top horses going to stud there and the powerful Coolmore operation in Co. Tipperary – headed by Vincent O'Brien's son-in-law John Magnier – has a veritable Debrett of stallions on its books. It can be firmly stated that Magnier controls more stallion shares than anyone else on the planet. Apart from Sadler's Wells, easily Europe's most successful sire for the past two decades, the Coolmore books have listed other internationally successful sires in Danehill, Grand Lodge, (sire of Sinndar), Night Shift, classic winners Dr. Devious and Entrepreneur, Montjeu and Giant's Causeway.

To some extent the Coolmore operation has for some time been a numbers game because there are bound to be a number which fail to live up to expectations. But buying potentially top-level horses on an in-depth basis is virtually bound to produce one or two who live up to expectations. The link-up between Coolmore,

THE CURRAGH

The Curragh is on Irish Department of Defence land 30 miles outside Dublin. It is Ireland's most important track and is also a major training ground, housing around 1,500 horses in the surrounding yards. Apart from the beach fixture at Laytown, the Curragh is the only course in the country which stages only flat racing. It is the home to all the Irish classics and many other major races, including the Moyglare Stud Stakes and the National Stakes for two-year-olds. Its classics take place about three weeks later than their British counterparts. It is a wide, sweeping right handed track, two miles around, with few undulations and long bends and a finishing straight of about 3½ furlongs. Races from five furlongs up to and including a mile are held on a virtually straight course with its starts to the right of the stands.

Michael Tabor, Magnier – many of whose horses race in the colours of his wife Susan – and trainer Aidan O'Brien rapidly propelled the latter on to national and worldwide stages. O'Brien, the master of Ballydoyle – the very yard where his namesake, but no relation, Vincent O'Brien pulled off so many outstanding achievements – trained his first winner at age 23 in the summer of 1993; he was champion jumps trainer in the next winter campaign. In 1998, Mick Kinane, the most successful jockey at home and abroad, left Dermot Weld's stable to join his operation.

Other jockeys have since risen to prominence in Ireland's ranks. Pat Smullen, who succeeded Kinane as Weld's top rider, was champion with 80 winners in 2000. Jamie Spencer, in his first year as stable jockey for Ballydoyle, led the rider standings with 93 victories in 2004 at a strike rate of 25.8 per cent.

The business of exporting horses between Ireland and Britain has thrived for a long time. Irish breeding promoters won an agreement from the Jockey Club in Britain so that horses foaled in Ireland should be so defined in official publications. Previously, horses foaled in countries outside the British Isles were defined with the suffixes Fr (France), Ger (Germany), USA, etc. with Irish-breds designated (Ire).

The thriving export trade between Ireland and Britain extends to jockeys as well as horses. Although Pat Eddery and Kieren Fallon are the only Irish-born champion flat jockeys since 1970, in the jumping world there have been five: Ron Barry, Tommy Stack, Jonjo O'Neill, Richard Dunwoody and Tony McCoy. Behind McCoy, the champion jockey every season since 1995–96, were many of his compatriots, including Norman Williamson, Mick FitzGerald, Tony Dobbin, Timmy Murphy and Adrian Maguire. Six Irishmen were in the top ten in 1999–2000.

Charlie Swan, the Irish champion jump jockey nine times in a row from 1989–98, started concentrating on training, though his career in the saddle seemed certain to last as long as Istabraq kept running. It left the way open for younger riders, such as Barry Geraghty, Paul Carberry and Ruby Walsh to move in at the top of the table. The latter two won the 1999 and 2000 Grand Nationals, riding for their fathers, Tommy and Ted (on BobbyJo and Papillon), respectively. Neither Walsh nor Geraghty showed any indication of wanting to ride full time in England, while Paul Carberry spent the 1997–98 season riding in Britain as retained jockey for owner Robert Ogden but did not renew the association at the end of that season and returned home.

In autumn 2000, a major split in Irish racing loomed when the Turf Club refused to join other bodies (racecourses, trainers, owners, etc.) and the overall Irish Horseracing Authority in agreeing to a new state-backed body – Horseracing Ireland. Eventually, however, agreement was reached, with the huge benefit that prize money for 2001 went up to Ir£34million – 40 percent more than in 2000. This followed the Government's decision, in line with the earlier agreement, that 80 percent of betting tax proceeds should be returned to racing. As evidenced by its bumper attendances in 2005, Irish racing remains buoyant.

Grandstand view: Leopardstown is Ireland's top dual-purpose course and spectators get a great view of the start.

FRANCE

REVOLUTION and the Napoleonic Wars slowed the arrival of racing in France. It was the 1830s before the sport was established on any scale and it owed its start to an Englishman, Lord Charles Seymour. He founded the Prix du Jockey Club in 1836 – and the organization which contributed its name – and added the Prix de Diane for fillies in 1843.

Seymour found natural turf for racing at Chantilly and on the riverside meadows at Maisons-Laffitte, both north of Paris. They also became the principal training centres. Chantilly has always been home to the greatest flat stables but it is only in the last quarter-century that Maisons-Laffitte has become almost entirely concerned with jumping. French racing bore a strong British character for many years. The best

known survivors of that era are the members of the Head family, which left Newmarket in the 19th century. Alec Head, himself the son of a successful trainer, was a fine jump jockey, a great trainer and a leading breeder, being one of the first Europeans to keep mares in Kentucky and use American sires. He is also the father of former champion jockey, Freddy, who now trains, as does his sister even more successfully, Criquette.

Paris dominates French racing. Four courses stage top-class flat meetings: Longchamp, Saint-Cloud, Chantilly and Maisons-Laffitte, and it was five until Evry was closed at the end of 1996. Auteuil is the main jumping course, supported by Enghien in the northern suburbs. Further out, Compiegne and Fontainebleau supply useful opportunities for the less talented horses.

Few of them ever have to travel far, except in August, when racing moves to Deauville or Vichy, leaving Paris to the trotters. Deauville, on the Normandy coast, was developed by the Duc de Morny, first minister to the Emperor Napoleon III, in the 1850s as a seaside and sporting resort. Deauville and the nearby course at Clairefontaine race throughout August and the town also stages the yearling sales at the end of that month. In recent years it has also become a full-time training centre.

Horses are trained throughout the country, with the greatest concentration in Normandy, which also has most of the major breeding farms.

Cream of racing: Chantilly hosts the Prix du Jockey Club and Prix de Diane and offers picturesque surroundings too.

The Vie River Valley is the site of the HH Aga Khan's stallion operation, Haras de Bonneval, which neighbours his Saint-Crespin farm, where he boards his broodmares. The two operations encompass approximately 810 acres.

Jacques Ortet and his jockey, Christophe Pieux, who led the way in jumping for most of the 1990s, are also based at Pau. Bordeaux, Lyon and Marseille each have two courses, staging worthwhile prizes throughout most of the year, but racing is strongest in spring and autumn, as it is at Nantes and Toulouse. There are over 200 smaller provincial courses, many with only a few holiday dates and often mixing flat racing, jumping and trotting on the same programme.

There is no thoroughbred racing in Paris between early December and the end of February. Pau, in the foothills of the Pyrenees, and Cagnes-sur-Mer, near Nice, race during this period. Both installed Fibresand tracks in 1999 and Pau staged France's first-ever flat programme on an artificial surface in January 2001. All the best racing there is over jumps but Cagnes has a jumping season followed by one on the flat. Some of these meetings are mixed with trotting.

French horses won many of the biggest races in Britain between 1946 and the late 1950s. However, prize money at home was poor. Marçel Boussac, the leading owner-breeder in France, and Jean Romanet, Director-General of the Societe d'Encouragement, the then ruling body of French racing (it is now France-Galop), introduced reforms. They centralized the organization of the sport and the distribution of prize money and introduced the tiercé, a bet which was so popular that it funded rapid increases in race values.

The Prix de l'Arc de Triomphe, first run in 1920, continues to retain its status as one of the world's greatest races. The 2004 winner, Bago, was a competitor with unique international connections, as he was bred in France by the people who campaigned him, the Famille Niarchos from Greece, was raised at Haras de Fresnay-Le Buffard in France (run by Englishman Tim Richardson) and trained by Englishman Jonathan Pease at Chantilly.

It would be impossible to understate the impact Famille Niarchos continues to have on French racing. In 2005, Bago accounted for the Prix Ganay. Another Niarchos homebred, Divine Proportions, won a trio of Group 1 events, including the Prix de Diane. In partnership with Michael Tabor and John Magnier, Famille Niarchos further campaigned Rumplestiltskin, who was Europe's champion two-year-old filly.

Some years back, French breeders were encouraged by the payment of premiums for finishers in the first three positions. This policy was extended with a second premium paid to all owners of French-bred horses who kept them in France. Strangely, these subsidies made many breeders less, rather than more, competitive. The industry reached a low point with the sale of Blushing Groom, Caro, Lyphard and Riverman to the USA around 1980, and others to Japan.

General turnover on betting – which has been by pari-mutuel only for more than 100 years but suffers from high deductions – has been falling and the years of steady increases in prize-money have ended.

There were calls to close both Chantilly, transferring its big races to Longchamp, and Maisons-Laffitte before the money-saving axe finally fell on Evry. Prizes for maiden and conditions races had always been the most important indicator of prosperity and Pattern-race purses were allowed to remain at a similar level to those in Britain. Pattern races are also the only ones which do not reward fifth place finishers and the result has been that many have become uncompetitive. Indeed they would be even weaker were it not for foreign runners. The anomaly of making the rewards less generous in the biggest races was finally ended in 2001.

Only Andre Fabre, who through 2005 had won 19 consecutive French training titles, is represented in almost every Pattern race. Hurricane Run's triumph is the 2005 Arc was the sixth for Fabre in that event. But France has other conditioners of note, one of whom is Alain du Royer-Dupre, who won the 2003 Arc with Dalakhani, and in 2005 was victorious with Shawanda in the Prix Vermeile Lucien Barriere,

Town and country: Paris tower blocks dominate the skyline behind Longchamp's grandstands in the Bois de Boulogne.

as well as the Irish Oaks. Pascal Barry won the Prix du Jockey Club five times between 1994 and 2004, and won a trio of Group 1 events in 2005 with Divine Proportions.

France probably has the finest group of jockeys of any European country. Olivier Peslier, Christophe Soumillon and Gerald Mosse are international racing stars and Thierry Jarnet has been home champion on several occasions.

Jumping recovered from a crisis period around 1980 and is now in excellent shape, with a strong concentration on young horses and a guarantee of soft or heavy going at Auteuil. French jumpers, as well as being more precocious than Anglo-Irish ones, are thoroughly schooled, which has made them popular with British buyers in recent years.

REST OF EUROPE

AUSTRIA

Vienna and its surrounding area are home to a pair of thoroughbred racetracks, the oldest and most prestigious being Rennbahn Freudenau, at Trapprenbahnplatz, which dates back to 1836. It is the home of the Vienna Derby, which is annually run in late June. Freudenau, because of its age, is expensive to maintain. The Magna Racing racetrack and casino complex, built by the company headed by Frank Stronach, is located 19 miles south of Vienna and commenced operations in 2004.

The Central European Breeders' Cup, a Stronach creation, was first staged at Freudenau in 2000. It consists of three races – run at sprint, mile and 2,400-metre distances – and now rotates between tracks in Austria, the Czech Republic, Poland, Slovakia and Hungary. Plans are for Switzerland to also become a Central European Breeders' Cup host country.

BELGIUM

An apparently thriving industry collapsed around 1990. The Derby, worth 1.5million BFr in 1988, dropped to 450,000 BFr by 1991 and was moved from Boitsfort to Groenendael. Now both those Brussels courses are closed and the race is run at Ostende, where the 2000 winner earned 110,000 BFr.

From 1978 to 1989, Ostende staged the Grand Prix Prince Rose, with a prize of 3million BFr. Now the course is open much longer and no winner earns more than 300,000BF. Only the annual day of jumping at Waregem has been able to maintain its excellent prizes, most of which fall to French raiders. Sterrebeek, one of Europe's first dirt tracks, is the only other in operation.

CYPRUS

Nicosia Race Club is in Ayios Dometios, a suburb of the capital city of Nicosia. The track races 84 days a year, and its racing events are simulcast to 100 off-site agencies. All races are broadcast live by Alpha TV. Nicosia's annual stakes programme includes the Cyprus Derby Cup, which is run over 2250 metres, and the Aphrodite Cup, contested by three-year-old fillies, also at the 2250-metre distance. A top event for horses aged four to seven is the 2250-metre Georghios Stavrakis Cup.

CZECH REPUBLIC

Pardubice is the one place everyone has heard of and the Velka Pardubicka Chase, over 4m 2½f and usually on the second Sunday in October, is one race jumping enthusiasts want to see. Pardubice, an industrial town a couple of hours east of Prague by road, is no longer just the home of cross-country chasing. It has introduced racing over more conventional fences, and started hurdling and flat racing, including its own Derby and St. Leger.

The real Czech Derby and St. Leger are at Velka Chuchle, Prague, but have only continued there with the help of the trotting association,

which shares the course. A remarkable 15 courses survived Communist rule in the old Czechoslovakia, 11 of them in the present Czech Republic. Prize money, except at Pardubice, is very modest but the Czechs have a fine racing tradition, particularly over jumps, and there is definite potential for growth.

DENMARK

One Danish official summed up the current state of racing in Scandinavia when he said: "The Norwegians have the money, the Swedes have

Making a splash: A horse comes to grief at the open water jump during the Velka Pardubicka in the Czech Republic.

the races and we have the jockeys." In 1999, Danes Mark Larsen (Denmark), Jacob Johansen (Norway) and Kim Andersen (Sweden) were champion jockeys. Andersen, who was also Scandinavian champion, retained his titles in 2000 and was also top in Norway. Sara Slot, an apprentice, led all rivals in Denmark but the performance of the year came from another Danish jockey, Nicholas Cordrey, who rode seven winners and a second in eight races at Jagersro, Sweden, on 22 June.

Klampenborg, the Copenhagen course where the Group 3 Scandinavian Open Championship is run each August, is the only one offering full flat-racing programmes. Odense, Aarhus and Aalborg all share their cards with trotters. Danish racing has always been a poor relation, even in Scandinavia. It would no doubt benefit from more investment but currently maintains its own modest level.

GERMANY

Betting turnover and prize money levels either stagnated or fell in Germany during the 1990s, although this had no immediate effect on the aesthetic appearance of the sport. Indeed, the quality of the horses, either bred or brought to race in Germany, improved throughout that period, and continued to do so through the opening years of the 21st century.

But the overall financial health of the racing industry in Germany is highly troublesome. The country has some 40 racecourses. All of them have financial problems, and at least half suffer from serious debt. Several are nearly bankrupt, and the problem appears to be growing. A number of Germany's courses have beautiful locations – Baden-Baden is set among the foothills of the Black Forest, and Dusseldorf borders the Grafenberg Forest. Quality is present, as well. Germany hosted 47 events in 2005 that bore group status, of which half-a-dozen had a designation of Group 1.

Hamburg annually conducts one of the country's most prominent meets, racing from late June through early July. It is here that the Deutsches Derby is run, a 2400-metre event that in 2005 went to Nicaron. Kolin Racecourse, near Cologne, is the site in late September of the Europa-Preis, a 2400-metre event won by Gonbarda in 2005.

Germany's most prominent race, though, remains the Grosser Preis von Baden at Baden-Baden. Its initial running in 1970 was won by Gestut Schlenderhan's Alpenkonig, and the same outfit repeated in the event the following year with Cortez. Gestut Schlenderhan is Germany's oldest privately owned stud – it dates back to

On the world stage: Baden Baden in Germany hosted an Emirates World Series race in 2000, the Grosser Preis von Baden.

1869, when it was founded by Baron Edouard von Oppenheim. Situated in Bergheim, 20 miles west of Cologne, Gestut Schlenderhan won its first Deutches Derby in 1908, and was subsequently triumphant in the race 15 times.

A fourth-generation relative of von Oppenheim, Baroness Karin von Ullmann, now has responsibility for Gestut Schlenderhan. She is assisted by her son, Baron George von Ullmann. The latter bagged consecutive runnings of the Grosser Preis von Baden in 1998–1999 with Tiger Hill, who, along with the stallion Monsun, have provided a powerful foundation for the Gestut Schlenderhan stud operation.

The Germans have not simply been content to earn top prizes at home. In fact, they have also been successful in Italy and elsewhere. Von Ullman's homebred, Shirocco won the Deutches Derby in July, 2004, was victorious three months later in the Gran Premio del Jockey Club at San Siro and in October, 2005, won the Breeders' Cup Turf at Belmont Park. Back in 1995, Lando, representing Germany's Gestut Ittlingen, was victorious in the Japan Cup. Epalo, a son of Lando, triumphed in the 2004 Singapore International Cup.

Of course, what's good for one side may be also good for the other. Foreign horses have made their invasions into Germany, too. For example, Mamoud, representing the Maktoum Family's Godolphin operation, accounted for both the Preis von Baden and the Preis von Europa in 2003. His Preis von Baden victory was

actually the second in a consecutive win streak of three for the Maktoums in the race.

GREECE

Phaleron, in Athens, a dirt course which is the country's only track, was due to close to make way for the equestrian centre for the 2004 Olympic Games.

However, delays in making arrangements for the proposed new course at Markopolou, outside the city, meant everything was behind schedule. Problems included future control of betting and the linking of the building at Markopolou to the construction of a second course at Thessaloniki.

BADEN-BADEN

Baden-Baden is a spa town and resort in the south west of Germany, close to the French border near Strasbourg. The racecourse, which was first used in 1858, is a few miles west of the town, between the River Rhine and the Black Forest. Nine furlongs around, the flat left-handed course has some tricky bends and a sharp dog-leg $1^1/_2$ furlongs from home. A holiday atmosphere pervades throughout the course, which is the most popular in Germany and has excellent facilities, yet maintains an old-fashioned charm. It stages just 12 days racing a year – six in late May and six at the end of August. The jewel in its crown is the Group 1 Grosser Preis von Baden, which was incorporated into the Emirates World Series in 2000.

HUNGARY

Few countries have a greater racing tradition or are currently so far from those days. Kisber, bred at the stud of that name in Hungary, won the Epsom Derby and Grand Prix de Paris in 1876. Kincsem was unbeaten in 54 races from 1876–79 and gave her name to the Budapest racecourse. It closed for rebuilding in 2000 but not before a historic performance from the jockey, Paul Kallai. He had won the Magyar Derby as a 17-year-old apprentice in 1950 and repeated the feat half a century later on Rodrigo. The winner was trained at Alayo, a course which closed in 1970 but was called back into existence as a replacement during the rebuilding of Kincsem Park.

CAPANNELLE

The Capannelle is approximately five miles south-east of the centre of Rome. It stages racing all year round apart from during the intense heat of June–August. All three of its courses are flat and right-handed. The biggest, which is $1^1/2$ miles long, has an alternative inner home bend which is used for the lesser races. Inside this is a dirt course and, tightest of all, a jumps course. There is also a straight six-furlong sprint course. It is home to three of the five classics, including the Derby Italiano, which begins at the top of $1^1/2$-mile chute so that only one, sweeping turn is negotiated. The five-furlong home straight puts the emphasis on stamina.

ITALY

Italian racing, like French, owes much of its foundation to the British and Irish, both those living in the country and the trainers and jockeys they imported. The Derby Italiano was first run in 1884 and won by Andreina, owned and trained by Thomas Rook. The filly was ridden by W. Wright, who won the race another three times up to 1900, and it was 1916 before an Italian jockey broke the foreign domination.

Federico Tesio and his wife, Donna Lydia, established Italian racing as an international force. The Tesios produced great racehorses in spite of modest resources, developing an intimate knowledge of the character of their animals. Tesio won his first Derby Italiano with Guido Reni in 1911 and he, either independently or in partnership, or his heirs racing under the name of his stud, Razza Dormello-Olgiata, won the race another 25 times up to 1969. Winners included Nearco (1938), who is male line ancestor of many of the horses racing today, but not Ribot – by Tesio – who missed the race through injury but won the Prix de l'Arc de Triomphe in 1955 and 1956 as well as the 1956 King George VI And Queen Elizabeth Stakes.

These champions, and others, came from a country which was producing no more than 400 foals a year. Even now, when racing is much more competitive, Italy produces a relatively small number of foals (1,950 in 2005). But Italy's pool of horses in training is augmented by breeders who board their mares elsewhere, particularly in Ireland, and by owners who purchase racehorses from foreign markets.

There are two premier racetracks in Italy. One is Capannelle, which was built in 1926 and is situated eight miles from the Colosseum in Rome. It has a turf course and an interior dirt course, along with a trio of training tracks, and conducts race meets from March through mid-June and from September through November.

San Siro, Italy's other major track, is in the northern sector of Milan and has a history that dates back to 1886. San Siro has three overlapping turf courses, of 2800, 2000 and 1800 metres, and five training surfaces – two grass, two consisting of sand and one of all-weather constitution. San Siro races from mid-March through July and from September through mid-November. It is the home of the Premio Oaks d'Italia, an 11-furlong event won in 2005 by Gyreka. San Siro also annually hosts the Gran Criterium, an eight-furlong event for two-year-olds, and the Gran Premio de Milan and the Gran Primio del Jockey Club, both of which are for three-year-olds and upwards.

All told, Italian racing featured nine Group 1 events in 2005, along with 17 other races of either Group 2 or Group 3 stature. The country's impressive stakes programme is a plus not only for its native horsemen, but for German racing interests as well, who have began conducting raids with regularity on Italy's more prominent events since the early 1980s. Kallistro provided the Germans with their first success in the Derby

Italiano in 2000. A tradeoff of sorts is occurring in that during past decade German stallions have increased in popularity among Italian breeders.

UNIRE is the ruling body for Italian racing, taking over the responsibilities of the Jockey Club, Societa des Steeple Chases and the trotting authorities. Prize money in Italy, however, is distributed by the Ministry of Finance. But UNIRE officials have their hands full given that approximately 23,000 races are conducted in the country annually. Of these, approximately 5,300 are held on the flat, and slightly fewer than 400 are jumping events. French horses continue to dominate the prominent jumping events at Rome, Milan and Merano.

THE NETHERLANDS

Attempts to establish a full-time dirt course at Schaesberg, in the south-east, in the 1970s, failed, leaving Duindigt as the only home of the tiny Dutch thoroughbred industry. Even Duindigt, near The Hague, usually stages only two or three flat races on its trotting cards. The Derby, run in early July, has no trouble attracting a big field but that is the exception. It was won by the German-trained Scarface in 2000 but most of the equine traffic is in the opposite direction and Dutch horses have enjoyed steady success in minor races in Germany.

For the whole of 2004, only 130 thoroughbred races were run in The Netherlands, and the country's breeders produced only 16 registered foals.

Global picture: Courses vary from right-handed to left, flat to jumps, sand to turf, but every one has a weighing room.

NORWAY

Ovrevoll offers the only thoroughbred racing in Norway, a country with ten harness racing tracks. The Oslo course prospered in the 1960s and 1970s and recovered its old confidence at the end of the century, applying for two of its big races, the Polar Million Cup and Marit Sveaas Minnelop, to become European Group 3 in 2001. It has good sponsors, some ambitious owners who pay big prices, not least 120,000gns for Pretty Girl, runner-up in the Tattersalls Houghton Sales Stakes at Newmarket in September 2000, and an excellent record in the top Swedish and Danish races.

Wido Neuroth, perennially the champion Scandinavian trainer, was involved in a messy doping scandal in 2005 – when his horses drew five positive samples in Norway and two more in Sweden. Neuroth blamed his veterinarian, and issued a statement: "This has nothing to do with me and nobody can provide evidence that I recognised any of the medicines that the vet was using on my horses." The vet, who was allowed to continue running his practice, blamed Neuroth. Regardless, Neuroth got off by paying some small fines. He kept his licence and his status intact for (among other things) having sent Valley Chapel out in 1999 to win Scandinavia's Triple Crown, the first time any horse had accomplished the feat in 37 years.

POLAND

It was Warsaw's misfortune that its new racecourse, Sluzewiec, opened only a few months before the German invasion of Poland started World War II. The handsome grandstand survived hostilities and the breeding industry was revived but it gradually lost the necessary investment under Communist rule.

There is still little money for new stallions but at least Poland produced a good horse in 2000. Dzamajka, a filly by Juror, won the 2,000 Guineas, Derby, Oaks, St. Leger and the principal weight-for-age race, the Wielka Warszawska. In 2004, Poland produced 493 thoroughbred foals, and it remains a country with potential.

RUSSIA

The Soviet Union was once proud of its racing, winning the Preis von Europa at Cologne three times with Anilin (1955–57) and with Aden in 1978. Soviet horses also challenged for the Prix de l'Arc de Triomphe, Washington DC International, Grand National and other great races around the world. Interest and investment gradually waned, however, and the Russian Stud Book is currently unacceptable, partly because of the use of artificial insemination and partly because no one could afford to update it.

Racing returned to the Moscow Hippodrome in 2000 for the first time in nine years. Moscow had become too expensive and the sport was restricted to Pyatigorsk, in the Caucasus, and Rostov-on-Don. The Moscow Derby, which dates back to 1892, now anchors the annual Nasibov Memorial Cup which is named after the heralded Russian jockey Nikolai Nasibov. The 2005 Russian Derby went to the two-year-old colt Smertin, who prevailed by seven and a half lengths under jockey Magomed Kappuschev.

Inside out: Horses tend to run rather wider than normal when negotiating the bushy bends at Merano.

SLOVAKIA

Slovakia – which gained its independence when Czechoslovakia split up – is the only former Communist country where racing still receives some support from the State. Bratislava staged 18 days in 2000 with another seven divided between Topolcianky, Novy Tekov, Senica and Surany. Bratislava has attracted owners from elsewhere and the 1998 Slovak Derby was won by the Russian-owned Temirkanov. It also likes to feature top jockeys and Michael Kinane rode Temirkanov while Gerald Mossé rode the German-trained Lauf nach vorn to win the 2000 Derby. In 2004, Slovakia introduced 136 registered thoroughbred foals.

SPAIN

It can be argued that an impressive revival of horse racing is occurring in Spain. At the turn of the 20th century, the Hipodromo Costa del Sol in Mijas became the first new Spanish racecourse to open in 25 years. It primarily races during the winter, serving as a haven for horsemen throughout Northern Europe, and offers the highest prize money in the country. It is the home of the Spanish Derby, Spanish Oaks, the Mijas Grand Premio and the Spanish 2000 Guineas. The Seville Hipodromo, which now operates under the same management as the Mijas track, is on an upswing.

Meanwhile, racing in Spain's capital and largest city, Madrid, has yet to recover fully from a downturn that reached its nadir in 1996 with the closing of the Hipodromo de la Zarzuela, which had once been the focal point of Spanish racing. After a fiscal shakeup and renovations, Zarzuela reopened, and it currently runs in the spring and in the fall. San Sebastian, in Spain's Basque Country, may be the best located facility for Spanish horsemen, in that it allows jockeys, trainers and owners regular opportunities to make raids on French prizes.

In 2004, Spain conducted 395 thoroughbred races, and the country's breeders produced 203 thoroughbred foals. Both figures reflect an improving economic climate for the sport.

SWEDEN

While harness racing is the dominant equine sport in Sweden, the thoroughbreds certainly have their moments of glory. Taby Galopp, located in the northern suburbs of Stockholm, opened in 1960 and now stages about 50 days of racing per year, spread out over ten months, with March and April being dark. Floodlights were installed at Taby in 1965, and it is one of Europe's main pioneers concerning evening racing.

Border raids: San Sebastian, in Spain's Basque region, gives local trainers easy access to France and the rest of Europe.

Taby resembles American racecourses. It has left-handed turns and a dirt track approximately eight furlongs in circumference, with a grass course on the inside. Taby is the home of a pair of Group 3 events, the 12-furlong Stockholm Cup International and the Taby Open Sprint Championship. Recent Stockholm Cup winners include Labirinto, who shipped in from France in 2003, and the English invader Collier Hill, who took the top prize in 2004.

The Lordagskomben is a handicap event run every Saturday at either Taby or at Jagersro. It draws small on-site crowds, but is part of a weekly jackpot bet that wins valuable exposure for flat racing. The Jagersro track is in Husie, which is a district on the eastern side of the city of Malmo. Jagersro was one of the first European tracks to install an all-weather surface. It races 25 days per year, from April through mid-November, and is home to the Svenskt Derby.

SWITZERLAND

Enthusiasm carried the small world of Swiss racing quite a way in the last quarter of the 20th century. Many of those in the sport have full-time jobs elsewhere while the return on investment for owners is lower even than that in Britain. Switzerland did not even have a Derby until 1981, when the first winner was Beyssac, Swiss-owned but trained in France, the typical profile of most of his successors. Tiger Groom, in 2000, was the sixth winner in nine years trained at Chantilly by Robert Collet.

The Derby is held at Frauenfeld, Zurich, on the day of the Grand Steeple Chase de Paris, guaranteeing the availablity of top French jockeys. Katoleme, who won it in 1987, became the first Swiss-trained winner of a Group race the following year. More important was the victory of La Sylphide, one of just 76 thoroughbreds foaled in Switzerland in 1996, in the Group 3 Prix Penélope at Saint-Cloud in April 1999.

Zurich has a second course, Dielsdorf, where the manager, Markus Graff, is also an owner with Mark Johnston and regularly brings horses from England. The 10 Swiss courses include Avenches, opened in 1999 and now the headquarters of the Swiss Jockey Club, and one which everyone should see, St. Moritz. The year begins with three Sundays on one frozen lake at Arosa and then moves on to three more at St. Moritz, ending with the Grosser Preis. Racing consists of a mixture of flat racing, trotting and skijoring, in which thoroughbreds pull drivers on skis.

TURKEY

One of the success stories of recent years, Turkish racing first showed its progress with the creation of four international races at Veliefendi,

Istanbul, in 1991. This ambitious programme was soon trimmed to two and even those opportunities were denied in 1998–99 by a ban on the import of horses to Turkey. But they resumed in September 2000, when Caitano won the Bogazici (Bosphorus) Trophy and Huambo the Topkapi Trophy. Both victors were trained by Andreas Schutz in Germany.

Veliefendi races from mid-April to mid-November, supported by Bursa from June to September. Izmir and Adana each race twice a week when Veliefendi is shut. A minor course opened at Sanliurfa in the 1990s and a more significant one at Ankara in 1999. The Elazig Hipodrumo hosted its first race in 2000.

For a long time all horses had to be homebred. The only way to improve was to import in-foal mares. George Thomas (by Godswalk) arrived in this way and won the 1990 Gazi Kosusu (Derby) in record time. He went on to sire Caprice, the 2000 winner of that race. Important changes had taken place in the meantime. The importation of foreign-bred foals was allowed from 1995 and a new stallion policy introduced in 1997.

The Turkish Jockey Club founded the National Stud at Izmit in 1971. Rich from a huge expansion in off-course betting, it bought the 1986 Breeders' Cup Turf winner, Manila, in 1997. Since then it has added two Kentucky Derby winners Sea Hero and Strike the Gold, the 2,000 Guineas winner Doyoun, and many others. In 2004, Turkish breeders produced 1,381 registered thoroughbred foals.

Former YUGOSLAV STATES

Some racing was conducted on the dirt at Belgrade throughout the dismemberment of the former Yugoslavia. With more settled conditions in **Serbia** in 2000, Group races were also run on turf courses at Karadjordjevo, Sabac, Bogatic, Pozarevac and Zobnatica. A race meeting was held at Sarajevo, **Bosnia**, as soon as possible after the lifting of the siege of the city. Another breakaway republic, **Croatia**, attracted Slovakian runners to Zagreb and Sinj in 1996 but Samuel Sokol, the trainer involved, did not repeat the experiment. **Slovenia** has a fledgling breeding industry with 28 mares in 1999, in which year it staged 14 races.

Winter racing: Playground of the rich and famous, St. Moritz's snow season provides racing in stunning scenery.

UNITED STATES OF AMERICA

MORE THOROUGHBRED RACES are run annually in the United States than in any other country. The U.S.A. boasts over one hundred tracks in some 30 states. Year-round live racing takes place in many jurisdictions, including New York, Pennsylvania, West Virginia Florida, Kentucky, Louisiana and California. In addition, the simulcasting of races from other locations takes place at tracks and off-site wagering parlours throughout the land. A few states such as California offer only simulcasts. But the vast majority of states where pari-mutuel betting is legal offer a mixture of live and simulcast events.

Six furlongs is the distance run most often in the U.S.A. The majority of horses are bred for speed, and races are carded accordingly. Middle-distance events ranging from seven furlongs to 1⅟₁₆ miles rank second in frequency. Route distances of 1⅛ miles or further are typical in stakes, although the number of exceptions to this has grown in recent times. Approximately 53,400 races are contested in the U.S.A. each year. About 1,880 of these are stakes, of which 475 bore graded status in 2006, including 104 that were designated as Grade 1.

The most prominent meeting in the U.S.A. is the one annually staged at Saratoga, between the Catskill and Adirondack mountain ranges in upstate New York. The meet comprises 36 racing days from late July to Labor Day (the first Monday in September). In 2006, the Saratoga schedule included 31 graded stakes, of which 13 bore Grade 1 status.

Saratoga runs when the weather is warm and the trees and meadows are in full bloom, attracting a large crowd. In downstate New York, however, Aqueduct conducts live racing six months each year, including the whole of the winter, when the harsh wind snaps off Jamaica Bay, snowfall is often heavy and on-site crowds often number fewer than 3,000.

Such are the contrasts of U.S. racing, which now operates year-round in northern and southern climates alike, and in the west too. The only day when tracks are universally dark in the U.S.A. is at Christmas.

The Western counterpart to Saratoga is Del Mar, founded in 1937 by a group that included

Around the clubhouse turn: Saratoga, in upstate New York, annually hosts North America's most prestigious meet.

CHURCHILL DOWNS

Founded in 1875, the Louisville track annually hosts the Kentucky Derby, and is one of the most revered facilities in all of North American sports. In recent years, Churchill has undergone a $121-million renovation, but it has also dramatically altered its historic appearance – Churchill's famed twin spires are now flanked by corporate suites and give the impression they've shrunk. Churchill's one mile dirt oval includes a 1,234-foot stretch run, which is one of the longest in North America. Inside is a seven-furlong turf course. In 2006, Churchill was host to the Breeders' Cup for the sixth time.

Golden State: Santa Anita, California, home of the Santa Anita Handicap, exemplifies the excellence of west coast racing.

the movie star and singer, Bing Crosby. Del Mar races 42 days per annum, from late July to mid-September. It is located within a mile of the Pacific Ocean, and has long advertised itself with the slogan, "Where the surf meets the turf." Del Mar joins with Hollywood Park and Santa Anita to make a powerful Southern California circuit.

Since 1971, North American racing has annually honoured its equine and human champions with Eclipse Awards, which are named after the great 19th century stallion. Award recipients are determined by representatives from three organizations: the National Thoroughbred Racing Association (also known as the NTRA); the Daily Racing Form; and the National Turf Writers Association. Winners are determined by whoever receives the majority (or plurality) of the ballots cast.

Although Eclipse Awards are intended to herald the achievements of performers across North America, it is virtually impossible to receive one without competing in the U.S.A., particularly in the major racing centres of New York and/or Southern California.

Tracks in these two areas hosted 239 (more than half) of the graded events staged in the U.S.A. in 2006, including 71 (more than two-thirds) of the Grade 1 stakes.

Next in line of significance are stakes at Kentucky's tracks, primarily Churchill Downs and Keeneland, which in 2006 hosted 30 Grade 1 events between them. The Kentucky Derby, of course, is America's most prominent race, and Kentucky Derby weekend, with the Friday

Kentucky Oaks card and the Saturday Derby programme, quite arguably constitutes the premier racing festival on the planet. The Oaks card in 2006 lured an on-site crowd of 108,065; the following afternoon's Derby drew 157,536. On both days, the vast majority of the crowd was jammed into the Churchill infield, where the general admission price was $40.

Central Kentucky is the headquarters of the Keeneland Association Inc., a not-for-profit organization situated on 921 acres on the western outskirts of Lexington. Keeneland conducts annual three-week race meetings in April and October – its average daily purse distribution for the spring session in 2006 was $652,894, a figure unmatched by any other track (including Saratoga) in North America. Keeneland is also the world's most prominent thoroughbred auction house. In 2005, gross receipts for horses auctioned at Keeneland totalled $744.41 million.

Responsibility for maintenance of The American Stud Book, which ensures integrity of the breed in the U.S.A., Canada and Puerto Rico, is entrusted to the Jockey Club, which was founded in 1894, and has major offices in Lexington and New York City. Administration of the regulatory aspects of American racing is largely left to the individual states, although all derive their codes from the Jockey Club's Rules of Racing. Reciprocity exists among states, and an individual ruled ineligible to participate in one U.S. racing jurisdiction is often denied access in all others as well.

In recent years many of the major U.S. tracks have come under the control of consortiums. Churchill Downs Inc, a publicly held company, now also owns and operates Arlington Park near Chicago (home of the Arlington Million), Calder Race Course in South Florida, Ellis Park in western Kentucky, Hoosier Park in neighbouring Indiana, Fair Grounds in New Orleans and co-owns Kentucky Downs. Frank Stronach's Magna Entertainment owns and operates several tracks, including Santa Anita, Golden Gate Fields in Northern California, Gulfstream Park in South Florida, Lone Star Park in Texas, and Laurel Park and Pimlico in Maryland.

In New York, the major tracks – Saratoga, Aqueduct and Belmont Park – are operated by the New York Racing Association Inc. (NYRA), which is charted by the state, pays taxes but awards no dividends. NYRA has been subjected to intense scrutiny and criticism in recent years for unsound business practices, and may soon be under new operational control.

In 1998, the NTRA was founded, with the mission of increasing "thoroughbred racing's public awareness, fan base and total pari-mutuel handle and to improve the economic conditions of the thoroughbred racing industry as a whole". On 1 January, 2001, the NTRA and Breeders' Cup Ltd merged to create one of the most powerful organizations in the sport.

THE SEVEN MOST INFLUENTIAL LEADERS IN THE U.S. THOROUGHBRED INDUSTRY

◆ James E. Bassett III, trustee emeritus and director, Keeneland Association Inc; member, the Jockey Club; director, Breeders' Cup Limited.

◆ Robert N. Clay, member, the Jockey Club; director, Breeders' Cup Limited; director, National Thoroughbred Racing Association; master, Three Chimneys Farm.

◆ William S. Farish, vice chairman, the Jockey Club; Former chairman, Churchill Downs Inc., director, Breeders' Cup Limited; master, Lane's End Farm.

◆ Thomas H. Meeker, president and CEO, Churchill Downs Inc., director, National Thoroughbred Racing Association; president, Triple Crown Productions Inc.

◆ Ogden Mills Phipps, chairman, the Jockey Club; Trustee, New York Racing Association Inc.; director, Breeders' Cup and National Thoroughbred Racing Association.

◆ Frank H. Stronach, chairman, Magna Entertainment; Director, Breeders' Cup Limited; master, Stronach Stables and Adena Springs Farm.

◆ Daniel G. Van Clief Jr., chairman emeritus, Breeders' Cup and National Thoroughbred Racing Association; President, Fasig-Tipton; member, the Jockey Club; Board member, American Horse Council.

CANADA & CENTRAL AMERICA

No bunching needed: The track at Woodbine, which was reconstructed for the 1996 Breeders' Cup, is up to 120 feet wide.

CANADA

Woodbine, the Toronto course which staged the 1996 Breeders' Cup, dominates Canadian racing just as the province of Ontario dominates Canadian breeding. The first Woodbine opened in 1874 but was replaced by the present version – on the north-western edge of the city – in 1956, although it continued to race under the name of Greenwood until 1993. Now the only other Ontario course is Fort Erie, across the U.S. border from Buffalo.

Woodbine was reconstructed for the Breeders' Cup with a 1¹/₂-mile turf course, compared to the seven furlongs or mile circuits at most of its North American rivals. It is also the only one on the continent which surrounds the dirt track. That was also rebuilt in 1994 while the inner turf course was converted for harness racing, making Woodbine the only racetrack in North America capable of staging both sports on the same day.

It is also the home of most of Canada's great races, starting with the Queen's Plate, for Canadian-bred three-year-olds on the first Sunday of July. First run in 1860, it is the oldest race in North America. Three Grade 1 events, mid-September's Woodbine Mile and the Canadian International and E.P. Taylor Stakes, one month later, all attract international runners.

E.P. Taylor (1901–89) was the driving force behind the development of Woodbine and the breeder of Canada's greatest horses, Northern Dancer, winner of the 1964 Kentucky Derby and

Queen's Plate, and his son Nijinsky, the last winner of the English Triple Crown (in 1970).

Canada has always been overshadowed by the United States and many of its best horses, trainers and jockeys race there at least part of the time. The weather is an important factor, because no racing is possible at Woodbine from early December to the end of March. Canadian breeding is governed by the U.S. Stud Book authority but, so far, demands for greater recognition have been directed more against American control of the Graded race programme. Canada established an independent system in 1999.

In recent years, Ontario tracks have been allowed to add slot machines and casino table games to their gambling menu, and the resulting revenues have allowed for huge increases in purses at Woodbine.

Race tracks in western New York, such as Finger Lakes and Buffalo (harness) Raceway, now have slot machines, too, as does the Senaca Niagara Casino in Niagara Falls. These operations have cut deeply into Fort Erie's business – traffic no longer freely flows there from the U.S. side of the bridge, and Fort Erie's purses dropped by 46 per cent in 2005.

What Fort Erie does continue to have is the Prince of Wales Stakes, sandwiched between Woodbine's Queen's Plate and Breeders' Stakes. The three races constitute Canada's Triple Crown, which has been swept seven times, by the likes of With Approval in 1989 and Dance Smartly in 1991 and most recently by Wando in 2003.

MEXICO

American influence has always been strong in Los Estados Unidos de Mexico. Agua Caliente, in Tijuana – where the Australian champion Phar Lap won his first, and only, race in North America in March 1932 – relied on visitors from California. Ciudad Juarez was another track relying on cross-border custom. And, when racing was revived in Mexico City at the Hipodromo de las Americas in 1943, it thrived because wartime restrictions had halted the sport in California, sending many of the horses south.

Agua Caliente fell on hard times and ceased live racing about 1990, switching to betting on other tracks, while betting and business taxes caused problems in the capital. Racing there came to an abrupt halt in August 1996. It restarted under the part management of Lone Star Park, Texas, in 2000 but made only a halting recovery.

PANAMA

One of the first countries to establish a school for jockeys, Panama has a remarkable record in that field. Laffit Pincay Jr, the world's most successful rider, who passed the 9,000 mark at Santa Anita in October 2000, is just the best known of a steady flow of good jockeys, many of whom imitate him and seek their fortune in the U.S. Racing at the Hipodromo Presidente Remon, is a mixture of events for local-breds and (mostly cheap) imports from the States. Robert Perez, who is one of the leading owners in New York, usually brings a few of these U.S.-

> ## WOODBINE
>
> Woodbine, near Toronto, is Canada's leading racecourse and its refurbished turf course, opened in 1994, is widely-regarded as the best in North America. The main, left-handed dirt oval is nothing special – one mile round, it has chutes for seven-furlong and 1¹/₄-mile races. In contrast, the turf course is fully 1¹/₂ miles around and – in places – up to 120 feet wide. In June and August, Woodbine stages the first and last legs of the Canadian Triple Crown – the Queen's Plate on dirt and the Breeders' Stakes on the turf. It is also home to a pair of top-class international events – the Atto Mile in mid-September and, four weeks later, the 1¹/₂-mile Canadian International.

breds home each year after they have shown some ability.

BARBADOS

Garrison Savannah, a tight, right-handed, six-furlong turf circuit just outside Bridgetown, is well known to tourists. They run 22 times a year in three seasons although racing is pretty continuous, mainly on Saturdays and at fortnightly intervals, between October and April. The third season, of which the Barbados Derby is the climax, is between June and August. The big race is the Gold Cup, currently sponsored by Sandy Lane, on the first Saturday of March. Three raiders from Trinidad won it in the 1980s and Iron Lover from Martinique was successful in 1983, but the locals have kept the prize at home since 1989.

Incitatus, the 1997 winner, went on to take the Grade 2 Connaught Cup at Woodbine two years later and become the first ever Barbados-bred winner of a North American Graded race. Both his trainer and jockey, Ronald Burke and Slade Callaghan, respectively, are from Barbados. Another Bajan, Patrick Husbands, was 1999's champion jockey at Woodbine.

JAMAICA

Caymanas Park, in St. Catherine, Kingston, is an American-style track – though on a slightly larger scale – in a country that is increasingly American-influenced. It races about eight times a month, usually on Wednesdays and Saturdays, and offers betting on simulcast racing from a range of American tracks the rest of the time.

Caymanas Park is a nine-furlong dirt circuit with a two-furlong straight. In addition, chutes allow a straight five-furlong course and nine-furlong events to be run round a single turn, the former unknown in the U.S. and the latter only at Belmont Park. The classics are for local-breds, mostly sired by American horses. But the biggest day features the Red Stripe Superstakes in November. Red Stripe sponsors four big races that day, restricted to horses bred in Jamaica, Barbados or Trinidad, plus an international jockeys competition.

MARTINIQUE

Flat racing started at the Hippodrome de Carrere, at Fort-de-France, in the 1970s. Horses are either local-breds or imported from France and, since the island is still considered part of France, they are entitled to run there without restrictions and to be handicapped on their Martinique form. Many leading French jockeys ride in the Grand Prix de Martinique in early January.

There is a little racing on the neighbouring island of **Guadeloupe**.

PUERTO RICO

Opened in 1976, El Nuevo Comandante lies in Canovanas, 12 miles east of San Juan. It is a typical American dirt track, with a one-mile oval and a 300-yard straight. Entrance, parking and racecard are all free, but the course can afford it because betting has increased steadily since the modernization of off-course facilities in 1991. They race five days a week with Tuesdays and Thursdays blank. Racing is divided between local-breds, who have their own Triple Crown, and imported horses. Just occasionally a cheap import turns out to be something exceptional as Bold Forbes did with five wins from five runs in 1975. Sent back to the U.S., and ridden by Puerto Rico's greatest jockey – Angel Cordero Jr. – Bold Forbes won the Kentucky Derby and Belmont Stakes.

El Comandante hosted the Caribbean's two international races, the Clasico del Caribe and Clasico Confraternidad in December 2000, when they were both won by Venezuelan horses, My Own Business and High Security. The course is operated by Equus Entertainment, an American company. The same corporation built the Hipodromo V Centenario in the **Dominican Republic**, opened in 1992 to celebrate the quincentenary of the arrival of Christopher Columbus, and also has courses in Colombia, Panama and Uruguay.

TRINIDAD

Racing in Trinidad, formerly conducted on three courses, was centralized at Santa Rosa Park, Arima, after its reopening in 1994. What had been a right-handed turf course, was relaid as a left-handed, 1m ¹/2f American-style oval.

However, turf racing was restored to the calendar in April 2000, depriving Barbados' Garrison Savannah's claim of possessing the only turf course in the Caribbean, but firing local trainers with the ambition to win the big race on that island, the Sandy Lane Gold Cup. There are about 400 horses in training in Trinidad, but Santa Rosa has capacity for another 200. They race about 40 days a year.

Racing went through a bad patch in the 1990s, when most of the betting was with bookmakers and on simulcasts from the U.S., ignoring the local product. However the Arima Race Club, which operates the track, agreed to co-operate with the bookies and also gained television coverage. They now want to celebrate their renewed prosperity with a Caribbean Championship Day, on the first Saturday of December.

Bajan sunshine: Garrison Savannah in Barbados is on the tourist trail and has the best racing in the Caribbean.

SOUTH AMERICA

ARGENTINA

Argentina has the grandest racing tradition in South America. However, inflation caused chaos throughout Argentine life in the final 30 years of the 20th century and the currency was not stabilized until the peso was linked to the U.S. Dollar in 1992. Off-course betting was developed at about the same time and racing entered an era during which the ratio of prize money to costs was one of the world's best. However, betting turnover declined by more than 20 percent in 2000, and the relatively high levels of prize money are unlikely to be maintained.

San Isidro, in the suburbs of Buenos Aires, is owned by the Jockey Club and races mainly on turf, although it has installed a dirt course for minor races. Palermo, otherwise known as the Hipodromo Argentino, is a dirt track in the city. Both are left-handed courses. Argentines expect their horses to handle both and to run in the big events at each course. Classic horses have a choice of Guineas races on turf and dirt at the two courses before the Gran Premio del Jockey

SAN ISIDRO

San Isidro, Argentina's leading racecourse, is 14 miles north of Buenos Aires, deep in the heart of the Pampas. It stages 120 days racing throughout the year on its left-handed turf course, which is over 1¹/₂ miles around. There is a straight five-furlong sprint course plus chutes for seven-furlong and 1¹/₂-mile races. The course has an unhurried atmosphere yet early morning training sees some 4,000 horses using the track. A day's racing can contain anything up to 14 races, beginning in mid-afternoon and ending under floodlights. San Isidro's biggest race is the Gran Premio Carlos Pellegrini, run over 1¹/₂ miles in mid-December.

Club, over 1¹/₄ miles on turf at San Isidro, and the 1⁹/₁₆-mile Gran Premio Nacional, on dirt at Palermo. The two courses form a circuit which is completed by La Plata, about one hour's drive from Buenos Aires. Between them they race all week and all year, with plenty or races and

runners. Two-year-olds do not begin racing until April or May. They change age on July 1 but the season keeps right on, with the classics being run between August and November. Good horses have their first break after the big races in December. Statistics are kept by the year rather than by season.

Argentina has another 30 courses but they are strictly local with the exception of Rosario, which has produced some good horses. Palermo has one meeting with races restricted to the best provincial horses. Argentine horses thrived in the U.S. but their record in the Gran Premio Latinoamericano, which visits a different country each year, is unimpressive away from home. Many of the best jockeys are foreigners, but there is opposition to them. Pablo Falero, the top rider in the 1990s, is from Uruguay.

BRAZIL

American owners paid little attention to Brazil until Romarin, Sandpit and Siphon began winning big races in the USA in the 1990s. Those

three were sent north by their owners and alerted bloodstock agents to what U.S. racing needs most, tough older horses. After Riboletta won five Grade 1 races in California and New York in 2000, her younger brother Super Power, Quari Bravo and Straight Flush – all big-race winners – were quickly snapped up.

Rio de Janeiro and Sao Paulo are not far apart but their racing might as well be in neighbouring countries, for they do not compete, except in the big races. The Jockey Club Brasileiro at Gavea, in Rio, and the Jockey Club de Sao Paulo at Cidade Jardim have matching rather than clashing programmes, catering for the same type of horses at different times.

Thus the Paulista Triple Crown takes place between October and December while that at Gavea follows between February and April. And the GP Sao Paulo and accompanying big races are in mid-May while the GP Brasil weekend is early in August. Both courses race four or five times a week, all year round and using both turf and dirt tracks.

There is still much less racing of two-year-olds than usual although *pencas* – short distance contests for young horses which have not competed in an official race – are popular in country districts. There is some good racing at

Cristal, in Porto Alegre, capital of Rio Grande do Sul, and at Taruma, in Curitiba, but the sport is dominated by the two great cities.

CHILE

Racegoers face a punishing experience if they stay for a full programme at either of the courses in Santiago, the Club Hipico or Hipodromo Chile. Cards of 18 races, normally with ten or more horses, rarely longer than six furlongs and with a high proportion of handicaps, are the standard fare. The Club Hipico races on Mondays and the Hipodromo Chile on Saturdays while they share Thursdays. Antofagasta, Concepcion and the Valparaiso Sporting Club – in the neighbouring seaside resort of Vina del Mar rather than Valparaiso itself – complete the circuit.

Valparaiso, where the principal season is in January and February, presents the only racing of significance outside the capital. Its big race is El Derby on the first Sunday of February, attracting good three-year-olds, but the real Chilean Derby is El Ensayo, run at the Club Hipico in November. Club Hipico and Valparaiso are right-handed turf courses. The Hipodromo de Chile is a left-handed dirt track. It offers more races over distances beyond one mile. It also has its own classic series of Guineas, Gran Criterium and St. Leger ending in mid-December.

Jose Santos has been the most consistent Chilean rider of recent years in the U.S. His brothers, Manuel, Pedro and Luis, have all been regular visitors to Scandinavia and Manuel has been Norway's champion several times. Fernando Diaz rides in Sweden most summers and Sweden has a Chilean trainer, Francisco Castro. Chilean-born Richard Castillo, was raised in the States and was already established as a jockey when he came home in 1997, followed by his brother Freddy, who arrived with his American wife, Michelle – who rode 176 winners in her first full season – late in 1999. Juan Cavieres has been the dominant trainer, setting a record of 185 wins in 1995 and surpassing it in 2000.

COLOMBIA

Racing vanished for eight years until it was revived at Los Comuneros, about 15 miles outside Medellin, in 1996. The course, which had no grandstand until the following year, is a 6½-furlong dirt oval. It became part of the Equus group, which operates in three other countries in the region, in 1998. Los Comuneros races every Saturday and on alternative Thursdays. Other tracks have been projected for Bogota and Cali.

Keeping busy: Not only does San Isidro in Argentina race on 120 days per year, some cards contain 14 races.

ECUADOR

Quito racecourse was snapped up for an extension to the airport in the early 1980s and no substitute was built. Racing at 9,000 feet must have been very testing in any case. The sport is now confined to sea level at Buijo, outside Guayaquil. Señorita won 1999's Clasico Confraternidad at Presidente Remon, Panama City, the greatest achievement of any Ecuador-bred horse.

PERU

Monterrico, a suburb of Lima, is Peru's only racecourse. It has both turf and dirt courses, including a straight five furlongs. It races four days a week, under lights on weekdays, all the year round. Peru is south of the equator but briefly experimented with switching its breeding season to Northern Hemisphere time in 1970. Peruvian horses had an excellent record in the continent's international races, but today, many of the best horses at Monterrico are imported as yearlings. Most top jockeys go abroad for richer pickings too.

URUGUAY

Uruguay's racing was still in good enough shape to host the first running of the Gran Premio Latinoamericano at Maroñas, in Montevideo, in 1981. Maroñas was already in decline, however, and closed altogether in 1997. It may be rebuilt by Bakery s.a., but the government and the sport will have to cede control of off-course betting for 30 years. Uruguay still has 11 provincial tracks, a large number for such a small country, and Las Piedras, north east of the capital, has ensured that the big races were not discontinued.

VENEZUELA

Oil made Venezuela rich and racing at La Rinconada, Caracas, once offered some of the best prizes in the world. Owners like Robert Sangster and the Aga Khan were both tempted briefly to place horses there. Those days are long gone. Venezuela's greatest horse was Canonero II. He arrived in the U.S., unknown and unconsidered, only days before taking the 1971 Kentucky Derby and Preakness Stakes. Canonero II was fourth in the Belmont Stakes and went home. High Security, who won 17 races in a row, did most of his winning at Santa Rita, on the eastern side of the mouth of the Lago de Maracaibo, near the Colombian border, rather than in Caracas. The only other course is at Valencia, between the two. La Rinconada races Saturday, Sunday and Monday and the others during the week. Jockeys travel between them regularly but horses stay mostly at their home base.

MIDDLE EAST

DUBAI

From informal beginnings in the late 1980s, racing in Dubai grew to be among the most significant in the world in the space of a few years. It has also forced a quick change in European attitudes to racing on dirt even though Nad Al Sheba now has a top-class turf course of its own.

Nad Al Sheba was originally laid out in 1986, but was moved and rebuilt before the first official race meeting in 1992. It owes its fame to the creation of the Dubai World Cup in 1996. World Cup Day 2006 (March 25) offered prizes of $21.25 million, richer even than the Breeders' Cup. Its appeal had also been widened progressively to include two valuable races on turf while the four dirt races had been augmented by the UAE Derby worth $2 million

in 2006, making it as rich as rich as the contest for which it was meant as a preparation, the Kentucky Derby. In fact, Dubai has added a fanfare for the start of a racing year which had become overloaded with huge autumn prizes.

Basic racing there belongs to horses with wonderful pedigrees but only modest abilities, sharpening up only when the Godolphin team begins to sort out which horses will later compete in Europe. But this is changing too. Les Benton, formerly in charge of Flemington racecourse, Melbourne, is now chief executive of the Emirates Racing Association and has introduced new influences.

The first sale of unraced New Zealand-bred horses was held late in 2000 and supported by the Pearls of Dubai Sales Graduate Stakes, run on dirt the following March with a prize of 1 million

dirhams (approximately $250,000). Graeme Rogerson, who already held trainers' licences in New Zealand and Australia, set up a subsidiary stable, which included many Pearls of Dubai horses, and a similar South African stable is planned.

There were also an increased number of amateur races in which the brothers, Sheikh Rashid and Sheikh Hamdan, two sons of the most important man in Dubai, Sheikh Mohammed, were regular participants. The future of Dubai as a racing country, and the worldwide involvement of the Maktoum family, will be in their hands.

LEBANON

One of the miracles of the troubles in Lebanon was the speed with which a meeting was

organized in Beirut. The racecourse is on the demarcation line between the warring factions. Another miracle was the emergence of racehorses from shell-damaged buildings and other unlikely shelters. Most of the horses are Arabians and they ran in 393 races in 1999.

SAUDI ARABIA

Prince Khalid Abdullah is one of the greatest owner-breeders in the world, with large strings racing in America, Britain and France, all produced by his Juddmonte Farms. Other Saudi owners, such as Prince Sultan al-Kabeer and Ahmed Salman's Thoroughbred Corporation, have also played a significant part. But what they accomplished abroad had little bearing on the conduct of the sport at home.

Racehorses were imported but however able or expensive – often they were both – they began again as maidens. Well-bred stallions were imported to cover Bedouin-owned mares free of charge. That the Stud Book was not recognized did not matter because the existence of African

Studying form: Racegoers scour the newspapers looking for likely winners on Dubai Gold Cup day at Nad Al Sheba in 1999.

Horse Sickness on the Yemeni border – though hundreds of miles from any thoroughbred – made export impossible.

Changes have begun. The Stud Book is now recognized and the export rules have changed. Markan became the first Saudi-trained horse to race abroad when he ran twice in Dubai early in 2000. Several trainers were brought in from America, notably John Veitch, whose season in Riyadh restored his career at home.

Good horses contest the two great races at Riyadh, the Crown Prince Cup and King's Cup, both run over 3,353 metres (2m 147y). Two events for Saudi-breds, the particular interest of Prince Sultan, with the same names but over shorter distances, are staged on the same days. Most racing is at Riyadh, all on Fridays, but the horses move to Taif in the western mountains in the hottest part of the year. After a rest, the new season begins there.

UNITED ARAB EMIRATES

Dubai, which is the headquarters of the Emirates Racing Association, is such an important country in racing terms that it is dealt with separately. However it is one of seven sheikhdoms in the UAE and, politically, it is junior to **Abu Dhabi**. Nad Al Sheba and Jebel Ali, the two courses in Dubai, staged 35 of the 55 fixtures in the 2000–01 season which lasted from 9 November to 14 April. Of those, Nad Al Sheba staged 26 days and most of the big races. The Abu Dhabi Equestrian Club ran 15 days on its turf course but the underused Ghantoot (in Abu Dhabi) turf course only one. **Sharjah**, the first emirate to have racing, in 1983, reopened after a rebuilding

On his own: High-Rise on the Al Quoz gallops with the Dubai skyline shimmering in the early-morning heat haze.

programme with four meetings in 2000.

Abu Dhabi sponsored the Prix du Jockey Club (French Derby) for several years and still sponsors two races for Arabians at Chantilly on that day. This is the part of the sport which interests this emirate most and the big races in Abu Dhabi are all for Arabians, many of which are imported from France and the United States. There are regular challengers from neighbouring **Oman** in Arabian races and, less frequently, from Qatar.

Arabians also dominate at Al Rayyan, in **Qatar**, and a typical card includes only two thoroughbred races, one for homebreds and one for imported horses. Qatar already has an international day, at which one of the first runners from Saudi Arabia was a winner in 2000.

There is also racing up the coast in **Bahrain** and, perhaps, an extension of the ERA circuit could happen one day. That said, Oman, Qatar and Bahrain are independent of the UAE.

JAPAN

Looking for a clue: Racing papers in hand, spectators watch the horses parade before the 1999 Japan Cup at Tokyo (Fuchu).

NO OTHER RACING COUNTRY can match the superlative prize money in Japan, and only Hong Kong can rival the huge crowds and remarkable betting volumes that accompany Japanese racing on a regular basis. However, recent economic problems have reminded horsemen in Japan that sport cannot rely on endlessly rising income. Other forms of gambling, including casinos, threaten racing's pre-eminence, while the rigid control of the sport's ruling body, the Japan Racing Association (JRA), is also being questioned.

The JRA was established in 1954 under the control of the Ministry of Agriculture, Forestry and Fishery. It runs ten principal courses, two giant training centres and all the subsidiary activities that support racing. The three premier JRA courses are Tokyo, which is 20 miles west of the centre of the city whose name it bears, Kyoto, which is six miles south of that city, and Hanshin, which is 12 miles from Osaka. The JRA actually operates only nine of its tracks per annum, as one is always closed for refitting. Tokyo Race Course, originally constructed in 1933, recently underwent major renovations, a circumstance that necessitated the country's most prominent event, the Japan Cup, being run at nearby Nakayama Race Course in 2002.

A second tier of Japanese tracks exists – lumped under the title of Regional Public Racing – run by local municipal governments under the National Association of Racing (NAR). Japan has a population of approximately 128 million, and the country's only other sport that generates as much interest as racing is baseball.

Tokyo is also the home of the Japanese Derby and Japanese Oaks. Its turf course is 2,116 metres in length, and its interior dirt course has a length of 1,878 metres. Tokyo, Nakayama, Kyoto and Hanshin are all on Japan's main island of Honshu, as are Chukyo, Fukushima and Niigata. The JRA's Hakodate and Sapporo courses are on the northern island of Hokkaido, which is also home to 80 per cent of Japan's breeding industry. Kokura is on the southwestern island of Kyushu. The combined JRA meetings add up to a 40-week season with 288 days of racing per year, nearly all of which are conducted on Saturdays and Sundays.

Regional racing, which takes place on 30 courses, has fewer limitations. Much of it occurs on weekday evenings, and it varies from small country tracks to Ohi in the Tokyo Bay area, which attracts large crowds to its night meetings. Chukyo, Niigata and Sapporo are all leased from the JRA for NAR meetings. Most NAR racing is on

dirt, while racing on JRA courses is divided between dirt and turf. Regular Member, a son of the 1993 Epsom and Irish Derby winner Commander in Chief, earned $516,000 for his victory in the Derby Grand Prix at Morioka in 2000. For comparison, that same year, Sinndar's prize for winning the Epsom Derby was $918,981, and Fusaichi Pegasus' prize for winning the Kentucky Derby was $888,400.

At one time, the division between JRA racing and NAR racing was rigid, but horses can now transfer en masse from JRA to regional racing at the end of each year, and there is increasing cooperation and competition between the two levels. Winning certain NAR races now qualifies horses to compete in JRA graded events. In addition, Japan has become keen to play a part in international racing on the dirt. Japan introduced a new graded stakes programme in 1997, comprising 12 JRA events and 35 on NAR courses. The Japan Cup Dirt was created in 2000, to be annually run at Tokyo on the day prior to the Japan Cup itself. In 2005, the Japan Cup Dirt, won by Kane Hekili, had a purse of $2.07 million, making it the world's fourth-richest race on dirt.

The Japan Cup, whose first running in 1981 was won by the American-trained Mairzy Doates, was the country's first step into international racing. Even now, foreigners are not allowed to have horses in training in Japan, and domestic owners are not allowed to import horses that have already competed elsewhere. Prior to 1993, only the Japan Cup and the insignificant Fuji Stakes were open events. Since then, the number has risen so that 24 were open in 2005.

At the same time, the number of races open to foreign-breds has increased. The permitted proportion was set at 15 per cent in 1984, rose to 20 per cent in 1989 and is now well over 50 per cent. Some of the major races, including the classics, were restricted to homebreds, but foreign-foaled horses are now granted a limited number of places.

Foreign-born sires, however, constitute the mainstay of Japan's breeding industry. Sunday Silence, who won the Kentucky Derby, Preakness Stakes and Breeders' Cup Classic and was North America's Horse of the Year in 1989, stood at Shadai Stallion Station on Hokkaido and sired 75 stakes winners prior to his death in 2002. Sunday Silence's first crop had yielded the Japanese Champions Dance Partner and Marvelous. In the years immediately following his passing, Sunday Silence continued to rank at the top of Japan's general sire list. Silver Charm and Charismatic, who each captured a pair of jewels in North America's Triple Crown in 1997 and 1999, respectively (Charismatic was also Horse of the Year), went on to become anchoring forces at the Japan Bloodhorse Breeders' Association's Shizunai Stallion Station.

Horses from foreign countries finished 1-2-3-4 in the first two runnings of the Japan Cup. Katsuragi Ace, in 1984, and Symboli Rudolf, in 1985, were the only two home-trained winners in the Japan Cup's initial 11 runnings. But in the ensuing years, the home team has become a formidable opponent. TM Opera O, who triumphed in 2000, was the sixth Japanese winner in nine years. In 2001, Japanese horses, led by victorious Jungle Pocket, swept the top five positions in the Japan Cup. Japanese representative Tap Dance City raced to victory in 2003, and Japanese horses, led by the victorious Zenno Rob Roy, took the top three positions in the Japan Cup in 2004.

One of Japan's most interesting races is the Arima Kinen. Run annually at the end of the year at Nakayama, its field is selected partly by popular vote. In April, 2000, Nakayama was also the venue for Japan's first international steeplechase event, with local favourite Gokai defeating Boca Boca from France and The Outback Way from England. Like the Japan Cup, the chase is an invitational event, with all expenses paid. Foreign owners have to pay their own way to Japan's other international races, and tend to take into account the considerable risks and costs more than the enormous prize monies on offer.

Many of the JRA's restrictions weigh most heavy on trainers. They have excellent facilities, but if headquartered on the island of Honshu, they must train either at Miho, which serves Tokyo and the east, or Ritto, which serves Kyoto and the west. There are some excellent private training facilities in Japan – the Yamamoto Centre owned by the Shadai Group being one of them – but horses conditioned there must then spend at least ten days at Miho or Ritto before they can compete. A different situation now prevails on the island of Hokkaido, where horses can ship directly from approved training centres to the regional racecourses.

Jockeys in Japan are also under restriction, both as to movements and contacts, from the day before racing. But their financial rewards are bountiful, and many of the best, including national hero Yutaka Take, also ride abroad during the quiet summer months.

Glittering prizes: Fuchu, 20 miles from Tokyo, hosts Japan's most valuable races including the £1.5million Japan Cup.

REST OF ASIA

CHINA

No one knows what the future holds for racing in China but a lot of people want to be ready to sell horses there the instant the opportunity arises. Japan helped to equip Longtou Farm with 19 mares and two stallions, Mejiro Ardan and Thrill Show, in a project which also has British finance and technical help. Australians have exported over 700 horses but failed in attempts to begin joint racecourse-building ventures. Ireland, in the shape of Coolmore, has a joint breeding enterprise.

How the Chinese will react remains uncertain. People have been sent to England and Japan to train as stud book officials and a China Stud Book could be recognized by 2002. Vets have also been sent abroad for further experience. But no one from China attended the Asian Racing Conference held in Singapore in March 2000 and they are in no hurry to take the obvious course of using the knowledge built up in Hong Kong. Everything depends on attitudes towards betting and the balance of power between the regions, some of which are strongly in favour, and central government, which is generally against. Development has been slow and the first and biggest course, at Guangzhou, was closed by official order in 2000 though reopening was anticipated.

HONG KONG

Hong Kong is one of the wonders of the racing world. Pre-war it was a junior partner of Shanghai, where huge sums were bet on Mongolian ponies ridden by amateur jockeys – and the word shamateur was invented. This was the tradition Hong Kong inherited but the HK Jockey Club announced in August 1971 that the sport would become completely professional, importing trainers and jockeys, and racing only thoroughbreds.

Happy Valley was the sole course until Sha Tin – built partly on land reclaimed from the sea – was opened in 1978. Sha Tin became the principal venue and stages the four International races, all but one with Group 1 status, in December and the Queen Elizabeth II Cup in April. These are invitational events and the HKJC pays all expenses for the visitors as well as offering huge prizes.

Balanced judgement: Jockeys need to keep their horses under control as they take the sharp bends of Happy Valley.

For many years, local horses tended to be outclassed in Hong Kong's international races. But this ceased to be the case with Fairy King Prawn's victory in the 1999 Hong Kong Sprint. The following year, Industrialist defeated the French runner Jim And Tonic in the QEII Cup. Most significant of all, in 2002 Precision accounted for the Hong Kong Cup, Olympic Express won the Hong Kong Mile and All Thrills won the Sprint, providing the home team with three triumphs in the four December events.

Industrialist had formerly raced in Britain under the name of Mensa. Owners have to win a place in a ballot to be allowed to import a horse but, once successful, they are free to change the name to something more propitious. Most choices concern money, winning or luck with a generous addition of superlatives. Robert Ng, who races as Lucky Stable, bought the British-trained Daliapour days before he won the 2000 International Vase and transferred him to Ivan Allan, trainer of Fairy King Prawn, after the race.

Hong Kong is keen to raise the quality of its horses, about 80 percent of which arrive without previous experience. The active population is about 1,200 and they contest 658 races at 78 meetings. Nearly all racing is on Wednesdays and either Saturday or Sunday, but never both. Sha Tin stages 48 meetings and Happy Valley the remaining 30, of which 25 are on Wednesday

nights. All but three Saturdays at Happy Valley are run under lights but Sha Tin's programme is more varied, though it does include a dozen night meetings. There is no racing from mid-June to early September.

Betting reaches gigantic levels, the biggest of all being the final day of the season and the most frenetic the final race. Turnover on this otherwise ordinary handicap in 2000 was $HK269,066,160 (£21,153,000 – US$31,700,000) but even this sensational sum was 5.1 percent down on the previous year.

Racing is still very international but six of the top 10 trainers, in terms of winners, in the

Reclamation project: The turf for Sha Tin racecourse in Hong Kong was taken from the mountain in the background, the land was reclaimed from the sea surrounding the Chinese dependency.

1999–2000 season were locally born, including the champion, and former champion jockey, Tony Cruz. Judged on earnings, however, he was only third behind the Australian David Hayes and Ivan Allan. Five South Africans, led by Robbie Fradd, topped the jockeys followed by two from France and four from Britain. The top Chinese rider was only 12th.

INDIA

Racing was not among national priorities after independence, although it still provided welcome winter work for British jockeys. Like most other sports, though, it has become increasingly popular as industry and business prosper.

The distances between racing centres are huge, which maintains the relative independence of India's nine courses, but a national sport is developing even if taking a horse from Calcutta to run in Bangalore involves a two-day train journey. Not many do so but

three big races, headed by the Wills Indian Turf Invitation Cup, require such a journey. These races should take place at a different course each year, in late February or early March, but Calcutta had problems in 2000 and the meeting was rescheduled for Bangalore in April.

Each course has its own classic series and, in some cases, more than one. Calcutta has its Monsoon Derby as well as the Wills Calcutta Derby in January. And there are Derbys at Bangalore in January and July. Indian courses love Derbys and the grand sounding Nilgiris Derby, at Udhagamandalam (Ootacamund), and North India Derby, at Delhi, both turn out to be relatively minor events at one mile.

The classics that really matter, and which all have Indian in their title, are at Mahalaxmi, Mumbai (Bombay). The Derby, for just-turned four-year-olds at the beginning of February, is sponsored by McDowell, a brewery owned by Vijay Mallya, whose UB Group also owns another big sponsor, Kingfisher. Mr. Mallya is one of

India's biggest owners. But not as big as Dr. MAM Ramaswamy, who won the Derby in 2000 with Smart Chieftan, ridden by Richard Hughes. He has over 1,000 horses, including breeding stock while Cyrus Poonawalla, who bred Smart Chieftan, has a still larger breeding operation. Hughes has enjoyed several good seasons in India but plentiful winter opportunities nowadays mean only a few foreign jockeys choose India.

Breeders are able to import well-bred stallions like Placerville, a Group 2 winner at Royal Ascot and sire of Smart Chieftan, and the current champion Razeen, beaten favourite in the 1990 Epsom Derby. More recent arrivals include Don't Forget Me and Tirol, two winners of both the English and Irish 2,000 Guineas. Few horses are imported to race, however, thanks to a combination of customs duties and the fact that they have to concede nine pounds to local-breds. Indian horses rarely compete abroad so there is little indication as to their current standard.

In at the top: Kranji racecourse officially opened in March 2000 and it immediately vaulted Singapore into the upper echelon of the Asian racing world.

MACAU

Macau is only half an hour by water taxi from Hong Kong, but this former Portuguese colony started professional racing later and there was never any chance that the two would form a circuit. Standards are lower all round. However, though the number of horses in training is similar to Hong Kong, Taipa racecourse operates at least twice a week and is open all year. Macanese horses have 1,200 chances a season compared to 660, admittedly much richer ones, in Hong Kong. Taipa races on Tuesdays and at weekends, using whichever day Hong Kong is inactive during the season there. Of the 110 meetings, 65 are at night, while 49 are on turf, 51 on sand and the remaining 10 are a mixture.

MALAYSIA

The loss of Singapore removed much of the talent, both human and equine, from the Malayan Racing Association circuit. Fixtures clash each Saturday

KRANJI

Kranji opened in March 2000 to replace Bukit Timah. A state-of-the-art facility which is connected to the city centre, some 12 miles to the south, by excellent road and rail links, it stages over 60 racedays throughout the year, with two six-week breaks at the start of March and end of August. The main course is a 1¹/4-mile, flat, left-handed oval. The turf is reinforced with netlon fibres and its sand base prevents waterlogging despite Singapore's high rainfall. The inner 7¹/2-furlong dirt course is used for Friday night fixtures. Kranji's big races include two international events – the Singapore Cup in early March and the Singapore Airlines International Cup and Sprint in May.

while a Singaporean ban on the import of horses from the mainland, because of an outbreak of disease, prevents competition. Three clubs remain in the MRA circuit, Selangor (at Kuala Lumpur), Perak (at Ipoh) and Penang and they still operate on both days of consecutive weekends, turn and turn about. Each course simulcasts its racing to the other two for betting, as they have done, originally with just sound, since 1961.

Kuala Lumpur has a new course of its own, at Sungei Besi, which opened in October 1993. At present, the MRA has lower prizes than Singapore and cannot attract the same quality of horses or jockeys. It is encouraging a wider selection of native-born riders, though. The big race is the Yang di Pertua Negeri Gold Cup, for Malaysian-trained horses, around the turn of the year.

SINGAPORE

By the single device of building a new course, Singapore repositioned itself in the racing world. The island had been independent of Malaysia since 1965 but its racing at Bukit Timah continued to be one-quarter of the Malayan Racing Association circuit. Work on the dazzling new course at Kranji began in 1996 and it opened in September 1999, although the grand opening was delayed until the first running of the Singapore Airlines International Cup on 4 March 2000. The Singapore Turf Club showed it wanted independence with the announcement of a new programme of international and local feature races. But the break was made complete by an outbreak of disease on the mainland, which closed the frontier to equine traffic.

Singapore needed new horses, trainers and jockeys to support its ambitions, and all arrived from Australia and New Zealand, although there were some horses and jockeys from South Africa

and Zimbabwe too. Half a dozen European jockeys also fly in on three-month contracts in the winter.

However, the champion trainer and jockey of 2000, Malcolm Thwaites and Jumaat Saimee, respectively, gained their experience on the MRA circuit. They also combined to win the first International Cup with Ouzo, who beat the French-trained favourite, Jim And Tonic, by a neck. Godolphin won the Singapore Plate with Timahs and the Derby with All The Way, both of which travelled from Dubai. Kranji stages 62 days' racing a year, with six-week breaks in March–April and September–October. Singapore's future on the international stage seems assured.

SOUTH KOREA

Until the economies of the Asian tigers crashed, South Korean racing was expanding rapidly. The sport was introduced in 1920 and there were nine tracks when the Japanese seized control in 1937. A decline was halted by the introduction of a computerized Tote in 1985 and the building of a new course at Kwachon, on the old equestrian centre site from the 1988 Seoul Olympics. There has been only one other course in Korea in recent years and that races mainly locally bred ponies.

Kwachon opened in 1989 and attracts average crowds of 50,000. It operates 94 days a year, all on weekends and usually with 12-race cards. Horses were imported cheaply, mostly from New Zealand, to establish the sport but the Korean Racing Association opened Wondong Stud in 1984. It imports stallions and offers free services to breeders, with the eventual aim of producing 75 percent of the horses needed. Another course is planned at Kwang Ju, near Pusan.

Opposite: **Under starter's orders:** The start of this race on a dirt track in Morocco could not be called an even break.

AFRICA

KENYA

Ngong, six miles west of Nairobi, is the country's only course. Opened in 1951, it races on 30–35 Sundays a year with a close season from July to September. There is a local breeding industry but Zimbabwe-breds have become popular. They are generally superior so buyers have to pay a levy. Women have long played an important role as trainers and, more recently, as jockeys. Patsy Sercombe has been champion trainer and her daughter, Leslie, champion jockey more than once. Julie Andrade was one of the first women to ride a Derby winner.

MAURITIUS

Champ de Mars, in Port Louis, is one of the oldest courses in the world. Racing has been staged there since 1810, shortly after British forces ousted the island's previous French rulers. The course is showing its age, however, and the latest project is a new track at Les Pailles, either

in competition or as a new home for the Mauritius Turf Club.

The MTC season consists of 26 Saturdays between May and November. Most of the horses, and many jockeys, are imported from South Africa, including the 2000 champion Mark Khan. Other riders come from Australia, France and Zimbabwe, while home-produced pilots, led by Yashin Emamdee and Dinesh Sooful, had their best-ever seasons in 2000. Racing attracts wide interest but has been badly affected by a ten percent betting tax, plus an extra two percent on winnings, introduced in 1997.

MOROCCO

Royal support has made Morocco the leading racing nation in north Africa and the only one with significant thoroughbred racing. Two Frenchmen, Joel Seyssel and Gerard Rivases, have been trainer and jockey for the royal Ecurie Les Sablons since the 1970s. Morocco was under French control until 1956 and racing is run to French rules. Four courses offer pari-mutuel betting, Anfa (Casablanca), Souissi (Rabat), El Jadida and Settat.

There are another seven provincial courses, at Fez, Kenitra, Khemisset, Khenifra, Marrakech, Meknes and Oujda. All are non-betting meetings on Saturday mornings, usually starting at nine. Oujda is just three miles from the frontier with Algeria.

Morocco's richest races are the Grand Prix Hassan II, for local-breds at Souissi in early November, and the Grand Prix Mohammed V, in which imported horses can run, at Anfa at the end of that month. Anfa races mainly on Fridays and Souissi on Sundays. Admission is free.

TURFFONTEIN

A city-centre racecourse, Turffontein is just 3km from the heart of Johannesburg in South Africa. It is the jewel in the crown of the Phumelela group, the larger of two organizations which operate most of the country's courses. The most important race staged there is the Summer Handicap, which was revived in 2000. Turffontein is a right-handed track with a circuit covering approximately 2600 metres. There is also a 1200-metre straight course, which meets the round one about 800 metres from the post. It is generally acknowledged to be one of the stiffer courses in the country, because there is a steady 400-metre climb from 1200 metres out. There is a 1400-metre start just off the tight final turn into the straight. The straight course, however, almost is flat and Turffontein's 1200-metre races are fairly undemanding as sprints go.

SENEGAL

Senegal is not included for the quality of its racing but for two other reasons. As one of the most advanced countries in West Africa, it is important to the Pari-Mutuel Urbain (off course tote) in Paris, which promotes betting on French racing throughout the former French empire. It is also merits mention for the sheer joy of the crowds, who festoon winning jockeys with notes. Their style may be rudimentary but the riders return with money in their mouths, their boots and anywhere else it will fit.

SOUTH AFRICA

London News, winner of the Queen Elizabeth II Cup in Hong Kong in 1997, and Horse Chestnut, successful by $5^1/2$ lengths in the Broward Handicap, on his American debut at Gulfstream Park in January 2000, gave South Africans the proof they needed that they could still produce top-class horses. Unfortunately Horse Chestnut, who had won eight of his nine races at home, broke down and was retired to stud in Kentucky rather than travelling on for the Dubai World Cup as planned.

His route was so indirect because of an outbreak of African Horse Sickness in the Cape, the one province which had long been clear of the disease. He had to spend 60 days in quarantine in the U.S. but would not have been accepted in Dubai without doing so. The outbreak also caused the abandonment of plans to attract international runners to the J & B Met, a Group 1 event at Kenilworth, Cape Town, at the end of January.

South Africans are keen to promote their stock abroad when the ban is lifted. As well as selling throughout the Southern Hemisphere there are plans to establish stables of South African-owned and bred horses in Singapore and Dubai.

Standards dropped during the latter years of apartheid. Both racing and the country generally need economic stability and ways to minimize inter-racial violence. In the meantime, the price of land and horses must appear cheap to anyone with confidence in the future. Although prize money is moderate, training costs are also relatively low.

Racing is managed by two groups, Gold Circle, responsible for the three courses in KwaZulu-Natal and two in Cape Town, and Phumelela, which runs the remaining eight. But only 13 courses in such a huge country means that the sport is a mystery to most people outside the cities, although racing does now have its own television channel. Discussions aimed at achieving a merger between Phumelela and Gold Circle began in 2000. Success would produce national tote and marketing strategies.

South Africa was the first country to start a jockeys' school and all hopefuls must attend its five-year course, which begins with education but ends almost entirely on horseback. The school at Summerveld, the largest training centre in the southern hemisphere, has produced many good riders. Michael Roberts and Basil Marcus are based in England while South Africans dominate racing in Hong Kong, where Marcus was champion five times. The top five jockeys in Hong Kong in 1999–2000 were all South Africans. To be champion at home requires endless travelling and, once they have proved themselves, many jockeys look elsewhere. The school has begun producing more black and more girl apprentices and in June 2000, Gift Funeka, 17, became the first black rider to win a Group race.

Phumelela revived the Summer Handicap at Turffontein, Johannesburg, in November 2000 as the country's richest race. Like the Rothmans July Handicap and other big races, it is dominated by older horses. Horse Chestnut dominated his contemporaries in the classics but it was his defeat of older horses in the J & B Met which established his reputation. Only six of the top 20 earners in 1999–2000 were three-year-olds while the highest earning two-year-old was 22nd. In comparison, there were two juveniles and 12 three-year-olds among the top 20 in Britain and Ireland in 1999. Four of the South African top 20 earners were imported from New Zealand while the leader, El Picha, is an Argentine-bred.

ZIMBABWE

Political chaos has taken its toll on all aspects of life. Owners have emigrated, trainers and jockeys look for work elsewhere and sponsors withdraw. The number of trainers at Borrowdale Park, Harare, almost halved between 1995 and 2000 while only two or three remained at Ascot, Bulawayo. Rothmans dropped sponsorship of the Zimbabwe Derby, won in 2000 by Willscore, a son of the leading stallion, Tilden, a former Irish sprinter. Zimbabwe-breds have become popular in South Africa and they are becoming more familiar to backers there, too, after an agreement which made Borrowdale the sole betting shop fodder on 19 Mondays. Racing continues most of the year except August.

REST OF AFRICA

Algeria has flat racing on the six courses, Djelfa, El Eulma, Msila, Oran, Tiaret and Zemmouri, but it is more heavily biased towards Arabians. Algeria is also the only north African country to have trotting.

Racing at Kassar Said in Tunis, **Tunisia**, is almost entirely for Arabians.

AUSTRALIA

THERE WAS A SIGNIFICANT development when racing started at Moonee Valley on 15 September 1883; W.S. Cox designated it a proprietary venture. When the Victorian government subsequently signalled its opposition to proprietary racing, Cox sold the site to the Moonee Valley Racing Club in 1917.

Five years after this the MVRC first conducted the W.S. Cox Plate, which has since come to be regarded as the weight-for-age championship of Australasia. Run over 2040 metres, the event has been won by the greatest racehorses of Australia and New Zealand including Phar Lap, Chatham, Rising Fast, Noholme, Tulloch, Tobin Bronze, Gunsynd, Kingston Town, Strawberry Road, Better Loosen Up, Super Impose, Octagonal, Saintly, Might And Power and Sunline. The Cox Plate was won on a record seven occasions by legendary trainer Tommy Smith, who headed the Sydney training premiership an incredible 33 times between 1952–53 and 1988–89.

The winding-up of the last of the remaining proprietary clubs in New South Wales in 1943 led to the formation of the Sydney Turf Club, which races at Rosehill and Canterbury. In 1957 the STC launched the Golden Slipper Stakes – an event Smith captured a record six times – over 1200 metres for two-year-olds at Rosehill in the autumn. Now respected as the third most important event in Australia – behind the Melbourne Cup and the Cox Plate – the Golden Slipper Stakes has been won by some of Australia's most brilliant speedsters.

Remarkably, Star Kingdom, who, racing as Star King won the Gimcrack Stakes and eight races in England, sired the Golden Slipper Stakes' first five winners, Todman, Skyline, Fine And Dandy, Sky High and Magic Night. The race has also had a noteworthy impact on the

Calm before the storm: The field parades in the enclosure before going down to the start at Rosehill Gardens, Sydney.

Australian breeding industry with former winners Todman, Vain, Luskin Star, Marscay, Rory's Jester, Marauding and Canny Lad later becoming influential sires.

During those formative years there were a number of important innovations. Among these was the publication of the Australian Stud Book in 1878 and a year later a weight-for-age scale was uniformly adopted by all leading Australian clubs. However, Australia's sheer size – 7,686,900 square kilometres – made a cohesive administration for the industry difficult as the 20th century dawned.

It led to the formation of the organization known as the Australian Principal Clubs on 5 April 1904. Renamed the Australian Racing Board in the 1990s, the principal clubs, which

Upper Hunter Valley, has a heritage as a thoroughbred farm that dates back to 1842. Arrowhead's modern-day operation, however, was founded two decades ago when the stallions Bellotto, Kenmare, Prego and Rancher arrived for stud duty. All four became sires of Group 1 winners. Perhaps most importantly, Arrowhead became the Southern Hemisphere base for Danehill, who sired more stakes winners than any other stallion in the world.

Shuttle sires (those who do service during both the Northern and Southern Hemisphere breeding seasons) continue to carry a major workload at Arrowhead – the 1995 Breeders' Cup Juvenile winner, Unbridled's Song, has in recent years served dual duties at Arrowhead and at Taylor Made Farm in Central Kentucky. Shuttle sires also hallmark John Magnier's Coolmore operation, which has established a powerful foothold in Australia's Hunter Valley, making sires such as Danehill Dancer, the 2000 Kentucky Derby winner Fusaichi Pegasus, Galileo, Johannesburg, Rock of Gibraltar, Royal Academy and Tale Of The Cat available to Australian breeders. And, going into 2006, the stud fee for Encosta De Lago – who also stands for Coolmore – was $176,000, making him Australia's most expensive stallion.

In 2004–2005, 364 racecourses operated in Australia, which is an enormous number, considering the country has only 20.24 million inhabitants. Race days (days when individual meets were conducted) totalled 2,745, and a total of 19,968 races was run. Crowd figures at the meets total about two million annually, making racing Australia's third-most-attended

Top two-year-old: The Golden Slipper Stakes at Rosehill Gardens is the most valuable juvenile race in Australia.

meet on a regular basis, have since remained responsible for the rules of racing operating around the nation. Local rules of racing may be adopted by individual principal clubs provided that no such rule is contrary to an ARB one.

The upward spiral in the fortunes of the racing industry was accompanied by an enormous improvement in Australia's thoroughbred breeding stock in the late 20th century. The Woodland Studs Syndicate, headed by the Ingham brothers, remains at the

forefront of this expansion despite Jack's death. Going into 2006, the Woodlands stud colony was anchored by Octagonal, who had carried the Inghams' all-cerise colours to Horse of the Year honours in Australia in 1995–1996; and by Octagonal's son, Lonhro, referred to by racing fans as "the Black Flash", who was crowned Australia's Horse of the Year for 2003–2004, and whose first-season stud fee of $66,000 was the highest ever for a colonially-bred stallion.

But Woodlands had plenty of competition. Arrowhead Stud, located in Scone in Australia's

FLEMINGTON

The first official race meeting was held at Flemington's present site, then known as Melbourne Racecourse, on 3 March 1840. It adopted the name of Flemington after a butcher, Bob Fleming, who had his premises on an adjoining road. Flemington – six kilometres from the centre of Melbourne – was controlled by the Governor of New South Wales and administered by six trustees until 1851, when the Port Phillip District became a separate entity. The rivalry that existed between Victoria and New South Wales was so intense that Flemington, and other Victorian courses, defiantly began racing left-handedly, while New South Wales continued to race right-handed. Australia's most famous horse race, the Melbourne Cup, was first run there in 1861. Flemington has a straight 1,200-metre course to go with the oval, which is 2,314 metres miles) round, with a straight of 453 metres. Other big races include the Victoria Derby, Victoria Racing Club Oaks, Australian Cup and Newmarket Handicap.

sport. At any one time, 10,000 racehorses are in training in Australia. Group 1 races were 66 in number in 2004–2005, and were complemented by 195 other events bearing either Group 2 or Group 3 status. The principal governing body is the Australian Racing Board, which oversees enforcement of the Australian Rules of Racing.

The actual conducting of the sport is divided into eight sectors: Victoria, where the Victoria Racing Club operates Flemington, home of the Melbourne Cup, and where the Melbourne Racing Club operates Caulfield and Sandown, and the Moonee Valley Racing Club annually stages the Cox Plate; New South Wales, where the Australian Jockey Club races at Royal Randwick and Warwick Farm, and the Sydney Turf Club conducts meets at Canterbury Park and Rosehill Gardens; South Australia, where the South Australian Jockey Club runs meets at Cheltenham, Morphettville and Victoria Park; Queensland, where the Brisbane Turf Club races at Doomben and the Queensland Turf Club conducts meets at Eagle Farm; Western Australia, where the Western Australian Turf Club operates Ascot Racecourse and Belmont Park; Tasmania, where the Tasmanian Turf Club races at Elwick Racecourse and Mowbry; the Northern Territory, where Thoroughbred Racing NT (formerly the Darwin Turf Club) conducts meets at Fannie Bay; and the Australian Capital Territory, where the Canberra Racing Club operates Thoroughbred Park.

A rich heritage resides at the heart of Australian racing – the names of famous horses, trainers and jockeys are familiar to schoolchildren throughout the country. On-track betting at Australia's racecourses includes pari-mutuel systems and a total of 610 licensed bookmakers, the latter of whom offer fixed

odds. Off-track betting is also extensive, with its venues including licensed pubs. In 2004–2005, legal betting on horse races throughout the country totalled $11.71 billion, which represented a slight decrease in action over a period of five years, but was still a healthy figure nonetheless. Prize monies for the season totalled $362 million.

Below: **Party time:** The city of Melbourne effectively shuts down on Melbourne Cup day.
Bottom: **Down the straight:** Flemington is the home of the Melbourne Cup, Australia's most important race.

NEW ZEALAND

IT IS GENERALLY BELIEVED that horse racing in New Zealand dates back to the early 1840s, when meets were held at Auckland, Onehinga and Epsom. Participants, both human and equine, were largely from the military. The Auckland Town Plate, run on January 5, 1841, had a subscription fee of three sovereigns for each participating horse. At Petone Beach on October 20, 1842, an imported horse named Figaro defeated a rival named Calmac Tartar for a purse of ten guineas in a sweepstakes that involved a series of 1-mile heats.

From these very modest beginnings has emerged, more than 160 years later, a New Zealand horse breeding and racing industry that annually produces 4,700 thoroughbred foals and has 52 active racecourses, many of which have heritages that date back well into the 19th century. Hawkes Bay, near the cities of Napier and Hastings on the eastern shore of New Zealand's North Island, was founded in 1845. It is the home of the Kelt Capital Stakes, a Group 1, weight-for-age event contested over 2,040 metres. With a $1-million purse, the Kelt Capital

Stakes is New Zealand's richest horse race – its 2005 winner was Xcellent, who the previous season had been victorious in the New Zealand Derby at Ellerslie.

Riccarton Park, founded in 1854, is home to the New Zealand 1,000 and 2,000 Guineas, both of which are run over 1,600 metres. Avondale, which was founded in 1889, is near Auckland, New Zealand's largest city. The Avondale course is the annual site of the 2,200-metre Avondale Gold Cup Handicap.

Trentham, located about 20 miles north of the New Zealand capital of Wellington, was founded in 1870. It is the annual site of the 3,200-metre Wellington Cup Handicap and 2,400-metre New Zealand Oaks, both of which also have Group 1 status. Trentham's grass course surrounds a figure-eight steeplechase course. For more than six decades, Trentham was also the location of New Zealand's most prominent yearling sale – the graduates of which include the great Phar Lap, who is best known for his racing exploits in Australia, but was actually a New Zealand-bred.

Breeding operations in New Zealand range from the very small to the extremely large. Graham Gimblett, a dairy farmer in Southern Hawke's Bay, owns only one thoroughbred broodmare, but she happens to be Excelo, the dam of the aforementioned Xcellent. On the other end of the scale, Cambridge Stud, owned by Sir Patrick Hogan and his wife, Lady Justine Hogan, has bred nearly 60 individual Group 1 winners during its 34 years of operation. Sir Patrick is credited with having made the biggest impact on New Zealand breeding during at least the past half-century – with his importing of Sir Tristram to do stud duty at Cambridge, commencing in the late 1970s.

Sir Tristram, a son of the 1968 Epsom Derby winner, Sir Ivor, became a nine-times winner of the Dewar Stallion Award, presented each season to the New Zealand-based sire with the greatest progeny earnings throughout New Zealand and Australia. His haul included 45 individual Group 1/Grade 1 winners, which in that category ranks him behind only Sadler's Wells worldwide. Six times, Sir Tristram was Australia's leading sire. His son Brew, out of the 1989 Japan Cup winner, Horlicks, was victorious in the Melbourne Cup in 2000, with New Zealand-bred and trained horses also third and fourth. This actually occurred three years after Sir Tristram's death, but his son, Zabeel, now anchors the Cambridge stallion colony, and has equalled Sir Tristram's record with nine Dewar trophies of his own.

Zabeel's son, Might And Power, led all the way to win the 1997 Melbourne Cup, and went on to win the 1998 Cox Plate in track-record time. But great New Zealand-breds of recent years, however, are not limited to Sir Tristram's family. Sunline, a daughter of Kiwi, won 32 stakes during her five seasons of racing, including consecutive runnings of the Cox Plate in 1999–2000 and the 2000 edition of the Hong Kong Mile. Dubbed "the Queen of the Turf", Sunline is arguably the most popular racemare ever to come out of New Zealand.

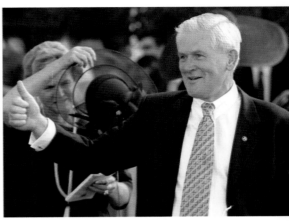

All smiles: Cambridge Stud owner Sir Patrick Hogan.

The country's racing industry has its star human participants, some of whom work in teams. The father-and-son combination of Stephen and Trevor McKee shared training chores for Sunline.

In March, 2006, the initial 14 honours winners were inducted into the New Zealand Bloodstock Racing Hall of Fame in Auckland. Among them were Dave O'Sullivan, who won 11 training premierships titles, and whose 1,877 winners trained in New Zealand remains a record; Lance O'Sullivan, who won a record 12 jockey premierships, and whose New Zealand tally of 2,358 victories is a record as well; Bill Broughton, who won 11 jockey premierships, and was New Zealand's leading rider during the 1940s; Bill Skelton, who was the first New Zealand jockey to record 2,000 career wins; and Richard John Mason, "the Prince of Trainers", who trained 30 Derby winners (which is believed to be a world record) during a career that spanned the years 1880–1932.

Rising stars in recent years include Michael Walker, who, at the age of only 16 won his first New Zealand jockey premiership during the 1999–2000 season.

Coiled spring: The jockeys at Ellerslie have their mounts tense before the starting gates spring open.

ELLERSLIE

Founded in 1874, Ellerslie is New Zealand's premier racecourse, staging 26 days of racing throughout the year, largely on Saturdays. The Auckland track's feature events are the New Zealand Derby (on Boxing Day), New Year's Day's Auckland Cup and, over jumps, the Great Northern Steeplechase, run over four miles and 25 fences in early June. The flat, turf course is level and right-handed, with a home straight of just over two furlongs. The chase course runs close to its flat counterpart but encompasses a number of sharp bends, plus a steep climb, followed by two fences, then a downhill section, on the home turn.

CHAPTER 3

THE MAJOR RACES

If imitation is the sincerest form of flattery, then the Epsom Derby must be the world's most important race. Almost everywhere there is racing can boast of staging a "Derby". Yet, two of England's five classics are older than the race first won by Diomed in 1780, including the fillies' classic, the Oaks, run at the same meeting.

TO AN OWNER, trainer or jockey, a one-mile claimer at a small, country track in front of 100 spectators, may be the biggest race in the world – if their horse wins it. The reality is that there are elite races to which most of the racing world can only dream of being a part. Around the world, life almost comes to a halt on these days as millions of people betting billions watch the race. Many of these 17 races merit places here on prestige, more than the winner's prize-money.

To avoid confusion with similarly-named races, Epsom's Derby is the Derby and the Gold Cup is the Ascot Gold Cup. Sadly, contemporary reports from the early days did not always record the names of the winning trainers or jockeys. However, the winners of 2,250 races are on the next few pages.

St. Leger – the world's oldest classic
The Oaks – fillies only need apply
The Derby – the classic of classics for three-year-olds
(Ascot) Gold Cup – Royal Meeting's gem
1,000/2,000 Guineas – springtime classics
Grand National – testing horse and jockey
Melbourne Cup – Australia stops for this race
Irish Derby – Ireland's biggest race
Belmont Stakes – "Triple Crown" marathon
Preakness Stakes – will Derby form stand up?
Kentucky Derby – one they all want to win
Breeders' Cup Classic – America's richest race
Prix de l'Arc de Triomphe – Europe's champion race
Cheltenham Gold Cup – chasing's real championship
Japan Cup – attracts 150,000 punters
Dubai Cup – world's richest race
Hong Kong Cup – spectacular festival

On the nod: Mark Of Esteem and Frankie Dettori (right) win the 1996 2,000 Guineas from Bijou D'Inde (3) and Even Top.

ST. LEGER

The St. Leger – the oldest of the five British classics for three-year-olds – is run over 1m 6f 132y at Town Moor, Doncaster, usually on the second Saturday in September. It makes up the final leg of the Triple Crown, though the days when it was traditionally contested by the colt who had won the Derby are something of a fading memory.

IT HAS BECOME fashionable in recent years to denigrate the St. Leger as a race of increasingly diminishing status. But one must remember it is Britain's oldest classic, an event richly endowed with well over two centuries of history. There is merit in enjoying it for its longevity alone, and the St. Leger's profile has received boosts in recent years - with Brian Boru honoured as Ireland's champion three-year-old colt in 2003, Rule of Law honoured as England's champion three-year-old colt in 2004 and the front-running victory by Scorpion in the 2005 St. Leger helping to garner him divisional champion status in both countries.

After the introduction of the 2,000 Guineas and 1,000 Guineas in the early 19th century, it became the formula for horses of classic potential to try to win the Guineas, Derby and St. Leger to prove their versatility and toughness through a season. To land the Triple Crown was the hallmark of a top-class colt who would then stay in training at four, with the Gold Cup at Ascot as the big ambition, and then start life at stud as a five-year-old.

But from the 1960s onward stamina became a

Perfect timing: John Reid on Nedawi (blue) comes alongside High And Low and goes away to win the 1998 St. Leger.

- ◆ For three-year-olds
- ◆ Held on the second Saturday in September, at Doncaster
- ◆ Inaugurated 1776

RACE DISTANCES
2 miles, 1776–1812
1m 6f 193y, 1813–25
1m 6f 132y 1826–date

COURSES HOSTING THE ST. LEGER
Cantley Common 1776–77 ◆ Doncaster 1778–1914, 1919–38, 1946–88,1990–date ◆ Newmarket 1915–18, 1942–44 ◆ Thirsk 1940 ◆ Manchester 1941 ◆ York 1945 ◆ Ayr 1989 ◆ No race 1939

TRAINER WITH MOST WINS
16 John Scott

JOCKEYS WITH MOST WINS
9 W. Scott
8 John Jackson and Lester Piggott

dirty word in fashionable flat racing circles and races like the St. Leger and the Gold Cup went through a very barren spell. There was talk on more than one occasion of reducing the distances of both races and, in the case of the St. Leger, opening the race up to horses above the age of three as happened in France and Ireland. Happily this was resisted and the final classic is less beleaguered than once looked likely, and it retains the support of many top owners and trainers.

The race was introduced in 1776 by Colonel Anthony St. Leger, after whom it is named, and was run over two miles at Cantley Common, very close to the site of what is now the racecourse at Doncaster. The winner was an unnamed filly – she was later given the name of Allabaculia – owned by Lord Rockingham and ridden by John Singleton, Sr.

Two years later the venue for the race was switched to the Town Moor where it has been staged ever since, apart from during the two World Wars when it was variously staged at Newmarket, Manchester, Thirsk and York, and in 1989 when it was switched to Ayr when the course at Doncaster subsided during the meeting

due to problems with the drainage.

The first jockey to make an impression on the race was John Mangle, who won it five times, 1780–92, and was first home on another occasion only to be disqualified. His tally was surpassed soon after the turn of the 19th century by John Jackson, who recorded eight successes, 1791–1822, and W. Scott with nine 1822–45.

There were two runnings of the race in 1819 when the local stewards acceded to a request from the disgruntled crowd that the first attempt should be dismissed as a false start, but in the end the Jockey Club ruled that the first attempt was valid and the winner remained the 33–1 chance Antonio. How much of the alleged false start was down to villainy on the part of jockeys is debatable, but there is no doubt that in 1827, when there were 26 starters, a number of jockeys conspired to stage a number of false starts in the hope that the Derby winner and favourite Mameluke would be left at the gate. He was, and in spite of valiant efforts was beaten a length.

There was even worse villainy in 1834, when Derby winner Plenipotentiary was so badly got at that he could barely get to the start, let alone come

ST. LEGER 1776–2005

YEAR	HORSE	JOCKEY	TRAINER
1776	Allabaculia	J Singleton	
1777	Bourbon	J Cade	
1778	Hollandaise	G Hearon	
1779	Tommy	G Lowry	
1780	Ruler	J Mangle	
1781	Serina	R Forster	
1782	Imperatrix	G Searle	
1783	Phoenomenon	A Hall	
1784	Omphale	J Kirton	
1785	Cowslip	G Searle	
1786	Paragon	J Mangle	
1787	Spadille	J Mangle	
1788	Young Flora	J Mangle	
1789	Pewett	J Singleton	
1790	Ambidexter	G Searle	
1791	Young Traveller	J Jackson	
1792	Tartar	J Mangle	
1793	Ninety-Three	W Peirse	
1794	Beningbrough	J Jackson	
1795	Hambletonian	Boyes	
1796	Ambrosio	J Jackson	
1797	Lounger	J Shepherd	
1798	Symmetry	J Jackson	
1799	Cockfighter	T Fields	
1800	Champion	F Buckle	
1801	Quiz	J Shepherd	
1802	Orville	J Singleton·Jr	
1803	Remembrancer	B Smith	
1804	Sancho	F Buckle	
1805	Staveley	J Jackson	
1806	Fyldener	T Carr	
1807	Paulina	W Clift	
1808	Petronius	B Smith	
1809	Ashton	B Smith	
1810	Octavian	W Clift	
1811	Soothsayer	B Smith	
1812	Ottrington	R Johnson	
1813	Altisidora	J Jackson	
1814	William	Shepherd	
1815	Filho Da Puta	J Jackson	
1816	The Duchess	B Smith	
1817	Ebor	Johnson	
1818	Reveller	Johnson	
1819	Antonio	Nicholson	
1820	St. Patrick	J Johnson	
1821	Jack Spigott	W Scott	
1822	Theodore	J Jackson	
1823	Barefoot	T Goodison	
1824	Jerry	B Smith	
1825	Memnon	W Scott	
1826	Tarrare	G Nelson	
1827	Matilda	J Robinson	
1828	The Colonel	W Scott	
1829	Bowton	W Scott	
1830	Birmingham	P Conolly	
1831	Chorister	J Day	
1832	Margrave	J Robinson	
1833	Rockingham	Darling	
1834	Touchstone	Calloway	
1835	Queen Of Trumps	T Lye	
1836	Elis	J Day	
1837	Mango	S Day	
1838	Don John	W Scott	
1839	Charles The Twelfth	W Scott	
1840	Launcelot	W Scott	
1841	Satirist	W Scott	
1842	Blue Bonnet	T Lye	
1843	Nutwith	J Marson	
1844	Faugh-A-Ballagh	H Bell	
1845	The Baron	F Butler	
1846	Sir Tatton Sykes	W Scott	
1847	Van Tromp	J Marson	
1848	Surplice	E Flatman	J Kent
1849	The Flying Dutchman	C Marlow	Fobert
1850	Voltigeur	J Marson	R Hill
1851	Newminster	S Templeman	
1852	Stockwell	J Norman	
1853	West Australian	F Butler	J Scott
1854	Knight Of St. George	Basham	
1855	Saucebox	J Wells	
1856	Warlock	E Flatman	
1857	Imperieuse	E Flatman	
1858	Sunbeam	L Snowden	
1859	Gamester	T Aldcroft	
1860	St. Albans	L Snowden	
1861	Caller Ou	T Chaloner	W I'Anson
1862	The Marquis	T Chaloner	
1863	Lord Clifden	J Osborne	
1864	Blair Athol	J Snowden	W I'Anson
1865	Gladiateur	H Grimshaw	T Jennings
1866	Lord Lyon	H Custance	J Dover
1867	Achievement	T Chaloner	
1868	Formosa	T Chaloner	
1869	Pero Gomez	J Wells	
1870	Hawthornden	J Grimshaw	
1871	Hannah	C Maidment	
1872	Wenlock	C Maidment	
1873	Marie Stuart	T Osborne	
1874	Apology	J Osborne	
1875	Craig Millar	T Chaloner	
1876	Petrarch	J Goater	
1877	Silvio	F Archer	M Dawson
1878	Jannette	F Archer	M Dawson
1879	Rayon D'Or	J Goater	
1880	Robert The Devil	T Cannon	
1881	Iroquois	F Archer	J Pincus
1882	Dutch Queen	F Archer	M Dawson
1883	Ossian	J Watts	
1884	The Lambkin	J Watts	
1885	Melton	F Archer	M Dawson
1886	Ormonde	F Archer	J Porter
1887	Kilwarlin	J Robinson	
1888	Seabreeze	J Robinson	
1889	Donovan	F Barrett	G Dawson
1890	Memoir	J Watts	
1891	Common	G Barrett	J Porter
1892	La Flèche	J Watts	
1893	Isinglass	T Loates	J Jewitt
1894	Throstle	M Cannon	
1895	Sir Visto	S Loates	M Dawson
1896	Persimmon	J Watts	R Marsh
1897	Galtee More	C Wood	S Darling
1898	Wildfowler	C Wood	
1899	Flying Fox	M Cannon	J Porter
1900	Diamond Jubilee	H Jones	R Marsh
1901	Doricles	K Cannon	
1902	Sceptre	F Hardy	R Sievier
1903	Rock Sand	D Maher	G Blackwell
1904	Pretty Polly	W Lane	P Gilpin
1905	Challacombe	O Madden	A Taylor
1906	Troutbeck	G Stern	W Waugh
1907	Wool Winder	W Halsey	H Enoch
1908	Your Majesty	Wal Griggs	C Morton
1909	Bayardo	D Maher	A Taylor
1910	Swynford	F Wootton	G Lambton
1911	Prince Palatine	F O'Neill	H Beardsley
1912	Tracery	G Bellhouse	J Watson
1913	Night Hawk	E Wheatley	W Robinson
1914	Black Jester	Wal Griggs	C Morton
1915	Pommern	S Donoghue	C Peck
1916	Hurry On	C Childs	F Darling
1917	Gay Crusader	S Donoghue	A Taylor
1918	Gainsborough	J Childs	A Taylor
1919	Keysoe	B Carslake	G Lambton
1920	Caligula	A Smith	H Leader
1921	Polemarch	J Childs	T Green
1922	Royal Lancer	R Jones	A Sadler
1923	Tranquil	T Weston	C Morton
1924	Salmon-Trout	B Carslake	R Dawson
1925	Solario	J Childs	R Day
1926	Coronach	J Childs	F Darling
1927	Book Law	H Jelliss	A Taylor
1928	Fairway	T Weston	Fk Butters
1929	Trigo	M Beary	R Dawson
1930	Singapore	G Richards	T Hogg
1931	Sandwich	H Wragg	J Jarvis
1932	Firdaussi	F Fox	Fk Butters
1933	Hyperion	T Weston	G Lambton
1934	Windsor Lad	C Smirke	M Marsh
1935	Bahram	C Smirke	Fk Butters
1936	Boswell	P Beasley	C Boyd-Rochfort
1937	Chulmleigh	G Richards	T Hogg
1938	Scottish Union	B Carslake	N Cannon
1939	No race		
1940	Turkhan	G Richards	Fk Butters
1941	Sun Castle	G Bridgland	C Boyd-Rochfort
1942	Sun Chariot	G Richards	F Darling
1943	Herringbone	H Wragg	W Earl
1944	Tehran	G Richards	Fk Butters
1945	Chamossaire	T Lowrey	R Perryman
1946	Airborne	T Lowrey	R Perryman
1947	Sayajirao	E Britt	F Armstrong
1948	Black Tarquin	E Britt	C Boyd-Rochfort
1949	Ridge Wood	M Beary	N Murless
1950	Scratch II	WR Johnstone	C Semblat
1951	Talma II	WR Johnstone	C Semblat
1952	Tulyar	C Smirke	M Marsh
1953	Premonition	E Smith	C Boyd-Rochfort
1954	Never Say Die	C Smirke	J Lawson
1955	Meld	W Carr	C Boyd-Rochfort
1956	Cambremer	F Palmer	G Bridgland
1957	Ballymoss	TP Burns	MV O'Brien
1958	Alcide	W Carr	C Boyd-Rochfort
1959	Cantelo	E Hide	C Elsey
1960	St. Paddy	L Piggott	N Murless
1961	Aurelius	L Piggott	N Murless
1962	Hethersett	W Carr	W Hern
1963	Ragusa	G Bougoure	P Prendergast
1964	Indiana	J Lindley	J Watts
1965	Provoke	J Mercer	W Hern
1966	Sodium	F Durr	G Todd
1967	Ribocco	L Piggott	Jhnsn Houghtn
1968	Ribero	L Piggott	Jhnsn Houghtn
1969	Intermezzo	R Hutchinson	H Wragg
1970	Nijinsky	L Piggott	MV O'Brien
1971	Athens Wood	L Piggott	Thomson Jones
1972	Boucher	L Piggott	MV O'Brien
1973	Peleid	F Durr	W Elsey
1974	Bustino	J Mercer	WR Hern
1975	Bruni	A Murray	HR Price
1976	Crow	Y SaintMartin	A Penna
1977	Denfermline	W Carson	WR Hern
1978	Julio Mariner	E Hide	C Brittain
1979	Son Of Love	A Lequeux	R Collet
1980	Light Cavalry	J Mercer	H Cecil
1981	Cut Above	J Mercer	WR Hern
1982	Touching Wood	P Cook	Thomson Jones
1983	Sun Princess	W Carson	WR Hern
1984	Commanche Run	L Piggott	L Cumani
1985	Oh So Sharp	S Cauthen	H Cecil
1986	Moon Madness	Pat Eddery	J Dunlop
1987	Reference Point	S Cauthen	H Cecil
1988	Minster Son	W Carson	WR Hern
1989	Michelozzo	S Cauthen	H Cecil
1990	Snurge	T Quinn	P Cole
1991	Toulon	Pat Eddery	A Fabre
1992	User Friendly	G Duffield	C Brittain
1993	Bob's Return	P Robinson	M Tompkins
1994	Moonax	Pat Eddery	B Hills
1995	Classic Cliche	L Dettori	S bin Suroor
1996	Shantou	L Dettori	J Gosden
1997	Silver Patriach	Pat Eddery	J Dunlop
1998	Nedawi	J Reid	S bin Suroor
1999	Mutafaweq	R Hills	S bin Suroor
2000	Millenary	T Quinn	J Dunlop
2001	Milan	MJ Kinane	AP O'Brien
2002	Bollin Eric	K Darley	T Easterby
2003	Brian Boru	JP Spencer	AP O'Brien
2004	Rule Of Law	K McEvoy	S bin Suroor
2005	Scorpion	L Dettori	AP O'Brien

back from it. But the bookmakers, who were inevitably involved in such malpractice, were outwitted in 1836 by Lord George Bentinck, the leading racing administrator of his day and a man determined to clean up the sport as best he could.

His colt Elis was based at Goodwood, Sussex, and, in the days before horse transportation, it was a 15-day walk from there to Doncaster. When bookmakers discovered that Elis was still at Goodwood a week before the St. Leger, they laid the colt to lose vast sums. But they were unaware that Bentinck had built a precursor of the modern horsebox and Elis arrived at Doncaster in plenty of time to win the race, make his owner a lot of money and cost the bookies a small fortune.

Until 1930 it was possible to have a run-off after two horses dead-heated. This was the case with Derby winner Voltigeur in 1850, who beat Russborough at the second attempt and won the Doncaster Cup two days later from the previous year's dual classic winner The Flying Dutchman.

The dominant trainer during the first part of the 19th century was John Scott, who won the race on 16 occasions, starting with Matilda in 1827 and ending with The Marquis in 1862. Other winners included West Australian, who in 1853 became the first horse to win the Triple Crown. Scott regarded him as the best horse he trained; as he sent out the winners of 41 classics that was quite a compliment.

The next winner of the Triple Crown was the French-owned and bred Gladiateur III, who was nicknamed "the avenger of Waterloo" after his successes in 1865. He was followed by Lord Lyon the next year and other top class horses like Ormonde (1886), Isinglass (1893) and Galtee More (1897).

Diamond Jubilee carried the royal colours to Triple Crown glory in 1900 (there was another royal success with Dunfermline in 1977), but the only two colts to land the Triple Crown since Rock Sand, in 1903, were Bahram in 1935 and Nijinsky in 1970. Fillies such as Meld (1955) and Oh So Sharp (1985) have won the St. Leger after successes in the 1,000 Guineas and the Oaks.

THE OAKS

The Oaks was first staged in 1779 and was named after the nearby country house on which the 12th Earl of Derby had taken a lease a few years earlier. The previous year, he and his friends had decided to introduce a race for three-year-old fillies the following summer over the then comparatively short distance of 1½ miles.

THERE WERE 12 RUNNERS for the first Oaks and, appropriately, it was won by Lord Derby's filly Bridget, whose jockey Richard Goodisson won the next two runnings on Tetotum and Faith.

The first jockey to win the Oaks and the Derby in the same year was Sam Chifney, Sr., who did so in 1789 on Skyscraper in the Derby and Tag, one of his four winners of the race, in the Oaks. Chifney, who invented a bit which carries his name, was a talented but conceited jockey who was the first to use come-from-behind tactics, but who may be best remembered for the Escape affair, involving him and the then Prince Regent.

Frank Buckle, who for many years held the record for the number of classic winners by a jockey (27), until Lester Piggott beat it, enjoyed the first of his record nine winners in the Oaks when Niké was successful in 1797, and two years later Eleanor, owned by Sir Charles Bunbury and ridden by J. Saunders, became the first filly to win the Derby, for which she started 5–4 favourite, and the following day she took the Oaks at 1–2.

Niké was the first of 11 Oaks winners trained by Robert Robson, whose exploits earned him the nickname of the "Emperor of Trainers". He won the Derby seven times and the two Guineas races on a total of 15 occasions.

Crucifix, whose owner Lord George Bentinck won the St. Leger with Elis, added an Oaks victory to her wins in both Guineas in 1840 and eight years later her son Surplice won the Derby and the St. Leger, though this was after Bentinck had sold all his bloodstock.

Blink Bonny became the second filly to pull off the Derby–Oaks double in 1870. Owned and trained in Yorkshire by the Scotsman William I'Anson, she started at 20–1 when John Charlton rode her to Derby success over the 200–1 shot Black Tommy, but was a 4–5 shot when she won the fillies classic, two days later.

In 1865 Formosa, ridden by George Fordham, won the Oaks and every other classic apart from the Derby – she dead-heated in the 2,000 Guineas. When Spinaway won the 1,000 Guineas and Oaks in 1875 she set an example which was to be followed by her half-sister Wheel Of Fortune four years later. Fred Archer, who rode both fillies for Lord Falmouth and Matt Dawson, said that Wheel Of Fortune was the best filly he ever rode.

La Flèche, who won the Oaks in 1892, also won the 1,000 Guineas and the St. Leger and may have won the Derby if George Barrett had not ridden an injudicious race. The Derby winner, Sir Hugo, was no match for her at Doncaster. The 1896 winner, Canterbury Pilgrim put her bad temper aside to get the better of the 1,000 Guineas winner Thais, but her real claim to fame is as the dam of Swynford and Chaucer and thus the ancestress of a number of top-class winners, such as Fairway, Colorado, Pharos and Sansovino.

The early years of the 20th century saw Oaks success for some outstanding fillies and the first win for an American-bred filly when Cap And Bells II was successful in 1902. The next three winners were Sceptre, Our Lassie and Pretty Polly. Sceptre raced for her first two seasons for the gambler and adventurer Bob Sievier, who bought her as a yearling for a then staggering 10,000gns. He took over her training as a three-year-old when, having begun her season in the Lincoln Handicap, she won both Guineas, finished fourth in the Derby, for which she started favourite two days before romping home in the Oaks, and she added the St. Leger to her tally in September.

Strange though it sounds nowadays, running a potential classic filly in the Lincoln was not that unusual a century ago. The 1903 Oaks winner Our

Not so fast: Aliysa lost the 1989 Oaks on a failed dope test.

Lassie was also beaten in that handicap (her owner Jack Joel had backed her to win £100,000). She won the Oaks with ease and later became an ancestress of Mill Reef. Pretty Polly did not run in the 2,000 Guineas, but won the 1,000, the Oaks (at odds of 8–100, roughly 1–12 today) and the St. Leger in a career which brought 22 wins worth more than £37,000. Though not a great success at stud, her descendants include Brigadier Gerard and two Derby winners, St. Paddy and Psidium.

One of the biggest shocks in Derby history was the 100–1 success of Signorinetta in 1908. She was owned, trained and bred by the Italian Chevalier Odorado Ginistrelli, but she showed it had been no fluke as she took the Oaks two days later. The 1910 winner, Rosedrop, was the dam of Gainsborough – the 1918 Triple Crown winner and an outstanding sire – while Jest, who claimed the 1913 Oaks, bred the Derby winner Humorist.

Rosedrop was the first of eight Oaks winners trained at Manton by Alec Taylor. Seven of those came in the ten-race period 1917–26, and included My Dear in 1918, one of the few to win a classic on a disqualification and promoted to first when Stony Ford was ruled out. During World War I the classics were run at Newmarket, where, in 1916, the bad-tempered Fifinella became the last filly to win the Derby and the Oaks, the former narrowly and the fillies' classic with ease.

The 1930 winner, Rose of England, provided a first classic success for Gordon Richards, who also won on King George VI's Triple Crown filly Sun Chariot in 1942. The Queen has won the Oaks on two occasions, with Carrozza, in 1957, and with Dunfermline in her Silver Jubilee year, 1997.

Other top post-War Oaks winners include fillies' Triple Crown winner Meld in 1955;

◆ For three-year-old fillies carrying 9st
◆ Held on the first or second Friday in June, at Epsom
◆ Inaugurated 1779

RACE DISTANCE
1½ miles, 1779–date

COURSES HOSTING THE OAKS
Epsom 1779–1914, 1919–39, 1946–date
Newmarket 1915–18, 1940–45

TRAINERS WITH MOST WINS
11 Robert Robson
8 Alec Taylor

JOCKEYS WITH MOST WINS
9 Frank Buckle
6 F. Butler, Lester Piggott

THE OAKS 1779–2006

YEAR	HORSE	JOCKEY	TRAINER
1779	Bridget	R Goodison	
1780	Tetoum	R Goodison	
1781	Faith	R Goodison	
1782	Ceres	S Chifney Sr	
1783	Maid Of The Oaks	S Chifney Sr	
1784	Stella	C Hindley	
1785	Trifle	J Bird	
1786	unnamed filly	J Edwards	
1787	Annette	D Fitzpatrick	
1788	Nightshade	D Fitzpatrick	
1789	Tag	S Chifney Sr	
1790	Hippolyta	S Chifney Sr	
1791	Portia	J Singleton	
1792	Volantè	C Hindley	
1793	Caelia	J Singleton	
1794	Hermione	S Arnull	
1795	Platina	D Fitzpatrick	
1796	Parissot	J Arnull	
1797	Niké	F Buckle	R Robson
1798	Bellissima	F Buckle	
1799	Bellina	F Buckle	
1800	Ephemera	D Fitzpatrick	
1801	Eleanor	Saunders	
1802	Scotia	F Buckle	
1803	Theophania	F Buckle	
1804	Pelisse	W Clift	R Robson
1805	Meteora	F Buckle	
1806	Bronze	W Edwards	
1807	Briseis	S Chifney Jr	
1808	Morel	W Clift	R Robson
1809	Maid Of Orleans	J Poss	
1810	Oriana	W Peirse	
1811	Sorcery	S Chifney Jr	
1812	Manuella	W Peirse	
1813	Music	T Goodison	R Robson
1814	Medora	S Barnard	R Robson
1815	Minuet	T Goodison	R Robson
1816	Landscape	S Chifney Jr	
1817	Neva	F Buckle	
1818	Corinne	F Buckle	
1819	Shoveler	S Chifney Jr	
1820	Caroline	H Edwards	
1821	Augusta	J Robinson	
1822	Pastille	H Edwards	
1823	Zinc	F Buckle	
1824	Cobweb	J Robinson	
1825	Wings	S Chifney Jr	
1826	Lilias	T Lye	
1827	Gulnare	F Boyce	
1828	Turquoise	J Day	
1829	Green Mantle	G Dockeray	
1830	Variation	G Edwards	
1831	Oxygen	J Day	
1832	Galata	P Conolly	
1833	Vespa	J Chapple	
1834	Pussy	J Day	
1835	Queen Of Trumps	T Lye	
1836	Cyprian	W Scott	
1837	Miss Letty	J Holmes	
1838	Industry	W Scott	
1839	Deception	J Day	
1840	Crucifix	J Day	
1841	Ghunznee	W Scott	
1842	Our Nell	T Lye	
1843	Poison	F Butler	
1844	The Princess	F Butler	
1845	Refraction	H Bell	
1846	Mendicant	S Day	J Day
1847	Miami	S Templeman	
1848	Cymba	S Templeman	
1849	Lady Evelyn	F Butler	
1850	Rhedycina	F Butler	
1851	Iris	F Butler	
1852	Songstress	F Butler	
1853	Catherine Hayes	Marlow	
1854	Mincemeat	Charlton	
1855	Marchioness	S Templeman	
1856	Mincepie	A Day	
1857	Blink Bonny	Charlton	W I'Anson
1858	Governess	T Ashmall	
1859	Summerside	G Fordham	
1860	Butterfly	J Snowden	
1861	Brown Duchess	L Snowden	
1862	Fue De Joie	T Chaloner	
1863	Queen Bertha	T Aldcroft	
1864	Fille De L'Air	A Edwards	
1865	Regalia	J Norman	
1866	Tormentor	J Mann	
1867	Hippia	J Daley	
1868	Formosa	G Fordham	
1869	Brigantine	T Cannon	
1870	Gamos	G Fordham	
1871	Hannah	C Maidment	
1872	Reine	G Fordham	
1873	Marie Stuart	T Cannon	
1874	Apology	J Osborne	
1875	Spinaway	F Archer	M Dawson
†1876	Enguerrande }	Hudson	
	Camelia }	Glover	
1877	Placida	H Jeffrey	
1878	Jannette	F Archer	M Dawson
1879	Wheel Of Fortune	F Archer	M Dawson
1880	Jenny Howlett	J Snowden	
1881	Thebais	G Fordham	
1882	Geheimniss	T Cannon	
1883	Bonny Jean	J Watts	
1884	Busybody	T Cannon	
1885	Lonely	F Archer	
1886	Miss Jummy	J Watts	
1887	Reve D'Or	C Wood	
1888	Seabreeze	J Robinson	
1889	L'Abbesse De Jouarre	J Woodburn	
1890	Memoir	J Watts	
1891	Mimi	P Rickaby	
1892	La Flèche	G Barrett	
1893	Mrs Butterwick	J Watts	
1894	Amiable	W Bradford	
1895	La Sagesse	S Loates	
1896	Canterbury Pilgrim	F Rickaby	
1897	Limasol	W Bradford	
1898	Airs And Graces	W Bradford	
1899	Musa	O Madden	
1900	La Roche	M Cannon	
1901	Cap And Bells II	M Henry	
1902	Sceptre	H Randall	R Sievier
1903	Our Lassie	M Cannon	C Morton
1904	Pretty Polly	W Lane	P Gilpin
1905	Cherry Lass	H Jones	W Robinson
1906	Keystone II	D Maher	G Lambton
1907	Glass Doll	H Randall	C Morton
1908	Signorinetta	W Bullock	E Ginistrelli
1909	Perola	F Wootton	G Davies
1910	Rosedrop	C Trigg	A Taylor
1911	Cherimoya	F Winter	C Marsh
1912	Mirska	J Childs	T Jennings
1913	Jest	F Rickaby	C Morton
1914	Princess Dorrie	W Huxley	C Morton
1915	Snow Marten	W Griggs	P Gilpin
1916	Fifinella	J Childs	R Dawson
1917	Sunny Jane	O Madden	A Taylor
*1918	My Dear	S Donoghue	A Taylor
1919	Bayuda	J Childs	A Taylor
1920	Charlebelle	A Whalley	H Braime
1921	Love In Idleness	J Childs	A Taylor
1922	Pogrom	E Gardner	A Taylor
1923	Brownhylda	V Smyth	R Dawson
1924	Straitlace	F O'Neill	D Waugh
1925	Saucy Sue	F Bullock	A Taylor
1926	Short Story	R Jones	A Taylor
1927	Beam	T Weston	Fk Butters
1928	Toboggan	T Weston	Fk Butters
1929	Pennycomequick	H Jelliss	J Lawson
1930	Rose Of England	G Richards	T Hogg
1931	Brulette	C Elliott	
1932	Udaipur	M Beary	Fk Butters
1933	Chatelaine	S Wragg	F Templeman
1934	Light Brocade	B Carslake	Fk Butters
1935	Quashed	H Jelliss	C Leader
1936	Lovely Rosa	T Weston	H Cottrill
1937	Exhibitionnist	S Donoghue	J Lawson
1938	Rockfel	H Wragg	O Bell
1939	Galatea II	R Jones	J Lawson
1940	Godiva	D Marks	W Jarvis
1941	Commotion	H Wragg	F Darling
1942	Sun Chariot	G Richards	F Darling
1943	Why Hurry	C Elliott	N Cannon
1944	Hycilla	G Bridgland	C Boyd-Rochfort
1945	Sun Stream	H Wragg	W Earl
1946	Steady Aim	H Wragg	Fk Butters
1947	Imprudence	WR Johnstone	J Lieux
1948	Masaka	W Nevett	Fk Butters
1949	Musidora	E Britt	C Elsey
1950	Asmena	WR Johnstone	C Semblat
1951	Neasham Belle	S Clayton	G Brooke
1952	Frieze	E Britt	C Elsey
1953	Ambiguity	J Mercer	RJ Colling
1954	Sun Cap	WR Johnstone	R Carver
1955	Meld	W Carr	C Boyd-Rochfort
1956	Sicarelle	F Palmer	F Mathet
1957	Carrozza	L Piggott	N Murless
1958	Bella Paola	M Garcia	F Mathet
1959	Petite Etoile	L Piggott	N Murless
1960	Never Too Late II	R Poincelet	E Pollet
1961	Sweet Solera	W Rickaby	R Day
1962	Monade	Y Saint-Martin	J Lieux
1963	Noblesse	G Bougoure	P Prendergast
1964	Homeward Bound	G Starkey	J Oxley
1965	Long Look	J Purtell	MV O'Brien
1966	Valoris	L Piggott	MV O'Brien
1967	Pia	E Hide	W Elsey
1968	La Lague	G Thiboeuf	F Boutin
1969	Sleeping Partner	J Gorton	Douglas Smith
1970	Lupe	A Barclay	N Murless
1971	Altesse Royale	G Lewis	N Murless
1972	Ginevra	A Murray	HR Price
1973	Mysterious	G Lewis	N Murless
1974	Polygamy	Pat Eddery	P Walwyn
1975	Juliette Marny	L Piggott	J Tree
1976	Pawneese	Y Saint-Martin	A Penna
1977	Dunfermline	W Carson	WR Hern
1978	Fair Salinia	G Starkey	M Stoute
1979	Scintillate	Pat Eddery	J Tree
1980	Bireme	W Carson	WR Hern
1981	Blue Wind	L Piggott	D Weld
1982	Time Charter	W Newnes	H Candy
1983	Sun Princess	W Carson	WR Hern
1984	Circus Plume	L Piggott	J Dunlop
1985	Oh So Sharp	S Cauthen	H Cecil
1986	Midway Lady	R Cochrane	B Hanbury
1987	Unite	WR Swinburn	M Stoute
1988	Diminuendo	S Cauthen	H Cecil
*1989	Snow Bride	S Cauthen	H Cecil
1990	Salsabil	W Carson	J Dunlop
1991	Jet Ski Lady	C Roche	J Bolger
1992	User Friendly	G Duffield	C Brittain
1993	Intrepidity	M Roberts	A Fabre
1994	Balanchine	L Dettori	H Ibrahim
1995	Moonshell	L Dettori	S bin Suroor
1996	Lady Carla	Pat Eddery	H Cecil
1997	Reams Of Verse	K Fallon	H Cecil
1998	Shahtoush	MJ Kinane	A O'Brien
1999	Ramruma	K Fallon	H Cecil
2000	Love Divine	T Quinn	H Cecil
2001	Imagine	MJ Kinane	AP O'Brien
2002	Kazzia	L Dettori	S bin Suroor
2003	Casual Look	M Dwyer	A Balding
2004	Ouija Board	K Fallon	E Dunlop
2005	Eswarah	R Hills	M Jarvis
2006	Alexandrova	K Fallon	AP O'Brien

* Winners. Stony Ford (1918) and Aliysa (1989), were disqualified
† Deadheat

Noblesse, who spread-eagled her rivals in 1963; and the French-trained Pawneese in 1976, who went on to win the King George VI And Queen Elizabeth II Stakes. Time Chatter won both those races and the Eclipse Stakes in 1982. Oh So Sharp swept the fillies' Triple Crown in 1985. Kazzia, the 2002 Oaks winner, also accounted for the Flower Bowl Invitational Stakes, a Grade 1 turf event at Belmont Park in New York."

Henry Cecil's seven victories in 16 runnings, 1985–2000, qualifies him as the Oaks' leading trainer of modern times.

Seven up: Richard Quinn drives Love Divine (left) up the hill in 2000 to give trainer Henry Cecil a seventh Oaks win.

THE DERBY

The Derby – although only third in terms of seniority to the St. Leger and the Oaks – remains the best-known flat race, certainly in Europe and probably in the world. It went through a very rocky patch in the late 20th century, but by the turn of the third millennium it appeared that things were on the mend.

THE RACE was first run in 1780, following the favourable reception given to the Oaks the year before. It was staged over a mile for its first four years before moving up in distance to join the fillies' race at 1 1/2 miles.

The story goes – and has never been contradicted – that the 12th Earl of Derby tossed a coin with Sir Charles Bunbury to decide on the name of the new race. Bunbury lost, but he has his name in the tale as the owner of the first winner, Diomed, who beat eight rivals in a race of which very few details were recorded.

Lord Derby won the race named after him with Sir Peter Teazle in 1787, but it was not until Sansovino's success in 1924 that a current holder of the earldom again had his colours carried to Derby success. Sir Thomas, in 1788, was the first royal and first odds-on winner; he was owned by the Prince of Wales, later King George IV.

Robert Robson, the first outstanding trainer, gained his first of seven Derby wins when Waxy, who was to sire four winners of the race, upset the odds-on Gohanna in 1793.

It was possible for horses to run without being named and it was not until 1946, by when it was applicable only to two-year-olds, that this practice was outlawed. The only Derby winner to have run without a name was the Duke of Bedford's Fidget colt, who had never run before his success in 1797 and was well beaten in his only start afterwards.

It was by no means unusual, even into the 19th century, for details of the Derby to be very scanty. Often no riders were listed for placed horses, distances did not go beyond that between first and second and, when Phantom, ridden by Frank Buckle, got up on the line in 1811, no horse was officially placed third even though there had been 16 runners. The 19th century was full of villains and racing was inevitably anything but exempt from their activities. In 1812 Manuella was pulled by Sam Chifney, Jr., who then backed her to win the Oaks, which she did at 20–1 after being well beaten behind Octavius in the Derby.

A second royal success in came in 1816 with the 20–1 chance Prince Leopold, who belonged to the Prince Regent's brother the Duke of York, though he raced in the name of Mr. Warwick Lake. The Duke was prepared to acknowledge

Flying finish: Sinndar, hard ridden by Johnny Murtagh (13), gets up to beat the longtime leader Sakhee in the 2000 Derby.

ownership of his second winner, Moses, in 1822.

One of the most successful owners in the early days was Lord Egremont, who gained the fifth and last of his wins with the 50–1 chance Lapdog in 1826. The first colt to win at that price was Azor, who gave his jockey Jem Robinson the first of six winners. Around this time there were a number of other long-priced winners: John Forth was more than 60 years old when he rode and trained Frederick to win in 1829 at odds of 40–1; there was another 50–1 winner in 1831, when Spaniel beat odds on Riddlesworth; Phosphorus was a 40–1 winner in 1837; followed by Amato (30–1), Bloomsbury (25–1) and Little Wonder (40–1) in the next three seasons.

There was more than a hint of wrongdoing about the two latter winners: many thought Bloomsbury was a four-year-old; while the runner-up, Deception, had been ridden to lose. With a different jockey, the filly won the Oaks two days later. It was also widely believed that Little Wonder was also aged four. But there is no doubt that the colt called Running Rein, who passed the post first in 1844, was in fact a four-year-old called

Maccabeus. This was proven in court and the race awarded to runner-up Orlando.

In 1853 West Australian became the first colt to win the Triple Crown. His example was followed quite regularly over the next half-

THE DERBY 1780–2006

YEAR HORSE	JOCKEY	TRAINER
1780 Diomed	S Arnull	
1781 Young Eclipse	C Hindley	
1782 Assassin	S Arnull	
1783 Saltram	C Hindley	
1784 Sergeant	S Arnull	
1785 Aimwell	C Hindley	
1786 Noble	J White	
1787 Sir Peter Teazle	S Arnull	
1788 Sir Thomas	W South	
1789 Skyscraper	S Chifney	
1790 Rhadamanthus	J Arnull	
1791 Eager	Stephenson	
1792 John Bull	F Buckle	
1793 Waxy	B Clift	R Robson
1794 Daedalus	F Buckle	
1795 Spread Eagle	A Wheatley	
1796 Didelot	J Arnull	
1797 unnamed colt	J Singleton	
1798 Sir Harry	S Arnull	
1799 Archduke	J Arnull	
1800 Champion	B Clift	
1801 Eleanor	J Saunders	
1802 Tyrant	F Buckle	R Robson
1803 Ditto	B Clift	
1804 Hannibal	W Arnull	
1805 Cardinal Beaufort	D Fitzpatrick	
1806 Paris	J Shepherd	
1807 Election	J Arnull	
1808 Pan	F Collinson	
1809 Pope	T Goodison	R Robson
1810 Whalebone	B Clift	R Robson
1811 Phantom	F Buckle	
1812 Octavius	W Arnull	
1813 Smolensko	T Goodison	
1814 Blucher	W Arnull	
1815 Whisker	T Goodison	R Robson
1816 Prince Leopold	Wheatley	
1817 Azor	J Robinson	R Robson
1818 Sam	S Chifney Jr	W Chifney
1819 Tiresias	B Clift	
1820 Sailor	S Chifney Jr	W Chifney
1821 Gustavus	S Day	
1822 Moses	T Goodison	
1823 Emilius	F Buckle	R Robson
1824 Cedric	J Robinson	
1825 Middleton	J Robinson	Edwards
1826 Lapdog	G Dockeray	Bird
1827 Marmeluke	J Robinson	Edwards
†1828 Cadland	J Robinson	
1829 Frederick	J Forth	J Forth
1830 Priam	S Day	W Chifney
1831 Spaniel	W Wheatley	
1832 St. Giles	W Scott	
1833 Dangerous	J Chapple	
1834 Plenipotentiary	P Conolly	
1835 Mündig	W Scott	J Scott
1836 Bay Middleton	J Robinson	
1837 Phosporous	G Edwards	
1838 Amato	J Chapple	R Sherwood
1839 Bloomsbury	S Templeman	W Ridsdale

YEAR HORSE	JOCKEY	TRAINER
1840 Little Wonder	W MacDonald	W Forth
1841 Coronation	B Conolly	
1842 Attila	W Scott	J Scott
1843 Cotherstone	W Scott	J Scott
1844*Orlando	N Flatman	Cooper
1845 Merry Monarch	F Bell	J Forth
1846 Pyrrhus The First	S Day	J Day
1847 Cossack	S Templeman	J Day
1848 Surplice	S Templeman	J Kent
1849 The Flying Dutchman	C Marlow	Fobert
1850 Voltigeur	J Marson	R Hill
1851 Teddington	J Marson	A Taylor
1852 Daniel O'Rourke	F Butler	J Scott
1853 West Australian	F Butler	S Scott
1854 Andover	A Day	J Day
1855 Wild Dayrell	R Sherwood	Rickaby
1856 Ellington	T Aldcroft	T Dawson
1857 Blink Bonny	J Charlton	W I'Anson
1858 Beadsman	J Wells	G Manning
1859 Musjid	J Wells	G Manning
1860 Thormanby	H Custance	M Dawson
1861 Kettledrum	R Bullock	Oates
1862 Caractacus	J Parsons	Zachary
1863 Macaroni	T Challoner	Godding
1864 Blair Athol	J Snowden	W I'Anson
1865 Gladiateur	H Grimshaw	T Jennings
1866 Lord Lyon	H Custance	J Dover
1867 Hermit	J Daley	Bloss
1868 Blue Gown	J Wells	J Porter
1869 Pretender	J Osborne	T Dawson
1870 Kingcraft	T French	M Dawson
1871 Favonius	T French	J Hayhoe
1872 Cremorne	C Maidment	W Gilbert
1873 Doncaster	F Webb	R Peck
1874 George Frederick	H Custance	T Leader
1875 Galopin	J Morris	J Dawson
1876 Kisber	C Maidment	J Hayhoe
1877 Silvio	F Archer	M Dawson
1878 Sefton	H Constable	A Taylor
1879 Sir Bevys	G Fordham	J Hayhoe
1880 Bend Or	F Archer	R Peck
1881 Iroquois	F Archer	J Pincus
1882 Shotover	T Cannon	J Porter
1883 Blaise	C Wood	J Porter
†1884 Gatien } Harvester }	C Wood S Loates	R Sherwood J Jewitt
1885 Melton	F Archer	M Dawson
1886 Ormonde	F Archer	J Porter
1887 Merry Hampton	J Watts	M Gurry
1888 Ayrshire	F Barrett	G Dawson
1889 Donovan	T Loates	G Dawson
1890 Sainfoin	J Watts	J Porter
1891 Common	G Barrett	J Porter
1892 Sir Hugo	F Allsopp	T Wadlow
1893 Isinglass	T Loates	J Jewitt
1894 Ladas	J Watts	M Dawson
1895 Sir Visto	S Loates	M Dawson
1896 Persimmon	J Watts	R Marsh
1897 Galtee More	C Wood	S Darling

YEAR HORSE	JOCKEY	TRAINER
1898 Jeddah	O Madden	R Marsh
1899 Flying Fox	M Cannon	J Porter
1900 Diamond Jubilee	H Jones	R Marsh
1901 Volodyovski	L Reiff	J Huggins
1902 Ard Patrick	J Martin	S Darling
1903 Rock Sand	D Maher	G Blackwell
1904 Amant	K Cannon	A Hayhoe
1905 Cicero	D Maher	P Peck
1906 Spearmint	D Maher	P Gilpin
1907 Orby	J Reiff	J Allen
1908 Signorinetta	W Bullock	E Ginistrelli
1909 Minoru	H Jones	R Marsh
1910 Lemberg	B Dillon	A Taylor
1911 Sunstar	G Stern	C Morton
1912 Tagalie	J Reiff	D Waugh
1913*Aboyeur	E Piper	T Lewis
1914 Durbar II	M MacGee	T Murphy
1915 Pommern	S Donoghue	C Peck
1916 Fifinella	J Childs	R Dawson
1917 Gay Crusader	S Donoghue	A Taylor
1918 Gainsborough	J Childs	A Taylor
1919 Grand Parade	F Templeman	F Barling
1920 Spion Kop	F O'Neill	P Gilpin
1921 Humorist	S Donoghue	C Morton
1922 Captain Cuttle	S Donoghue	F Darling
1923 Papyrus	S Donoghue	B Jarvis
1924 Sansovino	T Weston	G Lambton
1925 Manna	S Donoghue	F Darling
1926 Coronach	J Childs	F Darling
1927 Call Boy	C Elliott	J Watts
1928 Felstead	H Wragg	O Bell
1929 Trigo	J Marshall	R Dawson
1930 Blenheim	H Wragg	R Dawson
1931 Cameronian	F Fox	F Darling
1932 April The Fifth	F Lane	T Walls
1933 Hyperion	T Weston	G Lambton
1934 Windsor Lad	C Smirke	M Marsh
1935 Bahram	F Fox	Frank Butters
1936 Mahmoud	C Smirke	Frank Butters
1937 Mid-day Sun	M Beary	Fred Butters
1938 Bois Roussel	C Elliott	F Darling
1939 Blue Peter	E Smith	J Jarvis
1940 Pont L'Eveque	S Wragg	F Darling
1941 Owen Tudor	W Nevett	F Darling
1942 Watling Street	H Wragg	W Earl
1943 Straight Deal	T Carey	W Nightengall
1944 Ocean Swell	W Nevett	J Jarvis
1945 Dante	W Nevett	M Peacock
1946 Airborne	T Lowrey	R Perryman
1947 Pearl Diver	G Bridgland	C Halsey
1948 My Love	WR Johnstone	R Carver
1949 Nimbus	C Elliott	G Colling
1950 Galcador	WR Johnstone	C Semblat
1951 Arctic Prince	C Spares	W Stephenson
1952 Tulyar	C Smirke	M Marsh
1953 Pinza	Sir G Richards	N Bertie
1954 Never Say Die	L Piggott	J Lawson
1955 Phil Drake	F Palmer	F Mathet
1956 Lavandin	WR Johnstone	A Head
1957 Crepello	L Piggott	N Murless

YEAR HORSE	JOCKEY	TRAINER
1958 Hard Ridden	C Smirke	J Rogers
1959 Parthia	W Carr	C Boyd-Rochfort
1960 St. Paddy	N Murless	L Piggott
1961 Psidium	R Poincelet	H Wragg
1962 Larkspur	N Sellwood	MV O'Brien
1963 Relko	Y Saint-Martin	F Mathet
1964 Santa Claus	A Breasley	J Rogers
1965 Sea-Bird II	P Glennon	E Pollet
1966 Charlottown	A Breasley	G Smyth
1967 Royal Palace	G Moore	N Murless
1968 Sir Ivor	L Piggott	MV O'Brien
1969 Blakeney	E Johnson	A Budgett
1970 Nijinsky	L Piggott	MV O'Brien
1971 Mill Reef	G Lewis	I Balding
1972 Roberto	L Piggott	MV O'Brien
1973 Morston	E Hide	A Budgett
1974 Snow Knight	B Taylor	P Nelson
1975 Grundy	Pat Eddery	P Walwyn
1976 Empery	L Piggott	M Zilber
1977 The Minstrel	L Piggott	MV O'Brien
1978 Shirley Heights	G Starkey	J Dunlop
1979 Troy	W Carson	WR Hern
1980 Henbit	W Carson	WR Hern
1981 Shergar	WR Swinburn	M Stoute
1982 Golden Fleece	Pat Eddery	MV O'Brien
1983 Teenoso	L Piggott	G Wragg
1984 Secreto	C Roche	D O'Brien
1985 Slip Anchor	S Cauthen	H Cecil
1986 Shahrastani	WR Swinburn	M Stoute
1987 Reference Point	S Cauthen	H Cecil
1988 Kahyasi	R Cochrane	L Cumani
1989 Nashwan	W Carson	WR Hern
1990 Quest For Fame	Pat Eddery	R Charlton
1991 Generous	A Munro	P Cole
1992 Dr Devious	J Reid	Chapple-Hyam
1993 Commander In Chief	MJ Kinane	H Cecil
1994 Erhaab	W Carson	J Dunlop
1995 Lammtarra	WR Swinburn	S bin Suroor
1996 Shaamit	M Hills	W Haggas
1997 Benny The Dip	W Ryan	J Gosden
1998 High-Rise	O Peslier	L Cumani
1999 Oath	K Fallon	H Cecil
2000 Sinndar	J Murtagh	J Oxx
2001 Galileo	MJ Kinane	AP O'Brien
2002 High Chaparral	JP Murtagh	AP O'Brien
2003 Kris Kin	K Fallon	MR Stoute
2004 North Light	K Fallon	MR Stoute
2005 Motivator	JP Murtagh	M Bell
2006 Sir Percy	M Dwyer	M P Tregoning

* Winners Running Rein (1844) and Craganour (1913) were disqualified
† Dead heat (or run-off after dead-heat)

century: in 1865, the French-owned and bred but Newmarket-trained Gladiateur III did so, and his statue has pride of place at Longchamp; as did Lord Lyon a year later; the oustanding Ormonde was next, in 1886; Diamond Jubilee, owned by the then Prince of Wales, followed, in 1900; and Rock Sand completed the run in 1903.

In 1881 the American owner-breeder Pierre Lorillard's Iroquois gave Fred Archer the third of his five Derby successes. In 1894 Lord Rosebery became the first serving Prime Minister to own a winner of the Derby when he won with Ladas. A year later Lord Rosebery won again with Sir Visto.

The only dead heat in the Derby came in 1884 between St Gatien and Harvester. In 1828 the judge had been unable to split Cadland and The Colonel before Cadland won the run-off; the 1884 duo settled to share the spoils.

The Prince of Wales (later Edward VII) won with Persimmon in 1896, and won the race as King with Minoru in 1909, a year after the 100–1 chance Signorinetta had become the third filly to win the Derby following Eleanor in 1801 and Blink Bonny in 1857.

A most sensational race came in 1913, when the stewards awarded the race to 100–1 chance Aboyeur by disqualifying the hot favourite Craganour. Three exceptional winners came in successive years 1933–35: Hyperion, Windsor Lad and Bahram, the last of whom gained the penultimate Triple Crown of the 1900s. Nijinsky, in 1970, was the last colt to claim three classics.

One of the most popular winners was Pinza, who gave Sir Gordon Richards his first and only Derby win at the 28th attempt in 1953, and a year later Lester Piggott had the first of a record nine Derby victories on the 33–1 shot Never Say Die.

Sea-Bird II, the 1965 winner, was one of the supreme horses of the 20th century. Lammtara (1995) went on to become a Prix de l'Arc de Triomphe winner. The subsequent success of Sinndar in the 2000 Arc helped re-fortify the Derby's reputation, as did High Chapparal's victories in the 2002–2003 renewals of the Breeders' Cup Turf.

THE GOLD CUP

The Gold Cup – it is often wrongly called the Ascot Gold Cup – is the most important flat race in the world over a distance in excess of two miles. It is staged over 2½ miles on the third day, the Thursday (Ladies' Day), of the Royal Ascot meeting in mid-June. The Gold Cup is Ascot's most historic race.

Head first: Unusual headwear worn by lady racegoers is one of the attractions of Gold Cup, Ladies' Day, at Royal Ascot.

IT WAS FIRST RUN in 1807 with the cup worth 100gns as its prize and was won by the three-year-old Master Jackey, carrying 6st 12lb. The Prince Regent, whose father had commissioned the building of a permanent stand shortly before the end of the 18th century, was among the spectators – despite the Escape affair he maintained his enthusiasm for racing, though his horses ran as the property of nominees rather than in his own name.

It did not take long for the Gold Cup, and the Royal meeting in general, to become extremely popular with competitors and spectators alike, and one of the best early races for the Cup was that of 1829. It attracted the 1827 Derby winner Mameluke as well as Cadland and The Colonel, who had deadheated at Epsom in 1828 before Cadland won the run-off, but all three were beaten by Zinganee.

Zinganee had been unplaced in the 1828 Derby, but was suffering from a throat infection. At that time he belonged to the Chifney family (Sam Chifney rode him at Ascot), but they sold him shortly before the Gold Cup to Lord Chesterfield, with the agreement that they would keep the prize money and the new owner could have the cup.

King George IV had long wanted to win the Gold Cup – he had declined to pay 2,500gns for Zinganee when that colt was on offer –

and in a fit of pique shortly before he died he decreed that only members of the Jockey Club, or of the London men's clubs White's and Brooks's would be allowed to compete for it. His successor, William IV, soon repealed that rule.

Bizarre became the first horse to win the Cup two years in a row, accomplishing the feat in 1824-1825. Since then 15 other horses have duplicated his success, the most recent being Royal Rebel in 2001–2002. And another horse, Sagaro, went one step better than Bizarre, triumphing in the Cup in three successive years from 1975–1977.

There was a Russian element to the race for a decade from 1844 when the Czar of Russia was at Ascot during a state visit. He was so delighted when Lord Albermarle, whose unnamed colt won the Cup and was immediately called Emperor in honour of the visitor, that he put up a plate of £500 as the prize in future. This prompted the race to be re-named the Emperor's Plate, but such felicity came to an abrupt halt with the outbreak of the Crimean War in 1854.

When the Cup reverted to its original name the first winner was West Australian, who had taken the Triple Crown the year before, and in the next decade another Triple Crown winner, Gladiateur III, won the Cup by 40 lengths.

Although Queen Victoria largely gave up on public life after the death of Prince Albert in 1861, their son the Prince of Wales (later Edward VII) was a great racing enthusiast.

His Persimmon won the Gold Cup in the Diamond Jubilee year of 1897 and three years later the eight-year-old Merman, ridden by the American Tod Sloan in the colours of the Prince's mistress Lily Langtry, came home at 100–7 (approximately 14–1 in modern parlance).

In 1906 the outstanding mare Pretty Polly made her final racecourse appearance in the Gold Cup, but there was no fairytale ending as she was beaten by Bachelor's Button. There was much controversy in 1907 when The White Knight gained the first of his two wins. He had in fact only dead-heated with the French challenger Eider, but the latter was disqualified due to rough riding by his jockey George Stern, and while all this was going on the cup was stolen, so that the winning owner had to receive a substitute trophy.

The top-class Bayardo won in 1910, followed, in 1912 and 1913, by Prince Palatine. When the race was run at Newmarket in 1917 and 1918 during World War I (there was no race in 1915 or 1916), it was won by the Derby winners of those years, Gay Crusader and Gainsborough. There were two more dual winners in Invershin in 1928 and 1929 and Trimdon three years later and in 1934 the previous season's Derby winner Hyperion was galloped into the ground by Felicitation.

At the Double: Double Trigger and Jason Weaver won the Gold Cup at Ascot in 1995.

THE GOLD CUP 1807–2005

YEAR	HORSE	JOCKEY	TRAINER
1807	Master Jackey		
†1808	Brighton		
1809	Anderida		
1810	Loiterer		
1811	Smallhopes		
1812	Flash		
1813	Lutzen		
1814	Pranks		
1815	Aladdin		
1816	Anticipation		
1817	Sir Richard		
1818	Belville		
1819	Anticipation		
1820	Champohnon		
1821	Banker		
1822	Huldibrand		
1823	Marcellus	W Wheatley	
1824	Bizarre	W Arnull	
1825	Bizarre	W Arnull	
1826	Chateau Margaux	G Dockeray	
1827	Memnon	S Chifney	
1828	Bobadilla	T Lye	
1829	Zinganee	S Chifney	
1830	Lucetta	J Robinson	
1831	Cetus	J Robinson	
†1832	Camarine	J Robinson	
1833	Galata	W Arnull	
1834	Glaucus	W Scott	
1835	Glencoe	J Robinson	
1836	Touchstone	J Day	J Scott
1837	Touchstone	W Scott	J Scott
1838	Grey Momus	W Day	JB Day
1839	Caravan	J Robinson	
1840	St Francis	S Chifney	
1841	Lanercost	W Noble	T Dawson
1842	Beeswing	Cartwright	
1843	Ralph	J Robinson	
1844	The Emperor	Whitehouse	
1845	The Emperor	Whitehouse	
1846	Alarm	E Flatman	
1847	The Hero	A Day	JB Day
1848	The Hero	A Day	JB Day
1849	Van Tromp	C Marlow	
1850	The Flying Dutchman	C Marlow	J Fobert
1851	Woolwich	J Marson	
1852	Joe Miller	G Mann	
1853	Teddington	J Marson	
1854	West Australian	A Day	J Scott
1855	Fandango	T Ashmall	
1856	Winkfield	Bartholomew	
1857	Skirmisher	J Charlton	

YEAR	HORSE	JOCKEY	TRAINER
1858	Fisherman	J Wells	T Parr
1859	Fisherman	Cresswell	T Parr
1860	Rupee	H Grimshaw	M Dawson
1861	Thormanby	H Custance	M Dawson
1862	Asteroid	J Wells	G Manning
†1863	Buckstone	A Edwards	M Dawson
1864	The Scottish Chief	H Covey	M Dawson
1865	Ely	H Custance	T Olliver
1866	Gladiateur	H Grimshaw	T Jennings
1867	Lecturer	G Fordham	
1868	Blue Gown	Cameron	J Porter
1869	Brigantine	Butler	W Day
1870	Sabinus	Rowell	
1871	Mortemer	G Fordham	
1872	Henry	G Fordham	
1873	Cremorne	C Maidment	W Gilbert
1874	Boiard	Carver	
1875	Doncaster	G Fordham	R Peck
1876	Apology	J Osborne, jun	J Osborne, sen
1877	Petrarch	T Cannon	J Cannon
1878	Verneuil	J Goater	T Jennings
1879	Isonomy	T Cannon	J Porter
1880	Isonomy	T Cannon	J Porter
1881	Robert The Devil	T Cannon	R Blanton
1882	Foxhall	T Cannon	W Day
1883	Tristan	G Fordham	T Jennings
1884	St. Simon	C Wood	M Dawson
1885	St. Gatien	C Wood	R Sherwood
1886	Althorp	T Cannon	
1887	Bird of Freedom	W Warne	
1888	Timothy	WT Robinson	J Jewett
1889	Trayles	WT Robinson	
1890	Gold	F Webb	
1891	Morion	J Watts	R Marsh
1892	Buccaneer	G Barrett	
1893	Marcion	S Chandley	
1894	La Flèche	J Watts	R Marsh
1895	Isinglass	T Loates	J Jewett
1896	Love Wisely	S Loates	A Taylor
1897	Persimmon	J Watts	R Marsh
1898	Elf II	E Watkins	In France
1899	Cyllene	S Loates	W Jarvis
1900	Merman	JF Sloan	W Robinson
1901	Santoi	F Rickaby	Davis
1902	William The Third	M Cannon	J Porter
1903	Maximum II	A McIntyre	R Count
1904	Throwaway	W Lane	PP Gilpin
1905	Zinfandel	M Cannon	C Beatty
1906	Bachelor's Button	D Maher	C Peck
1907*	The White Knight	W Halsey	H Sadler
1908	The White Knight	W Halsey	A Taylor
1909	Bomba	F Fox	F Pratt

YEAR	HORSE	JOCKEY	TRAINER
1910	Bayardo	D Maher	A Taylor
1911	Willonyx	W Higgs	S Darling
1912	Prince Palatine	F O'Neill	H Beardsley
1913	Prince Palatine	W Saxby	H Beardsley
1914	Aleppo	C Foy	A Taylor
1915	No race		
1916	No race		
1917	Gay Crusader	S Donoghue	A Taylor
1918	Gainsborough	J Childs	A Taylor
1919	By Jingo!	G Hulme	J Rhodes
1920	Tangiers	G Hulme	R Dawson
1921	Periosteum	F Bullock	B Jarvis
1922	Golden Myth	EC Elliott	J Jarvis
1923	Happy Man	V Smyth	T Hogg
1924	Massine	A Sharpe	In France
1925	Santorb	S Donoghue	J Rhodes
1927	Foxlaw	B Carslake	R Day
1928	Invershin	B Carslake	G Digby
1929	Invershin	R Perryman	G Digby
1930	Bosworth	T Weston	Frank Butters
1931	Trimdon	J Childs	J Lawson
1932	Trimdon	J Childs	J Lawson
1933	Foxhunter	H Wragg	J Jarvis
1934	Felicitation	G Richards	Frank Butters
1935	Tiberius	T Weston	J Lawson
1936	Quashed	R Perryman	C Leader
1937	Precipitation	P Beasley	C Boyd-Rochfort
1938	Flares	RA Jones	C Boyd-Rochfort
1939	Flyon	E Smith	J Jarvis
1940	No Race		
1941	Finis	H Wragg	O Bell
1942	Owen Tudor	G Richards	F Darling
1943	Ujiji	G Richards	J Lawson
1944	Umiddad	G Richards	F Butters
1945	Ocean Swell	E Smith	J Jarvis
1946	Caracalla II	EC Elliott	C Semblat
1947	Souverain	M Lolleriou	H Delavaud
1948	Arbar	EC Elliott	C Semblat
1949	Alycidon	D Smith	W Earl
1950	Supertello	D Smith	JC Waugh
1951	Pan II	R Poincelet	E Pollet
1952	Aquino II	G Richards	F Armstrong
1953	Souepi	EC Elliott	G Digby
1954	Elpenor	J Doyasbere	EC Elliott
1955	Botticelli	E Camici	I Della Rochetta
1956	Macip	S Boullenger	EC Elliott
1957	Zarathustra	L Piggott	C Boyd-Rochfort
1958	Gladness	L Piggott	MV O'Brien
1959	Wallaby II	F Palmer	P Carter
1960	Sheshoon	G Moore	A Head
1961	Pandofell	L Piggott	F Maxwell
1962	Twilight Alley	L Piggott	N Murless

YEAR	HORSE	JOCKEY	TRAINER
1963	Balto	F Palmer	M Bonaventure
1964	Race abandoned		
1965	Fighting Charlie	L Piggott	F Maxwell
1966	Fighting Charlie	G Starkey	F Maxwell
1967	Parbury	J Mercer	D Candy
1968	Pardallo II	W Pyers	C Bartholomew
1969	Levmoss	W Williamson	S McGrath
1970	Precipice Wood	J Lindley	Mrs R Lomax
1971*	Random Shot	G Lewis	A Budgett
1972*	Erimo Hawk	Pat Eddery	G Barling
1973	Lasalle	J Lindley	R Carver
1974	Ragstone	R Hutchinson	J Dunlop
1975	Sagaro	L Piggott	F Boutin
1976	Sagaro	L Piggott	F Boutin
1977	Sagaro	L Piggott	F Boutin
1978	Shangamuzo	G Starkey	M Stoute
1979	Le Moss	L Piggott	H Cecil
1980	Le Moss	J Mercer	H Cecil
1981	Ardross	L Piggott	H Cecil
1982	Ardross	L Piggott	H Cecil
1983	Little Wolf	W Carson	WR Hern
1984	Gildoran	S Cauthen	B Hills
1985	Gildoran	B Thomson	B Hills
1986	Longboat	W Carson	WR Hern
1987	Paean	S Cauthen	H Cecil
1988*	Sadeem	G Starkey	G Harwood
1989	Sadeem	W Carson	G Harwood
1990	Ashal	R Hills	Thomsn Jones
1991	Indian Queen	WR Swinburn	Ld Huntingdon
1992	Drum Taps	L Dettori	Ld Huntingdon
1993	Drum Taps	L Dettori	Ld Huntingdon
1994	Arcadian Heights	M Hills	G Wragg
1995	Double Trigger	J Weaver	M Johnston
1996	Classic Cliche	M Kinane	S bin Suroor
1997	Celeric	Pat Eddery	D Morley
1998	Kayf Tara	L Dettori	S bin Suroor
1999	Enzeli	J Murtagh	J Oxx
2000	Kayf Tara	M Kinane	S bin Suroor
2001	Royal Rebel	JP Murtagh	M Johnston
2002	Royal Rebel	JP Murtagh	M Johnston
2003	Mr Dinos	K Fallon	P Cole
2004	Papineau	L Dettori	S bin Suroor
2005	Westerner	O Peslier	E Lellouche

* Winners, Eider (1907), Rock Roi (1971 and 1972),
Royal Gait (1988) were disqualified
† Dead-heat (or run-off after dead heat)

The Gold Cup has not been much of a race for fillies, but in 1936 Quashed, who had won the Oaks in 1935, got the better of the American Triple Crown winner Omaha by a nose after a splendid battle. For much of World War II, the Cup again moved to Newmarket, where Owen Tudor followed his Derby win of 1941 by taking the trophy. Ocean Swell did likewise when the race returned to Ascot in 1945, becoming the first Derby winner to win the Gold Cup on the Royal Heath in the same year since Persimmon in 1897.

There was a host of winners trained in France in the years after the War, with raiders like Caracalla, Souverain, Pan and Arbar proving successful, and there was also a success for Italy with Botticelli in 1955. Against them the home team mustered successes from the oustanding stayer Alycidon, as well as Souepi and Supertello.

Another fine mare, Gladness, won in 1958 and was the last of her sex to do so until Indian Queen in 1991. Sadeem's first of two Gold Cup triumphs in 1988 is somewhat marred in that he was awarded top position only after the panel of stewards disqualified Royal Gait, in what many believe was an outrageous decision.

Towards the end of the 20th century, the Jockey Club feared that the Gold Cup was losing appeal and prestige because, at least in part, of its long distance. It was suggested that the race should be dropped to two miles and relegated from Group 1 status. Fortunately wiser counsel prevailed and the Gold Cup has regained its popularity as well as keeping to its proper distance and status.

In 2005, with major renovations underway at Ascot, the Gold Cup was run at York. The Royal Family attended and they were treated to a quality winner. Westerner had twice been champion older male in France in previous seasons, and his Gold Cup victory gained him the honour of champion older male in England.

◆ For three-year-olds and upwards
◆ Held on the Thursday of the Royal Meeting, in mid-June, at Ascot
◆ Inaugurated 1807
◆ Known as the Emperor's Plate 1845–54

RACE DISTANCE
2 1/2 miles, 1807–date

COURSES HOSTING THE GOLD CUP
York 2005
Ascot 1807-1914, 1919-39, 1945-2004
Newmarket 1917-18, 1941-44
No race 1915-16, 1940, 1964

TRAINERS WITH MOST WINS
6 Alec Taylor

JOCKEYS WITH MOST WINS
11 Lester Piggott

THE GOLD CUP 61

2,000 AND 1,000 GUINEAS

In view of the way in which racing had been ruled from Newmarket by the Jockey Club from almost the moment there had been an attempt at a controlling body, it was surprising that none of the first three classic races should have been run there. This was remedied in 1809, with the arrival of the 2,000 Guineas, over the distance of one mile. It was followed five years later by the 1,000 Guineas, an equivalent race for fillies only.

THE INAUGURAL RUNNINGS of both races were won by Wizard and Charlotte respectively, both being owned by Christopher Wilson and ridden by William Clift. They had tasted classic glory together earlier when Champion took the Derby and St. Leger in 1800 – although Frank Buckle had been the winning jockey at Doncaster.

The first horse to win the Guineas and then the Derby was the black colt Smolensko, who did so in 1813 for Sir Charles Bunbury, and the first filly to be successful was Pastille in 1822. Her owner, the Duke of Grafton, won the 1,000 Guineas that year with Whizgig.

In 1828 Cadland preceded his Derby success by taking the 2,000 Guineas, an example followed by Bay Middleton eight years later before in 1840 Crucifix became the first filly to win both 2,000 and 1,000 Guineas. She also won the Oaks.

Stockwell, who went on to earn the title of the 'Emperor of Stallions' won the 2,000 Guineas in 1852, a year before the first Triple Crown winner, West Australian, whose career of three classic wins was followed by those of Gladiateur in 1865 and Lord Lyon the year after that.

2,000 GUINEAS
- For three-year-olds colts and fillies
- Held in late April or early May, at Newmarket
- Inaugurated 1809

1,000 GUINEAS
- For three-year-olds fillies
- Held in late April or early May, at Newmarket
- Inaugurated 1814

RACE DISTANCE
1 mile, 1809–date (2,000 Guineas)
1 mile, 1814–date (1,000 Guineas)

COURSE HOSTING 2,000 GUINEAS
Newmarket 1809–date

COURSE HOSTING 1,000 GUINEAS
Newmarket 1814–date

Majestic show: Kieren Fallon (spotted cap) pushes King's Best clear to win the 2,000 Guineas at Newmarket in May 2000.

In 1868, Formosa dead-heated for the 2,000 Guineas before winning every other classic except for the Derby, as did Sceptre in 1902, though she was an outright winner of the 2,000. The first royal winner of the 2,000 Guineas was the Prince of Wales's Diamond Jubilee in 1900. Nine years later he won the race again – this time as King Edward VII – with Minoru. Both colts went on to win the Derby and Diamond Jubilee took the Triple Crown.

The 2,000 Guineas success of the next Triple Crown winner, Gainsborough in 1918, meant that Lady James Douglas became the first woman to own a classic winner, and her example was not emulated for a further 15 seasons when the French-trained Rodosto won for the Princess de Faucigny-Lucinge.

There were other royal wins: in 1942, Big Game won for King George VI; and in 1958, Pall Mall carried The Queen's colours to victory. A year earlier, Lester Piggott had landed the first of his 2,000 Guineas victories aboard Crepello.

The biggest shock came in 1961 with a pair of 66–1 long-shots Rockavon and Prince Tudor the first two home. Rockavon was the first, and remains the only, horse trained in Scotland to have won a British classic.

One of the most dramatic afternoons came in 1980, when the hot favourite Nureyev finished first only to be disqualified for interference and the race awarded to Known Fact. Since then, only that fine colt, Nashwan in 1989, has followed 2,000 Guineas victory with Derby success.

THE FIRST GUINEAS for fillies was staged five years after the introduction of the 2,000 and, like its male counterpart, is run over the straight eight furlongs of Newmarket's Rowley Mile course at the second meeting of the season there. William Clift, the winning jockey on Charlotte in the first race, also landed the second 1,000 Guineas on Selim.

The first filly to follow Newmarket classic success by taking the Oaks was Neva in 1817, shortly before the Duke of Grafton established a near monopoly on the 1,000 Guineas, with eight wins in nine years, including the Oaks winner Zinc. The only time he did not win between 1819 and 1827 was when Cobweb was scored in 1824.

In 1840 Crucifix won both Guineas and the Oaks for Lord George Bentinck. He was successful again two years later with Firebrand.

In 1871, Hannah became the first to pull off

the fillies' Triple Crown by taking the 1,000 Guineas, the Oaks and the St. Leger. Six other fillies have landed this treble, with the most recent being Oh So Sharp in 1985 when her double short-head success in the 1,000 Guineas was the closest classic finish in history. The others are La Flèche, Pretty Polly, Sun Chariot, Meld and Apology.

When Mayonnaise was successful in 1849 she was the first of a record seven wins in the race for George Fordham. Strangely, though Lester Piggott, who rode the winners of more classics in Britain than anyone else, won the 1,000 only twice – on Humble Duty, whose seven lengths success in 1970 remains a record winning margin for the race, and on Fairy Footsteps in 1981 only a few days after he nearly lost an ear in a starting stalls accident at Epsom.

Coincidentally, Fred Archer, the outstanding jockey of the 19th century, also won the race

Closest ever: Oh So Sharp won the 1,000 Guineas in 1985 but she was just two short-heads from third place.

only twice – on Spinaway and Wheel of Fortune, who both went on to win the Oaks, in 1875 and 1879 – and Sir Gordon Richards, whose classic strike rate was nowhere near on a par with his overall tally, landed the 1,000 Guineas but thrice.

In 1896 the 1,000 Guineas success was part of an excellent year for the Prince of Wales (later Edward VII), who also won the Derby and the St Leger with Persimmon, and the superb Sceptre added the 1,000 to her 2,000 success in 1902 and went on to land the Oaks and the St Leger.

For many years the longest priced winners of the race were Cecilia and Siffleuse, who won at 100–3 and 33–1 respectively in 1873 and 1893, but they were surpassed by the 50–1 victory of Ferry in 1918.

There have been other Royal successes, with Scuttle for King George V in 1928, Sun Chariot and Hypericum (1946) for King George VI and Highclere in 1974.

From 1983, fillies owned by members of the Maktoum family achieved extraordinary success in the 1,000 Guineas, winning 11 of the subsequent 23 renewals. In 1995, when the race was won by Sheikh Hamdan al-Maktoum's Harayir, the 1,000 Guineas became the first British classic to be run on a Sunday.

2,000 GUINEAS / 1,000 GUINEAS WINNERS

YEAR	2,000 GUINEAS	1,000 GUINEAS	YEAR	2,000 GUINEAS	1,000 GUINEAS	YEAR	2,000 GUINEAS	1,000 GUINEAS	YEAR	2,000 GUINEAS	1,000 GUINEAS
1809	Wizard	no race	1861	Diophantus	Nemesis	1912	Sweeper II	Tagalie	1964	Baldric II	Pourparier
1810	Hephestion	no race	1862	The Marquis	Hurricane	1913	Louvois	Jest	1965	Niksar	Night Off
1811	Trophonius	no race	1863	Marconi	Lady Augusta	1914	Kennymore	Princess Dorrie	1966	Kashmir II	Glad Rags
1812	Cwrw	no race	1864	General Peel	Tomato	1915	Pommern	Vaucluse	1967	Royal Palace	Fleet
1813	Smolensko	no race	1865	Gladiateur	Siberia	1916	Clarissimus	Canyon	1968	Sir Ivor	Caergwrle
1814	Olive	Charlotte	1866	Lord Lyon	Repulse	1917	Gay Crusader	Diadem	1969	Right Tack	Full Dress II
1815	Tigris	unnamed filly	1867	Vauban	Achievement	1918	Gainsborough	Ferry	1970	Nijinsky	Humble Duty
1816	Nectar	Rhoda	†1868	Moslem }		1919	The Panther	Roseway	1971	Brigadier Gerard	Altesse Royale
1817	Manfred	Neva		Formosa }	Formosa	1920	Tetratema	Cinna	1972	High Top	Waterloo
1818	Interpreter	Corinne	1869	Pretender	Scottish Queen	1921	Craig An Eran	Bettina	1973	Mon Fils	Mysterious
1819	Antar	Catgut	1870	Macgregor	Hester	1922	St. Louis	Silver Urn	1974	Nonoalco	Highclere
1820	Pindarrie	Rowena	1871	Bothwell	Hannah	1923	Ellangowan	Tranquil	1975	Bolkonski	Nocturnal Spree
1821	Reginald	Zeal	1872	Prince Charlie	Reine	1924	Diophon	Plack	1976	Wollow	Flying Water
1822	Pastille	Whizgig	1873	Gang Forward	Cecilia	1925	Manna	Saucy Sue	1977	Nebbiolo	Mrs McArdy
1823	Nicolo	Zinc	1874	Atlantic	Apology	1926	Colorado	Pillion	1978	Roland Gardens	Enstone Spark
1824	Schahriar	Cobweb	1875	Camballo	Spinaway	1927	Adam's Apple	Cresta Run	1979	Tap On Wood	One In A Million
1825	Enamel	Tontine	1876	Petrarch	Camelia	1928	Flamingo	Scuttle	1980	*Known Fact	Quick As Lightning
1826	Devise	Problem	1877	Chamant	Belpheobe	1929	Mr. Jinks	Taj Mah	1981	To-Agori-Mou	Fairy Footsteps
1827	Turcoman	Arab	1878	Pilgrimage	Pilgrimage	1930	Diolite	Fair Isle	1982	Zino	On The House
1828	Cadland	Zoe	1879	Charibert	Wheel Of Fortune	1931	Cameronian	Four Course	1983	Lomond	Ma Biche
1829	Patron	Young Mouse	1880	Petronel	Elizabeth	1932	Orwell	Kandy	1984	El Gran Senor	Pebbles
1830	Augustus	Charlotte West	1881	Peregrine	Thebais	1933	Rodosto	Betty Brown	1985	Shaheed	Oh So Sharp
1831	Riddlesworth	Galantine	1882	Shotover	St. Marguerite	1934	Colombo	Campanula	1986	Dancing Brave	Midway Lady
1832	Archibald	Galata	1883	Galliard	Hauteur	1935	Bahram	Mesa	1987	Don't Forget Me	Miesque
1833	Clearwell	Tarantella	1884	Scot Free	Busybody	1936	Pay Up	Tide-Way	1988	Doyoun	Ravinella
1834	Glencoe	May-Day	1885	Paradox	Farewell	1937	Le Ksar	Exhibitionnist	1989	Nashwan	Musical Bliss
1835	Ibrahim	Preserve	1886	Ormonde	Miss Jummy	1938	Pasch	Rockfel	1990	Tirol	Salsabil
1836	Bay Midleton	Destiny	1887	Enterprise	Reve d'Or	1939	Blue Peter	Galatea II	1991	Mystiko	Shadayid
1837	Achmet	Chapeau D'Espange	1888	Ayrshire	Briarroot	1940	Djebel	Godiva	1992	Rodrigo De Triano	Hatoof
1838	Grey Momus	Barcarolle	1889	Enthusiast	Minthe	1941	Lambert Simnel	Dancing Time	1993	Zafonic	Sayyedati
1839	The Corsair	Cara	1890	Surefoot	Semolina	1942	Big Game	Sun Chariot	1994	Mister Baileys	Las Meninas
1840	Crucifix	Crucifix	1891	Common	Mimi	1943	Kingsway	Herringbone	1995	Pennekamp	Harayir
1841	Ralph	Potentia	1892	Bona Vista	La Flèche	1944	Garden Path	Picture Play	1996	Mark Of Esteem	Bosra Sham
1842	Meteor	Firebrand	1893	Isinglass	Siffleuse	1945	Court Martial	Sun Stream	1997	Entrepreneur	Sleepytime
1843	Cotherstone	Extempore	1894	Ladas	Amiable	1946	Happy Knight	Hypericum	1998	King of Kings	Cape Verdi
1844	The Ugly Buck	Sorella	1895	Kirkconnel	Galeottia	1947	Tudor Minstrel	Imprudence	1999	Island Sands	Wince
1845	Idas	Picnic	1896	St. Frusquin	Thias	1948	My Babu	Queenpot	2000	King's Best	Lahan
1846	Sir Tatton Sykes	Mendicant	1897	Galtee More	Chelandry	1949	Nimbus	Musidora	2001	Golan	Ameerat
1847	Conyngham	Clementina	1898	Disraeli	Nun Niver	1950	Palestine	Camaree	2002	Rock of Gibraltar	Kazzia
1848	Flatcatcher	Canezou	1899	Flying Fox	Sibola	1951	Ki Ming	Belle Of All	2003	Refuse To Bend	Russian Rhythm
1849	Nunnykirk	The Flea	1900	Diamond Jubilee	Winifreda	1952	Thunderhead II	Zabara	2004	Haafhd	Attraction
1850	Pitsford	Lady Orford	1901	Handicapper	Aida	1953	Nearula	Happy Laughter	2005	Footstepsinthesand	Virginia Waters
1851	Hernandez	Aphrodite	1902	Sceptre	Sceptre	1954	Darius	Festoon	2006	George Washington	Speciosa
1852	Stockwell	Kate	1903	Rock Sand	Quintessence	1955	Our Babu	Meld			
1853	West Australian	Mentmore Lass	1904	St. Amant	Pretty Polly	1956	Gilles De Retz	Honeylight	† Dead heat		
1854	The Hermit	Virage	1905	Vedas	Cherry Lass	1957	Crepello	Rose Royale II	* Winner Nureyev was disqualified		
1855	Lord Of The Isles	Habena	1906	Gorgos	Flair	1958	Pall Mall	Belle Paola			
1856	Fazzoletto	Manganese	1907	Slieve Gallion	Witch Elm	1959	Taboun	Petite Etoile			
1857	Vedette	Imperieuse	1908	Norman III	Rhodora	1960	Martial	Never Too Late			
1858	Fitzroland	Governess	1909	Minoru	Electra	1961	Rockavon	Sweet Solera			
1859	Promised Land	Mayonaise	1910	Neil Gow	Winkipop	1962	Privy Councillor	Abermaid			
1860	The Wizard	Sagitta	1911	Sunstar	Atmah	1963	Only For Life	Hula Dancer			

GRAND NATIONAL

It is the most famous steeplechase in the world, very probably the most famous race, and certainly no other day compares with it as far as interest for the non-racing man is concerned. There have been so many fairytales and dramas, that each race is almost worth a book in its own right.

On his way: Bobbyjo (far right) clears one of the Aintree obstacles on his way to winning the 1999 Grand National.

RUN OVER 4½ miles and 30 fences in the Aintree district of Liverpool, almost always on the first Saturday in April, it is hardly surprising that the race has thrown up so many long-priced winners.

But in spite of its immense popularity, the National has not been without problems. The severity of the fences and its very high profile mean that whenever a horse is killed in the race which, sadly but inevitably, happens sometimes, the death receives far more publicity than if it had happened in any other race.

There have been demonstrations at Liverpool by people claiming to support animal rights; there was the farce of two false starts and a void race in 1993 and the IRA bomb scare of 1997 which resulted in the race being eventually staged 48 hours later. But realistic advice about making the fences less daunting without taking away too much of their difficulty and trying to ensure that every horse and rider is competent to take part, have done much to restore the race's prestige.

The first Grand National was run in 1837, almost certainly over a course at Maghull, though there is a body of opinion which suggests that it

has always been staged at Aintree. It has unarguably taken place at Aintree since 1839, when the very appropriately named Lottery won. He was ridden by Jem Mason who, along with Tom Olliver (winner of three Aintree Nationals on Gay Lad, Vanguard and Peter Simple), was one of the two top jumping riders of the era.

Until 1843, the Grand National was a level-weights affair, but it then became a handicap with horses having to carry burdens in proportion to their ability. In the early days of steeplechasing the sport was almost a hand-to-mouth affair, subject to all sorts of villainy and in need of a ruling body.

Records were very erratically kept, so much so that although the winners in 1849 and 1853 were both called Peter Simple, there is serious doubt as to whether it was the same horse or two different ones who were successful, not least as different personnel were involved in the two successes. Nor are things helped by the fact that for many years horses over the age of six were referred to simply as "aged". Undoubtedly, though, the first horse to win the Grand National twice was the little Abd-el-Kader, who won in 1850 and the following season. No starting price (as was the

case with some early National winners) was recorded for him on the first occasion, but he was a 7–1 chance when he won for the second time.

The victory of the 25–1 shot Free Trader in 1856 was the first of a record five in the race for George Stevens, who also rode the sisters Emblem and Emblematic in 1863 and 1864 and partnered The Colonel to his double victories in 1869–70. He was killed in a fall when riding his hack on Cleeve Hill, above Cheltenham, in 1871.

The Colonel's two successes sandwiched those of the grey The Lamb, in 1868 and 1871, and in the same decade James Machell, who also prepared Hermit to win the 1867 Derby, won the race three times in four years with Disturbance, Reugny and Regal.

Despite the very testing nature of the race, the National initially did not produce many very long-priced winners. Salamander, in 1866, Playfair, 22 years later, and The Soarer, in 1896, were all 40–1 shots; in contrast Cloister, one of the best winners of the race, was 9–2 favourite when he made light

◆ For seven-year-olds and upwards
◆ Held in late March or early April, at Aintree
◆ Inaugurated 1837

RACE DISTANCE
4½ miles, 1839–date

COURSES HOSTING THE GRAND NATIONAL
Maghull 1837–8 ◆ Aintree 1839–1915, 1919–40, 1946–date ◆ Gatwick 1916–18 (1916 The Racecourse Association Steeplechase; 1917–18 The War National) ◆ No race 1941–45, 1993

TRAINERS WITH MOST WINS
4 Fred Rimell, Donald McCain
3 Neville Crump, Harry Escott, William Holman, Willie Moore, Vincent O'Brien

JOCKEYS WITH MOST WINS
5 George Stevens
3 Tommy Beasley, Brian Fletcher, Arthur Nightingall, Tom Olliver, Ernie Piggott, Tommy Pickernell

GRAND NATIONAL WINNERS 1837–2006

YEAR	HORSE	JOCKEY	TRAINER
1837	The Duke	Potts	unknown
1838	Sir Henry	T Olliver	unknown
1839	Lottery	J Mason	unknown
1840	Jerry	B Bretherton	unknown
1841	Charity	A Powell	unknown
1842	Gay Lad	T Olliver	unknown
1843	Vanguard	T Olliver	unknown
1844	Discount	H Crickmere	unknown
1845	Cure-All	Mr W Loft	W Loft
1846	Pioneer	W Taylor	unknown
1847	Matthew	D Wynne	J Courtenay
1848	Chandler	J Little	T Eskrett
1849	Peter Simple	T Cunningham	T Cunningham
1850	Abd-El-Kader	C Green	J Osborne
1851	Abd-El-Kader	T Abbot	J Osborne
1852	Miss Mowbray	A Goodman	G Dockeray
1853	Peter Simple	T Olliver	T Olliver
1854	Bourton	J Tasker	H Wadlow
1855	Wanderer	J Hanlon	unknown
1856	Freetrader	G Stevens	W Holman
1857	Emigrant	C Boyce	C Boyce
1858	Little Charley	W Archer	W Holman
1859	Half Caste	C Green	C Green
1860	Anatis	T Pickernell	W Holman
1861	Jealousy	J Kendall	C Balchin
1862	The Huntsman	H Lamplugh	H Lamplugh
1863	Emblem	G Stevens	E Weever
1864	Emblematic	G Stevens	E Weever
1865	Alcibiade	Capt H Coventry	Cornell
1866	Salamander	A Goodman	J Walters
1867	Cortolvin	J Page	H Lamplugh
1868	The Lamb	G Ede	B Land
1869	The Colonel	G Stevens	R Roberts
1870	The Colonel	G Stevens	R Roberts
1871	The Lamb	T Pickernell	C Green
1872	Casse Tete	J Page	A Cowley
1873	Disturbance	J Richardson	J Richardson
1874	Reugny	J Richardson	J Richardson
1875	Pathfinder	T Pickernell	W Reeves
1876	Regal	J Cannon	J Jewitt
1877	Austerlitz	F Hobson	R I'Anson
1878	Shifnal	J Jones	J Nightingall
1879	The Liberator	G Moore	J Moore
1880	Empress	T Beasley	H Linde
1881	Woodbrook	T Beasley	H Linde
1882	Seaman	Ld Manners	J Machell
1883	Zoedone	Count Kinsky	W Jenkins
1884	Voluptuary	T Wilson	W Wilson
1885	Roquefort	T Wilson	A Yates
1886	Old Joe	T Skelton	G Mulcaster
1887	Gamecock	W Daniells	J Gordon
1888	Playfair	G Mawson	T Cannon
1889	Frigate	T Beasley	M A Maher
1890	Ilex	A Nightingall	J Nightingall
1891	Come Away	H Beasley	H Beasley
1892	Father O'Flynn	R Owen	G Wilson
1893	Cloister	B Dollery	A Yates
1894	Why Not	A Nightingall	W Moore
1895	Wild Man	J Widger	J Gatland
1896	The Soarer	D Campbell	W Moore
1897	Manifesto	T Kavanagh	W McAuliffe
1898	Drogheda	J Gourley	R Dawson
1899	Manifesto	G Williamson	W Moore
1900	Ambush II	A Anthony	A Anthony
1901	Grudon	A Nightingall	B Bletsoe
1902	Shannon Lass	D Read	J Hackett
1903	Drumcree	P Woodland	Sir C Nugent
1904	Moifaa	A Birch	W Hickey
1905	Kirkland	F Mason	E Thomas
1906	Ascetic's Silver	A Hastings	A Hastings
1907	Eremon	A Newey	T Coulthwaite
1908	Rubio	H Bletsoe	F Withington
1909	Lutteur III	G Parfrement	H Escott
1910	Jenkinstown	R Chadwick	T Coulthwaite
1911	Glenside	J Anthony	R H Collis
1912	Jerry M	E Piggott	R Gore
1913	Covertcoat	P Woodland	R Gore
1914	Sunloch	B Smith	T Tyler
1915	Ally Sloper	J Anthony	A Hastings
*1916	Vermouth	J Reardon	J Bell
*1917	Ballymacad	E Driscoll	A Hastings
*1918	Poethlyn	E Piggott	H Escott
1919	Poethlyn	E Piggott	H Escott
1920	Troytown	J Anthony	A Anthony
1921	Shaun Spadah	F Rees	G Poole
1922	Music Hall	L Rees	O Anthony
1923	Sergeant Murphy	Capt G Bennett	G Blackwell
1924	Master Robert	B Trudgill	A Hastings
1925	Double Chance	J Wilson	F Archer
1926	Jack Horner	W Watkinson	H Leader
1927	Sprig	T Leader	T Leader
1928	Tipperary Tim	W Dutton	J Dodd
1929	Gregalach	R Everett	T Leader
1930	Shaun Goilin	T Cullinan	F Hartigan
1931	Grakle	B Lyall	T Coulthwaite
1932	Forbra	J Hamey	T Rimell
1933	Kellsboro'	JD Williams	I Anthony
1934	Golden Miller	G Wilson	B Briscoe
1935	Reynoldstown	F Furlong	N Furlong
1936	Reynoldstown	F Walwyn	N Furlong
1937	Royal Mail	E Williams	I Anthony
1938	Battleship	B Hobbs	R Hobbs
1939	Workman	T Hyde	J Ruttle
1940	Bogskar	M Jones	Lord Stalbridge
1941	No Race		
1942	No Race		
1943	No Race		
1944	No Race		
1945	No Race		
1946	Lovely Cottage	R Petre	T Rayson
1947	Caughoo	E Dempsey	H McDowell
1948	Sheila's Cottage	A Thompson	N Crump
1949	Russian Hero	L McMorrow	G Owen
1950	Freebooter	J Power	B Renton
1951	Nickel Coin	J Bullock	J O'Donoghue
1952	Teal	A Thompson	N Crump
1953	Early Mist	B Marshall	MV O'Brien
1954	Royal Tan	B Marshall	MV O'Brien
1955	Quare Times	P Taaffe	MV O'Brien
1956	ESB	D Dick	F Rimell
1957	Sundew	F Winter	F Hudson
1958	Mr What	A Freeman	T Taaffe
1959	Oxo	M Scudamore	W Stephenson
1960	Merryman II	G Scott	N Crump
1961	Nicolaus Silver	H Beasley	F Rimell
1962	Kilmore	F Winter	R Price
1963	Ayala	P Buckley	K Piggott
1964	Team Spirit	GW Robinson	F Walwyn
1965	Jay Trump	Mr T Smith	F Winter
1966	Anglo	T Norman	F Winter
1967	Foinavon	J Buckingham	J Kempton
1968	Red Alligator	B Fletcher	D Smith
1969	Highland Wedding	E Harty	G Balding
1970	Gay Trip	P Taaffe	F Rimell
1971	Specify	J Cook	J Sutcliffe
1972	Well To Do	G Thorner	T Forster
1973	Red Rum	B Fletcher	D McCain
1974	Red Rum	B Fletcher	D McCain
1975	L'Escargot	T Carberry	D Moore
1976	Rag Trade	J Burke	F Rimell
1977	Red Rum	T Stack	D McCain
1978	Lucius	R Davies	GW Richards
1979	Rubstic	M Barnes	J Leadbetter
1980	Ben Nevis	C Fenwick	T Forster
1981	Aldaniti	R Champion	J Gifford
1982	Grittar	CR Saunders	F Gilman
1983	Corbiere	B De Haan	Mrs J Pitman
1984	Hallo Dandy	N Doughty	GW Richards
1985	Last Suspect	H Davies	T Forster
1986	West Tip	R Dunwoody	M Oliver
1987	Maori Venture	S Knight	A Turnell
1988	Rhyme 'N' Reason	B Powell	D Elsworth
1989	Little Polveir	J Frost	G Balding
1990	Mr Frisk	M Armytage	K Bailey
1991	Seagram	N Hawke	D Barons
1992	Party Politics	C Llewellyn	N Gaselee
1993	Void race		
1994	Miinnehoma	R Dunwoody	M Pipe
1995	Royal Athlete	J Titley	Mrs J Pitman
1996	Rough Quest	M Fitzgerald	T Casey
1997	Lord Ghyllene	A Dobbin	S Brookshaw
1998	Earth Summit	C Llewellyn	Twiston-Davies
1999	Bobbyjo	P Carberry	T Carberry
2000	Papillon	R Walsh	T Walsh
2001	Red Marauder	R Guest	NB Mason
2002	Bindaree	J Culloty	N Twiston-Davies
2003	Monty's Pass	BJ Geraghty	JJ Mangan
2004	Amberleigh House	G Lee	D McCain
2005	Hedgehunter	R Walsh	W Mullins
2006	Numbersixval-verde	N Madden	M Brassil

* The race, run at Gatwick from 1916–18, was organised by the National Hunt Committee without input from the Aintree executive. None of the three races was called the Grand National.

of 12st 7lb in 1893 and won by 40 lengths. He had been second in the two previous seasons.

The only royal winner came in 1900 when the Prince of Wales's Ambush II won; the Prince also owned that years's flat-racing Triple Crown winner Diamond Jubilee. In 1901 the race was held in a snowstorm and the successful Grudon was much helped by his owner Bernard Bletsoe filling the horse's feet with butter to stop the snow balling up inside them.

This was one year in which the National was run without Manifesto who, until the advent of Red Rum in the 1970s, was the outstanding Grand National horse. He ran for 13 consecutive seasons and won the National in 1897 and 1899, was third in 1900, 1902 and 1903, fourth in 1895 and sixth at the age of 16 in 1904. But the story of this last race revolves about the winner Moifaa. The huge New Zealand-bred horse – so legend has it – was shipwrecked and swam ashore before being found on a beach by a fisherman in Ireland.

The one-eyed Glenside was the only horse to complete the course without falling in the appalling conditions of 1911. He carried only 10st 3lb, but Jerry M, who won the following season,

made light of 12st 7lb, as did Poethlyn when, ridden by Lester Piggott's grandfather, Ernie, he followed his wartime success at Gatwick by winning at Aintree in 1918. The oldest horse to win the National was Sergeant Murphy, who was 13 years old when he scored in 1923. The first 100–1 winner came when Tipperary Tim beat the American horse Billy Barton in 1928, after the latter fell at the last. No other horse finished.

In 1934 Golden Miller became the only horse to win the National and the Cheltenham Gold Cup in the same season – L'Escargot later won the two races in different years – and in the following two seasons Reynoldstown became the last horse until Red Rum to win the race twice. Bruce Hobbs, who rode the diminutive Battleship to win in 1938 at the age of 17, is the youngest man to win the National, and when the race resumed after World War II there was another 100–1 winner, Caughoo prevailing in thick fog in 1947.

Vincent O'Brien, who first made his training name with jumpers before turning his attentions to the flat, won three times in a row with Early Mist, Royal Tan and Quare Times from 1953 to 1955. The following year, E.S.B. was the winner,

but this was the occasion on which the Queen Mother's Devon Loch collapsed on the run-in with the race at his mercy.

An extraordinary pile-up at the 23rd fence – the smallest on the course – created a shock in 1967. Every surviving horse except the tailed-off 100–1 chance Foinavon was appallingly impeded by two riderless horses. He found a way through the mayhem to record one of the most amazing triumphs even by Grand National standards.

A few years later, Red Rum became a celebrity as the only horse to win the race three times (1973, 1974 and 1977 – he was second twice in between). Red Rum was trained by Donald "Ginger" McCain who in 2004, at the age of 73, won his fourth Grand National with Amberleigh House.

Jenny Pitman was the first woman to train Grand National winners, Corbiere in 1983 and Royal Athlete in 1995. In 1999 and 2000, there were wins for Irish father/son, trainer/jockey teams – Tommy and Paul Carberry, with Bobbyjo, and Ted and Ruby Walsh, with Papillon. Numbersixvalverde, the 2005 winner, was ridden by 20-year-old Niall "Slippers" Madden, son of the famed Irish rider Niall "Boots" Madden.

MELBOURNE CUP

"The World's Greatest Handicap", the Melbourne Cup – first run in 1861 – is a phenomenon. Evolved from a suggestion by Captain Robert Standish, an Englishman who arrived in the colonies with the reputation of being astute in racing matters, the Cup is truly unique.

THE MELBOURNE CUP is unlike any other major flat race. For a start, it does not possess the classic tradition of the English Derby, the French Prix de l'Arc de Triomphe or the American Kentucky Derby. And, unlike those and other celebrated events, the Melbourne Cup does little, if anything, to enhance the stud value of the winner. In fact more often than not the Cup is won by a New Zealand-bred, but Australian-trained, gelding.

Yet over the years the race has come to be recognised as the world's greatest all-aged handicap and has done more than anything else to publicize the State of Victoria and its capital. Traditionally, the Cup is the richest race on the Australian calendar as well as being the nation's most revered thoroughbred competition.

With speed applied from the moment the starting gates spring open it is an exacting test of stamina and willpower that can only be won by the hardiest of performers. The betting – with plenty of wagering on doubles with the 2400-metre Caulfield Cup run 17 days before – begins as soon as the Cup entries close at the beginning of August, and is another not inconsiderable factor behind the race's popularity.

It is possibly, though, the egalitarian nature of the Melbourne Cup that has most captured the imagination. For each year hundreds of horses, ranging from the lowliest of stayers with battling owners to fashionably-bred weight-for-age horses raced by the rich, are nominated. Under the handicapping system all, theoretically anyway, become equal.

But whatever the reason, the Melbourne Cup, run religiously on the first Tuesday of November, has become a festive ritual involving millions of people around Australia as well as overseas. Significantly, internationally renowned owner and breeder Robert Sangster soon joined those captured by the aura which surrounds the Melbourne Cup.

In recent times, a champagne culture and social whirl has also developed around the Cup, which has added to the revelry of the occasion. Parties abound around the length and breadth of the country as the popuation enters into the spirit of the day and the celebrations at Flemington begin as dawn breaks and lasts deep into the night. Even torrential downpours, like that in 1976, when New Zealander Van Der Hum virtually swam to victory, only serve to strengthen the feeling of camaraderie and good fellowship which prevails among the 100,000 or so spectators.

It is all a long way from the first Melbourne Cup run on 7 November 1861, when 2,100 paid for their day's enjoyment. But even with that initial running the race seemed destined to become part of Australia's folklore with the winner Archer being walked from Nowra on the south coast of New South Wales – a distance of some 500 miles – by his owner and trainer Etienne de Mestre.

Archer won again the following year and de Mestre went on to train another three Melbourne Cup winners to establish a record, which stood until the legendary Bart Cummings came along a century later. After a crisis in 1863, when only seven runners contested the race, the newly-formed Victoria Racing Club took over the event. That marked a beginning of an upward spiral in its history and as Melbourne boomed in the 1880s so did the Cup's fortunes.

By 1890, when Carbine – one of the immortals of the Australian turf and sire of the 1906 Epsom Derby winner Spearmint – was successful, the race was becoming known world-wide. Caught in the fervour of times the VRC added Aus£10,000 to the owners' sweepstakes in Carbine's year to make the Cup the richest race in the world. The nation responded enthusiastically and the largest field ever, of 39 runners, vied for the prize money before a then record crowd of 85,000. As the VRC had hoped, it was a truly memorable running with Carbine setting a weight-carrying record by lumping 10st 5lb, to a 2½ lengths victory in record time of 3min.28.25sec.

Prize-money slipped back to lower levels as the 20th century began and was Aus£6,000 when, in 1906, Poseidon became the first horse to complete the Caulfield and Melbourne Cups

Drink to it: The Melbourne Cup had another surprise winner in 2000 when New Zealand bred stayer Brew won at 14–1.

◆ 3200m Handicap for three-year-olds and upwards
◆ Run at Flemington, six kilometres west of Melbourne
◆ First run 1861

MOST SUCCESSFUL TRAINERS

11 Bart Cummings
5 Etienne de Mestre, DL Freedman
4 J Tait, WS Hickenbotham, R Bradfield, J Scobie

MOST SUCCESSFUL JOCKEYS

4 Bobby Lewis, Harry White
3 WH McLachlan, D Munro, J Purtell, J Johnson, G Boss

MELBOURNE CUP 1861–2005

YEAR	HORSE	JOCKEY	TRAINER
1861	Archer	J Cutts	E de Mestre
1862	Archer	J Cutts	E de Mestre
1863	Banker	H Chifney	S Waldock
1864	Lantern	S Davis	S Mahon
1865	Toryboy	E Cavanagh	P Miley
1866	The Barb	J Tait	J Tait W Davis
1867	Tim Whiffler	J Driscoll	E de Mestre
1868	Glencoe	J Tait	J Tait C Stanley
1869	Warrior	J Morrison	R Sevoir
1870	Nimblefoot	J Day	W Lang
1871	The Pearl	J Tait	J Tait J Cavanagh
1872	The Quack	J Tait	J Tait W Enderson
1873	Don Juan	W Wilson	J Wilson
1874	Haricot	R Piggott	S Harding
1875	Wollomai	R Batty	S Moon
1876	Briseis	P St Albans	J Wilson
1877	Chester	R Piggott	E de Mestre
1878	Calamia	T Brown	E de Mestre
1879	Darriwell	S Cracknell	WE Dakin
1880	Grand Flaneur	T Hales	T Brown
1881	Zulu	James Gough	T Lamond
1882	The Assyrian	C Hutchens	JE Savill
1883	Martini-Henri	J Williamson	M Fennell
1884	Malua	A Robertson	I Foulsham
1885	Sheet Anchor	M O'Brien	T Wilson
1886	Arsenal	W English	H Rayner
1887	Dunlop	T Sanders	J Nicholson
1888	Mentor	M O'Brien	WS Hickenbotham
1889	Bravo	J Anwin	T Wilson
1890	Carbine	R Ramage	WS Hickenbotham
1891	Malvolio	G Redfearn	J Redfearn
1892	Glenloth	G Robson	M Carmody
1893	Tarcoola	H Cripps	J Cripps
1894	Patron	H Dawes	R Bradfield
1895	Auraria	J Stevenson	JH Hill
1896	Newhaven	HJ Gardiner	WS Hickenbotham
1897	Gaulus	S Callinan	W Forrester
1898	The Grafter	John Gough	W Forrester
1899	Merriwee	V Turner	J Wilson Jnr
1900	Clean Sweep	A Richardson	J Scobie
1901	Revenue	F Dunn	H Munro
1902	The Victory	R Lewis	R Bradfield
1903	Lord Cardigan	ND Godby	AE Cornwell
1904	Acrasia	T Clayton	AE Willis
1905	Blue Spec	F Bullock	WS Hickenbotham
1906	Poseidon	T Clayton	I Earnshaw
1907	Apologue	W Evans	I Earnshaw
1908	Lord Nolan	J Flynn	EA Mayo
1909	Prince Foote	WH McLachlan	F McGrath
1910	Comedy King	WH McLachlan	J Lynch
1911	The Parisian	R Cameron	C Wheeler
1912	Piastre	A Shanahan	R O'Connor
1913	Positanus	A Shanahan	J Chambers
1914	Kingsburgh	G Meddick	J Foulsham
1915	Patrobas	R Lewis	C Wheeler
1916	Sasanof	F Foley	M Hobbs
1917	Westcourt	WH McLachlan	J Burton
1918	Night Watch	W Duncan	R Bradfield
1919	Artilleryman	R Lewis	PT Heywood
1920	Poitrel	K Bracken	HJ Robinson
1921	Sister Olive	E O'Sullivan	J Williams
1922	King Ingoda	A Wilson	J Scobie
1923	Bitali	A Wilson	J Scobie
1924	Backwood	P Brown	R Bradfield
1925	Windbag	J Munro	G Price
1926	Spearfelt	H Cairns	V O'Neill
1927	Trivalve	R Lewis	J Scobie
1928	Statesman	J Munro	W Kelso
1929	Nightmarch	R Reed	A McAulay
1930	Phar Lap	JE Pike	HR Telford
1931	White Nose	N Percival	EJ Hatwell
1932	Peter Pan	W Duncan	F McGrath
1933	Hall Mark	CB Kellow	J Holt J O'Sullivan
1934	Peter Pan	D Munro	F McGrath
1935	Marabou	K Voitre	L Robertson
1936	Wotan	O Phillips	J Fryer
1937	The Trump	A Reed	SW Reid
1938	Catalogue	F Shean	AW McDonald
1939	Rivette	E Preston	H Bamber
1940	Old Rowley	A Knox	JA Scully
1941	Skipton	W Cook	J Fryer
1942	Colonus	H McCloud	F Manning
1943	Dark Felt	V Hartney	R Webster
1944	Sirius	D Munro	E Fisher
1945	Rainbird	W Cook	S Evans
1946	Russia	D Munro	E Hush
1947	Hiraji	J Purtell	JW McCurley
1948	Rimfire	R Neville	S Boyden
1949	Foxami	W Fellowes	D Lewis
1950	Comic Court	P Glennon	JM Cummings
1951	Delta	N Sellwood	MM cCarten
1952	Dalray	W Williamson	CC McCarthy
1953	Hiraji	J Purtell	R Sinclair
1954	Rising Fast	J Purtell	IJ Tucker
1955	Toporoa	N Sellwood	TJ Smith
1956	Evening Peal	G Podmore	ED Lawson
1957	Straight Draw	N McGrowdie	JM Mitchell
1958	Baystone	M Schumacher	J Green
1959	MacDougal	P Glennon	RW Roden
1960	Hi Jinx	WA Smith	TH Knowles
1961	Lord Fury	R Selkrig	FB Lewis
1962	Even Stevens	L Coles	A McGregor
1963	Gatum Gatum	J Johnson	HG Heagney
1964	Polo Prince	RW Taylor	JP Carter
1965	Light Fingers	R Higgins	JB Cummings
1966	Galilee	J Miller	JB Cummings
1967	Red Handed	R Higgins	JB Cummings
1968	Rain Lover	J Johnson	ML Robins
1969	Rain Lover	J Johnson	ML Robins
1970	Baghdad Note	EJ Didham	R Heasley
1971	Silver Knight	RB Marsh	E Temperton
1972	Piping Lane	J Letts	GM Hanlon
1973	Gala Supreme	F Reys	RJ Hutchins
1974	Think Big	H White	JB Cummings
1975	Think Big	H White	JB Cummings
1976	Van Der Hum	RJ Skelton	LH Robinson
1977	Gold And Black	J Duggan	JB Cummings
1978	Arwon	H White	GM Hanlon
1979	Hyperno	H White	JB Cummings
1980	Beldale Ball	J Letts	CS Hayes
1981	Just A Dash	P Cook	TJ Smith
1982	Gurner's Lane	L Dittman	GT Murphy
1983	Kiwi	J Cassidy	ES Lupton
1984	Black Knight	P Cook	GM Hanlon
1985	What A Nuisance	P Hyland	J Meagher
1986	At Talaq	M Clarke	CS Hayes
1987	Kensei	L Olsen	LJ Bridge
1988	Empire Rose	T Allan	LK Laxon
1989	Tawrrific	RS Dye	DL Freedman
1990	Kingston Rule	D Beadman	JB Cummings
1991	Let's Elope	S King	JB Cummings
1992	Subzero	G Hall	DL Freedman
1993	Vintage Crop	MJ Kinane	DK Weld
1994	Jeune	W Harris	DA Hayes
1995	Doriemus	D Oliver	DL Freedman
1996	Saintly	D Beadman	JB Cummings
1997	Might And Power	J Cassidy	J Denham
1998	Jezabeel	C Munce	B Jenkins
1999	Rogan Josh	J Marshall	JB Cummings
2000	Brew	K McEvoy	M Moroney
2001	Ethereal	S Seamar	S Laxon
2002	Media Puzzle	DM Oliver	D Weld
2003	Makybe Diva	G Boss	D Hall
2004	Makybe Diva	G Boss	DL Freedman
2005	Makybe Diva	G Boss	DL Freedman

double. The heady years of Carbine's time were only distant memories when another immortal – Phar Lap – entered the annals of the Melbourne Cup. Despite the depression 72,358 people packed into Flemington to see the Red Terror, as Phar Lap was known, win the Cup of 1930. Although asked to establish a weight-carrying record for a four-year-old of 9st 12lb, Phar Lap started at odds of 8–11, the only odds-on favourite ever in the Cup, and justified his supporters' confidence, romping home by three lengths.

Four years later the redoubtable Peter Pan lumped 9st 10lb to victory as a five-year-old – he had also been triumphant in 1932 – to become the first stayer since Archer to capture two Melbourne Cups. But it was not until the beginning of the 1950s that a horse of class was to win the Cup again. Then in the space of five years – Comic Court (1950), Delta (1951), Dalray (1952) and Rising Fast (1954) – restored much prestige to the honour of winning the Melbourne Cup.

It was in 1965 that Bart Cummings began to exert his influence on the Cup when his gallant four-year-old mare Light Fingers edged out stablemate Ziema by a half-head after a desperate struggle over the concluding stages.

Cummings, then 37, had been the attendant for his father's runner Comic Court when he had raced away with the Cup 15 years earlier. He prepared the outstanding performer Galilee to win in 1966 as well as Red Handed in 1967 and equalled de Mestre's record when Think Big scored consecutive wins – Archer and Rain Lover (1968–69) are the only others to achieve this feat – in 1974 and 1975 (the two-mile race became a metric event – 3200m – in 1973). Cummings became the record holder in 1977, when Gold And Black scored a courageous win and he notched another victory in 1979, when jockey Harry White equalled Bobby Lewis's record of four wins aboard Hyperno.

Tragically that year, the favourite Dulcify – ridden by Brent Thomson and the winner, ten days earlier, of the coveted W.S. Cox Plate – had to be destroyed after being injured and that disaster marked one of the most depressing points in the distinguished training career of Colin Sidney Hayes. But the determination of Hayes, who was beginning to fear the Melbourne Cup was a jinx race for him, was fired by the ghastly experience he endured with Dulcify. Hayes returned in 1980 with four horses. His perseverance was rewarded when Sangster's Bedale Ball became the first imported runner in 56 years to win the Cup.

Then in 1986 it was the turn of Colin Hayes again when the Roberto horse At Talaq scored for Sheikh Hamdan bin Rashid al-Maktoum, who was to win again in 1994 with Jeune, trained by C.S.'s son David.

As the 1990s began to unfold, the Melbourne Cup underwent a dramatic change as the VRC, primarily through the efforts of racing manager Les Benton, began to court Northern Hemisphere participation. This led through to the memorable victory of the dour stayer Vintage Crop, prepared by Ireland's Dermot Weld and ridden by Michael Kinane. Vintage Crop was also to be placed behind Doriemus and Nothin' Leica Dane in his third attempt at the race in 1995.

While Northern Hemisphere involvement became an accepted part of the Melbourne Cup's format, it did not prevent Bart Cummings from dominating the race. Cummings captured the event in 1990 with the Secretariat horse Kingston Rule, who established a time record of 3min. 16.1sec. – it was the first running of the Cup with a winner's prize of $1 million. Further, Cummings was victorious in 1991 with Let's Elope, who had previously won the Caulfield Cup; and in 1996 with the Sky Chase gelding Saintly, whom he had also bred and campaigned in partnership with Malaysia's Dato Tan Chin Nam; and in 1999, with the nondescript seven-year-old Rogan Josh.

But Makybe Diva – who won the Cup in three consecutive years, from 2003–2005 – brought true definition to the word "brilliant". Her record may be one that stands for the ages.

IRISH DERBY

The Irish Derby, run over 1½ miles at the Curragh in Co. Kildare, now on the last Sunday in June or first in July, is markedly younger than its counterpart at Epsom as it was not staged until 1866, by which time the Derby was 86 years old. It is Ireland's most prestigious race and many of its winners have been of the highest class.

FOR MANY YEARS it was much in the shadow of the world's most famous classic at Epsom. It only became a level-weights race after World War II – before then winners had carried as much as 9st 8lb, as did Orby in 1907, and as little as 7st 13lb, as did Wild Bouquet in 1908. Orby was one of the best early winners of the race. Having become the first Irish-trained horse to win at Epsom, when he won by two lengths from Wool Winder, he had no problems in completing the double at the Curragh, but broke down irretrievably after finishing last in his only other run.

Very unusually for a classic, the Irish Derby boasts two dead heats. In 1924 the judge could not separate Haine and Zodiac, though as Haine was trying to concede 4lb he emerges as the moral winner, and ten years later Primero had to settle for a share of the spoils with Patriot King, to whom he was giving 10lb.

In 1932 the Aga Khan won the race with Dastur, whose half-brother Bahram was to land the Triple Crown in Britain three years later. Dastur, who also won the Sussex Stakes at Goodwood and the King Edward VII Stakes at Ascot, deserved his name on a list of classic winners as he was runner-up in the Derby, the St. Leger and the 2,000 Guineas in England.

The Phoenix, who came from the same family as Bahram and Dastur, won in 1943. He won all his three starts as a two-year-old, when he was

Double top: Sinndar and Johnny Murtagh follow their Epsom success by completing a Derby double at the Curragh in 2000.

rated top of his generation, as well as the Irish 2,000 and was second in the Irish St. Leger on the only occasion that he was beaten – good going for a horse whose yearling purchase price (even allowing for the exigencies of wartime) was only 290gns.

Sayajirao, who at 28,000gns was the most expensive yearling at the time, won the 1947 race en route to being rated the top three-year-old of the season. He also won the St. Leger and the Lingfield Derby Trial and was third in the Derby and the 2,000 Guineas.

Vincent O'Brien won the race for the first time in 1953 with Chamier, and four years later sent out arguably its first really top-class winner in Ballymoss. The colt had shown how good he might be when he was second to Crepello in the Derby at Epsom and he won the St. Leger later that year. As a four-year-old he had an outstanding career with wins in the Prix de l'Arc de Triomphe, the King George VI And Queen Elizabeth Stakes, the Eclipse and the Coronation Cup.

There should have been further cause for celebration in the O'Brien camp three years later when Chamour upset the odds on Alcaeus, who had finished second to St Paddy at Epsom three weeks earlier, but the fact that his success is officially credited to O'Brien's brother Phonsie indicates that all may not have been well.

Neither was it. Earlier in the season Chamour had won a maiden race at the Curragh, but post-race analysis revealed indications of a prohibited substance and, as the rules stood in those days,

not only were horses disqualified in such circumstances, but trainers lost their licences as well. Vincent O'Brien's was initally withdrawn for 18 months, though this was later reduced to a year. Fortunately his brother was able to take over official running of the yard, and the reaction from the crowd when Chamour won the Irish Derby left no doubt about what they thought of the stewards' decision.

The advent of sponsorship in the early 1960s was followed by a conspicuous advance in the quality of the fields, and it started to become the norm rather than the exception for the Derby winner to go to the Curragh after Epsom. Things, though, did not always go according to plan and in 1962 Larkspur, who had admittedly been a very fortuitous winner at Epsom when seven horses were brought down, could finish only fourth behind the French-trained Tambourine II.

The dual Derby was also the plan for the 1963 winner Relko, but he was withdrawn at the start in highly dramatic circumstances in Ireland and Ragusa, who had been third to him at Epsom, swept to a victory which was followed by successes in the King George VI And Queen Elizabeth Stakes and the St. Leger.

Santa Claus doubled up in 1964 and Meadow Court, who had been second to Sea-Bird at Epsom, went one better at the Curragh the following year, to be followed by the full brothers Ribocco and Ribero, both of whom were owned by Charles Engelhard, trained by Fulke Johnson Houghton and ridden by Lester Piggott.

IRISH DERBY 1866–2005

YEAR HORSE	JOCKEY	TRAINER	YEAR HORSE	JOCKEY	TRAINER	YEAR HORSE	JOCKEY	TRAINER	YEAR HORSE	JOCKEY	TRAINER
1866 Selim	C Maidment	J Cockin	1903 Lord Rossmore	J Dillon	J Fallon	1938 Rosewell	M Wing	A Blake	1974 English Prince	Y Saint-Martin	P Walwyn
1867 Golden Plover	C Maidment	J Cockin	1904 Royal Arch	F Morgan	M Dawson	1939 Mondragon	Joe Canty	James Canty	1975 Grundy	Pat Eddery	P Walwyn
1868 Madeira	D Wynne	Holland	1905 Flax Park	P Hughes	James Dunne	1940 Turkhan	C Smirke	F Butters	1976 Malacte	P Paquet	F Boutin
1869 The Scout	W Miller	J Johnstone	1906 Killeagh	C Aylin	M Dawson	1941 Sol Oriens	G Wells	A Blake	1977 The Minstrel	L Piggott	MV O'Brien
1870 Billy Pitt	W Canavan	T Connolly	1907 Orby	W Bullock	F McCabe	1942 Windsor Slipper	M Wing	M Collins	1978 Shirley Heights	G Starkey	J Dunlop
1871 Maid of Athens	T Broderick	P Doucie	1908 Wild Bouquet	P Hughes	James Dunne	1943 The Phoenix	Joe Canty	F Myerscough	1979 Troy	W Carson	WR Hern
1872 Trickstress	W Miller	T Moran	1909 Bachelor's Double	A Sharples	M Dawson	1944 Slide On	J Moylan	Fetherstnhaugh	1980 Tyrnavos	A Murray	B Hobbs
1873 Kyrle Daly	T Broderick	P Doucie	1910 Aviator	John Doyle	P Behan	1945 Piccadilly	J Moylan	Fetherstnhaugh	1981 Shergar	L Piggott	M Stoute
1874 Ben Battle	E Martin	T Connolly	1911 Shanballymore	John Doyle	J Dwyer	1946 Bright News	M Wing	D Rogers	1982 Assert	C Roche	D O'Brien
1875 Innishowen	G Ashworth	J Toon	1912 Civility	D Maher	B Kirby	1947 Sayajirao	E Britt	F Armstrong	1983 Shareef	WR Swinburn	M Stoute
1876 Umpire	P Lynch	J French	1913 Bachelor's Wedding	S Donoghue	HS Persse	1948 Nathoo	WR Johnstone	F Butters	1984 El Gran Senor	Pat Eddery	MV O'Brien
1877 Redskin	F Wynne	D Broderick	1914 Land of Song	S Donoghue	HS Persse	1949 Hindostan	WR Johnstone	F Butters	1985 Law Society	Pat Eddery	MV O'Brien
1878 Madame Dubarry	F Wynne	E Martin	1915 Ballaghtobin	W Barrett	J Hunter	1950 Dark Warrior	J Thompson	P Prendergast	1986 Shahrastani	WR Swinburn	M Stoute
1879 Soulouque	J Connolly	T Connolly	1916 Furore	H Robbins	V Tabor	1951 Fraise Du Bois II	C Smirke	H Wragg	1987 Sir Harry Lewis	J Reid	B Hills
1880 King of the Bees	F Wynne	D Broderick	1917 First Flier	W Barrett	J Parkinson	1952 Thirteen Of Diamonds	J Mullane	P Prendergast	1988 Kahyasi	R Cochrane	L Cumani
1881 Master Ned	T Broderick	P Doucie	1918 King John	H Beasley	PP Gilpin	1953*Chamier	W Rickaby	MV O'Brien	1989 Old Vic	S Cauthen	H Cecil
1882 Sortie	N Behan	P Doucie	1919 Loch Lomond	E Quirke	J Parkinson	1954 Zarathustra	P Powell, jun.	M Hurley	1990 Salsabil	W Carson	J Dunlop
1883 Sylph	J Connolly	James Dunne	1920 He Goes	F Templeman	F Butters	1955 Panaslipper	J Eddery	S McGrath	1991 Generous	A Munro	P Cole
1884 Theologian	J Connolly	W Behan	1921 Ballyheron	M Wing	J Hunter	1956 Talgo	E Mercer	H Wragg	1992 St. Jovite	C Roche	J Bolger
1885 St Kevin	H Saunders	James Dunne	1922 Spike Island	G Archibald	PP Gilpin	1957 Ballymoss	TP Burns	MV O'Brien	1993 Commander In Chief	Pat Eddery	H Cecil
1886 Theodemir	J Connolly	G Moore	1923 Waygood	M Wing	W Halsey	1958 Sindon	L Ward	M Dawson	1994 Balanchine	L Dettori	H Ibrahim
1887 Pet Fox	T Kavanagh	H Linde	†1924 Haine	Joe Canty	C Davis	1959 Fidalgo	J Mercer	H Wragg	1995 Winged Love	O Peslier	A Fabre
1888 Theodolite	W Warne	G Moore	Zodiac	G Archibald	PP Gilpin	1960 Chamour	G Bougoure	AS O'Brien	1996 Zagreb	P Shanahan	D Weld
1889 Tragedy	Mr T Beasley	T Gordon	1925 Zionist	H Beasley	R Dawson	1961 Your Highness	H Holmes	H Cottrill	1997 Desert King	C Roche	AP O'Brien
1890 Kentish Fire	M Dawson	R Meredith	1926 Embargo	S Donoghue	Bartholomew Jr	1962 Tambourine II	R Poincelet	E Pollet	1998 Dream Well	C Asmussen	P Bary
1891 Narraghmore	Mr T Beasley	C Archer	1927 Knight Of The Grail	M Beary	R Farquharson	1963 Ragusa	G Bougoure	P Prendergast	1999 Montjeu	C Asmussen	J Hammond
1892 Roy Neil	M Dawson	R Meredith	1928 Baytown	F Fox	N Scobie	1964 Santa Claus	W Burke	JM Rogers	2000 Sinndar	J Murtagh	J Oxx
1893 Bowline	M Dawson	R Meredith	1929 Kopi	FN Winter	W Earl	1965 Meadow Court	L Piggott	P Prendergast	2001 Galileo	MJ Kinane	AP O'Brien
1894 Blairfinde	W Garrett	S Darling	1930 Rock Star	M Wing	W Nightingall	1966 Sodium	F Durr	G Todd	2002 High Chaparral	MJ Kinane	AP O'Brien
1895 Portmarnock	W Clayton	S Jeffrey	1931 Sea Serpent	Joe Canty	P Behan	1967 Ribocco	L Piggott	Jhnsn Houghtn	2003 Alamshar	JP Murtagh	J Oxx
1896 Gulsalberk	A Aylin	S Jeffrey	1932 Dastur	M Beary	F Butters	1968 Ribero	L Piggott	Jhnsn Houghtn	2004 Grey Swallow	PJ Smullen	DK Weld
1897 Wales	T Fiely	W Cullen	1933 Harninero	C Ray	R Dawson	1969 Prince Regent	G Lewis	E Pollet	2005 Hurricane Run	K Fallon	A Fabre
1898 Noble Howard	T Moran	R Exshaw	†1934 Primero }	C Ray	R Dawson	1970 Nijinsky	L Ward	MV O'Brien			
1899 Oppressor	A Anthony	S Jeffrey	Patriot King }	G Bezant	F Pratt	1971 Irish Ball	A Gibert	P Lallie	† Dead heat		
1900 Gallinaria	G Lushinton	D McNally	1935 Museum	S Donoghue	JT Rogers	1972 Steel Pulse	W Williamson	A Breasley	* Winner, Premonition, was disqualified		
1901 Carrigavalla	A Anthony	D McNally	1936 Raeburn	T Burns	J Lawson	1973 Weaver's Hall	G McGrath	S McGrath			
1902 St. Brendan	D Condon	M Dawson	1937 Phidias	S Donoghue	JT Rogers						

There were other French successes with Prince Regent in 1969 and Irish Ball in 1971, and in between those two, Vincent O'Brien won the race for the third time with Nijinsky, who was ridden by Liam Ward. The agreement was that Ward would ride the colt in all races in Ireland and Lester Piggott outside that country.

In 1975 Grundy became the first horse since Santa Claus to complete the Epsom–Curragh double, but this achievement then became the norm with victories in Ireland for The Minstrel, Shirley Heights, Troy, Shergar, Shahrastani and Kahyasi. Generous and Commander in Chief accomplished the feat during the 1990s, as did Sinndar, Galileo and High Chaparral during the opening years of the 21st century.

The O'Brien name has continued to make major Irish Derby impacts. Vincent's son, David, sent out the 1982 winner, Assert, and Vincent himself saddled consecutive winners, El Gran Senor and Law Society, in 1984–1985. More recently, Aidan O'Brien – who is unrelated to either Vincent or David – won the 1998 race with Desert King and the 2001 and 2002 renewals with the aforesaid Galileo and High Chaparral.

Other important Irish Derby participants were the Maktoums. Sheikh Mohammed won with Shareef Dancer in 1983, and in the ensuing 12 years Maktoum horses triumphed on four more occasions. Steve Cauthen won on Old Vic for Sheikh Mohammed in 1989. The following year, Sheikh Hamdan bin Rashid al Maktoum won with the filly Salsabil, paying a Ir60,000-pound supplemental entry fee to get her in.

Salsabil was the first of her gender to win the Irish Derby in 90 years. The Maktoums' Godolphin operation won again with the filly Balanchine in 1994, and Sheikh Mohammed was victorious with Winged Love in 1995 – the first big success outside of France for jockey Olivier Peslier.

No charity: Generous, ridden by Alan Munro, goes clear to win his second major Derby at the Curragh in 1981.

BELMONT STAKES

The final event in North America's Triple Crown series, the Belmont Stakes is also the oldest of the classics, predating the Preakness Stakes by four years and the Kentucky Derby by eight. The Belmont does not have an uninterrupted history, for it was on hiatus from 1911–12, a period when anti-betting legislation closed down racing in New York.

NAMED AFTER AUGUST BELMONT, the Belmont Stakes was originally run at Jerome Park, then Morris Park from 1890–1904. In 1905, it was moved to Belmont Park, which had been constructed at a cost of $2.5 million. With the exception of the years 1963–67, when the race was run at Aqueduct while Belmont Park was being demolished and rebuilt, the Belmont Stakes has hence been run at the track whose name it shares.

There are unique features in the Belmont Stakes' heritage that differ from those of the other Triple Crown events. Its inaugural winner, Ruthless, was a filly. From 1905–20, the race was run in a clockwise direction, over what historical accounts refer to as "a fish-hook course" that blended the training track with the main dirt oval.

From 1919 through 1956, geldings were not allowed to participate in the Belmont. The only gelding to win the race to date is Creme Fraiche in 1985. The ridgling, A.P. Indy, accounted for the 1992 renewal, and was subsequently named divisional champion and Horse of the Year.

In 1993, Julie Krone became the first female jockey to win a Triple Crown event, guiding the 13.40–1 shot, Colonial Affair, to a 2 1/4-length Belmont victory. This accomplishment figured

heavily in Krone becoming the first woman elected to the National Museum of Racing's Hall of Fame in 2000.

Early on, the Belmont was dubbed "the breeders' race," and older racing participants often still refer to it as such. Three-year-olds produced by Kentucky have accounted for 88 runnings of the event, but other locales have various claims to fame. Scottish Chieftain, the 1897 Belmont winner, was bred in Montana. Secretariat, whose 31-length Belmont victory in 1973 is regarded as one of the greatest performances ever witnessed on an American racetrack, was a Virginia-bred.

Colts imported from Europe have won the Belmont eight times. The first to do so was English-bred Saxon in 1874. The most recent was Irish-bred Go and Go in 1990. Afleet Alex, in 2005, became the fifth Florida-bred Belmont winner, and the first produced by that state's breeding programme since Conquistador Cielo in 1982.

In 1919, Sir Barton became the first horse to sweep the Triple Crown, completing the feat by drawing off in the Belmont by five lengths in a new American record of 2:17 2/5 for 11 furlongs. But the phrase Triple Crown, coupling the trio of races, had yet to be coined. Sir Barton's accomplishment later became gigantic, albeit in retrospect.

The following year, Man o' War won the Belmont by 20 lengths, eclipsing Sir Barton's standard by more than three seconds. At stud, Man o' War sired three other Belmont Stakes winners: American Flag, who captured the race in 1925; Crusader, who did the same the following year; and War Admiral, who swept the Triple Crown events in 1937. All told, 11 Belmont winners, Count Fleet, Secretariat and Seattle Slew among them, have sired one or more colts who also won the race.

Only 21 fillies have competed in the Belmont, including Ruthless, the race's inaugural winner. Eight years after her Belmont victory, she was bred to her own sire. The result was a foal so deformed it couldn't stand. The most recent distaff winner was Tanya, who drew clear early,

Sad ending: Charismatic's bid for a Triple Crown ended with an injury suffered in the stretch run of the 1999 Belmont.

- ◆ For three-year-olds
- ◆ Held on the third Saturday following the Preakness Stakes at Belmont Park in Elmont, N.Y.
- ◆ Inaugurated 1867

RACE DISTANCES
1⅝ miles, 1867–73
1½ miles, 1874–89, 1926–date
1⅜ miles, 1896–1903, 1906–25
1¼ miles, 1890–92, 1895, 1904–05
1⅛ miles, 1893–94

TRACKS HOSTING BELMONT STAKES
Jerome Park 1867–89
Morris Park, 1890–1904
Belmont Park, 1905–10, 1913–62, 1968–date
Aqueduct, 1963–67
Not held 1911–12

TRAINERS WITH MOST WINS
8 James Rowe Sr.
7 Sam Hildreth
6 James "Sunny Jim" Fitzsimmons.

JOCKEYS WITH MOST WINS
6 Eddie Arcaro, James McLaughlin
5 Earl Sande, Bill Shoemaker
3 Braulio Baeza, Pat Day, Laffit Pincay, Jr., GL Stevens, James Stout

WINNING FILLIES
Ruthless (1867)
Tanya (1905)

then held on to win by a half-length at the inaugural Belmont Park meet in 1905.

Sixty runnings of the Belmont have been won by favourites, for a win ratio of 43.8 per cent. The shortest price, 1–20, was returned by Count Fleet in 1943. The longest, 70.25–1, was returned by Sarava under Edgar Prado in 2002. The previous longest-priced winner, Sherluck, who was 65.05–1 in 1961, was ridden by Braulio Baeza, who has the distinction of being a Belmont winner over three different surfaces: at old Belmont Park with Sherluck; at Aqueduct with Chateaugay in 1963; and at new Belmont Park with Arts and Letters in 1969.

Secretariat's margin of victory in the Belmont remains the largest recorded in any Triple Crown event. His final time, 2:24, still stands as the world record for 12 furlongs on a dirt surface. The smallest victory margin in the Belmont, a nose, was first registered by Granville in 1936,

BELMONT STAKES 1867–2006

YEAR	HORSE	JOCKEY	TRAINER
1867	Ruthless	J Gilpatrick	AJ Minor
1868	General Duke	R Swim	A Thompson
1869	Fenian	C Miller	J Pincus
1870	Kingfisher	E Brown	R Colston
1871	Harry Basset	W Miller	D McDaniel
1872	Joe Daniels	J Rowe	D McDaniel
1873	Springbok	J Rowe	D McDaniel
1874	Saxon	G Barbee	W Prior
1875	Calvin	R Swim	A Williams
1876	Algerine	W Donohue	TW Doswell
1877	Cloverbrook	C Holloway	J Walden
1878	Duke of Magenta	L Hughes	RW Walden
1879	Spendthrift	S Evans	T Puryear
1880	Grenada	L Hughes	RW Walden
1881	Saunterer	T Costello	RW Walden
1882	Forester	J McLaughlin	L Stuart
1883	George Kinney	J McLaughlin	J Rowe
1884	Panique	J McLaughlin	J Rowe
1885	Tyrant	P Duffy	W Claypool
1886	Inspector B	J McLaughlin	F McCabe
1887	Hanover	J McLaughlin	F McCabe
1888	Sir Dixon	J McLaughlin	F McCabe
1889	Eric	W Hayward	J Huggins
1890	Burlington	S Barnes	A Cooper
1891	Foxford	E Garrison	M Donavan
1892	Patron	W Hayward	L Stuart
1893	Commanche	W Simms	G Hannon
1894	Henry of Navarre	W Simms	B McClelland
1895	Belmar	F Taral	E Feakes
1896	Hastings	H Griffin	JJ Hyland
1897	Scottish Chieftain	J Scherrer	M Byrnes
1898	Bowling Brook	F Littlefield	RW Walden
1899	Jean Bereaud	RR Clawson	SC Hildreth
1900	Ildrim	N Turner	HE Leigh
1901	Commando	H Spencer	J Rowe
1902	Masterman	J Bullman	JJ Hyland
1903	Africander	J Bullman	R Miller
1904	Delhi	G Odom	J Rowe
1905	Tanya	E Hildebrand	JW Rogers
1906	Burgomaster	L Lyne	JW Rogers
1907	Peter Pan	G Mountain	J Rowe
1908	Colin	J Notter	J Rowe
1909	Joe Madden	E Dugan	SC Hildreth
1910	Sweep	J Butwell	J Rowe
1911	No Race		
1912	No Race		
1913	Prince Eugene	R Troxler	J Rowe
1914	Luke McLuke	M Buxin	JF Schorr
1915	The Finn	G Byrne	EW Heffner
1916	Friar Rock	E Haynes	SC Hildreth
1917	Hourless	J Butwell	SC Hildreth
1918	Johren	F Robinson	A Simons
1919	Sir Barton	J Loftus	HG Bedwell
1920	Man o' War	C Kummer	L Feustel
1921	Grey Lag	E Sande	SC Hildreth
1922	Pillory	CH Miller	TJ Healey
1923	Zev	E Sande	SC Hildreth
1924	Mad Play	E Sande	SC Hildreth
1925	American Flag	A Johnson	GR Tompkins
1926	Crusader	A Johnson	G Conway
1927	Chance Shot	E Sande	P Coyne
1928	Vito	C Kummer	M Hirsch
1929	Blue Larkspur	M Garner	C Hastings
1930	Gallant Fox	E Sande	J Fitzsimmons
1931	Twenty Grand	C Kurtsinger	J Rowe Jr
1932	Faireno	T Malley	J Fitzsimmons
1933	Hurryoff	M Garner	H McDaniel
1934	Peace Chance	WD Wright	P Coyne
1935	Omaha	W Saunders	J Fitzsimmons
1936	Granville	J Stout	J Fitzsimmons
1937	War Admiral	C Kurtsinger	G Conway
1938	Pasteurized	J Stout	GM Odom
1939	Johnstown	J Stout	J Fitzsimmons
1940	Bimelech	FA Smith	W Hurley
1941	Whirlaway	E Arcaro	BA Jones
1942	Shut Out	E Arcaro	JM Gaver
1943	Count Fleet	J Longden	GD Cameron
1944	Bounding Home	GL Smith	M Brady
1945	Pavot	E Arcaro	O White
1946	Assault	W Mehrtens	M Hirsch
1947	Phalanx	R Donoso	SE Veitch
1948	Citation	E Arcaro	HA Jones
1949	Capot	T Atkinson	JM Gaver
1950	Middleground	W Boland	M Hirsch
1951	Counterpoint	D Gorman	SE Veitch
1952	One Count	E Arcaro	O White
1953	Native Dancer	E Guerin	WC Winfrey
1954	High Gun	E Guerin	M Hirsch
1955	Nashua	E Arcaro	J Fitzsimmons
1956	Needles	D Erb	HL Fontaine
1957	Gallant Man	W Shoemaker	JA Nerud
1958	Cavan	P Anderson	TJ Barry
1959	Sword Dancer	W Shoemaker	JE Burch
1960	Celtic Ash	W Hartack	TJ Barry
1961	Sherluck	B Baeza	H Young
1962	Jaipur	W Shoemaker	WF Mulholland
1963	Chateaugay	B Baeza	P Conway
1964	Quadrangle	M Ycaza	E Burch
1965	Hail to All	J Sellers	E Yowell
1966	Amberoid	W Boland	L Laurin
1967	Damascus	W Shoemaker	FY Whiteley Jr
1968	Stage Door Johnny	H Gustines	JM Gaver
1969	Arts and Letters	B Baeza	E Burch
1970	High Echelon	JL Rotz	JW Jacobs
1971	Pass Catcher	W Blum	E Yowell
1972	Riva Ridge	R Turcotte	L Laurin
1973	Secretariat	R Turcotte	L Laurin
1974	Little Current	MA Rivera	TL Rondinello
1975	Avatar	W Shoemaker	AT Doyle
1976	Bold Forbes	A Cordero Jr	LS Barrera
1977	Seattle Slew	J Cruguet	WH Turner Jr
1978	Affirmed	S Cauthen	LS Barrera
1979	Coastal	R Hernandez	DA Whiteley
1980	Temperence Hill	E Maple	JB Cantey
1981	Summing	G Martens	L Barrera
1982	Conquistador Cielo	L Pincay Jr	W C Stephens
1983	Caveat	L Pincay Jr	WC Stephens
1984	Swale	L Pincay Jr	WC Stephens
1985	Creme Fraiche	E Maple	WC Stephens
1986	Danzig Connection	CJ McCarron	WC Stephens
1987	Bet Twice	C Perret	WA Croll Jr
1988	Risen Star	E Delahoussaye	LB Roussel III
1989	Easy Goer	P Day	C McGaughey III
1990	Go And Go	MJ Kinane	DK Weld
1991	Hansel	JD Bailey	FL Brothers
1992	A P Indy	E Delahoussaye	N Drysdale
1993	Colonial Affair	J Krone	FS Schulhofer
1994	Tabasco Cat	P Day	DW Lukas
1995	Thunder Gulch	GL Stevens	DW Lukas
1996	Editor's Note	RR Douglas	DW Lukas
1997	Touch Gold	CJ McCarron	D Hofmans
1998	Victory Gallop	GL Stevens	WE Walden
1999	Lemon Drop Kid	J Santos	FS Schulhofer
2000	Commendable	P Day	DW Lukas
2001	Point Given	GL Stevens	B Baffert
2002	Sarava	E Prado	KG McPeek
2003	Empire Maker	JD Bailey	R. Frankel
2004	Birdstone	E Prado	NP Zito
2005	Afleet Alex	J Rose	TF Ritchey
2006	Jazil	F Jara	K McLaughlin

then matched by Jaipur at the completion of his brilliant stretch duel with Admiral's Voyage in 1962. A nose was also the margin recorded by Victory Gallop in 1998, when he got up in the final strides to deprive Real Quiet of a Triple Crown sweep.

One of the most-heralded Belmont accomplishments was the five consecutive victories registered by Woodford C. "Woody" Stephens. His streak began with Conquistador Cielo's 14-length triumph in 1982, and culminated with Danzig Connection's win in 1986. Yet, even Stephens' record can't compare with that of James Rowe Sr., who rode the 1872–73 Belmont winners, Joe Daniels and Springbok, then subsequently trained eight winners of the race, beginning with George Kinney in 1883 and ending with Prince Eugene in 1913.

On-site attendance figures on Belmont Stakes Day tend to vary with the potential of a Triple Crown winner, while the New York Racing Association officials are also willing to exaggerate. Most certainly, the announced crowd of 120,139 for the Belmont's 2004 renewal, when Birdstone thwarted Smarty Jones' Triple Crown bid, seemed generous – with a gathering of about 90,000 closer to reality. Betting from all sources on the card that afternoon was a verifiable $114.89 million, a record for any New York track. The Belmont offered a $2,150 purse when it was initially run, the winning owner receiving $1,850, along with "a beautiful saddle made by Merry of England", according to reports of the day. The purse is now $1 million, from which the victorious owner receives $600,000.

But it can be a heart-breaking race. From 1997–2004, six horses – Silver Charm, Real Quiet, Charismatic, War Emblem, Funny Cide and Smarty Jones – won the Kentucky Derby and Preakness, but were denied Triple Crown sweeps in the Belmont.

Untouchable: Secretariat (Ron Turcotte up) in 1973 became the first horse to sweep the Triple Crown in a quarter-century.

PREAKNESS STAKES

The middle jewel in North America's Triple Crown, the Preakness Stakes is the strong link that joins the series together. Hosted by the Maryland Jockey Club, an organization dating back to 1743, the Preakness is an event of international stature that annually draws the largest crowds for any sporting event in its home region.

THE "MIDDLE JEWEL" of North America's Triple Crown series, the Preakness Stakes actually predates the Kentucky Derby by two years, but does not have an uninterrupted history. Named after the colt who won the Dinner Party Stakes at the inaugural meet of Pimlico Race Course in 1870, the race was transferred to New York's Morris Park in 1890, where it was open to three-year-olds and upwards, and run on the same day as the Belmont Stakes. From 1891–93, there is no record of the Preakness Stakes being renewed anywhere. In 1894, it was revived at the Gravesend track in New York. In 1909, the Preakness returned to Pimlico, which has remained its home ever since.

Confirming the form: Affirmed beats Alydar in the 1978 Preakness.

While it lacks the national and international acclaim of the Kentucky Derby, the Preakness is an event of extraordinary local and regional importance. The Maryland Jockey Club, which owns and operates the Pimlico track, dates back to 1743, and the Preakness has become the foundation of the state's racing heritage. The City of Baltimore annually stages a 30-day festival surrounding event. The announced record attendance figure for the 2006 Preakness, 118,402, is a suspect number, but it seems reasonable that the race annually draws crowds in excess of 90,000, the vast majority whom jam into the Pimlico infield. The 2005 Preakness card generated verified wagering from all sources totalling $88.1 million, a Maryland record.

In its early days, the Preakness was sometimes run prior to the Derby. This was the case in 1888, 1910, and from 1923–1931. Thus, the Triple Crown sweep by Gallant Fox in 1930 involved his winning the Preakness Stakes, Kentucky Derby and Belmont Stakes in that order. In 1917 and 1922, the Preakness and Derby were run on the same days. From 1896–1908, the Belmont was run from 4–10 days before the Preakness. The modern system, in which the Derby is run on the first Saturday in May, the Preakness on the third Saturday of that month, and the Belmont three weeks later, actually only dates back to 1962.

There's no doubt about the importance of the Preakness Stakes in contemporary times. In effect, it is the link that merges America's classics (for three-year-olds) into the continent's equine Holy Grail. No one is sure who first coined the phrase, "Triple Crown", in reference to the Kentucky Derby, Preakness Stakes and Belmont Stakes but it has been a fixture in American sports terminology since at least the 1920s. Even the most casual thoroughbred observer knows what the Triple Crown represents. Only 11 horses have ever swept the three races, and all, obviously, had to be Preakness winners in the process.

The first Preakness winner, Survivor, received a $1,850 share of a gross purse of $2,050. The 2005 winner, Afleet Alex, received a $650,000 share of the gross purse of $1 million. In between, the Preakness has offered many splendid moments: the effort by Hindus, who passed seven other horses in the final 3/16 mile to win by a head in 1900; the seasonal debut of Man o' War, in 1920, when he rushed to the lead on the first turn and held off the late charge by Upset (who had handed Man o' War his only career defeat the year before); the wire-to-wire, 5½-length score by Citation in 1948; Secretariat's brilliant rush down the backstretch in 1973; the three-horse photo finish involving Silver Charm, Free House and Captain Bodgit, in that order, in 1997.

Smarty Jones, in 2004, recorded the largest margin of victory in the Preakness – 11½ lengths, with jockey Steward Elliott aboard. A nose has separated the winner from the second-place horse six times, most recently when Sunday Silence defeated Easy Goer in 1989. The longest shot ever to win the Preakness was Master Derby, who

◆ For three-year-olds
◆ Held the third Saturday in May at Pimlico Race Course in Baltimore, Maryland
◆ Inaugurated 1873

RACE DISTANCES
1½ miles, 1873–88
1¼ miles, 1889–90
1 1/16 miles, 1894–1900, 1908
1 mile, 70 yards, 1901–07
1 mile, 1909–10
1⅛ miles, 1911–24
1 3/16 miles, 1925–date

TRACKS HOSTING PREAKNESS STAKES
Pimlico 1873–89; 1909–date ◆ Morris Park, 1890 ◆ Gravesend, 1894–1908 ◆ Not held 1891–93

TRAINERS WITH MOST WINS
7 Robert Wyndham Walden
5 Thomas J. Healey, D. Wayne Lukas
4 James "Sunny Jim" Fitzsimmons, H. A. "Jimmy" Jones, Bob Baffert

JOCKEYS WITH MOST WINS
6 Eddie Arcaro Jr.
5 Pat Day
3 G. Barbee, Bill Hartack, L. Hughes.

WINNING FILLIES
Flocarline (1903), Whimsical (1906), Rhine Maiden (1915), Nellie Morse (1924)

triumphed at 23.40–1 in 1975. The shortest price for a Preakness winner was 1–10, shared by Citation in 1948 and Spectacular Bid in 1979. All told, 68 post-time favourites have won the Preakness. Allowing for the two divisions of the 1918 renewal (the only time a North American Triple Crown event has been split), the win ratio of betting choices is 51.5 per cent.

In 1985, Tank's Prospect set the prevailing stakes-record time for the Preakness, 1:53⅖. The clocking was matched by Louis Quatorze in 1996. Tank's Prospect closed from more than eight lengths behind to do this; Louis Quatorze, conversely, took the lead a just few strides out of the gate and never surrendered it. Both colts were ridden by Pat Day, who also scored his third consecutive Preakness triumph (and fifth overall)

PREAKNESS STAKES 1873–2006

YEAR HORSE	JOCKEY	TRAINER	YEAR HORSE	JOCKEY	TRAINER	YEAR HORSE	JOCKEY	TRAINER	YEAR HORSE	JOCKEY	TRAINER
1873 Survivor	G Barbee	AD Pryor	1910 Layminster	R Estep	JS Healey	1943 Count Fleet	J Longden	GD Cameron	1977 Seattle Slew	J Cruguet	WH Turner Jr
1874 Culpepper	M Donohue	H Gaffney	1911 Watervale	E Dugan	J Whalen	1944 Pensive	C McCreary	BA Jones	1978 Affirmed	S Cauthen	LS Barrera
1875 Tom Ochiltree	L Hughes	RW Walden	1912 Colonel Holloway	C Turner	D Woodford	1945 Polynesian	WD Wright	MA Dixon	1979 Spectacular Bid	RJ Franklin	GG Delp
1876 Shirley	G Barbee	W Brown	1913 Buskin	J Butwell	J Whalen	1946 Assault	W Mehrtens	M Hirsch	1980 Codex	A Cordero Jr	DW Lukas
1877 Cloverbrook	C Holloway	J Walden	1914 Holiday	A Schuttinger	JS Healy	1947 Faultless	D Dodson	HA Jones	1981 Pleasant Colony	J Velasquez	JP Campo
1878 Duke of Magenta	C Holloway	RW Walden	1915 Rhine Maiden	D Hoffman	F Devers	1948 Citation	E Arcaro	HA Jones	1982 Aloma's Ruler	JL Kaenel	JJ Lenzini Jr
1879 Harold	L Hughes	RW Walden	1916 Damrosch	L McAtee	AG Weston	1949 Capot	T Atkinson	JM Gaver	1983 Deputed Testamony	DA Miller Jr	JW Boniface
1880 Grenada	L Hughes	RW Walden	1917 Kalitan	E Haynes	W Hurley	1950 Hill Prince	E Arcaro	JH Hayes	1984 Gate Dancer	A Cordero Jr	JC Van Berg
1881 Saunterer	W Costello	RW Walden	1918 (Div1) War Cloud	J Loftus	WB Jennings	1951 Bold	E Arcaro	PM Burch	1985 Tank's Prospect	P Day	DW Lukas
1882 Vanguard	W Costello	RW Walden	1918 (Div2) Jack Hare Jr	C Peak	FD Weir	1952 Blue Man	C McCreary	WC Stephens	1986 Snow Chief	A Solis	MF Stute
1883 Jacobus	G Barbee	R Dwyer	1919 Sir Barton	J Loftus	HG Bedwell	1953 Native Dancer	E Guerin	WC Winfrey	1987 Alysheba	CJ McCarron	JC Van Berg
1884 Knight of Ellerslie	SH Fisher	TB Doswell	1920 Man o' War	C Kummer	L Feustel	1954 Hasty Road	J Adams	H Trotsek	1988 Risen Star	E Delahoussaye	LJ Roussel III
1885 Tecumseh	J McLaughlin	C Littlefield	1921 Broomspun	F Coltilettii	J Rowe	1955 Nashua	E Arcaro	J Fitzsimmons	1989 Sunday Silence	PA Valenzuela	C Whittingham
1886 The Bard	SH Fishe	J Huggins	1922 Pillory	L Morris	T J Healey	1956 Fabius	W Hartack	HA Jones	1990 Summer Squall	P Day	NJ Howard
1887 Dunboyne	W Donohue	W Jennings	1923 Vigil	B Marinelli	T J Healey	1957 Bold Ruler	E Arcaro	J Fitzsimmons	1991 Hansel	JD Bailey	FL Brothers
1888 Refund	F Littlefield	RW Walden	1924 Nellie Morse	J Merimee	AB Gordon	1958 Tim Tam	I Valenzuela	HA Jones	1992 Pine Bluff	CJ McCarron	T Bohannan
1889 Buddhist	G Anderson	J Rogers	1925 Coventry	C Kummer	W Duke	1959 Royal Orbit	W Harmatz	R Cornell	1993 Prairie Bayou	ME Smith	T Bohannan
1890 Montague	W Martin	E Feakes	1926 Display	J Maiben	TJ Healey	1960 Bally Ache	R Ussery	HJ Pitt	1994 Tabasco Cat	P Day	DW Lukas
1894 Assignee	F Taral	W Lakeland	1927 Bostonian	A Abel	F Hopkins	1961 Carry Back	J Sellers	JA Price	1995 Timber Country	P Day	DW Lukas
1895 Belmar	F Taral	E Feakes	1928 Victorian	R Workman	J Rowe Jr	1962 Greek Money	JL Rotz	VW Raines	1996 Louis Quatorze	P Day	NP Zito
1896 Margrave	H Griffin	B McClelland	1929 Dr Freeland	L Schaefer	TJ Healey	1963 Candy Spots	W Shoemaker	MA Tenney	1997 Silver Charm	GL Stevens	B Baffert
1897 Paul Kauvar	C Thorpe	TP Hayes	1930 Gallant Fox	E Sande	J Fitzsimmons	1964 Northern Dancer	W Hartack	HA Luro	1998 Real Quiet	KJ Desormeaux	B Baffert
1898 Sly Fox	W Simms	H Campbell	1931 Mate	G Ellis	JW Healy	1965 Tom Rolfe	R Turcotte	FY Whiteley Jr	1999 Charismatic	CW Antley	DW Lukas
1899 Half Time	R Clawson	F McCabe	1932 Burgoo King	E James	HJ Thompson	1966 Kauai King	D Brumfield	H Forrest	2000 Red Bullet	JD Bailey	J Orseno
1900 Hindus	H Spencer	J H Morris	1933 Head Play	C Kurtsinger	TP Hayes	1967 Damascus	W Shoemaker	FY Whiteley Jr	2001 Point Given	GL Stevens	B Baffert
1901 The Parader	F Landry	TJ Healey	1934 High Quest	R Jones	RA Smith	1968 Forward Pass	I Valenzuela	H Forrest	2002 War Emblem	V Espinoza	B Baffert
1902 Old England	L Jackson	GB Morris	1935 Omaha	W Saunders	J Fitzsimmons	1969 Majestic Prince	W Hartack	J Longden	2003 Funny Cide	JA Santos	B Tagg
1903 Flocarline	W Gannon	HC Riddle	1936 Bold Venture	G Woolf	M Hirsch	1970 Personality	E Belmonte	JW Jacobs	2004 Smarty Jones	S Elliott	J Servis
1904 Bryn Mawr	E Hildebrand	WF Presgrave	1937 War Admiral	C Kurtsinger	G Conway	1971 Canonero II	G Avila	J Arias	2005 Afleet Alex	J Rose	TF Ritchey
1905 Cairngorm	W Davis	AJ Joyner	1938 Dauber	M Peters	RE Handlen	1972 Bee Bee Bee	E Nelson	DW Carroll	2006 Bernardini	J Castellano	T Albertrani
1906 Whimsical	W Miller	TJ Gaynor	1939 Challedon	G Seabo	LJ Schaefer	1973 Secretariat	R Turcotte	L Laurin			
1907 Don Enrique	G Mountain	J Whalen	1940 Bimelech	FA Smith	W Hurley	1974 Little Current	MA Rivera	TL Rondinello			
1908 Royal Tourist	E Dugan	AJ Joyner	1941 Whirlaway	E Arcaro	BA Jones	1975 Master Derby	DH McHargue	WE Adams			
1909 Effendi	W Doyle	FC Frisbie	1942 Alsab	B James	A Swenke	1976 Elocutionist	J Lively	PT Adwell			

aboard Louis Quatorze. Secretariat may have also clocked a 1:53²/5 with his 1973 Preakness win – that was the time according to *Daily Racing Form* clockers, but Pimlico officials, relying on their own watches, recorded a time for him of 1:54²/5.

One of the most memorable runnings of the Preakness took place in 1962, when the 11–1 shot Greek Money, ridden by John Rotz, engaged favoured Ridan, with Manuel Ycaza aboard, in a length-of-the-stretch duel at extremely close quarters. Greek Money prevailed by a nose, but Ycaza lodged a claim of foul. The Pimlico stewards dismissed it, and allowed the result to stand. Photographs subsequently revealed that Ycaza, who had lost his whip, was actually the transgressor. Approaching the finish line, he stuck his left elbow into Rotz's stomach. Ycaza was suspended for 30 calendar days.

Horses bred in Maryland have occasionally won the Preakness, and when this happens, it generates immense local pride. This was the case with Challedon, who defeated heavily favoured Johnstown in 1939; with Bee Bee Bee, who defeated the 3–10 choice, Riva Ridge, in 1972; and with Deputed Testamony, who defeated favoured Sunny's Halo in 1983. Fifty-two fillies have gone postward in the Preakness, and four have won. Of particular note among distaffers is the 1924 winner, Nellie Morse, who became one of the foundation broodmares of Calumet Farm.

The winning owner's trophy, the Woodlawn Vase, is said to be the most valuable in American sports, but it is not given away. It was created in 1860 by Tiffany and Company, and was valued at $1 million in 1983. The Woodlawn Vase is brought by armed guard to Pimlico each year at Preakness time and a sterling silver replica, valued itself at $30,000, is annually presented to the owner of the Preakness winner. The original is otherwise kept on display at the Maryland Historical Society.

In the mix: Tabasco Cat, ridden by Pat Day, edges out Go For Gin and Chris McCarron in the Preakness Stakes of 1994.

KENTUCKY DERBY

Held on the first Saturday in May, the Kentucky Derby ranks among the greatest of all sporting events in the United States. Dubbed "the Run for the Roses", it is the one event beyond all others that every North American horseman dreams of winning and perennially draws crowds unmatched by any other race on the continent.

UNIVERSALLY RECOGNIZED as North America's most prominent race, the Kentucky Derby was first run on the day Churchill Downs initially opened its gates on 17 May 1875. Dubbed "the Run for the Roses", the Kentucky Derby is the only American Triple Crown event that has not only an uninterrupted history but also has always been contested at the same track. A Derby field going around the clubhouse turn, with Churchill's grandstand and twin spires providing the background, is one of the most revered sights in all of sports.

The Derby's founding father was Churchill's first president, Colonel M. Lewis Clark. The person generally credited with the race's greatest growth period, however, is Colonel Matt J. Winn, who took managerial control of Churchill in 1902, and held it until his death in 1949. Under Winn, Churchill became profitable. Pari-mutuel machines replaced bookmakers in 1908. The Derby was broadcast on radio (specifically by WHAS in Louisville) for the first time in 1925. The first international radio broadcast of the Derby took place in 1931, when the British Broadcasting Corporation (BBC) carried the race.

In 1952, CBS offered the first national telecast of the Derby. The race was simulcast for the initial time to a trio of outside wagering outlets in 1981. For its 2005 edition, though, the Derby was sent to thousands of national and international simulcast sites. On-track attendance of 156,435 was the second highest in history (topped only by the 163,628 for the Derby's centennial year in 1974). Wagering from all sources on the 2005 Derby card totalled $155.79 million, an all-time North American record.

Aristides, the first Derby winner, was bred and owned by Henry Price McGrath. It is said that McGrath wanted Aristides' stablemate, Chesapeake, to win the race. But after watching Chesapeake start poorly and trail throughout, McGrath grandiosely waved and shouted to jockey Oliver Lewis, who had the lead aboard Aristides in the stretch, to "Go on!" Lewis was black, as were 12 of the other 14 jockeys who rode in the first Derby. Indeed, 15 of the first 28 runnings of the race were won by horses with African-American riders aboard.

On May 16, 1896, Ben Brush was the first horse to win the Derby at its now familiar

Long shot: The 50–1 outsider, Giacomo (left), on the way to winning the 131st Kentucky Derby in May 2005.

distance of 1¼ miles. In 1914, Old Rosebud won the race by eight lengths which remains the largest Derby margin of victory, although it is has been matched by Johnstown in 1939, Whirlaway in 1941, and Assault in 1946. The smallest margin of victory, a nose, has been recorded eight times, most recently by Grindstone in 1996.

Eight geldings have won the Derby, the first being Vagrant in 1876, the most recent being Funny Cide in 2003. Although by a Kentucky sire, Funny Cide is officially a New York-bred, and is the first representative of that state to be a Derby winner. Regret's two-length triumph in 1915 made her the first filly to win the Derby. She has since been joined by Genuine Risk and Winning Colors. Five fillies, including Regret, have been favourites in the race. All told, fillies have made 38 starts in the Derby, winning thrice, finishing second once and third on five occasions.

Post-time favourites have won 50 of the 131 runnings up to 2005, an overall win ratio of 38.2 per cent. But theirs has been a largely inconsistent heritage. Favourites won six consecutive runnings of the race from 1891–96, five of six runnings from 1926–31 and six of eight runnings from 1972–79. From then onwards, though, the burden of favouritism has proven disadvantageous, and during the most recent 26 runnings of the Derby only two wagering choices – Fusaichi Pegasus in 2000 and Smarty Jones in 2004 – have been victorious. The 2005 Derby winner, Giacomo, was sent off at 50.30–1 odds.

Big Noise: Real Quiet (right) held Victory Gallop clear in 1998.

KENTUCKY DERBY 1875–2006

YEAR	HORSE	JOCKEY	TRAINER
1875	Aristides	O Lewis	A Williamson
1876	Vagrant	R Swim	J Williams
1877	Baden-Baden	W Walker	E Brown
1878	Day Star	J Carter	L Paul
1879	Lord Murphy	C Shauer	G Rice
1880	Fonso	G Lewis	T Hutsell
1881	Hindoo	J McLaughlin	J Rowe Sr
1882	Apollo	B Hurd	GB Morris
1883	Leonatus	W Donohue	J McGinty
1884	Buchanan	I Murphy	W Bird
1885	Joe Cotton	E Henderson	A Perry
1886	Ben Ali	P Duffy	J Murphy
1887	Montrose	I Lewis	J McGinty
1888	Macbeth II	G Covington	J Campbell
1889	Spokane	T Kiley	J Rodegap
1890	Riley	I Murphy	E Corrigan
1891	Kingman	I Murphy	D Allen
1892	Azra	A Clayton	JH Morris
1893	Lookout	E Kunze	W McDaniel
1894	Chant	F Goodale	E Leigh
1895	Halma	J Perkins	B McClelland
1896	Ben Brush	W Simms	H Campbell
1897	Typhoon II	F Garner	JC Kahn
1898	Plaudit	W Simms	JE Madden
1899	Manuel	F Taral	RJ Walden
1900	Lieut Gibson	J Boland	CH Hughes
1901	His Eminence	J Winkfield	FB Van Meter
1902	Alan-a-Dale	J Winkfield	TC McDowell
1903	Judge Himes	H Booker	JP Mayberry
1904	Elwood	F Prior	CE Durnell
1905	Agile	J Martin	R Tucker
1906	Sir Huon	R Troxler	P Coyne
1907	Pink Star	A Minder	WH Fizer
1908	Stone Street	A Pickens	JW Hall
1909	Wintergreen	V Powers	C Mack
1910	Donau	F Herbert	G Ham
1911	Meridian	G Archibald	A Ewing
1912	Worth	CH Shilling	EM Taylor
1913	Donerail	R Goose	TP Hayes
1914	Old Rosebud	J McCabe	FD Weir
1915	Regret	J Notter	J Rowe Sr
1916	George Smith	J Loftus	H Hughes
1917	Omar Khayyam	C Borel	CT Patterson
1918	Exterminator	W Knapp	H McDaniel
1919	Sir Barton	J Loftus	HG Bedwell
1920	Paul Jones	T Rice	W Garth
1921	Behave Yourself	C Thompson	HJ Thompson
1922	Morvich	A Johnson	F Burlew
1923	Zev	E Sande	DJ Leary
1924	Black Gold	JD Mooney	H Webb
1925	Flying Ebony	E Sande	WB Duke
1926	Bubbling Over	A Johnson	HJ Thompson
1927	Whiskery	L McAtee	F Hopkins
1928	Reigh Count	C Lang	BS Michell
1929	Clyde Van Dusen	L McAtee	C Van Dusen
1930	Gallant Fox	E Sande	J Fitzsimmons
1931	Twenty Grand	C Kurtsinger	J Rowe Jr
1932	Burgoo King	E James	HJ Thompson
1933	Brokers Tip	D Meade	HJ Thompson
1934	Cavalcade	M Garner	RA Smith
1935	Omaha	W Saunders	J Fitzsimmons
1936	Bold Venture	I Hanford	M Hirsch
1937	War Admiral	C Kurtsinger	G Conway
1938	Lawrin	E Arcaro	BA Jones
1939	Johnstown	J Stout	J Fitzsimmons
1940	Gallahadion	C Bierman	R Waldron
1941	Whirlaway	E Arcaro	BA Jones
1942	Shut Out	WD Wright	JM Gaver
1943	Count Fleet	J Longden	GD Cameron
1944	Pensive	C McCreary	BA Jones
1945	Hoop Jr	E Arcaro	IH Parke
1946	Assault	W Mehrtens	M Hirsch
1947	Jet Pilot	E Guerin	T Smith
1948	Citation	E Arcaro	BA Jones
1949	Ponder	S Brooks	BA Jones
1950	Middleground	W Boland	M Hirsch
1951	Count Turf	C McCreary	S Rutchick
1952	Hill Gail	E Arcaro	BA Jones
1953	Dark Star	H Moreno	E Hayward
1954	Determine	R York	W Molter
1955	Swaps	W Shoemaker	MA Tenney
1956	Needles	D Erb	HL Fontaine
1957	Iron Liege	W Hartack	HA Jones
1958	Tim Tam	I Valenzuela	HA Jones
1959	Tomy Lee	W Shoemaker	F Childs
1960	Venetian Way	W Hartack	VJ Sovinski
1961	Carry Back	J Sellers	JA Price
1962	Decidedly	W Hartack	HA Luro
1963	Chateaugay	B Baeza	JP Conway
1964	Northern Dancer	W Hartack	HA Luro
1965	Lucky Debonair	W Shoemaker	F Catrone
1966	Kauai King	D Brumfield	H Forrest
1967	Proud Clarion	R Ussery	L Gentry
*1968	Forward Pass	I Valenzuela	LC Cavalaris Jr
1969	Majestic Prince	W Hartack	J Longden
1970	Dust Commander	M Manganello	D Combs
1971	Canonero II	G Avila	J Arias
1972	Riva Ridge	R Turcotte	L Laurin
1973	Secretariat	R Turcotte	L Laurin
1974	Cannonade	A Cordero Jr	WC Stephens
1975	Foolish Pleasure	J Vasquez	L Jolley
1976	Bold Forbes	A Cordero Jr	LS Barrera
1977	Seattle Slew	J Cruguet	WH Turner Jr
1978	Affirmed	S Cauthen	LS Barrera
1979	Spectacular Bid	RJ Franklin	GG Delp
1980	Genuine Risk	J Vasquez	L Jolley
1981	Pleasant Colony	J Velasquez	JP Campo
1982	Gato Del Sol	E Delahoussaye	E Gregson
1983	Sunny's Halo	E Delahoussaye	DC Cross Jr
1984	Swale	L Pincay Jr	WC Stephens
1985	Spend a Buck	A Cordero Jr	C Gambolati
1986	Ferdinand	W Shoemaker	C Whittingham
1987	Alysheba	CJ McCarron	JC Van Berg
1988	Winning Colors	GL Stevens	DW Lukas
1989	Sunday Silence	FA Valenzuela	C Whittingham
1990	Unbridled	C Perret	CA Nafzger
1991	Strike the Gold	CW Antley	NP Zito
1992	Lil E Tee	P Day	LS Whiting
1993	Sea Hero	JD Bailey	M Miller
1994	Go for Gin	CJ McCarron	NP Zito
1995	Thunder Gulch	GL Stevens	DW Lukas
1996	Grindstone	JD Bailey	DW Lukas
1997	Silver Charm	GL Stevens	B Baffert
1998	Real Quiet	KJ Desormeaux	B Baffert
1999	Charismatic	C W Antley	DW Lukas
2000	Fusaichi Pegasus	KJ Desormeaux	N Drysdale
2001	Monarchos	J Chavez	JT Ward, Jr.
2002	War Emblem	V Espinoza	B Baffert
2003	Funny Cide	JA Santos	B Tagg
2004	Smarty Jones	S Elliott	J Servis
2005	Giacomo	ME Smith	J Shirreffs
2006	Barbaro	E Prado	M Matz

* Winner, Dancer's Image, was disqualified after a dope test.

The longest shot ever to win the Derby was Donerail, who scored at 91.45–1 in 1913 (the same year the Derby at Epsom provided a 100–1 winner in Aboyeur). The longest price ever accorded to any Derby participant was 294.40–1 by A Dragon Killer in 1958. A Dragon Killer slayed no dragons that day, but he did manage to finish seventh in the 14-horse field.

Triple Crown victors Count Fleet, in 1943, and Citation, in 1948, share the record for shortest-priced Derby winners; both were sent off at 2–5. The shortest-priced Derby favourite to fail also started at odds 2–5, but Honest Pleasure was second to Bold Forbes in 1976.

Citation and Secretariat probably are the most famous Derby winners. Both subsequently went on to Triple Crown sweeps. Of Citation's five rivals in 1948, only his Calumet Farm stablemate, Coaltown, was considered a serious competitor and Citation beat Coaltown by 3½ lengths on a sloppy track. He is one of eight Calumet homebreds to win the race. Calumet also bred the 1991 Derby winner, Strike the Gold.

Secretariat's 2½-length Derby triumph was accomplished in the time of 1:59²⁄₅, which remains Churchill's track record for the 1¼-mile distance. Astoundingly, as the race progressed, each quarter registered by Secretariat was quicker than the prior one; in effect, the further he went, the faster he ran. The previous Derby standard of 2:00 had been set in 1964 by Northern Dancer, who subsequently became the most prominent thoroughbred sire in the world.

There has been controversy aplenty at the Derby. In 1933, jockeys Donald Meade (on Brokers Tip) and Herbert Fisher (Head Play), slapped, swung at, and shoved each other as their horses neared the wire. Brokers Tip won by a nose, but the two jockeys were subsequently suspended. This is referred to in Derby lore as "The Fighting Finish".

In 1968, Dancer's Image won the Derby by 1½ lengths, but was subsequently disqualified when post-race testing discovered the then prohibited medication phenylbutazone (Bute) in his system. Despite four years of appeals the disqualification was ultimately upheld.

On 22 occasions, horses have led wire-to-wire in the Derby. They include the Triple Crown winner, Sir Barton, who broke his maiden with his Derby win in 1919; and the Triple Crown winner, Count Fleet, who cruised to an easy three-length win in 1943. A truly electrifying flag-fall-to-finish performance was turned in by five-length winner Spend A Buck in 1985 in what is still the fourth fastest Derby clocking ever, 2:00 1/5. War Emblem, in 2002, is the most recent Derby participant to register a wire-to-wire win.

In 1996, the Derby became the first Triple Crown event to offer a $1 million-added purse, and in 2005 its purse money was raised to $2-million-added, of which Giacomo received a $1,639,600 share. Along with football's Super Bowl, baseball's World Series, automobile racing's Indianapolis 500 and college basketball's NCAA Final Four, the Derby ranks as one of the top five sporting events annually staged in the USA.

◆ For three-year-olds
◆ Held the first Saturday in May at Churchill Downs in Louisville, Kentucky
◆ Inaugurated 1875

RACE DISTANCES
1½ miles, 1875–95
1¼ miles, 1896–date

TRACK HOSTING KENTUCKY DERBY
Churchill Downs, 1875–date

TRAINERS WITH MOST WINS
6 Ben A. Jones
4 D. Wayne Lukas, H.J. "Dick" Thompson
3 Bob Baffert, James "Sunny Jim" Fitzsimmons, Max Hirsch

JOCKEYS WITH MOST WINS
5 Eddie Arcaro, Bill Hartack
4 Bill Shoemaker;
3 Angel Cordero Jr, Isaac Murphy, Earl Sande, Gary Stevens

WINNING FILLIES
Regret (1915)
Genuine Risk (1980)
Winning Colors (1988)

BREEDERS' CUP CLASSIC

Although its history stretches barely beyond two decades, the Breeders' Cup Classic has already become one of the most valued prizes on the globe. Anchoring a championship day of racing involving eight events, it is now the premier determinant for North American Horse of the Year honours.

THE RICHEST RACE run in North America, the Breeders' Cup Classic highlights an end-of-the-year championship that includes nine Grade 1 events. The others are the Breeders' Cup Steeplechase (run separately), Breeders' Cup Sprint, Breeders' Cup Juvenile, Breeders' Cup Juvenile Fillies, Breeders' Cup Distaff, Breeders' Cup Filly and Mare Turf, Breeders' Cup Mile and Breeders' Cup Turf. In 2005, their aggregate purse values totalled $14.45 million. The Breeders' Cup Classic alone had a purse of $4,291,560.

Host tracks for the Breeders' Cup are chosen by its founding organization, Breeders' Cup Limited, which is now merged with the National Thoroughbred Racing Association and is headquartered in Lexington, Kentucky. Churchill Downs has been the most frequent host, doing it six times, including the 2006 renewal. Belmont Cup has hosted the Breeders' Cup on four occasions, as has Santa Anita. Gulfstream Park and Hollywood Park have each thrice served as hosts – Hollywood was the site of the inaugural Breeders'

Cup in 1984. In 1996, Woodbine in Toronto, Canada, hosted the only renewal of the event that, to date, has been run on foreign soil. Aqueduct, Arlington Park and Lone Star Park have each hosted the event once, and Monmouth Park on the New Jersey shore is scheduled to be the host track in 2007.

Perfect timing: Jockey Chris McCarron raises his whip in triumph as Tiznow edges out Giant's Causeway in the 2000 Breeders' Cup Classic at Churchill Downs.

BREEDERS' CUP CLASSIC 1984–2005

YEAR	HORSE	JOCKEY	TRAINER	YEAR	HORSE	JOCKEY	TRAINER
1984	Wild Again	P Day	V Timphony	1995	Cigar	JD Bailey	WI Mott
1985	Proud Truth	J Velasquez	JM Veitch	1996	Alphabet Soup	CJ McCarron	D Hofmans
1986	Skywalker	L Pincay Jr	M Whittingham	1997	Skip Away	ME Smith	H Hine
1987	Ferdinand	W Shoemaker	C Whittingham	1998	Awesome Again	P Day	PB Byrne
1988	Alysheba	CJ McCarron	JC Van Berg	1999	Cat Thief	P Day	DW Lukas
1989	Sunday Silence	CJ McCarron	C Whittingham	2000	Tiznow	CJ McCarron	JM Robbins
1990	Unbridled	P Day	CA Nafzger	2001	Tiznow	CJ McCarron	JM Robbins
1991	Black Tie Affair	JD Bailey	ET Poulos	2002	Volponi	JA Santos	PG Johnson
1992	A P Indy	E Delahoussaye	N Drysdale	2003	Pleasantly Perfect	A Solis	R Mandella
1993	Arcangues	JD Bailey	A Fabre	2004	Ghostzapper	JJ Castellano	R Frankel
1994	Concern	JD Bailey	RW Small	2005	Saint Liam	JD Bailey	RE Dutrow, Jr.

Big shock: Arcangues' 1993 Classic win remains the most stunning in Breeders' Cup history.

From 1984–2005, 155 of 198 Eclipse Award winning horses (excluding steeplechase competitors) ran in Breeders' Cup races. On 12 occasions, the Breeders' Cup Classic winner was named divisional champion. Ten of them – Ferdinand (1987), Alysheba (1988), Sunday Silence (1989), Black Tie Affair (1991), A. P. Indy (1992), Cigar (1995), Skip Away (1997), Tiznow (2000), Ghostzapper (2004) and Saint Liam (2005) – were further honoured as North America's Horse of the Year. Other than the Triple Crown events, the Breeders' Cup Classic has unquestionably become the most prominent race on the continent.

Favourites have not always fared well in the Classic. During its first 22 runnings, only seven wagering choices have prevailed, for a win ratio of 31.8 per cent, which is well below that of most other major races. The Classic's initial winner, Wild Again in 1984, scored at 31.30–1 odds. In 1993, the shipper from France, Arcangues, won at the incredible odds of 133.60–1. Jerry Bailey, who rode him, said afterwards that the first time he ever set eyes on the horse was in the paddock just prior to the race. When trainer Andre Fabre gave him pre-race instructions, Bailey could not understand him because he didn't speak French. Not only was Arcangues the longest shot on the board, he remains the longest-priced horse ever to win any Breeders' Cup event.

Volponi, the 2002 Breeders' Cup Classic winner, was also the longest shot on the board, at 43.50–1. Conversely, the shortest-priced Classic winner was Cigar, who at 7–10 odds prevailed by 2½ lengths in 1995. That year's Breeders' Classic was Cigar's 12th straight win in a streak that would ultimately extend to 16 races.

Three-year-olds have triumphed in the Breeders' Cup Classic seven times, although the last time it happened was with Tiznow in 2000, who triumphed by a neck over the European challenger and fellow three-year-old, Giant's Causeway. In 2001, Tiznow became the only repeat Classic winner, in consecutive years or otherwise. He is also one of nine horses to have won the Classic during their four-year-old seasons. Five-year-olds have won the race six times, with the most recent being Saint Liam at Belmont in 2005. A gelding has yet to win the Classic, although a ridgling, A.P. Indy, was triumphant in 1992.

Skip Away set a stakes record for the Breeders' Cup Classic's ten-furlong distance in 1997, clocking 1:59. The race was held at Hollywood that year, and race times were recorded to a fifth of a second. Ghostzapper registered a time of 1:59.02 at Lone Star Park in 2004, with race times being recorded to a hundredth of a second. Skip Away and Ghostzapper, therefore, for all intents and purposes share the status of co-record holders.

- ◆ For three-year-olds and upwards
- ◆ Held in either late October or early November at a track selected by Breeders' Cup Limited
- ◆ Inaugurated 1984

RACE DISTANCE
Run at 1¼ miles

TRAINER WITH MOST WINS
2 John M. Robbins, Charles Whittingham

JOCKEYS WITH MOST WINS
5 Jerry Bailey, Chris McCarron
4 Pat Day

Volponi's margin of victory, 6½ lengths, is the largest in the Classic. The shortest margin of victory, a nose, was first recorded by Ferdinand at Hollywood in 1987, and subsequently matched by Alphabet Soup in 1996 at Woodbine and by Tiznow in 2001 at Belmont. Eleven of its runnings have been decided by a length or less, and nine of these required photos to determine winners.

On-site crowd figures for the Breeders' Cup have often been suspect. The record attendance, an alleged 80,452 at Churchill Downs in 1998, may have been inflated by as many as 20,000.

Much more reliable indicators of growth are provided by simulcast and wagering statistics. In 1984 total wagering on the Breeders' Cup races from all sources was $16.4 million.

Yet, the Breeders' Cup has never been able to approach the domestic popularity of the Kentucky Derby, Preakness or Belmont Stakes. One of the reasons for this is its place on the calendar – from 2001–2005 it was held in late October, at the same time as baseball's World Series, and when college football (which is primarily played on Saturdays, the same day of the week as the Breeders' Cup) is at its peak. This has resulted in a real struggle for media coverage. In 2006, the Breeders' Cup will revert to the first Saturday in November, which at least will avoid a clash with the World Series.

Memorable moments have become a forte of the Breeders' Cup Classic. There was the stretch duel between the threesome of Ferdinand, Alysheba and Judge Angelucci at Hollywood in 1987, with Ferdinand prevailing and securing Horse of the Year honours. The following year, a late post and murky weather at Churchill resulted in the Classic being run in near darkness. This time, Alysheba emerged from the deep shadows for a half-length win over Seeking the Gold.

In 1989, a pair of three-year-olds, Sunday Silence and Easy Goer, went postward in the Breeders' Cup Classic at Gulfstream as the two favourites, with divisional and Horse of the Year honours in the balance. Sunday Silence took the lead inside the final furlong, and then withheld Easy Goer's late charge to prevail by a neck.

The Classic has had two wire-to-wire winners, Black Tie Affair in 1991 and Ghostzapper in 2004. Proud Truth, on the other hand, came from last position in an eight-horse field to win by a head in 1985. Concern came from last position in a 14-horse field to win by a neck in 1994. Black Tie Affair and Concern were both ridden by Bailey, and with Arcangues, Cigar and Saint Liam added in, Bailey rode a total of five Classic winners. Only Chris McCarron can match Bailey's total.

PRIX DE L'ARC DE TRIOMPHE

The Prix de l'Arc de Triomphe vies with the King George VI And Queen Elizabeth Stakes as the premier all-aged 1 1/2-mile race in Europe. The senior of the two races by 31 years – the first running was in 1920 – apart from a brief hiatus and two years at Le Tremblay during World War II, it has always been run at Longchamp.

THE PRIX DE L'ARC DE TRIOMPHE, run over 2400 metres at Longchamp in Paris's Bois de Boulogne on the first Sunday in October, is one of the two most important middle-distance races run in Europe. Its rival for that title is the King George VI And Queen Elizabeth Stakes at Ascot in July and it is pointless to try to justify claims that one is a more important race than the other, not least because they are staged well over two months apart. There can, however, be no doubting a top-class horse when he wins both races in the same season as has been managed, for example, by Mill Reef and Dancing Brave.

The Arc was first run in 1920 and its first winner, Comrade, was trained at Newmarket by Peter Purcell Gilpin, the man whose earlier career had included the top-class filly Pretty Polly. Comrade made a very inauspicious start in life as he was held in such low regard as a yearling that he changed hands for only 25gns. Having won all three of his juvenile starts, he listed the Grand Prix de Paris as well as the Arc among his second season successes and his earnings came to more than £25,000.

Comrade was ridden by Frank Bullock, who won the race for the second time in 1922 when the previous year's winner, Ksar, gained his second victory. On the first occasion he was ridden by George Stern, who was one of the top jockeys of his time in France and also won

Trusted trainer: Saeed bin Suroor, a triple Arc winner.

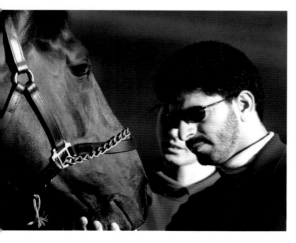

English classics on Sunstar, Kennymore and Troutbeck.

Although there was a long later spell when challenges for the Arc by horses trained in England met with ignominious failure, they held their own in the early years and the 1924 winner, Parth, was trained by John Crawford and ridden by the American Frank O'Neill, champion jockey in France every year except one between 1910 and 1922 and winner of the 1920 Derby on Spion Kop.

The first jockey to win the Arc three times was Charles Semblat, who also subsequently trained a quartet of Arc winners. John Watts, a member of a famous racing family whose ancestors and descendants all won classics and who sent out Call Boy to win the Derby in 1927, trained in Germany as well as England before he took up the role of private trainer to Marcel Boussac in the mid-1930s. In 1936–37, Watts sent out Corrida to become the second horse to win the Arc in consecutive years. Tantieme, Ribot and Alleged eventually duplicated that feat, but a period has now elapsed where no horse has twice won the Arc, in consecutive years or otherwise, in over a quarter of a century.

The German occupation of France resulted in there being no Arc renewals in 1939–40, although the race was run during the remainder of World War II. The early to mid-1940s belonged to Boussac and his trainer Semblat, as Djebel won in 1942, Ardan won in 1944 and Caracalla won in 1946. La Paillon, who was victorious in the Arc in 1947, had finished second in the Champion Hurdle earlier in the year. His trainer, Willie Head, again won the race with Bon Mot III in 1966. Willie's son, Alec, trained three Arc winners – Nuccio in 1952, Saint Crespin (via disqualification) in 1959 and Ivanjica in 1976. And Willie's granddaughter, Criquette, trained the 1979 Arc winner Three Troikas.

There was another Boussac/Semblat victory with Coronation in 1949 before François Mathet and Jacko Doyasbere enjoyed consecutive wins with the top-class Tantieme in 1950 and 1951, a few years before dual success for one of the top horses of the century, Ribot, in 1955 and 1956. Ribot was unbeaten in 16 starts in three seasons and won his Arcs first by three lengths and then

◆ For three-year-olds and upwards
◆ Held the first Sunday in October, at Longchamp
◆ Inaugurated 1920

RACE DISTANCE
2400 metres, 1920–38; 1941–date

COURSE HOSTING THE PRIX DE L'ARC DE TRIOMPHE
Longchamp 1920–38, 1941–42, 1945–date
No race 1939–40; Le Tremblay 1943–44

TRAINERS WITH MOST WINS
6   Andre Fabre
4   C Semblat
3   F Carter, F Mathet, E Pollet, S bin Suroor

JOCKEYS WITH MOST WINS
4   J. Doyasbère, P. Eddery, F.Head, Y. Saint-Martin

by six, and in his only other venture away from Italy he had five lengths to spare in the King George VI and Queen Elizabeth Stakes.

Vincent O'Brien won the race for the first time with Ballymoss in 1958, three years before another win for Italy with Molvedo who, like Ribot, was ridden by Enrico Camici. Four years after that came victory for maybe the best horse ever to win the race, Sea-Bird, who spreadeagled as good a field as has ever been assembled for an Arc, winning by six lengths from Reliance.

Pollet won the race again in 1968 when Vaguely Noble, who had changed hands at the end of the previous season for a then record auction price of 136,000gns, beat Sir Ivor, and his jockey Bill Williamson was successful again 12 months later when Levmoss beat the filly Park Top, whom some people felt was an unlucky loser.

Following Nijinsky's shock defeat by Sassafras the next year, there was an end to the lean spell endured by horses trained in Britain when Mill Reef won in tremendous style. Apart from Migoli in 1948 he was the first British-trained Arc winner since the early days and two years later there was another when Lester Piggott won the race for the first time on Rheingold.

The filly Allez France, who was runner-up to Rheingold, emulated her sire Sea-Bird by taking the race in 1974, followed by its longest-priced

PRIX DE L'ARC DE TRIOMPHE 1920–2005

YEAR HORSE	JOCKEY	TRAINER	YEAR HORSE	JOCKEY	TRAINER	YEAR HORSE	JOCKEY	TRAINER	YEAR HORSE	JOCKEY	TRAINER
1920 Comrade	F Bullock	PP Gilpin	1943 Verso II	G Duforez	C Clout	1966 Bon Mot III	F Head	W Head	1989 Carroll House	M Kinane	M Jarvis
1921 Ksar	G Stern	W Walton	1944 Ardan	J Doyasbère	C Semblat	1967 Topyo	W Pyers	C Bartholomew	1990 Saumarez	G Mossé	N Clement
1922 Ksar	F Bullock	W Walton	1945 Nikellora	WRJohnstone	R Pelat	1968 Vaguely Noble	W Williamson	E Pollet	1991 Suave Dancer	C Asmussen	J Hammond
1923 Parth	F O'Neill	J Crawford	1946 Caracella	C Elliott	C Semblat	1969 Levmoss	W Williamson	S McGrath	1992 Subotica	T Jarnet	A Fabre
1924 Massine	Sharpe	E Cunnington	1947 La Paillon	F Rochetti	W Head	1970 Sassafras	Y Saint-Martin	F Mathet	1993 Urban Sea	E Saint-Martin	J Lesbordes
1925 Priori	M Allemand	P Carter	1948 Migoli	C Smirke	F Butters	1971 Mill Reef	G Lewis	I Balding	1994 Carnegie	T Jarnet	A Fabre
1926 Biribi	D Torterolo	J Torterolo	1949 Coronation	R Poincelet	C Semblat	1972 San San	F Head	A Penna	1995 Lammtarra	WR Swinburn	S Bin Suroor
1927 Mon Talisman	C Semblat	F Carter	1950 Tantieme	J Doyasbère	F Mathet	1973 Rheingold	L Piggott	B Hills	1996 Helissio	O Peslier	E Lellouche
1928 Kantar	A Esling	R Carver	1951 Tantieme	J Doyasbère	F Mathet	1974 Allez France	Y Saint-Martin	A Penna	1997 Peintre Célèbre	O Peslier	A Fabre
1929 Ortello	P Caprioli	W Carter	1952 Nuccio	R Poincelet	A Head	1975 Star Appeal	G Starkey	T Grieper	1998 Sagamix	O Peslier	A Fabre
1930 Motrico	M Fruhinsholtz	M d'Okhuysen	1953 La Sorellina	M Larraun	E Pollet	1976 Ivanjica	F Head	A Head	1999 Montjeu	M Kinane	J Hammond
1931 Pearl Cap	C Semblat	F Carter	1954 Sica Boy	WR Johnstone	P Pelat	1977 Alleged	L Piggott	MV O'Brien	2000 Sinndar	J Murtagh	J Oxx
1932 Motrico	C Semblat	M d'Okhuysen	1955 Ribot	E Camici	I Della Rocchetta	1978 Alleged	L Piggott	MV O'Brien	2001 Sakhee	L Dettori	S bin Suroor
1933 Crapom	P Caprioli	F Regoli	1956 Ribot	E Camici	U Penco	1979 Three Troikas	F Head	C Head	2002 Marienbard	L Dettori	S bin Suroor
1934 Brantôme	C Bouillon	L Robert	1957 Oroso	S Boullenger	D Lescalle	1980 Detroit	P Eddery	O Douieb	2003 Dalakhani	C Soumillon	A de Royer-Dupre
1935 Samos	W Sibbritt	F Carter	1958 Ballymoss	A Breasley	MV O'Brien	1981 Gold River	G Moore Jr	A Head			
1936 Corrida	C Elliott	J Watts	1959*Saint Crespin	G Moore	A Head	1982 Akiyda	Y Saint-Martin	F Mathet	2004 Bago	T Gillet	J Pease
1937 Corrida	C Elliott	J Watts	1960 Puissant Chef	M Garcia	C Bartholomew	1983 All Along	WR Swinburn	PL Biancone	2005 Hurricane Run	K Fallon	A Fabre
1938 Eclair Au Chocolat	C Bouillon	L Robert	1961 Molvedo	E Camici	A Maggi	1984 Sagace	Y Saint-Martin	PL Biancone			
1939 No race			1962 Soltikoff	M Depalmas	R Pelat	1985 Rainbow Quest	P Eddery	J Tree	*Midnight Sun dead-heated but was disqualified.		
1940 No race			1963 Exbury	J Deforge	G Watson	1986 Dancing Brave	P Eddery	G Harwood			
1941 La Pacha	P Francolon	J Cunnington	1964 Prince Royal II	R Poincelet	G Bridgland	1987 Trempolino	P Eddery	A Fabre			
1942 Djebel	J Doyasbère	C Semblat	1965 Sea-Bird II	P Glennon	E Pollet	1988 Tony Bin	J Reid	L Camici			

Fantastic hat-trick: Johnny Murtagh's *annus mirabilis* continued as dual Derby winner Sinndar leaves Egyptband trailing at the end of the 2000 Prix de l'Arc de Triomphe at Longchamp.

(110–1) and first German-trained win with Star Appeal and, two years after that, wins for Vincent O'Brien and Lester Piggott with Alleged in 1978 and 1979.

Pat Eddery won his first Arc on Detroit, in the same colours as Alleged but trained by Olivier Douieb, in 1979, and was to follow that with a hat-trick which began in 1985 when Rainbow Quest was awarded the race at the expense of the previous season's winner Sagace. Eddery's other wins were on Dancing Brave, whose defeat of the French star of the year Bering was one of the highlights of 1986, and Trempolino, a first Arc success for André Fabre.

Fabre's victory with Hurricane Run in the 2005 Arc was his sixth, a record for a trainer. It was also one of three Group 1 wins at Longchamp that day for jockey Kieren Fallon. Fabre's triumph with Trempolino in 1987 had culminated in a hat trick for jockey Pat Eddery, and Fabre's victories with Peintre Celebre and Sagamix in 1997–98 provided Olivier Peslier with a hat trick as well. Peintre Celebre's final time, 2:25, remains the Arc record.

Hurricane Run was the tenth three-year-old to win the Arc in its most recent 12 runnings – the only older horses to triumph during that period were Sakhee in 2001 and Marienbard in 2002, both representing the Maktoum family's Godolphin stable, both trained by Saeed bin Suroor and both ridden by Frankie Dettori. Drama has always gone hand-in-glove with the Arc. The 2004 victor, Bago, had to recover from an early-season virus before gaining his victory for the Niarchos family, trainer Jonathan Pease and jockey Thierry Gillet.

CHELTENHAM GOLD CUP

For many years the Grand National stood head and shoulders above every other race in the steeplechasing calendars and any horse worth even a pinch of salt was aimed at it, not least because there were precious few other chances for steeplechasers to collect even a decent prize. The Cheltenham executive decided that there should be a counter attraction to the Grand National, a weight-for-age race rather than a handicap, and the Cheltenham Gold Cup came into existence in 1924.

EARLY IN THE 20TH CENTURY, the Cheltenham Festival was, up to a point, an established part of the season, but its main event was the four-mile National Hunt Chase for amateur-ridden maidens, which had settled there since 1911 after a nomadic existence before that. Although to start with the Cheltenham Gold Cup was regarded by many as a prep race en route to Liverpool, it was not long before it stood firmly on its own and it has long been the most important chasing prize of the season.

There were nine runners for the first race, which produced a thrilling finish as the five-year-old Red Splash, ridden by Dick Rees, won by a neck and a head from Conjuror II and Gerald. Rees had been going to ride the apparent good thing, Alcazar, but that horse was taken out on the morning of the race and Fred Withington, Red Splash's trainer, ensured that Rees was on his five-year-old.

Alcazar was able to run the following season when he was ridden by Rees and started at odds-on in a field of four, but was no match for the Irish-trained mare Ballinode, whose jockey Ted Leader had won the Grand Sefton Chase on her earlier in the season. Leader was champion jockey in 1925–26 and rode Sprig to take the 1927 Grand National.

The first amateur to win was Hugh Grosvenor on Thrown In, who had been bought for him by his father Lord Stalbridge, and Dick Rees became the first man to win the race twice when Patron Saint, another five-year-old, was successful in 1928.

For the next seven years the race was dominated by two of the very best chasers of their or any other era – Easter Hero and Golden Miller. Easter Hero, owned by the anglophile American Jock Whitney and trained by Jack Anthony, won by 20 lengths in 1929 and 1930, ridden by Dick Rees on the first occasion and Tommy Cullinan on the second. Cullinan was to have ridden Easter Hero in the Grand National of that year, but the horse went lame shortly before the race which

Cullinan then won on Shaun Goilin, becoming the first man to win National, Gold Cup and Champion Hurdle (Brown Tony) in the same year.

Then came Golden Miller, owned by Miss Dorothy Paget, who won the Cup in five consecutive years, 1932–36. He was denied the chance of six in a row when the meeting was abandoned in 1937 and went down by two lengths to Morse Code on his final appearance in 1938.

World War II meant that there was no race in 1943 and 1944 and when things resumed Lord Stalbridge, who had won with Thrown In in 1927 and took the 1940 Grand National with Bogskar, won the Cup again with Red Rower, whose jockey Davy Jones was much more a flat-race rider and who carried about three stones of lead.

There were some outstanding winners immediately after the war. Prince Regent, whose career might have scaled even greater heights but for the conflict, had a deserved win in 1946 and the following year Fortina, who went on to become a high class sire, became the only full horse to win the race when he beat Happy Holme in a race delayed until April by bad weather.

Vincent O'Brien sent out Cottage Rake and

Record breaker: Golden Miller's five consecutive victories in the early 1930s will probably never be beaten.

Aubrey Brabazon for a hat-trick in the next three seasons and Knock Hard to win in 1953. Between those two horses there was a trememdous finish in 1951 when Silver Fame short headed Greenogue and another success for Miss Paget with Mont Tremblant the next season.

The biggest shock of that era came with the 33–1 success of Gay Donald in 1955 and three years after that Kerstin beat Polar Flight to become the second mare to triumph, preceding another Irish success with Roddy Owen in 1959. Pas Seul would almost certainly have won that year had he not fallen when in front at the final fence. He made no such mistake 12 months later.

Fred Winter rode the next two winners, on Saffron Tartan and the remarkable Mandarin, before the latter's trainer Fulke Walwyn won the race for the third time with Mill House in 1963. Mill House was for a short time regarded as the oustanding horse of his time, but he was no match for the great Arkle, who won the next three Gold Cups and might well have emulated Golden Miller had not injury in the King George VI Chase at Kempton at the end of 1966 ended his career.

His trainer Tom Dreaper had won in 1946 with Prince Regent and would do so again with Fort Leney in 1968 and Dreaper's son Jim sent out Ten Up to carry the colours of Arkle's owner, Anne, Duchess of Westminster, to victory in 1975, during a period when Irish-trained horses

- ◆ For five-year-olds and upwards
- ◆ Held on the Thursday of the Festival Meeting at Cheltenham in mid March
- ◆ Inaugurated 1924

RACE DISTANCE
About 3¼ miles, 1924–date

COURSE HOSTING THE CHELTENHAM GOLD CUP
Cheltenham 1924–date
No race 1931, 1937, 1943-44, 2001

TRAINERS WITH MOST WINS
5　Tom Dreaper
4　B Briscoe, MV O'Brien

JOCKEYS WITH MOST WINS
4　Pat Taafe
3　A Brabazon, T Carberry, J Culloty, D Rees

CHELTENHAM GOLD CUP 1924–2006

YEAR	HORSE	JOCKEY	TRAINER
1924	Red Splash	F Rees	FE Worthington
1925	Balinode	E Leader	F Morgan
1926	Koko	J Hamey	A Bickley
1927	Thrown In	H Grosvenor	O Anthony
1928	Patron Saint	F Rees	H Harrison
1929	Easter Hero	F Rees	J Anthony
1930	Easter Hero	T Cullinan	J Anthony
1931	No race		
1932	Golden Miller	T Leader	B Briscoe
1933	Golden Miller	W Scott	B Briscoe
1934	Golden Miller	G Wilson	B Briscoe
1935	Golden Miller	G Wilson	B Briscoe
1936	Golden Miller	E Williams	O Anthony
1937	No race		
1938	Morse Code	D Morgan	I Anthony
1939	Brendan's Cottage	G Owen	G Beeby
1940	Roman Hackle	E Williams	O Anthony
1941	Poet Prince	R Burford	I Anthony
1942	Medoc	H Nicholson	R Hobbs
1943	No race		
1944	No race		

YEAR	HORSE	JOCKEY	TRAINER
1945	Red Rower	D Jones	Lord Stalbridge
1946	Prince Regent	T Hyde	T Dreaper
1947	Fortina	R Black	H Christie
1948	Cottage Rake	A Brabazon	MV O'Brien
1949	Cottage Rake	A Brabazon	MV O'Brien
1950	Cottage Rake	A Brabazon	MV O'Brien
1951	Silver Fame	M Molony	G Beeby
1952	Mont Tremblant	D Dick	F Walwyn
1953	Knock Hard	T Molony	MV O'Brien
1954	Four Ten	T Cusack	J Roberts
1955	Gay Donald	A Grantham	J Ford
1956	Limber Hill	J Power	W Dutton
1957	Linwell	M Scudamore	C Mallon
1958	Kerstin	S Hayhurst	C Bewicke
1959	Roddy Owen	H Beasley	D Morgan
1960	Pas Seul	W Rees	R Turnell
1961	Saffron Tartan	F Winter	D Butchers
1962	Mandarin	F Winter	F Walwyn
1963	Mill House	GW Robinson	F Walwyn
1964	Arkle	P Taaffe	T Dreaper
1965	Arkle	P Taaffe	T Dreaper

YEAR	HORSE	JOCKEY	TRAINER
1966	Arkle	P Taaffe	T Dreaper
1967	Woodland Venture	T Biddlecombe	F Rimell
1968	Fort Leney	P Taaffe	T Dreaper
1969	What A Myth	P Kelleway	R Price
1970	L'Escargot	T Carberry	D Moore
1971	L'Escargot	T Carberry	D Moore
1972	Glencaraig Lady	F Berry	F Flood
1973	The Dikler	R Barry	F Walwyn
1974	Captain Christy	H Beasley	P Taaffe
1975	Ten Up	T Carberry	J Dreaper
1976	Royal Frolic	J Burke	F Rimell
1977	Davy Lad	D Hughes	M O'Toole
1978	Midnight Court	J Francome	F Winter
1979	Alverton	JJ O'Neill	M Easterby
1980	Master Smudge	R Hoare	A Barrow
1981	Little Owl	AJ Wilson	M Easterby
1982	Silver Buck	R Earnshaw	M Dickinson
1983	Bregawn	G Bradley	M Dickinson
1984	Burrough Hill Lad	P Tuck	Mrs J Pitman
1985	Forgive N'Forget	M Dwyer	J FitzGerald
1986	Dawn Run	JJ O'Neill	P Mullins

YEAR	HORSE	JOCKEY	TRAINER
1987	The Thinker	R Lamb	WA Stephenson
1988	Charter Party	R Dunwoody	D Nicholson
1989	Desert Orchid	S Sherwood	D Elsworth
1990	Norton's Coin	G McCourt	S Griffiths
1991	Garrison Savannah	M Pitman	Mrs J Pitman
1992	Cool Ground	A Maguire	G Balding
1993	Jodami	M Dwyer	P Beaumont
1994	The Fellow	A Kondrat	F Doumen
1995	Master Oats	N Williamson	K Bailey
1996	Imperial Call	C O'Dwyer	F Sutherland
1997	Mr Mulligan	AP McCoy	N Chance
1998	Cool Dawn	A Thornton	R Alner
1999	See More Business	M Fitzgerald	P Nicholls
2000	Looks Like Trouble	R Johnson	N Chance
2001	No race		
2002	Best Mate	J Culloty	HC Knight
2003	Best Mate	J Culloty	HC Knight
2004	Best Mate	J Culloty	HC Knight
2005	Kicking King	B Geraghty	T Taaffe
2006	War of Attrition	C O'Dwyer	M Morris

dominated the race. L'Escargot was the last horse to win the race in consecutive years, in 1970 and 1971 and went on to take the Grand National in 1975, the mare Glencaraig Lady won in 1972, Captain Christy in 1974 and Davy Lad in 1977.

Davy Lad tried to add the Grand National of the same year to his laurels but fell at Liverpool as, sadly fatally, did the 1979 Gold Cup winner Alverton, whose jockey Jonjo O'Neill rode Dawn Run to her emotional success in 1986 when she thus became the first horse to win both the Gold Cup and the Champion Hurdle.

Michael Dickinson sent out Silver Buck to win in 1982 and the following season pulled off the amazing feat of having the first five finishers – Bregawn, Captain John, Wayward Lad, Silver Buck and Ashley House – before Jenny Pitman became the first woman to train a winner with Burrough Hill Lad. She also won with Garrison Savannah, in 1991 after 100–1 Norton's Coin became the race's longest priced winner. Two years earlier, the hugely popular Desert Orchid sent the crowd into raptures with his defeat of Yahoo. In fact, the 1990s saw ten different winning horses, trainers and jockeys. The Gold Cup winner in 2000, Looks Like Trouble, seemed aptly-named, as a foot and mouth outbreak caused the abandonment of the 2001 Cheltenham Festival.

It resumed, thankfully, in 2002, seeing the first of three consecutive victories in the Cheltenham Gold Cup by Best Mate, trained by Henrietta Knight and ridden by Jim Culloty. A burst blood vessel prevented Best Mate from competing in the 2005 renewal of the race, and he subsequently died of a suspected heart attack the following autumn. In 2005, another appropriately named jumper, Kicking King, proved best going over Cheltenham's 22-fence course, as was the case with War of Attrition in 2006.

Triple success: Jim Culloty and Best Mate clear the last in 2004 on their way to their third successive Gold Cup win.

JAPAN CUP

Japan's racing authorities attempt to put themselves at the forefront of the international scene resulted in the first Japan Cup in 1981. Previously their involvement had been largely limited to sending occasional horses to run in big races in Europe and America. The race's growing importance is, in part, due to its vast prize money.

THE JAPAN CUP, which made its first appearance in 1981, is annually run at Tokyo Race Course at the end of November, and is called a world championship by its promoters. It is not one, of course, as there really is no such thing in thoroughbred racing, but the Japan Cup has quickly attained a position of major significance in the international calendar. Its 2005 renewal, won by the British invader Alkaased under jockey Frankie Dettori, was accomplished in a world record time of 2:22.1 for the 2,400 metres on the grass.

When the Japan Cup was inaugurated, horses from only a select handful of countries were allowed to compete. The 1981 running pretty much turned into a showcase for North American horses, as Mairzy Dotes, trained by John Fulton and ridden by American Cash Asmussen, won by a length over Canada's Frost King. The nearest of the Japanese contenders was Gold Spencer, who finished fifth.

The international restrictions were lifted in 1982, but once again the winner came from the United States as Half Iced, ridden by Don

Macbeth, proved the better of two challenging mares from France, All Along and April Run. Another European-based filly, the Irish-trained Stanberry, was fourth in the field of 14. And once again, no Japanese runner made an impact.

Fast forward to the year 2001, however, and one can see how much the Japan Cup has changed, and how major a factor Japanese horses have become. That year, Japanese-bred runners occupied a sweep of the top five positions. The victor, ridden by Olivier Peslier, was Jungle Pocket, who overtook T.M. Opera O in the

JAPAN CUP 1981–2005

YEAR	HORSE	JOCKEY	TRAINER
1981	Mairzy Dotes	C Asmussen	J Fulton
1982	Half Iced	D Macbeth	S Hough
1983	Stanerra	B Rouse	F Dunne
1984	Katsuragi Ace	K Nishiura	K Domon
1985	Symboli Rudolf	Y Okabe	Y Nohira
1986	Jupiter Island	Pat Eddery	C Brittain
1987	Le Glorieux	A Lequeux	R Collet
1988	Pay The Butler	C McCarron	R Frankel
1989	Horlicks	L O'Sullivan	D O'Sullivan
1990	Better Loosen Up	M Clarke	D Hayes
1991	Golden Pheasant	G Stevens	C Whittingham
1992	Tokai Teio	Y Okabe	S Matsumoto
1993	Legacy World	H Koyauchi	H Mori

YEAR	HORSE	JOCKEY	TRAINER
1994	Marvelous Crown	K Minai	M Osawa
1995	Lando	M Roberts	H Jentzsch
1996	Singspiel	L Dettori	M Stoute
1997	Pilsudski	M Kinane	M Stoute
1998	El Condor Pasa	M Ebina	Y Ninomiya
1999	Special Week	Y Take	T Shirai
2000	TM Opera O	R Wada	I Iwamoto
2001	Jungle Pocket	O Peslier	S Watanabe
2002	Falbrav	L Dettori	L Brogi
2003	Tap Dance City	T Sato	S Sasaki
2004	Zenno Rob Roy	O Peslier	K Fujisawa
2005	Alkaased	L Dettori	L Cumani

Down the stretch: A huge crowd watches the horses storm down the straight in 1993.

stretch to win by a length. The best that any American invader could do was an eighth-place finish. Jungle Pocket's victory was the fourth straight for a Japanese representative in the race, and the seventh in ten years. The home team had turned into formidable hosts.

But foreign challengers have not shirked from the Japan Cup – rather, many now point to it as a major objective. In 2002, Fulcra, an Irish-bred who was raised in Italy and became one of the finest international runners ever to represent that country, took the lead in the stretch under Debtor and then held on to prevail by a nose over the American challenger Sara fan.

In 2003, the Japanese runner Tap Dance City rolled to a wire-to-wire victory in the Japan Cup. His nine-length margin of victory under jockey Testis Sato remains the record for the race. The following year, before a crowd of 119,362, Japanese horses occupied the top three positions, with Zenno Rob Roy prevailing by three lengths under Peskier. With Alkaased's successful invasion in 2005, the Japan Cup has, indeed, become a merry free-for-all.

The Japanese had first landed their own race when Katsuragi Ace came home 1½ lengths to the fore of the British hope Bedtime in 1984. The following year, the home team finished one-two as Symboli Rudolf proved the better of his compatriot Rocky Tiger, with the New Zealand contender The Filbert finishing third. The initial success in the Japan Cup for a horse trained in Britain came in 1986, with Jupiter Island, trained by Clive Brittain and ridden by Pat Eddery, outperforming his compatriot Allez Milord.

In 1987, a horse trained in France became the first and, to date, only Japan Cup winner to represent that country, when Le Glorieux triumphed by three-quarters of a length over the

Opposite: **Sandwich filling:** TM Opera O and Ryuji Wada (blue cap, middle) come home to win the 2000 Japan Cup.

American representative, Southjet. Trained by Robert Collet and ridden by Alain Lequeux, Le Glorieux was also the first three-year-old to win the race. The following year, the United States recorded its third success in the Japan Cup when Pay The Butler, trained by Bobby Frankel and ridden by Chris McCarron, came home three-quarters of a length in front of the Japan-based favourite Tamamo Cross.

Horses from lands Down Under took the next two Japan Cup renewals. In 1989, Horlicks, a six-year-old grey mare from New Zealand, narrowly defeated the Japanese representative, Oguri Cap. In 1990, Loosen Up, representing Australia, produced a whirlwind late run to catch Cacoethes near the line and then held on to prevail by a head over another strong finisher, the French-trained mare Ode. In 1991, it was the USA's turn again when Golden Pheasant, trained by Charlie Whittingham and ridden by Gary Stevens, outran the French representative, Magic Night. This culminated in a six-year stretch when the Japan Cup was won by foreign runners.

From a Japanese standpoint, the situation was righted in 1992, with Tokai Teio's victory.

- ◆ For three-year-olds and upwards
- ◆ Held on the last weekend in November at Tokyo Race Course
- ◆ Inaugurated 1981

RACE DISTANCE
2,400 metres, 1981-2001, 2003-date
2,200 metres, 2002

TRACKS HOSTING JAPAN CUP
Tokyo Race Course 1981-2001, 2003-date
Nakayama Race Course 2002

TRAINERS WITH MOST WINS
2   Michael Stoute

JOCKEYS WITH MOST WINS
3   L Dettori
2   Y Okabe, O Peslier

Tokai Teio's sire was Symboli Rudolf, the aforesaid 1985 Japan Cup winner, and they thus became the first sire/son duo to triumph in the race. Controversy enveloped the 1993 Cup when jockey Kent Desormeaux, riding the American-trained favourite Kotoshaan, mistook the finish line and lost the race to Japan's Legacy World. The following year, Japan triumphed again with Marvelous Crown, who got up at the finish line to thwart the efforts of the American horse Paradise Creek.

Germany, which had been unsuccessful with several earlier attempts in the Japan Cup, won the race for the first time in 1995 when Lando, trained by Heinz Jentzsch and ridden by South African Michael Roberts, outgamed Japan's Hishi Amazon. In 1996, Singspiel, trained in Newmarket by Michael Stoute, held on by a whisker under Dettori against Fabulous La Fouine. And in 1997, another horse trained at Newmarket by Stoute, Pilsudski, was brilliantly ridden by Mick Kinane to a narrow victory over Japan's Air Groove.

The following season, the home country's El Condor Pasa won the Japan Cup, finishing 2½ lengths in front of Air Groove, who again was the runner-up. Special Hero, ridden by Japanese folk hero Yutaka Take, secured victory for the home country once more in 1999, as did T.M. Opera O in 2000.

In 2002, the Japan Cup was run over 2,200 metres at Nakayama Race Course, while major renovations were taking place at the race's traditional host site. In 2000, a sister Group 1 race, bearing the rather inelegant name Japan Cup Dirt, was inaugurated. It is run on the same weekend as the Japan Cup over the surface its name suggests. Dettori, whose three Japan Cup victories are the most by any jockey, set a historic precedent by winning both the Japan Cup and the Japan Cup Dirt (the latter with a horse named Eagle Café) in 2002.

DUBAI WORLD CUP

Although it is the youngest of the events of prime international importance, since its inception the Dubai World Cup has carried the status of being the richest horse race on the globe. And although annually it lures competitors from many far-away lands, to date it has been dominated by two forces - the home team and the Americans.

THE DUBAI WORLD Cup is not the most prominent horse race on the globe, but it is undeniably the richest. The 2006 running, won by Electrocutionist, had a purse of $6.02 million. Run at a distance of 2,000 metres on the Maktoum family's Nad Al Sheba racecourse, the event regularly lures competitors from North America, Europe, the Far East and Australia. More often than not, however, the Dubai World Cup has been taken by members of the home team.

Indeed, six times in its initial 11 runnings the Dubai World Cup has gone to Maktoum horses.

They include Singspiel, who was victorious for Sheikh Mohammed bin Rashid Al-Maktoum in 1997; Almutawakel, who triumphed for Sheikh Hamdan bin Rashid Al-Maktoum in 1999; Dubai Millennium, who won for the Maktoums' Godolphin operation in 2000; Street Cry and Moon Ballad, who won back-to-back runnings for Godolphin in 2002-03, respectively; and Electrocutionist, who is still another bearer of the royal blue Godolphin silks. Of the six, Singspiel was trained by Sir Michael Stoute, and the others have been trained by Saeed bin Suroor.

Yet the home team has experienced significant defeats as well - all of them at the hands of the Americans. The inaugural running of the Dubai World Cup in 1996 went to Cigar – it was the fourteenth triumph in what eventually would be a 16-race winning streak for Allen Paulson's American-based champion. Trained by Bill Mott and ridden by Jerry Bailey, Cigar prevailed by half a length over another American-

Racing riches: Jockey Jamie Spencer walks back after winning the Dubai Duty Free at the 2006 Dubai World Cup.

DUBAI WORLD CUP 1996–2006

YEAR	HORSE	JOCKEY	TRAINER
1996	Cigar	JD Bailey	WI Mott
1997	Singspiel	JD Bailey	M Stoute
1998	Silver Charm	G Stevens	B Baffert
1999	Almutawakel	R Hills	S bin Suroor
2000	Dubai Millennium	L Dettori	S bin Suroor
2001	Captain Steve	JD Bailey	B Baffert

YEAR	HORSE	JOCKEY	TRAINER
2002	Street Cry	JD Bailey	S bin Suroor
2003	Moon Ballad	L Dettori	S bin Suroor
2004	Pleasantly Perfect	A Solis	R Mandella
2005	Roses In May	J Velazquez	D Romans
2006	Electrocutionist	L Dettori	S bin Suroor

based runner, Soul Of The Matter. The Dubai World Cup purse that year was $4 million, with a $2.4 million share going to Cigar (which would constitute 24 per cent of his career earnings).

Other American horses would subsequently perform brilliantly in the Dubai World Cup, too. Silver Charm, victorious in the 1997 Kentucky Derby and Preakness Stakes, was shipped by trainer Bob Baffert to Nad Al Sheba in March 1998 and defeated the Godolphin star, Swain, by a nose. Gary Stevens was aboard Silver Charm for that trip. Another Baffert trainee, Captain Steve, won the Dubai World Cup under Bailey in 2001. Pleasantly Perfect, who had registered an upset victory in the Breeders' Cup Classic at Santa Anita the prior November, won the Dubai World Cup for jockey Alex Solis and trainer Richard Mandella in 2004. And Roses In May won for jockey John Velazquez and trainer Dale Romans the following year.

Nad Al Sheba's dirt track is 20 metres wide and 2,254 metres in length, and has left-handed turns - the lattermost factor is also the case at racetracks throughout North America, which may constitute a reason why horses from those shores have fared so well. But the Maktoums' runners still hold overall advantages, not least of which is the vast opportunities many of them have throughout their careers to train and engage in preparatory races over the Nad Al Sheba surface.

Through the first 11 runnings, the fastest time registered by a Dubai World Cup winner was 1:59.5, compliments of Dubai Millennium, who was guided by Frankie Dettori. This was the first of a trio of victories Dettori has had in the race - the others came with Moon Ballad and Electrocutionist. There are no such things as on-

site favourites or long shots winning the Dubai World Cup, because no wagering is allowed at Nad Al Sheba. The race, however, is simulcast to numerous sites on other continents where wagering activity on the race is extensive.

There are other races of prominence on the Dubai World Cup card. The Dubai Sheema Classic is run at 2,400 metres on the turf. In 2006, it had a purse of $5 million and was won by Heart's Cry, a competitor from Japan. The Dubai Duty Free Stakes is run at 1,800 metres on the turf. In 2006, it also had a purse of $5 million, and was won by David Junior, a representative from England. These are the two richest stakes run anywhere in the world over a grass course.

The Dubai Golden Shaheen is run at 1,200 metres on the dirt. In 2006, it had a purse of $2 million, and was won by Proud Tower Too, an American-based runner. As is also true of the Dubai World Cup, Dubai Sheema Classic and Dubai Duty Free Stakes, these races bear Group 1 status.

Bearing Group 2 status are the UAE Derby and the Godolphin Mile. The former is run over 1,800 metres on the dirt, had a $2 million purse in 2006 and was won by the Godolphin colt, Discreet Cat. The latter is run at 1,600 metres on the dirt, had a $1 million purse in 2006 and was won by the Japanese runner, Utopia. All told, purses for the 2006 Dubai World Cup card total more than $21 million, a figure unmatched by any single day or night of racing anywhere else. Horses from a

dozen countries competed.

It is said that Sheikh Mohammed was the founding force behind the Dubai World Cup. His countrymen have certainly embraced the concept. Racing fans in excess of 70,000 regularly come to Nad Al Sheba for the event. They have been known to chant loudly, "Go-dol-phin! Go-dol-phin!," much like a football crowd when one of the Sheikhs' horses wins, which is both the nationalistic and wise thing to do, considering that the Maktoums are also Dubai's rulers. The international press turns out in large numbers, too, from as many as six continents (Antarctica being the sole exception).

While it does seem incongruous that a country as small as the United Arab Emirates (32,000 square miles, 2.56 million inhabitants) is the host of a racing event that has no peer regarding purse money awarded, an economy that remains enormously wealthy in oil and natural gas reserves has allowed this to become possible. The future of the Dubai World Cup appears as guaranteed as that of any major international race. The emirate of Dubai itself, which is the centre point of the Maktoum empire, is fast developing into a major thoroughbred breeding locale. As evidenced by the Dubai World Cup programme, its prominence as a major racing centre is already established.

Golden triumph: Jockey John Velazquez holds aloft the winner's golden riding crop for taking the 2005 Dubai Cup.

◆ For three-year-olds and upwards
◆ Held in late March at Nad Al Sheba in the United Arab Emirates
◆ Inaugurated 1996

RACE DISTANCE
Run over 2,000 metres

TRAINER WITH MOST WINS
5   Saeed bin Suroor
2   Bob Baffert

JOCKEYS WITH MOST WINS
4   Jerry D. Bailey
3   Lanfranco Dettori

HONG KONG CUP

Since its inaugural running in 1988, the Hong Kong Cup has grown from a modest regional affair into the anchoring event of a spectacular international festival, annually luring participants from both the Northern and Southern Hemispheres.

THE HK$18-MILLION Hong Kong Cup is one of the world's premier 2000-metre turf races. It is hosted by the Hong Kong Jockey Club at Sha Tin Racecourse, and is the anchoring event of an international racing festival that further includes the 2400-metre Hong Kong Vase, the 1600-metre Hong Kong Mile and the 1000-metre Hong Kong Sprint. All four of these races have gained the classification of Group 1, which is the highest rating a racing event can achieve on the global scale.

Year after year, the Hong Kong International Races programme lures competitors from such countries as England, Ireland, France, Germany, the United Arab Emirates, Japan, Australia, the United States, Denmark and Australia. The festival further includes an international jockeys' contest, involving a trio of races at the Hong Kong Jockey Club's other track, Happy Valley, which is located in the downtown sector of the city. In conjunction with its international races, the Jockey Club further annually conducts an auction of two-year-old horses who have been primarily obtained at yearling sales in England, the United States and Australia.

A great deal of fanfare accompanies the Hong Kong Cup – speeches, drum rolls, the waving of flags, bagpipes, marching bands, fireworks, dancing dragons, numerous renditions of "God Save the Queen" (Hong Kong was a British colony until 1997) and so forth. One year, an 88-member troupe was brought in on the day of the Cup to give a Kung Fu demonstration on Sha Tin's turf course. On-site crowds in excess of 50,000 are the norm for the Hong Kong Cup, and wagering is further conducted at Happy Valley, more than a hundred off-track-betting facilities throughout the city and via hundreds of thousands of telephone wagering accounts.

A select group of horses stationed in Hong Kong is invited to participate in the international races each year. One of them, Precision, achieved a photo-finish triumph in the Hong Kong Cup in 2002. Precision's odds were a generous 65–1, and his victory secured him a niche as one of the greatest runners from the local ranks in the city's history.

When the Hong Kong Cup was inaugurated (as the Hong Kong Invitational Cup) in January, 1988, its distance was 1800 metres and invitations were extended only to Hong Kong, Singapore and Malaysian horses. The winner was Flying Dancer, owned by Lim Por Yen and trained by Ping Chee Kan. Flying Dancer stalked the early pace, took the lead in the final 100 metres and drew off to a 1½ length victory.

In 1989, the Hong Kong Cup's invitational list was expanded to include horses from Australia and New Zealand. The following year, horses from Europe were added to the list of invited participants, as were horses from the United States in 1991 and from Canada and Japan in 1992.

Horses aged three years and older are eligible to run in the Hong Kong Cup. No horse has ever won it twice, although several

Fabulous festival: Frankie Dettori and Falbrav win the Hong Kong Cup at Sha Tin racecourse in December 2003.

◆ For three-year-olds and upwards
◆ Held in mid-December at Sha Tin in Hong Kong
◆ Inaugurated 1988

RACE DISTANCE
1800 metres, 1988-1998
2000 metres, 1999-date

COURSE HOSTING THE HONG KONG CUP
Sha Tin, 1988-date

TRAINER WITH MOST WINS
1 Held by 19 different trainers

JOCKEYS WITH MOST WINS
2 Lanfranco Dettori, Gerald Mosse

HONG KONG CUP 1988-2005

competitors have tried. Colonial Chief, who won the second running of the race in 1989, finished unplaced and third, respectively, in subsequent renewals. River Verdon, victorious in the 1991 renewal, finished unplaced in a pair of subsequent Hong Kong Cup efforts. Jim And Tonic, the 1999 Hong Kong Cup winner, finished third in the 2000 renewal, and was unplaced in 2001.

Midnight Bet, the 1998 Hong Kong Cup winner, was the stakes record holder when the race was run at 1800 metres, clocking a final time of 1:46.9. The Hong Kong Cup's current 2000-metre distance was adopted in 1999. The winner that year was Jim And Tonic, who is something of a folk hero among Hong Kong racing fans, as he also shipped in from France to win the Hong Kong Bowl in 1998 and the Queen Elizabeth II Cup at Sha Tin in the spring of 1999.

Certainly one of the most memorable performances in the Hong Kong Cup was turned in by Fantastic Light, who in the year 2000 raced on four continents, and won or placed in major stakes on all of them. Fantastic Light's 1½ length victory in the Cup was achieved under jockey Frankie Dettori, who three years later registered another Hong Kong Cup win with Falbrav.

In 2001, a Japanese representative, Agnes Digital, won the Hong Kong Cup in a photo finish. He was actually one of three horses based in Tokyo to be victorious in a major event on the card, as Japan's Stay Gold won the Hong Kong Vase and Eishin Preston won the Hong Kong Mile. These circumstances inspired one scribe to quip, "Not since the Japanese invaded Manchuria in 1937 have they fared so well on Chinese soil."

Falbrav's triumph is the 2003 Hong Kong Cup was his eighth in Group 1 company, and his career finale as well. He had a widening two-length lead at the finish, and his time, 2:00.9, remains the fastest for the Cup at its current 2000-metre distance. The victory by Falbrav came the day prior to Dettori's 33rd birthday, and he was whooping and hollering in the weighing room afterwards. Luca Cumani, who trained Falbrav, had provided Dettori with his initial career winner 16 years earlier.

Alexandra Goldrun, with her photo-finish triumph in 2004, became the first filly to win the Hong Kong Cup. Prior to shipping to Sha Tin, she had been a Group 1 winner in France, and the fact that experienced and proven male horses constituted her Cup competition didn't faze Alexandra Goldrun's trainer, Jim Bolger. "The greatest thing about her is she knows how to scrap," Bolger said.

Vengeance of Rain, the 2005 Hong Kong Cup winner, achieved his victory in workmanlike fashion, taking the lead in mid-stretch, opening up a daylight margin and then holding off the late charge of the mare Pride. A gelded son of Zabeel representing Australia, Vengeance of Rain was ridden by Anthony Delpech, a former leading jockey in South Africa who had relocated to Hong Kong.

No trainer or owner has yet achieved two Hong Kong Cup wins, although Saeed bin Suroor and Godolphin Stable came very close, winning with Fantastic Light in 2000 and just missing victory by a head with Tobougg in 2001. Aside from Dettori, the only jockey to win the Hong Kong Cup twice is Gerald Mosse, who prevailed with River Verdon in 1991 and with Jim And Tonic in 1999.

Major companies have not been reluctant to partner with the Hong Kong International Races. In recent years, Cathay Pacific Airlines has been the title sponsor of the Hong Kong Cup. The Hong Kong Jockey Club helps underwrite the travel and lodging expenses for members of the foreign press who visit to cover the Hong Kong Cup, which always results in an impressive media turnout.

Asian spectacular: Sha Tin draws crowds in excess of 50,000 for its International Races.

CHAPTER 4
LEGENDARY HORSES

The Olympic ideals of swifter, higher, stronger does not translate into horse racing, not least because records for race times have been – the U.S. excepted – haphazard at best. Rarely is it a performance in one race that creates a racing legend; in racing most careers last three seasons, or less, but the results can be exceptional.

THE 20 LEGENDS included here have little in common, other than their continued successes. Breeding – that most inexact of sciences – proves nothing because some legends came from undistinguished sires and dams, others were equine blue-bloods; and the same scenario continued when, in the case of mares and stallions, they passed on their genes – for example, Cigar proved to be impotent, costing his owner and prospective breeders a large fortune.

In terms of pure quality, one horse in this list does not belong. However, it would be a travesty of justice to omit the only three-time Grand National winner. Red Rum was probably burdened with the bets of a greater percentage of British people in the 1977 Grand National than any horse has had to carry – with the possible exception of Irishmen backing Arkle at Cheltenham in 1966. His performances at Aintree were the stuff of legend.

The inclusion of others here, such as Secretariat, is obvious. In 1973, Secretariat set a track record at Belmont Park for 1 1/2 miles in winning the Belmont Stakes (by an astonishing 31 lengths). His time for the third U.S. Triple Crown classic is the best ever over for the race by a clear two seconds.

World traveller: Cigar (8) wins the inaugural Dubai World Cup in 1996, one of his 16 consecutive victories in 21 months.

ARKLE

ALTHOUGH HE WAS NEVER entered for, let alone ran in, the most famous steeplechase in the world, the Grand National, Arkle was beyond dispute the outstanding European steeplechaser of the second half of the 20th century and very probably of all time. No other horse in the history of racing has been so superior to his contemporaries that the rules of racing had to be altered to give the opposition some sort of a chance.

Trained by Tom Dreaper for Anne, Duchess of Westminster, Arkle won 27 of the 35 races in which he took part and accumulated first-place prize money of £75,207. He could well have done even better than this as there had been no sign that his powers were diminishing when an injury in the King George V1 Chase in 1966 resulted in one of his rare defeats and in due course led to his retirement.

The first of his successes came in a novice hurdle worth £133 to the winner, at Navan in January 1962. Amazingly, in view of what was to come, he started at 20–1 and his stablemate Kerforo, who was later to win the Irish Grand National, started even-money favourite and was

> "In Arkle's case, it is the combination of speed, stamina and jumping ability in a degree so far unequalled, which has produced the champion steeplechaser of all time" Ivor Herbert, Arkle, The Story of a Champion, **1966**

beaten nearly 10 lengths into third place.

Two more wins over hurdles followed the next season before Arkle was sent over fences and he made his first appearance in England at Cheltenham in November 1962. He then annihilated a field, which included two horses, Milo and Time, who were to win at the National Hunt Festival the following March, by 20 lengths and more.

Arkle was back for that meeting as well and won the Broadway (now Royal & SunAlliance) Chase by 20 lengths, giving every indication that he was a horse of Cheltenham Gold Cup potential. He just swept on to victory after victory and in this and the following season his only defeat came in unfortunate circumstances when he was third to Mill House in the Hennessy Gold Cup at Newbury after slipping badly on landing four fences from home.

At that time Mill House was the top staying

chaser in England and many were prepared to believe that he would give the lie to stories about Arkle having been unlucky at Newbury when they met again in the Gold Cup at Cheltenham. Mill House started at odds-on, but Arkle swept him aside and won by five lengths.

He then went on to land the Irish Grand National under top weight and the following season left no doubt about his superiority to Mill House when he won the Hennessy Gold Cup by 10 lengths under 12st 7lb. Mill House, receiving 3lb, was 28 lengths behind him.

Though he could not quite give lumps of weight to Flying Wild and Buona notte in the Massey-Ferguson Gold Cup at Cheltenham later that month, Arkle returned there the following spring and won his second Gold Cup He was unbeaten in five starts in 1965–66, when he started at 1–10 as he completed a hat trick in the Cheltenham Gold Cup. He looked set to take Kempton's King George VI Chase for the second time in December 1966, only to fracture a bone in his foot as he failed by a length to give 21lb to Dormant.

When he first went out of training to recover from this injury there were high hopes that Arkle would be able to race again, but in October 1968 it was announced that he would never be able to do so. The following May, with the arthritic lesions he had in his hind feet making life increasingly painful for him, the inevitable decision was taken to have him humanely put down.

b g			
By Archive out of Bright Cherry			
(Knight of the Garter)			
Foaled 1957			
Died 1969			

Career record	Starts	1st	2nd	3rd
	35	27	2	3

True champion: Arkle and Pat Taaffe clear the last fence in the 1965 Cheltenham Gold Cup well clear of Mill House.

BAHRAM

BAHRAM WAS THE FOURTH SON of his sire to win the Derby in a period of seven years when he completed Britain's Triple Crown in 1935 – the last colt to do so until Nijinsky 35 years later. His dam cost his owner-breeder the Aga Khan (the grandfather of the present holder of that title) 240gns and Bahram alone repaid that judgement by being unbeaten in nine races and winning more than £43,000.

He was never a horse to overexert himself, which is possibly why when he made his debut as a two-year-old in the National Breeders' Produce Stakes at Sandown Park in 1934, he started at 20–1. His stablemate Theft – both were owned by the Aga Khan and trained by Frank Butters – was second favourite after having won at Royal Ascot.

Bahram, admittedly receiving 9lb from Theft, won by a neck and there was never any more 20–1 about him in his other eight races. His next success came in the Rous Memorial Stakes at Goodwood and by the end of that season he had added three more victories, including the Gimcrack and the Middle Park.

He was then rated the top two-year-old in the country and was given 9st 7lb (133 pounds) in the Free Handicap, which is how what is now the British part of the International Classifications was then known. Two other of the Aga Khan's horses, Theft and Hairan, were next in the list.

In spite of his outstanding juvenile career, Bahram did not start favourite for the 2,000 Guineas the following season, maybe because he had had a temperature and been unable to have a race before the classic. It made no difference, though, as he once again proved superior to Theft, whom he beat by 1¹/₂ lengths, this time, of course, at level weights.

He started hot favourite against 15 rivals in the Derby and duly did what was expected of him as he beat Robin Goodfellow by two lengths. Then came success at 1–8 in the St. James's Palace Stakes at Royal Ascot before he wound up his racing career by taking the St. Leger at Doncaster, ridden on this occasion by Charlie Smirke as his regular jockey Freddie Fox had been injured.

The Aga Khan then decided that Bahram would race no more and, to wide regret as there was every indication that the colt, who had never had a day's unsoundness, would continue as a major force as a four-year-old, would go to stud.

At the same time he declared that he would

Perfect champion: HH Aga Khan leads Bahram and Freddie Fox back to the unsaddling enclosure after winning the Derby.

never sell the horse, but he changed his mind about that five years later and a bid of £40,000 secured Bahram for an American syndicate. At the end of World War II he was on the move again, this time to Argentina, where he died in 1956. Nothing he sired was as good as he, though his son Big Game won a wartime 2,000 Guineas for King George VI. Another, Turkhan, took the St. Leger during the same period and a third son, Persian Gulf, sired another Derby winner in Parthia.

b c			
By Blandford out of Friar's Daughter (Friar Marcus)			
Foaled 1932			
Died 1956			
Career record	**Starts**	**1st**	**2nd**	**3rd**
	9	9	0	0

"Bahram is a splendid horse. He is a racing machine. It seems he must win."

Bahram's trainer Frank Butters, June 1935 after the Derby

BRIGADIER GERARD

RIGADIER GERARD was a vivid example that, even in the days of huge stallion fees and some elements apparently trying to take an almost monopolistic grip on racing, it is still possible for the small man to enjoy top-level success. He was by an unfashionable sire out of a mare who never won a race and his owner-breeders, the British husband and wife team of John and Jean Hislop, could not afford to be among the top league of spenders.

But in the Brigadier they produced a horse whom at least some experts rate as the best horse to have raced in Great Britain in the 20th century and whose achievements bear the closest inspection. He won from two years old to four, over distances from five furlongs to 1 1/2 miles and was beaten in only one of his 18 starts.

He was, by the most exacting of standards, a horse of the highest quality, but though he had been shaping well on Dick Hern's gallops at West Ilsley before his first appearance, at Newbury in the summer of 1970, he still went off as the outsider of five at odds of 100–7 (14–1). He won that race by five lengths and such a price was never available again.

Three more successes followed that season, at Salisbury, Newbury and finally the Middle Park Stakes at Newmarket which he won by three lengths. This was very smart form, but at the end of the season My Swallow and Mill Reef were rated respectively 2lb and 1lb above him.

The trio met the following season in one of the highest-quality runnings there can ever have been for the 2,000 Guineas. Both Mill Reef and My Swallow, who had won earlier in the year, were preferred to him in the betting, but Brigadier Gerard beat Mill Reef by three lengths, handsomely vindicating the decision by the Hislops to turn down a winter offer of £250,000.

He went on through that season by winning the St. James's Palace, Sussex and Champion Stakes and as a four-year-old began by taking the Lockinge Stakes at Newbury. He followed that by winning at Sandown, in the Prince of Wales's Stakes at Ascot and back at Sandown for the Eclipse before tackling 1 1/2 miles for the first and only time in the King George VI and Queen Elizabeth Stakes at Ascot.

He had to survive a stewards' inquiry after beating Parnell by a length and a half, but there was to be even bigger drama next time when he started at 1–3 for the first running of the Benson & Hedges Gold Cup at York. Brigadier Gerard broke the track record but still finished three lengths behind all-the-way winner Roberto, winner of that year's Derby but later beaten out of sight in the Irish Derby. The result is as inexplicable now as it was then.

Brigadier Gerard won his last two races, Ascot's Queen Elizabeth II Stakes and the Champion Stakes at Newmarket, before going to stud the following season. He died in 1989 but his record as a sire was not a patch on his as a racehorse; by far his best winners were Light Cavalry in the St. Leger and Vayrann in the Champion Stakes.

"He proved himself one of the outstanding horses of this century, combining power and quality to an unusual degree."

Biographical Encyclopedia of British Flat Racing, 1978

b c
By Queen's Hussar out of La Paiva
(Prince Chevalier)
Foaled 1968
Died 1989

Career record	Starts	1st	2nd	3rd
	18	17	1	0

Fifteen straight: Brigadier Gerard (ridden by Joe Mercer) lost his perfect record to Derby-winner Roberto at York.

CARBINE

Improved with age: In winning the 1890 Melbourne Cup, five-year-old Carbine carried a record 10st 5lb.

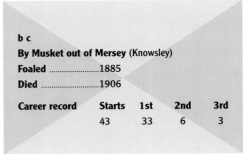

b c
By Musket out of Mersey (Knowsley)
Foaled 1885
Died 1906

Career record	Starts	1st	2nd	3rd
	43	33	6	3

BRED BY the New Zealand Stud Company, Carbine was sold to Dan O'Brien for the then substantial sum of 620 guineas as a yearling. Carbine, who originally raced as Mauser, demonstrated exceptional ability from his first start when after being left 60 yards he was still able to win the Hopeful Stakes, over five furlongs, by a length.

He went on to win the Middle Park Stakes, Dunedin (New Zealand) Jockey Club Champagne Stakes, Christchurch Champagne Stakes and Challenge Stakes at four subsequent appearances as a two-year-old. At his first appearance in Australia he was beaten, but not disgraced, in finishing second to Ensign in the 1888 Victoria Derby at Flemington after his jockey dropped his whip close to home.

Following his win in the Flying Stakes five days later, he was purchased for 3,000 guineas by Donald Wallace and entered the stables of Walter Hickenbotham, in whose care Carbine recorded eight wins, two seconds and a third in 11 remaining races at three. The most important of these was in the 1889 Sydney Cup, in which he carried 9st to a decisive victory over the the hot favourite Abercorn.

Although suffering from heel trouble Carbine won a further nine races – including a second Sydney Cup under 9st 9lb – as a four-year-old. By then known as "Old Jack" he soared to even greater heights as a five-year-old. He began the 1890–91 season with wins in the A.J.C. Spring Stakes, A.J.C. Craven Plate and V.R.C. Flemington Stakes leading through to the Melbourne Cup, in which he had been beaten a length by Bravo the previous year.

Carbine was burdened with 10st 5lb (145 pounds) in the 1890 Cup and whether he could cope with the demanding assignment became the subject of considerable speculation around Australia. Amid the debate novelist Nat Gould wrote,

"Back a good horse and a good jockey and damn the weight."

With Bob Ramage replacing the horse's regular jockey Mick O'Brien, Carbine was sent out as a 4–1 favourite even though he had to contend with 38 rivals. "Old Jack" proved more than equal to the task, coming through an opening in the straight to score by 2^1/$_2$ lengths from Highborn, who had only 6st 8lb (92 pounds) and was to win the following year's Sydney Cup. The winning time was 3:28^1/$_4$, which was the fastest ever run in the colony.

Carbine went on capture the Essendon Stakes, Champion Stakes, All-Aged Stakes and Autumn Stakes in Melbourne before a second to Marvel in the A.J.C. All-Aged Stakes brought an end to a winning streak extending over 15 races. He completed his career in glorious fashion, however, by winning the A.J.C. Cumberland Stakes, over two miles, and the A.J.C. Plate, over three miles, at his last two racecourse appearances in the autumn of 1891.

After being retired to stud Carbine was sold privately for 13,000 guineas to the Duke Of Portland in March of 1895 and stood alongside St. Simon at Welbeck Abbey Stud, where he sired the Derby winner of 1906, Spearmint.

> "There was never a Melbourne Cup like Carbine's. Those who saw it are never likely to forget it. The tumult after his victory was unbelievable. The great horse stood, quivered a little and took the tumult as his due. Thus was a legend born, for he became a symbol of courage, the great-hearted stayer, who triumphed while carrying a punishing load."

Melbourne Punch, **November, 1890.**

CIGAR

WAITING PATIENTLY for a horse to fulfil his potential can be an exercise in futility. In the case of Cigar, patience brought extraordinary dividends. Winning just twice, in maiden and allowance company, in his initial 13 career starts, the bay colt was switched from the grass to the dirt in October of his three-year-old campaign. Cigar immediately embarked on a 16-race winning streak, which included ten Grade 1 triumphs. It further included a trip to the United Arab Emirates, where he won the inaugural running of the Dubai World Cup, the richest ever race worldwide.

A U.S. homebred representing the late Allen E. Paulson, Cigar was backed by one of the finest teams of handlers in existence. Hall of Famer Bill Mott was his trainer; Hall of Fame jockey Jerry Bailey was aboard Cigar from the second start of the streak through the remainder of his racing career. Cigar's career earnings, which came to just short of $10 million, constitute the all-time record for any horse of any breed who ever raced.

Early on, Cigar's accomplishments were modest. He graduated in maiden sprint company second time out, at Hollywood Park on May 9, 1993. Mott then put Cigar on the turf, where he was once an allowance winner and twice placed in graded stakes, but displayed a reluctance to fire in the stretch. Some fine jockeys tried to bring the best out of Cigar, Hall of Famers Chris McCarron and Julie Krone among them. The colt continued to disappoint.

> "Over the span of 21 months, Cigar ran in 16 increasingly high-profile races from coast to coast and continent to continent. He faced 116 opponents, beating every one … Cigar is the very model of the modern major thoroughbred." **John Lee**, Cigar Aficionado, **Winter 1996/1997**

On October 28, 1994, Mott put Cigar back on the dirt. The result was an eight-length victory in a Belmont Park allowance. The following month, Cigar became a Grade 1 winner, triumphing by seven lengths in the NYRA Mile.

In January 1995, Cigar won an allowance race at Florida's Gulfstream Park. From thereon, he competed in nothing but major stakes company. His 1995 campaign, which included nine stakes victories at six different tracks in as many states, culminated with an easy win in North America's richest event, the Breeders' Cup Classic, at Belmont Park.

Cigar's unbeaten streak continued through four more stakes, including the World Cup, during the opening seven months of 1996. He won both the Donn and Massachusetts Handicaps for the second consecutive year, and also triumphed in an event especially created for him, the Citation Challenge at Arlington Park.

But in the Pacific Classic on August 10 at California's Del Mar racetrack, Cigar was defeated by a horse named Dare and Go. Cigar promptly rebounded by winning Belmont's Woodward Stakes, but was beaten in his final two career starts, completing his racing days with a third-place finish in the Breeders' Cup Classic, which in 1996 was run at Woodbine in Toronto.

Voted North America's Horse of the Year in both 1995 and 1996, Cigar was also champion handicap competitor during those seasons. He was subsequently booked to some of the finest broodmares on the continent, but was infertile at stud. Cigar is now a pensioner at the Kentucky Horse Park near Lexington. Tens of thousands of people visit him annually.

b c				
By Palace Music out of Solar Slew (Seattle Slew)				
Foaled 1990				
Raced...............1993–96				
Career record	**Starts**	**1st**	**2nd**	**3rd**
	33	19	4	5
Earnings	$9,999,815			

Smoking: Cigar, with Jerry Bailey up, scores by 2½ lengths in the 1995 Breeders' Cup Classic at Belmont Park.

CITATION

IN ITS HEYDAY, Kentucky's Calumet Farm was the most prominent single thoroughbred breeding and racing operation in the world. Horses carrying devil red and blue silks won the Kentucky Derby eight times, the Preakness Stakes six times, and the Belmont Stakes twice. Whirlaway (the 1941 U.S. Triple Crown winner), Armed, Bewitch, Coaltown – all were homebreds who campaigned for Calumet.

But the Calumet torch-bearer who stands out among all others is Citation. With Man o' War and Secretariat, he is easily a consensus choice among racing experts as one of the three greatest horses to compete in North America during the 20th century.

Bay in colour, swift as a sudden wind, Citation was trained by the father and son team of Ben and H. A. "Jimmy" Jones. Citation broke his maiden at first asking at the Havre de Grace track in Maryland on April 22, 1947. He was the betting favourite in 43 of his 44 career starts for which wagering was allowed.

The first horse to ever reach the seven-figure plateau in career earnings, Citation won 28 of his initial 30 career starts. His only loss at age two was to stablemate Bewitch. At age three, his only defeat was administered by the colt, Saggy, who Citation annihilated in a rematch five days later.

Citation's 1948 Triple Crown sweep was among the most authoritative in the series' history. He won the Derby by a widening 3 1/2 lengths, the Preakness by a widening 5 1/2 lengths, and the Belmont by a widening eight lengths. In the hiatus between the Preakness and Belmont, he won the Jersey Stakes in track-record time.

From mid-April 1948 through mid-January 1950, Citation won 16 consecutive starts, including 13 in stakes. The streak constitutes a 20th century record for a North American horse, matched only by Cigar from 1994–96 and the Louisiana-based sprinter, Hallowed Dreams, in 1999–2000.

Many consider the 1948 Pimlico Special

b c				
By Bull Lea out of Hydroplane II (Hyperion)				
Foaled 1945				
Died 1970				
Raced 1947–48, 1950–51				
Hall of Fame 1959				
Career Record	**Starts**	**1st**	**2nd**	**3rd**
	45	32	10	2
Earnings $1,085,760				

Citation's most extraordinary performance. No challengers came forth. Hall of Famer Eddie Arcaro, galloped Citation around the track in what is regarded as a "walkover". Arcaro held the reins tightly until they reached the Pimlico Race Course stretch. At that point, Citation's strength overwhelmed Arcaro's hold and the colt stormed down the lane to the wire, completing the final one and one-half furlongs of the 1 3/16-mile distance in 17 3/5 seconds.

Albert Snider, the first jockey to regularly ride Citation, disappeared during a fishing trip in the Florida Keys in the winter of 1948. Neither he nor his two companions were ever found. Arcaro then got the mount. Because of an osselet on his left ankle, Citation missed the 1949 racing season. When he returned in 1950, riding chores were primarily handled by Steve Brooks.

At age five, Citation set a world record for one mile at Golden Gate Fields in northern California. He came in second to the Irish-bred import, Noor, four times at West Coast tracks that year. Noor had to set two world records, one North American record and one track record to do this.

Citation's final career start brought a victory in the 1951 Hollywood Gold Cup. Subsequently standing at stud for Calumet, he sired the 1956 Preakness winner, Fabius, and Silver Spoon, North America's 1959 three-year-old filly champion, but otherwise his offspring were largely undistinguished.

Sitting pretty: Citation gave jockey Eddie Arcaro plenty to smile about, including a Triple Crown sweep in 1948.

"At a mile and a quarter or thereabouts, Citation can win over slop, dust, sand, goo, plowed fields, broken bottles or swampland. With Arcaro up he flows along in front with the smooth grace that is the admiration and despair of any man who has ever saddled a horse."

Joe Palmer, New York Herald Tribune, **1948**

DR. FAGER

SPEED AND THE ABILITY TO CARRY WEIGHT are two of the pre-eminent traits of great racehorses. Only the rare racehorse blends both into his performances. Dr. Fager was one of those rarities.

His 10-length triumph in the 1968 Washington Park Handicap was accomplished in a world record clocking for one mile, 1:32 1/5, under 134 pounds (9st 8lb). In his career finale, the 1968 Vosburgh Handicap at Aqueduct, Dr. Fager set a track record for seven furlongs, 1:20 1/5, under 139 pounds (9st 13lb). The world mark has since been several times surpassed (by horses carrying less prohibitive imposts). Dr. Fager's Aqueduct standard stood for 31 years – the colt who finally lowered it, Artax, was carrying only 114 pounds (8st 2lb).

Dr. Fager is one of a half-dozen horses (Twilight Tear, Citation, Bold Ruler, Buckpasser, and Damascus are the others) to be honoured with four North American championships in one season. This happened in 1968, when he was Horse of the Year, sprint champion handicap champion, and champion grass runner.

A homebred representing William L. McKnight's Tartan Stable, Dr. Fager was exceptional the first time he ran, breaking his maiden by seven lengths at Aqueduct on July 15, 1966.

"He has the smoothest, longest stride I've ever seen on any of my horses," said the colt's Hall of Fame trainer, John A. Nerud.

That stride carried Dr. Fager to 17 stakes triumphs, including seven under imposts of 130 pounds or more. Hall of Fame jockeys Manuel Ycaza and Bill Shoemaker rode Dr. Fager early on. For 12 of his final 14 starts, though, the bay colt had Hall of Famer Braulio Baeza aboard, and it was during this period, from June of 1967 into November of the following year, that Dr. Fager registered his greatest feats.

He set track records in the 1967 editions of the 1 1/8-mile Rockingham Special and the 1 1/4-mile New Hampshire Sweepstakes at Rockingham Park. He equaled another track record in the 1968 running of Aqueduct's 1 1/4-mile Suburban Handicap, defeating Damascus before a July 4th crowd of 54,336.

The only criticism of Dr. Fager was that sometimes, despite Baeza's efforts, he failed to control his speed, particularly when Damascus

b c				
By Rough'n Tumble out of Aspidistra (Better Self)				
Foaled	1964			
Died	1976			
Raced	1966–68			
Hall of Fame	1971			
Career Record	**Starts**	**1st**	**2nd**	**3rd**
	22	18	2	1
Earnings	$1,002,642			

was aided by a stablemate named Hedevar. It was Hedevar's role to be a "rabbit", engaging Dr. Fager in a duel while blazing through the opening quarters. Twice this resulted in Damascus defeating Dr. Fager, including a 10 1/2-length thumping in Aqueduct's 1967 Woodward Stakes.

"No one horse can beat Dr. Fager doing anything," was Nerud's response. Subsequent efforts proved him correct.

> "Three decades have passed, and Dr. Fager's feats and records are still beyond reach, swirling about in the wind. And how do you catch the wind?" **Steve Haskin**, Daily Racing Form, **1998**

Dr. Fager was named after a Boston, Massachusetts, surgeon, an irony in that a blood infection, a chronically troublesome right knee, and bouts with colic kept the colt away from the races for various periods. The knee prevented his participation in the 1967 Triple Crown events, and although Dr. Fager finished first in the Jersey Derby that spring, he was disqualified to fourth for crowding other horses in the early part of the race.

Upon retiring from the races, Dr. Fager returned to his roots at Tartan Farms in Florida. As a stallion, Dr. Fager was most prominent as a sire, and his progeny included 35 stakes winners, with two North American champions – Dearly Precious and Dr. Patches – and the Canadian champion, L'Alezane, among them.

Flat out: When at the top of his game, Dr. Fager was capable of outrunning any other horse at any distance.

FANTASTIC LIGHT

A HORSE'S ABILITY ability to deliver top-rate performances is often in question when shipping long distances to race, particularly against world-class competition. But not in the case of Fantastic Light. In 2000, he won the Man o' War Stakes at Belmont Park in New York and the Hong Kong Cup at Sha Tin. In 2001, Fantastic Light was victorious in the Gold Cup at the Curragh, the Prince of Wales Stakes at Ascot, the Champion Stakes at Leopardstown, and he set a course record of 2:24.36 in winning the 1½-mile Breeders' Cup Turf at Belmont. That all adds up to six Grade 1 and Group 1 victories at five different courses in four different countries on three continents during a two-year period. Fantastic Light was the horse of the hour everywhere he went.

His exploits twice earned Fantastic Light a $1 million bonus for capturing the Emirates World Series racing title. Bred by Sheikh Maktoum al Maktoum's Gainsborough Farm, Fantastic Light campaigned for the Maktoum family's Godolphin stable - a circumstance that inspired one turf handicapper to dub him, "The Godolphin Globetrotter." Trained by Saeed bin Suroor, Fantastic Light was ridden by Jerry Bailey for his Man o' War victory, but Frankie Dettori handled the riding assignments for all his other major triumphs.

Fantastic Light raced from ages two to five. Cautiously handled as a juvenile, at age three he was a 1½-length winner of the Great Voltigeur Stakes at York, and he also accounted for the Thresher Classic Trial Stakes at Sandown Park. Fantastic Light commenced his four-year-old campaign with a three-length victory in the Dubai Sheema Classic at Nad Al Sheba. He had thus established unqualified credentials as a distance performer at the Group 2 and Group 3

> "Fantastic Light's superb qualities only received due recognition towards the end of a career that saw him race on into the twilight …"
>
> **Julian Muscat, Pacemaker, December 2001**

levels. But Fantastic Light's initial five attempts in top-level company were not successful. At age three, he had finished 12th of 14 in the Prix de l'Arc de Triomphe. And while Fantastic Light had finished a close second or third in three of his other four Group 1 efforts, he had yet to be victorious.

That status changed when Bailey guided Fantastic Light from last position in a field of seven to a one-length victory in the 2000 Man o' War. A little over three months later, under Dettori, Fantastic Light was a 1½-length winner of the Hong Kong Cup. He had now risen to the status of a formal international competitor, and it was a status he maintained through the remainder of his racing days.

In 2001, at age five, Fantastic Light arguably became the finest runner on the globe. He made six starts, winning four of them, and his two defeats were by a nose to Stay Gold in his seasonal debut, the Dubai Sheema Stakes, and by two lengths to the highly talented Galileo in the King George VI and Queen Elizabeth Diamond Stakes at Ascot – a race in which Fantastic Light carried 12 more pounds (4.8kg) than the victor. His victory in the Breeders' Cup Turf brought Fantastic Light the honour of being named champion male turf competitor in North America. He was also champion older male in Ireland that season, and Horse of the Year at the Cartier Racing Awards gala in London.

Fantastic Light ended his racing career as the all-time money earner among European-trained horses. Upon retiring, he was sent to the Maktoums' Dalham Hall Stud in Newmarket. His first crop included the English Group 3 winner Prince of Light and the Japanese stakes winner Jalisco Light.

Globe trotter: Fantastic Light and Frankie Dettori power home to take the 2001 Prince of Wales Stakes at Ascot.

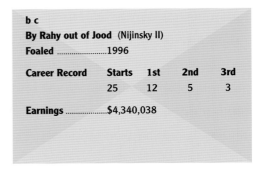

b c
By Rahy out of Jood (Nijinsky II)
Foaled 1996

Career Record	Starts	1st	2nd	3rd
	25	12	5	3

Earnings $4,340,038

GIANT'S CAUSEWAY

HEART-STOPPING IS AN often overused description in the sporting world, but it applies, again and again, to the performances by Giant's Causeway during his three-year-old campaign in 2000. From late July to early September, he won five consecutive Group 1 races - the St. James Palace Stakes at Ascot, the Eclipse Stakes at Sundown, the Sussex Stakes at Goodwood, the Juddmonte International Stakes at York and the Irish Champion Stakes at Leopardstown. His margins of victory in these events were, respectively, a head, a head, three-quarters of a length, a head and a half-length.

The running style of Giant's Causeway was equally consistent. He would stalk, then go into the lead and dare others to try to go past. During his two racing campaigns, Giant's Causeway faced 118 opponents, and only four of them were able to finish in front of him. When he made his initial career start at Ireland's Naas course in July, 1999, Giant's Causeway won by seven lengths. In his second career start, he was a 2½-length winner in Group 3 company. And Giant's Causeway finished his two-year-old season by triumphing by two lengths in his first Group 1 effort, the Prix de la Salamandre at Longchamp.

From there on, Group 1 events were all that Giant's Causeway pursued. In his three-year-old debut, he finished second in the 2000 Guineas at Newmarket. His streak of five straight wins followed, with the last four of them coming against older runners. In September, he finished second, missing by just half a length to his fellow three-year-old Observatory, in the Queen Elizabeth II Stakes at Ascot. Giant's Causeway then ventured across the Atlantic to Louisville, Kentucky - for the 17th running of the Breeders' Cup Classic at Churchill Downs in Louisville.

Giant's Causeway had never competed on a dirt surface before, but he performed valiantly, finishing second by a neck to Tiznow, who would be honoured at the season's end as North America's champion three-year-old colt and Horse of the Year. Giant's Causeway was elected champion three-year-old colt in both England and Ireland for that season, and he also earned the ultimate honour of being named Europe's Horse of the Year.

A son of the near-peerless Storm Cat, Giant's Causeway was purchased for $300,000 as a yearling. He campaigned for Michael B. Tabor

and Mrs. John Magnier, and was trained by Aidan P. O'Brien. With the exception of his Eclipse Stakes effort, Giant's Causeway was ridden in all his races by Mick Kinane. Go back four generations and one finds a paternal-maternal Bold Ruler cross in the pedigree of Giant's Causeway. It has been said that only excellence can beget true excellence, and Giant's Causeway appears to be proof of that theory.

In the breeding shed, Giant's Causeway quickly established himself as a sire in high demand. Standing for a syndicate at Ashford Stud in Central Kentucky, he was North America's leading juvenile and second crop sire in 2005, and his live foal stud fee for 2006 was $300,000. His first foal crop included Shamardal, a multiple Group 1 winner who was elected champion two-year-old colt in England, and Footstepsinthesand,

> "Horses with (Giant's Causeway's) indomitable will to win, superb consistency and tough-as-teak soundness - not to mention connections prepared to use those qualities to full advantage - come along all too rarely."
>
> **Jeremy Early,** Pacemaker, **2000**

ch c				
By Storm Cat out of Mariah's Storm (Rahy)				
Foaled 1997				
Raced...........................1999-2000				
Career record	**Starts**	**1st**	**2nd**	**3rd**
	13	9	4	0

who was a 2000 Guineas winner. Indeed, the excellence of Giant's Causeway is now flowing through the blood of his own sons and daughters - ensuring further glory for the sport.

Giant effort: Tiznow just edges out Giant's Causeway in the Breeders' Cup Classic at Churchill Downs in 2000.

HYPERION

THOUGH HE NEVER STOOD HIGHER than 15.1 hands, Hyperion was the outstanding three-year-old of his era when he won the Derby and the St. Leger. Yet at one time in his early days he was so small and weedy that there was serious discussion about having him put down on the grounds that he would never have the strength to make a racehorse.

He did not take long to prove that idea wrong, though, as on his second attempt he won the New Stakes at Ascot by three lengths from 21 rivals. He then dead-heated at Goodwood and ended his first season with victory in the Dewhurst Stakes at Newmarket. In the Free Handicap he was the second highest-rated colt; the top three in the list were fillies.

Hyperion's first race as a three-year-old resulted in convincing success in the Chester Vase, though not for the first time he showed clear signs of idleness and Tommy Weston had to give him a sharp crack with his whip to make him go about his business.

This victory resulted in Hyperion starting as 6–1 favourite for the Derby and he did all that was expected of him as he beat King Salmon by four lengths. The result was very well received, not only because he started favourite, but his lack of inches had made him particularly popular with the racing public who were delighted to see

> "It was a case of 'Eclipse first, the rest nowhere,' with Hyperion filling the role of Eclipse. He scored by four lengths, which was more than sufficient for the purposes of the case." Augur after the Derby in the Sporting Life, **June 1933**

the black jacket and white cap of Lord Derby carried to victory in the race named after his ancestor. This has not happened at Epsom since, though Watling Street won a wartime Derby at Newmarket.

Hyperion went on to win at Ascot and ended the year by making all the running to win the St. Leger at Doncaster by three lengths from Felicitation. For these first two seasons he had been trained by George Lambton, but a difference of opinion between him and Lord Derby resulted in Colledge Leader taking charge of Hyperion for his final season.

In those days the traditional plan was for Derby winners to try to win the Gold Cup at Ascot the next year, but though Hyperion began well enough by taking two minor races at Newmarket, he was not at his best at Ascot and was a well-beaten third behind Felicitation.

Sadly he was beaten on his final appearance as well, but his career at stud more than made up for that. He was an oustanding sire, champion on six occasions. The last of these was in 1954, six

years before he died. At the end of 1960 his stock had won 752 races worth £633,520 in the British Isles alone. They included the King George VI And Queen Elizabeth Stakes winner and Derby runner-up Aureole, and classic winners in Sun Chariot, Owen Tudor and Godiva, while Khaled and Heliopolis represented him well in the United States.

ch c			
By Gainsborough out of Selene (Chaucer)			
Foaled 1930			
Died 1960			
Career record	**Starts**	**1st**	**2nd**	**3rd**
	13	9	2	1

Photo finish: Hyperion, under Tommy Weston, is four lengths clear of King Salmon at the end of the 1933 Derby.

JOHN HENRY

JOHN HENRY was one of those unique competitors who really did get better as he got older. A gelding of undistinguished breeding, he commenced his career at age two at small tracks in southern Louisiana, spent a period in the claiming ranks, and ultimately matured into a winner of 30 stakes, including 16 of the Grade 1 classification. Formidable on both the dirt and grass, his career earnings at the time of his retirement constituted an all-time record for any horse of any breed.

At the apex of his abilities, John Henry consistently took on the best horses from more than one continent. He won the inaugural running of the Arlington Million in 1981, bettering The Bart in the final stride by a nose. In 1984, John Henry registered a second triumph in the Million, this time leaving Royal Heroine and Gato Del Sol in his immediate wake. John Henry twice received Eclipse Awards as North America's Horse of the Year, and was honoured four times as champion male on the grass, and once as champion male handicapper.

"There have been innumerable good and great geldings in the annals of the American turf ... but not one of the truly great ones was still whipping first-rate horses in major stakes at so advanced an age." William Nack, Sports Illustrated, 1984

His career journeys brought John Henry to 18 tracks in nine states, spanning all major points on the compass. He was ridden by 19 different jockeys, including Hall of Famers Chris McCarron (14 times), Bill Shoemaker (11 times), Laffit Pincay Jr. (seven times), and Angel Cordero Jr. (twice). Five different trainers took care of his conditioning chores, but John Henry's greatest exploits took place with Hall of Famer Ron McAnally in charge.

The maiden career score for John Henry was achieved at first asking on May 20, 1977, at Jefferson Downs in New Orleans. Bred in Kentucky, he initially campaigned for a Louisiana horsewoman, Colleen Madere, who had purchased him privately for $10,000. During

Fan favourite: John Henry, in retirement at the Kentucky Horse Park, was a crowd pleaser during and after his racing days.

a two-month period in the spring of 1978, John Henry went through a pair of ownership changes – the second involved his being purchased for $25,000 by Sam and Dorothy Rubin's Dotsam Stable after a race at Keeneland. "It was the best investment I ever made," Sam Rubin was to say later, in an understatement worthy of *Bartlett's Book Of Quotations*.

In September 1977, John Henry scored his first stakes win, in the Lafayette Futurity at Evangeline Downs. Yet he subsequently made five starts in claiming races. Rubin ran John Henry twice for claiming tags (he won by 2 1/2 and 14 lengths), and from there ever after sought more illustrious company. In September 1978, John Henry became a Grade 3 winner, scoring by 12 lengths in the Round Table Handicap at Arlington Park. By the time he registered his first Grade 1 triumph, in the 1980 San Luis Rey at Santa Anita, he was strictly a stakes horse.

The career finale for John Henry came in the Ballantine Handicap at The Meadowlands in

northern New Jersey on October 13, 1984. Under McCarron, he won by 2 3/4 lengths, equaling the turf course record of 2:13 for 1 3/8 miles. A bowed tendon forced the gelding into retirement. At age ten in 1985, John Henry briefly returned to training, but subsequently was retired to the Kentucky Horse Park near Lexington. He remains one of the park's most beloved inhabitants, and is happily photographed by thousands of people each year.

b g			
By Ole Bob Bowers out of Once Double (Double Jay)			
Foaled	1975		
Raced	1977–84		
Hall of Fame	1990		

Career Record	Starts	1st	2nd	3rd
	83	39	15	9
Earnings	$6,597,947			

KELSO

HONOURED FIVE TIMES, from 1960–64, as North America's Horse of the Year, Kelso was one of the greatest running machines of the 20th century. From age three through six, he won at least three major stakes per year. Kelso won five consecutive runnings of the Jockey Club Gold Cup in New York.

All told, the dark bay gelding accumulated 31 stakes triumphs, at seven different distances ranging from one to two miles. At the time of his retirement, Kelso was the all-time North American leader in career earnings, having topped the previous record achieved by Round Table.

A homebred representing Mrs. Richard duPont's Bohemia Stable, Kelso was as formidable on grass surfaces as he was on the dirt. Following a trio of close, second-place finishes in the Washington DC International in 1961–63, he won that race in 1964, establishing a world record of 2:23 4/5 for the 1 1/2-mile distance. Wet going didn't hamper Kelso; his first Gold Cup triumph, in 1960, was achieved over a sloppy surface at Aqueduct in a North American record time of 3:19 2/5 for two miles.

Kelso broke his maiden at first asking at Atlantic City on September 4, 1959. His trainer at age two was Dr. John M. Lee. Commencing with Kelso's three-year-old campaign, though, conditioning chores were entrusted to Carl Hanford, a former jockey with modest training credentials, who nonetheless had been recommended by several respected horsemen to Mrs. duPont.

Under Hanford's care, Kelso became a powerhouse. His initial black-type victory came in the Choice Stakes at Monmouth Park in August 1960, with Hall of Fame jockey Bill Hartack aboard. Fellow Hall of Famer Eddie Arcaro was put aboard Kelso for his next 14 starts. The result was 12 more wins, including 11 in stakes. Arcaro would have kept the mount had he not chosen to retire from riding.

Yet another Hall of Fame jockey, Bill Shoemaker, rode Kelso in the first four starts of his 1962 campaign. The gelding only scored once, in a tune-up allowance event. A less heralded rider, Ismael Valenzuela, was then given the opportunity to ride him. Valenzuela remained in the irons for 35 of Kelso's final 38 career starts.

Challengers did not uniformly shy away from Kelso. A New York-based horse, Beau Purple, beat him three times during a period extending from July 1962 to February '63. Carry Back beat him twice, as did Mongo. The weight assigned him was often a factor – as Kelso's career went on, his imposts grew heavier. It is one of many indications of his greatness that in 1963 he won six consecutive stakes while carrying 130 pounds (9st 4lb) or more.

> "Few horses in history could beat Kelso at any distance, and in the opinion of his admirers, no horse that ever lived could beat him going two miles."
>
> **Russ Harris,** The Racing Times, **1991**

During his winter breaks, Mrs. duPont often took Kelso for strolls through the woods, fording streams, jumping over light brush, on her Chesapeake, Maryland, farm. Following his retirement, Kelso made public appearances at racetracks for charitable purposes. On October 15, 1983, at the age of 26, he made a final visit to Belmont Park, parading on the track and posing for photographs with two other Hall of Fame geldings, Forego and John Henry. The strain of the occasion proved too much for him, and Kelso died the following day.

db g				
By Your Host out of Maid of Flight (Count Fleet)				
Foaled 1957				
Died 1983				
Raced 1959-66				
Hall of Fame 1967				
Career record	**Starts**	**1st**	**2nd**	**3rd**
	63	39	12	2
Earnings $1,977,896				

Truly peerless: Kelso was named North America's Horse of the Year an unprecedented five times.

MAKYBE DIVA

dk b m			
By Desert King out of Tugela (River Man)			
Foaled 1999			
Raced 2002-2005			
Career record	**Starts**	**1st**	**2nd**	**3rd**
	36	15	4	3
Earnings ....Aus$14,426,685			

Triple triumph: Makybe Diva and jockey Glen Boss after a record-breaking third successive victory in the Melbourne Cup.

THE MELBOURNE CUP possesses a heritage that spans 146 years, but no horse had ever won it three times, consecutively or otherwise. Then, along came Makybe Diva, ascending from champion to greatness to true legendary status. Her victories in the 2003, 2004 and 2005 renewals of Australia's greatest race – and what many believe is the premier handicap race in the world – constitute a historic triple that may never be duplicated. In the words of trainer Lee Freedman, who prepared Makybe Diva for her second and third Cup triumphs, "She transcends the sport."

Transcendence, of course, rarely occurs among athletes. The great South American star Pele met that designation in football, as did America's Babe Ruth in baseball and Muhammad Ali in boxing. But many an Australian sporting fan believes that their names should be joined by Makybe Diva's. The two-mile Melbourne Cup is often referred to as "the race that stops a nation", and the onsite Flemington crowd that witnessed Makybe Diva's career-culminating victory in 2005 numbered over 130,000. During the post-race

celebration, Freedman suggested to reporters that they seek out the youngest children at the track, because "they're the only (ones) who will live long enough to ever see this happen again."

Conceived in Ireland and foaled near Somerset, England, Makybe Diva campaigned for the South Australian tuna fisherman Tony Santic, who designed her name by using the first two letters in the names of five of his female employees - Maureen Dellar, Kylie Bascomb, Belinda Grocke, Dianne Tonkin and Vanessa Parthenis. These ladies, the turf scribe Larry Rivera has noted, "are now part of Australian racing history."

Makybe Diva debuted as a racehorse in August, 2002, and her maiden effort was uninspiring as she finished a well-beaten fourth at Benalla Racecourse in Victoria. David Hall was training her back then, and with his guidance she quickly matured into a provincial winner, an open handicap winner at Flemington and subsequently a listed stakes winner. From there, she continued to climb the success ladder with a victory in the Group 2 Queen Elizabeth II Stakes. But much more

substantial achievements were in the offing, particularly once the Sydney-based jockey Glen Boss was entrusted with regular riding chores.

Several months after Makybe Diva's initial Melbourne Cup victory, Hall left Australia to train in Hong Kong. Freedman, who had won the Melbourne Cup with Tawrrific in 1989 and with Doriemus in 1995, became Makybe Diva's new conditioner. Whereas she had been the second favourite in her first Melbourne Cup try, Makybe Diva was sent off in the 2004 renewal as the 5–2 wagering choice, despite the inclusion in the field of the 2002 Melbourne Cup winner Media Puzzle, the multiple Irish St. Leger winner Vinnie Roe and the Caulfield Cup winners Mummify and Elvstroem.

During her final season of racing, Makybe Diva's victories included the Turnbull Stakes and the Cox Plate – the latter was achieved despite having to go around a wall of horses on the final turn. Following her 2005 Melbourne Cup win, Santic waved the solid gold, three-handled loving cup trophy high over his head and announced to the Flemington multitude, "This is for you." The same can be said for the whole of Makybe Diva's exploits. Among all the great fillies and mares who have raced around the globe, Makybe Diva is the one who has accumulated the highest career earnings.She will forever be an Australian treasure, her brilliance preserved in the mind's eye.

"Without wimping out, Carbine was Australia's horse of the 19th century, Phar Lap the 20th and Makybe Diva the 21st, even with the latter in only its sixth year."

Peter Tonkes, The Blood-Horse, 2005

MAN o' WAR

EW ATHLETES set standards so sublime they achieve the status of peerless. Man o' War is an exception. His deeds were accomplished during "the Golden Age of American Sports", when Babe Ruth was bashing baseballs into distant seats, Jack Dempsey became boxing's undisputed heavyweight champion, and Knute Rockne's Notre Dame teams were vanquishing their football foes. All remain unchallenged, even today, as to what they represent for their respective sports. The same is true for Man o' War.

Man o' War's career earnings would be considered good, though not exemplary, in modern times. But his bankroll was considered astonishing for the era in which he competed. On three occasions, Man o' War was sent off at odds-on one cent on the dollar (1–100). He won one of those races, the 1920 Lawrence Realization at Belmont Park, by 100 lengths. His talents were so formidable that during the final 10 starts of his career, an average of only 1.5 other horses per race came forth to take him on.

When fully extended, Man o' War's stride measured nearly nine metres. This, itself, might provide many a racehorse with an edge over his competition, but when combined with this great chestnut's speed and power, it made him nearly unbeatable.

Indeed, the only horse ever to defeat Man o' War was a colt appropriately named Upset. This came during their two-year-old season in the 1919 Sanford Memorial Stakes at Saratoga. The margin was a quickly diminishing half-length.

The four other times they ran against each other, Man o' War was victorious.

Bred in Kentucky by August Belmont, Man o' War was purchased at a Saratoga auction for $5,000 by Samuel D. Riddle in the summer of 1918. The colt broke his maiden at Belmont Park on June 6 of the following year, winning by six lengths at odds of 3–5. Man o' War, in fact, was the odds-on favourite for every trip he ever made postward. He registered eight stakes triumphs at two, and 11 more as a three-year-old, the Preakness and Belmont Stakes among them. Man o' War set five North American records during his three-year-old campaign. His clocking for 1 5/8 miles in the Lawrence Realization, 2:40 4/5, is still the Belmont standard for that distance.

Man o' War's final career start took place on October 12, 1920, in the Kensington Park Gold Cup in Windsor, Ontario. His sole opponent in this match was the 1919 Triple Crown winner, Sir Barton. Leading throughout the 1 1/4-mile contest, Man o' War won by seven lengths. Film footage of the event shows the crowd stampeding onto the track and running after the two horses as they headed down the stretch.

Louis Feustal was Man o' War's trainer throughout his career. Four jockeys rode the colt: Charles Loftus rode Man o' War during his two-year-old campaign; Clarence Kummer was aboard for all but two of his efforts at age three.

Man o' War was retired to stud at Faraway Farm in Kentucky's Bluegrass region. He was North America's leading sire in 1926, and sired a grand total of 61 stakes winners during his 22 years at stud. Among them was War Admiral, who swept the 1937 Triple Crown. Man o' War's remains are buried at the Kentucky Horse Park. A life-sized bronze statue stands over his grave.

> "The world is full of hero-worshippers. But in most cases the worship has to be cut and trimmed and carefully patched according to the assorted imperfections of the hero. Thrice heroic, then, was Man o' War, for which no qualification was necessary." **Joe A. Estes,** The Blood-Horse, **1947**

ch c
By Fair Play out of Mahubah (Rock Sand)

Foaled	1917		
Died	1947		
Raced	1919–20		
Hall of Fame	1957		

Career record	**Starts**	**1st**	**2nd**	**3rd**
	21	20	1	0

Earnings	$249,465

Battle hardened: Man o' War, shown here with Clarence Kummer up, represented America's "Golden Age" of sports.

MILL REEF

THE FIRST TIME MILL REEF appeared on a racecourse he faced an opponent who was regarded as unbeatable for the race in question. It was only a run-of-the-mill two-year-old heat at Salisbury in May 1970 but Fireside Chat, who had won his previous start at Newmarket, started at 2–9, with Mill Reef at 8–1. Mill Reef won in style by four lengths to launch an outstanding career.

He then won the Coventry Stakes at Ascot by eight lengths before going down by a short head to the season's top juvenile, My Swallow, in the Prix Robert Papin at Maisons-Laffitte, but that hard race left no mark on him as he showed when he almost literally walked on water when winning the Gimcrack Stakes at York in very heavy going by 10 lengths. He won his final two races in that first season, not impressively at Kempton Park, but with authority in the Dewhurst Stakes at Newmarket.

Having won his first three-year-old start, Mill Reef started favourite against My Swallow in the 2,000 Guineas. He beat his old rival well enough, but neither was any match for Brigadier Gerard; for the rest of their careers there was hope that there might be a re-match between Mill Reef and the Brigadier, but the circumstances never worked out.

Though there was some doubt as to whether he would stay 1¹/₂ miles in the Derby, his next race, Mill Reef had no problem with that distance and beat Linden Tree by two lengths to start a truly purple passage in his career.

The following month he took on his seniors for the first time in the Eclipse Stakes at Sandown Park and swept home by four lengths from the very smart French-trained four-year-old Caro, and he did even better later in July with a six lengths defeat of Ortis in the King George VI And Queen Elizabeth Stakes at Ascot.

Then came the highlight of Mill Reef's career when he became the first horse trained in England for 23 years to win the Prix de l'Arc de Triomphe, which he did from the fillies Pistol Packer and Cambrizzia.

Mill Reef began his final season with a ten lengths success in the Prix Ganay at Longchamp.

Lucky 13: Geoff Lewis is out of the saddle as Mill Reef comes home clear of the 1971 Prix de l'Arc de Triomphe field.

He then only scrambled home in the Coronation Cup at Epsom, but was found to be suffering from a virus when he returned to Ian Balding's stables. Though in due course he recovered from that, his career came to an end at the end of August 1972 when he broke a bone in his foreleg while exercising.

Happily his life was saved and Mill Reef stood at the National Stud at Newmarket until he had to be put down at the beginning of 1986 because of a heart condition. While it may have been impossible for him to do as well at stud as he had done on the track, he still proved a top-class sire and produced English and French Derby winners in Shirley Heights (who sired two more in Slip Anchor and Darshaan), Reference Point and Acamas and other top winners in Lashkari, Wassl, Glint of Gold, Diamond Shoal and Fairy Footsteps.

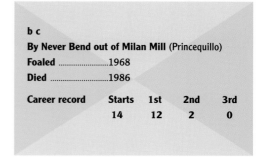

b c
By Never Bend out of Milan Mill (Princequillo)
Foaled 1968
Died 1986

Career record	Starts	1st	2nd	3rd
	14	12	2	0

> "This great horse, apart from his ability, was blessed with a perfect racing temperament."

Roger Mortimer, History of The Derby Stakes, 1973

NIJINSKY

THE INTERNATIONAL PRE-EMINENCE of the Northern Dancer stallion line owes a huge amount to Nijinsky, who, in 1970, became the first colt to win the British Triple Crown since Bahram 35 years earlier. He was bred to be a star as his sire won the Kentucky Derby and the Preakness Stakes and his dam was a top-class racemare, but even so it was inspired advice from Vincent O'Brien which persuaded Charles Engelhard to buy the colt as a yearling for $84,000.

Nijinsky won all his five races as a two-year-old, the first four of them in Ireland, including three of the most significant juvenile heats at the Curragh, the Railway Stakes, Angelsey Stakes and Beresford Stakes, and he ended his first year with a three lengths defeat of Recalled in the Dewhurst Stakes at Newmarket, for which he started at 1–3. He was placed at the top of the Free Handicap, 2lb above Approval.

In his second season he swept from victory to victory, taking the 2,000 Guineas at 4–7 by 2^{1}/$_{2}$ lengths from Yellow God and then showing a hugely impressive turn of acceleration to beat Gyr by the same distance in the Derby. Gyr had been well fancied to beat him but simply had no answer to Nijinsky's pace. In his races in England Nijinsky was ridden by Lester Piggott, but the arrangement was that Liam Ward should be the colt's partner in Ireland and so he was in the saddle when Nijinsky took the Irish Derby by three lengths from Meadowville.

Then followed success against his seniors when he beat the previous year's Derby winner Blakeney in the King George VI And Queen Elizabeth Stakes at Ascot, but complications developed as he was being prepared for the St. Leger in an attempt to land the Triple Crown. Nijinsky developed ringworm and though he made it to Doncaster and confirmed his superiority over Meadowville, he was not as impressive as he had been against the same colt at the Curragh.

Sadly, Nijinsky lost his last two races and it is highly likely that the effort involved in getting him to Doncaster took its toll. In the Prix de l'Arc de Triomphe he could not quite get the better of

Poetry in motion: Nijinsky, ridden by Lester Piggott, wins the 1970 Derby, the middle leg of his Triple Crown.

Sassafras and then, when he attempted to end his career with a win, he found Lorenzaccio too good for him in Newmarket's Champion Stakes.

Nijinsky retired to stud in Kentucky as the winner of 11 of his 13 races with earnings of £246,132 in the British Isles and ff480,000 in France, and with a value of $5.5million. He was an immediate success with his first crop including classic winners in Green Dancer and Caucasus, and that trend was maintained until he died in April 1992.

By then he had sired 145 stakes winners on both sides of the Atlantic, of whom more than

30 scored in Group/Grade 1 company. They included Golden Fleece, Ferdinand, Niniski, Shadeed, Caerleon and Shahrastani. There was posthumous glory for him, when Lammtarra – foaled out of 1989 Oaks winner Snow Bride – took the 1995 renewals of Epsom's Derby, the King George VI And Queen Elizabeth Stakes and the Prix de l'Arc de Triomphe at Longchamp.

b c
By Northern Dancer out of Flaming Page (Bull Page)
Foaled 1967
Died 1992

Career record	Starts	1st	2nd	3rd
	13	11	2	0

> "There is no denying that at his peak, Nijinsky was a very great racehorse indeed."

Biographical Encyclopedia of British Flat Racing, 1978

NORTHERN DANCER

WITH ALL THE magnificence attributed to Northern Dancer as a sire, it is sometimes forgotten that he was an outstanding racehorse. During his two seasons of campaigning he was triumphant in ten stakes, including the 1964 Kentucky Derby and Preakness Stakes. In the final start of his racing career, Northern Dancer was a 7½-length winner of the Queen's Plate, historically the most prominent racing event in his country of breeding, Canada. Honours accumulated by Northern Dancer during his racing days include recognition as North America's three-year-old champion in 1964, and the Sovereign Award as Canada's Horse of the Year in the same season.

Northern Dancer's victory in the Kentucky Derby was achieved in a track record clocking of 2:00, and that standard wasn't lowered until Secretariat's Derby in 1973. And, to this day, Northern Dancer's Derby remains the third fastest ever run. Bred and owned by Edward P. Taylor's Windfield Farms and trained by Horatio A. Luro, Northern Dancer was guided through his Classic and Queen's Plate efforts by jockey Bill Hartack. Northern Dancer's maternal grandsire, Native Dancer, was defeated only once in his 22 career starts at the races. That loss came by a diminishing head in the 1953 Kentucky Derby – but 11 years later, Northern Dancer provided restitution for this lone blemish.

But, Northern Dancer's exploits as a sire are what truly sets him apart. No other North American horse, regardless of breed, had such an impact at stud during the 20th century. From 1967-89, a grand total of 297 of Northern Dancer's sons and daughters were sold at public North American yearling auctions, fetching a cumulative $184,091,718 in gross receipts. This divides out to an astonishing average for each horse sold of $619,837, which is approximately 20 times the average price for all thoroughbred yearlings auctioned in North America during that period.

Standing 15.2 hands, Northern Dancer was what breeders call a "blocky" horse, possessed of powerful quarters. He initially stood for a $10,000 fee, but as his prominence quickly increased the cost of breeding to him multiplied and eventually became by private contract only. Northern Dancer's profound impact was not limited to the boundaries of North America's shores. Indeed, he was recognized four times as

Speedy success: Northern Dancer, under jockey Bill Hartack, claims the 1964 Kentucky Derby in a new track record.

the leading sire of horses who campaigned in England. The Maktoum family of Dubai, Robert Sangster, Stavros Niarchos, Allen Paulson – all competed aggressively at sales, frequently making bids that were well into seven figures, for Northern Dancer's progeny.

American and European champions among Northern Dancer's offspring number more than two dozen. They include Ajdal, Antheus, Broadway Dancer, Dance Act, Dance in Time, Danzatore, El Gran Senor, Franfreluche, Giboulee, Lauries Dancer, Minsky, Nice Dancer, Nijinsky II, Northernette, Northern Trick, Nureyev, One for All, Sadler's Wells, Secreto, Shareef Dancer, Storm Bird, The Minstrel, Try My Best, Unfuwain, Viceregal and Woodstream.

Further, Northern Dancer is a sire of other highly prominent sires. Seattle Dancer, a son of the aforesaid Nijinsky II, was sold at Keeneland in July, 1985, for $13.1-million. This remains a world-record price for a yearling at public auction. Danzig, Lyphard, Nureyev, Sadler's Wells – all of them also manifested excellence in their breeding duties. Indeed, while Northern Dancer himself is no longer with us, his influence promises to continually span future generations.

b c			
By Nearctic out of Natalma (Native Dancer)			
Foaled 1961			
Died 1990			
Raced......................1963–64			
Hall of Fame 1976			
Career Record	Starts	1st	2nd	3rd
	18	14	4	4
Earnings $580,806			

PHAR LAP

IRONICALLY, PHAR LAP'S BEGINNINGS could hardly have been less auspicious. Bred at Timaru in New Zealand, he was bought on behalf of struggling Sydney trainer Harry Telford, who was attracted by his pedigree, for a mere 160 guineas at the 1928 Trentham Yearling Sales.

Unable to raise the purchase price Telford sold him on to American David Davis, who was so unimpressed with the horse that he would not pay any training or nomination fees.

A massive individual – he grew to be 17 hands high – Phar Lap at first showed little inclination to gallop and was unplaced in four races as a two-year-old before winning over six furlongs at Rosehill on 27 April 1929. Another four unplaced outings at three led through to a fast-finishing second to high-quality performer Mollison in the weight-for-age Chelmsford Stakes, over nine furlongs, at Randwick in September 1929.

That was to be the beginning of an incredible series of performances over the following 2¹/₂ years in which he registered 36 wins, three seconds and two thirds from 41 starts. Phar Lap's first major success was in the Rosehill Guineas, before he easily won the A.J.C. Derby in record time when partnered by Jim Pike, who was to ride him to victory on another 25 occasions.

After capturing the Victoria Derby he raced fiercely in the Melbourne Cup, over two miles, at Flemington and could only finish third behind Nightmarch and Paquito. Beaten into second place in the St. George Stakes, over nine furlongs, at Caulfield when resuming in the autumn he won at his nine subsequent outings for the season in Melbourne, Sydney and Adelaide.

Again beaten first time out the following spring, Phar Lap then put together 14 consecutive wins including victories in the prestigious W.S. Cox Plate, over 9¹/₂ furlongs at Moonee Valley, and the Melbourne Cup. Three days before the Melbourne Cup Phar Lap won

the Melbourne Stakes, over 10 furlongs, at Flemington. Hidden away after a failed attempt to shoot him while he was being returned to his stables, Phar Lap arrived at Flemington for the Cup under an armed guard.

Carrying 9st 12lb (138 pounds), the chestnut was being asked to establish a weight-carrying record for a four-year-old but was still sent out as an 8–11 favourite. He completely justified the confidence of his supporters by cruising home a winner by three lengths from the dour stayers Second Wind and Shadow King.

"He just cantered along in fourth or fifth place all the way," Pike reported. "I never felt I was on anything but a winner."

Displaying his strength and versatility, two days after the Cup Phar Lap easily won the Linlithgow Stakes, over a mile, and another two days later won the C.B.Fisher Plate, over 1¹/₂ miles. That meant he had won four races run over a total of 5³/₄ miles in the space of eight days. His winning sequence finally came to an end with a second in the Lloyd Stakes, over a mile, at his last appearance as a four-year-old.

At five he won seven successive races – featuring a second Cox Plate – before an eighth behind White Nose under 10st 10lb (150 pounds) in the 1931 Melbourne Cup after a request to scratch the horse was denied.

Only 17 days later Phar Lap was loaded onto a ship for the United States in quest of the richer prize-money on offer

in America. At his overseas debut he strode home a two lengths winner in the Agua Caliente Handicap over 1¹/₄ miles at Tijuana, Mexico, in course record time of 2min.2.8sec. The gelding was seemingly about to establish his authority as a racehorse on the world but 16 days later Phar Lap became ill and died in circumstances which have since remained a mystery.

Dynamic duo: Handled by Tommy Woodcock, Phar Lap, was Australia's most famous horse and whose death, in the U.S. remains shrouded in controversy.

> "The best I've ridden. In fact I don't think there has ever been his equal, certainly not during my time and before that either. I would say that up to a mile-and-a-half Phar Lap is the best horse Australia's ever had and one of the best the world's ever had. It's sacrilege, really, to ride some horses after once having been on Phar Lap's back." **Jim Pike, Jockey**

ch g
By Night Raid out of Entreaty (Winkie)
Foaled 1926
Died 1932

Career record	Starts	1st	2nd	3rd
	51	37	3	2

RED RUM

IN TERMS OF ACTUAL ABILITY Red Rum does not figure among the top steeplechasers of his or any other time; he would never have won a top-class weight-for-age chase such as the Cheltenham Gold Cup or the King George V1 Chase, but his performances in the Grand National at Liverpool from 1973–77 guarantee his place in racing history.

Red Rum ran in the National in every one of those five years – that alone is quite some achievement – and he is the only horse to have won the race three times, which he did in 1973, 1974 and 1977. He was runner-up in the two seasons in between, and though one of the dual winners, Manifesto, was also third twice and fourth once, it is highly unlikely that Red Rum's achievements will ever be equalled.

Curiously, it was at Liverpool, which was to be the scene of his great triumphs, that Red Rum made his first appearance on a racecourse. This came in the very humble surroundings of the Thursby Selling Plate in April 1967 when Red Rum dead-heated with Curlicue (there was no photo finish camera at Liverpool in those days) and earned £133 for owner Maurice Kingsley, who had earlier owned the triple Champion Hurdle winner Sir Ken.

Later he became the property of Mrs. Lurline Brotherton, whose Freebooter won the 1950 Grand National, but neither she nor Freebooter's trainer Bobby Renton could see him as another Aintree hero, and Red Rum was sold at Doncaster in August 1972, to the little-known Southport trainer Donald McCain, who was nicknamed

"Ginger" due to his conspicuous head of hair.

McCain bought Red Rum, who had suffered from pedalostitis, for veteran owner Noel Le Mare, who had long expressed an ambition to win the National. It was an inspired purchase and for whatever reason – maybe the sea breeze and exercising on the Southport beach had more than a bit to do with it – Red Rum went from strength to strength.

In the 1973 Grand National he caught Crisp, who had at one time been 30 lengths clear and was trying to give Red Rum 23lb, in the final 50 yards and won by 3/4 length in a time which shattered the race record by more than 18 seconds, and 12 months later Red Rum, this time carrying 12st (168 pounds), beat the dual Cheltenham Gold Cup winner L'Escargot by seven lengths. A strict interpretation of those results suggests that Crisp would have won the 1974 race with 13st 8lb (190 pounds) on his back!

L'Escargot took revenge the following year when on much more favourable terms he beat Red Rum by 15 lengths, and in 1976 Red Rum had to give best to Rag Trade. By now his long time partner Brian Fletcher had had a row with McCain and been replaced by Tommy Stack, who had ridden and briefly trained the horse in earlier years, and it was Stack who had the thrill

of riding the horse to his record-breaking third success when he beat Churchtown Boy by 25 lengths in 1977.

Red Rum was forced into retirement shortly before what would have been his sixth Grand National venture in 1978. He had run 100 times over jumps – winning 24 races (including the Scottish Grand National and the Grand National Trial at Haydock Park) and being placed in 45 – and 10 times on the flat (succeeding thee times). He became something of a celebrity, opening fêtes, appearing on television and leading the Grand National parade, but *anno domini* took its toll and he had to be put down in October 1995.

b g			
By Quorum out of Mared (Magic Red)			
Foaled 1965			
Died 1995			
Career record	**Starts** **1st** **2nd** **3rd**		
	110	27	15	22

Into legend: Red Rum, under Tommy Stack, wins the 1977 Grand National, his record-breaking third win.

RIBOT

IBOT WAS A GIANT of a horse both on the racecourse and at stud, one of the two best horses ever to be trained in Italy, where he represented the combination of Federico Tesio and the Marchese Incisa della Rochetta, in whose colours he raced. He was trained by Ugo Penco and ridden by Enrico Camici as he won all his 16 starts, including the Prix de l'Arc de Triomphe in successive years and the King George V1 And Queen Elizabeth Stakes, as well as many of the top races in his home land.

His best wins in Italy came in the Gran Premio di Milano, the Premio del Jockey Club and Emanuele Filiberto and the Gran Criterium, but it was on his ventures outside that country that Ribot really impressed himself on the racing world.

The first of these came in the 1955 Prix de l'Arc de Triomphe, when he beat Beau Prince II by three lengths with 21 others behind, and the following year he trounced Talgo and 18 other opponents by six lengths in one of the most dominating displays in the history of the race. In between those two Longchamp victories, Ribot won the King George VI And Queen Elizabeth Stakes at Ascot when, undistressed by the long delay at the start after the Belgian horse Todrai unseated his rider and bolted, he beat the Queen's horse High Veldt by five lengths.

He went to stud at the end of his four-year-old season after setting an earnings record for a horse in Europe, and after standing for one season in England and three in Italy, he was leased by the Darby Dan Farm in Kentucky of John Galbreath. The initial theory of this deal was that Ribot would return after a five-year spell in the United States, but this never happened as it was felt that his temperament would not be suited by the travelling.

He was an outstanding success on both sides of the Atlantic and by the time of his death in 1972 he had sired more than 50 top-level winners. Two of his sons, Molvedo and Prince Royal II, emulated their sire and won the Arc, and other classic winners in Europe by Ribot

Italian stallion: Ribot won in his native Italy, France and England, then sired big-race winners all around the world.

were the brothers Ribocco and Ribero, both of whom won the Irish Derby at the Curragh and the St. Leger at Doncaster; another St. Leger winner in Ragusa, who also took the King George VI And Queen Elizabeth Stakes, Eclipse Stakes and Irish Derby; Boucher (St. Leger), Regal Exception (Irish Oaks) and the Oaks d'Italia winner Alice Frey.

It was generally agreed that his stock were better suited by racing in Europe than in the United States, but in spite of that he sired a number of top winners in the U.S. These included Arts And Letters, who won the Belmont Stakes and was voted Horse of the Year in 1969, Tom Rolfe – the 1965 Preakness Stakes winner, Belmont Stakes runner-up and Kentucky Derby third – Dapper Dan, second in that Kentucky Derby and Preakness Stakes, and Graustark, who was beaten only once in eight races.

> ## "A big bay horse with an honest, sensible head, Ribot was was beyond doubt one of the greatest racehorses of this century."
> **Biographical Encyclopedia of British Flat Racing, 1978**

b c

By Tenerani out of Romanella (El Greco)

Foaled	1952
Died	1972

Career record	Starts	1st	2nd	3rd
	16	16	0	0

ROUND TABLE

IT CAN BE argued that no other horse in 20th-century North American racing matched the versatility of Round Table. During his four-year career he either set or equalled sixteen time standards, 12 of which were achieved on the dirt and four of which were accomplished on grass courses. Round Table recorded 32 stakes triumphs, and they came at eight different distances, ranging from four furlongs to 1⅝ miles. He won on dirt surfaces when they were dry and when they were sloppy. Round Table won when the turf footing was firm and when it was soft. And he was victorious carrying weights as high as 136 pounds (61.8 kg).

When he retired from racing following his 1959 campaign, Round Table had accumulated purse earnings of $1,749,869 – at the time the highest total ever achieved by any racehorse. Round Table proved to be top-rate at stud as well. Standing at the place where he was bred and born, Claiborne Farm, Round Table was North America's leading sire in 1972. His influence extended through generations. Among Round Table's get were Targowice, who sired the European champion and 1983 North American Horse of the Year, All Along; and Poker, who was the broodmare sire of the 1977 Triple Crown winner, Seattle Slew.

A son of the two-time North American leading sire, Princequillo, Round Table initially campaigned for Claiborne, but in February of his three-year-old season a majority interest in him was sold to Oklahoma oilman Travis M. Kerr. Two months later, Round Table established the first of his track standards in the Blue Grass Stakes at Keeneland, clocking a winning time of 1:47⅖ for 1⅛ miles. During a period spanning five months and three days that season, Round Table won 11 consecutive races, and he subsequently had another streak of eight straight victories.

Ten different jockeys partnered with Round Table during his racing efforts. But his most frequent companion was Bill Shoemaker, who guided Round Table to the majority of his stakes wins. Among them were the 1957 and 1959 editions of the United Nations Handicap at Atlantic City Race Course, and standard-setting performances in the 1958 renewals of the Santa Anita and Hawthorne Gold Cup Handicaps, both of which were run at 1⅝ miles.

Round Table didn't have geographic limitations. His stakes victories were achieved at tracks in Kentucky, Florida, California, New Jersey, Illinois and New York, and below the United States border, too – in 1958, he registered a 9¼-length win in the Caliente Handicap at Tijuana, Mexico, setting a track record of 1:41⅕ for 1¹⁄₁₆ miles. Four times during his career, Round Table seemed such a formidable force that betting was cancelled on races he entered. When betting was allowed, he had a streak spanning 32 races in which he was the post-time favourite.

Honoured as North America's Horse of the Year and champion handicap horse in 1958, and for the consecutive years from 1957–1959 as champion grass runner, Round Table was trained for his early efforts by Moody Jolley, and subsequently for the major portion of his career by William Molter, Jr. When Queen Elizabeth II toured Central Kentucky in 1984, she amended her schedule, allowing time for a visit to Claiborne to see Round Table.

> "RoundTable is a scant 15.3 hands at the withers. But rivals a hand taller have found (him) an opponent of unremitting courage in stretch duels."
>
> **Charles Hatton,** The American Racing Manual, **1958**

b c

By Princequillo out of Knight's Daughter (Sir Cosmo)

Foaled 1954			
Died 1987			
Hall of Fame 1972			

Career record	Starts	1st	2nd	3rd
	66	43	8	5
Earnings	$1,749,869			

All-rounder: The versatile Round Table, a stakes winner at eight different distances, being walked by his handlers.

SEABISCUIT

THERE MAY NEVER be another horse whose story is quite the same as Seabiscuit's. It wasn't until his eighteenth career start that he broke his maiden — this took place on June 22, 1935, at Rhode Island's now-defunct Narragansett Park. Prior to that effort, Seabiscuit had failed in just about every sort of company that a juvenile can try, including four times amongst claimers.

Before his two-year-old campaign was completed, though, Seabiscuit was thrice a stakes winner. By the time his race career was over, he had won 27 stakes and had either set or equalled 13 track records at distances ranging from five furlongs to 1 1/4 miles.

Seabiscuit, bred by Wheatley Stable, was foaled at Kentucky's Claiborne Farm. The bay colt possessed impressive bloodlines. His paternal grandsire was Man o' War. His maternal grandsire, Whisk Broom II, included Victorian, John P. Grier, Whiskery, and Upset among his progeny. Yet the Wheatley people didn't seem to think very much of Seabiscuit. The stable's trainer, Hall of Famer James "Sunny Jim" Fitzsimmons, used Seabiscuit during his three-

"The achievement of Seabiscuit is one strictly abnormal. For which the main explanation is that he is an abnormal race horse … and since he found himself his consistency has been remarkable."

John Hervey, American Race Horses, **1937**

year-old season as a workmate for Omaha, who had swept the Triple Crown in 1935.

Small and slight of build, Seabiscuit ultimately ran for two ownerships, had four trainers, and was ridden by 13 jockeys during his half-dozen seasons of campaigning. His greatest exploits took place from late August 1936 onward, when he raced for Mr. and Mrs. Charles S. Howard, was conditioned by Thomas Smith, and primarily was ridden by Johnny "Red" Pollard and Hall of Famer George Wolfe.

Seabiscuit's constitution belied his physique. In quest of his maiden-breaking victory, there were four occasions when he ran twice in just four calendar days. In 1937, he won seven consecutive stakes in the space of five months, journeying across the country. Later that season, Seabiscuit won the Continental Handicap in New York, then

journeyed to Maryland where he dead-heated for first in the Laurel Stakes four days later.

In November of 1938, Seabiscuit engaged the previous year's Triple Crown winner, War Admiral, in the Pimlico Special. Despite being staged on a Tuesday, the match race drew a crowd of 40,000 to Maryland's Pimlico Race Course. With Wolfe aboard, Seabiscuit led at every call, drawing away by four lengths at the wire, while clocking a track record 1:56 3/5 for the 1 3/16-mile distance.

An inflamed suspensory ligament kept Seabiscuit away from racing for most of 1939. Howard bred him to seven mares that year, then rested him. Seabiscuit returned to competition in 1940 and won a pair of stakes, closing out his racing career with a victory in the Santa Anita Handicap, clocking a track record 2:01 1/5 for 1 1/4 miles.

The book, Seabiscuit, An American Legend, by Laura Hillenbrand, became a cultural phenomenon in the United States and elsewhere, rising to the top of the New York Times best-seller list in 2001. A movie, starring Tobey Maguire and Jeff Bridges, was subsequently made based on Hillenbrand's material, and it was one of five nominees for the Academy Award as Best Picture for 2003. An earlier film, The Story of Seabiscuit, starring Barry Fitzgerald and Shirley Temple, was released in 1949 — while containing some splendid racing scenes, much of the story it told was actually fictional.

b c

By Hard out of Tack Swing On (Whisk Broom II)

Foaled	1933			
Died	1947			
Raced	1935–40			

Career record	**Starts**	**1st**	**2nd**	**3rd**
	89	33	15	13
Earnings	$437,730			

Enduring tale: From claimer to stakes hero — the story of Seabiscuit is one of the most extraordinary in racing.

SECRETARIAT

IT'S AN ODDS-ON WAGER that at least nine out of ten Americans who have never considered attending a horse race know who Secretariat was. North America's Horse of the Year at both ages two and three, winner of the 1973 Triple Crown, a champion on both the dirt and the grass, he has achieved a status in the sport's history books that is rivalled only by Man o' War and Citation.

Secretariat's racing career spanned just 16 months, but during that period he won 15 stakes. His triumph in the 1 1/4-mile Kentucky Derby was accomplished in a track record time of 1:59 2/5 at Churchill Downs.

Two weeks later, in the 1 3/16-mile Preakness Stakes, the *Daily Racing Form's* clockers caught him in a final time of 1:53 2/5, also a track record had Pimlico Race Course officials decided to accept it (they relied, instead, on an adjusted clocking from a malfunctioning teletimer).

Three weeks later, Secretariat provided what many consider the most powerful performance in American horse racing annals, winning the Belmont Stakes at New York's Belmont Park by 31 lengths. His time for the 1 1/2-mile event, 2:24, was a world record for that distance on the dirt, and, as is also true with his Churchill mark, still serves as the stakes and track standard. Secretariat's Triple Crown sweep was the first since Citation's a quarter-century earlier.

A Meadow Stable homebred foaled at Christopher Chenery's farm in Virginia, Secretariat scored his first career win at second asking on July 15, 1972, at Aqueduct. Trainer Lucien Laurin then took him to Saratoga, where he named the journeyman jockey, Ron Turcotte, to replace the apprentice, Paul Feliciano, on the chestnut colt.

> "Longdon tells me Count Fleet was the greatest … I'm going to tell you Citation was the greatest. It's a matter of opinion. I will say this, though. don't think any that horse could have beaten Secretariat on Belmont Day. I've never seen a horse do the things that he did."

Eddie Arcaro, The Way It Was, **PBS broadcast, 1977**

ch c				
By Bold Ruler out of Somethingroyal (Princequillo)				
Foaled 1970				
Died 1989				
Raced 1972-73				
Career record	Starts	1st	2nd	3rd
	21	16	3	1
Earnings $1,316,808				

At Saratoga, Secretariat won a pair of stakes, including the Hopeful Stakes. He went from there to win Belmont's Futurity Stakes, finished first but was disqualified to second for interference in the Champagne Stakes, then closed out the season with authoritative triumphs in the Laurel Futurity Stakes and Garden State Stakes. He was the first two-year-old to receive the Eclipse Award as champion among all divisional leaders.

Early in his three-year-old campaign, Secretariat won Aqueduct's Gotham Stakes, equalling the track record for seven furlongs. His post-Triple Crown efforts included a victory over older horses in Belmont's inaugural Marlboro Cup, during which he set a world record of 1:45 2/5 for 1 1/8 miles.

Secretariat wasn't invincible that season. Onion and Prove Out, both trained by Hall of Famer H. Allen Jerkens, beat him in a pair of New York stakes. Secretariat closed out that season, though (and his race career), by winning Belmont's 1 1/2-mile Man o' War Handicap in a turf course record time, 2:24 4/5, that stood for 19 years, and the Canadian International Stakes at Toronto's Woodbine Race Course. In the latter case, Eddie Maple was his jockey, as Turcotte was undergoing a brief suspension.

Crowned three-year-old champion, grass champion, and overall champion for 1973, Secretariat thereafter stood at Kentucky's Claiborne Farm. While Secretariat was never able to duplicate himself at stud, his offspring did include North America's 1986 Horse of the Year, Lady's Secret, and the 1988 three-year-old champion colt, Risen Star. More than a decade after his death, Secretariat's name continues to appear high on the annual lists of leading broodmare sires.

Out of sight: Ron Turcotte looks back at the field as Secretariat wins the 1973 Belmont Stakes by 31 lengths.

TULLOCH

BRED IN NEW ZEALAND, Tulloch was one of Australia's greatest racehorses, fully deserving of a ranking alongside Carbine, Phar Lap and Makybe Diva. Tulloch earned this status despite not having raced as a four-year-old and missing the majority of his five-year-old season because of a near fatal stomach ailment.

Although of medium size – he stood 15.2 hands – Tulloch appealed to trainer Tommy Smith because of his conformation and comportment, as emphasized by his head that seemed to reflect determination, and his swinging, almost swaggering walk. However, at the 1956 New Zealand National Yearling Sale at Trentham, there was little interest in the horse and Smith was able to purchase him for just 750 guineas for owner E. A. Haley.

From such modest circumstances, legends can emerge, and that was the case with Tulloch. After breaking his maiden by winning the 1000-metre Canonbury Stakes at Randwick on 6 October, 1956 – with George Moore in the saddle – Tulloch continued onward to victories in six additional races as a two-year-old. He made half-a-dozen other starts that season as well, and finished second in all of them.

At age three, Tulloch made 16 starts, won 14 of them and placed in the other two. His victory in the 1957 AJC Derby at Randwick was achieved in a course-record of 2:29.1 for 12 furlongs, eclipsing a standard that had been set by Phar Lap in 1929. Also at age three, Tulloch set a world record for 12 furlongs on the grass of 2:26.1 while defeating older horses in the Caulfield Cup. Tulloch's winning margins that season extended as far as 20 lengths.

But Tulloch did not race at age four – a debilitating stomach disease brought about a near catastrophic decline in his weight, along with recurring infections, and almost claimed his life. Nearly two years elapsed from the time Tulloch first became ill until his return to the races, which occurred on 12 March, 1960, when Tulloch won the ten-furlong Queen's Plate at Flemington, edging out the high-quality weight-

Prize performer: Tulloch, with regular jockey George Moore aboard, sprints down Sydney's Royal Randwick track in 1960.

for-age performer Lord in a photo finish, to the absolute delight of the 80,000 spectators in attendance.

The Queen's Plate was the first of five victories in what turned out to be an undefeated season for Tulloch at age five. At age six, he was victorious in ten of his 19 trips postward. In winning the Cox Plate at Moonee Valley, Tulloch set a course record for ten furlongs of 2:01. He closed out his racing career on 12 June, 1961, by narrowly defeating the classy stayer Sharply in the two-mile Brisbane Cup at Eagle Farm.

Of Tulloch's 36 career wins, 19 of them came in races that now bear Group 1 status. Seven others now bear Group 2 status, and two others have Group 3 rankings. Twice, Tulloch won the 12-furlong Autumn Stakes at Randwick, a race that has since been discontinued, but also listed Peter Pan and Carbine among its victors. The Queen's Plate is also no longer run – joining

Tulloch on the list of winners of that event are Carbine and Phar Lap.

Only once in Tulloch's 53 career efforts did he fail to win or place. This happened in the 1960 Melbourne Cup, when he finished seventh to the victorious Hi Jinx. Much blame for the defeat was directed towards the jockey, Neville Selwood. But it should be noted that Selwood rode Tulloch in a grand total of 15 races and won 12 of them. It was Selwood who was aboard for the world record Caulfield Cup performance and the Cox Plate triumph. Moore, though, was Tulloch's most frequent partner, riding him 30 times, on 19 of those occasions to victory.

Disappointingly, after retiring to Haley's Te Koona Stud, Tulloch sired only two stakes winners, Dahma Star and Valide.

"On my recent trip to France and England I did not see a three-year-old who would get anywhere near Tulloch. I would say that at this stage he is the best horse of his age in the world, perhaps even the greatest horse in the world." **Jockey George Moore in 1957**

b c
By Khorassan out of Florida (Salmagundi)
Foaled 1954
Died 1969

Career record	Starts	1st	2nd	3rd
	53	36	12	4

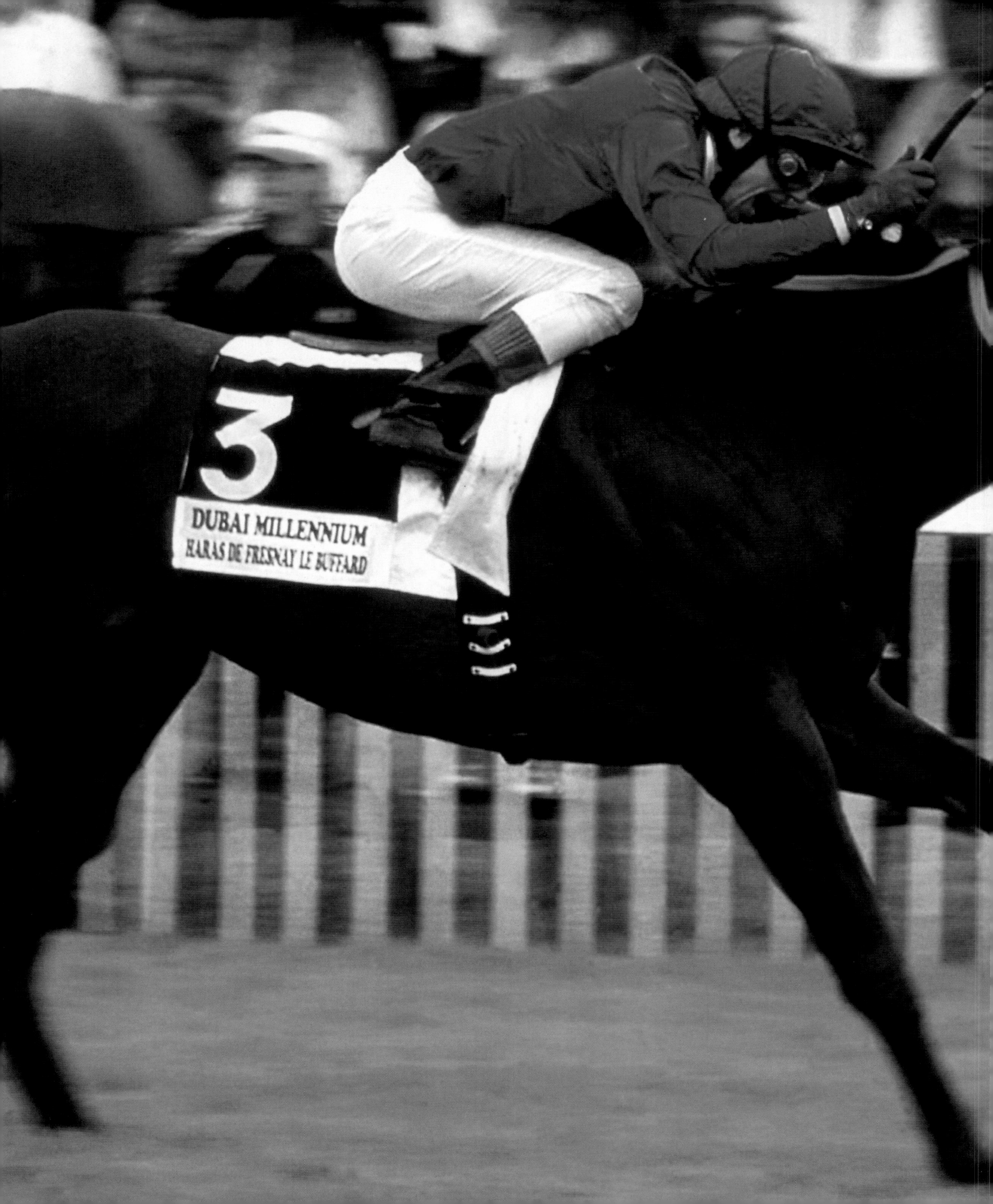
3
DUBAI MILLENNIUM
HARAS DE FRESNAY LE BUFFARD

CHAPTER 5

A–Z OF FAMOUS HORSES

From Abernant to Zev, this is truly an A–Z of famous horses (only U, X and Y are unrepresented). Many of the great horses of the 19th and last centuries could have appeared in the previous chapter without demeaning the word legend. Many of these equine superstars won more often than not.

IF, AS WAS SEEN in the last chapter, breeding cannot give a hard and fast guide to a horse's potential, so great horses are not exclusive to the best racing nations. The animals in this chapter would be exceptional wherever they ran and in any era. Some horses appear not to know when they are beaten and always, somehow, find a way to get their neck out in front when it really matters – in the shadow of the winning post.

As many great horses' careers rarely last beyond three or four years, every decade will provide many outstanding examples of equine talent. It has been a thankless task for the authors to limit themselves to these champions from around the world when the claims of hundreds more were equally compelling.

Part of racing's great attraction is that the stars of the track live in almost identical conditions to those of a humble conditional horse, they live in similar-sized boxes, eat the same type of food, have similar training regimens exercise and receive the same undying love from the stable staff. The only difference is talent level.

Fin de siècle: Dubai Millennium wins the 1999 Prix Jacques le Marois at Deauville for the all-conquering Godolphin stable.

A

ABERNANT

- gr c
- Foaled: 1946, by Owen Tudor out of Rustom Mahal (Rustom Pasha)

Abernant was an oustanding sprinter who very nearly won the English 2,000 Guineas and went on to prove an extremely successful sire. He won five of his six starts as a two-year-old, including the Champagne Stakes and Middle Park Stakes. He was caught only in the final yards of the 2,000 Guineas by the subsequent Derby winner Nimbus. It proved to be his only defeat in his second season, a campaign in which he took the July Cup, King's Stand Stakes and Nunthorpe Stakes. In his last year, he again won the Nunthorpe and also took the July Cup, though he just failed to give 23lb to the three-year-old Tangle in the King's Stand Stakes, before retiring to the Egerton Stud at Newmarket of his owner-breeder Lady Macdonald-Buchanan. He died in July 1970, by which time he had sired the winners of nearly 500 races in the British Isles. His daughter Abermaid won the 1,000 Guineas and his other best winners included Abelia, Liberal Lady, Favorita and Welsh Rake.

AFFIRMED

- ch c
- Foaled: 1975, by Exclusive Native out of Won't Tell You (Crafty Admiral)

Sweeping North America's Triple Crown in 1978, Affirmed thrice outduelled rival Alydar, annexing the Kentucky Derby by 1½ lengths, the Preakness Stakes by a neck, and the Belmont Stakes by a head. His career record against Alydar included seven victories in 10 attempts. Affirmed was two-year-old champion in 1977, three-year-old champion and Horse of the Year in 1978, and handicap champion and Horse of the Year in 1979. A homebred representing Louis Wolfson's Harbor View Farm, Affirmed was trained by Lazaro S. Barrera. The chestnut colt was primarily ridden by Steve Cauthen during his juvenile and sophomore seasons. Following four straight losses with Cauthen aboard, riding responsibilities were entrusted to Laffit Pincay Jr. in February 1979. Affirmed completed his racing career with seven consecutive victories under Pincay. The finale was the 1979 Jockey Club Gold Cup Stakes. All told, Affirmed registered 19 career stakes triumphs, 14 of them in Grade 1 events. He won the 1979 Santa Anita Handicap in track-record time.

ALCIDE

- b c
- Foaled: 1955, by Alycidon out of Chenille (King Salmon)

It is widely believed that Alcide would have won Epsom's 1958 Derby had not foul play prevented him from running. A form line through Nagami, who was third in the Derby and when racing against Alcide, give credence to that theory. At the time there was an alarming amount of villainy in racing and there seems no doubt that he had been hit when in his stable and sustained a broken rib. As a two-year-old Alcide had won the Horris Hill Stakes at Newbury and his first success in his second season was in the Chester Vase. He then romped home in the Lingfield Derby Trial and

Eurostar: Alleged's only defeat was when he came second to Dunfermline in the 1977 St. Leger.

after he had recovered from his injury he won the Great Voltigeur by 12 lengths and the St. Leger by eight. He was held up in his preparation for the Ascot Gold Cup the following season but even so was only just beaten by Wallaby II. Six weeks later he won the King George VI And Queen Elizabeth Stakes and retired to stud as the winner of eight races worth £56,042. His stud career was not as successful as had been expected, though he sired good winners in Oncidium, Approval, Atilla and Remand. He died in 1973.

ALL ALONG

- b f
- Foaled: 1979, by Targowice out of Agujita (Vieux Manoir)

During a six-week period in the fall of 1983, All Along put together one of the most breathtaking skeins of Group 1 and Grade 1 triumphs by a filly ever witnessed on the turf. On 2 October, she won the Prix de l'Arc de Triomphe at Longchamp. Two weeks later she won the Rothmans International Stakes at Woodbine. Thirteen days after that she was an 8¾-length winner of the Turf Classic Invitational at Belmont Park. And on 12 November, All Along was a 3¼-length winner of the Washington, D.C., International at Laurel Race Course. Rarely had any equine competitor put together such a transcontinental assault, and at the season's end All Along was honoured as Horse of the Year in both Europe and North America. Bred and owned by Daniel Wildenstein and trained by Patrick-Louis Biancone, All Along had a career record that included 21 starts, nine victories, six placings and earnings of $3.02 million. Jockey Walter R. Swinburn piloted her in the autumn of 1983. In the breeding shed the best

Affirmation: Affirmed with jockey Steve Cauthen proved unbeatable in the 1978 Triple Crown events

foal that All Along produced was Along All (by Mill Reef), a Group 2 and Group 3 winner in France.

ALLEGED

◆ b c
◆ **Foaled: 1974, by Hoist The Flag out of Princess Pout (Prince John)**

Alleged was perhaps the best horse to carry Robert Sangster's colours when horses trained for him by Irishman Vincent O'Brien were almost invariably in the forefront of every big race. He was good enough to win the Prix de l'Arc de Triomphe in 1977 and 1978, and the only time he was beaten in ten starts was when he was outstayed by the Queen's filly Dunfermline in the St. Leger. Not a great deal was expected of him in his early days and he was a 33–1 chance when he won the Royal Whip at the Curragh on his second three-year-old appearance, but by the time he won his first Arc, by 1½ lengths from New Zealand-bred Balmerino, with Dunfermline fourth, his merits were fully appreciated. A year later he beat Trillion and Dancing Maid by two lengths and the same. By the time of his death in 2000 Alleged had proved himself a top sire with classic winners such as Shantou, Law Society, Leading Counsel, Midway Lady and Sir Harry Lewis. His other top winners included Miss Alleged, Legal Case and Muhtarram.

ALLEZ FRANCE

◆ b f
◆ **Foaled: 1970, by Sea-Bird II out of Priceless Gem (Raise A Native)**

Allez France was the outstanding racemare in Europe in the mid-1970s, at the time when her owner-breeder Daniel Wildenstein seldom let a big race go by unattacked. She did him proud and really never looked back from the moment she won the Criterium des Pouliches in her first season. As a three-year-old, she won three of seven starts, the Prix Vermeille and two classics, the Prix de Diane and the Poule d'Essai des Pouliches. She was beaten only by Rheingold in the Prix de l'Arc de Triomphe, but made up for that in the following season's race, when she got the better of Comtesse du Loir. Allez France also won the Prix d'Harcourt, Prix Ganay and Prix Foy. Having been trained by Albert Klimscha for her first two seasons, she was under the care of Angel Penna for the other two and in her final year she won the Prix Ganay, Prix Dollar and Prix Foy, retiring with 13 wins from 21 races worth £493,100. Her broodmare record was very disappointing before she was put down after an accident in the paddocks aged 19. Of her five foals, only Action Francaise won a decent race.

Not this time: Alysheba (right) was second to Ferdinand in the 1987 Breeders' Cup Classic, but won the 1998 renewal.

ALYCIDON

◆ ch c
◆ **Foaled: 1945, by Donatello II out of Aurora (Hyperion)**

Alycidon was a top-class British stayer who became a champion sire despite suffering from low fertility and a relatively short career at stud. After he had whipped around at the start of his first outing as a three-year-old, Alycidon always raced in blinkers, but there was nothing irresolute about his racing. His first important success came in the 1948 Princess of Wales's Stakes at Newmarket and later that year, in spite of starting at 20–1, he was beaten only by Black Tarquin in the St. Leger. He won two more races that year and two more as a four-year-old before meeting with Black Tarquin again in the Ascot Gold Cup. He won by five lengths after Black Tarquin had seemed not to stay the distance, and completed his career by adding the Goodwood and Doncaster Cups – to make a tally of 11 wins worth £37,201. At stud, his crop included Alcide, the Triple Crown filly Meld, who enabled him to be top stallion in 1955, the fine stayer Grey of Falloden and other high-class fillies such the Oaks winner Homeward Bound and Almeria. Alycidon was put down in 1962.

ALYSHEBA

◆ b c
◆ **Foaled: 1984, by Alydar out of Bel Sheba (Lt. Stevens)**

Winner of the Kentucky Derby and Preakness Stakes, Alysheba was North America's champion three-year-old in 1987. But the bay colt truly achieved his potential the following season, when he triumphed in a half-dozen Grade 1 stakes, the finale of which was the Breeders' Cup Classic at Churchill Downs. Campaigning for the mother-and-daughter partnership of Dorothy and Pam Scharbauer, Alysheba was a touch slow in his early development, winning just one of his first 10 career starts. The Scharbauers and trainer Jack Van Berg were patient, though, and called on Chris McCarron to take the mount in spring 1987. With McCarron aboard, Alysheba went on to score 10 stakes wins. He was North America's champion handicapper and Horse of the Year in 1988. Possessed of a strong closing kick, Alysheba, at age four, set track records for 1 1/4 miles in Belmont Park's Woodward Handicap and the Meadowlands Cup Handicap at The Meadowlands in New Jersey.

ARCHER

◆ b c
◆ **Foaled: 1856, by William Tell out of Maid of Oaks (Vagabond)**

Archer bears the dual distinctions of being the first Melbourne Cup winner, achieving the feat in 1861, and also being the first horse to win Australia's most prestigious race two years in succession. His triumph in the 1862 renewal was achieved by ten lengths. Foaled near Nowra in New South Wales, Archer was a grandson of the 1834 St. Leger Stakes victor, Touchstone. It is said that because no rail service existed during Archer's time between his home base of Sydney and the Flemington racecourse, his trainer, Etienne de Mestre, had him walked (and/or ridden) the entire 600-mile distance - through rain, heat and mountainous terrain - to participate in the race. Such legendary exploits constitute the source material for movies, and one was made about Archer in 1997. Jockey Johnnie Cutts rode Archer to both of his Melbourne Cup wins. The day following the first one, Archer was victorious in the Melbourne Town Plate, which was also contested at a distance of 3,200 metres. An injury to Archer in 1865 ended his racing days. He remains one of the most historic figures in the archives of Australian sports.

ARD PATRICK

- br c
- Foaled: 1899, by St Florian out of Morganette (Springfield)

Ard Patrick emerged victorious in what was one of the notable battles of the early 20th century when he and Sceptre, 1902's top middle-distance colt and filly, respectively, faced the year's Derby winner Rock Sand in the 1903 Eclipse Stakes. Rock Sand could not stay with his seniors and Ard Patrick wore down Sceptre near the line to win by a neck. This was the second time in three attempts that he had beaten the oustanding filly. Ard Patrick had finished third to Sceptre in the 2,000 Guineas, but reversed that in the 1902 Derby, with the filly – who started favourite – only fourth. After the Derby, he was awarded the Prince of Wales's Stakes on an objection. Ard Patrick missed the St. Leger because of leg trouble and broke down so badly after that great Eclipse Stakes that he could not race again. Before that race he had been sold as a stallion to the German government for £21,000 but despite siring a Deutsches Derby winner, Ariel, and the successful mare Antwort, he did not achieve much as a stallion.

ARDROSS

- b c
- Foaled: 1976, by Run The Gantlet out of Le Melody (Levmoss)

Ardross's head defeat by Akiyida in the 1982 Prix de l'Arc de Triomphe, the final race of his career, showed that in spite of being a top class stayer he was more than capable of holding his own at top level over middle distances. Ardross first raced for Ireland's Paddy Prendergast and, after his death, was bought by Charles St. George and trained by Henry Cecil in England, winning 14 of his 24 starts, 13 of them coming at Pattern level. He twice won the Gold Cup at Ascot and the Yorkshire Cup, and his other major successes came in the Prix Royal-Oak and the Doncaster and Goodwood Cups. Before moving to Newmarket he had been runner-up to the Henry Cecil-trained Le Moss at Ascot. When he went to stud Ardross was syndicated for £2 million, but none of his progeny came anywhere near his level of ability. His best flat horses were Karinga Bay and the filly Filia Ardross. Overall he did better as a sire of jumpers

with the Champion Hurdle winner Alderbrook, Anzum, Young Kenny and Ackzo to his credit.

ARMED

- br g
- Foaled: 1941, by Bull Lea out of Armful (Chance Shot)

A brown gelding of exceptional durability, Armed campaigned for seven seasons, with his journeys taking him to 13 tracks all across the United States. Calumet Farm homebred, trained by the father-and-son team of Ben and H.A. "Jimmy" Jones, Armed registered 21 career stakes triumphs, including consecutive runnings of Hialeah's Widener Handicap in 1946–47. Armed also set track records at Florida's Tropical Park and Gulfstream Park, and Havre de Grace in Maryland. The Gulfstream Park effort came in his career finale. Ridden by Douglas Dodson in the majority of his races, Armed had the services of 13 other jockeys as well. A weight carrier, Armed was successful 12 times under imposts of 130 pounds (9st 4 lb) or more. Twice, Armed had six-race winning streaks. He commenced his five-year-old campaign with four wins in the space of 22 calendar days. Armed was North America's champion handicapper in 1946. He received that same honour in 1947, when he was also Horse of the Year.

ASSAULT

- ch c
- Foaled: 1943, by Bold Venture out of Igual (Equipoise)

So lightly regarded was Assault at age two that he was sent off at odds of 79–1 in maiden company (and finished fifth). The following season, however, he matured into one of the finest three-year-olds in the history of US racing, sweeping the Triple Crown, winning five other stakes, including the Pimlico Special, securing divisional honours and the 1946 Horse of the Year title as well. Bred in Texas by King Ranch, Assault represented that stable throughout his six seasons of campaigning, registering 15 stakes triumphs all told. The chestnut colt was trained by Maxwell Hirsch through all but his final three career starts (when Max's son, W. J. "Buddy" Hirsch, handled those chores). Assault's greatest triumphs at age three were achieved with jockey Warren Mehrtens in the irons. Eddie Arcaro, though, was the winner in six stakes with him during the period from November 1946–July 1947. Assault defeated the great handicapper, Stymie, five times, conceding weight in four of those efforts.

AUREOLE

- ch c
- Foaled: 1950, by Hyperion out of Angelola (Donatello II)

Despite some serious problems of temperament and the fact that British trainer Cecil Boyd-Rochfort's stable jockey Harry Carr lost the ride on him halfway through his career, Aureole is widely regarde as the best horse to have raced for the Queen. Eph Smith had taken over the ride when he had his outstanding success, in the 1954 King George VI And Queen Elizabeth Stakes, beating Vamos and Darius. Smith was also on board for Aureole's victories in the Coronation Cup, the Hardwicke Stakes and Cumberland Lodge Stakes. Carr had ridden him when he was second to Pinza in 1953's Derby and King George and claimed the 1953 Lingfield Derby Trial. Aureole died in 1975 after having proved an oustanding success at stud – far better than Pinza. He was twice champion sire with his best winners including St. Paddy, Aurelius, Provoke, Hopeful Venture (who also carried the Queen's colours), Vienna and Buoy.

AZERI

- ch m
- Foaled: 1998, by Jade Hunter out of Zodiac Miss (Abonoora)

A late bloomer, Azeri didn't make her career debut until three years old, when on 1 November, 2001, she claimed a victory by six lengths in maiden company at Santa Anita. For her exploits in each of her subsequent campaigns, Azeri received the Eclipse Award as North America's leading older female, becoming the first three-time champion of her division. Her career record included 24 starts, 17 victories and four placings, and earnings of $4.1 million. At age four, Azeri was triumphany in five Grade 1 events, the Breeders' Cup Distaff at Arlington Park, the Apple Blossom Handicap at Oaklawn Park and the Santa Margarita Invitational Handicap at Santa Anita among them. At age five she repeated in the Apple Blossom and claimed two other Grade 1 events. And at six years old Azeri was successful in her third consecutive Apple Blossom, along with the Spinster Stakes at Keeneland and Go for Wand Stakes at Saratoga – giving her 11 career Grade 1 triumphs all told, nine with Mike Smith as her jockey and two with Pat Day aboard. Bred by Allen Paulson, for whose family she campaigned, Azeri was trained in her first three seasons by Laura De Seroux and at the age of six by D. Wayne Lukas.

Arlington joy: Mike Smith celebrates after riding Azeri to victory in the 2002 Breeders' Cup Distaff.

B

BADSWORTH BOY

- ◆ ch g
- ◆ Foaled: 1975, by Will Hays out of Falcade (by Falcon)

The Queen Mother Champion Chase has for some reason produced a remarkable number of double winners in its comparitively short existence, far more than the Cheltenham Gold Cup, and one of the very best of that group was Badsworth Boy who completed a hat-trick from 1983–85. In so doing he also became a winner for all three members of the Dickinson family as Tony, Michael and Monica all trained him in their turn and he became the 12th horse in jumping history to pass the £100,000 earnings mark. In all he claimed victory eight times over hurdles and 18 times over fences, in spite of the fact that his very fast jumping sometimes led to disaster. In the first of his three Champion Chase triumphs Badsworth Boy won by a distance from Artifice with his stablemate and favourite Rathgorman – the 1982 winner – well behind. In 1984 he had ten lengths to spare over Little Bay, and in his final success he finished the same distance in front of Far Bridge. His final trip into the winner's circle came in January, 1987.

BALLYMOSS

- ◆ ch c
- ◆ Foaled: 1954, by Mossborough out of Indian Call (by Singapore)

In 1957, Ballymoss became the first Irish-trained horse to win the St. Leger at Doncaster. He was one of the first top-level flat horses to be trained by Vincent O'Brien. Ballymoss cost only 4,500gns as a yearling and his dam once changed hands for only 15gns. Despite this low profile he came to prominence when finishing second to Crepello in the 1957 Derby. As a four-year-old Ballymoss had an outstanding season, which contained victories in the King George VI And Queen Elizabeth Stakes and the Prix de l'Arc de Triomphe, following his wins in the Eclipse Stakes and the Coronation Cup. His career earnings of £107,165 were a British record at the time. When he went to stud, Ballymoss sired the top class Royal Palace, whose wins included the King George VI And Queen Elizabeth Stakes, the Eclipse Stakes, the Derby and the 2,000 Guineas, and two winners of the Irish Oaks in Ancasta and Merry Mate. The latter was out of Gladness who, like Ballymoss, raced for John McShain.

THE BARB

- ◆ bl c
- ◆ Foaled: 1863., by Sir Hercules out of Fair Ellen (Doctor)

Regarded as the "First Australian Champion", The Barb had the distinction of winning the Nursery Handicap, over six furlongs, at the Australian Jockey Club's inaugural autumn carnival at Randwick in 1866. Owned and trained by "Honest" John Tait, who has been described as the "Father of the Australian Turf", The Barb won the A.J.C. Derby the following spring. Then, carrying only 6st 11lb, he raced to victory in the 1866 Melbourne Cup, over two miles at Flemington. As a four-year-old The Barb's successes featured the Launceston Town Plate, over 2^1/2 miles, and the Sydney Cup, over two miles, carrying 8st 12lb in record time of 3:40. The following season he was triumphant at each of his seven appearances at distances from 10 furlongs to three miles, at which he was most effective. He produced his finest performance in winning the 1869 Melbourne Cup under 10st 8lb – a weight-carrying record which still stands – equalling his time of the previous year. The Barb retired after racing away with the Queen's Plate, over three miles, two days later.

BAYAKOA

- ◆ b f
- ◆ Foaled: 1984, by Consultant's Bid out of Arlucea (by Good Manners)

Bred by Haras Principal in Argentina, Bayakoa was a Grade 1 winner in her homeland under the training regimen of Jorge Machado prior to being purchased late in her three-year-old season by Frank and Jan Whitman of Leoti, Kansas. She was brought to the United States, where training responsibilities were turned over to Ron McAnally, and at age four Bayakoa was modestly successful. But at age five she triumphed in seven Grade 1 races, ending the season with a one-length success in the Breeders' Cup Distaff at Gulfstream Park. The following year, Bayakoa claimed five more Grade 1 events, ending her season with another Breeders' Cup Distaff victory, this time at Belmont Park. The latter score was marred by the fatal breakdown of the filly Go For Wand, with whom Bayakoa was engaged in a furious stretch duel. In both 1989 and 1990, Bayakoa was honoured as champion of her North American division. Her career record included 39 starts, 21 victories, nine placings and earnings of $2.82 million. Of the dozen North American Grade 1 victories Bayakoa achieved, Laffit Pincay Jr. was her jockey for ten of them, and Chris McCarron the other two. As a broodmare, Bayakoa has produced undistinguished foals.

BAYARDO

◆ b c
◆ foaled: 1906, by Bay Ronald out of Galicia (by Galopin)

Although Bayardo won only one of the three British classics in which he competed, there is a strong case for stating that he was the best colt of his generation. A dry spring at Manton in 1909, where he was trained by Alec Taylor, made it impossible for him to be ready for the 2,000 Guineas and he was not at his best for the Derby either. However, when he won the St. Leger, he proved markedly superior to the Derby winner Minoru. As a two-year-old Bayardo won all his seven races, including the Middle Park Stakes, Dewhurst Stakes, Richmond Stakes and New Stakes. His other three-year-old successes apart from the final classic, took in the Prince of Wales's Stakes, the Eclipse and the Champion. In his final year he landed the Chester Vase and the Gold Cup at Ascot, but his career ended on a low note when he failed by a neck at 1–20 to give 36lb to the three-year-old Magic in the Goodwood Cup after being set a ludicrous amount to do by Danny Maher. Though he died at the age of only 11, he sired two Triple Crown winners in Gainsborough and Gay Crusader, with the former going on to sire Hyperion.

BELLA PAOLA

◆ br f
◆ Foaled: 1955, by Ticino out of Rhea II (by Gundomar)

During the 1950s and 1960s, the combination of French owner-breeder François Dupré and his trainer François Mathet was to be feared in all the major races, and one of their best horses was Bella Paola. She was the second-best two-year-old in France when her three successes included the Grand Criterium and only her stablemate Texana was rated superior to her. Dupré and Mathet were always keen to attack the top prizes in England and Bella Paola did them proud, winning the 1,000 Guineas and the Oaks. In the former she was ridden by Serge Boullenger, but because of military service he was not allowed to ride at Epsom and Max Garcia replaced him. An unlucky second in the Prix du Jockey Club, she won the Prix Vermeille, ran disappointingly in the Prix de l'Arc de Triomphe, but ended her career by landing the Champion Stakes. At stud her best foal was Pola Bella, who won the Poule d'Essai des Pouliches and was second in the Prix de Diane before breeding several winners, including Val Divine.

Brilliant Best: Jim Culloty rides Best Mate to his third successive Cheltenham Gold Cup triumph in 2004.

Home from home: Bernborough raced in Australia and later stood at the Spendthrift Farm Stud in Kentucky, U.S.

BERNBOROUGH

◆ b c
◆ Foaled: 1940, by Emborough out of Bern Maid (Bernard)

A dispute over his ownership forced Bernborough to race at Toowoomba – 125km west of Brisbane, and the only place where his nomination was accepted – as a two, three, four and five-year-old. Sparingly raced, he won 11 times from 19 starts at Toowoomba, before being sold at auction. He was purchased for 2,600 guineas in October 1945 by Sydney restauranteur Azzelin Romano, who was bidding on the advice of leading trainer Harry Plant. Following the change of ownership Bernborough was then allowed to race in the major Australian centres. After being unplaced at his first outing in Sydney for Mr. Romano he put together a series of 15 successive victories, mostly being brought with devastating finishing bursts by his jockey Athol Mulley. Bernborough's most notable successes were registered in premier events such as the Futurity Stakes, at Caulfield; the Newmarket Handicap, at Flemington, in which he carried 9st 13lb; and the All-Aged Stakes, at Randwick. Most memorable of all were his victories in the Doomben 10,000, over 6½ furlongs, carrying 10st 5lb, and the Doomben Cup, over 1m 3f, carrying 10st 11lb. These two impressive performances came just a week apart in June 1946.

BEST MATE

◆ br g
◆ Foaled: 1995, by Un Desperado out of Katday (Miller's Mate)

One of the all-time great steeplechasers from Ireland, Best Mate won three consecutive runnings of the Cheltenham Gold Cup from 2002–2004. He was owned by Jim Lewis and trained by Henrietta Knight, who was assisted by her husband, Terry Biddlecombe – a former three-time champion jump rider. Jim Culloty was the jockey who guided Best Mate through his Cheltenham efforts for each of his Gold Cup successes. Best Mate's career record further included victories in the Scilly Isles Chase in 2001, the Peterborough Chase and the King George VI Chase in 2002 and the Ericsson Chase in 2003. Overall, he made 22 starts, was triumphant in 14 of them and earned £1.02 million. Best Mate was also scheduled to run in the 2001 Cheltenham Gold Cup, but was withdrawn because of the outbreak of Foot and Mouth disease. A burst blood vessel during a gallop prompted his withdrawal from the 2005 Cheltenham Gold Cup just eight days before the race. Best Mate died of heart failure after being pulled up by jockey Paul Carberry in the William Hill Haldon Gold Cup at Exeter on November 1, 2005. Best Mate's remains were cremated, and on December 10 of that year his ashes were fittingly buried adjacent to the winning post at Cheltenham Racecourse.

BEWITCH

◆ br f
◆ Foaled: 1945, by Bull Lea out of Potheen (Wildair)

One of the finest homebred distaffers to ever represent Calumet Farm, Bewitch was a U.S. stakes winner every season she campaigned. At age two she handed stablemate Citation his only defeat as a juvenile, drawing clear of him by a length in the Washington Futurity. All told, Bewitch registered 16 career stakes triumphs. Six of them came at age two, when she was North America's juvenile filly champion. Four came at age four, when Bewitch was honoured as champion handicap mare. Trained by the father and son team of Ben and and H.A. "Jimmy" Jones, Bewitch broke her maiden at first asking and equaled the Keeneland track record for four furlongs in her second career start. She ran her best at sprint and middle distances. Bewitch's seven-length triumph in the 1950 running of the $1\frac{1}{8}$-mile Black Helen Handicap at Hialeah is often viewed as her finest effort.

BLUE PETER

◆ ch c
◆ Foaled: 1936, by Fairway out of Fancy Free (Stefan The Great)

The outbreak of World War II prevented what should have been a fascinating battle for the St. Leger between the English colt Blue Peter and France's Pharis II. It denied Lord Rosebery's colt a chance of the Triple Crown. He had won the 2,000 Guineas and the Derby, as well as the Eclipse Stakes, after a juvenile career in which he did not win either of his two races but had shown enough when fifth in the Imperial Stakes and second in the Middle Park Stakes. Because of the War and the inevitable uncertainty surrounding racing, Lord Rosebery decided that Blue Peter, who was trained by Jack (later Sir) Jarvis and ridden by Eph Smith, should be sent to stud forthwith. Like so many top-class horses, Blue Peter was unable to sire one of his own merit, but his first crop did include the Derby and Ascot Gold Cup winner Ocean Swell, and he also produced another Ascot Gold Cup winner in Botticelli, the talented but unsound Blue Train and the Hardwicke Stakes and Champion Stakes winner Peter Flower.

BOLD RULER

◆ db c
◆ Foaled: 1954, by Nasrullah out of Miss Disco (Discovery)

Better known, today, as the sire of Secretariat, Bold Ruler won 17 stakes during his own U.S.

Final hurrah: Bosra Sham won the Prince of Wales's Stakes at Royal Ascot in 1997, but it was the filly's last victory.

racing career, including the 1957 Preakness Stakes. Whether the race surface was dry or wet mattered not. In the 1957 Benjamin Franklin Handicap, Bold Ruler carried an impost of 136 pounds (9st 10lb), including regular jockey Eddie Arcaro, to a 12-length triumph in the slop. A Wheatley Stable homebred, Bold Ruler was trained by James "Sunny Jim" Fitzsimmons. Speed was the dark bay colt's forte, but Bold Ruler could maintain it for sizable distances. Thrice he scored wire-to-wire over middle distances, including the 1958 renewal of the $1\frac{1}{4}$-mile Monmouth Handicap. In 1957, Bold Ruler was the champion of one of the finest three-year-old crops in North American racing history – his classmates included Round Table, Gen. Duke, Gallant Man and Iron Liege. During one stretch of his career, Bold Ruler won 11 of 14 stakes tries, carrying imposts of 130 pounds (9st 4lb) or higher in 10 of those efforts

BOLDBOY

◆ b g
◆ Foaled: 1970, by Bold Lad out of Solar Echo (Solar Slipper)

There have been few better examples of the benefits of gelding recalcitrant horses than that of the Lady Beaverbrook-owned, Dick Hern-trained Boldboy, who was a temperamental nightmare as a two-year-old until his operation, but so reformed after it. By the time Boldboy retired, aged nine, he had set an earnings record for a gelding in the British Isles after winning 14 of his 45 starts. The success of the unkindest cut of all was apparent immediately he started racing as a three-year-old when he won the Greenham Stakes at Newbury. Later in 1973 he added the Prix de la Porte Maillot,

Diadem Stakes and Challenge Stakes to his laurels, and as a four-year-old he took the Lockinge Stakes and Abernant Stakes. He went on to win the latter race four times in all. Other victories came in the Duke of York Stakes and the Vernons Sprint Cup and he was also placed in the Waterford Crystal Mile, Victoria Cup and Beeswing Stakes. He lived in retirement at the Warren Stud at Newmarket until he had to be put down in the autumn of 1998.

BOSRA SHAM

◆ ch f
◆ Foaled: 1993, by Woodman out of Korveya (Riverman)

Words like "the best I have ever trained" are often fated. Henry Cecil said them of Bosra Sham after she had won the Prince of Wales's Stakes at Royal Ascot in 1997, and the filly never won another race. Bosra Sham was beaten in controversial circumstances in her next start, in the Eclipse Stakes, in which she was given a widely (though not entirely justifiably) criticised ride and could finish only third behind Pilsudski. She only made one more start, in the Juddmonte International at York, because the foot problem which had been with Bosra Sham through her entire career reoccurred. After finishing only fourth she was retired to stud. Bosra Sham cost 530,000gns as a yearling and was the highest-priced of that season in the British Isles. She won her only two juvenile starts, the second being in the Fillies' Mile at Ascot. In 1996, Bosra Sham won the Fred Darling Stakes and the 1,000 Guineas before missing almost four months. She returned to finish second to Mark Of Esteem in the Queen Elizabeth II Stakes, then proved too strong for Halling in the Champion Stakes.

BROWN JACK

- br g
- Foaled: 1924, by Jackdaw out of Querquidella (Kroonstad)

Brown Jack, who changed hands in his early days for £275, has his place in the annals of the turf due to his achievement in winning Royal Ascot's Queen Alexandra Stakes for six years in a row, from 1929 through 1934. He was 10 years old when he did so for the final time to the unstinted delight of the crowd. Originally Brown Jack had been bought to England from Ireland as a jumper for Sir Harold Wernher and he finished third in a novice hurdle at Bournemouth in his first appearance in England. He ended that season by winning the second running of the Champion Hurdle at Cheltenham in 1928 and never went over hurdles again. Before he started his Queen Alexandra sequence, Brown Jack won the Ascot Stakes and he also won the Goodwood, Doncaster and Chester Cups (the latter with 9st 6lb – 132 pounds), and the Ebor Handicap with 9st 5lb. His flat career netted 18 wins, worth £21,646, from 55 starts. He died in 1948.

BUCKPASSER

- b c
- Foaled: 1963, by Tom Fool out of Busanda (War Admiral)

One of the most stout-hearted closers in United States racing history, Buckpasser's strongest strides came inside the final furlong. The majority of his career triumphs measured less than a length. At age two, Buckpasser won eight consecutive races. At ages three and four, he had an extraordinary streak of 15 straight victories. Altogether, Buckpasser registered 22 stakes triumphs for his owner-breeder, Ogden Phipps. Among them were the 1965 Hopeful and Champagne, the 1966 Brooklyn Handicap and Travers, and the 1967 Metropolitan Handicap. At age three, Buckpasser won the 5 1/2-furlong Tremont Stakes. At age four, he won the 2-mile Jockey Club Gold Cup. He displayed brilliance at both those distances, and virtually all points between. Buckpasser was trained at ages three and four by Eddie A. Neloy and for all but three of the bay colt's career starts, jockey Braulio Baeza was his rider. Buckpasser's race career included four divisional championships. He was North America's Horse of the Year in 1966.

BULA

- b g
- Foaled: 1965, by Raincheck out of Pongo's Fancy (Golden Chain)

Until Dawn Run managed to do so in 1986, no horse who had won the Champion Hurdle at Cheltenham had managed also to win the Gold Cup there, but Bula came closer than most of those who tried. He won the Champion Hurdle in 1971 and 1972 and was third to Ten Up in the Gold Cup three years later. For all his racing career Bula was trained by Fred Winter and ridden mainly by Paul Kelleway, who seemed to set the horse some apparently formidable tasks. Nevertheless, Bula was almost invariably equal to them all, coming to win from almost impossible positions. He ran 51 times, winning 34 of those races for prize money worth £69,672. Apart from his two Champion Hurdles, he won the Kingwell Hurdle, the Welsh Champion Hurdle and the Kirk & Kirk Hurdle. His best successes over fences came in the Black & White Gold Cup and the Blue Circle Chase. Two years after his Gold Cup third he had a heavy fall in the Champion Chase and two months later he had to be put down after the injured foreleg became paralysed.

BUSTED

- b c
- Foaled: 1963, by Crepello out of Sans Le Sou (Vimy)

Busted came from Ireland to England in 1967, ostensibly as a workmate at Noel Murless' Warren Place yard for the previous year's Derby winner Royal Palace. He belonged to Stanhope Joel, whose cousin Jim owned Royal Palace, and Busted soon proved far better in England than he had been in Ireland, where his best victory in two seasons was in the Gallinule Stakes. In England he began by winning the Coronation Stakes at Sandown, returned there to claim the honours in the Eclipse Stakes and then was a most impressive winner of the King George VI and Queen Eizabeth Stakes. He then triumphed in the Prix Foy but could not run in the Prix de l'Arc de Triomphe and retired to stud as the winner of £51,911 in the British Isles and ff104,625 in France. By the time of his death in 1988 Busted had proved a huge success at stud. His first classic winner came from his second crop with the Irish Derby winner Weavers' Hall, but the best horse he sired was Bustino. Other top winners by Busted included Mtoto, Crash Course, Opale and Erin's Isle.

BUSTINO

- b c
- Foaled: 1971, by Busted out of Ship Yard (Doutelle)

Bustino's victory in England's 1974 St. Leger was the high point of Lady Beaverbrook's racing career. She had spent a fortune in pursuit of classic glory. But the race for which Bustino will be most remembered is the 1975's King George VI And Queen Elizabeth Stakes at Ascot, in which he had a titanic duel with that year's dual Derby winner Grundy before going down by half a length. It has been called the race of the century. Apart from his Doncaster success, he had won the Lingfield Derby Trial before coming fourth in the Derby. Bustino also won the Coronation Cup in record time, but was injured during the the the epic King George and never ran again. His stallion career produced the Derby runner-up and Juddmonte International Stakes winner Terimon, and Height Of Fashion, who was a smart racemare for the Queen and an outstanding broodmare for Sheikh Hamdan al-Maktoum, for whom she has produced Nashwan and Unfuwain. Bustino was put down because of kidney trouble in 1997.

C

CAPTAIN CHRISTY

- b g
- Foaled: 1967, by Mon Capitaine out of Christy's Bow (Bowsprit)

In spite of an alarming tendency to make mistakes, Captain Christy was one of the very best Irish chasers of his era and his 30 lengths demolition of Bula in the 1975 King George VI Chase at Kempton Park was a performance of the highest standard. Gerry Newman rode him in that race, but for most of his other successes his jockey was Bobby Coonan. Throughout his career Captain Christy was trained by Pat Taaffe, and that victory over Bula was the second time he had beaten the dual Champion Hurdle winner. He had outgalloped him in the 1972 Irish Sweeps Hurdle. But Captain Christy's most important success came in the 1974 Cheltenham Gold Cup, when he beat the previous year's winner The Dikler. He also went beyond the British Isles and other valiant efforts saw him finish runner-up in the Grand Steeplechase de Paris and fourth in the Colonial Cup in the USA.

COALTOWN

- b c
- Foaled: 1945, by Bull Lea out of Easy Lass (Bienheim II)

Had Coaltown not been a classmate of his fellow Calumet Farm homebred, Citation, he might have swept North America's Triple Crown in 1948; he certainly had the ability. Five times a stakes winner at age two, Coaltown prepped for the 1948 Kentucky Derby with a track record triumph in Keeneland's Blue Grass Stakes. Coaltown raced against Citation just once, finishing second to him in the Derby. Thereafter, Calumet's father-and-son training team of Ben and H.A. "Jimmy" Jones campaigned the two bay colts separately. Coaltown's career record included 16 stakes triumphs. Blessed with exceptional speed, he had staying power as well, winning four stakes at $1^1/4$ miles, including a track record performance in the 1949 Gulfstream Park Handicap. North America's champion sprinter in 1948, Coaltown was also voted champion handicapper in 1949. Primarily ridden by Steve Brooks, Coaltown had one streak of 12 victories in 13 starts, including a walkover in the 1949 Edwin Burke Handicap at Havre de Grace. He was less successful at stud, never siring a stakes winner.

COLIN

- b c
- Foaled: 1905, by Commando out of Pastorella (Springfield)

Perfection is elusive, but Colin's race record was unblemished. The winner of 12 starts, including 11 stakes, at two, he completed his undefeated racing career with three more stakes triumphs at age three. Favoured every trip postward, the bay colt won at various distances ranging from five furlongs on a straight track to $1^3/8$ miles going clockwise around turns. Speedy and enduring, Colin was never worse than fourth place at any call in any race. A homebred campaigning for James R. Keene, Colin was trained by James Rowe Sr., and ridden for most of his juvenile efforts by Walter Miller. As a two-year-old, Colin was twice a stakes winner under 129 pounds. He was unhampered by wet tracks, and claimed the honours in the 1908 Belmont Stakes under a new jockey, Joe Notter, in a heavy rainstorm. Colin completed his racing days with a track-record performance in the Tidal Stakes at Sheepshead Bay. Leg problems brought about his early retirement.

COLORADO

- b c
- Foaled: 1923, by Phalaris out of Canyon (Chaucer)

Although he was beaten more than five lengths in the 1926 Epsom Derby – for which he started favourite – by Coronach, Colorado beat that colt in the other three races in which they met and is entitled to be rated superior to him. His jockey, for one, was certain that he would have at least been closer at Epsom if he had not been tied down by waiting orders. Colorado, whose two-year-old successes included the Coventry Stakes at Ascot, finished ahead of Coronach by five lengths in the 2,000 Guineas and, after having taken a long time to re-find his form after the Derby, he was again much the better of the pair in the Princess of Wales's Stakes and Eclipse Stakes and he eventually retired to stud as the winner of nine races, worth £30,358. He died after only two seasons at stud, but in that short time he sired the Ascot Gold Cup winner Felicitation, Eclipse Stakes winner Loaningdale, Scarlet Tiger, who was third in the St. Leger, the top sprinter Coroado and the very versatile Colorado Kid.

COTTAGE RAKE

- br g
- Foaled: 1939, by Cottage out of Hartingo (Hartford)

Before he embarked on his spectacular jumping career, Cottage Rake was failed by a veterinarian on no fewer than three different examinations. On the last of these three occasions the vet was working for Frank Vickerman, who had just become one of the first patrons of a new Irish trainer named Vincent O'Brien. But the deal still went through and Cottage Rake ultimately set his trainer on the route to the top of the training ladder by becoming only the second horse to win the Cheltenham Gold Cup three years in a row. He achieved the impressive hat-trick from 1948–50, with his most imposing victory being the last of the trio when he beat Finnure by ten lengths. His hardest-won triumph had come the previous year when he only got the better of Cool Customer in the final 100 yards. Such was his partnership with jockey Aubrey Brabazon that a verse was composed about their success. Sadly, Cottage Rake completely lost his form after his third Gold Cup triumph. He moved over to Gerald Balding's stable in England but the change of scenery could not resurrect it.

COUNT FLEET

- b c
- Foaled: 1940, by Reigh Count out of Quickly (Haste)

North America's sixth Triple Crown winner, Count Fleet completed his sweep of the 1943 classics with a 25-length triumph in the Belmont Stakes. The champion two-year-old in 1942, this bay colt was an easy selection as three-year-old divisional champ and Horse of the Year. The Belmont was Count Fleet's 10th consecutive victory, and his ninth overall in stakes. His owner-breeder, Mrs. John D. Hertz, promptly retired him to stud. Trained by G. Don Cameron, Count Fleet was ridden throughout his racing career by John Longden. Although he didn't break his maiden until his third time out, Count Fleet moved quickly from there into top-rate company, winning the Wakefield Stakes at New York's Empire City track in late July 1942. Count Fleet closed out his two-year-old season with a 30-length triumph in the Walden Stakes at Pimlico Race Course. Never seriously challenged thereafter, he remains one of the greatest horses never to race beyond age three.

CREPELLO

- ch c
- Foaled: 1954, by Donatello II out of Crepuscule (Mieuxce)

Crepello was a British horse of huge ability but chronic unsoundness prevented him from achieving all he might have done. He won the last of his three two-year-old starts, beating Doutelle, and he began his second season in the 1957 2,000 Guineas, in which he proved to be too good for Quorum and Pipe of Peace. In the Derby he again beat Pipe of Peace into third place, but this time it was Ballymoss who split the pair. Crepello's racing career ended on a controversial note when Noel Murless withdrew him from the King George VI And Queen Elizabeth Stakes at Ascot only on the afternoon of the race, stating that the ground was unsuitable. Crepello was a great success at stud until he was put down in 1974. He was leading sire in 1969 and produced classic winners in Caergwrle, Mysterious, Celina and Crepellana, as well as other top horses in Busted, Lucyrowe and The Creditor. Crepello was so immensely popular a horse that in the early 1960s British Railways renamed one of their fleet of 22 Deltic lomotives operating on the famous East Coast Mainline – D9102 – in his honour.

D

DAHLIA

- ch f
- Foaled: 1970, by Vaguely Noble out of Charming Alibi (Honey's Alibi)

Dahlia had the constitution of an ox and great talent to go with it. She raced all over the world until the end of her fifth year, won races in five different countries and when she retired her win earnings of £497,710 was a record for a horse trained in Europe. In this respect she comfortably eclipsed her contemporary Allez France, but on the six occasions that the two fillies met Allez France was always the better. Dahlia won once as a two-year-old and the following season she took the Prix de la Grotte, the Prix Saint-Alary and the Irish Oaks before winning the King George VI And Queen Elizabeth Stakes by six lengths. She ended that year with victory in the Washington DC International at Laurel Park and preceded a second King George success by taking the Grand Prix de Saint-Cloud. Having won the Benson & Hedges Gold Cup at York, she crossed the Atlantic again, winning the Man o' War Stakes and the Canadian International, and she gained the last of her 15 wins (from 48 starts) with a second success in the Benson & Hedges Gold Cup as a five-year-old.

DAMASCUS

- b c
- Foaled: 1964, by Sword Dancer out of Kerala (My Babu)

Victorious in the 1967 Preakness and Belmont Stakes, Damascus also registered a 22-length score in the Travers Stakes, and went on to thrice beat older horses (including Buckpasser) in the late summer and fall of that season. These triumphs gained him the honours of champion three-year-old, champion handicapper, and Horse of the Year in North America – a remarkable feat for a single campaign. Bred and owned Mrs. Edith W. Bancroft, Damascus was trained by Frank Y. Whiteley Jr. Damascus was primarily ridden by Bill Shoemaker during the bay colt's first two racing seasons, Manuel Ycaza and Braulio Baeza handled most of the riding chores thereafter. He won 17 stakes, at distances ranging from seven furlongs to two miles. A strong closer, Damascus benefited several times from the efforts of his entrymate, Hedevar, whose job

Grey flash: Daylami, ridden by Frankie Dettori, wins the 1999 King George VI And Queen Elizabeth Stakes at Ascot.

was to lead the competition through swift early fractions. A bowed tendon effected an early retirement by Damascus from the races.

DANCING BRAVE

- b c
- Foaled: 1983, by Lyphard out of Navajo Princess (Drone)

Many, but not all, people feel that Dancing Brave should have won the 1986 Epsom Derby instead of finishing second to Shahrastani. He was superior to his Epsom conqueror in their subsequent meetings and maybe jockey Greville Starkey, who later lost the ride to Pat Eddery, left the colt with too much to do. But that defeat took little gloss away from a career which included victories in the Prix de l'Arc de Triomphe, on which he produced an amazing surge to catch Bering in the final furlong, the King George VI And Queen Elizabeth Stakes, Eclipse Stakes and 2,000 Guineas, in all of which his hallmark was the power of his finishing dash. He ended 1986 with a rating of 141, the highest since the International Classifications were introduced in 1977. Dancing Brave retired to the Dalham Hall Stud but his early days were clouded by ill health and he was sold to Japan in 1991. His son Commander in Chief won the Derby, the filly Wemyss Bight landed the Irish Oaks and another son, White Muzzle, won Derby Italiano.

DANEHILL

- b c
- Foaled: 1986, by Danzig out of Razyana (His Majesty)

Long distances didn't suit Danehill during his racing days, but shorter ones most definitely did, as proven at age three by his triumph in the Group 1 Sprint Cup at Haydock Park and his course record victory in the Cork and Orrery Stakes at Ascot. At the culmination of the 1989 season, he was honoured as Europe's champion sprinter. But Danehill's extraordinary record in the breeding shed is what truly makes him stand out. He is the only stallion in thoroughbred history to have sired 300 stakes winners - that plateau was achieved when his daughter, Nevis, won the Australian Toy Show Quality Stakes at Royal Randwick on 20 August, 2005. By that time Danehill had actually been deceased for over two years, the victim of a paddock accident at Coolmore Stud in County Tipperary, Ireland, in May, 2003. Danehill was a shuttle stallion, doing service in both the Northern and Southern Hemispheres. Twice he was France's leading sire, and he was seven times the leading sire in Australia. Included among Danehill's get are approximately 200 group and graded stakes winners, and nearly 1,400 winners overall.

DAWN RUN

- b f
- Foaled: 1978, by Deep Run out of Twilight Slave Arctic Slave)

The scenes at Cheltenham on 13 March 1986, were some of the most exuberant ever seen on a British racecourse. The crowd had just witnessed Dawn Run become the first horse in the 60-odd year history of the two races to follow Champion Hurdle success by winning

Foot perfect: Desert Orchid's fine jumping brought him four King George VI Chase wins and the 1989 Cheltenham Gold Cup.

the Gold Cup. To top things, not only was she Irish-trained (by Paddy Mullins), but she was also ridden by the hugely popular Jonjo O'Neill. Dawn Run had won both the Cheltenham Hurdle and its French equivalent. She had run only four times over fences when she lined up for the Gold Cup, with three wins and an "unseated rider" in the other. When she dropped back to third place approaching the final Gold Cup fence, there seemed little prospect of the double. But she fought back tenaciously to regain the lead in the last 50 yards and beat Wayward Lad by a length. Sadly she was to race only twice more. Having finished second in a prep race for a crack at a second French championship, she subsequently fell and broke her neck. She had earned a record for a jumper based in the British Isles of £259,868.

DAYJUR

◆ br c
◆ **Foaled: 1987, by Danzig out of Gold Beauty (Mr Prospector)**

Asking a jockey which is the best horse he has ridden may not elicit a simple answer. Willie Carson, for example, has difficulty in splitting Epsom Derby winners Nashwan and Troy, but as to the best sprinter he has no doubt – Dayjur. He was beaten only four times in 11 starts and of those one was because he did not stay the trip, and another in the most freakish circumstances. That was in his final race, the

Breeders' Cup Sprint at Belmont Park, in 1990, when Dayjur looked set for victory only to attempt to jump the shadow of the grandstand near the line which allowed Safely Kept to beat him by a neck. Before that he had carried almost all before him as a three-year-old, once his best distance and running style were sorted out, and he blazed to victory in the Temple Stakes, the Nunthorpe, the Ladbroke Sprint Cup and the Prix de l'Abbaye before he went to Belmont. He retired to the Shadwell Farm in Kentucky of his owner Sheikh Hamdan al-Maktoum, from where he has sired fast horses like Tipsy Creek, Hawriyah, Hayil and Millstream.

DAYLAMI

◆ gr c
◆ **Foaled: 1994, by Doyoun out of Daltawa (Miswaki)**

Daylami, unusually, won Group 1 races for two major owners. He landed the Poule d'Essai des Poulains for his breeder, the Aga Khan but, at the end of his second season, was sold to Sheikh Mohammed for his Godolphin operation, where he did even better. Daylami won at the first time of asking for Godolphin in the 1998 Tattersalls Gold Cup at the Curragh. He then won the Eclipse Stakes (in which Godolphin horses filled the first three places), and the Man o' War Stakes at Belmont Park. His season ended with a disappointing third in the Champion Stakes. He took a couple of races to find his form as a five-

year-old, but did so in the Coronation Cup at Epsom before putting up a sparkling show to win the King George VI And Queen Elizabeth Stakes by five lengths. He then romped home in the Irish Champion Stakes, but could not cope with the very soft ground in the Prix de l'Arc de Triomphe before ending his racing days in a blaze of glory in the Breeders' Cup Turf. He retired to stand at the Aga Khan's Gilltown Stud in Ireland.

DESERT ORCHID

◆ gr g
◆ **Foaled: 1979, by Grey Mirage out of Flower Child (Brother)**

With his grey coat, flamboyant style of jumping and unlimited enthusiasm for competition, Desert Orchid was the ultimate crowd-puller and no modern British horse has attracted the public in the way that he did. His exploits made him known well outside the narrow confines of racing and people who had never had a bet were aware of him. Though he was a good hurdler, it was really as a chaser that he made his name, not least through the dramatic way in which he attacked his fences. Though to begin with he was kept to races around two miles, his trainer David Elsworth always said he would stay further and Desert Orchid vindicated that judgement by winning the 1989 Cheltenham Gold Cup, the King George VI Chase (on a record-breaking four occasions), the Irish Grand National and the Whitbread Gold Cup. He retired after falling in an attempt for a fifth King George in 1991 with career earnings of £652,802. But far from disappearing from view, he is still in constant demand for celebrity appearances, which he fulfils with all the zest he showed when he was racing.

DIAMOND JUBILEE

◆ b c
◆ **Foaled: 1897, by St. Simon out of Perdita (Hampton)**

Diamond Jubilee was so foul-tempered as a juvenile it was felt he should be gelded, despite being a full brother to the highly successful Persimmon. The idea was shelved, and Diamond Jubilee went on to win the British Triple Crown in 1900, enabling his owner-breeder, the Prince of Wales (later King Edward VII), to be one of the lucky few to own winners of both the Derby and the Grand National – his Ambush II won the latter event in 1900. Diamond Jubilee took a serious dislike to Richard Marsh's stable jockey, Jack Watts, and replacement Mornington Cannon decided to give him up after the horse had attacked him. The ride thus went to one of

Driven home: Dubai Millennium found the Derby distance too far for him, but not the mile of the Queen Elizabeth II Stakes.

Marsh's lads, Herbert Jones, who rode him regularly at home. They won the Triple Crown of 2,000 Guineas, Derby and St. Leger, as well as the Eclipse Stakes. Diamond Jubilee was also very difficult when he first retired to the Sandringham Stud, but he was sold to a breeder from Argentina for £31,500 in 1906, proving very successful there until his death at the age of 26.

DISCOVERY

◆ ch c
◆ Foaled: 1931, by Display out of Ariadne (Light Brigade)

A career winner of 22 stakes, including eight straight at age four, Discovery ranks among the great handicappers in North American racing annals. From 1934–36, he won three consecutive runnings of both the Brooklyn Handicap and Whitney Stakes. His match race margin over Azucar in the 1935 Detroit Challenge Cup was 30 lengths. Discovery won the 1935 Bunker Hill Handicap by 15 lengths, and the 1935 Cincinnati Handicap by 12. Displaying promise, but not stardom, at age two, Discovery was purchased for $25,000 in November of that season by Alfred Gwynne Vanderbilt. Training duties were entrusted to J.H. "Bud" Stotler. John Bejshak rode the chestnut colt in 43 of his subsequent 50 career starts. Discovery won Saratoga's 1935 Merchants And Citizens Handicap under 139 pounds. Nine other times, he won carrying 130 pounds or more. Discovery was

champion handicapper in 1936 and, with the exception of three starts at Santa Anita (where he won the 1936 San Carlos Handicap), he spent his career east of the Mississippi River.

DUBAI MILLENNIUM

◆ b c
◆ Foaled: 1996, by Seeking The Gold out of Colorado Dancer (Shareef Dancer)

The Godolphin policy of buying horses once they have proved their ability does not always go down well with observers, but there are no complaints on that score with homebred Dubai Millennium, whose name was changed from Yaazer before he ran. He won his only start as a two-year-old and, after winning the Predominate Stakes at Goodwood on his reappearance, he started favourite for the Epsom Derby only to fail to stay. Dropped back in distance, he won the Prix Eugene Adam at Maisons-Laffitte before winning the Prix Jacques le Marois at Deauville and the Queen Elizabeth II Stakes at Ascot in very soft ground at 4–9. His final season began with two wins in Dubai, including the Dubai World Cup by six lengths. He then won the Prince of Wales's Stakes by eight lengths from Sumitas after apparent chief rival Sendawar ran way below form. There was then talk of a match between Dubai Millennium and Montjeu, but before this could get anywhere near concrete Dubai Millennium broke a bone in his leg and had to be retired.

DUNFERMLINE

◆ b f
◆ Foaled: 1974, by Royal Palace out of Strathcona (St. Paddy)

Dunfermline managed to give extra cause for celebration during the Queen's Silver Jubilee year by carrying the royal colours to two British classic victories, although her owner-breeder was not able to be present for either of them. Though she did not win as a two-year-old, Dunfermline was placed in the May Hill at Doncaster and the Fillies' Mile at Ascot, and showed her appreciation of a longer distance when she won the Pretty Polly Stakes at Newmarket on her three-year-old debut. She then won the Oaks to give Dick Hern his third royal classic following two wins with Highclere in 1974. After being beaten in the Yorkshire Oaks, thanks mainly to the race's muddling pace, she had a pacemaker in the St. Leger. Here she showed great tenacity to upset the odds-on Alleged. She was then fourth in the Prix de l'Arc de Triomphe and second in the Hardwicke Stakes as a four-year-old, but did not win again. She made no impression at stud and died after the birth of her final foal in 1988.

E

EASTER HERO

◆ ch g
◆ Foaled: 1920, by My Prince out of Easter Week (Outbreak)

Easter Hero was the first horse to win the Cheltenham Gold Cup on two occasions, which he did in 1929 and 1930, but that race was then only in its infancy – 1924 was its first running – and the Grand National stood head and shoulders above all other steeplechases in terms of prestige. Easter Hero ran in the Grand National three times and put up a superb display when second to Gregalach in 1929, trying to give the winner 17lb and having to race with a twisted shoe for the final mile. He had a dramatic effect on the 1928 Grand National by landing on top of the Canal Turn fence and effectively ruling out most of the field. Only nine horses got past him and the 100–1 shot Tipperary Tim finished alone. Apart from his two Gold Cups, both of which were by 20 lengths, Easter Hero won the Molyneux and Becher Chases at Aintree. After dead-heating for Aintree's 1931 Champion Chase he was retired. His owner, John Hay Whitney, took him to his farm in Virginia where Easter Hero died at the age of 28.

EL GRAN SENOR

◆ b c
◆ Foaled: 1981, by Northern Dancer
   out of Sex Appeal (Buckpasser)

The field which El Gran Senor beat to win the 2,000 Guineas in 1984 was one of the best ever assembled for the race. The three horses who finished immediately behind him, Chief Singer, Lear Fan and Rainbow Quest, went on to prove themselves top-level performers, but on the day El Gran Senor's finishing speed was all too much for them. This was his sixth success from six starts – as a two-year-old he had won four including the National Stakes at the Curragh and the Dewhurst Stakes. Despite doubts about his stamina, El Gran Senor's form meant that he was sent off at odds-on for the Derby. He was worried out of the race by Secreto, but went on to win a very slowly-run Irish Derby before retiring to stud in Maryland at a value of $32 million. He has sired more than a dozen Grade 1 winners, with his best progeny including Rodrigo de Triano, Saratoga Springs, Santillana and Signorina Cattiva.

EQUIPOISE

◆ ch c
◆ Foaled: 1928, by Pennant out of Swinging
   (Broomstick)

Plagued with a quarter crack for much of his six seasons of racing, Equipoise nonetheless registered 25 career U.S. stakes triumphs. Included were consecutive victories in the Metropolitan Handicap at Belmont Park in 1932–33, and in the Philadelphia Handicap at Havre de Grace in 1933–34. Equipoise won at distances ranging from four furlongs to 1^3/4 miles. Bred and owned by Harold Payne Whitney and his son, Cornelius Vanderbilt Whitney, Equipoise engaged in streaks, winning four consecutive stakes at age two, seven consecutive races

(including five stakes) at age four, and seven stakes in a row at age five. He won the 1933 Arlington Handicap under 135 pounds (9st 9lb). In an unusual situation for a horse with 50-plus career starts, only two jockeys rode Equipoise. Raymond "Sonny" Workman was aboard for 45 of his races, Alfred Robertson for the remainder. Fred Hopkins handled the chestnut colt's training chores through his four-year-old season. Thomas J. Healey was in charge thereafter.

EXTERMINATOR

◆ ch g
◆ Foaled: 1915, by McGee out of Fair Empress
   (Jim Gore)

A stakes winner at ten distances ranging from 6–18 furlongs, Exterminator competed at 19 different North American tracks. His career stakes triumphs numbered 33 all told, 19 of which were achieved at 10 furlongs or further. Trained by eight different conditioners and ridden by 18 different jockeys, the chestnut gelding established durability standards that rarely have been approached. Exterminator's initial stakes score came in the 1918 Kentucky Derby. It was his seasonal debut, and the first start he made for the second of his two owners, Willis Sharpe Kilmer. Exterminator won the 2^1/4-mile Pimlico Cup Handicap thrice and the 1^3/4-mile Saratoga Cup four times. Exterminator also registered multiple victories in the 1^1/4-mile Toronto Autumn Cup Handicap and the 1^1/8-mile Long Beach Handicap. The imposts he carried to victory were as high as 138 pounds. Eight track records were either set or equaled by Exterminator and when he retired, only Zev had higher career earnings.

F

FAIRWAY

◆ b c
◆ Foaled: 1925, by Phalaris out of Scapa Flow
   (Chaucer)

Fairway might have won all three legs of Britain's 1928 Triple Crown had things gone his way. As it was, he had only the St. Leger to his credit. He developed an abcess in his mouth on the day before the 2,000 Guineas and was mobbed by the crowd on his way to the Derby start, so that he totally boiled over. But away from such problems,

Victory kiss: The Fellow, jockey Adam Kondrat and trainer François Doumen won the 1994 Cheltenham Gold Cup.

Fairway was a top-class horse as he showed at Doncaster as well as in the Eclipse Stakes that year and the Champion Stakes and the Jockey Club Cup the following season. He won 12 races worth £42,722, three of them as a two-year-old, and retired to stud at a fee of 400gns. He was an outstanding sire, topping the list on four occasions and being thrice second. His best son was Blue Peter, who succeeded in the Derby where Fairway could not. He sired another (albeit wartime) Derby winner in Watling Street, and other classic winners in Pay Up, Kingsway and Garden Path. He died in 1948 by which time he had produced the winners of almost 400 races worth nearly £300,000.

FALBRAV

◆ b c
◆ Foaled: 1998, by Fairy King out of Gift Of The
   Night (Slewpy)

Falbrav spent the first half of his career racing in Italy, and is the finest international competitor to emerge from that country. In 2002, he registered a photo-finish victory in the Japan Cup. In 2003 he registered a 1½-length triumph in the Prix d'Ispahan at Longchamp, a three-quarter-length triumph in the Eclipse Stakes at Sandown Park, a two-length triumph in the Juddmonte International Stakes at York and a two-length victory in the Hong Kong Cup at Sha Tin - all bear Group 1 status. In the spring of 2002, Falbrav had also accounted for a pair of Group 1 events in Italy, the Premio Pres della Repubblica at Campannelle and the Gran Permio di Milano at San Siro. All told, Falbrav made 26 career starts, won 13, placed in ten others and earned $5.83 million. He was bred in Ireland by Italian businessman Luciano Salice, who campaigned him in partnership with the Japanese breeder Teruya Yoshida. Falbrav was trained by Luca Cumani. Dario Vargiu rode Falbrav to his two most prominent scores in Italy. Frankie Dettori, Kieron Fallon and Darryll Holland handled Falbrav in major global events. He now stands at Yoshida's Shadai Farm in Japan.

THE FELLOW

◆ b g
◆ Foaled: 1985, by Italic out of L'Oranaise
   (Paris Jour)

Although there have always been a good number of French-bred jumping winners in Britain, French-trained winners have been nothing like as frequent. But for the efforts of The Fellow's trainer François Doumen that situation might have remained the case for longer. Doumen first made an impression on the British scene when

Spot on: Gallant Fox (Earl Sande up) blended speed with endurance while sweeping to the U.S. Triple Crown in 1930.

Nupsala won the King George VI Chase in 1987, but by far his most successful challenger was The Fellow, who, as a six-year-old in 1991, became the youngest winner of the Kempton Park race since Mandarin 18 years earlier. Previously that year he had been beaten only a short head by Garrison Savannah in the Cheltenham Gold Cup. He was again beaten a short head in the Cheltenham Gold Cup by Cool Ground in 1992, but repeated his success in the following season's King George, before running disappointingly at Cheltenham. It was not until 1994, at the fourth attempt, that he finally managed to win the Cheltenham Gold Cup, getting the better of the previous year's winner Jodami. He also won the Grand Steeplechase de Paris, but retired after failing in that race in 1995.

FOREGO

◆ b g
◆ Foaled: 1970, by Forli out of Lady Golconda
　 (Hasty Road)

Winner of three consecutive North American Horse of the Year titles from 1974–76, Forego was one of the great weight carriers of his generation, winning under imposts as high as 137 pounds (9st 11lb). A homebred representing Mrs. Martha Gerry's Lazy F Ranch, the bay gelding registered 24 career stakes victories. The first of these didn't come until late in his three-year-old campaign. Large and awkward early on, Forego was a classmate of Secretariat, whom he raced against once, finishing fourth to the 1973 Triple Crown winner in the Kentucky Derby. Forego's overall

record, though, requires no apologies. He won 14 times in Grade 1 company. Included were multiple triumphs in the Brooklyn, Widener, Woodward, and Metropolitan Handicaps. Trained by Sherrill Ward and Frank Y. Whiteley Jr., Forego most often had Heliodoro Gustines in his irons, although his final seven career wins were achieved with Bill Shoemaker up. Champion sprinter at age four, Forego was also North America's champion handicapper from 1974–77.

G

GAINSBOROUGH

◆ b c
◆ Foaled: 1915, by Bayardo out of Rosedrop
　 (St Frusquin)

Gainsborough was the first English Derby winner to be owned by a woman when he carried the colours of Lady James Douglas to Triple Crown success in 1918, starting at odds-on and beating his stablemate Blink by 1 1/2 lengths in the Derby. He again beat stablemates My Dear and Prince Chimay in the St. Leger, but the latter took revenge in the Jockey Club Cup and Gainsborough retired to stud. He might have achieved his victories for a different owner had Lady James been prepared to accept a bid of 1,800gns for him as a yearling after the colt had failed to make his reserve, which was only 200gns more. He was

initally trained by Colledge Leader but spent most of his career with Alec Taylor. He was a great success as a stallion, finishing top of that list in 1932 and 1933 and in the top four on six other occasions. His outstanding son was Hyperion, who won the 1933 Derby, and he sired other classic winners in Singapore, Solario and Orwell. He died in 1945 by which time his progeny had earned £340,144 in winning stakes.

GALILEE

◆ b or br g
◆ Foaled: 1962, by Alcimedes out of Galston
　 (Balloch)

Despite being pigeon-toed and plagued with foreleg problems, Galilee proved himself to be an Australian racehorse of immense ability. Trained by Bart Cummings, who appreciated his sloping shoulders, deep girth and powerful hindquarters, Galilee was allowed every opportunity to develop and mature. After having only one start as a two-year-old he won seven of his 11 races at three. It was as a four-year-old, in 1966, that he became a dominant force. Ridden by John Miller he won the Toorak Handicap, over a mile, and the Caulfield Cup, over 12 furlongs, on his way through to the Melbourne Cup, over two miles. Carrying 8st 13lb, Galilee stormed by his stablemate Light Fingers, who had won the Cup the previous year, about a furlong from home to score easily by two lengths. In the autumn he impressively won the Queen's Plate, over 10 furlongs, and the Queen Elizabeth Stakes, over 12 furlongs, by 10 lengths from the 1966 Sydney Cup winner Prince Grant. Galilee then made light of his weight of 9st 7lb to score a six-length victory, again from Prince Grant, in the Sydney Cup, over two miles. He is the only horse to have completed the Australian Stayers' Triple Crown of Caulfield Cup, Melbourne Cup and Sydney Cup in the one season.

GALLANT FOX

◆ b c
◆ Foaled: 1927, by Sir Gallahad III out of
　 Maguerite (Celt)

In 1930, Gallant Fox became the second horse to sweep North America's Triple Crown. Back then, the series opened with the Preakness Stakes, followed by the Kentucky Derby and Belmont Stakes. A homebred representing William Woodward's Belair Stud Stable, the bay colt graduated in the Flash Stakes at Saratoga in July, 1929. Every subsequent triumph was achieved in stakes as well. Gallant Fox's performances blended speed with endurance. In the 1 1/2-mile Belmont, he led at every call from the opening quarter-mile onward. The winner of just one of his first six starts, Gallant Fox won ten of his subsequent 11 races, his final effort resulting in a three-length victory in the Jockey Club Gold Cup. Trained by James "Sunny Jim" Fitzsimmons, Gallant Fox conducted the whole of his three-year-old campaign with jockey Earl Sande aboard. His initial career win came at odds of 10–1 odds, but in the Gold Cup, he went off at four cents on the dollar (1–25).

GAY CRUSADER

◆ b c
◆ Foaled: 1914, by Bayardo out of Gay Laura (Beppo)

Gay Crusader was the first of back-to-back British Triple Crown winners sired by Bayardo and trained by Alec Taylor. Having won once from two starts as a two-year-old, he beat his stablemate Magpie in the 2,000 Guineas before winning the Derby, which was run as late as July 31 that year, by four lengths from Dansellon. Later that year he added four more wins, including the St. Leger and the Champion Stakes, but he broke down when being prepared for the wartime Gold Cup as a four-year-old. Steve Donoghue, who rode many big race winners, reckoned Gay Crusader was the best he had ridden. He was very well supported at stud after his owner Alfred Cox, who raced as Mr. Fairie, had turned down an offer of £100,000, but he was not a great success. His best offspring were the Derby and St. Leger runner-up Hot Night, and Hurstwood and Kincardine, who were placed in the Derby and the 2,000 Guineas respectively.

GENEROUS

◆ ch c
◆ Foaled: 1988, by Caerleon out of Doff The Derby (Master Derby)

Generous became the longest-priced winner of Newmarket's Dewhurst Stakes when he won the 1990 race at 50–1, but his exploits the following season made it quite clear that was no fluke. He fourth in the 2,000 Guineas before romping home in the Epsom Derby, seven lengths ahead of Marju. Between those two classics, Generous had acquired a new jockey. His owner Prince Fahd Salman retained Alan Munro to ride for him and Richard Quinn, who enjoyed a long and successful association with the colt's trainer, Paul Cole, took the hard blow in exemplary fashion. Generous went on to win the Irish Derby by three lengths from Suave Dancer and the King George VI And Queen Elizabeth Stakes by a race record six lengths. His career ended on a low note when he was well beaten behind Suave Dancer in the Prix

de l'Arc de Triomphe. He stood at stud for four years in England before being exported to Japan. His best winners include Blueprint, Teapot Row, Windsor Castle and Fahris.

GENUINE RISK

◆ ch f
◆ Foaled: 1977, by Exclusive Native out of Virtuous (Gallant Man)

One of only three fillies to win the Kentucky Derby (the others were Regret and Winning Colors), Genuine Risk registered a career record of 15 starts, ten victories, five placings and earnings of $646,587. Campaigning for Bertram and Diane Firestone and trained by LeRoy Jolley, Genuine Risk was a multiple graded stakes winner competing against members of her own sex at age two. The following year, 1980, she finished third against male runners in the Wood Memorial Stakes at Aqueduct in New York. Two weeks later, at 13.30-1 odds, Genuine Risk was a one-length winner of the 106th running of the Derby. Second-place finishes in the Preakness and Belmont Stakes followed. In October of that year, Genuine Risk registered a photo-finish victory against older fillies and mares in the Ruffian Stakes at Belmont, and at the season's end she was honoured as champion of North America's three-year-old filly division. With great fanfare, Genuine Risk was subsequently bred to prominent stallions, the 1973 Triple Crown winner Secretariat among them, but of the few foals she produced, none of them ever raced.

GLADNESS

◆ b/br f
◆ Foaled: 1953, by Sayajirao out of Bright Lady (April The Fifth)

In the late 1950s the American owner John McShain was fortunate enough to have two top-class horses with Irish trainer Vincent O'Brien. One was Ballymoss and the other Gladness, and when the pair were mated in later years they produced his Irish Oaks winner Merry Mate. Gladness gained her first win in a maiden race at Manchester as a three-year-old and her first major success came in the Irish Champion Stakes. As a five-year-old she won Ascot's Gold Cup, taking revenge on Scot II, who had just beaten her in the Prix du Cadran, and then won the Goodwood Cup before making light of 9st 7lb in the Ebor Handicap. Her final race saw her finish second to Alcide in the 1959 King George VI And Queen Elizabeth Stakes. In all, she won eight races worth £27,528. Apart from Merry Mate, she also bred Glad One, who was placed in three classics, and Bally Joy. She died in 1968.

High flyer: Mick Kinane aboard High Chaparral wins the 2002 Breeders' Cup Turf race at Arlington Heights.

GOLDEN MILLER

◆ b g
◆ Foaled: 1927, by Goldcourt out of Miller's Pride (Wavelet's Pride)

Golden Miller's record in winning five Cheltenham Gold Cups from 1932–36 (he would probably have made it six had the weather allowed the race to be run in 1937) will almost certainly never be equalled, and he remains the only horse to win that race and the Grand National in the same season, as he did in 1934. He won 28 of 52 races over nine seasons without falling once despite the volatile displays by his owner Miss Dorothy Paget, who changed her trainers with alarming frequency. In his early days Golden Miller was trained by Basil Briscoe, but Miss Paget later moved her horses to Donald Snow and then Owen Anthony. The first switch came after Golden Miller's thrilling Gold Cup success over Thomond II in 1935, when he ran twice at Liverpool in two days (first in the Grand National) and refused both times. His final race saw him finish second to Morse Code in the 1938 Cheltenham Gold Cup. He died in 1957.

GRUNDY

◆ ch c
◆ Foaled: 1972, by Great Nephew out of Word From Lundy (Worden II)

Grundy was the outstanding British colt of his

The greatest: Grundy's King George VI And Queen Elizabeth Stakes battle with Bustino was one of racing's greatest ever.

generation at two and three. He claimed victory in all four of his two-year-old starts, climaxing with a six-length success in the Dewhurst Stakes, but lost his unbeaten record first time out in 1975, when, probably not at his peak after having been kicked in the face by a stablemate, he finished second behind Mark Anthony. Grundy was then second to Bolkonski in the strike-disrupted 2,000 Guineas but gained his first classic success when winning the Irish 2,000 Guineas. He followed this with a defeat of Nobiliary in the Derby, another decisive victory in the Irish Derby and the tremendous battle between him and four-year-old Bustino in the King George VI And Queen Elizabeth Stakes, which the younger horse won by half a length. That race took a fearful toll on both horses: Bustino didn't run again and Grundy was well beaten in the Benson & Hedges Gold Cup. Although he sired the Oaks winner Bireme and the Gold Cup and Goodwood Cup winner Little Wolf, Grundy was not greatly supported at stud and was exported to Japan in 1983.

H

HALLING

- ◆ ch c
- ◆ Foaled: 1991, by Diesis out of Dance Machine, by Green Dancer)

Halling was not nearer than fourth in his first three starts, but once he started claiming victory, which he did in a minor handicap at Ripon in August 1994, he went from strength to strength. He was triumphant three times more at the age of three, including in the Cambridgeshire Handicap. By the start of his 1995 campaign, he had become part of the Godolphin operation and he did them proud, winning four consecutive races, including the Eclipse Stakes at Sandown Park and the Juddmonte International at York and a pair in Dubai. Although he failed in his quest for the the Breeders' Cup Classic, he came back with zest as a five-year-old to repeat his successes at Sandown in the Eclipse Stakes and at York in the Juddmonte International, with another success in Dubai and the Prix d'Ispahan also to his credit. He finished second to Bosra Sham in the Champion Stakes on his final appearance and his first crop of runners in 2000 have included useful winners in Baaridd, Halland and Chancellor.

HATTON'S GRACE

- ◆ b g
- ◆ Foaled: 1940, by His Grace out of Hatton (Mr Jinks)

Hatton's Grace was a very smart handicapper on the flat where he won the Irish Lincoln in 1949 and the Irish Cesarewitch a year later, but it was over hurdles that he really made his mark and helped to set Vincent O'Brien out on his oustanding career as a trainer. He was the first horse to win Cheltenham's Champion Hurdle more than once when he completed a hat-trick from 1949–51. In the first two of those races he was ridden by Aubrey Brabazon and in the last by Tim Molony. He was a relatively aged 11 years old when he won the title for the third time. In all he won ten times over hurdles, putting up notable displays when winning handicaps at Naas and Leopardstown under 12st 7lb (175 pounds).

HIGH CHAPARRAL

- ◆ b c
- ◆ Foaled: 1999, by Sadler's Wells out of Kasora (Darshaan)

During his three racing seasons, Irish-bred High Chaparral made only two starts in the United States, but they resulted in back-to-back triumphs in the Breeders' Cup Turf in 2002 at Arlington Park and in 2003 at Santa Anita. The latter win came via a dead-heat for first position with Johar, the only time this has happened in Breeders' Cup history. But High Chaparral remains the only repeat winner of the Breeders' Cup Turf. Co-owned by Michael Tabor and Susan Magnier and trained by Aidan O'Brien, High Chaparral was a Group 1 winner every year he raced, accounting for the Racing Post Trophy Stakes at Doncaster at age two, the English and Irish Derbies at age three and the Champion Stakes at Leopardstown at age four. Overall, he had a career record of 13 starts, ten victories, three placings and earnings of $5.33 million. High Chaparral was America's champion male grass runner for both 2002 and 2003. Mick Kinane piloted him through most efforts, although Kevin Darley was aboard in the Post Trophy and John Murtagh rode him in the English Derby. High Chaparral now stands at Coolmore Stud in Ireland.

HOLY BULL

- ◆ gr c
- ◆ Foaled: 1991, by Great Above out of Sharon Brown (Al Hattab)

Honoured as North America's champion three-year-old colt and Horse of the Year in 1994, Holy Bull won eight of ten starts that season. Among them were a 5¾-length score in the Florida Derby at Gulfstream Park, a 5½-length score in the Metropolitan Handicap against older horses at Belmont Park, a 1¾-length victory in the Haskell Invitational Handicap at Monmouth Park, a photo-finish victory in the Travers Stakes at Saratoga and a five-length score against older runners in Belmont's Woodward Stakes - all were Grade 1 events. Overall, Holy Bull won 13 of his 16 career efforts, and his earnings totalled $2.48 million. Owned and trained by Warren A. Croll Jr., Holy Bull won his maiden effort under Luis Rivera Jr., and was ridden by Mike Smith thereafter. In the wake of severely injuring his left front leg while running in Gulfstream's Donn Handicap in February, 1995, Holy Bull was retired and sent to stud at Jonabell Farm in Lexington, Kentucky. He is now the property of the Maktoum family's Darley stud operation in Lexington, and is the sire of the 2005 Kentucky Derby winner, Giacomo.

HURRY ON

- ◆ ch c
- ◆ Foaled 1913, by Marcovil out of Toute Suite (Sainfoin)

For a trainer who conditioned as many top winners as England's Fred Darling, the observation that Hurry On was the best horse he ever trained is high praise indeed. Hurry On never ran as a two-year-old and was not entered for the Derby, but he was unbeaten in all his six starts as a three-year-old, including the wartime St. Leger at Newmarket and the Jockey Club Cup. He cost his owner James Buchanan (the Scotch whisky producer and later Baron Woolavington) only 500 guineas as a yearling. In view of the relatively low quality of the field for the 1916 Derby, including the winning filly Fifinella, it seems highly likely that Hurry On would have won it had he entered. He sired the Derby winner Captain Cuttle from the first mare he covered at stud, and was champion sire in 1926, the year his colt Coronach emulated Captain Cuttle at Epsom. He sired a third Derby winner in Call Boy, as well as a pair of Oaks winners in Pennycomequick and Toboggan and two 1,000 Guineas winners in Plack and Cresta Run. Hurry On's death in 1935 followed the passing of Buchanan by only a year. The impacts of the duo on British racing extend through generations.

I

ISTABRAQ

◆ b g
◆ Foaled: 1992, by Sadler's Wells out of Betty's Secret (Secretariat)

Despite his stellar flat-race pedigree, it is as a hurdler that Ireland's Istabraq has made his mark, becoming the latest horse to land a hat-trick in the Champion Hurdle, from 1998–2000. He won a couple of times on the flat when trained by John Gosden and was bought for J.P. McManus for 38,000gns in mid-1996. His first major success over timber came in the 1997 Sun Alliance Hurdle at Cheltenham and he ended that first jumping season with a runaway victory in another Group 1 race at Punchestown. Allaying fears that two miles at top level might be a bit sharp for him, Istabraq won his first Champion Hurdle the following year with a 12-length trouncing of Theatreworld. He was beaten in his final start that season, but swept through seven races unbeaten in 1998–99 and once again beat Theatreworld at Cheltenham, though this time by only 3 1/2 lengths. His winning sequence was interrupted by Limestone Lad at Fairyhouse in December 1999. An overnight scare only improved his odds at Cheltenham in March 2000, as he beat Hors La Loi III by four lengths.

J

JERRY M

◆ b g
◆ Foaled: 1903, by Walmsgate out of (*unnamed mare*) (Luminary)

In the days when the Grand National dominated the steeplechasing world, every horse worth his salt was aimed at it, and there were some oustanding winners. One of these was Jerry M, who won the race in 1912, ridden by Lester Piggott's grandfather Ernie, and carrying top weight of 12st 7lb. He won by six lengths and four from Bloodstone and Axle Pin. Two years earlier he had been runner-up in the Grand National, also carrying 12st 7lb, failing by just three lengths to give 30lb to Jenkinstown. In all, Jerry M won 14 of his 20 races over four seasons before having to be put down in the autumn of 1914. Four of those wins came in Ireland from five starts before his sixth birthday. Despite an unfavourable veterinary report, he was bought by Sir Charles Assheton-Smith for £1,200. Sir Charles had first won the National in 1893 with Cloister, who was also burdened with 12st 7lb.

JIM AND TONIC

◆ ch g
◆ Foaled: 1994, by Double Bed out of Jinka (Jim French)

Jim And Tonic was a splendid example of a global warrior. Bred in France, he competed in major events in his home country, England, Hong Kong, Singapore, Dubai, Canada and the United States. He made 39 starts during his career, winning 13 of them and earning $4.98 million. The Sha Tin Course in Hong Kong hosted several of Jim And Tonic's finest performances - his 1¾-length victory in the Hong Kong International Bowl in December, 1998, his course-record victory (2:00.3 for 2,000 metres) in the Queen Elizabeth II Cup in April, 1999, and his 3¾-length victory in the Group 1 Hong Cup in December 1999. Three times Jim And Tonic was a champion in France, and his victory in the 2001 Group 1 Dubai Duty Free Stakes at Nad Al Sheeba secured him a championship in Dubai as well. Jim And Tonic campaigned for John David Martin, a London stockbroker, and was trained by Francois Doumen. Riding chores were regularly handled by Gerald Mosse. Upon retiring from racing in March, 2003, Jim And Tonic was pensioned at the place of his birth, Haras d'Ecouves, in Normandy, France.

K

KINGSTON TOWN

◆ bl g
◆ Foaled: 1977, by Bletchingly out of Ada Hunter (Andrea Mantegna)

Retained by his breeder David Hains after being passed-in for Aus$5,000 as a yearling, Kingston Town finished 10 lengths last at his racing debut in March 1979. Subsequently gelded at the insistence of trainer Tommy Smith, he made a further 40 starts until his retirement as a six-year-old. "The King", as he was known, was the dominant three-year-old of his era with 12 victories at that age featuring the Spring Champion Stakes, A.J.C. Derby and Sydney Cup at Randwick as well as the Tancred Stakes at Rosehill. Troubled by foreleg problems he raced only six times as a four-year-old but his wins included the W.S.Cox Plate, over 2050m at Moonee Valley, which is regarded as Australasia's weight-for-age championship. On 19 September 1981, he became the first horse in Australia to exceed $1 million in prizemoney in taking the S.T.C. Cup, over 2400m at Rosehill. Although uncomfortable around Melbourne's anti- (counter) clockwise way of racing, Kingston Town followed up by winning the Cox Plate again in 1981 and 1982 to become the first horse to win the event on three occasions. But arguably his best performance was his second to Gurner's Lane in the 1982 Melbourne Cup, when carrying 59kg and being sent for home 800m out he was beaten only in the last few strides.

L

L'ESCARGOT

◆ ch g
◆ Foaled: 1963, by Escart III out of What a Daisy (Grand Inquisitor)

L'Escargot is one of only two horses to have won the Grand National and the Cheltenham Gold Cup, though unlike Golden Miller, his triumphs came in different seasons. His owner, Raymond Guest, is also in a select band as one of a handful to have owned winners of the Grand National and the Derby – Sir Ivor and Larkspur were his Epsom heroes. L'Escargot, who was trained by Dan Moore and invariably ridden by Tommy Carberry, gained his first important success in a division of the Gloucestershire Hurdle in 1968. He was a 33–1 chance when he claimed victory in the 1970 Gold Cup, beating French Tan by 1 1/2 lengths. A year later, he justified joint favouritism with a 10-length beating of Leap Frog. He had four cracks at the Grand National, falling at the first attempt and finishing third, then second to Red Rum in 1973 and 1974 before ending that winner's hat-trick attempt in 1975. He was supposed to have retired after that, but in fact had one more race the following season before retiring to his owner's home in the United States. Guest served as Ambassador to Great Britain. A video, L'Escargot, The Snail and the Diplomat and the Chase, can be purchased on the internet.

LADY'S SECRET

◆ gr f
◆ Foaled: 1982, by Secretariat out of Great
Lady M. (Icecapade)

Unquestionably the greatest daughter of Secretariat, Lady's Secret registered 22 career stakes triumphs, half of them coming in Grade 1 company. She defeated male horses in the 1986 renewal of Saratoga's Whitney Handicap, and culminated that season's campaign with a 2 1/2-length victory in the Breeders' Cup Distaff at Santa Anita. Lady's Secret was champion of North America's older filly and mare division in 1986. She was also Horse of the Year, a rare distinction for a distaffer. Purchased privately as a weanling, Lady's Secret campaigned for Mr. and Mrs. Eugene V. Klein. Training chores were entrusted to D. Wayne Lukas. Ten jockeys were aboard Lady's Secret during her four seasons of racing, Pat Day guiding her through most of her championship campaign, including the Whitney and Breeders' Cup triumphs. Stakes that Lady's Secret twice annexed include the Maskette, Ruffian, and Beldame. Upon retiring, she had the highest career earnings of any filly or mare in North American racing history.

LAMMTARRA

◆ ch c
◆ Foaled: 1992, by Nijinsky out of Snow Bride
(Blushing Groom)

Lammtarra is one of the very few examples of the son of Epsom Derby and Oaks winners

No snail: L'Escargot (Tommy Carberry up) is led in by owner Raymond Guest after winning the 1975 Grand National.

Top of the crop: Lady's Secret, the greatest filly by Secretariat, won 11 Grade 1 events, including the Breeders' Cup Distaff.

producing another Derby winner – though Snow Bride was only awarded the 1989 Oaks after Aliysa was disqualified. But Lammtarra, the son of Triple Crown winner Nijinsky, did everything to live up to his illustrious parentage, winning all four races he contested, including the Derby, the King George VI And Queen Elizabeth Stakes and the Prix de l'Arc de Triomphe. For those three races Lammtarra was trained by Godolphin's Saeed bin Suroor, but in his first season, when he won his only start at Newbury, he was trained by Alex Scott who had backed him at 33–1 for the 1995 Derby. Tragically, Scott was shot dead by a disgruntled employee within weeks of the first win. Having come from a long way back to win the Derby in record time by a length from Tamure, Lammtarra wore down Pentire to take the King George by a neck. In the Arc, he held off Freedom Cry by a 3/4-length margin to complete a very rare treble. He then went to the Dalham Hall Stud, but amid stories of an unsatisfactory temperament he was exported to Japan after one season.

LEVMOSS

◆ b c
◆ Foaled: 1965, by Le Levanstell out of Feemoss
(Ballymoss)

Levmoss's defeat of Park Top in the 1969 Prix de l'Arc de Triomphe was a bodyblow to those who claim that horses who win long-distance races are too slow to do anything else. He had already won the Gold Cup at Ascot and the Prix du Cadran that year, but he had enough pace when dropped back to 1 1/2 miles to beat not

only Park Top, but three other classic winners in Blakeney, Prince Regent and Crepellana. He had also beaten Park Top in 1968, in the Oxfordshire Stakes at Newbury, and that year also won the two-mile Leopardstown Handicap and was placed in the French St. Leger, the Queen's Vase and the Lingfield Derby Trial. As a two-year-old he won once from two starts. Levmoss went to stud as a five-year-old after accumulating eight wins worth £142,226. He stood for most of his life in Ireland, where he had been trained by Seamus McGrath, but moved to France for the 1977 season and died that year. The Irish St. Leger winner M-Lolshan and Prix du Cadran winner Shafaraz were his best winners.

LOCHSONG

◆ b f
◆ Foaled: 1988, by Song out of Peckitts Well
(Lochnager)

Lochsong's rise to the top of the British sprinting tree in the early- to mid-1990s was one of the most remarkable progress stories of the time. Her first two wins came in an ordinary maiden race at Redcar and an apprentice handicap. She became hugely popular throughout racing, not least because of her sheer enthusiasm for going as fast as she could for as long as she could, a quality which saw her win top sprints like the Prix de l'Abbaye in successive years, the Nunthorpe Stakes, King's Stand Stakes. Temple Stakes and Ayr Gold Cup. It did not matter who rode her, Frankie Dettori, Willie Carson or the apprentice Francis Arrowsmith, she invariably did all she could. She was undoubtedly better at five furlongs rather than six and her career ended on an untypically low note when she was last in the Breeders' Cup Sprint having injured herself in the process. Life at stud has been disappointing so far and neither of her two foals to race has yet won.

M

MANIFESTO

- ◆ b g
- ◆ Foaled: 1888, by Man O'War out of Vae Victis (King Victor)

No horse may ever equal Red Rum's achievements in winning three Grand Nationals, but for durability as far as Liverpool was concerned, it will be very hard to match the record of Manifesto, who ran in the race eight times, the last time at the age of 16, in the late 19th–early 20th century. He finished first twice, third three times and fourth once. Even allowing for the fact that in his day the National stood well above its contemporary races, that record is testament to Manifesto's power and strength. He raced for 13 consecutive seasons and gained his first National triumph in 1897 when, starting 6–1 favourite, he beat Filibert by a head. Two years later he had five lengths to spare over Ford of Fyne. He is one of the very few winners of the race to have carried 12st 7lb (175 pounds) to victory, which he did on the occasion of his second success. In other years he carried 12st 8lb and as much as 12st 13lb.

Manifesto's other notable wins came in the Lancashire Chase at Manchester and the Irish Champion Chase.

MANIKATO

- ◆ ch g
- ◆ Foaled: 1976, by Matrice out of Markato (Natural Bid)

A wilful gelding, Manikato, who cost only Aus$3,500 as a yearling, was a brilliant performer right from the beginning of his career. Displaying blistering speed, he won Rosehill's Golden Slipper Stakes and Caulfield's Blue Diamond Stakes – Australia's premier two-year-old races. At three – after being moved to the stables of Bob Hoysted after the death of his brother Bon – Manikato scored a series of memorable victories including the Caulfield Guineas, over 1600m. He also overcame weight disadvantages to defeat the older horses in the Marlboro Cup, over 1400m at Caulfield, and the Rothmans 100,000, over 1350m at Doomben. Manikato registered the first of three successive wins in the 1400m weight-for-age Futurity Stakes, at Caulfield. He was most effective, however, around the tight, turning Moonee Valley circuit where he registered wins in seven of eight appearances. Among them were the weight-for-age William Reid Stakes, over 1200m, in which he was triumphant on an unprecedented five occasions in 1979, 1980, 1981, 1982 and 1983.

MANILA

- ◆ b c
- ◆ Foaled: 1983, by Lyphard out of Dona Ysidra (Le Fabuleux)

Uninspired on dirt surfaces at age two, Manila was switched to the greensward early in his three-year-old campaign and by the end of the season he had become North America's foremost grass competitor, winning six consecutive graded stakes. Manila's photo-finish triumph over Theatrical in the 1986 Breeders' Cup Turf at Santa Anita remains one of the most heralded in that event's heritage. It secured the 1986 male turf championship title. Manila initially raced for his breeder, Eduardo M. Conjuangco Jr. In late 1985, ownership of the the bay colt was leased to Bradley M. Shannon and it was in Shannon's name that Manila raced thereafter. Trained by Leroy Jolley, Manila was ridden by seven different jockeys. Jose Santos had the mount in the Breeders' Cup, while Angel Cordero Jr. was aboard for the colt's career finale, a 1 1/2-length victory in the 1987 Arlington Million. Altogether, Manila won 10 stakes, including consecutive runnings of the United Nations Handicap in 1986–87.

MANNA

- ◆ b c
- ◆ Foaled: 1922, by Phalaris out of Waffles (Buckwheat)

The 6,300gns which Fred Darling paid on behalf of owner Henry Morriss, a Shanghai-based bullion broker for Manna when the British colt was a yearling was quite an outlay by the standards of the time (the Derby was worth less than twice that sum), but it proved money well spent. Manna won twice as a two-year-old, including the Richmond Stakes at Goodwood. A very wet spring led – Darling felt – to an unsatisfactory preparation for the 1925 2,000 Guineas and he started at the price of 100–8. Nevertheless Manna led all the way and won by two lengths. He then galloped away with the Derby, again in soft ground, and won by eight lengths. Sadly, Manna was denied a fair crack at the Triple Crown when he broke down running in the St. Leger. His best winners at stud were Colombo, who won the 2,000 Guineas and the Eclipse Stakes winner Miracle.

MELD

- ◆ b f
- ◆ Foaled: 1952, by Alycidon out of Daily Double (Fair Trial)

When Meld completed the British fillies' Triple Crown by beating Nucleus in the 1955 St. Leger, she enabled Cecil (later Sir Cecil) Boyd-Rochfort to become the first trainer in England to have

Flying filly: For Lochsong, one of Britain's fastest-ever sprinters, even six furlongs was almost too far

Repeat the dose: Miesque (left) goes clear of Warning to win her second Prix Jacques le Marois at Deauville in 1988.

won more than £1 million for his patrons. In view of the way in which she had dominated her rivals in the 1,000 Guineas and the Oaks, Meld was rather disappointing in the style of her Doncaster success in which she was taking on colts for the first time that year. She won by only ³/4 length, and then had to survive an objection from Lester Piggott, who had ridden Nucleus. But there was a lot of coughing about at the time and it was rumoured that Meld herself had coughed on the morning of the race. Like a number of top-class racemares, Meld had a very low-key career at stud, which was saved from complete obscurity by the 1966 Derby success of her son Charlottown who, like Meld, carried the colours of Lady Zia Wernher. Another son, Mellay, also did well as a sire in New Zealand.

MIESQUE

◆ **b f**
◆ **Foaled: 1984, by Nureyev out of Pasadoble (Prove Out)**

Since the advent of the Breeders' Cup in the mid-1980s, success for horses trained in Europe in this very valuable series has been nothing like as frequent as the protagonists would like. For Miesque, however, winning at Churchill Downs in Kentucky or at Hollywood Park in California, was no different from doing so at Longchamp or Deauville in France, where she was trained by François Boutin. Miesque won the Breeders' Cup Mile at those tracks in 1987 and 1988, respectively, and when she retired after the second of those successes she had won ten Group/Grade 1 races around the world. She won all three starts as a two-year-old, including the Prix de la Salamandre and Prix Marcel Boussac, and in her second season victories came in the 1,000 Guineas, Poule d'Essai des Pouliches, Prix Jacques le Marois and Prix du Moulin, before her first successful sortie to America. As a four-year-old she had only three

races before her second transatlantic venture, winning the Prix Jacques le Marois (again) and Prix d'Ispahan before narrowly going down to Soviet Star in an attempt for a second Prix du Moulin.

MIGHT AND POWER

◆ **b c**
◆ **Foaled: 1993, by Zabeel out of Benediction (Day Is Done)**

Like many of the progeny by champion Australian sire Zabeel, Might And Power needed the chance to develop and mature. After being a winner over 1400m, at two he indicated his potential at three by winning the Group 3 Frank Packer Plate, over 2000m, at Randwick and finishing second to Intergaze in the Group 1 Canterbury Guineas, over 1800m. However, even those closest to Might And Power were surprised at the heights he attained as a four-year-old in the spring of 1997. A series of encouraging performances led through to a blistering exhibition of sustained power in the Caulfield Cup, over 2400m. Leading throughout, he charged away from his rivals over the final 400m to score by 7¹/2 lengths in 2min 26.20sec, which bettered the record Tulloch had set 30 years earlier. He again led all the way – under 56kg – to win the Melbourne Cup, over 3200m at Flemington, by a nose from Doriemus, who had completed the Cups double in 1995. Might And Power produced another awesome performance in the 1998 in the BMW Cox Plate, over 2040m, when he again successfully defied the attempts by his rivals to overhaul him to win in record time of 2min 03.54sec. He was acclaimed as Australia's Champion Racehorse in 1997–98 and 1998–99.

THE MINSTREL

◆ **ch c**
◆ **Foaled: 1974, by Northern Dancer out of Fleur (Victoria Park)**

Those who dislike chestnut horses with plenty of white about them would have had a splendid time with The Minstrel. They would, though, have had to admit that his courage and determination more than saw off any prejudice which suggested lack of resolution. The Minstrel was one of the chief standard bearers for the Robert Sangster, Vincent O'Brien, Lester Piggott team, which at that time seemed to carry almost all before them. He won all three races as a two-year-old, most notably the Dewhurst Stakes, but when he was beaten in the 2,000 Guineas at Newmarket and in the

Irish version at the Curragh, his detractors were rubbing their hands. The Minstrel put them in their place by winning the Derby – after an amazingly strong ride from Piggott to beat Hot Grove by a neck – then the Irish Derby and the King George VI And Queen Elizabeth Stakes – the latter by a short-head from Orange Bay. He was sent to stud in the United States and when he died in 1990 he had sired top winners in L'Emigrant, Kanz, Musical Bliss, Palace Music and Opening Verse.

MONKSFIELD

◆ **b c**
◆ **Foaled: 1972, by Gala Performance out of Regina (Tulyar)**

There was never much of Monksfield, but his small frame hid an attitude of great determination. If it came to a fight Monksfield would not only want to be in it, he would expect to win it. This was more than clear through a career which saw him win two Champion Hurdles and the Aintree Hurdle at Liverpool thrice – including a dead-heat with Night Nurse, one of his two greatest rivals. Monksfield cost his Irish trainer Dessie McDonogh only 740gns as a yearling, but he won five times on the flat to add to his hurdling triumphs. He won four times in his first season hurdling, as well as finishing second in the Triumph Hurdle at Cheltenham. He was runner-up in the 1977 Champion Hurdle behind Night Nurse, but triumphed in 1978, ahead of Sea Pigeon and Night Nurse. The rivalry between Monksfield and Sea Pigeon reached its peak in 1979 and 1980 with Monksfield winning the 1979 Champion Hurdle, and the latter reversing the decision – by a comprehensive seven lengths – a year later. Monksfield died in 1989 after nine years at stud; his best winners included Lackendara, Garrylough and It's A Snip.

MONTJEU

◆ **b c**
◆ **Foaled: 1996, by Sadler's Wells out of Floripedes (Top Ville)**

At his best Monteju was a top-class horse, as was proved by his wins around Europe in the Prix de l'Arc de Triomphe, King George VI And Queen Elizabeth Stakes, Irish Derby and Prix du Jockey Club. The fact that his racing days ended on a rather downbeat note with defeat in his last three runs should not detract from what he had achieved. Having won both his starts as a two-year-old, Montjeu began his second season by landing the Prix Greffulhe at Longchamp before being amazingly beaten in the Prix Lupin after starting at 1–10. He took revenge on that race's winner, Gracioso, in the Prix du Jockey Club, won the Irish Derby in style and then took the Prix Niel en route to the Arc, in which he caught the Japanese horse El Condor Pasa well inside the final furlong. He then disappointed in the Japan Cup, but showed that he was back to form as a four-year-old with wins in the Tattersalls Gold Cup and the Grand Prix de Saint-Cloud before his King George success. He retired to stud in 2001 as part of the Coolmore team.

MTOTO

- ◆ b c
- ◆ Foaled: 1983, by Busted out of Amazer (Mincio)

Mtoto recovered so well from the foot problems which dogged his early career that when he went to stud, he did so as the winner of the King George VI And Queen Elizabeth Stakes, and double winner of both the Eclipse Stakes and Prince of Wales's Stakes. He very nearly added the Prix de l'Arc de Triomphe to this illustrious list too. All this from a horse who, by the end of his three-year-old campaign, had won only once, and that was a small maiden race at Haydock Park. His first important success came as a four-year-old in the Brigadier Gerard Stakes at Sandown. He really blossomed in his final year, 1988, showing he was as good over 1 1/2 miles as he was over 10 furlongs and ending his racing life with a neck second to Tony Bin in the Arc. He stood at Aston Upthorpe Stud at a fee of £18,000, where he sired the Derby winner Shaamit, the Ascot Gold Cup hero Celeric and other smart horses like Arbatax and Maylane.

French fast: Montjeu bypassed the Epsom Derby to enter – and win – the Prix du Jockey Club at Chantilly in June 1999.

N

NASHUA

- ◆ b c
- ◆ Foaled: 1952, by Nasrullah out of Segula (Johnstown)

Triumphant in track-record time in the 1955 Preakness Stakes, Nashua was also a nine-length winner of the Belmont Stakes. But he's better known for his 6 1/2-length victory over his fellow three-year-old, Swaps, in the Washington Park Match Race in August 1955, thus avenging his loss to the same horse in the Kentucky Derby. All told, Nashua registered 19 career stakes wins. Bred by Belair Stud Inc., Nashua conducted a homebred campaign through age three. He was then sold to a syndicate headed by Leslie Combs II, in whose name he raced thereafter. James "Sunny Jim" Fitzsimmons trained Nashua throughout his race career. Eddie Arcaro was his regular rider. Nashua was North America's male two-year-old champion in 1954, and three-year-old champ and Horse of the Year the following season. Lengthy distances suited Nashua. He won consecutive runnings of the two-mile Jockey Club Gold Cup in 1955–56. The latter effort, his final career start, was also accomplished in track-record form.

NASHWAN

- ◆ ch c
- ◆ Foaled: 1986, by Blushing Groom out of Height of Fashion (Bustino)

The success story of Nashwan is entwined around the Queen. She sold the colt's dam, Height Of Fashion, to his owner-breeder Sheikh Hamdan al-Maktoum and Nashwan swept through his *annus mirabilis* of 1989 on the heels of Hern's dismissal as a royal trainer. Nashwan's 2,000 Guineas success, in particular, gave the British racing public their chance to express their feelings and they needed no second bidding. He had won both his juvenile starts in satisfactory style, and once more Hern showed he could get a horse ready for a classic first time out, as Nashwan beat Exbourne at Newmarket, before romping to a five-length Derby victory over Terimon. He then had a hard race in the Eclipse Stakes before beating Opening Verse and an even harder one to account for Cacoethes in the King George VI And Queen Elizabeth Stakes. Nashwan's last

race saw him finish only third in the Prix Foy. At stud Nashwan sired Swain, a double King George winner, the top US filly Wandesta and Juddmonte International Stakes winner One So Wonderful.

Just enough: Willie Carson (striped cap) drives Nashwan past his rivals to win 1989's 2,000 Guineas at Newmarket.

NATIVE DANCER

- ◆ gr c
- ◆ Foaled: 1950, by Polynesian out of Geisha (Discovery)

A winner in all but one of his career efforts, Native Dancer registered 18 stakes triumphs during three seasons of racing, including the 1953 Preakness and Belmont Stakes. His sole defeat came in that year's Kentucky Derby, by a diminishing head to a 25–1 shot named Dark Star. Favoured every time he ran, from his maiden outing onward, Native Dancer won four Saratoga stakes races at age two, and went from there to Belmont Park where he equaled the 6 1/2-furlong track record on the Widener Course. Native Dancer was crowned North America's male two-year-old champion at season's end. The following season, he was three-year-old male champion and Horse of the Year. Bred and owned by Alfred Gwynne Vanderbilt, Native Dancer was trained by William C. Winfrey, and ridden in 21 of his starts by Eric Guerin. Decades later, Guerin relived the 1953 Derby numerous times in his dreams. "I always saw the finish line coming, knowing we'd end up short," he said.

NEARCO

- ◆ br c
- ◆ Foaled: 1935, by Pharos out of Nogara (Havresac II)

Only once in his racing days did Nearco venture outside his native Italy. He was unbeaten in 13 races there from five furlongs to nearly two miles, and when he went to France for the

Grand Prix de Paris he beat that year's Derby winner, Bois Roussel, into third place. So superior was he to his own age group in Italy that he won the Derby Italiano by a distance, and a few days after his Longchamp success he was bought by the British bookmaker Martin Benson, who operated under the name of Duggie Stewart and with the claim that "Duggie never owes." Nearco was a huge success as a stallion and by the time he died in 1957 his progeny had won almost 600 races and he was in the top 10 sires (champion twice) for 15 years in a row. His classic winners included two pairs of full brothers, Dante and Sayajirao, Nimbus and Neasham Belle, and he got other high-level winners in Hafiz II, Neolight and Narrator.

NEVER SAY DIE

◆ ch c
◆ **Foaled: 1951, by Nasrullah out of Singing Grass (War Admiral)**

Even if he had achieved nothing else, Never Say Die would be in the racing history books as the first Derby winner ridden by Lester Piggott, who was 18 years old when he rode the colt to a 33–1 success at Epsom in 1954. But Never Say Die was a great deal more than a one-race wonder. As a two-year-old, he won once and was placed in the Richmond Stakes and Dewhurst Stakes. Although Never Say Die was beaten in a very rough race for the King Edward VII Stakes at Ascot (Piggott received a very harsh six months suspension for his riding in the

All strung out: Never Say Die, ridden by 18-year-old Lester Piggott, left the field trailing in his wake at the 1954 Derby.

race), he ended his career with a 12-length success in the St. Leger. On retirement, his owner, American Robert Sterling Clark, presented him to the National Stud and he was champion sire in 1962, thanks to Larkspur's Derby victory. He also sired the Oaks and 1,000 Guineas winner Never Too Late and other good winners in Die Hard and Sostenuto. He was put down in 1975, by when his stock had won 309 races worth more than £400,000 in Great Britain.

NIGHT NURSE

◆ b g
◆ **Foaled: 1971, by Falcon out of Florence Nightingale (Milesian)**

There were some outstanding hurdlers during the 1970s and Night Nurse, who won the 1976 and 1977 Champion Hurdle, was very much one of them. And after his hurdling days were over he took to fences with almost equal success, coming very close to being the first horse to win the Champion Hurdle and the Cheltenham Gold Cup when second to stablemate Little Owl in 1981. Night Nurse, who was trained throughout his career by Peter Easterby, had respectable form on the flat but made an immediate impression over hurdles with his flamboyant jumping and determined front-running. In his first season he won six times from seven starts, before beating Birds Nest in his first Champion Hurdle and Monksfield in his second. He also won the Scottish and Welsh editions of the Champion Hurdle, the Irish Sweeps Hurdle and Fighting Fifth Hurdle, as well as dead-heating with Monksfield at Liverpool. He did very well over fences, winning races such as the Buchanan Gold Cup at Ascot and the Mandarin Chase at Newbury in addition to his Gold Cup second. He had to be put down in 1998.

NOOR

◆ b c
◆ **Foaled: 1945, by Nasrullah out of Queen of Baghdad (Bahram)**

A four-time conqueror of Citation in 1950, Noor set two world records in the process, registering 1:46⁴/5 for 1¹/8 miles in the Forty-Niners Handicap on 17 June and 1:58¹/5 for 1¹/4 miles in the Golden Gate Handicap on 24 June. Both efforts came at California's Golden Gate Fields. Earlier that season, Noor set a North American standard for 1³/4 miles in Santa Anita's San Juan Capistrano Handicap. He also set a 1¹/4-mile track record in the Santa

Anita Handicap. Bred in Ireland, Noor campaigned for two years in England. He was then brought to the United States by Charles S. Howard, who had purchased the bay colt in a $175,000 package with Narullah. Trainer Burley Parke sent Noor out to win six U.S. stakes including his career finale, the 1950 Hollywood Park Gold Cup. Noor set a 1¹/4-mile track record in that race, too. Altogether, Noor set world, North American, or track records in six of his final 10 career starts. John Longden was the jockey aboard each time.

Record breaker: Irish-bred Noor, who defeated Citation four times, set a pair of world records in the process.

O

OH SO SHARP

◆ ch f
◆ **Foaled: 1982, by Kris out of Oh So Fair (Graustark)**

Oh So Sharp became the first classic winner for her owner-breeder Sheikh Mohammed al-Maktoum when she came out best in a double short-head finish to the 1985 1,000 Guineas. It extended her unbeaten run to five races and she went on to win the English Oaks by six lengths from the Irish 2,000 Guineas winner Triptych. Her first two defeats then followed, initially when she was beaten a neck by Petoski in the King George VI And Queen Elizabeth Stakes, and then when she found the 1984 St. Leger winner, Commanche Run, too strong in the Benson & Hedges Gold Cup at York. However, she ended her racing days with a hard-won defeat of Phardante in the St. Leger to complete the fillies' version of the Triple Crown. None of her progeny have been anywhere near as successful on the track as she was, but she has produced winners in Rosefinch, who won the Prix Saint-Alary, Shaima, Sacho and Felitza.

OMAHA

◆ ch c
◆ Foaled: 1932, by Gallant Fox out of Flambino (Wrack)

The only Triple Crown winner whose sire also swept North America's classics, Omaha won just once in nine starts at age two. At three, he registered his initial career stakes triumph in the Kentucky Derby, followed that with an easy win in the Preakness, and, after a hard-closing second in the Withers, scored a 1¹/₂-length triumph in the Belmont Stakes. A homebred representing William Woodward's Belair Stud Stable, Omaha was trained for his North American campaigns by James "Sunny Jim" Fitzsimmons. At age four, the chestnut colt was sent to England, where Cecil Boyd-Rochfort handled conditioning chores. Omaha won the 1936 Victor Wild Stakes and the Queen's Plate at Kempton. Subsequently, he recorded close second-place finishes in Ascot's Gold Cup and Newmarket's Prince of Wales Stakes. Seven jockeys rode Omaha during his three seasons racing, with William "Smokey" Saunders partnering him to the Triple Crown. Curiously, Omaha was Saunders' only Kentucky Derby ride.

P

PAN ZARETA

◆ ch f
◆ Foaled: 1910, by Abe Frank out of Caddie Griffith (Rancocas)

A great sprinter of the early 20th century, Pan Zareta had a career record of 151 starts, 76 wins and earnings of $39,082. Her five-furlong world time record at Juarez in 1915 stood for 36 years. Campaigning in Mexico, Canada, and at various United States tracks from New York to Salt Lake City, the chestnut distaffer won under imposts as high as 146 pounds (10st 6lb). Early on, Pan Zareta was four times triumphant in claiming company. Unusually quick as a filly, downright formidable as a mare, she did most of her running in overnight handicaps. Pan Zareta also registered six stakes scores. She campaigned during an era when purses were spartan. A competitor of her ability would earn millions of

dollars today. Pan Zareta had four trainers, a quartet of owners, and was ridden by more than 30 jockeys. She died of pneumonia in the winter of 1918, and is buried under the grass course at the Fair Grounds race track in New Orleans.

PAPPA FOURWAY

◆ b c
◆ Foaled: 1952, by Pappageno II out of Oola Hills (Denturius)

Pappa Fourway was one of two very smart British sprinters trained in the 1950s by Bill Dutton – Right Boy was the other. The former's performances were all the more meritorious, because so little had been expected of him as a yearling that he had changed hands at that stage for less than £200. Pappa Fourway won four times from seven starts as a two-year-old, but his brilliance really came to the fore in his second season when he was unbeaten in eight attempts, starting in May and going on to

November. His biggest successes came in the July Cup, the King's Stand Stakes, Diadem Stakes and the Gosforth Park Cup. He carried 9st 7lb (133 pounds) or 9st 6lb in the three handicaps which he won. Pappa Fourway had won 12 races worth £9,889 when he was exported to America in 1956.

PARK TOP

◆ b f
◆ Foaled: 1964, by Kalydon out of Nellie Park (Arctic Prince)

Park Top had an unfashionable pedigree, cost only 500gns as a yearling and did not run as a two-year-old. Her grand-dam Oola Hills was the dam of Pappa Fourway, but unlike him Park Top was at her best over middle distances, as she showed when gaining her first important success in the Ribblesdale Stakes at Ascot in 1967. She won the Brighton Cup (then a good handicap) that year and as a four-year-old, when she also took the Prix d'Hedouville at

Hard and fast: The fleet racemare Pan Zareta made 151 career starts and won an incredible 76 times.

Longchamp. But it was as a five-year-old that she really shone. A victory at Longchamp in May was followed by success in the Coronation Cup, Hardwicke Stakes and King George VI And Queen Elizabeth Stakes. She was beaten in controversial circumstances in the Prix de l'Arc de Triomphe and Eclipse Stakes, when many felt that her jockeys had not shone. Park Top went on racing at age six, when she won twice more, bringing her career tally to 13 races worth £136,440. Her record as a broodmare was very disappointing and her few foals had shown minimal talent before she was retired in 1979.

PEBBLES

◆ ch f
◆ **Foaled: 1981, by Sharpen Up out of La Dolce (Connaught)**

Pebbles became the first English-trained winner of a Breeders' Cup race when she won the Breeders' Cup Turf at Aqueduct, New York, in 1985. She had already proved to be one of the best fillies of her time. She originally raced for Captain Marcos Lemos, for whom she won the 1984 1,000 Guineas. Later that year, however, she was sold to Sheikh Mohammed al-Maktoum, though she was still trained by Clive Brittain. Her first big win for her new owner was in the 1985 Eclipse Stakes, and she went on to take the Champion Stakes before her Breeders' Cup triumph. Her only defeat in that final season was when she was beaten by Bob Back in an extraordinary race for the Prince of Wales's Stakes at Ascot. Unfortunately, like so many top-class racemares, Pebbles proved to be far less successful at stud.

PEINTRE CELEBRE

◆ ch c
◆ **Foaled: 1994, by Nureyev out of Peinture Bleue (Alydar)**

With a better run in one of his races, Peintre Celebre would have carried all before him in 1997; as it was he ended the year with a brilliant future after claiming victory in four of his five starts. That culminated in a superb display in the Prix de l'Arc de Triomphe, which he won by five lengths. Peintre Celebre won one of two starts in his two-year-old season and began his second year with a two-lengths victory in the Prix Greffulhe before he went on to triumph in the Prix du Jockey Club by two lengths from Oscar in what was, surprisingly, a first success in that race for his owner Daniel Wildenstein and trainer André Fabre. There then followed success in the Grand Prix de Paris before his somewhat controversial defeat in the Prix Niel after a clear run came all too late. That misfortune was forgotten, however, when he toyed with his rivals in the Arc and won by five lengths from Pilsudski. The plan was for him to run again at the age of four but injury put paid to that idea and he was retired to stud at Coolmore.

PENDIL

◆ b g
◆ **Foaled: 1965, by Pendragon out of Diliska (Distinctive)**

The description "the best horse never to win a Gold Cup" has been applied to many chasers and one who certainly qualifies for it is Pendil. He was beaten a short head by The Dikler in 1973 and brought down at the third last 12 months later, having started at odds-on each time. Pendil, who was trained for most of his career by Fred Winter, was one of the most brilliant jumpers of fences and won 21 chases and six times over hurdles. His best victories came in the Arkle Chase at Cheltenham in 1972, the Massey-Ferguson Gold Cup the following year and the King George VI Chase at Kempton in those two years. He broke down in 1975 and though he came back to triumph in three more races, another injury forced him into retirement. He lived on a farm in Wiltshire until he had to be put down in 1995, but the photograph of him standing many yards off a fence at Kempton and soaring over it is a memory of his talent.

Rolling stone: Pebbles (ridden by a happy Philip Robinson) leaves the 1984 1,000 Guineas field trailing in her wake.

PERSIAN WAR

◆ b g
◆ **Foaled: 1963, by Persian Gulf out of Warning (Chanteur II)**

Persian War was the third horse, following Hatton's Grace and Sir Ken, to win the Champion Hurdle three years in a row which he did from 1968–70. There were a number of truly top-class hurdlers in the 1960s and 1970s and he was one of them. Having shown respectable form on the flat, Persian War won 18 times over hurdles during a career which brought him a number of trainers due to the volatile temperament of his owner Henry Alper. At various stages Tom Masson, Brian Swift, Colin Davies, Arthur Pitt, Dennis Rayson and Jack Gibson were in charge of him. It was Davies who trained him during the glory days when he won his three Champion Hurdles, as well as the Schweppes Gold Trophy and the Triumph Hurdle, invariably ridden at that stage by Jimmy Uttley. Sadly, his owner insisted on him racing for far too long after he should have retired.

PERSONAL ENSIGN

◆ b f
◆ **Foaled: 1984, by Private Account out of Grecian Banner (Hoist the Flag)**

In a most dramatic fashion, Personal Ensign kept her record unblemished with a come-from-behind, nose victory in her final career start, the 1988 Breeders' Cup Distaff at Churchill Downs. This gave the American filly 13 wins in as many tries – perfection. It was also Personal Ensign's tenth career stakes triumph, seven of which came in Grade 1 events. Flawless against the best in her division, she also whipped male horses in Saratoga's 1988 Whitney Handicap. An Ogden Phipps homebred, Personal Ensign was trained by Claude "Shug" McGaughey III, and ridden in all but one of her efforts by Randy Romero. Carefully spotted and a touch fragile, Personal Ensign averaged barely more than four starts per campaign. Twice she beat Winning Colors, who in 1988 had become only the third filly to win the Kentucky Derby. Personal Ensign was North America's champion handicap mare for 1988. She remains one of only a handful of competitors who competed at the top, yet never lost a race.

PETER PAN

◆ ch c
◆ **Foaled: 1929, by Pantheron out of Alwina (St. Alwyn)**

A rangy chestnut, with a silver mane and tail,

Peter Pan proved himself to be one of Australia's greatest stayers with 23 wins from 39 starts. Trained by Frank McGrath he was unplaced in his only two-year-old appearance, but won nine of his 11 races at three, including the A.J.C. Derby, the Melbourne Cup and the A.J.C. St. Leger. His four-year-old campaign was restricted when he was troubled by muscular rheumatism, which caused him to miss the 1933 Melbourne Cup, in which he was scheduled to shoulder the top weight of 9st 7lb. He recovered and was prepared for the Melbourne Cup the following year in which he was saddled with 9st 10lb. Peter Pan won the weight-for-age Melbourne Stakes, over 10 furlongs, three days before the Cup but his chances seemed doomed when Flemington Park was saturated by heavy rain. His jockey Darby Munro decided to race wide in the Cup, where the going was firmer. After reaching the lead about two furlongs from home he went on to win comfortably by three lengths. Only three other horses – Archer (1861–62), Rain Lover (1968–69) and Think Big (1974–75) – have been able to win the Melbourne Cup on two occasions. Peter Pan was asked to carry 10st 6lb in the 1935 Melbourne Cup but found the task beyond him.

PETITE ETOILE

- gr f
- Foaled: 1956, by Petition out of Star of Iran (Bois Roussel)

Petite Etoile was a filly of the highest quality, but her success would hardly have been anticipated by those who saw her in her first race as a two-year-old when she was beaten by eight lengths in a two-horse race. After that, though, she never looked back and Petite Etioile claimed the honours in the Free Handicap on her first appearance at three, before taking the 1,000 Guineas. Not everyone was sure she would stay the 1½ miles of Epsom's Oaks but she did so without problem and went on to triumph in the Sussex Stakes, Yorkshire Oaks and Champion Stakes. In 1960 she easily beat the 1959 Derby winner, Parthia, before losing the King George VI And Queen Elizabeth Stakes to Aggressor in what has long been regarded as a race in which other jockeys combined to make things difficult for Lester Piggott. As a five-year-old Petite Etoile claimed a second Coronation Cup and was also victorious in three other races. She retired as the winner of 14 races worth £72,626. However, in subsequent years, her career as a broodmare was nothing short of disastrous.

As pleased as punch: Walter Swinburn waves his stick with joy as Pilsudski wins the 1996 Breeders' Cup Turf at Woodbine.

PILSUDSKI

- b c
- Foaled: 1992, by Polish Precedent out of Cocotte (Troy)

Pilsudski was one of those admirable horses who never ran a bad race and the longer he continued racing the better he seemed to get. As a three-year-old he was no more than a good handicapper, though clearly one improving all the time, and when he moved into Pattern company at four he continued his upward march. His first win at black-type level came in the Brigadier Gerard Stakes at Sandown and later in the year he won the Royal Whip at the Curragh, the Grosser Preis von Baden Baden and the Breeders' Cup Turf at Woodbine in Toronto. He was also runner-up to Helissio in the Prix de l'Arc de Triomphe. There was more of the same when he was five with wins in the Eclipse Stakes and Champion Stakes (both the Leopardstown and Newmarket versions). He was again second in the Arc, this time to Peintre Celebre, before ending his career with victory in the Japan Cup. He is now at stud in that country having been bought for a reported $20million.

PINZA

- b c
- Foaled: 1950, by Chanteur II out of Pasqua (Donatello II)

If Pinza's soundness had matched his ability there is no saying what he might have achieved. His talent is well illustrated by the fact that when he won the Derby he beat Aureole by four lengths and Aureole went on to prove himself one of the top horses in Europe the following

year, by which time injury had forced Pinza into retirement. He was an especially popular Derby winner, not only because he was one of the most fancied contenders, but also because he enabled the recently knighted Gordon Richards finally to win the race after 27 previous failures. As well as the Derby, Pinza also won the King George VI And Queen Elizabeth Stakes, again beating Aureole, and the Newmarket Stakes. However, he failed to live up to the hopes held out for him as a stallion. His best winner was Pindari, who won the King Edward VII Stakes, Great Voltigeur Stakes and Craven Stakes, and maybe Pinturischio would have lived up to high expectations had he not been nobbled.

PRETTY POLLY

- ch f
- Foaled: 1901, by Gallinule out of Admiration (Saraband)

Pretty Polly won her first race by ten lengths and never looked back, establishing herself as one of the very best fillies ever to have raced in Britain. At the time of her retirement, she had won 22 of her 24 starts and collected more than £37,000 in prize money. She won eight more races in her first season and as a three-year-old won the fillies' Triple Crown as well as the Coronation Stakes, Nassau Stakes and Park Hill Stakes before being beaten by the outsider Presto II in testing conditions in the Prix du Conseil Municipal at Longchamp. She won four more times at four, including the Coronation Cup and Champion Stakes and took the Coronation Cup again in her final season before being beaten in the Gold Cup at Ascot on her final appearance. She was not a great success at stud but two of her fillies, Molly

Desmond and Polly Flinders, won good races and she is ancestress of top horses like Brigadier Gerard and Supreme Court.

PRINCE PALATINE

◆ b c
◆ Foaled: 1908, by Persimmon out of Lady Lightfoot (Isinglass)

Prince Palatine was one of those horses who illustrated the point that being able to win over long distances, as he frequently did, was no bar to success over shorter trips. Having won over six furlongs as a two-year-old, he went on to take the Eclipse Stakes as a four-year-old to add to his wins in the major British staying races. These included two wins in the Gold Cup at Ascot, as well as the St. Leger, the Doncaster Cup, Coronation Cup and Jockey Club Stakes. As a result of these successes, Jack Joel bought the horse for £45,000 – a very considerable sum for the time – on condition Prince Palatine won the Goodwood Cup, reduced to £40,000 if he failed. As Prince Palatine had been suffering very badly from foot trouble, he didn't win. His stud career was not much of an improvement as he stood in England, France and the USA before being burned to death in 1924. Prince Palatine sired only the Cesarewitch Handicap and Queen Alexandra Stakes winner Rose Prince of any consequence.

Q

QUASHED

◆ b f
◆ Foaled: 1932, by Obliterate out of Verdict (Shogun)

For many years the Verdict family was not accepted into the British Stud Book because Quashed's dam was effectively a half-bred and it was not until the 1960s era of the July Cup winner Lucasland that the family's merit persuaded the authorities to review their opinion about its eligibility. But though Quashed may not have been granted a presence in the GSB, she could not be prevented from racing and by the time she retired at the end of 1937 she had won ten races worth £18,997. Chief among these was the Gold Cup at Ascot in 1936, when she beat the American horse Omaha by a short head after a tremendous battle, but she also won the Oaks – having started at 33–1 – the Ormonde Stakes and Jockey Club Cup. Her record at stud was one of total failure.

R

RAGUSA

◆ b c
◆ Foaled: 1960, by Ribot out of Fantan II (Ambiorix II)

So small and weedy was Ragusa when he first went into training with Irishman Paddy Prendergast that he was called "the Ribot rat", but in spite of his lack of inches in his younger days, when Prendergast paid a modest 3,800 guineas for him, he went on to prove himself a formidable racehorse. His first sign of real merit came when he finished third behind Relko in the Derby and then, when Relko was withdrawn at the start of the Irish Derby, Ragusa won that classic and followed up by taking the honours in the King George VI And Queen Elizabeth Stakes by four lengths and the St. Leger by six. His final triumph came in the following season's Eclipse Stakes and before he died in 1973 he had sired the Derby winner Morston, Ballymore, who claimed the Irish 2,000 Guineas, the Ascot Gold Cup hero Ragstone and Caliban, who beat Park Top in the Coronation Cup.

RAINBOW QUEST

◆ b c
◆ Foaled: 1981, by Blushing Groom out of I Will Follow (Herbager)

Prince Khalid Abdullah has owned an impressive number of top-class horses since he first became involved in racing in Britain in the 1970s, but very few have done better for him than Rainbow Quest, who followed a top-class racing career by going on to become an extremely successful sire. Rainbow Quest's biggest victory came when he was awarded the 1985 Prix de l'Arc de Triomphe on the disqualification Sagace who had passed the post in first place, but he also claimed the Coronation Cup and the Great Voltigeur Stakes, as well as being placed in the King George VI And Queen Elizabeth Stakes, Irish Derby, Eclipse Stakes, and Prix du Jockey Club. At stud he has done even better, siring a Derby winner in Quest For Fame, a Prix de l'Arc de Triomphe winner in Saumarez, Spectrum, who claimed the Irish Guineas and Champion Stakes (whose first crop, in turn, made a very bright start in 2000), the St. Leger winner Nedawi, Sunshack, a Coronation Cup winner, and the Prix Lupin winner Croco Rouge.

REFERENCE POINT

◆ b c
◆ Foaled 1984, by Mill Reef out of Home On The Range (Habitat)

Reference Point gave English trainer Henry Cecil and U.S.-born jockey Steve Cauthen their second Derby win in three years when he led just about from start to finish, a fitting reward after the serious sinus operation which had held up his work in the spring. As a two-year-old, he had ended his first season with a runaway success in the Racing Post Trophy at Doncaster. After the Derby, he was just outpaced by Mtoto over the shorter distance of the Eclipse Stakes, but he then made all the running in the King George VI And Queen Elizabeth Stakes to win by three lengths, and then added the Great Voltigeur Stakes before getting the better of Mountain Kingdom in the St. Leger. Reference Point's career ended on a low note with a poor display in the Prix de l'Arc de Triomphe, for which an abcess was probably responsible. He was retired to stud in 1988, but stood for only a very short time before having to be put down after he broke a leg at Dalham Hall in 1991.

RIGHT BOY

◆ gr c
◆ Foaled: 1954, by Impeccable out of Happy Ogan (Ballyogan)

Right Boy, who cost only 575gns as a yearling, was the second top sprinter of the 1950s to be trained in Yorkshire by Bill Dutton – the first was Pappa Fourway, who cost even less, and when Dutton died in 1958 the horse was taken over by his late trainer's son-in-law Pat Rohan. Perhaps rather surprisingly, his early career was of no particular significance, but he certainly made his mark later on with 16 wins including the Nunthorpe Stakes (twice), and the July Cup, King George Stakes and Cork And Orrery Stakes, as well as the King's Stand Stakes. At stud he fell a long way below expectations and the only decent winners he produced by the time he was put down in 1977 were Reet Lass, who won the Molecomb Stakes at Goodwood, and Village Boy, who landed the Richmond Stakes at the same course.

RISING FAST

◆ b c
◆ Foaled: 1949, by Alonzo out of Faster (Mr. Standfast)

A fast-running stayer who needed time to

mature, Rising Fast had seven wins from 23 starts in New Zealand before his training was taken over in Australia by Ivan Tucker in April 1954. He suddenly emerged as a performer of the highest class as a five-year-old. After winning the Turnbull Stakes, over 10 furlongs at Flemington, and the Caulfield Stakes at the same trip, he comfortably took the Caulfield Cup, over 12 furlongs, carrying 8st 10lb in the spring of 1954. A week later he won the weight-for-age W.S.Cox Plate, over 10 furlongs at Moonee Valley. Ten days after his Cox Plate triumph, Rising Fast carried 9st 5lb to victory in the Melbourne Cup, over two miles, to become the only horse to have won those three premier races in the one year. With Tucker suspended by New Zealand racing authorities, Rising Fast was transferred to leading Melbourne trainer Fred Hoysted. Under Hoysted's care Rising Fast carried 9st 10lb to a comprehensive three lengths victory in the 1955 Caulfield Cup. Sent out a 2–1 favourite in the Melbourne Cup – despite being burdened with 10st – he just failed to complete the Cups double again when he was beaten by Toparoa, who was in receipt of 34 pounds.

ROBERTO

- ◆ b c
- ◆ **Foaled: 1969, by Hail To Reason out of Bramalea (Nashua)**

Roberto's career was one of extraordinary contrasts, with its highlight coming in the inaugural running of the Benson & Hedges Gold Cup at York in 1972, when he became the only

horse ever to beat Brigadier Gerard. The crack American rider Braulio Baeza sent Roberto flying out of the stalls and they led all the way, setting a track record in the process. Prior to that, he had responded with great courage to one of Lester Piggott's most powerful finishes to win the Derby at Epsom by a short head from Rheingold. Between the successes at Epsom and York, Roberto produced an abysmal effort in the Irish Derby at the Curragh. Before he was retired to stud, he enjoyed further success at the Epsom Derby meeting by winning the Coronation Cup. He was a great success at stud with his best winners including Touching Wood, Celestial Storm, the top Canadian horse of his era Driving Home, At Talaq, Robellino (who got the 2,000 Guineas winner Mister Baileys) and Silver Hawk (sire of Derby winner Benny The Dip). He died in 1988.

ROCK OF GIBRALTAR

- ◆ b c
- ◆ **Foaled: 1999, by Danehill out of Offshore Boom (Be My Guest)**

Winning five Group 1 races at five different racecourses during a period of less than five months constitutes a stunning achievement. That's what Rock Of Gibraltar accomplished during his three-year-old campaign in 2002. In chronological order, they were the English 2000 Guineas at Newmarket, the Irish 2000 Guineas at The Curragh, the St. James Palace Stakes at Ascot, the Sussex Stakes at Goodwood and the Prix du Moulin de Longchamp. Couple these with Rock Of Gibraltar's victories at age two in the Grand Criterium at Longchamp and the Dewhurst Stakes

at Newmarket - both achieved within a 13-day period - and there stands a competitor who registered a record seven consecutive Group 1 wins. Overall, Rock of Gibraltar's career statistics included 13 starts, ten victories, two placings and earnings of $2.03 million. Bred by Joe Crowley in partnership with Aidan and Anne-Marie O'Brien, trained by Aidan O'Brien and co-owned by Manchester United manager Sir Alex Ferguson and Susan Magnier, Rock of Gibraltar scored most of his major victories under jockey Mick Kinane. Following his 2002 campaign, Rock of Gibraltar was retired to Coolmore Stud in Ireland.

ROCK SAND

- ◆ br c
- ◆ **Foaled: 1900, by Sainfoin out of Roquebrune (St Simon)**

Rock Sand may neither have been good enough to beat his seniors, 1902 Epsom Derby and Oaks winners Ard Patrick and Sceptre, respectively, when they met in the 1903 Eclipse Stakes, nor to hold Sceptre when they met again in the Jockey Club Stakes later that year, but he was still good enough to pull off the 1903 Triple Crown. He won five times in six starts as a two-year-old, culminating in the Dewhurst Stakes and, having won the 2,000 Guineas the following spring he started at 6–4 for the Derby and won by two lengths from Vinicius. Later that year he won the St. James's Palace Stakes at Ascot and completed his Triple Crown by landing the odds of 5–2 in the St. Leger. His four-year-old wins included the Hardwicke Stakes, Jockey Club Stakes and Princess of Wales's Stakes. At stud he sired the St. Leger and Eclipse winner Tracery and Mahubah, who went on to breed the star U.S. horse Man o' War. He stood in England and America but was based in France when he died in 1914.

ROOSTER BOOSTER

- ◆ gr g
- ◆ **Foaled: 1994, by Riverwise out of Came Cottage (Nearly A Hand)**

Winner of the Champion Hurdle at Cheltenham Racecourse in 2003, and a close runner-up in the same race the following year, Rooster Booster remains one of the most popular steeplechasers in the annals of racing in the British Isles. Owned by Terry Warner and trained by Philip Hobbs, Rooster Booster made 46 career starts, winning ten of them and finishing in second position 14 times, while amassing earnings of £687,541. His

All the way: Steve Cauthen on Reference Point (16) led almost from the start to win the 1987 Derby at Epsom.

Masterstroke: 54-year-old Lester Piggott (white cap) drives Royal Acadamy past Itsallgreektome (6) to win the Breeders' Cup Mile at Belmont Park in 1990.

regular riding partner was Richard Johnson, who guided Rooster Booster to seven of his victories, the Champion Hurdle among them. Rooster Booster's initial major triumph came in the County Hurdle at the Cheltenham Festival in 2002. In 2003, Rooster Booster exploded into the public spotlight - he registered five wins, including one in the Bula Hurdle, which were followed by his Champion Hurdle effort. The following season, Rooster Booster won the Champion Hurdle Trial at Haydock. His effort for a repeat Champion Hurdle victory was short by just a nose. In late 2005, while preparing to compete in the Stan James Christmas Hurdle at Sandown, Rooster Booster collapsed and died of a suspected heart attack.

ROYAL ACADEMY

- ◆ b c
- ◆ Foaled: 1987, by Nijinsky out of Crimson Saint (Crimson Satan)

In view of the fact that he cost $3.5million as a yearling, Royal Academy had an awful lot to live up to on the racecourse. With his victories in two Group 1 races, over six furlongs and a mile, he achieved the sort of things which were expected of him. His success over the longer trip came in the 1990 Breeders' Cup Mile at Belmont Park, New York, when he got up near the line to complete the amazing return to the saddle by Lester Piggott, who was thus linking up once more with Irishman Vincent O'Brien. Royal Academy also won the July Cup and was runner-up to Dayjur in the Ladbroke Sprint Cup at Haydock. He has sired

a lot of winners since retiring to stud, first in Ireland and then in Kentucky. Among the best of his progeny are Ali-Royal, Sleepytime, Oscar Schindler, Bolshoi and Lavery.

ROYAL PALACE

- ◆ b c
- ◆ Foaled: 1964, by Ballymoss out of Crystal Palace (Solar Slipper)

Royal Palace's wins in the 1967 2,000 Guineas and the Derby were the highlights of the year when top Australian jockey George Moore rode as stable jockey to Noel Murless at Newmarket. He just pipped Taj Dewan at Newmarket but was then far too good for his Epsom rivals. He ran only once more at age three, but came back in style the next year, winning the Eclipse Stakes in a superb battle with Taj Dewan and Sir Ivor (who, like Royal Palace had recorded the 2,000 Guineas and Derby double) and then, in spite of sustaining the injury which prematurely ended his racing career, taking the King George VI And Queen Elizabeth Stakes. His career at stud was not quite on a par with his exceptional racing level, but he did sire the Oaks and St. Leger heroine Dunfermline and other good fillies in Royal Hive and Escorial, and he also got the triple Champion Hurdle winner See You Then. He was put down at the National Stud at the age of 27.

RUFFIAN

- ◆ db f
- ◆ Foaled: 1972, by Reviewer out of Shenanigans (Native Dancer)

Arguments are made that Ruffian was the greatest filly in North America's racing history. Undefeated, and barely challenged in her first 10 starts, she broke down during a $350,000 match race against that year's Kentucky Derby winner, Foolish Pleasure, on 6 July 1975, at Belmont Park. The following day, Ruffian was euthanized, her remains buried in Belmont's infield. Bred and owned by the Locust Hill Farm of Mr. and Mrs. Stuart S. Janney Jr., Ruffian was trained by Frank Y. Whiteley Jr., and ridden in all but two of her career starts by Jacinto Vasquez. Ruffian broke her maiden by 15 lengths. At age two, she won four stakes and was champion of her division. In 1975, Ruffian was North America's three-year-old filly champ, as she won four stakes including New York's Triple Tiara – the Beldame, Mother Goose, and Coaching Club American Oaks. Then came the match race, crack filly against crack colt, and a tragic end to a splendid story.

S

SADLER'S WELLS

- ◆ b c
- ◆ Foaled: 1981, by Northern Dancer out of Fairy Bridge (Bold Reason)

Sadler's Wells was a very good racehorse, as he showed when winning the Eclipse Stakes, Irish Guineas and Irish Champion Stakes, as well as being placed in the Prix du Jockey Club and the King George VI And Queen Elizabeth Stakes. However, it is as a sire that he has really made his mark. Since he was retired to stud in 1985, at Coolmore, he has sired top winner after top winner. Montjeu, Barathea, Salsabil, Kayf Tara, Dream Well, King Of Kings, Entrepreneur and Ebadiyla are just a few among his top-level winners. Sadler's Wells is the most in-demand stallion in the world. His fee is not published but it is reported to be Ir200,000gns and he regularly covers about 200 mares a season. He was champion sire in the British Isles for the tenth time in 2000 when one of his yearlings was sold for a European record of 3.4million gns and his tally of 44 individual Group 1 winners equals the world record set by Sir Tristram.

SAGARO

◆ ch c
◆ **Foaled: 1971, by Espresso out of Zambara (Mossborough)**

There was a time when the brown and white colours of Gerry Oldham and his Citadel Stud were regularly to be seen in big races, almost all on horses which he had bred, first when they were trained by Harry Wragg and then by François Boutin. There were some good ones, too, and among the best was Sagaro, who became the first horse to win the Gold Cup at Ascot three times when he triumphed in 1975, 1976 and 1977. He also won the Prix du Cadran and the Grand Prix de Paris. After his third Gold Cup win he was bought by the National Stud for £175,000 but the fact that he stayed long distances damned him as far as breeders were concerned and he moved about a good deal in his short time at stud. He died of a heart attack in 1986, leaving Super Sunrise and Sagamore among his best winners.

SAKHEE

◆ b c
◆ **Foaled: 1997, by Bahri out of Thawakib (Sadler's Wells)**

Sakhee made just14 starts during his four racing campaigns, but he won eight of them, placed in four others and achieved £2.21 million in earnings. At age four he was Europe's champion older horse, winning the Juddmonte International Stakes at York by seven lengths and registering an equally annihilating triumph by six lengths in the Prix de l'Arc de Triomphe at Longchamp. The only blemish on Sakhee's record that season was a second-place finish in the Breeders' Cup Classic, a race which he lost by a nose to Tiznow - it was Sakhee's first career effort on a dirt surface. Bred

by the Maktoum family under their Shadwell Farm name and campaigned by the Maktoums' Godolphin stable, Sakhee registered his maiden victory at the second time of asking at England's Nottingham course. Trained by Saeed bin Suroor, he was ridden during his four-year-old campaign by Frankie Dettori - Sakhee's Arc win was also Dettori's 100th Group 1 triumph. At the culmination of his five-year-old season, Sakhee was sent to the Maktoums' Shadwell Estate subsidiary, Nunnery Stud, in Norfolk, England.

SALSABIL

◆ b f
◆ **Foaled: 1987, by Sadler's Wells out of Flame of Tara (Artaius)**

Salsabil was an oustanding filly, more than capable of holding her own against her male contemporaries, as she showed when winning the 1990 Irish Derby. Her owner, Sheikh Hamdan al-Maktoum, had to pay a supplementary entry fee of £60,000 for her to take part, but she rewarded him by beating Deploy by 3/4 length. Before that Salsabil had won the Oaks at Epsom – disproving any doubts held by her trainer John Dunlop regarding her stamina – by five lengths, and the 1,000 Guineas and Prix Marcel Boussac. She went on to take the Prix Vermeille before running the only bad race of her career in the Prix de l'Arc de Triomphe, when connections felt that she had done enough for the season. Sadly, she died after only six seasons at stud, from cancer of the colon. By far the best of her foals on the racecourse was the Nashwan filly Bint Salsabil, who won four races including the Rockfel and Sweet Solera Stakes.

SCEPTRE

◆ b f
◆ **Foaled: 1899, by Persimmon out of Ornament (Bend Or)**

Sceptre was not only an outstandingly good filly, she was also an extremly tough one. Her British owner Robert Sievier, who bought her for 10,000gns and trained her for much of her career, was in almost constant need of funds and betting on Sceptre was one way to keep himself afloat. She won twice at two and, staggeringly by modern standards, began her three-year-old life in the Lincoln. She was second in that, then won both the 1,000 and 2,000 Guineas, finished fourth in the Derby, won the Oaks two days later, then had two losing races before winning the St. James's Palace Stakes. Sceptre lost the Sussex Stakes but won the Nassau and won her fourth classic, the St. Leger. In early 1903 Sievier sold her for £25,000. Sceptre won the Jockey Club Stakes and Champion Stakes and ended with 13 victories to

her name. She died in 1926 and although none of her foals were anywhere near as good as she was, her bloodline could be found in classic winners Relko, April The Fifth and Craig An Eran.

SEA-BIRD II

◆ ch g
◆ **Foaled: 1962, by Dan Cupid out of Sicalade (Sicambre)**

The Prix de l'Arc de Triomphe has historically been one of the defining horse races in the world. Sea-Bird II's six-length victory under jockey Pat Glennon in the 1965 edition of the Arc remains one of the greatest performances ever witnessed on the international turf. Sea-Bird II's racing career encompassed just two campaigns, during which he made eight starts and won seven of them, while finishing second in his only defeat. At age two, he won the Criterium de Maison-Laffite and the Prix de Blaison at Chantilly, and placed in the Grand Criterium (in his only career effort when Glennon wasn't aboard). At age three, Sea-Bird II was undefeated in five starts – in addition to his Arc victory, he was a 2½-length winner of the Derby at Epsom (in his only career start outside of France). A homebred who campaigned for Jean Ternynck, Sea-Bird II was trained by Etienne Pollet. Standing at John W. Galbreath's Darby Dan Farm in Kentucky, Sea-Bird II sired the 1974 Arc winner, Allez France. Sea-Bird II returned to France to do stud duty at Paul Chedeville's Haras du Petit Tellier near Argentan in 1973, but the breeding season had barely started when he died on March 15 from an intestinal blockage.

SEA PIGEON

◆ b g
◆ **Foaled: 1970, by Sea-Bird II out of Around The Roses (Round Table)**

Sea Pigeon was one of the most oustandingly versatile horses of his or any other generation. Though he began life with high expectations in the classics, it was as a jumper that he hit the real highspots, though he proved well capable of showing top-class handicap form on the flat. He made his mark as a hurdler virtually from the moment he started jumping and finally landed the Champion Hurdle he had long promised to win when he beat Monksfield by seven lengths in 1980. He returned to Cheltenham the following year and won the Champion Hurdle for the second time. His best flat successes came in the Chester Cup, which he won twice, and the Ebor Handicap. He retired in 1982 after having won 21 of 40 starts over hurdles for £130,395 and 16 of 45 flat ventures with earnings from them of £96,985, and lived happily on a farm in Yorkshire until he died in October 2000.

SEATTLE SLEW

- ◆ db c
- ◆ **Foaled: 1974, by Bold Reasoning out of My Charmer (Poker)**

Unbeaten as a juvenile, Seattle Slew swept the 1977 Kentucky Derby, Preakness, and Belmont Stakes, stretching his career-opening win streak to nine. He also won five of his final seven career outings. When he defeated Affirmed in the 1978 Marlboro Cup Handicap at Belmont Park, Seattle Slew became the only North American Triple Crown winner to defeat a horse who had also swept the classics. Seattle Slew was a $17,500 yearling purchase by the partnership of Mickey and Karen Taylor, and James Hill, DVM. The dark bay colt was trained by William Turner Jr. and ridden by Jean Cruguet through the Triple Crown. Following a fourth-place effort in the 1977 Swaps Stakes at Hollywood Park, Turner was replaced by Douglas Peterson. For his final four career outings in 1978, two of which were Grade 1 victories, Angel Cordero Jr. was aboard. Champion male juvenile in 1976, Seattle Slew was champion three-year-old and Horse of the Year in 1977, and champion handicap horse in 1978.

SEE YOU THEN

- ◆ br g
- ◆ **Foaled:, 1980, by Royal Palace out of Melodina (Tudor Melody)**

Although his pedigree was entirely one of flat racing – his sire was a dual classic winner – and he won four flat races in Ireland, it was over hurdles that See You Then made his name. He was the outstanding horse in that sphere in the mid-1980s, winning three Champion Hurdles in a row, 1985–87. He won his first two titles by seven lengths, but had to work much harder for the third, when he was all out to beat the U.S. horse Flatterer by 1½ lengths. This he achieved despite increasing problems of unsoundness and by the time of his third success at Cheltenham he was having to be restricted to just three or even two outings in a season. Not only did his injuries become more common, they also took longer and longer to heal, which resulted in his appearances on the racecourse diminishing year by year. Attempts to re-kindle his top-level form in later years were finally abandoned when he retired during the 1989–90 season.

SHARPO

- ◆ ch c
- ◆ **Foaled: 1977, by Sharpen Up out of Moiety Bird (Falcon)**

Sharpo was the champion British sprinter of 1981. He won seven races and more than £230,000 in prize money during a career which was restricted by his marked preference for soft ground. He developed a particular liking for York, winning the William Hill Sprint Championship – then known as the Nunthorpe Stakes – three times from 1980, becoming the first to do so since Tag End in the 1920s. He also won the July Cup at Newmarket and the Prix de l'Abbaye de Longchamp, as well as twice being second in the major French sprint. Sharpo went on to become a very successful sire before his death in June 1994, siring the winners of 216 races on the flat worth £1.7million. His best winners were College Chapel (who is now proving to be a successful sire in his own right), Risk Me, Cutting Blade and Lavinia Fontana.

SHERGAR

- ◆ b c
- ◆ **Foaled: 1978, by Great Nephew out of Sharmeen (Val de Loir)**

Shergar was an outstanding racehorse whose 10-length trouncing of Glint Of Gold in 1981's Epsom Derby represents the widest winning margin in the history of the race. There is a story that he was so far ahead of the field at the winning post that the jockey on the runner-up thought he had won! But if Shergar was a sensation in life, he became even more of one in death and the mystery of his disappearance from the Aga Khan's stud in Ireland remains officially unsolved. As well as the Derby, Shergar also won the King George VI And Queen Elizabeth Stakes, the Irish Derby, the Chester Vase and the Sandown Classic Trial. As he was about to start his second season at stud, he was kidnapped by a gang who, it is widely felt, were involved with the IRA and planned to hold the horse to ransom. But no such serious demand ever came to light and Shergar was never seen again. A body found in 2000 and claimed to be his proved not to be so.

SHIROCCO

- ◆ b c
- ◆ **Foaled: 2001, by Monsun out of So Sedulous (The Minstrel)**

During the initial 21 years of the Breeders' Cup, no German-bred runner had ever emerged victorious. But that circumstance changed in 2005 with Shirocco's 1¾-length triumph in the Breeders' Cup Turf at Belmont Park. It was his third career win in Grade 1/Group 1 company. In 2004, Shirocco had been a four-length victor of the Deutsches Derby at Hamburg, and had also registered a photo-finish score in the Gran Premio del Jockey Club at San Siro in Italy. These triumphs gained him honours as the champion male three-year-old in the countries where the wins occurred. Shirocco's Breeders' Cup Turf triumph, however, elevated his status to international stardom. Bred and campaigned by Baron Georg von Ullmann, whose family owns Gestut Schlenderhan, Germany's oldest and most prominent stud farm, Shirocco is trained by Andre Fabre. Jockey Andreas Suborics handled his riding chores at Hamburg and San Siro, and Christophe Soumillon was aboard at Belmont. Shirocco completed his 2005 campaign with career statistics that included nine starts, four wins, four placings and earnings of $2.02 million.

SINNDAR

- ◆ b c
- ◆ **Foaled: 1997, by Grand Lodge out of Sinntara (Lashkari)**

Sinndar was the fourth Derby winner in 20 years for his owner-breeder the Aga Khan, though the first for his trainer John Oxx, who has charge of the owner's horses which are trained in Ireland. He was the oustanding middle distance colt of his generation. Having won both his races as a two-year-old he progressed all through his second season, following his success in the Leopardstown Derby Trial by taking the Derby, in which he wore down Sakhee close home, and then the Irish Derby at the Curragh by no fewer than nine lengths. He won the Prix Niel by eight lengths, and though the Prix de l'Arc de Triomphe was billed as a match between him and the previous year's winner, Montjeu, it was very much one-way trafic with Sinndar beating the filly Egyptband by 1½ lengths, with Montjeu, maybe below par, only fourth. Although there were hopes that he might race in his fourth year, Sinndar was retired to stand at stud for 2001.

SIR BARTON

- ◆ ch c
- ◆ **Foaled: 1916, by Star Shoot out of Lady Sterling (Hanover)**

In 1919, Sir Barton became the first horse to sweep North America's Triple Crown. Winless at age two, he registered his maiden triumph in the Kentucky Derby, then won the Preakness,

European marvels: German-bred Shirocco and French jockey Christophe Soumillon win the 2005 Breeders' Cup Turf race.

Withers, and Belmont Stakes in that order. The whole of Sir Barton's race career included 12 stakes scores. In winning the 1920 Saratoga Handicap, he set a track record for 1¼ miles. That same meet, he won the Merchants & Citizens Handicap, setting a track record for 1³/16 miles. Owned by the Canadian, J.K.L. Ross, and trained by H. Guy Bedwell, Sir Barton campaigned in Man o' War's shadow. The two colts met once, in the Kenilworth Park Gold Cup, a match race, on October 12, 1920. Though a year younger, Man o' War won by seven lengths. Sir Barton was race ridden by nine jockeys. John Loftus guided him through the Triple Crown. During the 1920 season, Earl Sande registered four consecutive stakes scores with Sir Barton, including the aforesaid track records.

SIR IVOR

◆ **b c**

◆ **Foaled: 1965, by Sir Gaylord out of Attica (Mr Trouble)**

Sir Ivor was one of those admirable horses who proved not only top class on the track but also very successful at stud. He was regarded by Lester Piggott as the best horse he ever rode. That was some compliment, especially from a judge not known for effusive praise. Piggott rode him to win the Derby, the Washington DC International, the 2,000 Guineas and the Champion Stakes and two other of the horse's eight wins, as well as to be second in the Prix de l'Arc de Triomphe. Sir Ivor was the first of two English champions to be owned by the American Raymond Guest; in the 1970s he would win the Cheltenham Gold Cup and Grand National with L'Escargot. When he went to stud, first in Ireland and then in Kentucky, where he had to be put down in 1995, Sir Ivor did particularly well as a sire of fillies with Ivanjica, Godetia and Lady Capulet among his best. Good colts he sired included Bates Motel and St Hilarion.

SIR KEN

◆ **b g**

◆ **Foaled: 1947, by Laeken out of Carte Grise, (unknown)**

Sir Ken was a truly outstanding hurdler at a time when such horses were almost the norm rather than the exception. When he completed his hat-trick of Champion Hurdle victories in 1954, it meant that only he and two other horses (Hatton's Grace – the first three-time winner – and National Spirit) had won the race during an eight-year period. In all, Sir Ken won

20 races over hurdles, gaining his first championship in 1952 when he beat Noholme by two lengths. He was invariably ridden by the champion jockey Tim Molony and at one stage won 16 consecutive races. After his third Champion Hurdle victory, he was sent over fences. He began his career over the larger obstacles very promisingly and won the Cotswold Chase at Cheltenham, Liverpool's Mildmay Chase and two other races of similar prestige, but he fell in his final race of the 1955–56 season and was never the same horse again. He retired two years later.

SKIP AWAY

- ◆ r c
- ◆ Foaled: 1993, by Skip Trial out of Ingot Way (Diplomat Way)

A $30,000 auction purchase at age two, Skip Away matured into the second-highest money earner in North American racing history. The roan colt won 16 stakes, including consecutive runnings of the Jockey Club Gold Cup in 1996–97, and the 1997 renewal of the Breeders' Cup Classic at Hollywood Park. In the latter effort, Skip Away scored by six lengths, and registered a stakes record 1:59 for 1¼ miles. Owned by Carolyn H. Hine, and trained by by her husband, Hubert H. "Sonny" Hine, Skip Away won major stakes all across the United States and in Canada as well. Six jockeys rode him, with Shane Sellers and Jerry D. Bailey aboard most frequently. "Skippy", as Carolyn Hine called him, was an odds-on betting choice in six consecutive starts at age five. He won all of them. Champion handicapper in 1997, Skip Away received that honour again in 1998, when he was also Horse of the Year.

SMARTY JONES

- ◆ ch c
- ◆ Foaled: 2001, by Elusive Quality out of I'll Get Along (Smile)

One of the most beloved horses to race in North America in recent decades, Smarty Jones won all eight of his initial career starts, including the 2004 Kentucky Derby and Preakness Stakes. The only blemish on his record came in his career finale, when Birdstone caught and passed him in deep stretch in the Belmont Stakes, depriving Smarty Jones of a Triple Crown sweep. Smarty Jones' career earnings totalled $7.6 million. Although he was by a Kentucky sire, he was officially Pennsylvania-bred, and campaigned for his breeders, Patricia and Roy Chapman, whose nom de course was

Perfect timing: Sinndar (13) and Johnny Murtagh come with a late run to pass Sakhee and win the 2000 Derby.

Someday Farm. Early in his two-year-old season, Smarty Jones suffered multiple skull fractures and a broken left eye socket in a school gate accident, and extensive surgery was needed to save his life. Trained by John Servis, Smarty Jones was ridden throughout his two seasons of racing by Stewart Elliott. He now stands at Three Chimneys Farm near Versailles, Kentucky, where he services a book of 111 mares per season, continues to receive fan mail on a daily basis and is viewed by over 10,000 visitors per year.

SPEARMINT

- ◆ b c
- ◆ Foaled: 1903, by Carbine out of Maid Of The Mint (Minting)

Danny Maher, the first American rider to be champion jockey in Great Britain, reckoned that of all the winners he rode there, only Bayardo was superior to Spearmint. However, at an early stage in his career, his trainer Peter Purcell Gilpin regarded the colt as so short of promise as to be virtually worthless. He won once as a two-year-old and it was only because other horses in Gilpin's stable encountered problems that Spearmint became a Derby contender. After he had worked with Pretty Polly it became clear that Gilpin was going to have to reconsider

his early opinions. Spearmint duly won at Epsom by 1½ lengths from the amateur-ridden Picton. Spearmint broke down after winning the Grand Prix de Paris and when he went to stud, he sired the 1920 Derby winner Spion Kop, the St. Leger winner Royal Lancer and a pair of classic winners in Ireland in Zionist and Spelthorne.

SPECTACULAR BID

- ◆ gr c
- ◆ Foaled: 1976, by Bold Bidder out of Spectacular (Promised Land)

Many experts regard Spectacular Bid's campaign as a four-year-old the finest ever conducted in North America at that age. Champion male juvenile in 1978, the gray colt won the Kentucky Derby and Preakness Stakes, and was divisional champ again in 1979. In 1980, though, Spectacular Bid was undefeated in nine starts, all of which came in either Grade 1 or Grade 2 stakes. Spectacular Bid set seven track records, four of which came as four-year-old, including a world mark of 1:57⁴/₅ in the 1¼-mile Charles H. Strub Stakes at Santa Anita. Spectacular Bid's final career effort was a walkover in the Woodward Stakes at Belmont Park. A $37,000 yearling purchase by Harry, Teresa and Tom Meyerhoff, Spectacular Bid was trained by Grover "Buddy" Delp. A Delp protege, Ron Franklin, handled most riding chores through the 1979 Triple Crown. Thereafter, Bill Shoemaker was in the irons. All told, Spectacular Bid registered 23 stakes triumphs. Not surprisingly, he was the 1980 season's champion handicapper and Horse of the Year.

STORM CAT

- ◆ dkb/br c
- ◆ Foaled: 1983, by Storm Bird out of Terlingua (Secretariat)

The most expensive stallion in the world, Storm Cat stands at Overbrook Farm in Lexington, Kentucky. His live foal fee for 2006 was $500,000. A winner of the Grade 1 Young America Stakes at Meadowlands in New Jersey at age two, Pennsylvania-bred Storm Cat had a limited racing career that spanned barely beyond one season. He made eight starts, winning four times, placing thrice and earning $570,610. Breeder/owner William T. Young subsequently put him in the breeding shed, and the members of Storm Cat's first crop were foals of 1989. Since then, he has twice been North America's leading general sire and seven times the leading juvenile sire. Storm Cat has sired champions in England, Ireland, France, Italy, Germany, Canada and for the whole of North America. Through 2005, his get included over 140 stakes winners and nearly 90 graded/group stakes winners, of whom 30 had been victorious in Group 1/Grade 1 events. In September, 2005, a Storm Cat yearling colt was auctioned at Keeneland for $9.7 million. The year before, Keeneland had auctioned one for $8 million. Not surprisingly, Storm Cat's private barn at Overbrook is sturdy enough to withstand a direct strike from a category four tornado.

STYMIE

- ◆ ch c
- ◆ Foaled: 1941, by Equestrian out of Stop Watch (On Watch)

The epitome of the blue-collar equine workman, Stymie ascended from the ranks of maiden claimers to be North America's champion handicapper in 1947. Campaigning for seven seasons all told, he won 25 stakes at distances ranging from 1–2 1/2 miles. Claimed from King Ranch for $1,500 in his third career start, Stymie henceforth campaigned for Mrs. Ethel D. Jacobs. Maxwell Hirsch was the chestnut colt's trainer throughout his race career. It took Stymie 14 tries under six jockeys to break his maiden and he registered his first career stakes victory at age four, in the Grey Lag Handicap at Jamaica. From thereon, though, Stymie was a hugely tough competitor, famous for his closing rushes from off the pace. Stymie made one Florida sojourn at the start of his three-year-old campaign. Otherwise, he raced exclusively in the North-East and Mid-Atlantic regions. He registered two victories in the Metropolitan Handicap, the Gallant Fox Handicap and the Saratoga Cup.

SUN BEAU

- ◆ b c
- ◆ Foaled: 1925, by Sun Briar out of Beautiful Lady (Fair Play)

There have been horses who have run as well or better than Sun Beau, but none who tried harder. After breaking his maiden at odds of 17–1, the bay colt registered 17 career stakes triumphs. Among them were three consecutive runnings of the Hawthorne Gold Cup from 1929–31, and back-to-back runnings of the Washington Handicap at Laurel Park in 1929–30. A homebred representing Willis Sharpe Kilmer, who also campaigned Exterminator, Sun Beau had nearly as many trainers (11) as he did jockeys (13). Sun Beau won at distances ranging from 6–14 furlongs. At one point during his four-year-old season, he won five races, including four stakes, in the space of 29 calendar days. Sun Beau was a traveller, but he never seemed weary, venturing to tracks throughout the East and Midwest, in Canada, and in Mexico. Upon retiring, his career earnings were the highest ever achieved by a North American racehorse. Nine years passed before Seabiscuit eclipsed Sun Beau's standard.

SUN CHARIOT

- ◆ br f
- ◆ Foaled: 1939, by Hyperion out of Clarence (Diligence)

Sun Chariot, one of those horses who was bred by the National Stud and raced for King George VI, was a filly of great talent but very difficult temperament. Before she ever appeared on a racecourse, she displayed such a lack of promise that she was nearly returned to Ireland, where the stud then was. She topped the Free Handicap after winning the Middle Park Stakes, Queen Mary Stakes and two other races. However, in her first start as a three-year-old, she refused to make any effort and was beaten for what turned out to be the only time. She won the 1,000 Guineas, Oaks (despite steering a most wayward course) and the St. Leger, in which she beat the Derby winner Watling Street. In retirement she bred some good winners at stud before her death in 1963, including: Blue Train, whose unsoundness prevented him from doing himself justice; Landau, who inherited something of his dam's temperament but showed smart form in spite of this; and Pindari, whose successes included the King Edward VII Stakes and Great Voltigeur Stakes.

SUSAN'S GIRL

- ◆ b f
- ◆ Foaled: 1969, by Quadrangle out of Quaze (Quibu)

A winner of 24 stakes at ten different race tracks during her five seasons of racing, Susan's Girl was one of the most versatile female performers to grace North America's shores during the second half of the 20th Century. Bred and owned by Fred W. Hooper and trained by Russ Fenstermaker, Susan's Girl compiled an overall career record of 63 starts, 29 victories, 25 placings (for a 1st-2nd-3rd ratio of 85.7 per cent) and earnings of $1.25 million. She was twice a winner of the Spinster Stakes at Keeneland, the Delaware Handicap at Delaware Park and the Beldame Stakes at Belmont Park, all of which were Grade 1 events. At age three, Susan's Girl won the Kentucky Oaks at Churchill Downs. She was piloted by 14 different jockeys at various points in her career – Hall of Famers Braulio Baeza, Sandy Hawley, Laffit Pincay Jr. and Jorge Velasquez among them. Susan's Girl was honoured as North America champion handicap mare in both 1973 and 1975. In the breeding shed, she produced the multiple Grade 1 winning colt Copelan and the listed stakes winning colt Paramount Jet, both of whom were by the sire Tri Jet.

SWAIN

- ◆ b c
- ◆ Foaled: 1992, by Nashwan out of Love Smitten (Key To The Mint)

Swain is one of only two horses to win the King George VI And Queen Elizabeth Stakes for two years in a row, and he was six years old when he did so for the second time in 1998 when he beat the Derby winner High-Rise by a length. This time he was ridden by Frankie Dettori, who had deserted him 12 months earlier when John Reid rode Swain to victory over Pilsudski. Later in his final season Swain won the Irish Champion Stakes, but his career ended with a controversial third-place finish in the Breeders' Cup Classic and his jockey was widely criticized. In earlier seasons, apart from his first King George and when he was trained in France by André Fabre before joining Godolphin, Swain also won the Coronation Cup, the Prix Foy and the Grand Prix de Deauville. He retired and stands at stud at Shadwell Farm in Kentucky.

Chance ride: John Reid rode Swain (7) instead of Frankie Dettori and won the 1997 King George VI And Queen Elizabeth Stakes.

SWAPS

◆ ch c
◆ Foaled: 1952, by Khaled out of Iron Reward (Beau Pere)

Perhaps of the greatest of California-bred runners, Swaps registered 15 career stakes victories. Included was the 1955 Kentucky Derby, in which he defeated favoured Nashua, who had prepped at Atlantic seaboard tracks. Since the Derby represented the first start by Swaps outside his home state, an East/West rivalry was born. This resulted in the famous Washington Park Match race on 31 August 1955, which Nashua won by 6 1/2 lengths. Otherwise, Swaps almost always vanquished his opponents. A stakes winner at age two, he also annexed the Santa Anita and American Derbies at age three. In 1956, he set six track records at five different distances, ranging from 1–1 5/8 miles. That season, Swaps was North America's champion handicapper and Horse of the Year. Bred and owned by Rex C. Ellsworth, Swaps was trained by M.A. "Mesh" Tenney. Bill Shoemaker, who was aboard the chestnut colt for most of his major starts, calls Swaps the best horse he ever rode.

SYSONBY

◆ b c
◆ Foaled: 1902, by Melton out of Optime (Orme)

With only a single, third-place finish marring an otherwise perfect race record, Sysonby was one of the equine stars of the early 20th century. Four times a stakes winner at age two, including twice at Saratoga, the bay colt experienced his only career defeat when he broke poorly in the Futurity at Sheepshead Bay in New York. Subsequently, Sysonby won 10 straight races. His career victories ultimately numbered 14, including the 1905 Metropolitan Handicap at Belmont Park and Saratoga's Great Republic Stakes. Favoured every time he raced, Sysonby was sent off at odds as low as three cents on the dollar (1–33). He won at distances ranging from 5 1/2–18 furlongs. All his career starts came at New York tracks. Sysonby campaigned for James R. Keene, was trained by James Rowe Sr., and was ridden by four different jockeys during his relatively brief career, although David Nicol was up for seven of Sysonby's nine starts at age three.

T

TANTIEME

◆ b c
◆ Foaled: 1947, by Deux Pour Cent out of Terka (Indus)

Tantième was the fourth horse to win the Prix de l'Arc de Triomphe on two occasions, which he did in 1950 and 1951. If he had been a better traveller he might well have left no doubt that he was the best horse in Europe at the time. In his native France he also won the Poule d'Essai des Poulains, Prix Ganay, Prix Lupin and Grand Criterium. He was only third behind Supreme Court in the first running of what is now the King George VI And Queen Elizabeth Stakes, he won the Coronation Cup and beat the 1949 Arc winner Coronation V in a race at Ascot. At stud Tantième sired a number of top horses, including Match, who won the King George and the Washington DC International; Brioche, winner of the Yorkshire Cup and the Hardwicke Stakes; Reliance, who landed the Prix du Jockey Club, Prix Royal-Oak and the Grand Prix de Paris; and Tanerko, winner of the Prix Ganay and Prix d'Harcourt, who was the sire of the 1963 Derby winner Relko.

THEATRICAL

◆ b c
◆ Foaled: 1982, by Nureyev out of Tree of Knowledge (by Sassafras)

Victorious in the Group 2 Derrinstown Derby Trial at Leopardstown in his native Ireland in 1985, Theatrical continued to mature through his three-year-old and four-year-old campaigns, placing five times in Group 1/Grade 1 company in Ireland, Germany and Southern California. Meanwhile, Theatrical's breeder, Bertram Firestone, sold a half-interest in the colt to Allen Paulson. It was a complicated arrangement with Firestone retaining the position of managing owner. In early 1987, training chores were transferred from Bobby Frankel to Bill Mott and riding chores from Gary Stevens to Pat Day. Theatrical went on that season to win five Grade 1 events - the Hialeah Turf Cup Handicap, the Bowling Green Handicap and Turf Classic Stakes at Belmont Park, the Man o' War Stakes at Aqueduct and the Breeders' Cup Turf at Hollywood Park. Theatrical was honoured as North America's champion male turf competitor for 1987. His career record included 22 starts, ten wins, six placings and earnings of $2.94 million. He stands at Hill 'N' Dale Farms in Lexington, Kentucky, and during 2005 had sired 20 Grade 1 winners.

THE TETRARCH

◆ gr c
◆ Foaled: 1911, by Roi Herode out of Vahren (Bona Vista)

The Tetrarch was one of the most extraordinary horses in British racing history. He was so strangely marked on his coat that he was known as "The Rocking Horse" or "The Spotted Wonder". He possessed brilliant speed which saw him win all his seven races as a two-year-old. This was no surprise to his trainer Atty Persse as he had trounced decent older horses in trials at home. The best of his seven wins included the Champagne Stakes, Coventry Stakes and National Breeders' Produce Stakes (the last under extreme difficulties) but he was injured after winning at Doncaster and never ran again. He may have been a very shy coverer of mares when he went to stud but he produced some top-quality offspring, siring St. Leger winners in Salmon Trout, Caligula and Polemarch, the 2,000 Guineas winner Tetratema and the very speedy Mumtaz Mahal, who became an ancestress of Petite Etoile and Nasrullah. 80 of his 130 foals won. The Tetrarch died in 1935.

THINK BIG

◆ **b g**
◆ **Foaled: 1970, by Sobig out of Sarcelle (Oman)**

A product of the New Zealand breeding programme, Think Big was purchased for $10,000 by trainer Bart Cummings at the Trentham yearling sales. This proved to be one of the most brilliant transactions in Cummings' long and legendary career, for Think Big triumphed in the Melbourne Cup in both 1974 and 1975. But Think Big was something of a late bloomer. At age two, he managed just one victory in eight starts. At age three, his record improved to five wins in 15 starts. And at age four, he achieved the first of his Melbourne Cup triumphs, wearing down his favoured stablemate Leilani with a huge, sweeping drive in the final 50 metres to prevail by a length. The following year, Think Big became only the third horse at that point in history to register a repeat victory in the Melbourne Cup, this time fighting off a challenge by stablemate Holiday Waggon. It was actually Think Big's first score since his prior Cup win, and his odds were 33–1. It was also the fifth of Cummings' 11 Melbourne Cup triumphs. Jockey Harry White was aboard Think Big for both of his greatest efforts.

THREE TROIKAS

◆ **b f**
◆ **Foaled: 1976, by Lyphard out of Three Roses (Dual)**

Three Troikas was one the of seven fillies to claim victory in the Prix de l'Arc de Triomphe in a 12-year spell from 1972. Her success was in 1979, when she won by three lengths and one length respectively from Le Marmot and Troy, whose first defeat of the season this was and the final race of his career. It was Three Troikas' fifth victory of the season and the sixth of her career. Her other successes in her three-year-old season came in the Prix Vermeille, Prix Saint-Alary and the Poule d'Essai des Pouliches. She stayed in training at four and won the Prix d'Harcourt before being placed in the Prix Ganay. In her next race Three Troikas broke a bone in a foot and was off the course for almost four months. She came back to run fourth in the 1980 Arc, but her trainer, Criquette Head, thought she would have won with a satisfactory preparation.

TIME CHARTER

◆ **b f**
◆ **Foaled: 1979, by Saritamer out of Centrocon (High Line)**

Saritamer had been a good sprinter in his day – he won the July Cup and Diadem Stakes – but it was quite remarkable that he should have sired a filly who stayed as well as Time Charter. She won the Oaks at Epsom in 1982 and went on to claim the King George VI And Queen Elizabeth Stakes too. She got her stamina from her dam, Centrocon, but in spite of her staying ability she also had the pace to win the Champion Stakes as well as being being second in the Eclipse Stakes and fourth in the Prix de l'Arc de Triomphe. She ran until the end of her fourth campaign before going off to stud in 1985. There she has produced a number of winners, though none have proved to be quite as good as she was herself. Zinaad, Illusion and By Charter are among the best of them.

TIZNOW

◆ **b c**
◆ **Foaled: 1997, by Cee's Tizzy out of Cee's Song (Seattle Song)**

The only two-time winner of the Breeders' Cup Classic, Tiznow raced at ages three and four and made only 15 career starts. But he triumphed in eight of them, including four Grade 1 events, and he placed in six others, while accumulating career earnings of $6.43 million. Owned by the Cee's Stable partnership headed by the beer distributor Michael Cooper and trained by Jay Robbins, Tiznow was ridden to all his major victories by Chris McCarron. Among them were a track record-performance (1:59.84) in the 1¼-mile Super Derby at Louisiana Downs in 2000, a photo-finish triumph over Giant's Causeway in the Breeders' Cup Classic at Churchill Downs that same year, a five-length score in the 2001 Santa Anita Derby and another photo-finish victory in Tiznow's career finale, the 2001 Classic at Belmont. Tiznow was North America's champion three-year-old colt and Horse of the Year in 2000 and champion older horse in 2001. He stands at WinStar Farm (as a joint venture with Taylor Made Farm) in Versailles, Kentucky, and was North America's leading first-crop sire for 2005.

TM OPERA O

◆ **ch c**
◆ **Foaled: 1996, by Opera House out of Once Wed (Blushing Groom)**

The greatest equine beneficiary in history of the Japanese Racing Association's lucrative purses, TM Opera O is the world record-holder in career

earnings - having accumulated the equivalent of $16.2 million in US dollars. In 1999, TM Opera O was champion of his three-year male division, with the Japanese 2000 Guineas at Nakayama Racecourse among his victories. But during a stretch that extended from 20 February, 2000, through 29 April, 2001, TM Opera O won nine consecutive stakes at Japanese tracks. His most notable effort during the period was a photo-finish triumph in the 2000 renewal of the Japan Cup at Tokyo Race Course. As the 1-2 wagering choice, TM Opera O was the first favourite in 14 years to win Japan's most prestigious race, and he was honoured as Horse of the Year at the culmination of that season. All told, TM Opera O won seven Group 1 stakes. Bred in Japan by Kineusu Bokujo, owned by Masatsugu Takezono and trained by Ichizo Iwamoto, he was guided through his championship efforts by jockey Ryuji Wada. Retired from racing in January, 2002, TM Opera O was sent to East Stud in Hokkaido, Japan.

TOM FOOL

◆ **b c**
◆ **Foaled: 1949, by Menow out of Gaga (Bull Dog)**

As fine a horse as ever campaigned for historic Greentree Stable, Tom Fool was undefeated at age four. Registering 10 triumphs in that 1953 season, in races such as the Carter, Metropolitan, Suburban, Brooklyn and Whitney Handicaps, and the Pimlico Special, he proved so formidable that wagering was cancelled the final four times he ran. Altogether, the bay colt recorded 18 career stakes victories. Somewhat curiously, the Suburban was the only race Tom Fool ran in twice – and he won it both times. Trained by John M. Gaver, and ridden in all his starts by Ted Atkinson, Tom Fool was North America's champion two-year-old for 1951, when his victories included a pair of Saratoga stakes and the Futurity at Belmont Park. In 1953, he was champion handicapper and Horse of the Year. At age three, a cough accompanied by fever kept Tom Fool out of the Triple Crown. At age four, he won at six distances ranging from 5½ furlongs to 1¼ miles, under imposts as high as 136 pounds.

TRIPTYCH

◆ **b f**
◆ **Foaled: 1982, by Riverman out of Trillion (Hail To Reason)**

Triptych was an amazingly tough filly who went on racing until the age of six, travelling around the world always taking on the very best. She ran 41 times, of which she won 14; of those, 12 were Pattern races, including nine Group 1 events. She

Proud father: Tudor Minstrel was the son and grandson of English Derby winners and sire of Kentucky Derby winner Tomy Lee.

was placed another 19 times, all but one of them in Group 1 races, and her worldwide earnings amounted to more than £1,500,000. Her first big win came in the Prix Marcel Boussac, when she was trained by David Smaga in France, but she moved to David O'Brien in Ireland for her second season when she beat the colts in the Irish 2,000 Guineas and was runner-up in the Oaks. At four Triptych won the Champion Stakes and La Coupe, by which time she had joined Patrick Biancone. She was placed in the King George VI And Queen Elizabeth Stakes, Eclipse Stakes and Prix de l'Arc de Triomphe. The following season she excelled herself, winning the Coronation Cup (which she also won in 1987), Prix Ganay, Champion Stakes (both English and Irish versions) and the Matchmaker International Stakes. She retired after the following season.

TROYTOWN

◆ br g
◆ Foaled: 1913, by Zria out of Diane (Ascetic)

Troytown was a hugely powerful horse who scaled great heights in his all-too-brief career. He may have gone on to even better things had he not been fatally injured in a fall in his first race after claiming the Grand Steeplechase de Paris. However, the habit of bludgeoning his way through fences, which caused the fatal accident, had long been with Troytown. When he won the 1920 Grand National, he almost carted his amateur jockey, Jack Anthony, round the track and survived two appalling mistakes which would have defeated almost any other horse. Before that he had won once in his native Ireland, taken the Champion Chase at Liverpool in 1919 and made every yard to win the Grand Steeplechase de Paris that season.

TUDOR MINSTREL

◆ br c
◆ Foaled: 1944, by Owen Tudor out of Sansonnet (Sansovino)

Although his sire and his dam's sire both won the English Derby (Sansovino in 1924, Owen Tudor in 1941), Tudor Minstrel did not stay beyond a mile, though at that distance he was exceptionally talented. He won all four of his juvenile starts and galloped his rivals into the ground in 1947's 2,000 Guineas, which he won by eight lengths. He did not stay the 1 1/2-mile trip in the Derby, for which he started at 4–7. His lack of stamina made a fortune for the bookmaker William Hill, who was convinced that he would not get the trip and ran his book accordingly. Back at a mile, he won the St. James's Palace Stakes and he retired as the winner of eight races worth £24,629. His career at stud before he retired in 1970 was satisfactory rather than spectacular, though he got classic winners in Tomy Lee, who won the Kentucky Derby, the Poule d'Essai winner Toro as well as the very speedy Sing Sing and the Eclipse winner King of the Tudors.

TWILIGHT TEAR

◆ b f
◆ Foaled: 1941, by Bull Lea out of Lady Lark (Blue Larkspur)

Another of the superb Calumet Farm homebreds of the 1940s, Twilight Tear won her maiden at first asking, then won a stakes her next time out. She subsequently put together an 11-race win streak during her three-year-old campaign, completing the season with a six-length triumph over male competitors in the Pimlico Special. Bay in colour, stout in heart, Twilight Tear registered a total of 10

career stakes victories. In July 1944, she set a seven-furlong track record in the Skokie Handicap at Washington Park near Chicago. Five times, she won stakes in gate-to-wire fashion, the aforesaid Special among them. In 1944 Twilight Tear was three-year-old filly champion, handicap mare champion, and North America's Horse of the Year. Her father and son training team, Ben and H.A. "Jimmy" Jones, put eight different jockeys up on Twilight Tear. She won with seven of them aboard, most notably Con McCreary, under whom she went eight-for-eight.

V

VAGUELY NOBLE

◆ b c
◆ Foaled: 1965, by Vienna out of Noble Lassie (Nearco)

Vaguely Noble was never far away from drama. Having won the Observer Gold Cup at Doncaster by seven lengths he was put up for sale to help pay death duties on the estate of his first owner, Major Lionel Holliday. Amid extraordinary scenes at Newmarket, he went under the hammer for a record 136,000gns. As a three-year-old he was trained by Etienne Pollet and won three races in France before putting up a display of total authority to beat Sir Ivor and six other classic winners in the Prix de l'Arc de Triomphe. He had no classic engagements, which made his purchase for Dr. Robert Franklyn a real gamble, but he landed it in style. Vaguely Noble was champion sire in 1973 and 1974, and by the time of his death in 1989 he has sired top winners like Dahlia, Noble Decree, Ace of Aces, Empery, Exceller and Nobiliary.

VAIN

◆ ch c
◆ Foaled: 1967, by Wilkes out of Elated (Orgoglio)

Vain was only beaten in two of his 14 races and both times his trainer Jim Moloney blamed himself. An explosive sprinter, he won at his four starts leading up to Australia's richest two-year-old race, the 1969 Golden Slipper Stakes, over six furlongs at Rosehill. He won the Golden Slipper eased down by four lengths but Moloney felt he was "short of a gallop" when he was beaten by Beau Babylon in the A.J.C. Sires' Produce Stakes, over seven furlongs, at Randwick two weeks later. With a point to prove Moloney ensured Vain was 100 per cent fit for the Champagne Stakes, over six furlongs at Randwick, and he won by 10 lengths in record time of 1min 9.2sec. At three,

Vain won twice before having his colours lowered by Daryl's Joy in the Moonee Valley Stakes, over a mile, when wet tracks had interrupted his preparation. But with regular jockey Pat Hyland aboard he won the Caulfield Guineas, over a mile, and then the Craven A. Stakes, over six furlongs; the Linlithgow Stakes, over seven furlongs, and the George Adams Handicap, over a mile, in the space of eight days. A fetlock injury sustained in 1970 brought an end to Vain's racing career.

W

WAKEFUL

◆ b f
◆ **Foaled: 1896, by Trenton out of Insomnia (Robinson Crusoe)**

Intermittently lame, Wakeful was unable to begin her racing career until four years of age but she soon proved to be a sensation. Trained by Hugh Munro – the father of Melbourne Cup-winning jockeys Darby and Hugh – she won the prestigious 1900 Oakleigh Plate, over 5 1/2 furlongs at Caulfield at only her third start. At her next appearance she won Melbourne's premier sprint – the Newmarket Handicap, over six furlongs at Flemington – and followed up by taking Australia's most famous mile race the Doncaster Handicap, at Randwick. Two days after that, in only her sixth outing and on a sprinter's preparation, she was third behind San Fran and Australian Colours in the Sydney Cup, over two miles. At five, Wakeful won nine races including the 1902 Sydney Cup – carrying 9st 7lb (133 pounds) – and the weight-for-age All-Aged Stakes, over a mile, two days afterwards. She won ten races at age six, over distances from 10 furlongs to three miles. At age seven, Wakeful won thrice and finished second in the Melbourne Cup.

WAR ADMIRAL

◆ br c
◆ **Foaled: 1934, by Man o' War out of Brushup (Sweep)**

The finest competitor sired by Man o' War, War Admiral swept North America's Triple Crown in 1937. A stakes winner at age two, he registered an 11-race win streak over 14 months, beginning with his three-year-old debut. In total, War Admiral's career stakes triumphs numbered 15. Front-running victories were his forte; in the Kentucky Derby and Preakness Stakes, War Admiral took early leads and never surrendered them. Same, too,

in the Belmont Stakes, where he eclipsed his sire's 17-year-old track record for 1 1/2 miles. War Admiral's wins at age four included the Saratoga Handicap, Whitney Stakes, Saratoga Cup, and Jockey Club Gold Cup. His final stakes win came in the 1938 Rhode Island Handicap at Narragansett Park. Bred and owned by Samuel D. Riddle, He was trained by George Conway, and ridden mainly by Charles "the Flying Dutchman" Kurtsinger. In 1937, War Admiral was Horse of the Year.

WAYWARD LAD

◆ br g
◆ **Foaled: 1975, by Royal Highway out of Loughanmore (Bargello)**

Wayward Lad was one of the "Dickinson five" (Michael Dickinson trained all the horses which took the first five places in the 1983 Cheltenham Gold Cup). But there was far more than that to Wayward Lad's career, which ended in early 1987. By then he had won 28 of his 55 races on 16 different tracks and his final success, at the 1987 Grand National meeting, brought his career earnings to £218,732, at the time a sum beaten only by Dawn Run. His best wins came in that Liverpool race twice, the King George VI Chase, which he won for a third time in 1985, the Charlie Hall Chase and the Edward Hanmer Chase. Sadly a row between his owners resulted in him having to go to Doncaster sales where Tony Dickinson (Michael's father) bought him for 42,000gns and sent him into retirement with his son, who had begun a new career training in the USA.

WHIRLAWAY

◆ ch c
◆ **Foaled: 1938, by Blenheim II out of Dustwhirl (Sweep)**

Whirlaway swept North America's Triple Crown in 1941, and subsequently became the most formidable handicap competitor on the continent. A multiple stakes winner as a juvenile, he dominated his divisions in 1941 and 1942, winning Horse of the Year honours both seasons. A career winner of 24 stakes, at distances from 5 1/2–16 furlongs, Whirlaway avoided no challenges. Others often avoided him, notably his walkover in the 1942 Pimlico Special. Earlier that year, he set three track records in four starts. His Kentucky Derby and Preakness wins came just a week apart. In October 1942, he won two stakes within five days. A Calumet Farm homebred, Whirlaway was trained by the father/son team of Ben and H.A. "Jimmy" Jones. Eddie Arcaro rode Whirlaway to the Triple Crown, while others who helped him

to multiple stakes victories included George Woolf and John Longden.

WINDSOR LAD

◆ b c
◆ **Foaled: 1931, by Blandford out of Resplendent (By George!)**

Windsor Lad was one of the best Derby winners. He won the Epsom classic by a length and a neck from Easton and the arguably unlucky hot favourite Colombo. Although Windsor Lad was beaten in his next race, the Eclipse Stakes, when he finished third after getting badly boxed in, he never lost again. After the Eclipse, he was bought by the bookmaker Martin Benson (who operated under the name of Duggie Stewart and also bought Nearco), and won at York before equalling the track record when taking the St. Leger at 4–9. He won four more races aged four, including the Eclipse Stakes and the Coronation Cup. Sadly, he had little chance to pass on his ability when he retired to stud because he developed severe sinus trouble in 1938 and never really recovered. The best winners he produced were Windsor Slipper and Phase.

Z

ZEV

◆ br c
◆ **Foaled: 1920, by The Finn out of Miss Kearney (Planudes)**

Zev was the first horse to win a $100,000 race on North America's shores. It was a match race, on 20 October 1923, against the Epsom Derby winner, Papyrus and on a sloppy Belmont Park track, Zev won the 1 1/2-mile contest by five lengths. It was one of 15 career stakes victories the brown colt registered, at distances ranging from five furlongs to 1 5/8 miles. Included in this list of successes were the 1923 Kentucky Derby and Belmont Stakes. Four weeks following his effort against Papyrus, Zev won another match race. This time the opponent was the American colt, In Memoriam, and Zev defeated him by a nose at 1 1/4 miles at Churchill Downs. The following year, Zev set a one-mile track record at Kentucky's Latonia Race Course. At his peak, he triumphed in 17 of 21 starts. Owned by Harry F. Sinclair's Rancocas Stable, and trained by Samuel C. Hildreth, Zev performed best with jockey Earl Sande in the saddle. Zev retired having replaced Man o' War as the all-time leading money earner.

CHAPTER 6

LEGENDARY JOCKEYS

Jockeys are a special breed. They earn a living trying to steer a third of a ton/tonne of horse at 40mph (65 km/h) over a fence or through a gap a couple of yards/metres wide that may close at any moment, almost without thought, while wearing no more protection than a skateboarder.

THE 20 JOCKEYS who have earned legendary status encompass the whole of the 20th century. Their backgrounds could hardly have been more different, but they all shared one consuming passion: to get their mount safely past the winning post ahead of all their rivals. The tiniest error of judgement could not only cost them the race, the horse's and their safety could be jeopardized.

Eddie Arcaro – simply The Master

Jerry Bailey – rider of the 1990s

Scobie Breasley – artist in the saddle

Steve Cauthen – the Kentucky Kid

Angel Cordero – riding on the edge

Pat Day – never has a bad day

Frankie Dettori – shooting star

Steve Donoghue – "come on Steve"

John Francome – the greatest jump jockey

Mick Kinane – upholds the family tradition

John Longden – "I want to be the best"

Chris McCarron – 1,000 wins in two years

Tony McCoy – gives no-hopers a chance

George Moore – the man with "cotton fingers"

Lester Piggott – the housewives' choice

Laffit Pincay Jr. – racing's winningest jockey

Sir Gordon Richards – first knight of the turf

Yves Saint-Martin – France's best 15 times

Willie Shoemaker – 1,000 stakes wins

Yutake Take – Japanese genius

Hard at work: Pat Day drives Banshee Breeze home to win the 1999 Breeders' Cup Distaff at Gulfstream Park, Florida.

EDDIE ARCARO

"There were great jockeys before he came onto the scene. There are great ones – a few – riding today. There will be great ones in the future. But wherever men gather to speak of racing and race riding, Eddie Arcaro always will be 'The Master'." **Joe Hirsch,** Daily Racing Form, **1962**

NAMING THE GREATEST JOCKEY in North America's history will always be an exercise that inspires debate. But if a vote were to be taken among the sport's veteran chroniclers, Eddie Arcaro would be the consensus choice.

"The Master", as he was, indeed, known to his peers and the public, Arcaro won the Kentucky Derby five times – a record subsequently equaled by Bill Hartack, but never surpassed by any other rider. Arcaro was also triumphant in a record six editions of the Preakness Stakes and a record-equalling six editions of the Belmont Stakes, thus achieving an unmatched 17 victories in the American Classics. He is also the only jockey to twice sweep the American Triple Crown, achieving the feat with the Calumet Farm homebreds Whirlaway in 1941 and Citation in 1948.

Born in Cincinnati, Ohio, Arcaro began exercising horses at old Latonia Race Course in neighboring Kentucky in his early teens. His first race victory was registered aboard a gelding named Eagle Bird in a $500 claiming event at Mexico's Agua Caliente track on January 14, 1932. Arcaro's highest victory total for a single season, 236, was achieved in 1959, when he was 43 years old. During each of his final 16 full seasons of riding, Arcaro's mounts achieved over $1 million in earnings. They topped the $2 million plateau in 1956.

Hot-tempered and at times reckless in his youth, Arcaro, by his own description, began riding during the era of "setting traps, grabbing saddle cloths, and leg locking." In 1942, after being squeezed coming out of the starting gate in the Cowdin Stakes at Aqueduct, Arcaro forcefully bore over on fellow jockey Venancio Nodarse. The track's stewards suspended Arcaro indefinitely. The enforced hiatus lasted for a year, and ended after Mrs. Helen Whitney, the owner of Greentree Stable, pleaded for Arcaro's reinstatement in a letter to William Woodward Sr., president of the Jockey Club.

Thereafter, Arcaro was more self-disciplined, establishing standards only a few have ever approached. He won the Wood Memorial, the premier Derby prep of his era, nine times. He won the Jockey Club Gold Cup 10 times; the Suburban Handicap eight times; the Widener Handicap thrice; the Travers Stakes on four occasions; the Santa Anita Handicap twice. Arcaro's 554 career stakes victories in North America was a record until Bill Shoemaker broke it in 1972.

Seventeen years earlier, Arcaro, aboard Nashua, had defeated Shoemaker, aboard Swaps, in one of the most celebrated match races in racing history at Washington Park near Chicago. Most observers felt that Arcaro controlled that race from the start, "herding" Shoemaker to the outside whenever the latter attempted to make a move. Despite this, Arcaro and Shoemaker remained close friends.

Arcaro's riding career ended in 1962, with a worldwide tour that culminated in Australia. From the late 1960s through most of the 1970s, he worked as a racing commentator for the CBS and ABC television networks. Arcaro was twice married. His first wife, Ruth, with whom he had two children, Carolyn and Robert, passed away in 1988. His second wife, Vera, survives him. Heart ailments slowed Arcaro in his later years and he died at age 81, a victim of liver cancer.

Born	19 February 1916		
Died	14 November 1997		
Riding career	spanned 32 years		
Hall of Fame	1958		
Career record	Mounts	1st	2nd	3rd
	24,029	4,779	3,807	3,302
Earnings	$30,039,543		

The Master: Eddie Arcaro's 17 victories in American Triple Crown events constitute a record unmatched.

JERRY BAILEY

THE MULTIPLICITY OF Jerry Dale Bailey's career accomplishments is beyond the sublime. When he retired from race riding on January 28, 2006, Bailey was the all-time leader in Breeders' Cup victories, with 15. Five of them had come in the Breeders' Cup Classic, aboard Black Tie Affair, Arcangues, Concern, Cigar and Saint Liam. Four times he had won the Dubai World Cup, with Cigar, Singspiel, Captain Steve and Street City. Bailey had won the Kentucky Derby with Sea Hero and Grindstone, the Preakness Stakes with Hansel and Red Bullet, and the Belmont Stakes with Hansel and Empire Maker. Seven times, Bailey was honoured with Eclipse Awards as North America's champion journeyman jockey.

His North American purse earnings totalled $296.06 million, good for second position behind only his fellow Hall of Famer, Pat Day. Add in Bailey's earnings in international racing events, and his total of $311.36 million is unmatched by any North American-based rider. On March 12, 1995, Bailey won seven races on a single card at Florida's Gulfstream Park. He is the all-time leading jockey at Saratoga, where he won 693 races. In 2003, he set North American records for stakes wins during a single year, with 70, and Grade 1 victories, with 26.

Originally from Dallas, Bailey spent much of his youth in western Texas. At age 12 he was riding Quarter Horses in match races. His father, a dentist, owned a small string of claiming horses that raced just across the state line at Sunland Park in New Mexico. It was at Sunland where Bailey registered his initial career win, and it came aboard his first mount, an allowance runner named Fetch on November 3, 1974.

For much of the next eight years, Bailey travelled around the United States, riding at various tracks in the Southwest, Florida, Illinois, New Jersey and elsewhere. He set up a permanent base in New York in 1982. There, Bailey first gained national recognition by sweeping the New York Handicap Triple Crown,

> "If Bailey were a Broadway show, the reviews pasted on the billboards outside his theater would read, 'the rider of the 1990s.' ... He seems to go from one good horse to another the way a squirrel springs from limb to limb."
>
> **Bill Leggett,** Thoroughbred Daily News, **1996**

comprising the Metropolitan, Brooklyn and Suburban Handicaps, with Fit To Fight in 1984.

In the late 1980s, though, Bailey's career stalled, as he had to overcome chronic alcoholism. His fight against the disease is documented in his 2005 autobiography, "Against The Odds: Riding for My life." In 1994–96, Bailey was the rider aboard Cigar for 15 of that horse's record-tying 16-race win streak. Bailey later said that Cigar was the most genuine, charismatic equine athlete he had ever been around.

As Bailey's talents matured, he could frequently choose the best mounts for major stakes events. But he also scored on many a horse who was not a favourite. In the 1993 Derby, Sea Hero won at odds of 12.90–1 under Bailey. In the 1993 Breeders' Cup Classic, Arcangues won at 133.60–1 with Bailey aboard. Arcangues remains the longest shot ever to win any Breeders' Cup race. On August 19, 2000, he recorded a remarkable double at Arlington Park near Chicago by winning the Beverly D. Stakes on Snow Polina and the Arlington Million on the Juddmonte Farms homebred, Chester House.

Bailey's final career victory came on January 27, 2006 aboard a horse named Shakespearesister at Gulfstream. His future plans include working as a television analyst for major North American races on the ABC and ESPN networks.

Pleased as Punch: Jerry Bailey's quartet of Breeders' Cup Classic victories give him one of many reasons to smile.

Born	August 29, 1957
Riding career	spanned 33 years
Hall of Fame	1995

Career record	Mounts	1st	2nd	3rd
(through 2006)	30,901	5,900	3,849	3,388
Earnings	$311,356,757			

SCOBIE BREASLEY

AN ARTIST in the saddle, Arthur Edward Breasley's finesse and exquisite timing enabled him to achieve exceptional success as a jockey in Australia and England. Always modest and quietly spoken, Breasley, who was born in the New South Wales country town of Wagga Wagga in 1914, was the son of a cattle drover who trained horses as a hobby. Learning to ride at an early age, he was soon nicknamed Scobie after the legendary trainer James Scobie, whose wins were highlighted by three Melbourne Cup victories.

On leaving school at the age of 12 – two years before the law then permitted – Breasley became apprenticed the following year and in 1928 rode his first winner Noo Jee in Melbourne. His first feature race win came in 1930 when he rode Cragford to victory in The Metropolitan at Randwick in Sydney. After that major race luck pretty much deserted him until 1938, when he landed the Moonee Valley Gold Cup on Ortelle's Star.

In 1942 he registered the first of his record five Caulfield Cups on the high-class mare Tranquil Star and followed up by winning the event in the next three years on Saint Warden, Counsel and St. Fairy. Breasley's other important wins in the 1940s included the Victoria Racing Club Oaks on three occasions; the Caulfield Guineas three times; the Victoria Derby; the Epsom Handicap; a Sydney Cup; another Moonee Valley Cup; and a Brisbane Cup.

The nearest he came to winning Australia's most coveted horse race – the Melbourne Cup – was in 1933 when he went down by a head to Hall Mark when riding the grand old stayer Shadow King. His accomplishments led to J.V. Rank – the brother of film magnate J. Arthur Rank – offering Breasley a retainer in 1950 to ride in England.

At that stage he had ridden 1,091 winners in Australia – he returned in the spring of 1952 to win, among other races, his fifth Caulfield Cup on Peshawar and the Victoria Derby on Advocate – and he went on to compile a total of 2,161 wins from 9,716 rides in England. Remarkably, Breasley's rise to fame and fortune was achieved after a horrific fall at Alexandra Park in 1954. He

fractured his skull, went cross-eyed for a time and – worst of all – lost his sense of balance.

"The specialists said I wouldn't ride again and for a time I feared they were right," he said. "When I came out of hospital I couldn't get around without holding on to my wife Mae or my daughter Loretta's arm, because I couldn't keep my balance."

But, acting on his doctor's advice, Breasley began going for long walks and within three months he was riding again.

Demonstrating his resilience he won the English Jockeys' Championship three years later when he rode 173 winners. He had further reason to celebrate in 1958 when he produced a trademark rails ride to win the Prix de l'Arc de Triomphe at Longchamp on the Vincent O'Brien-trained Mossborough horse Ballymoss. Despite being involved in an intense competition with Lester Piggott, who was 21 years his junior, Breasley went on to win the jockeys' premiership on three more occasions with 171 wins in 1961; 179 in 1962; and 176 wins in 1963.

Australian jockey Ron Hutchinson, who followed Breasley to England, described his style, "He had a beautiful seat in the saddle and a lovely style. As well as that he was totally fearless and I remember that sometimes, when I was following him, he would take openings that weren't there and get up to win by a head."

The crowning glory to his days in the saddle came at age 50 when he brought Santa Claus home – "I always said he was my Father Christmas," he joked later – with a whirlwind finish to defeat Indiana and Dilettante II in the Derby at Epsom. He won the classic again in 1966 aboard Charlottown and with his record – apart from a Melbourne Cup win – complete, he retired from the saddle at the end of the 1968 season.

After deciding to become a trainer he set up stables at South Hatch on Epsom Downs, before moving to Chantilly in the early 1970s, and New York in 1977, before ultimately settling in Australia in the 1980s.

Early Christmas gift: Scobie returns to the unsaddling enclosure after winning the 1964 Derby on Santa Claus.

Born	7 May 1914, Australia			
Riding career	1928–68			
Career record	Starts	1st	2nd	3rd
		3,251		
English career (1950–68)	Starts	1st	2nd	3rd
	9,716	2,160		

"I couldn't speak more highly of Scobie as a jockey. In fact I've always regarded him as the ultimate, as far as jockeys are concerned."

Ron Hutchinson, former international rider who rode many races against him

STEVE CAUTHEN

Kentucky Kid: Steve Cauthen was a Transatlantic champion.

Born	Kentucky, U.S., 1 May 1960
Riding career	spanned 18 years
Hall of Fame	1994

Career record	Mounts	1st	2nd	3rd
	2,974			

N O JOCKEY ACHIEVED A GREATER level of success on both sides of the Atlantic Ocean than Steve Cauthen. He arrived in England, aged 18, in 1979 and proceeded to win almost every major race in the calendar for the top owners and trainers. Cauthen was champion jockey on three occasions, earned a reputation for integrity and became an ambassador for the sport.

When Cauthen came to England – at the instigation of Robert Sangster – and started riding for Barry Hills with whom Sangster then had many horses, he had already reached the top of the tree in U.S. He won the American Triple Crown on Affirmed in 1978 having set a U.S. record with 487 winners from 2075 rides, the previous year, aged 17 – all within barely two years of having had his first success. Affirmed's Belmont Stakes victory was one of America's greatest ever finishes and a tribute to Cauthen's horsemanship.

The combination of increasing weight and a losing run persuaded him to accept Sangster's offer to ride in Britain. He won on his very first mount in England, on Marquee Universal at Salisbury, and his career went from strength to strength thereafter. His first UK classic success came a month later when Tap On Wood won the 2,000 Guineas, and he enjoyed his 1,000th winner when the aptly-named Thousandfold won at Doncaster later in 1979. Among other top wins for Barry Hills were the Champion Stakes and Benson & Hedges Gold Cup on Cormorant Wood, the Lockinge Stakes on Motavato, Ascot's Gold Cup on Gildoran and the Cheveley Park Stakes on Desirable.

The liaison ended in 1985 when Cauthen joined Henry Cecil's stable. This new partnership was a great success. In their first season together Cecil and Cauthen won the fillies' triple crown with Oh So Sharp and the Derby with Slip Anchor. A second Derby followed with Reference Point in 1987. They also took the Irish Derby and the Prix du Jockey Club with Old Vic, the Oaks and the Irish Oaks with Diminuendo, another Oaks with Snow Bride (although she profited from the long-delayed disqualification of Aliysa on technical grounds), St. Legers with Reference Point and Michelozzo and the King George VI And Queen Elizabeth Stakes with Reference Point.

In 1991 he became the retained rider for Sheikh Mohammed, who owned many of those big winners like Old Vic and Oh So Sharp, and their subsequent successes included the Prix de Diane with Indian Skimmer, but after two years and 188 winners in this role they failed to agree terms to renew the contract.

Soon after that decision Cauthen retired after a career which earned him the highest international reputation as a jockey and a sportsman and his total of 197 winners for his final jockeys' championship in 1987 (when he beat Pat Eddery by two) was the highest such total since (Sir) Gordon Richards won with 231 in 1952. He is the only man to have won the Derby at Churchill Downs (Kentucky), Epsom (English), the Curragh (Irish) and Chantilly (French). A year after his 1993 retirement, he was honoured with election to the U.S. Horse Racing Hall of Fame.

Cauthen remained involved in racing and breeding – he bred one of his mares to Affirmed. He owns Dreamfields Training Center in Verona, Kentucky. Cauthen is one of three living jockeys (the others are Ron Turcotte and Jean Cruguet) who have won America's Triple Crown.

> "Steve Cauthen is no 18-year-old, he's an old man. Sometimes he makes me believe in reincarnation. Maybe he had another life when he was a leading rider for 50 years." Affirmed's trainer, Lazaro Barrera, **1978**

ANGEL CORDERO Jr

Seasons in the sun: Angel Cordero Jr., winner of over 7,000 races, was Saratoga's champion jockey 13 times.

Engaging and volatile, he was loved by many racing fans, hated by others, and, not surprisingly, inspired heavy wagering on most of the horses he rode.

Champions, some of them future Hall of Fame horses, were frequently sent Cordero's way. He guided Seattle Slew to his final three career triumphs. He was aboard Manila when the colt scored his final career victory in the 1987 Arlington Million. Cordero's rides aboard Bold Forbes in the 1976 Derby and Belmont are viewed by most racing experts as feats of brilliance. Neither the colt's pedigree nor his past performances offered guarantees he could run Classic distances. But Cordero had Bold Forbes on the lead throughout in both events, winning the 1 1/4-mile Derby by a length and the 1 1/2-mile Belmont by a diminishing neck.

Cordero won the Woodward Stakes, a premier race on Belmont Park's fall schedule, a record six times, including five consecutive runnings from 1981–85. In 1989, he rode Open Mind to a sweep of New York's Triple Tiara series (which is regarded as the Triple Crown for fillies). Groovy and Gulch became North American sprint champions with Cordero in the irons. He guided Slew O'Gold to a pair of championships, as North America's leading three-year-old in 1983 and leading handicap horse in 1984.

After being injured for the 24th time in a spill at New York's Aqueduct track in January, 1992, Cordero retired from riding. He subsequently trained horses, and is now an agent for the New York-based jockey, John Velasquez.

But in January 2001, Cordero's wife, Marjorie, was struck and killed by a hit-and-run automobile driver. Cordero has five children. Now a grandfather as well, he has expressed a desire to return to race riding, but his doctors have strongly advised against this.

"The riders, none of them weighing more than about 115 pounds ... (manoeuvre) brakeless half-ton race horses around dirt or grass tracks at 40 miles an hour. Nobody does it with more flair, dedication or consistent competence than Angel Cordero Jr." **Steve Cady,** New York Times, **1976**

TO DESCRIBE THE riding style of Angel Cordero Jr. in one word, "daring" is most apt. He would move his mounts through the smallest of holes, drift out or bear in on other horses to within a centimetre of what the rules permitted, always seeking the edge. Cordero's tactics brought frequent suspensions, but they also allowed him to score over 7,000 career victories, including three in the Kentucky Derby, two in the Preakness Stakes, one in the Belmont Stakes and four in Breeders' Cup competition.

Born in Santurce, Puerto Rico, Cordero received early schooling in riding skills from his father, who was also a jockey and later a trainer. Cordero registered his first career victory at

Puerto Rico's El Comandante track in 1960. The following year, he was the leading rider there with 123 wins. In 1962, Cordero brought his tack to New York. At Saratoga that summer, he slept in a car because he couldn't afford lodging. Cordero subsequently was the leading rider a record 13 times at the upstate track.

Cordero approached his riding chores with a swagger. He would sing to his horses during post parades, jabber away at other jockeys as fields approached the starting gate, and hop off his mounts with an acrobatic flourish in the winner's circle. He would stage press conferences, complaining to the media about what track stewards were allegedly doing to him.

Born	8 November 1942		
Riding career	spanned 33 years		
Hall of Fame	1988		
Career record	**Mounts** **1st**	**2nd**	**3rd**
	38,646 7,057	6,136	6,359
Earnings	$164,526,217		

PAT DAY

PAT DAY HAS said that when he first rode in pari-mutuel races in 1973, he didn't know the name of the track on which the Kentucky Derby was held. Ironically, Churchill Downs subsequently became his greatest showcase. When Day retired from race riding on August 4, 2005, he was the all-time leading jockey at Churchill in wins, with 2,471, and in stakes triumphs, with 155. The former figure is well over twice the number achieved by his closest rival, and the latter number is more than three times as many. Day is also the all-time leader at Keeneland in victories, with 918, and in stakes triumphs, with 95. Many decades will almost certainly pass before his standards are eclipsed.

Despite riding in the race 22 times, Day only won the Derby once, with 16.80–1 shot Lil E. Tee in 1992. But he won the Preakness Stakes five times, with Tank's Prospect, Summer Squall, Tabasco Cat, Timber Country and Louis Quatorze, and he won the Belmont Stakes thrice, with Easy Goer, Tabasco Cat and Commendable. Day further won 12 Breeders' Cup races, and ranks behind only Jerry Bailey among the all-time leaders in that department. In 1984, Day won the inaugural Breeders' Cup Classic with the 31.30–1 shot, Wild Again, and he further won the Classic three other times, with Unbridled, Awesome Again and Cat Thief.

Day is the all-time leading jockey in North American purses earned, with $297.9 million. He is also the leading Breeders' Cup jockey in purses earned, with $23 million. On September 14, 1989, he won eight races on a single card at Arlington Park near Chicago. On four occasions, Day received the Eclipse Award as North America's outstanding journeyman jockey. He was the leading rider at Oaklawn Park in Hot Springs, Arkansas, every year from 1983–94, and so profoundly did he influence the wagering patterns that he once went through a two-month period at Oaklawn when no horse he rode went off at odds as high as 7–1.

Born in Colorado's high country, Day spent his early youth on his family's ranch, where his father taught him basic horsemanship. Day's early goal was to become a rodeo rider, but his diminutive height – just four feet and 11 inches – brought about a major change in thinking, and

Safer conveyances: Four times honoured with Eclipse Awards, Pat Day originally wanted to be a rodeo rider.

during his teenage years he decided to pursue a racing career. His initial career victory came on July 29, 1973, in a $631 claiming race at Prescott Downs in Arizona aboard a horse named Forblunged.

It isn't unusual for modern-day athletes to go through raucous periods, and Day admits his wild side often prevailed when he was a young man. But for the past quarter-century, he has been a devout Christian, and neither consumes alcohol nor smokes. Day celebrated many a stakes triumph by sipping not champagne, but water from a fine-stemmed glass, and as he grew older he became a popular lecturer on religious topics.

There's a room at Day's home in Louisville, Kentucky where the hundreds of trophies, awards and citations he has received are displayed. Day himself says he is astounded whenever he walks in and gazes around. His final career win was achieved on July 10, 2005, aboard a horse named Ay Caramba at Churchill. Day plans to devote the remainder of his working life to the Race Track Chaplaincy programme.

> "(Day) was truly a credit, probably the one guy who has come along in my era that from top to bottom tried to improve the sport in every way."
>
> **Trainer D. Wayne Lukas, quoted in "The Thoroughbred Times," 2005**

Born	13 October 1953
Riding career	has spanned 33 years
Hall of Fame	1991

Career record (through 2006)	Mounts	1st	2nd	3rd
	36,016	8,803		

Earnings	$297,912,019

FRANKIE DETTORI

A NATIVE OF MILAN, Lanfranco "Frankie" Dettori is the son of the 13-time champion Italian jockey Gianfranco Dettori, and is the closest thing to a shooting star on the international racing scene. Famed for his "flying dismounts" after victories, Frankie has three times been the champion jockey in England. By the end of 2005, he had also participated in 39 Breeders' Cup races, the most for any foreign-based rider. Dettori was victorious in the 1994 Breeders' Cup Mile with Barathea, and has twice won the Breeders' Cup Turf, with Daylami and Fantastic Light. Dettori is also a two-time winner of the Hong Kong Cup, with Fantastic Light and Falbrav. He has won the Prix de l'Arc de Triomphe three times, with Lammtarra in 1995 and back-to-back runnings with Sakhee and Marienbard in 2001–02. And he has also won the Japan Cup three times, with Singspiel, Falbrav and Alkaased.

Dettori's mother was a professional circus performer. At age eight, he was given a Palomino pony, and for the next five years he practised his riding skills every day. At age 13, Dettori dropped out of school to pursue his own career as a jockey. He subsequently went to work for trainer Luca Cumani in Newmarket. On 16 November, 1986, Dettori won his first race, on a horse named Billy Pitt at Italy's Turin racecourse. On 9 June, 1987, Dettori achieved his first win at an English track with Lizzy Hare at Goodwood. In 1989, he was England's champion apprentice, with 75 wins, and in 1990 he became the first teenager since Lester Piggott to record 100 victories in one season.

Born.........................15 December, 1970
Riding career ....has spanned 24 years

It was also in 1990 that Dettori recorded his first Group 1 win, piloting the Cumani-trained MarkofDistinction to victory in the Queen Elizabeth II Stakes at Ascot. In 1992, Dettori registered his first classic victory with Polytain in the Prix du Jockey Club at Chantilly. Two years later, he began riding for the Maktoum family's Godolphin Racing operation, a situation that has provided many rewards for both parties. The aforesaid Lammtarra, Sakhee, Marienbard, Fantastic Light, the 2002 Oaks winner Kazzia, the 2004 Gold Cup winner Paineau – all are Maktoum horses that were ridden by Dettori.

In 1995, Dettori won the St. Leger Stakes on Godolphin's Classic Cliché to achieve his 1,000th winner in England. The following month he added Lammtarra's Arc de Triomphe victory to his expanding portfolio. It was also aboard Lammtarra that Dettori achieved the first of his quartet of victories in the King George VI and Queen Elizabeth Diamond Stakes, the others coming with Swain, Daylami and Doyen.

Ascot has been the scene of many notable Dettori moments, but none more so than when he rode all seven winners at accumulative odds of 25,095–1 on the Saturday (28 September) of the Ascot Festival in 1996. Four of the horses were Maktoum runners – but no jockey in all of Britain had ever before ridden more than six winners in one day at one meeting. The achievement made front-page headlines in all the British papers, a very rare occurrence for anything involving racing.

In June of 2000, Dettori and jockey Ray Cochrane survived the crash of a light aircraft at Newmarket that killed the pilot. Dettori broke his ankle and Cochrane, who pulled him from the wreckage, is credited with saving Dettori's life.

"Frankie Dettori has the best mechanics of any race rider I have ever seen. He also has the most 'come-and-watch-us' charisma of any jockey anywhere on the planet." **Brough Scott**, Injured Jockeys' Fund Calendar, **2001**

Jumping for joy: Frankie Dettori does his celebratory flying dismount from Daylami after the pair won the 1999 King George VI And Queen Elizabeth Stakes at Ascot.

STEVE DONOGHUE

STEVE DONOGHUE was the dominant rider of the first part of the 20th century, until the arrival of Gordon Richards. He was champion jockey in Great Britain for 10 consecutive years from 1914, sharing the title on the final occasion with Charlie Elliott, and won the Derby four times in five seasons.

His early racing life was somewhat chequered. The son of a steelworker from Warrington in Lancashire, Donoghue was attached, though never apprenticed, to three stables in England before taking up a job in France with the American trainer Edward Johnson.

He was 20 years old before he rode his first winner, on Hanoi at the small track of Hyères, and he did not return to ride in England until 1911 when, after riding in Ireland for Michael Dawson and Philip Behan, he joined Atty Persse's stables in Hampshire.

Success was almost immediate. In 1913, he rode the brilliant two-year-old The Tetrarch to all his victories and in 1914, he was champion jockey for the first time with a total of 129 winners. The following year he had his first classic victories when Pommern landed the wartime Triple Crown, an achievement he repeated on Gay Crusader in 1917.

Donoghue won the Oaks for the first time in 1918 on My Dear. It was from 1921 that he began his sequence of four Derby victories in five years with the ill-fated Humorist, who died a few days after the race. The other Derby winners in this run were Captain Cuttle (in 1922), Papyrus (in 1923) and Manna, who also won the 2,000 Guineas, in 1925.

During this time Donoghue became extremely popular with the racing public, so much so that the call of "come on, Steve" became almost a national expression, but his attitude to owners and trainers – who paid him retainers – was less than exemplary. He frequently asked to be released from agreements so that he could ride a horse which he thought had better prospects.

Although he rode only one classic winner after Manna and never regained the jockeys' championship after 1923, Donoghue remained very popular with racegoers, due to no small extent to his association with the hugely popular stayer Brown Jack, winner of Ascot's Queen Alexandra Stake for six years in a row from 1929.

His final classic success came on Exhibitionnist in 1937, and he retired from the saddle at the end of that season and started

training at Blewbury. Like so many top-class riders on the flat he was nowhere near as successful out of the saddle, and though he bred the winner of the 1919 Ascot Gold Cup in By Jingo!, his breeding ventures scaled no great heights, either.

Donoghue, whose son Pat rode King Of Clubs to win the Lincolnshire Handicap in 1926 and later had a brief spell as a trainer, died during a visit to London in 1945. Although he had earned a great deal of money at the peak of his riding days, he was hopelessly impulsive and generous and gave much of it away.

"As well as being a jockey of great tactical skill, Steve Donoghue was a horseman who had a deep love of horses. With his beautiful hands, he could settle the freest of runners, and he was absolutely fearless."

Biographical Encyclopedia of British Flat Racing, 1978

Win double: Steve Donoghue's first great partner was The Tetrarch, the "Spotted Wonder" whose career ended aged two.

Born	Lancashire, England, 8 November 1884
Died	23 March 1945
Riding career	spanned 35 years

JOHN FRANCOME

Setting the standard: John Francome's winners mark has been surpassed, but his talents as a jump jockey has not.

Born	...............Swindon, England, 13 December 1952		
Riding career	......spanned 15 years		

Career record	Mounts	1st	2nd	3rd
	5,072	1,138		

"His lasting legacy was to put horsemanship back to the top of the agenda. Wanting to make a horse jump and make yourself go with them like Francome became every jockey's ideal."

Brough Scott, Injured Jockeys' Fund Calendar, 2001

JOHN FRANCOME DOMINATED the jumping scene from the mid-1970s until he retired towards the end of the 1984–85 campaign. He later turned to training but that was not a success and he is now involved as a broadcaster and writer.

He first made his name in the equestrian world as a show jumper and was part of the British team which won the European junior championship in 1969. In the same year Francome had his first involvement with trainer Fred Winter at the start of a long and successful association. He rode his first winner on Multigrey at Worcester in December 1970.

It took just under three more years for Francome to reach a career tally of 50 wins, but progress became more rapid and he achieved his century when King Flame won at Folkestone in December 1974. Two seasons later he won the championship for the first time with a total of 96 winners. He retained his title the following season.

In 1978 he won the delayed Cheltenham Gold Cup on Midnight Court. Cheltenham had been covered in snow on the Thursday of the Festival, and the race was postponed from March to April. However, that success was surrounded by controversy as it was announced on the morning of the race that he and bookmaker John Banks were to face the Jockey Club to answer allegations of bribery and corruption.

At the hearing, later that month, Francome was found guilty and was fined £750 as well as being suspended for nine weeks. Banks was banned from racing for three years and fined £2,500. The jockey, though, was cleared of any charges of stopping horses from winning.

Three years later, Francome piloted Sea Pigeon to win the horse's second straight Champion Hurdle deputising for the regular jockey Jonjo O'Neill, who was injured. Francome's utter coolness in a race has never been better illustrated than when he deliberately restrained Sea Pigeon from going ahead until halfway up the run-in.

Francome rode his 700th winner in 1981–82, but he was fighting a losing battle with Peter Scudamore for a fourth jockeys' title that season. He was some 20 winners adrift when Scudamore broke his arm towards the end of April. In an amazing act of sportsmanship, Francome said that he would stop for the season if he reached Scudamore's score. He kept his promise and when he rode his 120th winner, he stopped riding and the title was shared.

He landed the title for the next three seasons and in May 1984 beat Stan Mellor's National Hunt record total of 1,035 winners when Don't Touch was successful at Fontwell. His career tally had reached 1,138 when he retired in April 1985.

Though he never won the Grand National – the best he managed was second on Rough And Tumble behind Ben Nevis in 1980 (he had finished third on him the year before) – his other top successes included two King George VI Chases on Wayward Lad and Burrough Hill Lad, the Schweppes Gold Trophy on Donegal Prince, the Sun Alliance Chase on Brown Chamberlin and the Stayers' Hurdle on Derring Rose.

In retirement from riding, Francome trained for a short time but never threatened to scale the heights he had hit in the saddle and gave up at the end of 1987. He has since written a number of racing thrillers and has become a regular member of the Channel 4 broadcasting team.

MICHAEL "MICK" KINANE

THIRTEEN IS SAID to constitute a baker's dozen, and it is also the number of times that Michael "Mick" Kinane has been the champion jockey in his native Ireland. But Kinane has displayed his immense talents in many other lands as well. In 1989, he registered his first Prix de l'Arc de Triomphe victory with Carroll House, and repeated the achievement with Montjeu a decade later. Kinane won the 1993 Melbourne Cup with Vintage Crop and the 1997 Japan Cup with Pilsudski. He won the 2002 Hong Kong Cup with Precision. Kinane registered an English Oaks/Derby double with Imagine and Galileo in 2001. Three times he has been victorious in Breeders' Cup events, scoring with Johannesburg in the Breeders' Cup Juvenile in 2001 and with High Chaparral in back-to-back running of the Breeders' Cup Turf in 2002–2003.

Originally from County Tipperary, Kinane comes from a famous racing family. His father, Tommy, won the 1978 Champion Hurdle on Monksfield. Kinane was apprenticed to Liam Browne, one of the top nurturers of young riding talent in Ireland, and at age 15 registered his first career win aboard a horse named Muscari at Leopardstown. The following season Kinane landed his initial pattern win on Reelin Jig. In 1982 he registered his first classic victory aboard Dara Monarch, who was trained by Browne, in the Irish 2000 Guineas.

In 1984, Kinane was retained by Dermot Weld, Ireland's leading flat trainer, starting a 15-year association that matured into one of Europe's most formidable teams. Kinane rode Flash Of Steel to victory in the 1986 Irish 2,000 Guineas for Weld, but they truly hit the jackpot with Carroll House's victory in the 1989 Arc. From then on, Kinane was in demand by trainers throughout England. In 1990, he won the 2,000 Guineas for Richard Hannon on Tirol, and rode Belmez to victory in the King George VI and Queen Elizabeth Diamond Stakes at Ascot for Henry Cecil.

Further, it was in 1990 when Kinane managed to win the third jewel of the US Triple Crown, the Belmont Stakes, with Weld's trainee, Go And Go. At odds of 7.50–1, Go And Go was an Irish homebred campaigning for Morglare Stud Farm, and won the Belmont by a widening 8 lengths – a most discouraging circumstance for American breeders.

As the 1990s progressed, Kinane's list of clients continued to expand. He won the 1996 Gold Cup with Godolphin's Classic Cliché and the 1997 Champion Stakes with Lord Weinstock's Pilsudski. It was during that time that Kinane started riding for Irish trainer Aidan O'Brien, with the latter's yard gradually becoming the most important in Ireland. After ending his retainer with Weld, Kinane became the stable jockey for O'Brien's powerful Ballydoyle operation.

In 2000, Kinane guided the O'Brien-trained colt Giant's Causeway to five consecutive Group 1 victories. And in 2001–2002, Kinane registered six more Group 1 wins aboard another O'Brien trainee, Rock of Gibraltar. Milan, Imagine, Galileo, High Chaparral – their performances were the product of the same jockey/trainer partnership, too. In 2003, Kinane won six of the ten Group 1 races on the Irish schedule.

But, in a move that was surprising to many, the Kinane/O'Brien partnership ended at the end of the 2003 season. Kinane then took a retainer for the stable of trainer John Oxx, for which he won the St. James Palace and Irish Champion Stakes with the Aga Khan's colt, Azamour, in 2004. The man never seems to pause for breath.

"Michael Kinane is in a class of his own in his native Ireland, where he is a regular record-breaker. He continues to be very much the man for the big occasion." **Graham Dench**, Turf Directory, **1994**

As keen as ever: Michael Kinane may be in his fourth decade in the the saddle, but he retains his boyish enthusiasm for racing.

Born	22 June, 1959
Riding career	has spanned 33 years

JOHN LONGDEN

Spoils of victory: English-born John Longden piloted Count Fleet to Kentucky Derby glory in 1943 and a Triple Crown sweep.

"Longden and retirement seemed a contradiction in terms. He defied death so many times he seemed indestructible; and his competitive spirit was so strong that friends joked he would refuse to dismount even for his own funeral." **Archie McDonald,** The Canadian Horse, **1966**

JOHN LONGDEN'S PHILOSOPHY towards his profession was summed up in two short sentences. "I don't want to be another race rider," he said. "I want to be the best race rider." For a good portion of his career he undoubtedly was, registering 6,026 victories at North American tracks and a half-dozen on other shores, for a grand total of 6,032 – an all-time record at the time of his retirement as a jockey in 1966.

Longden's greatest feat was sweeping the North American Triple Crown with Mrs. John D. Hertz's homebred, Count Fleet, in 1943. Count Fleet culminated his career with ten straight victories. All his career efforts came with Longden aboard. Longden won the Santa Anita Handicap four times. In 1950, he guided Irish-bred Noor to four victories over the greatest American champion of that era, Citation. At the age of 51, Longden booted T.V. Lark to a three-quarter-length upset of Kelso in the Washington DC International.

Originally from Pontefract (near Wakefield), England, Longden emigrated to Canada with his family in either 1909 or 1912. The exact date depends upon his year of his birth. Some historians contend it was 1907. In his biography, *The Longden Legend*, Longden said he was born in 1910. He also said he and his family were booked for passage on the Titanic, but their connecting train was late, and they missed the fated liner's maiden voyage.

What is certain is that the Longdens went to Halifax, Nova Scotia, via another ship, and migrated from there to the coal-mining fields of Alberta. At age 13, John went to work in the mines. But he was learning to ride horses at the same time, and eventually was competing in unsanctioned races in Montana, one of the northernmost of the United States.

In 1927, Longden journeyed to Salt Lake City, Utah. A Mormon, he wanted to see the faith's founding city. There was also a recognized fall race meet there at the local fairgrounds, and on October 4, a nine-year-old claiming horse named Hugo K. Asher scored with Longden aboard. The winner's share of the purse was $280.

One of Longden's most remarkable feats involved Rushaway, who in 1936 won two major stakes, the 1 1/8-mile Illinois Derby and 1 1/4-mile Latonia Derby, at tracks 300 miles distant from each other on successive days. Longden shared the box car for the overnight train ride from Chicago to northern Kentucky with the gelding.

At age two, Calumet Farm's Hall of Fame homebred, Whirlaway, was guided to the winner's circle four times by Longden. Busher, another Hall of Famer, gained eight of her career stakes triumphs with Longden aboard.

Longden won the final race he ever rode. The nose victory was achieved aboard Royal George in the San Juan Capistrano Invitational Handicap at Santa Anita. Following his riding career, Longden became a trainer. In 1969, he sent Majestic Prince out to win the Kentucky Derby and Preakness Stakes. He remains the only person to ride and condition Derby winners.

After retiring from training in 1982, Longden frequently visited race tracks. Crowds surrounded him whenever he did. Autographs were frequently requested, and Longden would graciously comply.

Born	14 February 1910
Died	14 February 2003
Riding career	spanned 40 years
Hall of Fame	1958

Career record	Mounts	1st	2nd	3rd
	32,413	6,032	4,914	4,273
Earnings	$24,665,800			

CHRIS McCARRON

DURING THE FIRST YEAR in which Chris McCarron regularly rode races, he scored 546 times, setting what was then an all-time record for a single season by a jockey. This was in 1974. The following year he recorded 468 wins, and in the early weeks of 1976 he achieved career triumph number 1,000 – thus reaching the four-figure plateau in what was actually just a 24-month period. When McCarron retired from riding in July 2002, his career victory total was the sixth highest in history for a North American jockey. Among them was a pair of Kentucky Derby triumphs, with Alysheba and Go for Gin, a pair of Preakness Stakes triumphs, with Alysheba and Pine Bluff, and two Belmont Stakes triumphs with Danzig Connection and Touch Gold.

McCarron's resume further included nine wins in Breeders' Cup events, five of which came in the Breeders' Cup Classic – with Alysheba, Sunday Silence, Alphabet Soup and twice with Tiznow. McCarron won the Eclipse Award as North American's outstanding apprentice jockey in 1974, and a second Eclipse as outstanding journeyman in 1980. His career purse earnings in

> "Far from being an adolescent hell-for-leather daredevil, McCarron rides thoughtfully, 'like an old man,' according to some. He has a mystical instinct that enables him to stay out of trouble and to move at the right time." **Frank Deford,** Sports Illustrated, **1975**

North America totalled $263.99 million, the third highest figure ever achieved. In 1992 alone, McCarron was the regular rider for three champions: Paseana, the leading older distaffer; Guilded Time, the leading juvenile male runner; and Flawlessly, the leading distaff grass performer.

Born in Dorchester, Massachusetts, McCarron has an older brother named Gregg who was also a jockey. The latter once told their mother that Chris wouldn't succeed in the business, but the prediction proved erroneous. McCarron initial career victory was achieved aboard a gelding named Erezev in a $6,500 claiming race at Maryland's now-defunct Bowie Race Course on February 9, 1974. He went on to be the leading

jockey at four East Coast race tracks that year.

In 1978, McCarron relocated to Southern California, and that became his base of operations for the remainder of his riding career. Three times he won the Santa Anita Handicap, with Alysheba, Free House and Tiznow. McCarron was also a four-time winner of the Santa Anita Derby, with Dinard, Cavonnier, The Deputy and Came Home. He also won the 1998 Pacific Classic at Del Mar Free House.

With McCarron aboard, the Hall of Fame gelding John Henry won six Grade 1 races, one of which was the 1984 Arlington Million. McCarron was also the regular rider of the Hall of Famer Alysheba, with whom he won eight Grade 1 events, including the first two jewels of the 1987 Triple Crown. In 1988, McCarron journeyed to Tokyo Race Course and won the Japan Cup with Pay the Butler. In 1992, a quick plane flight across the International Date Line allowed him to ride in the Japan Cup and win the Matriarch Stakes at Hollywood Park on the same day.

On June 23, 2002, McCarron recorded his final career victory aboard Came Home in the Grade 3 Affirmed Handicap at Hollywood. But retirement from the saddle brought new frontiers to explore, including a tenure as a race-track administrator. McCarron is now devoting considerable time to a jockey school he has founded at the Kentucky Horse Park near Lexington. He also continues his involvement with the Don MacBeth Memorial Jockey Fund, which he pioneered to provide relief to disabled riders and their families.

Spirited ride: The 1994 Kentucky Derby belonged to Chris McCarron, who booted Go For Gin to a two-length victory.

Born	27 March 1955		
Riding career	spanned 29 years		
Hall of Fame	1989		
Career record	Mounts	1st	2nd	3rd
(through 2006)	34,239	7,141	5,670	4,672
Earnings	$264,380,651		

TONY McCOY

FEW SPORTSMEN in any walk of life can have reached the top of their professions as quickly as Tony McCoy, who rode his first winner (on the flat) in March 1992 and was champion jump jockey in Great Britain just over four years later. His liaison with Martin Pipe, which effectively began in 1997, has resulted in a seemingly endless succession of records.

McCoy, whose father bred the 1993 County Hurdle winner Thumbs Up, was apprenticed to the leading Irish trainer Jim Bolger in 1991 and, with 13 (flat and jumping) winners to his name, he moved to England for the 1994–95 season, joining Toby Balding's stable. His first winner in Britain came on Chickabiddy at Exeter in September 1994, and he ended the 1994–95 season as leading conditional rider with a record in that sphere of 74 winners, 50 more than the score of his nearest rival. It would have placed him seventh in the senior table.

His first big-race success came when Kibreet won the Grand Annual Chase at the Cheltenham Festival in March 1996. He ended that season as champion jockey for the first time with 175 winners. At that time he was riding mainly for Paul Nicholls, but McCoy's decision to ride a horse for Martin Pipe – instead of one of Nicholls' – halfway through the 1996–97 season was the first firm step towards a partnership which has proved so rewarding for both men.

Born	Antrim, N. Ireland, 4 May 1974		
Riding career	8 years		

Career record (as of May 2000)	Mounts	1st	2nd	3rd
		1102		

McCoy had two lengthy spells on the sidelines in 1996–97, but still gained his second jockeys' title with 190 winners. The two most important of those came in March 1997, at the Cheltenham Festival, when Mr Mulligan won the Cheltenham Gold Cup and Make A Stand took the Champion Hurdle. The year continued to be memorable for him as he rode five winners at one meeting on two occasions and, in August, landed his 500th career success.

Less than three months later, he beat his own record for the fastest century in a season when Sam Rockett was successful at Newton Abbot. The records continued to fall – the fastest 150 in December and the fastest 200 in February. By the end of the 1997–98 season he was champion for the third time with a record 253 victories, beating by 32 the previous highest tally of Peter Scudamore.

With the benefit of having the pick of Martin Pipe's horses, he was champion jockey again in 1998–99, with 186 wins, including the Supreme Novices Hurdle – aboard Hors La Loi – and Mildmay of Flete Challenge Cup – riding Majadou – at the Cheltenham Festival.

In 1999–2000, McCoy blasted through the 200-win barrier again and retained his jockeys' championship with 245 winners. The highlight of his season was victory in the Queen Mother Champion Chase on Edredon Bleu, adding to his previous Cheltenham Festival successes.

Although McCoy's gaudy figures must be tempered by the fact that there is far more jump racing now than there was even 10 years ago, his skill and determination – marked by his willingness to travel the length and breadth of Great Britain and to keep his weight down to as near 10st as he can (sometimes he gets down to that minimum) – have earned him the highest praise.

"Tony McCoy is quite outstanding. McCoy is the best jockey I have ever seen, since the days of my career in the saddle or since I retired. He is unbelievable and I have never seen a better Gold Cup ride than the one he gave Mr. Mulligan." **John Francome,** The Sun, **1997**

Flood of winners: Tony McCoy, Martin Pipe's No.1 jockey, has Blowing Wind perfectly balanced as they clear a fence during 2000's National Hunt Handicap Chase at Cheltenham.

GEORGE MOORE

LEADING AUSTRALIAN TRAINER Neville Begg said of George Moore, "He rode with a long rein, which relaxed the horses he rode and helped them to reserve their energy for the last run. Besides he was able to make his own luck during races, which was also important."

The name of George Moore is one of the most revered in Australian racing. Renowned during his career as "cotton fingers" for his silken touch, he was born George Thomas Donald Moore in Queensland in 1923 and began his riding career in Mackay, north Queensland, at the age of 14. The following year he moved to Brisbane but his career did not begin to gather momentum until 1939 when his indentures were transferred from Louis Dahl to Jim Shean.

Not meeting the physical qualifications for active service, Moore joined the First Labour Company and on being invalided out of the unit in 1943 he moved to Sydney. Soon acknowledged as the leading apprentice he captured headlines in 1946 by winning the Sydney Cup and The Metropolitan, at Randwick, on Cordale.

At the invitation of American jockey John Longden, who had been in Sydney the year before, Moore rode in the United States for a time in 1950 where his 11 wins featured the San Diego Handicap at Del Mar on Manyunk. His career was completely disrupted in 1954 when he admitted to a charge of betting and was suspended at the pleasure of the stewards, which resulted in him spending considerable time in the wilderness. On his return, Moore quickly demonstrated that he still possessed all his skills by winning the Sydney jockeys' premiership in 1956–57 and 1957–58.

Not long after resuming his occupation he began riding in France for Alec Head and in 1959 rode a superlative race to win the Prix de l'Arc de Triomphe for the stable aboard Prince Aly Khan's Aureole horse Saint Crespin in sensational circumstances. Saint Crespin dead-heated for first with Midnight Sun, ridden by Jean Fabre, but Moore lodged an objection claiming his mount had been bumped several times in the

"George Moore was a great horseman, who had a touch of genius about him. He rode a lot of winners for me and I was amazed at the way he always placed his horses so well during races."

Neville Begg, leading Australian trainer.

straight and quite severely in the last 100 metres. After a lengthy hearing the stewards eventually disqualified Midnight Sun from first place for having hampered Saint Crespin and awarded him the race.

To his delight, 22 years later, he was to witness his son, Gary, also winning the Prix de l'Arc de Triomphe for Alec Head on the Riverman four-year-old Gold River. Commuting regularly between Australia and England in the 1960s Moore won the first of eight consecutive Sydney jockeys' championships in 1961–62, when he rode 85 winners. Many of those winners were prepared by leading Sydney trainer Tommy Smith, with whom he had a highly successful if tempestuous association.

They combined most successfully together with some wonderful horses including Tulloch, who won 36 races and ran 16 placings in 53 starts. Moore was aboard Tulloch in 19 of his wins including the Australian Jockey Club, Victoria and Queensland Derbys as well as the Brisbane Cup at his last appearance on 12 June 1961. While dominating the Sydney scene Moore was continuing to be eagerly sought-after in England and Europe.

In 1967, he had a vintage year riding for Noel Murless, winning the 2,000 Guineas and the Derby on Royal Palace; the 1,000 Guineas and Coronation Stakes on Fleet, and the King George VI And Queen Elizabeth Stakes on Busted. His other victories featured the Princess Of Wales's Stakes and the Geoffrey Freer Stakes for the Queen on Hopeful Venture. Appropriately, Moore ended his riding career in a blaze of glory. With his days in the saddle coming to a close he performed the extraordinary feat of capturing 15 of the 29 races decided at the 1969 A.J.C. autumn carnival at Randwick.

Then he won the Golden Slipper Stakes – Australia's premier two-year-old event – at Rosehill for the first time in 1970 on Baguette and again the following year on the Smith-trained Fairy Walk. His last year as a jockey, 1971, he was also triumphant on Baguette in the

Newmarket Handicap; on Rajah Sahib in the Doncaster handicap; and in the A.J.C. and Victoria Derbys on Classic Mission.

After turning to training he established stables in France before moving to Hong Kong where he won the championship 11 times in 13 years before retiring to Queensland's Gold Coast.

Born		5 July 1923		
Riding career		1937–71		
Career record (worldwide)	Starts	1st 2,278	2nd	3rd
In Sydney (1957–71)	Starts 3,403	1st 1,040	2nd 620	3rd 447

Fast track: George Moore unsaddles Fleet after the pair had combined to win the 1,000 Guineas at Newmarket in 1967.

LESTER PIGGOTT

LESTER PIGGOTT has scaled the pinnacle of fame throughout the world in spite of having to overcome a number of physical problems – poor hearing, a cleft palate and a permanent battle to keep his weight down – during a career in which controversy was never far away.

He was apprenticed to his father Keith, whose father Ernie won the Grand National on Poethlyn (twice) and Jerry M . Lester rode his first winner at the age of only 12 when The Chase was successful in a selling race at Haydock in 1948.

Two years later he rode 52 winners in the season, but his almost ruthless determination

Housewives' choice: Lester Piggott rode more winners around the world than any other European-based jockey.

> "Although he ceased to be champion in 1972, there was still no doubt that Lester Piggott was the greatest of contemporary jockeys."

Biographical Encyclopedia of British Flat Racing, 1978

to win was already leading him into trouble and he received his first lengthy suspension in the autumn of 1950. Piggott's first top-level success came when Mystery IX took the Eclipse Stakes in 1951 and three years later he won the Derby for the first time on the 33–1 chance Never Say Die. He was aged 18. The horse's name made him very popular with small punters and Piggott's success was a major step in gaining him the folk-hero status he was to enjoy for many years.

Just a few weeks after winning his first Derby, Piggott was suspended – by no means justly in a number of opinions – for six months after riding Never Say Die in a very rough race at Royal Ascot, but this was only a temporary setback and he began 1955 as first jockey to Noel Murless' powerful stable at Newmarket. The association lasted for 12 seasons and included 2,000 Guineas and Derby wins on Crepello (1957), the Oaks with Carrozza (1957) and Petite Etoile (1959), the Derby and St. Leger with St. Paddy (1960), and the St. Leger with Aurelius (1961).

He was champion jockey for the first of 11 times in 1960 with 170 winners.

By the mid-1960s Piggott became increasingly involved with Vincent O'Brien's stable in Ireland and he split with Murless to ride the successful Valoris in the 1966 Oaks for O'Brien with Murless' Varinia back in third. The link with O'Brien was outstandingly successful, highlighted by the 1970 Triple Crown – 2,000 Guineas, Derby and St. Leger – of Nijinsky and as well as the Derby with Roberto in 1972 and The Minstrel (1977).

It should be pointed out that both those two were ridden with maximum force by Piggott and he would have incurred long suspensions had the current rules on use of the whip been in force then.

Piggott rode the Derby winner for a record ninth time on Teenoso in 1983 and he set a classic-winning record of 29 when Shadeed took the 2,000 Guineas in 1985. At the end of that season he retired from the saddle and started training, landing a Royal Ascot winner in his first season, but it all went wrong the following autumn when he was jailed for three years for tax evasion.

He served a year of that sentence and in 1990 took up his riding career again. Within weeks of so doing he rode Royal Academy to win the Breeders' Cup Mile for O'Brien and, in 1992, he won the English and Irish 2,000 Guineas, Champion Stakes and Juddmonte International Stakes on Rodrigo de Triano.

Piggott retired for good in 1994 with a career tally in Britain of 4,493 winners, but he remains keenly interested in the sport and was particularly happy when his son-in-law William Haggas trained Shaamit to win the 1996 Derby at Epsom.

Born	Newmarket, England, 5 November 1935		
Riding career	spanned 47 years		
Career record	**Mounts**	**1st**	**2nd**	**3rd**
(Estimated)	5,300			

LAFFIT PINCAY JR.

L AFFIT PINCAY JR. began his racing career at the age of 15 as an unpaid hot walker at the Presidente Ramon race track in his hometown of Panama City, Panama. He also began attending a local race-riding school run by a former jockey, Bolivar Moreno. From humble beginnings major accomplishments can sometimes occur, and in Pincay's case the accomplishments were colossal. When he retired in April 2003, Pincay had accumulated 9,530 career wins, more than any other jockey in thoroughbred racing history.

Pincay was a marvel of strength and timing. No other rider could match his ability to close ground in the final furlongs of races, a factor made possible by the athleticism he possessed to be in perfect synchronisation with his mounts. Pincay's career earnings remain the fourth-highest ever achieved by a North American-based jockey. He was a five-time Eclipse Award winner as outstanding journeyman rider, and he was inducted into the National Museum of Racing's Hall of Fame in Saratoga Springs, New York, before his 29th birthday.

The celebrated owner-breeder, Fred Hooper, engaged Pincay to bring his riding tack to the United States in 1966. Pincay was already a star in his home country – he had won 448 races during his first two seasons in Panama. From 1970–74, he was the yearly leader among all North American riders in purses earned, and in 1971 led the standings with 380 victories as well. Based primarily in Southern California, he won the Santa Anita Handicap five times, with Cougar II, Crystal Water, Affirmed, John Henry and Greinton, and the Santa Anita Derby seven times, with Alley Fighter, Solar Salute, Sham, An Act, Affirmed, Muttering and Skywalker.

It wasn't until 1982, though, that Pincay won his first Triple Crown race – that victory was

"For years, Pincay has been the nation's most powerful finisher, throwing his muscular, 117-pound frame so fiercely into a horse's closing strides that he often gives the appearance of lifting his mount in the final jump and dropping the horse's nose on the wire." William Nack, Sports Illustrated, 1986

achieved with Conquistador Cielo in the Belmont Stakes. Pincay subsequently won the 1983 Belmont with Caveat, and the 1984 Kentucky Derby and Belmont with Swale. He was triumphant in seven Breeders' Cup events, the most prominent being the 1986 Breeders' Cup Classic, which he won with the 10.10–1 shot Skywalker. Pincay also twice won the Arlington Million, with Perrault and Tight Spot. A Preakness Stakes victory, however, never came his way, but he twice won the Travers Stakes at Saratoga, with Bold Reason and Carr de Naskra.

Tragedy and other adversities did not spare Pincay over the years. His first wife, Linda, committed suicide in 1985. Controlling his weight took decades of discipline. Santa Anita's media guide aptly described him as "a bantamweight in a welterweight's body", while further noting he "restricted himself to an average intake of 750 calories per day for most of his adult life".

On March 14, 1987, Pincay won seven races on a single card at Santa Anita. On two other occasions, he won six races on a card at Santa Anita, and he also recorded half-a-dozen victories during a single afternoon at both Del Mar and Hollywood Park. During the 1990s, Pincay was frequently the oldest jockey in the races in which he competed. In 1999, the industry honoured him with a sixth Eclipse, this one for his meritorious representation of racing.

Setting the standard: Laffit Pincay Jr. is congratulated by fellow riders after tying Bill Shoemaker's career win record of 8,833, 9 December 1999, at Hollywood Park racetrack.

Born	29 December 1946			
Riding career	spanned 41 years			
Hall of Fame	1975			
Career record	**Mounts**	**1st**	**2nd**	**3rd**
(through 2003)	48,486	9,530	7,784	6,650
Earnings	$237,120,625			

SIR GORDON RICHARDS

"I had four great things in my life: Abernant, Crepello, Petite Etoile and a game, honest and thoroughly genuine friend, my stable jockey until his retirement in 1954, Sir Gordon Richards." **Sir Noel Murless**, Trainer.

GORDON RICHARDS dominated flat racing through the middle part of the 20th century. He was champion jockey for the first time in 1925 and failed to land that crown in only three seasons until his final title in 1953. On two of those occasions he was unable to defend his crown due to illness or injury and by the time he retired he had 4,870 winners to his name from 21,843 rides.

He enjoyed an unsullied reputation throughout his career which began with his apprenticeship to Martin Hartigan; he rode his first winner in 1921 on Gay Lord at Leicester. He gained his first championship in 1925 with a total of 118 in his first season as a full jockey. However, he was diagnosed with tuberculosis the following season, and Tommy Weston was champion for the only time.

In his first championship season, Richards was retained by Thomas Hogg, who went on to provide him with his first classic success when Rose Of England won the Oaks in 1930. Hogg was private trainer to Rose of England's owner, Lord Glanely. It was also in 1930 that Richards lost his jockeys' title for the only time in level competition, Freddie Fox beating him by one on the last day of the season.

In 1932, Richards teamed up with trainer Fred Darling and, a year later, set a record of 259 winners in the season, beating the previous best of 246 set by Fred Archer in 1885. His classic winners for Darling's yard at Beckhampton included Pasch in the 2,000 Guineas of 1938, the royal horses Big Game and Sun Chariot (she won the fillies Triple Crown of 1,000 Guineas, Oaks and St. Leger in spite of becoming very temperamental), all in 1942, and the top miler Tudor Minstrel in 1947.

After the hostilities of World War II had ceased, Richards joined Noel Murless' stable and enjoyed continued success although well into his 40s. The Derby, though, eluded him for year after year until, at the 28th – and what turned out to be final – attempt he rode Pinza to beat the Queen's Aureole in 1953. He had been knighted for his services to horse racing only a few days earlier in Her Majesty's Coronation year. Sir Gordon was 49 years old.

Ironically, it was one of the Queen's horses, Abergeldie, who ended Richards' career by throwing and rolling on him at Sandown Park the following summer. He had already decided to retire and take up training, but though he did well in his new sphere, he was nowhere near as successful as he had been in the saddle. His most important victory came when Reform won the Champion Stakes in 1967. He sent out Pipe Of Peace, Dart Board and Court Harwell to be placed in classics and also won good races with Greengage and London Cry.

He retired in 1969 because he could not find suitable premises and became racing manager for Lady Beaverbrook and the Ballymacoll Stud team of Sir Michael Sobell and Lord Weinstock. In November 1986, at the age of 82, the first knight of horse racing, Sir Gordon Richards, died.

Worth waiting for: Sir Gordon Richards was 49 years old when he won his first and only Derby, on Pinza in 1953.

Born	Shropshire, England, 5 May 1904
Died	10 November 1986
Riding career	spanned 34 years

Career record	Mounts	1st	2nd	3rd
	21,843	4,870		

YVES SAINT-MARTIN

YVES SAINT-MARTIN was the outstanding French jockey of his era, during which time he was 15 times champion, as well as achieving great international success with major wins in Britain and the United States. He had anything but a conventional background for a top-class jockey. There was no family connection with the sport until he joined a local riding club at Agen in the South of France and he was apprenticed to the top trainer François Mathet at the age of 14.

The following year he broke both his wrists in a fall from a yearling he was helping to break in, but in July 1958 he rode his first winner when Royallic was successful in an apprentice race at the Paris track of Le Tremblay. Royallic was trained by Mathet and his association with the trainer was to scale much greater heights in years to come.

He was champion jockey for the first time in 1962, the year he made his first big impression on racegoers in Britain when Monade won the Oaks by a whisker from West Side Story. Dicta Drake took the Coronation Cup and Match III, whose owner François Dupré was the chief patron of Mathet's stable, won the King George VI And Queen Elizabeth Stakes at Ascot. He also gained his first home classic success when La Sega took the Prix de Diane (French Oaks).

Later that season Saint-Martin impressed himself on American audiences when Match won the Washington DC International at Laurel Park, Maryland. In 1963, he wore the Dupré colours to victory in the Derby on Relko. The pair won the Prix Royal-Oak that year and the Grand Prix de Saint-Cloud and the Prix Ganay the next season. In 1964 the Aga Khan had horses with Mathet for the first time and Saint-Martin set a

record for a French season with 184 winners. The first of his eight triumphs in the Prix du Jockey Club came on Reliance, also for Dupré and Mathet, in 1965.

Saint-Martin maintained his link with Mathet until 1970, in which season he gained his first victory in the Prix de l'Arc de Triomphe on Sassafras. He then linked up with the art dealer Daniel Wildenstein, who was about to make a major impression on racing all around the world. Their most successful season came in 1976, when they won three of the British classics: Flying Water took the 1,000 Guineas, Pawneese claimed the Oaks (and later the King George VI And Queen Elizabeth Stakes) and Crow won the St. Leger.

He also twice won the Prix de l'Arc de Triomphe for Wildenstein, on Allez France in 1974 and on Sagace ten years later. When Sagace was first home again a year later – only to be demoted to second place – it was not Saint-Martin who was aboard. He was on Sumayr for the Aga Khan, for whom he had won the Arc on Akiyda in 1982.

By the time he retired, at the end of 1987, he had included the Prix de Diane five times and the two French Guineas on a total of 12 occasions. Yves' son Eric has also won the Prix de l'Arc de Triomphe, on Urban Sea in 1993, but his career has not, yet at least, reached the heights of his father's.

Golden boy: Yves Saint-Martin rode in the 1986 Derby at Epsom, a year before he retired from the saddle.

Born	Agen, France, 8 September 1941
Riding career	spanned 30 years

Career record	Mounts	1st	2nd	3rd
	3,314			

WILLIE SHOEMAKER

RECORDING A THOUSAND CAREER WINS would be a fair feat for most jockeys, but Bill Shoemaker, during his four-plus decades of riding, accumulated 1,009 victories in stakes alone. Four of these triumphs came in the Kentucky Derby, two in the Preakness Stakes, and five in the Belmont Stakes.

Shoemaker won the Santa Anita Handicap a record 11 times; he won three consecutive runnings of the United Nations Handicap from 1957–59. He won the inaugural edition of the Arlington Million (aboard John Henry) in 1981. His winning ride, at age 56, aboard Ferdinand in the 1987 Breeders' Cup Classic is considered one of the most thrilling in that event's history.

Today, more than a decade after Shoemaker's retirement from riding, only Eddie Arcaro and Laffit Pincay Jr. are considered his equals among 20th century North American jockeys. Shoemaker's career wins in all North American races totaled 8,818. His victories at tracks in England, Ireland, Argentina, and South Africa brought the grand total to 8,833, an all-time world record until Pincay surpassed it in 1999. Based primarily in California, Shoemaker won 17 riding titles at Santa Anita, 18 at Hollywood Park, and seven at Del Mar. He twice received the Eclipse Award as North America's leading jockey, in 1976 and 1981.

Originally from Fabens, Texas, Shoemaker weighed 2½ pounds at birth – his grandmother put him in a shoe box and used the kitchen oven as a make-shift incubator to keep him alive. In his riding prime, Shoemaker weighed just 93 pounds. He scored his initial career win aboard a filly named Shafter V in a $2,000 claiming race at Golden Gate Fields near San Francisco on April 20, 1949. The following year, Shoemaker was co-leader on the continent with 388 victories. In 1953 he registered 485 wins, which stood as the all-time single-season record until Sandy Hawley broke it in 1973.

"The Shoe", as he was known to both racetrackers and fans, led all North American

The Shoe: Winner of 8,833 races, including 11 classics, Willie Shoemaker may be the most beloved jockey to compete in the U.S.

jockeys in money earned 10 times, including seven straight years from 1958–64. He was the first rider whose career mounts earned $100 million. Still, one of his most famous rides involved a defeat, when he mistook the sixteenth-pole for the finish line in the 1957 Derby, stood up in his irons early, and lost by a nose aboard Gallant Man.

Swaps, Round Table, Northern Dancer, Buckpasser, Damascus, Forego, Spectacular Bid – all were among the greatest horses of their generations, all are in the Hall of Fame, and all scored multiple major stakes wins under Shoemaker. Eight times he won six races on a single card. When Shoemaker retired from riding

in 1990, after a tour of racetracks throughout North America, his plans called for a lengthy tenure as a thoroughbred trainer, but it wasn't to be.

In April 1991, Shoemaker was in an automobile accident that left him a quadriplegic. With the help of dedicated assistants, he continued as a licensed trainer for another six years, before retiring to a life in the background of the racing world. Thrice divorced, Shoemaker, who died in October 2003, devoted his twilight years to making appearances for the Shoemaker Foundation, which continues to bear his name and solicits donations to financially assist injured racetrack workers.

Born	19 August 1931
Died	12 October 2003
Riding career	spanned 42 years
Hall of Fame	1958

Career record	Mounts	1st	2nd	3rd
	40,350	8,833	6,136	4,987
Earnings	$123,375,524			

"Class can be defined in any number of ways, from outstanding abilities to a person's way of walking head and shoulders above the rest. In Shoemaker, the blend is difficult to separate."

Maryjean Wall, Lexington Herald, **1982**

YUTAKA TAKE

S O DOMINANT A JOCKEY has Yutaka Take been in his native Japan that most of the standards he competes against are those of his own making. Each year from 1996-99, Take set a new single-season record for wins at Japan's race tracks. In 2003, he became the first Japanese jockey to crack the double-century mark, registering 204 victories. In 2004, he established yet another new Japanese riding standard, with 211 wins, and in 2005 he surpassed even that mark, winning 216. Take's popularity in his home country has reached cult status – the mere fact that he is riding at a track on a given day guarantees a high turnstile count.

Originally from Kyoto, Take is the son of former jockey Kunihiko Take, who was dubbed, "The Magician on Turf", during his own riding days. And Yutaka Take's brother Koshiro is also a professional race rider. Take is rather tall for a jockey – he stands 5ft 7in. (1.7m). His riding career commenced on 1 March, 1987, at Hanshin Race Course, and he recorded his initial career

"Take is known for making the best of the split-second decisions. 'Genius' is a word often used to describe him, but his real secret lies in hard work and study." **JRA News Topics, 2005**

victory six days later aboard a horse named Dyna Bishop. Take set a record for first-year riders in Japan that season with 69 wins, and was honoured as his country's champion apprentice.

In 1989, Take registered his first overall Japanese riding title. And it commenced a period when he led the Japanese standings in victories 14 times during a 16-year period. In 1997, Take became the youngest jockey in Japanese racing history to reach the 1,000 career-win plateau. In 1998–99, he became the first jockey to win back-to-back runnings of the Japan Derby, achieving the feat with Special Week and Admire Vega, respectively. And in 1999, he booted Special Week to victory in the Japan Cup, while in 2001 he was victorious with Kurofune in the Japan Cup Dirt.

Riders possessing exceptional skills are almost destined to try their luck overseas. In 1991, Take ventured to Saratoga in upstate New York, where he won the Grade 3 Seneca Stakes with a horse named El Senor. During the next decade, international Group 1 company became part of Take's domain. In 1994, he was victorious on Ski Paradise in France's Prix du Moulin de Longchamp. The following year, Take won the Prix Maurice de Gheest with Seeking the Pearl. In 1999, he won Europe's foremost sprinting event, the Prix de l'Abbaye de Longchamp, with Agnes World, and the following year he rode Agnes World to victory in the July Cup at Newmarket. Take won a second Prix de l'Abbaye de Longchamp with Imperial Beauty in 2001, and also in that year, he won the Hong Kong Vase with Stay Gold.

Take's attempts at establishing semi-permanent bases in other countries have not been as gainful. He had only modest success riding in Southern California in 2000. The following year, after registering a surprising front-running win with Stay Gold in the Dubai Sheema Classic, Take set up shop in Chantilly, France. But in July he suffered a broken wrist, which prevented him from making the critical contacts with trainers during the summer months that jockeys from other lands dearly need. In Japan, however, Take has no peer. In 2005, he swept that country's Triple Crown with Deep Impact. During 2005, Take had recorded 2,691 career victories at Japanese Racing Association tracks, and his overall win ratio was 20.8 per cent.

Cult hero: Yutaka Take celebrates victory on Time Paradox during the Japan Cup Dirt in November 2004.

Born .... 15 March, 1969
Riding career .... has spanned 20 years

CHAPTER 7

A–Z OF RACING GREATS

Racing's great personalities come in all shapes and sizes and from all walks of life. In Britain, for instance, Her Majesty The Queen owns and breeds thoroughbreds and her expertise is recognised worldwide. Phil Bull was a humble mathematics teacher whose calculations primarily were based on race times.

THE PREVIOUS CHAPTER focused on the greatest jockeys from around the world; this one looks at all the people who make horse racing the sport it is: administrators, breeders, owners, trainers, jockeys, even gamblers. There are tales of rags to riches, a few riches to rags too, heartwarming sagas and sob stories.

Nowhere else, at least in Britain, is the class society more adhered to than in a racing paddock. The stable lad looks up to the jockey, who is employed by the trainer, who does as the owner bids. And the jockey – even if he is the greatest rider of his generation – will probably tip his cap in deference to the owners before speaking to them.

At the same time, racing is the most egalitarian of sports because every professional jockey earns the same fee for riding in a race, be it the $1 million Derby watched by hundreds of millions worldwide or the £1,904 ($2,750) Yodel For Your Neighbours Day Selling Stakes in front of a few hundred hardy racegoers. The winning jockeys, Johnny Murtagh and Dean Mernagh, respectively, also collected identical winning percentages – although the actual amounts differed somewhat!

Royal Family: British racing's leading family in the late 20th century were the al-Maktoum sheiks, princes from Dubai.

A

PRINCE KHALID ABDULLAH
Owner/breeder

◆ **Born: 1937**

A six-time recipient of the Eclipse Award – on four occasions as North America's leading breeder and twice as leading owner – Khalid Abdullah is the master of Juddmonte Farms, which is now one of the most powerful racing and bloodstock empires in the world. Juddmonte has major racing and/or breeding divisions in England, Ireland, France and the United States. Abdullah purchased his first racehorse in 1977, and he was represented by his first classic winner in 1980, when Known Fact won the 2,000 Guineas at Newmarket. In 1986, Dancing Brave presented Abdullah with victories in the 2,000 Guineas, the King George VI and Queen Elizabeth Diamond Stakes and the Prix de l'Arc de Triomphe. Dancing Brave was Europe's champion racehorse that year, as were Warning in 1988 and Zafonic in 1993, both of whom also carried Abdullah's green, pink and white colours. Within North America's shores, Abdullah's major victories include the 2001 Breeders' Cup Fillies and Mares Turf with Banks Hill, the 2003 Belmont Stakes with Empire Maker and the 2005 Breeders' Cup Fillies and Mares Turf with Intercontinental.

FRANK D. "DOOLEY" ADAMS
Jockey

◆ **Born: 1927 Died: 2004**

His plaque in the National Museum of Racing's Hall of Fame states that Frank D. "Dooley" Adams rode in 1,312 steeplechase events, and triumphed in 337 of them, for a win ratio of 25.7 percent. For seven consecutive years, from 1949–55, he led all North American steeplechase riders in victories. In 1951,

Eclipse master: Prince Khalid Abdullah after the Jersey Stakes at Royal Ascot in June 2000.

Adams won with 35 percent of his mounts. In 1954, his win ratio was 36.9 percent. A native of New York, Adams won a race at Mexico's Agua Caliente track at age 14, and began riding in the United States two years later. Oedipus and Neji were North American steeplechase champions with Adams handling riding chores. Adams won both the Saratoga and Beverwyck Steeplechase Handicaps four times, the Harbor Hill and Temple Gwathmey three times each, and the American Grand National twice. Adams never incurred as much as a single penalty for a riding infraction. After retiring to his home in Southern Pines, North Carolina, he occasionally tutored young riders on the art of negotiating jumps.

SHEIKH HAMDAN BIN RASHID AL-MAKTOUM
Owner/breeder

◆ **Born: 1945**

Sheikh Hamdan, second of the four Maktoum brothers, has had impacts in major races on several continents. In 1989, his colt Nashwan, trained by Dick Hern, accounted for the 2,000 Guineas, the Derby, and the King George VI and Queen Elizabeth Diamond Stakes and Eclipse Stakes. Sheikh Hamdan has twice won the Melbourne Cup, with Al Talaq in 1986 and with Jeune in 1994. Additional prestigious triumphs have come with Salsabil in the 1990 editions of the 1,000 Guineas, Oaks and Irish Derby, and in subsequent renewals of the 1,000 Guineas with Shadayid, Harayir and Lahan. Sheikh Hamdan scored his second Derby win at Epsom with Erhaab in 1994. In 2004, he won the Juddmonte International Stakes at York with Nayef. Numerous other Group 1 winners, of course, have been campaigned under the nom de course, Godolphin Stable, which has bases in Newmarket and Dubai. Daylami, Dubai Millennium, Fantastic Light, Lammtarra, Swain – these are just a handful of the horses who have earned champion honours for Godolphin in recent years.In 2006, Sheikh Hamdan's Jazil was victorious in the finale of America's Triple Crown, the Belmont Stakes.

SHEIKH MAKTOUM BIN RASHID AL-MAKTOUM
Owner/breeder

◆ **Born: 1943 Died: 2005**

The eldest of the four Maktoum brothers, Sheikh Maktoum became involved with thoroughbreds during the 1970s. He was the owner of Gainsborough Stud, which remains headquartered near Newbury, Berkshire, England, and has major satellite operations in Ireland, Australia and near Versailles, Kentucky. Sheikh Maktoum succeeded

Multiple winner: Emirati Prime Minister and Ruler of Dubai, Sheikh Mohammed Bin Rashid Al-Maktoum.

his late father as the ruler of Dubai in November, 1990, and also was vice president and prime minister of the United Arab Emirates. He was the first of the Maktoums to win a UK classic when Touching Wood took the 1982 St. Leger Stakes at Doncaster. The following year, Sheikh Maktoum won the Irish Derby with Shareef Dancer. Hatoof won the 1,000 Guineas for him in 1992, along with the Champion Stakes the following year, and in 1994 she added the winner's trophy from the Beverly D. Stakes at Arlington Park to the Sheikh's collection as well. Three times, Sheikh Maktoum's fillies won the Oaks. More recently, he won the Dewhurst Stakes at Newmarket in 2004 with Shamardal. His Gainsborough Farm, Kentucky, operation remains the home of Elusive Quality, who sired the 2004 Kentucky Derby winner, Smarty Jones.

SHEIKH MOHAMMED BIN RASHID AL-MAKTOUM
Owner/breeder

◆ **Born: 1949**

It is widely acknowledged that Sheikh Mohammed, the third oldest of the Maktoum brothers, has been the primary force in the ascendancy of the family to the realm of the world's foremost thoroughbred breeders and owners. He is master of Darley Stud, which under its umbrella operates eight farms, the most prominent being Dalham Hall Stud in Newmarket and Kildangan Stud in County Kildare, Ireland. All told, though, Darley has stallions in eight countries – England, Ireland, France, Dubai, Japan, Australia, New Zealand and the United States. In 2001, Sheikh Mohammed established Darley at Jonabell Farm in Lexington, Kentucky. Sheikh Mohammed purchased his first horse in 1976. During the 15 year-period from 1985–1999, he was the leading owner in England 13 times. In 1994, the Maktoum brothers established the Godolphin Stable. Besides winning major Group 1 races worldwide under the Godolphin banner, they have established their home country as a major bloodstock centre. In 2006, Sheikh Mohammed's Bernardini won the Preakness Stakes, the first win in an American Triple Crown race for a Maktoum.

American abroad: Cash Asmussen at Chantilly in 1993.

CASH ASMUSSEN Jockey

◆ Born: 1962

Brian Keith Asmussen changed his name legally to Cash in 1977. From a racing family, he rode in his first race at the age of 12, breaking his maiden on Pirate Island at Sunland Park, New Mexico in 1978, the year he moved to ride in New York. Asmussen was that area's leading rider in the next two seasons with scores of 231 and 246 and in 1980 and 1981 his earnings topped $5million. His first major successes came when Waya won Belmont Park's Beldame Stakes in 1979 and the Japan Cup on Mairzy Doates in 1981. In 1982 he moved to Europe as retained rider for Stavros Niarchos and a year later became the first American to ride a winner for the Queen when Reflection won at Chepstow. Asmussen became the first jockey to ride 200 winners in a French season in 1988. His major victories included the Prix de l'Arc de Triomphe on Suave Dancer – the first of three French Derby winning rides – the Irish 2,000 Guineas on Spinning World, the Prix de Diane three times and the Prix du Moulin five times. Asmussen retired from competitive riding in 2001. He now devotes the bulk of his professional efforts to his family's thoroughbred training operation on the outskirts of Laredo, Texas.

LORD ASTOR Owner/breeder

◆ Born: 1879 Died: 1952

A member of a very wealthy New York family, Lord Astor came to England as a boy and became the owner of 11 classic winners, all of which were bred at his Cliveden Stud in Berkshire. He was MP for Plymouth until he inherited his father's peerage in 1919. His first classic victory was when Winkipop took the 1,000 Guineas in 1910. Her descendants included the 1929 Oaks winner Pennycomequick and the 2,000 Guineas victor Court Martial. Her sister Third Trick bred Lord Astor's fourth Oaks winner, Short Story. Lord Astor won the Oaks five times and was twice leading owner, in 1925 and 1936, but the Derby eluded him: he owned five runners-up, including his 1921 2,000 Guineas winner Craig an Eran. His trainers included Alec Taylor, Joe Lawson, Jack Colling and William Waugh. High Stakes was his most prolific winner, with no fewer than 34 wins from 55 tries over nine seasons. When Lord Astor retired in 1950, his horses had won almost 500 races.

TED ATKINSON Jockey

◆ Born: 1916 Died: 2005

The round-house style he employed with a whip earned Ted Atkinson the nickname, "The Slasher," which he always thought inappropriate. Never one to mark up a horse or strike in mid-stride, Atkinson spared the rod far more than he used it. At the time of his retirement in 1959, Atkinson ranked fourth in all-time career wins among world riders, trailing only John Longden, Sir Gordon Richards, and Eddie Arcaro. A Kentucky Derby victory eluded Atkinson, but he won the 1949 Preakness and Belmont Stakes aboard the Greentree Stable homebred, Capot. His most remarkable feat involved riding Tom Fool through an undefeated four-year-old campaign in 1953. One of eight children, the Canadian-born Atkinson moved with his family to the United States in 1920. Uncommonly conscientious, he kept written journals of every race he ever rode. The notations are secured in bound volumes in the study of the farm Atkinson shared with his wife, Martha, near Richmond, Virginia. Both Ted and

Ready to go: Ted Atkinson prepares to leave for a race.

Martha have passed away, but their surviving family members intend to keep it as a vacation place.

B

BRAULIO BAEZA Jockey

◆ Born: 1940

One of the greatest riders to ever emerge from Panama, Braulio Baeza first rode in the United States in 1960. By the end of the 1960s, he had led the North American jockey standings in earnings four times, and was the regular rider aboard a trio of Horse of the Year honourees – Buckpasser in 1966, Dr. Fager in 1968, and Arts and Letters in 1969. Quiet, dignified and exceptionally efficient in his professional approach, Baeza first gained notice when he guided Sherluck to victory in the 1961 Belmont Stakes. At 65–1, Sherluck remains the longest shot to ever win that event. Baeza won both the Kentucky Derby and Belmont with Chateaugay in 1963, and the Belmont a third time with Arts and Letters in 1969. A Preakness Stakes triumph, though, always eluded him. Baeza led all jockeys in earnings again in 1975. Upon retiring from riding, he became a trainer, and subsequently an official at New York Racing Association tracks.

BOB BAFFERT Trainer

◆ Born: 1953

Impressive streaks and skeins hallmark Bob Baffert's career. For three consecutive years, from 1997-99, he received the Eclipse Award as North America's outstanding trainer. And in a period starting with Silver Charm's victory in the 1997 Kentucky Derby and extending to War Emblem's triumph in the 2002 Preakness Stakes, horses trained by Baffert won eight of 17 Triple Crown events. Four times, with Silver Charm, Real Quiet in 1998, Point Given in 2001 and with War Emblem, Baffert has sent out a horse who accounted for two jewels in the Triple Crown. He has also thrice won Breeders' Cup races - the Breeders' Cup Sprint with Thirty Slews in 1992, the Breeders' Cup Juvenile Fillies with Silverbulletday in 1998 and the Breeders' Cup Juvenile with Vindication in 2002. Baffert began his career as a quarter horse trainer and switched full-time to thoroughbreds in 1991. He has twice won the richest race on the globe, the Dubai World Cup, with Silver Charm in 1998 and with Captain Steve in 2001. Baffert further sent out

Horse of the Year Point Given to win the 2001 Travers Stakes at Saratoga.

LAZARO BARRERA Trainer

◆ **Born: 1924 Died: 1991**

Cuban-born and one of 12 children – including fellow trainer Oscar – Lazaro Barrera began his racing career as a hotwalker at Havana's Oriental Park. In 1944, he emigrated to Mexico, and became the leading trainer at the Hipodromo de Las Americas track. Barrera moved his operational base to Southern California in the early 1960s. He subsequently received four consecutive Eclipse Awards, 1976–79, as North America's outstanding trainer. Barrera's best horse was Affirmed, who swept the 1978 Triple Crown, and was Horse of the Year in both 1978 and 1979. He also trained Bold Forbes, who won the 1976 Kentucky Derby and Belmont Stakes en route to divisional honours. In 1977, Barrera sent out J.O. Tobin to hand Seattle Slew his initial career defeat. Cuban and Mexican racing records are spotty, but it's estimated that Barrera achieved 3,000 career victories. Four times, from 1977 to 1980, Barrera led North American trainers in earnings. Lazaro and Oscar died within three weeks of each other in 1991.

BOBBY BEASLEY Jockey

◆ **Born: 1936**

Bobby Beasley was born into a famous Irish racing family and he maintained its tradition, being one of the few men to win the Grand National (on Nicolaus Silver), Cheltenham Gold Cup (Roddy Owen and Captain Christy) and Champion Hurdle (Another Flash). He began by riding on the flat, but soon became too heavy for that and switched to the obstacles. Beasley had successful associations with Fred Winter and

Grand old lady: Lady Beaverbrook (right) is congratulated by the Queen after her Petoski had won at Ascot in 1985.

Paddy Sleator, who trained Another Flash to his Cheltenham triumph, and was involved with Beasley's success on Black Ice in the Triumph Hurdle, though that success is officially credited to Arthur Thomas. Weight problems forced Beasley into what turned out to be a short retirement, 1969–70, but he finally hung up his boots in 1974, with around 700 winners to his name. Turning to training, his first victory came in 1976, when he was based in Ireland. He returned to England, but his training career never matched his riding achievements and he gave up in 1988.

PATRICK (RUFUS) BEASLEY
Jockey/trainer

◆ **Born: 1906 Died: 1982**

Rufus Beasley, whose father rode Come Away to win the Grand National in 1891 and nephew Bobby won the 1961 race on Nicolaus Silver, began riding in Ireland before moving to England in 1926. In 1930 he rode a treble for Victor Gilpin at Royal Ascot and he was later retained by Miss Dorothy Paget and Jack Colling before becoming stable jockey to Cecil Boyd-Rochfort in 1936. The combination was extremely successful with their biggest wins coming when Boswell won the 1936 St. Leger and 1937 Eclipse Stakes, Precipitation collected the Ascot Gold Cup and Flares took the Champion Stakes. In 1945, Beasley retired to train at Malton. He came closest to a classic win when Bounteous was second in the St. Leger, but he was very successful with his handicappers, winning the Cambridgeshire three times, plus the Magnet Cup, Vaux Gold Tankard and Manchester November Handicap. Beasley also took the Dewhurst Stakes and Middle Park Stakes before retiring in 1974.

LADY BEAVERBROOK Owner

◆ **Born: 1909 Died: 1994**

Lady Beaverbrook – born Marcia Christoforidi – was a major player at the yearling sales through the late 1960s and 1970s when every breeder hoped any horse they submitted might attract her attention. Her horses were first trained by Walter Nightingall. Lady Beaverbrook's first winner came at Epsom in 1967 with Rosebid, and a major triumph followed soon after, Hametus taking the Dewhurst Stakes. The best horse she owned was Bustino, who cost her 21,000gns as a yearling. He gave his owner her first classic victory when he won the 1974 St. Leger, having won the Lingfield Derby Trial. As a four-year-old, Bustino won the Coronation Cup before finishing second to Grundy in the King George VI And Queen Elizabeth Stakes in what has often been described as the race of the

century. Lady Beaverbrook also won the 2,000 Guineas with Mystiko, the St. Leger with Minster Son, the King George VI And Queen Elizabeth Stakes with Petoski and the Irish St. Leger with Niniski. Boldboy, who raced until the age of nine, contributed 14 of her tally of 241 winners.

HARRY GUY BEDWELL Trainer

◆ **Born: 1874 Died: 1951**

The trainer of North America's first Triple Crown winner, Sir Barton, H. Guy Bedwell began his racing career at a bush track in Grand Junction, Colorado. A jack-of-all-trades, he once rode four horses and drove in six harness races on the same day. Moving east, he became the continent's leading thoroughbred trainer seven times, including six consecutive years from 1912–17. Under the employ of the Canadian sportsman, J.K.L. Ross, Bedwell conditioned Sir Barton and the crack sprinter, Billy Kelly. The latter actually beat Sir Barton on eight occasions. Because of a dispute over his use of the banned jockey, Carroll Shilling, Bedwell was not allowed to race in New York from 1921–38. During that period, he confined most of his training activities to Maryland. Later on, he moved his stable to the New England circuit. Bedwell is credited with a grand total of 2,160 career victories. The last was with a $5,000 claimer named Supper Date at West Virginia's Waterford Park on June 14, 1951.

TERRY BIDDLECOMBE Jockey

◆ **Born: 1941**

Terry Biddlecombe was the younger of two farming brothers from Gloucestershire – the senior, Tony, retired in 1965 – who appeared on the scene in the late 1950s. Many of his best winners were for Fred Rimell, with whom he had a very succesful association and for whom he gained his most important success when Woodland Venture took the 1967 Cheltenham Gold Cup. Their other big successes included two Mackeson Gold Cups on Gay Trip and the Triumph Hurdle on Coral Diver. Injury deprived Biddlecombe of a victorious ride on Gay Trip in the 1970 Grand National but he did partner him to second to Well To Do in 1972. Biddlecombe gained his first title in 1964–65, then repeated that feat the following season – becoming the first jump jockey to ride more than 100 winners in consecutive seasons – and shared it with erstwhile brother-in-law Bob Davies in 1968–69. Weight problems forced his retirement in 1974 after riding 908 winners. However, his personal life has not always run smoothly. After two failed marriages he met trainer Henrietta Knight and became her assistant. They were married in 1995 and the partnership has proved extremely successful.

MARCEL BOUSSAC
Owner/breeder

◆ **Born: 1889 Died: 1980**

Marcel Boussac dominated flat racing in England and France immediately after World War II. He had made his fortune in the textile industry during World War I and the first big success came when Ramus took the Prix du Jockey Club in 1922. In England, he won the 1950 Derby, Oaks and St. Leger with Galcador, Asmena and Scratch II, respectively, while Talma II claimed the 1951 St. Leger. There were the Champion Stakes with Goyescas and Asterus, four Ascot Gold Cup winners (Caracalla II, Arbar, Elpenor and Macip), Djeddah won the Eclipse Stakes and Champion Stakes and, although all his horses were – from the 1940s – trained in France by Charles Semblat, he was leading owner in Britain in 1950 and 1951. In France his best wins included the 1956 Prix du Jockey Club and the Prix de Diane with Philius and Apollonia. Boussac was created President of the Société d'Encouragement but his empire was already crumbling. Crepellana took the Prix de Diane in 1969 and Acamas the Prix du Jockey Club in 1978, the year his textile business went bankrupt.

FRANÇOIS BOUTIN Trainer

◆ **Born: 1937 Died: 1995**

François Boutin was an outstanding trainer who won major races all over the world. In particular, he was champion in his native France on no fewer than seven occasions. Boutin began training in 1964 after having spent three seasons as assistant to Etienne Pollet. His first win came with Aravios at Saint-Cloud in 1965 and his first major victory was when La Lagune took the honours in the 1968 Oaks. Boutin's best horse was the filly Miesque, who won the Breeders' Cup Mile twice, the 1,000 Guineas in England and France, and the Prix Jacques le Marois twice; later her colt Kingmambo – sire of 2,000 Guineas winner in 2000 King's Best – took the Poule d'Essai des Poulains and Prix du Moulin while her filly East of the Moon won the Poule d'Essai des Pouliches and Prix de Diane. Boutin's other big wins included Nonoalco (1974's 2,000 Guineas), Sagaro (three Ascot Gold Cups), L'Emigrant and Hector Protector (Poule d'Essai des Poulains) and Arazi, who was the world's champion two-year-old in 1991.

Early riser: François Boutin supervises an early-morning workout at Chantilly in September 1987.

SIR CECIL BOYD-ROCHFORT
Trainer

◆ **Born: 1887 Died: 1983**

Cecil Boyd-Rochfort, the stepfather of Henry Cecil, trained for King George VI and then Queen Elizabeth II from 1943 until he retired in 1968, the same year in which he was knighted. His biggest royal wins were Pall Mall in the 1958 2,000 Guineas, Hypericum in the 1956 1,000 Guineas, Aureole in the 1954 King George VI And Queen Elizabeth Stakes and Canisbay in the 1965 Eclipse Stakes. He trained at Newmarket's Freemason Lodge stables from 1923 to 1968. Brown Betty's 1933 Oaks win was his first classic, but his particular flair was for training stayers; Boswell's 1936 St. Leger triumph was the first of six final classic wins (from 13 entries). Boyd-Rochfort's only success in the Derby came in 1959 with Parthia. He was champion trainer twice in the 1930s and thrice in the 1950s, and other top successes for his stable were the Gold Cup wins of Precipitation and Zarathustra, and in the later stages of his career he won the Goodwood Cup four times between 1962 and 1966.

COLONEL EDWARD RILEY BRADLEY Owner/Breeder/Racetrack Executive

◆ **Born: 1859 Died: 1946**

The first owner to win four Kentucky Derbys, Colonel Edward Riley Bradley was master of the 1,500-acre Idle Hour Stock Farm, one of the great breeding establishments in the Bluegrass region. Behave Yourself won America's premier

race for Bradley in 1921, as did Bubbling Over in 1926, Burgoo King in 1932, and Broker's Tip in 1933. All were homebreds. All, in the Bradley tradition, had names that started with "B". A real estate speculator, with large holdings in Chicago and Palm Beach, Bradley used the fortune gained from these ventures to underwrite his thoroughbred activities. From 1926–32, Bradley owned the Fair Grounds racetrack in New Orleans. Top homebreds he campaigned further included Blue Larkspur, Bimelech, Bee Mac, By Jimminy, and Busher. Bradley vowed that he'd be racing horses to his last day, a promise fulfilled. Upon his death, *The Thoroughbred Record* stated, "His permanent influence on the American turf … was as great as that of any man who lived in modern times."

EDGAR BRITT Jockey

◆ **Born: 1913**

Edgar Britt was one of the first of the many Australian jockeys who came to ride in Britain after World War II. He rode his first winner at Canterbury, in Sydney, in 1930, before riding for the Maharajah of Baroda in India for a decade from 1935. Britt moved to Britain to ride for the Maharajah, when his horses were trained by Sam Armstrong, winning the Cesarewitch Handicap on Kerry Piper and the substitute Manchester November Handicap on Oatflake in his first season in England. The Maharajah's Sayajirao provided his first classic winners in 1947, in the Irish Derby and St. Leger. In 1948, Britt lost the retainer with the owner, but found a job with Marcus Marsh and when Harry Carr broke a leg, Britt came in for a number of rides for Cecil Boyd-Rochfort's yard, winning the St. Leger on Black Tarquin. He rode Musidora to win the 1949 1,000 Guineas and Oaks, Frieze in the 1952 Oaks, Nearula in the 1953 2,000 Guineas and Honeylight in the 1956 1,000 Guineas, all for Charles Elsey's stable. Britt retired in 1959 and returned to Australia. In 2004, at the age of 90, Britt was inducted into the Racing Hall of Fame.

CLIVE BRITTAIN Trainer

◆ **Born: 1933**

Clive Brittain began training in 1972, having worked as an apprentice, then stable lad for Sir Noel Murless. He quickly acquired a reputation for optimism, running horses apparently way above their class, but his tactics have often been rewarded with victory. His first top-level success was with Averof in the 1974 St. James's Palace Stakes. He also won the 1978 St. Leger with Julio Mariner and was the first British-based trainer to win the Japan Cup, in 1986 with Jupiter Island. Brittain won the 1991 2,000 Guineas with Mystiko. The Derby remains elusive, but when Terimon was second at 500–1 in 1989 he was the longest-priced horse ever to be placed in that classic. Brittain has been particularly successful with fillies, among the best of whom have been Pebbles, winner of the 1,000 Guineas, Eclipse Stakes and Breeders' Cup Turf; User Friendly, the 1992 English, Irish and Yorkshire Oaks and St. Leger winner, and Crimplene, whose 2000 successes included the Irish and German 1,000 Guineas, Coronation Stakes and Nassau Stakes. In 2003–04, Brittain sent out Warrsan to win back-to-back runnings of the Coronation Cup. He also won the 2004 Prix de l'Abbaye de Longchamp with Var.

ARTHUR BUDGETT
Trainer/owner/breeder

◆ **Born: 1916**

Arthur Budgett is one of only two men to have owned, trained and bred two Derby winners which he did with half-brothers Blakeney in 1969 and Morston in 1973. Their dam, Windmill Girl, was herself trained by Budgett to be second in the Oaks. Budgett trained briefly in 1939 but made his mark immediately after World War II. In 1946 Arthur and brother Alan Budgett's Commissar won the Stewards' Cup; two years later, Budgett trained the then eight-year-old to win the Lincoln. In 1951 he moved to the Whatcombe estate – where he trained until he retired in 1976 – and in that year he produced one of the first important successes for Lester Piggott when Barnacle won the Great Metropolitan Handicap at Epsom. Other big races which he won were the Queen Elizabeth II Stakes with Derring-Do and Ascot's Gold Cup with Random Shot, though only on the disqualification of Rock Roi. Budgett was champion trainer in 1969, Blakeney's year, thanks also to Huntercombe, who won three big races, and Aggravate.

PHIL BULL
Gambler/owner/breeder/publisher

◆ **Born: 1910 Died: 1989**

Phil Bull founded the Timeform organisation which has become accepted as the most accurate and impartial assessment of horses' merits worldwide. The idea developed from his quest for backing winners, but he was also a

Number cruncher: Phil Bull turned numbers into winners.

successful owner and breeder. He was a mathematics teacher, but used such calculations primarily as a means of helping him to back winners at which, from the 1940s onwards, he did very well. He produced his racing annuals, first as *Best Horses of …* and then covering every horse that ran in Great Britain in a year. Timeform as an organisation came into existence in 1948. Bull's many winners as an owner, with a variety of trainers, were headed by Sostenuto, Philoctetes and Pheidippides, while the best horse he bred was Charles Engelhard's Romulus. Bull regularly professed almost passionate contempt for the Jockey Club and the way in which racing was run. He was at different times on the councils of the Racehorse Owners' Association and the Thoroughbred Breeders' Association.

FRANK BUTTERS Trainer

◆ **Born: 1877 Died: 1957**

Frank Butters first made his mark on British racing at age 50, but was outstandingly successful for more than 20 years, sending out the winners of 15 classics. He began his training career in his native Austria, moved to Italy and arrived in England in 1927 to train for Lord Derby. He trained a classic winner in his first season at Newmarket when Beam took the Oaks and ended the year as champion trainer. Butters was champion again in 1928, when Toboggan

won the Oaks and Fairway – the Derby's beaten favourite – took the St. Leger. Three years later Butters started training for the Aga Khan and, in 1932, sent out Udaipur to win the Oaks and Firdaussi the St. Leger. Butters won the Oaks again with Light Brocade in 1934, and the Derby with the Triple Crown winner Bahram in 1935 and Mahmoud a year later. He won wartime St. Legers with Turkhan and Tehran and gained his final two classic successes when Steady Aim and Masaka won the Oaks in 1946 and 1948.

C

HARRY CARR Jockey

◆ **Born: 1916 Died: 1985**

Harry Carr rode for Cecil Boyd-Rochfort's Freemason Lodge stable for 17 years and was the royal jockey from 1947 until his retirement in 1964. He was apprenticed to Bob Armstrong and rode his first winner at Ayr in 1930. Carr won every English classic apart from the 2,000 Guineas. The best horses Carr rode were Alcide, who would have started hot favourite for the 1958 Derby but was nobbled, and Meld, who landed the fillies' Triple Crown in 1955. Alcide won the 1958 St. Leger by eight lengths and the 1959 King George VI And Queen Elizabeth Stakes. Carr wore Alcide's colours – of owner Sir Humphrey de Trafford – to victory in the 1959 Derby on Parthia. He also won the 1962 St. Leger on Hethersett in the twilight of a career which included more than 1,000 winners in Great Britain and 300-plus in India, where he rode regularly through the winter and where his successes included the Indian Derby and the King Emperor's Cup. Carr operated his Genesis Green Stud on the outskirts of Newmarket for over 20 years before his death.

BROWNIE CARSLAKE Jockey

◆ **Born: 1886 Died: 1941**

Bernard "Brownie" Carslake was one of the first jockeys to come to Britain from Australia which he first did in 1906 and, after a spell riding in Eastern Europe, returned for good near the end of World War I. In 1918, he rode Ferry to win the 1,000 Guineas for George Lambton and he partnered Keysoe to St. Leger victory in 1919. A year later, Atty Persse retained him to ride Tetratema to 2,000 Guineas victory, and Silver Urn to take another 1,000 Guineas. In 1924 Carslake gained his second St. Leger victory on

Salmon Trout amid rumours that he had been bribed by the bookmaker Mo Tarsh to stop the colt from winning. Carslake was advised that the stewards would be watching him very closely; Salmon Trout won; Tarsh and other bookmakers had heavy losses. After a brief spell training, in 1929, Carslake returned to riding and won the 1934 Oaks on Light Brocade. He won the 1938 St. Leger on Scottish Union, but his constant battle with his weight took a heavy toll; he collapsed at Alexandra Park in 1940 and immediately retired.

WILLIE CARSON Jockey/breeder

◆ **Born: 1942**

Willie Carson had to wait for three years after he was apprenticed to Gerald Armstrong in 1959 before he rode his first winner, on Pinker's Pond at Catterick. His career was a conspicuous success for many years after that until injury forced him into retirement in 1997 after riding 3,828 winners in Great Britain alone. He was champion jockey on five occasions with a best score of 182 in 1978 and won every classic, beginning with High Top – for whose trainer Bernard van Cutsem he rode a lot of big winners – in the 1972 2,000 Guineas. Carson's first Derby came with Troy in 1979. By this time he was retained by Dick Hern at West Ilsley. Carson's fierce loyalty to Hern resulted in some outspoken and much admired comments when Hern was sacked as one of the Queen's trainers in 1989. His other Derby triumphs came on Nashwan (in 1989) who, like Troy, also won the

King George VI And Queen Elizabeth Stakes, Henbit (1980) and Erhaab (1994).

HENRY CECIL Trainer

◆ **Born: 1943**

The elder by ten minutes of twin brothers – and stepsons of Cecil Boyd-Rochfort – Henry Cecil began training in 1969 and his career has been one of almost uninterrupted success. In his first season, he won the Eclipse Stakes with Wolver Hollow and the Observer Gold Cup with Approval; his first classic came when Bolkonski took the 1975 2,000 Guineas. Cecil was leading trainer for the first of ten occasions in 1976, the year when Wollow won the 2,000 Guineas. In 1987 he set a record of 180 winners in a season, including the second of four Derby wins, this time with Reference Point, ridden by Steve Cauthen. Kieren Fallon was stable jockey, until controversially sacked, when completing the 1999 Derby/Oaks double on Oath and Ramruma. Cecil's other top winners include the fillies' Triple Crown in 1985 with Oh So Sharp; the King George VI And Queen Elizabeth Stakes with Reference Point, Belmez and King's Theatre; the Oaks on four other occasions; another five in the 1,000 Guineas; and the St. Leger four times.

JOE CHILDS Jockey

◆ **Born: 1884 Died: 1958**

Joe Childs was one of the oustanding riders in the first third of the 20th century, but the domination of Steve Donoghue and Gordon Richards,

Cups King: Bart Cummings shows off the 1999 Melbourne Cup with jockey John Marshall (left) and horse Rogan Josh.

successively, meant he was never champion jockey. His preferred tactic of riding only waiting races possibly prevented him from doing better. Nevertheless, he rode 15 classic winners, beginning with Fifinella, the last filly to win Derby and Oaks – in 1916 – and including the 1918 wartime Triple Crown hero Gainsborough. Childs, whose father and four brothers were also jockeys, began his riding career in England, had two spells in France and one in Germany before returning to England in 1914. His successes on Gainsborough started a long association with that colt's trainer Alec Taylor. Childs later became first jockey for King George V, for whom he won the 1,000 Guineas on Scuttle, and other top-level successes came with Coronach in the Derby and the St. Leger, Cameronian in the 2,000 Guineas and four Ascot Gold Cups.

NEVILLE CRUMP Trainer

◆ **Born: 1910 Died: 1997**

Neville Crump was an outstanding trainer of jumpers, particularly steeplechasers, from the end of World War II until he retired in 1989. He was a trainer of the old school, and though he possessed a formidable temper, he was a kindly man. Crump set up at Middleham in Yorkshire and gained the first of his three Grand National victories with the mare Sheila's Cottage in 1948. His other triumphs in the race came with Teal in 1952 and Merryman II in 1960; Teal's success was a major factor in his trainer's first championship and he also won the title five years later when Much Obliged was victorious in the first running of the Whitbread Gold Cup. Crump managed to claim just about every major chase in Britain; Wot No Sun, Merryman II and Arcturus won the Scottish Grand National; there were also other Whitbread successes with Hoodwinked and Dormant;

Number one: Willie Carson was champion jockey on five occasions and won the Derby four times in a 38-year riding career.

Skyreholme landed the Welsh National; and Cheltenham Festival successes included the Mildmay of Flete with Verona Forest and the Cathcart Challenge Cup with Hoodwinked.

LUCA CUMANI Trainer

◆ Born: 1949

The son of Sergio Cumani, who was ten times champion trainer in their native Italy, Luca Cumani is one of Europe's finest thoroughbred conditions. A former European amateur riding champion, Cumani received his trainer's licence in 1978. He has won the Derby twice, with Kahyasi in 1988 and with High-Rise in 1998, and has twice been victorious in the Juddmonte Stakes, with One So Wonderful in 1998 and with Falbrav in 2003. Further, Cumani has twice won the Fillies Mile at Ascot, with Glorosia in 1997 and with Gossamer in 2001. At tracks further afield, Cumani won the 1983 Arlington Million with Tolomeo, the 1994 Breeders' Cup Mile at Churchill Downs with Barathea and the 2003 Hong Kong Cup with Falbrav (the latter actually won five Grade 1/Group 1 stakes under Cumani's care). In 2005, Cumani was victorious in the Prix du Moulin de Longchamp and the Queen Elizabeth II Stakes at Newmarket with Starcraft, and he also won the Japan Cup with Alkaased. Cumani's base of operations is Bedford Lodge Stables at Newmarket. He is also director of Fittocks Stud in Newmarket, which bred the 2001 St. Leger Stakes winner, Milan.

BART CUMMINGS Trainer

◆ Born: 1927

James Bartholomew "Bart" Cummings is an Australian icon. Through Australia's 2005–06 racing season, he had won the Melbourne Cup 11 times – an extraordinary string of success that commenced with Light Fingers in 1965, and has since included Galilee, Red Handed, Think Big (twice), Gold And Black, Hyperno, Kingston Rule, Let's Elope, Saintly and Rogan Josh. All told, Cummings had also registered 245 career Group 1 victories, well over twice as many as any other Australian trainer. His father, James, conditioned the 1950 Melbourne Cup winner, Comic Court, for whom Bart was a handler. Cummings received his own training licence in 1953. He has won the Australian Cup 12 times and the Caulfield Cup on six occasions. He also has a trio of victories with Taj Rossi, Saintly and Dane Ripper in the Cox Plate. And he has trained nine Australian Horse of the Year honourees – Dayana, Taj Rossi, Leilani, Lord Dudley, Maybe Mahal, Hyperno, Beau Zam, Let's Elope and Saintly. Cummings was made a member of the Order of Australia in 1982. He was inducted into the Sport Australia Hall of Fame in 1991, and was an inaugural inductee into the Australian Racing Hall of Fame.

D

FRED DARLING Trainer

◆ Born: 1884 Died: 1953

Fred Darling's utter dedication to training winners ruled his life. He trained the winners of 19 classics and was champion trainer six times, the last being in 1947 – when Tudor Minstrel won the 2,000 Guineas – the year he retired. Darling rode a few winners as an apprentice (to his father) and began training in 1907, winning the Cesarewitch Handicap with Yentoi in his second season. After a five-year spell in Germany he returned to Britain in 1913, and won his first classic in 1916 when Hurry On took the wartime St. Leger. In 1922 Captain Cuttle provided Darling with the first of seven Derby victories; others followed with Guineas winners Cameronian, Manna and Coronach, the last of whom also won the St. Leger. He was the royal trainer when Sun Chariot and Big Game won four of the five classics for King George VI in 1942 – the Derby eluded them. In retirement Darling had a small stud, where he bred the 1953 Derby winner Pinza, ridden by his long-time stable jockey, Gordon Richards.

DICK DAWSON Trainer

◆ Born: 1865 Died: 1955

Dick Dawson moved to England from his native Ireland in 1897 to train at Whatcombe. His first major success came when Drogheda defied a snowstorm to win the 1898 Grand National; his first big flat win came with The Solicitor in the 1902 Royal Hunt Cup. In 1914 Dawson moved to Newmarket, becoming champion trainer for the first time in 1916 when Fifinella won the wartime Derby and Oaks. Dawson and his principal patron, Edward Hulton, split two years later and the trainer returned to Whatcombe. In 1919, he and his brother paid 750gns for the yearling Blandford, who would become an oustanding sire. Dawson became the Aga Khan's first trainer in 1922. Two years later Diophon and Salmon Trout won the 2,000 Guineas and the St. Leger, respectively, and Dawson was champion trainer for the second time. He topped that list for the third time in 1929 thanks to the Derby and St. Leger successes of Trigo. He won the Derby for the Aga with Blenheim in 1930 but they fell out soon afterwards and Dawson retired in 1945.

ETIENNE DE MESTRE
Trainer/owner

◆ Born: 1838 Died: 1916

An accomplished horseman in youth, Etienne De Mestre was Australia's first outstanding horse trainer. He established a fine horse stud

Turf wars: Kent Desormeaux winning the 1993 Breeders' Cup Turf on Kotashaan (11) at Santa Anita.

and a racetrack – Terara – on the Shoalhaven River of New South Wales in the late 1850s. In 1859 he won the first Inter-Colonial Challenge against Victoria with Veno. In 1861 and 1862, De Mestre took Archer 500 miles from Terara to Flemington to win the first two runnings of the Melbourne Cup. He won the Cup again, with Tim Whiffler in 1867, with Chester in 1877 and with Calamia in 1878. De Mestre built up a formidable record in many of the Australia's other important events. Financial problems led to a complete breakdown in his health in the 1880s. De Mestre was forced to sell Terara but the proceeds from a special race meeting at Randwick and gifts from friends enabled him to buy a small farm at Moss Vale in New South Wales. He was buried in the Church Of England cemetery at Bong Bong – the site of Australia's most famous picnic race meeting.

LORD HOWARD DE WALDEN
Owner/breeder/administrator

◆ **Born: 1912 Died: 1999**

Lord Howard de Walden was one of the leading lights in post-World War II British racing. He was one of the last home-based major owner-breeders and was three times senior steward of the Jockey Club. He enjoyed top-level success on both the flat and over jumps, with Slip Anchor winning the Derby and Lanzarote taking the Champion Hurdle. Lanzarote was later killed when trying to become the first horse to pull off the Champion Hurdle/Cheltenham Gold Cup double. Having succeeded his father to the peerage in 1946, Lord Howard had his first winner three years later when Jailbird won at Chepstow. He was trained by Jack Waugh, whose other top winners for him included Almiranta and Ostrya. Waugh also trained the temperamental Oncidium (later a top sire in Australia/New Zealand), though the colt had been switched to George Todd when he won the Coronation Cup. Later he had horses with Noel Murless and then Henry Cecil, who sent out Slip Anchor to Derby success as well as other good winners like Catalpa and Strigida, Sandy Island, Kris and Diesis.

17TH EARL OF DERBY
Owner/breeder

◆ **Born: 1865 Died: 1948**

The great-great-grandson of the man after whom the Derby was named, Lord Derby had an oustanding career as an owner-breeder in the first half of the 20th century when he owned and bred the winners of 20 classics. The

National pride: Richard Dunwoody, in owner Freddie Starr's colours, won the Grand National on Miinnehoma in 1994.

best horse to carry his colours was Hyperion, who won the 1933 Derby and St. Leger before becoming an outstanding sire. The Earl's other Derby winners were Sansovino and Watling Street, in 1924 and 1942, respectively. Lord Derby's first classic success was with Swynford in the 1910 St. Leger. That colt, like so many of his owner's best winners, was trained by George Lambton or Frank Butters until the end of 1933, when Lord Derby decided that Lambton was not well enough to continue. In subsequent years Colledge Leader and Walter Earl trained for him; Tommy Weston, Dick Perryman and Harry Wragg were his jockeys. Hyperion's Derby year was one of six in which Lord Derby was leading owner. Others included 1928, when Fairway won the St. Leger and Toboggan took the Oaks, and 1945 when Sun Stream landed the Oaks and the 1,000 Guineas.

KENT DESORMEAUX Jockey

◆ **Born: 1970**

Certain records do remain unbroken, and the 598 victories achieved by Kent Desormeaux in 1989 should long stand as the all-time single season mark for a jockey. Born and raised in Louisiana, where his father operated a bush track, Desormeaux registered his first pari-mutuel win at age 16. He moved to Maryland the following year, registering 450 wins as North America's leading apprentice in 1987. Desormeaux was further honoured as the continent's leading journeyman in both 1989

and 1992. In 1998, Desormeaux won the Kentucky Derby and Preakness Stakes with Real Quiet, and was nosed out of a Triple Crown sweep in the final strides of the Belmont Stakes. He won the 1993 Breeders' Cup Turf aboard Kotashaan, and the 1995 Breeders' Cup Sprint with Desert Stormer. Desormeaux also rode Fusaichi Pegasus to victory in the 2000 Derby. In 2001, Desormeaux spent ten weeks in Japan, where he won the Japanese Oaks with Lastel and also took the Japanese Racing Association jockey title in Tokyo. In 2004, he was inducted into the Racing Hall of Fame in Saratoga Springs, New York.

TOM DREAPER Trainer

◆ **Born: 1898 Died: 1975**

Tom Dreaper was an outstanding trainer of jumpers from 1931 until he handed over the licence to his son Jim 40 years later. He will be always associated with Arkle, the outstanding chaser of all time, but even without him Dreaper's career was one of almost endless success. The first top horse he trained was Prince Regent, who won the 1942 Irish Grand National, under 12st 7lb (175 pounds), and the Cheltenham Gold Cup in 1946, but found the task of conceding 25lb to Lovely Cottage and 31lb to Jack Finlay just beyond him in the Grand National. When Arkle won the Irish National in 1964, he was part of a seven-year winning sequence for his trainer. Arkle never ran at Liverpool, but won the Cheltenham Gold Cup three times and the King George VI Chase in 1965 before injury at Kempton the next year ended his career. Arkle's contemporary and stablemate Flyingbolt – rated only 2lb behind him – won the Two Mile Champion Chase and Cotswold Chase at Cheltenham. Dreaper also took the Two Mile Champion Chase with Fortria, twice, Ben Stack and Muir.

JOHN DUNLOP Trainer

◆ **Born: 1939**

John Dunlop has been one of the most successful trainers of the final 40 years of the 20th century, even though he has only once been champion. That was in 1995 when he earned the title thanks particularly to the successes of Bahri in the Queen Elizabeth II Stakes and of Beauchamp King in the Racing Post Trophy. After first working for jumps trainer Neville Dent, Dunlop moved to the Duke of Norfolk's Sussex stable in 1963 and took out a licence in 1966, Tamino giving him his first victory in the Palace House Stakes at Newmarket that season. His first British classic came when Shirley Heights won the 1978 Derby (and Irish

Derby); his second Derby was with Erhaab in 1994, four years after Salsabil had added the Irish Derby to her successes in the Oaks and 1,000 Guineas. He has taken the 1,000 Guineas on two other occasions and won the St. Leger three times, as well as winning a number of European classics. Dunlop's oldest son, Tim, died in France in 1987, but two other sons, Ed and Harry, also became racehorse conditioners.

RICHARD DUNWOODY Jockey

◆ **Born: 1964**

The stylish Richard Dunwoody, whose father George trained in their native Ulster, was one of the best jump jockeys in the late 20th century. He won the Grand National (West Tip, in 1986, and Miinnehoma, 1994), Cheltenham Gold Cup (Charter Party, 1988) and Champion Hurdle (Kribensis, 1990), and rode 100 or more winners a record ten times. His first winner was as an amateur on Game Trust at Cheltenham in 1983. Dunwoody turned professional before the 1984–85 season, when attached to Tim Forster's yard, and became first jockey to David Nicholson in 1986. His first top-level success for that stable was on Very Promising in the 1986 Mackeson Gold Cup, and at the end of the 1992–93 season he moved to Martin Pipe's yard. This coincided with his three championships, and included success on Miinnehoma in the Grand National. Dunwoody's best wins, apart from the big three races, came on Desert Orchid in the King George VI Chase twice and Irish Grand National, and on One Man twice in the King George VI Chase. He retired as the all-time leading jump jockey with 1,699 wins, at the end of 1999.

FRANÇOIS DUPRE Owner/breeder

◆ **Born: ?? Died: 1966**

François Dupré, one of the most successful owner-breeders in France for more than 30 years, died a day after Danseur gave him his third success in the Grand Prix de Paris. He first became involved in racing in 1921 and his first winner, the following season, was Rosy Cheeks – the grandam of Dante and Sayajirao. Dupré's first classic victory came when Yonne took the 1939 Poule d'Essai des Pouliches. His best horse was Tantieme, who won the Prix de l'Arc de Triomphe in1950 and 1951, as well as the Coronation Cup and the Poule d'Essai des Poulains. Tantieme proved a very successful sire, and his progeny included Match, who won the King George VI And Queen Elizabeth Stakes, Grand Prix de Saint-Cloud and Washington DC International; Match's full brother Reliance, a Prix du Jockey Club and Grand Prix de Paris winner;

and Relko, a three-parts brother to Match and Reliance, who won the Derby, Coronation Cup, Poule d'Essai des Poulains and Prix Royal-Oak. Dupré also had a top-class filly in Bella Paola, who landed the Champion Stakes, Prix Vermeille, Oaks and 1,000 Guineas.

E

PAT EDDERY Jockey

◆ **Born: 1952**

Pat Eddery, whose father Jimmy won the 1955 Irish Derby on Panslipper, was an outstanding jockey for well over three decades. Champion on 11 occasions – as well as Irish champion in 1982 – he is one of a select few to have ridden more than 200 winners in a season; his 1990 achievement was the first time since Gordon Richards in 1952. Eddery has been retained by Peter Walwyn's and Vincent O'Brien's stables and it was for Walwyn that he gained his first classic successes, on Polygamy in 1974's Oaks. The following season he rode Grundy to Epsom and Irish Derby victories. A year after riding Prince Khalid Abdullah's Dancing Brave to glory in the 1976 King George VI And Queen Elizabeth Stakes and Prix de l'Arc de Triomphe, the Saudi prince retained Eddery. That was the third of Eddery's four Arc wins. Abdullah's and Eddery's link ended officially in 1994, but Eddery's fortunes did not suffer as a freelance. He rode his 4,000th winner in Britain when Silver Patriarch won the St. Leger in 1997. In 2000, Eddery extended his own record with the 27th 100-win season of his career. When he retired in 2003, Eddery had over 4,600 career victories in Britain.

HM KING EDWARD VII Owner

◆ **Born: 1841 Died: 1910**

Very few people are fortunate enough to own winners of the Derby and Grand National; even fewer win both in the same year, but King Edward VII – as the Prince of Wales – was one of those. In 1900, a year before his accession to the throne, Ambush II won the Grand National and Diamond Jubilee took the Derby – the middle leg of his Triple Crown. Although he had his first runner in 1877, the King was not able to celebrate a winner until 1886. The advice of his trainer John Porter that the King should buy the mare Perdita II proved a turning point. Perdita cost 900gns but she repaid that many times over. The first good winner she bred was Florizel, whose wins included the Goodwood Cup and Jockey Club Cup. At that point

there was a split between the Prince and his trainer and Edward's horses went to Richard Marsh. Marsh thus trained Persimmon, another of Perdita's foals, who won the 1896 Derby and the St. Leger, and his full brother Diamond Jubilee, as well as Minoru, who won the 1909 2,000 Guineas and Derby.

CHARLIE ELLIOTT Jockey/trainer

◆ **Born: 1904 Died: 1979**

Charlie Elliott rode top-class winners in England and France for more than 30 years until retiring in 1953, after which he took up training for a decade. He achieved the considerable distinction of being champion jockey while he was still apprenticed to Jack Jarvis. In 1923 he shared the title with Steve Donoghue, and the following season won it outright to end Donoghue's 10-year reign. He won every British classic – apart from the St. Leger – the first being Ellangowan who took the 1923 2,000 Guineas. Elliott's three Derby wins came on Call Boy in 1927, Bois Roussel in 1938 and the 2,000 Guineas winner Nimbus in 1949. He also rode Supreme Court to win the first running of what is now the King George VI And Queen Elizabeth Stakes. Elliott also rode and trained top winners in France, mostly for Marcel Boussac. He won the Prix du Jockey Club four times as a jockey, and once as a trainer. He won other French classics with Macip and Apollonia, and sent Elpenor over from France to take the Ascot Gold Cup.

CHARLES ELSEY Trainer

◆ **Born: 1882 Died: 1966**

Charlie Elsey, whose father trained in Lincolnshire, followed the same career, briefly, before World War I, resuming in 1922. He was first based near Ayr and then at Malton, where he established a team powerful enough to take on and beat the leading stables in the South. Elsey was champion trainer in 1956 and only once out of the first six between 1948 and 1960. He did particularly well with long-distance horses, winning the Northumberland Plate and the Ebor Handicap three times apiece as well as the Chester Cup and the Cesarewitch Handicap, but his successes were by no means confined to handicaps and he gained his first classic victory when Musidora won the 1,000 Guineas in 1949. She went on to win the Oaks, in which Frieze was also successful in 1952. The following year Nearula won the 2,000 Guineas and in 1956 Honeylight took the 1,000 Guineas. Elsey's last classic winner came with Cantelo in the St. Leger of 1959. Charlie retired in 1960 – his son Bill took charge of the Highfield stable – and was awarded the CBE for his services to racing the following year.

CHARLES ENGELHARD Owner

◆ Born: 1917 Died: 1971

Charles Engelhard – an American of German descent who was chairman of a vast metals and minerals company – was a huge supporter of racing worldwide. He did not become involved until he was 40, but when he died he had 300 horses. For all his excellent winners, undoubtedly the best horse he owned was Nijinsky, trained by Vincent O'Brien, who won the Triple Crown in 1970. Nijinsky also won the Irish Derby and King George VI And Queen Elizabeth Stakes, but was somewhat controversially beaten in the Prix de l'Arc de Triomphe. Engelhard had three other winners of the St. Leger: Indiana was successful in 1964 and full brothers Ribocco and Ribero, trained by Fulke Johnson Houghton, won in 1967 and 1968, respectively. Johnson Houghton also trained the top class milers Habitat and Romulus, both of whom included the Prix du Moulin among their wins. His best winners in the U.S. were Assagai, whose successes included the United Nations Handicap and the Man o' War Stakes, and South African-bred Hawaii, who won 21 times in 28 attempts there and in America.

F

ANDRE FABRE Jockey/trainer

◆ Born: 1945

Andre Fabre won more than 250 races as a jump jockey, including a score aboard Corps A Corps in the 1977 Grand Steeple Chase de Paris. He took over the yard when Corps A Corps' trainer, Andre Adele, died in 1978, and he had his first winner

as a trainer early that season. By the end of the 20th Century, Fabre had become the most dominant force among France's thoroughbred conditioners, a situation that is continuing as the new century unfolds. Since 1987, Fabre has been the country's leading trainer for 19 consecutive years. He has won the Prix de l'Arc de Triomphe a record six times, with Trempolino, Subotica, Carnegie, Peintre Celebre, Sagamix and most recently with Hurricane Run in 2005. Elsewhere, from 1994–96, Fabre won three consecutive runnings of the Coronation Cup at Epsom. He has conditioned a quartet of Breeders' Cup winners: In the Wings, who accounted for the Breeders' Cup Turf in 1990; Arcangues, who at odds of 133.60–1 won the Breeders' Cup Classic in 1993; Banks Hill, who won the Breeders' Cup Filly and Mare Turf in 2001; and Shirocco, who won the Breeders' Cup Turf in 2005.

KIEREN FALLON Jockey

◆ Born: 1965

Kieren Fallon was first apprenticed to Kevin Prendergast in his native Ireland before moving to Jimmy FitzGerald in Yorkshire. He rose to the top of his profession during a stormy career in which sensation has seldom been far away. He was suspended for six months for dragging another jockey off his horse at the end of a race; five years later he was sacked from his position as stable jockey to Henry Cecil amid strenuously denied seamy rumours in a Sunday tabloid. He also won a libel case against a trade newspaper. For all the controversy Fallon proved himself a very capable jockey. He was a triple champion from 1997–99, reaching the 200 mark each time, but was denied the chance of a fourth consecutive title in 2000 when he was badly injured at Royal Ascot. After

leaving Cecil, Fallon was retained by Sir Michael Stoute, for whom he rode King's Best to win the 2,000 Guineas. Other classic wins were for Cecil – on Oath (Derby), Ramruma (Oaks) and Wince (1,000 Guineas) in 1999, plus Reams of Verse (Oaks) and Sleepytime (1,000 Guineas) in 1997. In 2003, Fallon was victorious in the Derby with Kris Kin and in the Gold Cup with Mr. Dinos. In 2004, he registered a Derby/Oaks double, with North Light and Ouija Board. In 2003–04, Fallon also won back-to-back runnings of the Breeders' Cup Filly and Mare Turf, with Islington and Ouija Board.

WILLIAM S. FARISH
Owner/Breeder

◆ Born: 1939

Master of Lane's End Farm near Versailles, Kentucky, William S. Farish is North America's most prominent horseman. Twice the recipient of Eclipse Awards as outstanding breeder, he is a close friend of fellow racing owner/breeder H.M. Queen Elizabeth II, and of presidents George H. and George W. Bush. From 2001–2004, Farish served as US Ambassador to Great Britain and Northern Ireland. Heir to the Standard and Exxon Oil empires, he treats everyone with courtesy and respect, be they the most prominent of statesmen or the humblest of grooms. Farish purchased his first thoroughbred in 1963. His first classic winner was Bee Bee Bee, who accounted for the 1972 Preakness Stakes. Farish co-bred Seattle Dancer, who fetched a world record auction price for a yearling of $13.1 million at Keeneland in July, 1985. Farish also co-bred and co-owned the 1992 Belmont Stakes and Breeders' Cup Classic winner, A. P. Indy, who was North America's Horse of the Year that season. More recently, Farish bred and raced Mineshaft, who was champion older male and Horse of the Year in 2003. During his Court of St. James tenure, Farish also won the 2003 Oaks, with Casual Look.

"SUNNY JIM" FITZSIMMONS
Trainer

◆ Born: 1874 Died: 1966

The trainer of two Triple Crown winners, Gallant Fox in 1930 and Omaha in 1935, "Sunny Jim" Fitzsimmons ranks among the finest conditioners in North America's racing history. He won 13 classics all told, along with ten runnings of the Saratoga Cup, and eight renewals

Double first: Kieren Fallon rode Oath to win 1999's Derby and Ramruma to complete an Epsom double in the Oaks.

of the Wood Memorial. Indeed, if there was a major East Coast stakes Fitzsimmons never won, it escapes recall. A native New Yorker, Fitzsimmons mucked out stalls at 11, subsequently became a jockey, and took out his first trainer's licence in 1899. Statistics from Fitzsimmons' early years are incomplete, but the respected turf writer, George Ryall, estimated he accumulated 2,500 career training victories, many of them for William Woodward's Belair Stud Stable. Johnstown, Nashua, Bold Ruler – all are Hall of Famers, all were trained by Fitzsimmons. Despite arthritis so severe it bent his back at a right angle, Fitzsimmons outlived his beloved wife, Jenny, by 15 years. The couple had six children, 17 grandchildren, and, at the time of Sunny Jim's death, 43 great-grandchildren.

TIM FORSTER Trainer

◆ **Born: 1934 Died: 1999**

Tim Forster was one of the outstanding trainers of steeplechasers of his era, winning the Grand National three times, with Well To Do in 1972, Ben Nevis (1980) and Last Suspect in 1985. A notorious pessimist, Forster had ridden a few winners while in the Army before becoming a pupil with Geoffrey Brooke and Derrick Candy. He took out a training licence in 1962 and his first success came when Baulking Green won the 1963 United Hunts Chase at Cheltenham. Baulking Green won the United Hunts Chase four times. There were Mildmay of Flete wins for Take Plenty and Mocharabuice, Martha's Son won the Queen Mother Champion Chase and Denys Adventure took the Arkle. Other top wins for Forster were those of Royal Marshal in the King George VI Chase and Hennessy Gold Cup and Dublin Flyer and Pegwell Bay in the Mackeson Gold Cup. Forster, who was awarded the OBE in 1998, moved from Letcombe Basset, where he had been since he started, to Downton Hall near Ludlow in 1994. He retired in 1998 with 1,346 wins to his name, but took out a permit and had one winner in that capacity.

FREDDIE FOX Jockey

◆ **Born: 1888 Died: 1945**

Freddie Fox was the only jockey to deny Gordon Richards the championship between 1925 and 1954 in level competition as Richards was ill for one of those the other two seasons when he was not top and badly injured in another. Fox's championship year was in 1929 (Tommy Weston

The family way: Arthur Hancock, with wife Tracy, briefly was the third generation to run the Claiborne Farm Stud.

won in 1926 and Harry Wragg won in 1941), when he beat Richards by one by winning two of the last three races of the season at Manchester. Fox's first classic winner was Atmah in the 1911 1,000 Guineas. In 1930 he rode Diolite to win the 2,000 Guineas and the following year he partnered Cameronian to Derby victory. Fox rode the Aga Khan's Firdaussi to St. Leger triumph in 1932. He had ridden Bahram to victory in the 1935 Derby and 2,000 Guineas, but an injury sustained in a fall on the eve of the race prevented him from riding the Aga Khan's colt to St. Leger and Triple Crown success. He retired from riding in 1936, but he suffered a heavy blow when his son was killed when serving with the Royal Air Force. Fox died in a car crash in late 1945.

JOHN A. FRANKS Owner/Breeder

◆ **Born: 1925 Died: 2003**

A four-time Eclipse Award recipient as North America's outstanding owner, John Franks owned and raced more thoroughbreds during the last two decades of the 20th Century than anyone else on the continent. An oil magnate, with extensive holdings in commercial real estate, cattle and pecan farms as well, Franks had as many as 900 horses in training at a single time. Franks established major breeding operations in both Florida and his home state of Louisiana, and as the years went on the great majority of the horses he campaigned were homebreds. Major stakes winners he raced included Dave's Friend, who in 1984 became North America's first

sprinter to amass career earnings of over $1 million; Heatherton, whose victory in the 1984 Apple Blossom Handicap at Oaklawn Park was the first Grade 1 triumph for Hall of Fame trainer Bill Mott; Kissin Kris, who won the Haskell Invitational Handicap at Monmouth Park in 1993; Halo America, who won the 1997 Apple Blossom; and Lady Tak, who was victorious in the Test Stakes at Saratoga in July, 2003, just five months prior to Franks' passing.

G

PETER PURCELL GILPIN
Trainer

◆ **Born: 1858 Died: 1928**

If he had never trained another horse, Peter Purcell Gilpin would have taken his place in racing's annals as the trainer of the outstanding filly Pretty Polly, winner of the fillies' Triple Crown in 1904 and 19 of her 21 other races; her classic wins enabled her trainer to top the list for the first time that year. Gilpin began training at Blandford, Dorset, but the money he won through Clarehaven's success in the 1900 Cesarewitch enabled him to move to Newmarket, from where he sent out the winners of six other classics. Spearmint, who also took the Grand Prix de Paris, and his son Spion Kop both won the Derby, Flair and Electra the 1,000 Guineas, St Louis the 2,000 and Snow Marten was successful in the Oaks.

JOHN GOSDEN Trainer

◆ **Born: 1951**

John Gosden's father, "Towser", trained with much success in Sussex – his horses included the 1960 King George VI and Queen Elizabeth Diamond Stakes winner, Aggressor. After having acted as an assistant to Noel Murless and Vincent O'Brien, John moved to the other side of the Atlantic and commenced training in California in 1980. Gosden's top horses in America included Bates Motel, who won a trio of Grade 1 events and was champion handicap runner in 1983, and Royal Heroine, the Robert Sangster representative who was victorious in the inaugural Breeders' Cup Mile in 1984. Gosden returned to England in 1989, being based at Stanley House in Newmarket, and gained his first classic success when Mashaallah won the Irish St. Leger in 1992. Gosden won the 1996 St. Leger with Shantou, and the 1997 Derby with Benny the Dip. He moved from Newmarket to Manton in 2000, which was the same year in which he won the Fillies Mile with Crystal Music, the Queen Elizabeth II Stakes with Observatory and the 1,000 Guineas with Lahan. In 2002 Gosden won the Middle Park Stakes with Oasis Dream. In 2003 he won the Nunthorpe Stakes with Oasis Dream, and in 2004 he was victorious again in the Fillies Mile with Playful Act.

RAYMOND GUEST Owner

◆ **Born: 1907 Died: 1992**

The United States' Ambassador to Ireland during the 1960s and 1970s, Raymond Guest owned top class winners on both sides of the Atlantic. He was among the few owners of Derby (Larkspur and Sir Ivor) and Grand National (L'Escargot) winners. Larkspur (1962) was a very lucky Derby winner as seven of the field failed to finish, but Sir Ivor (1968) was a top class colt, whose other wins included the 2,000 Guineas, Champion Stakes and Washington DC International. After winning the Cheltenham Gold Cup in 1970 and 1971 – the last horse in the 20th Century to win the race twice – L'Escargot was twice placed in the Grand National behind Red Rum before getting the better of his old rival in 1975. Raymond Guest's best horses in the U.S. were headed by Tom Rolfe, in 1965, who won the Preakness Stakes, Citation Handicap and American Derby; his half-brother Chieftain won the Arlington and Laurel Turf Club Handicaps. Raymond Guest's brother, Winston, owned Gyr, who was second in the Derby, and his sister the Comtesse de la Valdene, owned Pieces of Eight, Sea Hawk and Prince Regent.

ARTHUR BOYD HANCOCK
Owner/Breeder/Racetrack official

◆ **Born: 1875 Died: 1957**

With 1,300 acres of land inherited from his wife's father, Arthur Boyd Hancock founded Claiborne Farm in 1910. During the ensuing four decades, Claiborne grew to 2,100 acres, becoming one of the world's finest thoroughbred breeding establishments, a status it retains today. Sires Hancock stood at Claiborne included Wrack, Celt, Sir Gallahad III, Stimulus, Blenheim II, Gallant Fox, Nasrullah, Ambiorix, Princequillo, Hill Prince, and Double Jay. Nine times during the 1930s and 40s, Hancock led all North American breeders in races won. Four times he was the leading breeder in monies earned. Thirteen horses bred by Hancock earned more than $100,000 racing, an exceptional feat for his era. Hancock further served as a racing steward and race commissioner. In 1949, a stroke forced him to relinquish Claiborne's reins to his son, Arthur B. "Bull" Hancock Jr.

JOHN W. HANES
Adminstrator/Owner/Breeder

◆ **Born: 1892 Died: 1987**

The first board chairman of the New York Racing Association, John W. Hanes is one of five individuals to be recognized as one of the sport's

"Exemplars" by the National Museum of Racing's Hall of Fame. The Hanes family held stock in the American Tobacco and Hanes Hosiery companies. Hanes, himself, variously sold cigarettes and underwear, had a New York Stock Exchange seat, was on more than 30 corporate boards, served in Franklin D. Roosevelt's presidential administration, and was entrusted with the reorganization of William Randolph Hearst's business empire. Having served as a Belmont Park director, Hanes, in 1953, was given the challenge of revitalizing New York racing. Hanes consolidated the state's major meets from five tracks to three (Belmont, Saratoga, and a rebuilt Aqueduct) under an umbrella corporation that did not compensate trustees, paid no dividends, and gave almost all profits to the state. His plan saved the sport in New York, and remains effective today.

RICHARD HANNON Trainer

◆ **Born: 1945**

It was at one time possible that Richard Hannon would seek his career in the world of pop music but, having taken over the stable at East Everleigh when his father Harry retired in 1970, he made a major success out of that role and trained one of the biggest strings in England. He made his first big impression when the 50–1 chance Mon Fils won the 1973 2,000 Guineas and he has won that classic twice since, with Don't Forget Me (in 1987) and Tirol (1990) – both also won the Irish edition. Hannon has won races of all types and distances, from major handicaps like the Ebor Handicap with Another Sam and the Wokingham Handicap with Venture Capitalist, to pattern races such as the Prix du Cadran and Prix Royal-Oak with Assessor and the Lockinge Stakes with Swing Low. Champion trainer in 1992, Hannon's reputation was made thanks to his successes with sprinters and two-year-olds. These included Lyric Fantasy, Mr Brooks, Sharp N'Early, Rock City and River Falls.

BILL HARTACK Jockey

◆ **Born: 1932**

With five Kentucky Derby victories Bill Hartack is tied with Eddie Arcaro as the all-time leading jockey in that category. But while Arcaro had 21 career Derby mounts, Hartack received only 12. Three Preakness Stakes victories and a single triumph in the Belmont Stakes fortify Hartack's career record. For three consecutive years, from

Number two: Bill Hartack registers the second of his record-tying five Kentucky Derby wins aboard Venetian Way.

Famille royale: Freddie (far left) and sister Criquette (far right) are the fourth generation of Heads at the top of French racing.

1955–57, and again in 1960, he led all North American riders in wins. Immensely talented, charming when he so desired, but frequently boorish as well, Hartack remains a complex figure. Reared in Pennsylvania's farm country, he scored his first win at West Virginia's Waterford Park track aboard a $2,000 claimer named Nickleby on October 14, 1952. Within three years, Hartack was a national sports star. But tax problems forced him to ride in Hong Kong towards the end of his career. Now a steward, Hartack works from November to March at the Fair Grounds track in New Orleans. As was the case in his riding days, he declines most requests for media interviews.

SANDY HAWLEY Jockey

◆ **Born: 1949**

One of the most prominent Canadian-born jockeys, Sandy Hawley led all North American riders in victories in 1970, 1972, and 1973. His 515 victories in 1973 made him the first jockey to reach the 500 plateau in a single season. Hawley won the Queen's Plate a record four times. He registered five consecutive Canadian Oaks triumphs, 1970–74, subsequently won the Oaks three times more, and posted his 6,000th career win at Toronto's Greenwood track on November 26, 1992. Hawley credits an uncle, Web Bride, with initiating his interest in racing. At age 17, Hawley began grooming and exercising racehorses. He scored his first career win aboard a maiden claimer named Fly Alone at Woodbine on October 14, 1968. The following year, Hawley was North America's leading apprentice. In 1976, he was honoured with an Eclipse Award as the continent's leading journeyman. Headquartered for a decade during his prime in California, Hawley otherwise always used his home country as a base. Twice he was Canada's Athlete of the Year. Hawley retired from riding in 1998 with 6,449 career victories.

ALEC HEAD Trainer/jockey

◆ **Born: 1924**

Alec Head is a member of one of the most famous racing families in France. His grandfather Willie, who emigrated from England in the late 19th century and rode the Grande Course des Haies winner, became a successful trainer, succeeded by Willie junior – Alec's father. Alec was apprenticed to Willie Junior and began to train the year he rode Le Paillon to second in the 1947 Champion Hurdle. He rode about 300 winners on the flat and jumping and sent out Kwannin to win the Triumph Hurdle. His best successes were on the flat and he won top races in England as well as France until he retired and handed over the licence to his daughter Criquette in 1984. He won the Derby with Lavandin, the 1,000 Guineas with Rose Royale II, the 2,000 with Taboun and the King George VI And Queen Elizabeth Stakes with Vimy. In France he won the Prix de l'Arc de Triomphe four times, the Prix du Jockey Club three times and he had a total of eight successes in the two Poules d'Essai.

CRIQUETTE HEAD-MAAREK Trainer

◆ **Born: 1948**

Christiane (Criquette) Head-Maarek had only one success as a jockey, but has more than maintained the family standing as a trainer, a career on which she embarked in 1978. Her first group winner came that year when Sigy took the Prix d'Arenberg, and in 1979 she sent out her mother's filly, Three Troikas, to win the Prix de l'Arc de Triomphe. In 1982, Head-Maarek won the Prix de Diane with Harbour. Her first major success in England came when Ma Biche won the 1,000 Guineas in 1983. Head-Maarek subsequently landed that classic twice more with Ravinella and Hatoof. Many observers feel that her best horse has been Bering, winner of the Prix du Jockey Club in 1986. Head-Maarek's other classic successes in France include half-a-dozen victories in the Poule d'Essai des Pouliches, with Three Troikas, Silvermine, Baiser Vole, Ravinella, Matiara and Always Loyal. A more recent success came in 2004 when Head-Maarek landed the Poule d'Essai des Poulains with American Post – she had also won that race a decade earlier with Greene Tune. Head-Maarek is married to journalist Gilles Maarek.

FREDDIE HEAD Jockey/trainer

◆ **Born: 1947**

Freddie Head, son of Alec and brother of Criquette, was French champion jockey six times and rode almost 3,000 winners worldwide. He retired in 1997 and started training, renting four boxes from Lucy Boutin, with whose late husband François he had enjoyed a long and successful association. His first training winner was Mulahen at Fontainebleau in March 1998; his first Group success came when Northerntown won at Longchamp in 1999. Freddie rode his first winner at Fontainebleau in 1964 and enjoyed Group 1 success at home and in England, Ireland and the U.S. He won the Prix de l'Arc de Triomphe on Bon Mot III, San San, Ivanjica and Three Troikas, and the Prix du Jockey Club on Goodly, Roi Lear, Youth and Val de l'Orne. His best wins in England were on Ma Biche in the 1,000 Guineas and Cheveley Park Stakes, Miesque in the 1987 1,000 Guineas and Zino in the 1982 2,000 Guineas. He won the Irish 2,000 on King's Company. Miesque was the best horse he rode, enjoying successive Breeders' Cup Mile victories in 1987 and 1988.

WILLIE HEAD JR Jockey/trainer

◆ **Born: 1889 Died: 1980**

Willie Head was the second generation of a family of British origin which emigrated to France towards the end of the 19th century. His father rode the winner of the Grande Course de Haies in 1890, but injury ended his career ten years later. Willie junior rode about 500 jumping winners with a highest tally of 115 in 1911. Having served with the British Army during World War I, he rode Ballyboggan to victory in the 1918 Irish Grand National and to second to Poethlyn in the 1919 Grand National. He started training in 1922. He sent out Vatelys, ridden by his son Alec, to claim the Grande Course des Haies, but most of his big wins were on the flat. Bon Mot, ridden by his grandson Freddie, won the Prix de l'Arc de Triomphe; he won the Prix du Jockey Club with Goodly and Le Fabuleux and also took the Prix de Diane and Poule d'Essai des Poulains.

DICK HERN Trainer

◆ **Born: 1921 Died: 2002**

One of the oustanding trainers of his era, Dick Hern retired at the end of the 1997 season after sending out the winners of every British classic, even though he was confined to a wheelchair after a hunting fall in 1984, and being champion trainer four times between 1962 and 1983. The best horse he trained was Brigadier Gerard, winner of 17 of his 18 races over three seasons including the King George VI And Queen Elizabeth Stakes and the 2,000 Guineas. Hern was for five years assistant to Michael Pope before becoming private trainer to Major Lionel Holliday in 1957. At the end of 1962, during which he won the St. Leger with Hethersett, he moved to West Ilsley, where he was based until the end of 1990, when he was effectively dismissed by the Queen, who owned the stables. Hern had trained many royal winners including dual classic heroines Dunfermline and Highclere, and his sacking provoked much bitterness. Hern moved to Lambourn at a yard set up for him by Sheikh Hamdan al-Maktoum.

SAMUEL CLAY HILDRETH
Trainer/Owner/Jockey

◆ **Born: 1866 Died: 1929**

Nine times North America's leading trainer, including the consecutive years from 1921–24, Samuel Clay Hildreth rose from a bush league jockey, to a $40-per-month Kansas trainer, to a $40,000-a-year conditioner for Harry F. Sinclair's Rancocas Stable. In 1917, Hildreth sent out Hourless to defeat Kentucky Derby winner Omar Khayyam in a match race. Six years later, Hildreth sent out Zev to his match victory against Papyrus. Both rank among the great historic events in U.S. racing. Hildreth never, himself, won the Kentucky Derby or Preakness Stakes, but he saddled seven Belmont Stakes winners, the first being Jean Bereaud in 1899, and the last being Mad Play in 1924. Exact records were not kept in his day, but Hildreth estimated that the horses he trained earned $5million, an extraordinary sum for the era in which he worked. The Hall of Famer, Grey Lag, won 17 stakes with Hildreth as trainer, including the 1921 Belmont Stakes, the 1922 Saratoga Handicap, and the 1923 Metropolitan Handicap.

WILLIAM HILL
Bookmaker/breeder/owner

◆ **Born: 1903 Died: 1971**

William Hill was the outstanding bookmaker of his or any other era, starting in that profession at the age of 19. In the days when bookmakers bet to their opinions – rather than being run by accountants for shareholders – Hill took very firm views when so inclined, never more so that when he was convinced that the apparent "good thing" Tudor Minstrel, would not stay 1 1/2 miles in the 1947 Derby. His success as a bookmaker enabled him to buy Whitsbury Manor Stud in Hampshire and then Sezincote Stud in Gloucestershire, and on the advice of Phil Bull his early purchases included the mare Kong, who bred the 1949 2,000 Guineas and Derby winner Nimbus. Although Hill sold many of his stud's best products and was more interested in breeding horses than owning them, he enjoyed considerable success with some of those that he kept. Particularly among them was Cantelo, who won the 1959 St. Leger, and Be Careful, whose wins included the Gimcrack and Champagne Stakes. He also bought Chanteur II, the sire of 1953 Derby winner Pinza, on the eve of his success in the 1947 Coronation Cup.

MAX HIRSCH
Trainer/Jockey/Owner/Breeder

◆ **Born: 1880 Died: 1969**

Max Hirsch wasn't exactly sure of his birthday. "It is July 12 or July 30," he would say. "The records weren't good in Fredericksburg, Texas," Hirsch's birthplace. What is more certain is that he started off as a jockey, then became a trainer. The first winner Hirsch saddled was Gautama, at the New Orleans Fair Grounds track on March 21, 1902. Hirsch's racing career ultimately spanned seven decades, encompassing 12 U.S. presidential administrations. His training career started even before the Wright brothers flew their first aeroplane and ended the year men first walked on the moon in 1969. Hirsch's Classic runners included Bold Venture, who won the 1936 Kentucky Derby and Preakness Stakes, and Middleground, who won the 1950 Kentucky Derby and Belmont Stakes. Most noteworthy, though, was the King Ranch homebred, Assault, whom Hirsch sent out to sweep North America's Triple Crown in 1946. In 1968, his 88th year,

Winning smile: Jack Ingham and wife Sue wave to the crowd after Lovelorn won the 2000 Crown Oaks at Flemington.

Hirsch led all New York trainers with $914,356 in purse earnings. Records from the time are incomplete but it is estimated that he scored at least 2,000 career training wins.

BRUCE HOBBS Jockey/trainer

◆ **Born: 1920 Died: 2005**

Bruce Hobbs became the Grand National's youngest winning jockey when, as a 17-year-old in 1938, he partnered Battleship, who was trained by his father Reg. But the combination of World War II and increasing weight spelled the end of his riding career and, having had a spell as a private trainer, he worked for Cecil Boyd-Rochfort, George Beeby and Jack Clayton before becoming one of the private trainers for David Robinson in 1964. Two seasons later he became a public trainer and he achieved his only classic success when Tyrnavos won the Irish Derby in 1980. That success gave him particular pleasure as he had trained the colt's dam Stilvi and her other progeny with considerable success. Hobbs' other top winners included the juvenile fillies Cry Of Truth and Jacinth, who both won the Cheveley Park Stakes, with Jacinth taking the Coronation Stakes in her second season; Take A Reef, rated the top three-year-old of his year – despite never running in a classic; and Tromos, whose wins included the Dewhurst Stakes. Hobbs retired at the end of 1985 and died 20 years later.

MAJOR LIONEL HOLLIDAY
Owner/breeder

◆ **Born: 1880 Died: 1965**

Not even his nearest and dearest would claim that Lionel Holliday was an easy man to get on with – he was inclined to change trainers and jockeys at the drop of a hat – but he was undoubtedly a very successful owner-breeder for 20 years after World War II, thanks particularly to the descendants of the mare Lost Soul, whom be bought for 4,000 guineas. He won three classics: the 1951 Oaks with Neasham Belle; the St. Leger 11 years later with Hethersett, who would probably have won the Derby had he not been brought down; and the 1,000 Guineas of 1965 with Night Off. In the year of Hethersett's Doncaster success, Holliday was the leading owner and breeder in the country. His other good winners included Narrator, None Nicer and Cursorial, but the best horse he bred was Vaguely Noble, who raced after the Major's death. Having won the 1967 Observer Gold Cup, he was sold for a then staggering 136,000 guineas at the December sales; the following season he won the Prix de l'Arc de Triomphe and was later a very successful sire.

I

JACK AND BOB INGHAM
Owners/breeders

◆ **Born: 1928 (Jack), 1931 (Bob) Died: 2003 (Jack)**

When Walter Ingham passed away in 1953, he left his sons, Jack and Bob, a modest poultry business and a thoroughbred broodmare named Valiant Rose. The boys subsequently parlayed the poultry holdings into a $1-billion enterprise. And Valiant Rose became the foundation mare for Woodlands Stud, which became the largest privately owned breeding and racing operation in the Southern Hemisphere. Woodlands is in Denham, New South Wales, and by the year 2000 it had grown into an operation that included 900 broodmares, stallions and young racing stock. The Inghams' Woodlands Stud Syndicate colour bearer, Octagonal, was Australia's Champion Racehorse of the 1995–96 season – when he accounted for the Cox Plate, Australian Derby, Canterbury and Rosewell Guineas (thus sweeping the Australian Triple Crown) and the Australian Cup. Octagonal's career record included 28 starts, 14 victories, eight placings and earnings of $5.89 million. Jack, three years older than his brother, is now gone, but Woodlands' future remains potent. Lonhro, Australian Horse of the Year in 2003–04 and World Champion Miler of 2004, is a recent addition to the stallion roster.

J

HIRSCH JACOBS
Trainer/Owner/Breeder

◆ **Born: 19 Died: 1970**

The man who claimed Stymie for $1,500, Hirsch Jacobs was a native New Yorker who stepped off the sidewalks of Brooklyn to lead North American trainers in wins 11 times between 1933–44. For the whole of his career, Jacobs registered 3,596 career training victories. Among his charges was the racemare, Searching, who Jacobs purchased for $15,000 as a maiden from Ogden Phipps. Searching's career race earnings ultimately totalled $311,081. In the breeding shed, her produce included the champion Affectionately, and the stakes winners Admiring and Priceless Gem. Jacobs sent Stymie out to win

24 stakes. The horse's success allowed Jacobs and a partner, Isidore Bieber, to purchase a 283-acre farm near Monkton, Maryland, which they named Stymie Manor. The Jacobs/Bieber partnership bred the winners of over 3,500 races. Earnings compiled by these horses exceeded $20 million. Jacobs died in 1970, so he did not live to see homebreds Personality and High Echelon win the 1971 Preakness and Belmont Stakes, respectively. Both colts campaigned in the name of his widow, Ethel D. Jacobs.

SIR JACK JARVIS Trainer

◆ **Born: 1887 Died: 1968**

Knighted for his services to racing in the year he retired, 1967, Jack Jarvis was champion trainer three times, sent out the winners of almost 2,000 races and achieved the considerable feat at the time of winning more than £1million for his owners. A member of a leading racing family, he was apprenticed to his father William, rode his first winner in 1903 and gained his first important success on Hacklers Pride in the Cambridgeshire. But weight brought his riding career to a premature end and he started training in 1914. His first classic victory was the fifth Earl of Rosebery's Ellangowan, who won the 1923 2,000 Guineas, but the best horse belonged to the sixth Earl of Rosebery. That was Blue Peter, who won the Derby and the 2,000 Guineas in 1939. Jarvis also won a wartime Derby for Lord Rosebery with Ocean Swell, and other classic victories included the St. Leger with Sandwich, the 2,000 Guineas with Flamingo and the 1,000 Guineas with Plack, Campanula and Happy Laughter. He also won the Ascot Gold Cup four times and the Eclipse Stakes on three occasions.

WALTER JEFFORDS
Owner/Breeder

◆ **Born: 1883 Died: 1960**

A charter trustee of the New York Racing Association, Walter M. Jeffords was a collector of racing art and and a primary force behind the

World traveller: Rae Johnstone, French champion in 1933, rode in his native Australia, as well as India, and England.

creation of the National Museum of Racing in Saratoga Springs. His wife's uncle, Samuel D. Riddle, owned Man o' War, and Jeffords' breeding program strongly reflected that stallion's line. Sixteen of Jeffords' 59 stakes winners were by Man o' War. Thirteen others were out of Man o' War's daughters. Jeffords bred four winners of the Coaching Club American Oaks. His homebred, colt Pavot was unbeaten and champion of his North American division at age two, and won the Belmont Stakes in 1945. Another Jeffords homebred, Kiss Me Kate, was champion three-year-old filly in 1951. One of only five people to be recognized as an "Exemplar" of the sport by the racing museum's Hall of Fame, Jeffords was also a Master of Fox Hounds. From 1941–49, he served on the Jockey Club's Board of Stewards.

JACK JOEL Owner/breeder

◆ **Born: 1862 Died: 1940**

Jack Joel, whose father was a publican in London's East End, rose from humble origins to run the major diamond business in South Africa, where he also had many other successful interests. He went into racing in 1900 and gained his first classic winner when Our Lassie landed the 1903 Oaks. Glass Doll took that race in 1907 and Your Majesty won the St. Leger in 1908. Sunstar, who like all his owner's classic winners, was trained by Charles Morton, took the 1911 2,000 Guineas and the Derby, but was so injured after Epsom that he never ran again. Humorist, who provided his owner with his final classic victory in the 1921 Derby died of a haemorrhage a few days after the race. For most of his racing days, Mr Joel based his breeding operation at the Childwick Bury Stud in Hertfordshire, which he bought from Sir Blundell Maple in 1907, but its fortunes declined in later years and his son had to organise a major change of fortune when he inherited it.

JIM JOEL Owner/breeder

◆ **Born: 1894 Died: 1992**

Jim Joel was an outstanding supporter of racing in Britain under both codes for many years, having inherited the Childwick Bury Stud in Hertfordshire on his father's death in 1940. He revitalised the stud to such effect that he had his first classic success when Picture Play won the 1,000 Guineas in 1944 and though he had to wait until 1967 for his next, when Royal Palace won the Derby and the 2,000 Guineas, he had many big winners in the intervening years and Light Cavalry took the St. Leger in 1980 and Fairy Footsteps the 1,000 Guineas a year later. Royal Palace also won the Eclipse and the King George VI

And Queen Elizabeth Stakes, Welsh Pageant took the Queen Elizabeth II Stakes and Lockinge Stakes twice, West Side Story was beaten a whisker in the Oaks and won the Ribblesdale Stakes and Yorkshire Oaks, and Derby runner-up Connaught took the King Edward VII Stakes and Prince of Wales's Stakes twice. Jim Joel's best jumping success came when Maori Venture won the Grand National of 1987.

RAE JOHNSTONE Jockey

◆ **Born: 1905 Died: 1964**

Rae Johnstone was only moderately successful in Australia before moving briefly to India in 1931. Continuing on to Paris two years later he quickly demonstrated his ability by winning the 1933 French jockeys' championship. He registered the first two of his 12 British classic successes when he rode Colombo in the 2,000 Guineas and Campanula in the 1,000 Guineas in 1934. Soon after being released from internment by the Germans, during World War II, Johnstone signed a contract to be the number one jockey for French cotton magnate Marcel Boussac. In 1948 Johnstone, a smooth, polished horseman, became the first Australian jockey to win the Derby when he scored on the Aga Khan's My Love. He won the Derby again in 1950 on Boussac's Galcador and in 1956 on Lavandin, who was trained by Alec Head. His other important successes featured the Prix du Jockey Club on Bey and Auriban in 1948 and 1952, respectively, as well as the 1947 Prix de Diane on Montenica. He retired from riding to become a trainer in 1958, but died six years later.

BEN JONES Trainer

◆ **Born: 1882 Died: 1961**

Benjamin Allyn "Plain Ben" Jones was Calumet Farm's head trainer from 1939–53. During that period, the Calumet homebreds Whirlaway and Citation registered Triple Crown sweeps, and the farm recorded three additional triumphs in the Kentucky Derby and two in the Preakness Stakes. This remains the greatest run in the classics ever registered by a single North American stable. Originally from Missouri, Jones was the son of a cattle farmer, who also operated a local racetrack. He spent many years training at small Midwest and Southern tracks and it was not until Jones was in his 50th year that he got his big break. In 1932, he began conditioning thoroughbreds for Herbert M. Woolf, for whom he sent postward his first Derby winner, Lawrin, in 1938. The following year, Jones signed on with Calumet. Working as a team with his son, "Jimmy", Ben Jones helped Calumet become the most powerful racing entity

in the land. After turning over training chores to Jimmy in 1953, Jones became the farm's general manager. He retained that position until 1957, when failing health necessitated his retirement.

HERBERT JONES Jockey

◆ **Born: 1881 Died: 1951**

Herbert Jones, whose father Jack trained jumpers for Edward VII when the King was Prince of Wales, was apprenticed to the royal flat trainer Richard Marsh at the age of ten and came in for the ride on the foul-tempered Diamond Jubilee in the 1900 2,000 Guineas when the colt refused to co-operate with Jack Watts and Mornington Cannon. He rode Diamond Jubilee to win the Triple Crown and took over as the King's jockey when Watts retired that year. In 1909 he partnered Minoru to take the Derby and the 2,000 Guineas for His Majesty and he had other classic wins with Vedas and Gorgos in the 2,000 Guineas and Cherry Lass in the Oaks.

JIMMY JONES Trainer

◆ **Born: 1906 Died: 2001**

The son of Benjamin Allyn Jones, H.A. "Jimmy" Jones spent nearly his entire racing career in partnership with his father. During the 1920s, they operated Jones Stock Farm in Parnell, Missouri, where their stallion, Seth, ranked among North America's top 20 sires. Meanwhile, father and son raced at tracks from Chicago to New Orleans. In 1933, they had the leading stable at Arlington Downs in Texas. Six years later, they were recruited by Calumet Farm. Jimmy Jones' hand was involved in conditioning all the great Calumet homebreds of the 1940s – Whirlaway, Citation, Bewitch, Coaltown, Armed, Twilight Tear – each of whom became a Hall of Famer. When Ben was named Calumet's general manager in 1953, Jimmy became head trainer. In 1957, he sent out Iron Liege to win the Kentucky Derby. The following year, he sent out Tim Tam to win the Kentucky Derby and Preakness Stakes. After retiring in 1964, Jimmy Jones long remained a frequent Churchill Downs visitor at Derby time.

SIR GEORGE JULIUS Inventor

◆ **Born: 1873**

A consulting engineer, Sir George Julius, who was the son of an Anglican Archbishop, played a significant role in the advancement of Australian and world racing as the inventor of the automatic totalisator. Originally from Norwich, Julius was still at school when his family emigrated to Australia in the 1880s and

he completed his studies at Melbourne Grammar School. He was working at Western Australian Railways when a dispute arose over the counting of votes in an election. With that, Julius resigned from his job and moved to Sydney to develop an electrical vote counter. Over a period of five years his vote counter evolved into a machine that could accept bets and determine dividends with reliability. The equipment, which he constructed in a shed at his home, was first used at a meeting in Auckland in 1913. Four years later his totalisator was installed at Randwick racecourse and by 1920 his company, Automatic Totalisator Pty Ltd, was being used widely in Australia and New Zealand. Over the next decade the equipment was put into operation at racecourses in over 35 countries and Julius was eventually knighted for his inventiveness.

K

3rd AGA KHAN Owner/Breeder

◆ **Born: 1877 Died: 1957**

His Highness the Aga Khan, spiritual leader of the Ismaili sect of Shia Muslims, was a major figure in European flat racing for more than 30 years, during which he won 17 British classics. He saw Jeddah win the 1898 Derby at odds of 100–1 while on his first visit to England from his native India; his first top level wins were Diophon in the 1924 2,000 Guineas and Salmon Trout in the same year's St. Leger. After waiting six years for the next classic success, Blenheim's win in the 1930 Derby was the start of a purple patch for the Aga Khan, during which time Firdaussi won the St. Leger, Bahram achieved the Triple Crown in 1935 and Mahmoud took the 1936 Derby in record time. The Aga Khan's horses were trained in Britain first by Dick Dawson, Frank Butters from 1931 until 1949, and Marcus Marsh who sent out the owner's last classic winner, the 1952 Derby and St. Leger hero Tulyar. The Aga Khan, whose horses were almost entirely trained in France in the last years of his life, also owned the Arc and Eclipse winner Migoli.

4th AGA KHAN Owner/Breeder

◆ **Born: 1936**

When the third Aga Khan died in 1957, it was his grandson who succeeded him as the spiritual leader of the Shia Muslims, becoming His Highness the fourth Aga Khan. He showed little sign of his

Derby double: H.H. the 4th Aga Khan with the ill-fated Shergar, after winning the Irish Derby in 1981.

grandfather's – or father's – enthusiasm for racing until 1960, when the victory by Charlottesville in the Prix du Jockey Club at Chantilly seemed suddenly to convert him. Since then, the fourth Aga Khan has become one of the most prominent racehorse owners in the world. He has thrice won the Prix de l'Arc de Triomphe, with Akida in 1982, with Sinndar in 2000 and with Dalakhani in 2003. Controversy has not avoided him. Lashkari, who won the inaugural Breeders' Cup Turf in 1984, initially tested positive for a prohibited substance, but subsequent testing cleared her name. For many years, the fourth Aga Khan refused to have horses trained in Britain after a row with authorities over post-race testing procedures, following Alyisa's disqualification from first position in the 1989 Oaks. Alamshar won the King George VI and Queen Elizabeth Diamond Stakes for the fourth Aga Khan in 2003, as did Azamour in 2005.

ALY KHAN Owner/breeder

◆ **Born: 1911 Died: 1960**

The Aly Khan was the eldest son of the third Aga Khan, but his father bypassed him in nominating his successor in favour of the Aly's son, the current Aga. He may have not had the supreme family title, but he certainly maintained the family enthusiasm for, and success in, racing, and in 1959 he became the first owner to receive winning prize money of more than £100,000 in Great Britain. This came about after Petite Etoile had won the 1,000 Guineas, Oaks and Champion Stakes, Taboun had taken the 2,000 Guineas, Saint Crespin III the Eclipse Stakes and Venture VII took the Imperial Produce Stakes and Middle Park Stakes. He had been an accomplished amateur jockey, winning races in both England and France, and was prepared to back his judgement. When his father sent Stafaralla to the yearling sales in 1936, the Aly Khan bought her for 1,850 guineas, and she won the Cheveley Park Stakes before becoming dam of

the St. Leger winner Tehran. The Aly Khan died in a car crash in 1960.

L

GEORGE LAMBTON
Jockey/trainer

◆ **Born: 1860 Died: 1945**

George Lambton was a very capable rider, counting the Grand Steeplechase de Paris on Parasang among his successes, before becoming a top-class trainer in 1892. He single-handedly ran a crusade to persuade the Jockey Club of the dangers of doping horses. His first classic success came when Canterbury Pilgrim won the 1896 Oaks. She belonged to Lord Derby, to whom Lambton was private trainer and/or racing manager from 1893 to 1933. During this time he was champion trainer three times and sent out two Derby winners, Sansovino (in 1924) and Hyperion (1933), who also won the St. Leger – as had Swynford (1910) – and the 2,000 Guineas winner Colorado (1926). After splitting with Lord Derby, Lambton set up as a public trainer, winning the 1938 Irish 1,000 Guineas with Lapel. His last winner was Golden Cloud at Newmarket shortly before he died. His crusade against doping came in the early 20th century. The practice had been introduced to Britain by American trainers who landed some major gambles. The Jockey Club was unconcerned, until Lambton demonstrated how dramatically doping could affect horses' form. The practice was immediately barred.

GEOFF LEWIS Jockey/trainer

◆ **Born: 1935**

Geoff Lewis was a hotel pageboy before being apprenticed to Ron Smyth. The first of his 1,879 winners in Great Britain came on Eastern Imp in 1953. He rode for a number of top stables during 26 years in the saddle, including those of Noel Murless, Ian Balding and Bruce Hobbs. His first classic win came with Right Tack in the 1969 2,000 Guineas. The best horse he rode was Mill Reef, an outstanding horse in an era of equine stars such as Brigadier Gerard and Nijinsky, and though the Brigadier beat him in the 1971 2,000 Guineas, he won the Prix de l'Arc de Triomphe, King George VI And Queen Elizabeth Stakes, Derby and Eclipse Stakes. In the same year, Lewis rode Altesse Royale to win the Oaks for Noel Murless and he teamed up with him to win the race again on Mysterious in 1973, who also won the 1,000 Guineas. He started training in 1980 and enjoyed

considerable success with the smart sprinter Lake Coniston, who won the July Cup, and another Group 1 winner in Yawa (Grand Prix de Paris and Premio Roma) before retiring in 1999.

D. WAYNE LUKAS Trainer

◆ **Born: 1935**

The winner of 13 Triple Crown events and a record 18 Breeders' Cup races, D. Wayne Lukas was the premier North American trainer during the final two decades of the twentieth century. Lukas has trained 23 champions, the most recent of whom is Azeri, who led North America's older filly and mare division in 2004. A trio of Lukas runners has gained Horse of the Year honours – Lady's Secret in 1986, Criminal Type in 1990 and Charismatic in 1999. Lukas himself has been honoured four times with Eclipse Awards as North America's outstanding trainer. A former college and high school basketball coach, Lukas first trained quarter horses, then switched to thoroughbreds full-time in 1978. In 1981, he sent out his first classic winner, Codex, who was victorious in the Preakness Stakes. In 1988, Lukas recorded his first of four Kentucky Derby victories with the filly, Winning Colors. Commencing with Tabasco Cat's triumph in the 1994 Preakness, Lukas won six consecutive Triple Crown events. Through 2005, Lukas's career purse earnings total was $244.74 million, an all-time record for a North American trainer.

HORATIO LURO Trainer/owner

◆ **Born: 1901 Died: 1991**

Born into wealth and social position in his native Argentina, Horatio Luro spent portions of his early years travelling to Europe, attending veterinary school, and managing his father's

Amazing run: D. Wayne Lukas trained the winners of six straight classics, 1994–96, but not a Triple-Crown champion.

thoroughbred stable. In the mid-1930s, Luro migrated to the United States. In 1942, he entered a claim of $2,500 in New York for a horse named Princequillo, who, under Luro's handling, became one of the finest distance runners in the land. Thus commenced the Luro legend. It would eventually encompass Kentucky Derby victories with Decidedly and Northern Dancer (both accomplished in track record clockings – and the latter also won the Preakness Stakes), and the exploits of Iceberg II, Miss Grillo, Victoria Park, Grey Dawn II, and One For All, among others. Tall, handsome, cultured and charming, Luro was nicknamed "El Senor". In his later years, he campaigned a Grade 1 winner by that name, with training chores entrusted to his grandson, William Wright. Luro thrice won Canada's Queen's Plate.

M

DANNY MAHER Jockey

◆ **Born: 1881 Died: 1916**

Danny Maher was the first, and until Steve Cauthen, the only American rider to have been champion jockey in Britain, which he was in 1908 and 1913, with respective scores of 139 and 115, though in neither season did he ride any of his nine classic winners. He came to Britain in 1900, two years after being champion in the U.S. and gained his first classic success on Aida in the 1901 1,000 Guineas. In 1903 he rode Rock Sand to victory in the Derby and the St. Leger and he had consecutive Derby successes on Cicero and Spearmint (1905 and 1906). In 1909 he won the Eclipse and the St. Leger on Bayardo, on whom he won the 1910 Ascot Gold Cup, by which time he was being paid a total of £8,000 per annum for retainers to Lord Rosebery, the Australian A.W. Cox and Leopold de Rothschild. Danny Maher had to waste hard to ride at 8st and this took its toll. He returned to America at the outbreak of the World War II and died from tuberculosis in November 1916.

SIR CHESTER MANIFOLD
Adminstrator/owner

◆ **Born: 1897 Died: 1979**

After being a member of the Victorian Legislative Assembly, 1929–35, Sir Chester Manifold became a leader of the racing industry. He served on the Victoria Racing Club committee from 1937 to 1962, being the V.R.C.'s chairman 1953–62. Manifold was also principal of the Talindert Stud in Victoria's Western District, where he bred the magnificent steeplechaser Crisp, who won many of Victoria's top steeplechases before campaigning in England. There he produced a spectacular exhibition of jumping in the 1973 Grand National, but was caught close to home and narrowly beaten by Red Rum, who received 23 pounds. Manifold is best remembered for his efforts to have legalized off-course betting introduced. He recognised that the establishment of legal betting facilities away from the racecourse would be the best way of channelling back into racing the vast sums of money lost to illegal gambling. He fought for a number of years to have the Victorian Totalizator Board instituted; it came into being in 1961. TABs have since been introduced in all Australian states and territories and now harness vast amounts of money each year for the racing industry.

LUCILLE MARKEY Owner/Breeder

◆ **Born: 19 Died: 1982**

One of racing's grand dames, Mrs. Lucille Markey was originally married to Warren Wright Sr., the heir to Calumet Farm. From 1941 until Wright's death in 1950, Calumet homebreds twice swept the Triple Crown, winning four renewals of the Kentucky Derby all told. Under the leadership of his widow, Calumet homebreds subsequently won the Derby four more times. Mrs. Wright, who remarried in 1952 and was Mrs. Gene Markey thereafter, led all North American owners in purse earnings in 1952, from 1956–58 inclusive, and again in 1961. Over the decades, she watched the likes of Whirlaway, Armed, Citation, Coaltown, Bewitch, and Tim Tam (all Hall of Famers) compete in Calumet's blue and devil's red colours. From the mid-1960s onward, though, Calumet entered into a slow, consistent decline in prominence. In her twilight years, Mrs. Markey would watch her horses run at Keeneland from a chauffeured automobile on the clubhouse lawn. It was there that she watched her hombred Alydar win the 1978 Blue Grass Stakes.

MARCUS MARSH Trainer

◆ **Born: 1904 Died: 1983**

Having learned his trade from his father Richard and from Fred Darling, two masters of their craft, Marcus Marsh set up on his own account in 1929 and he had his first top level successes with Windsor Lad in the 1934 Derby and St. Leger. Marsh served in the RAF during World War II, and resumed training at the Newmarket yard where his father had been based, and in his first season there he won the Diadem Stakes and Nunthorpe Stakes with The Bug, who was sent to him on the advice of Windsor Lad's jockey Charlie Smirke. For the 1950 season he became trainer for the Aga Khan and the new partnership met with instant success when Palestine won the 2,000 Guineas. In 1952 he was champion trainer when the Aga Khan's Tulyar landed the King George VI And Queen Elizabeth Stakes, the Derby, the Eclipse and the St. Leger. He retired in 1964.

RICHARD MARSH Trainer/jockey

◆ **Born: 1851 Died: 1933**

Richard Marsh rode on the flat and over fences, winning Royal Ascot's New Stakes and Liverpool's Grand Sefton Chase, before starting a 52-year training career in 1872. His first classic success came when Ossian won the 1883 St. Leger. In 1886 he sent out Miss Jummy to take the 1,000 Guineas and the Oaks and in 1892 he became the royal trainer when the Prince of Wales (later Edward VII) split with John Porter. The Prince's Persimmon won the 1896 Derby and the St. Leger and, two years later, Marsh won the Derby with the 100–1 chance Jeddah. In 1900 Persimmon's bad-tempered brother Diamond Jubilee carried the royal colours to Triple Crown victory. Marsh gambled successfully by putting up the inexperienced Herbert Jones when the colt refused to co-operate with top jockeys. He also sent out Thais to win the 1900 1,000 Guineas. Marsh, a three-time champion trainer, also won the 2,000 Guineas with Gorgos, and in 1909 sent out the King's Minoru to win the 2,000 Guineas and the Derby for the only occasion the colours of a reigning monarch have been worn to Derby success.

BRYAN MARSHALL Jockey

◆ **Born: 1916 Died: 1991**

Bryan Marshall was one of the best and most stylish jump jockeys in the post-World War II years, becoming champion jockey in 1947–48 and winning the Grand National on Early Mist in 1953 and Royal Tan a year later. He rode 517 NH winners in Britain. Marshall was apprenticed on the flat with Atty Persse. He had trouble getting his weight down after the end of the War, but did so and soon struck up a successful partnership with Fulke Walwyn. Having ridden Roi d'Egypte to win the 1942 Cathcart Chase at Cheltenham – he was on leave – Marshall gained his first big post war success on Walwyn's Leap Man in that race's 1946 edition. He won that race three times more for Walwyn, with whom he also teamed up to take the 1947 King George VI Chase on Rowland Roy. He also rode big winners for Peter Cazalet, including the King George VI Chase on Manicou in 1950 and the first Mildmay Memorial Chase on Cromwell, after whose owner the race was named.

FRANCOIS MATHET Trainer

◆ **Born: 1903 Died: 1983**

François Mathet started training after World War II and from 1949–82, he was leading trainer in his native France for races and/or stake money won. He sent out more than 3,000 winners for

Big winner: Paul Mellon, one of five "Exemplars" of racing.

major owner-breeders such as the Duprés, de Rothschilds, Volterras and the Aga Khan. One of his first top-level successes came when Coronation Cup winner Tantieme won the 1950 and 1951 Prix de l'Arc de Triomphe. Mathet also won the Prix de l'Arc de Triomphe with Akiyda and Sassafras. Sassafras was one of Mathet's six Prix du Jockey Club winners, and also won the Prix Royal-Oak. Other Prix du Jockey Club winners included Reliance and Top Ville, while Match III and Relko also claimed the Prix Royal-Oak. Match and Relko were among Mathet's many big winners outside France. Match took the King George VI And Queen Elizabeth Stakes and Washington DC International, Relko won the Derby and Coronation Cup. Mathet won another Derby with Phil Drake, the 1,000 Guineas and the Oaks with Bella Paola and the Oaks alone with Sicarelle.

RON McANALLY Trainer

◆ **Born: 1932**

One of the all-time leading trainers at California's Del Mar and Oak Tree at Santa Anita meets, Ron McAnally has made major impacts

elsewhere as well. Three times he has won the Arlington Million, with John Henry in 1981 and 1984, and with Tight Spot in 1991. McAnally's resume further includes four triumphs in Breeders' Cup events, including back-to-back runnings of the Distaff with Bayakoa in 1989–90. Raised in a North Kentucky orphanage, McAnally credits an uncle, Reggie Cornell, for his start in racing. McAnally has thrice received Eclipse Awards as North America's outstanding trainer. He trained John Henry to a pair of Horse of the Year titles. Bayakoa, Paseana, Northern Spur and Tight Spot all gained divisional honors under McAnally's care. In 1989, McAnally sent out Hawkster to a world record clocking of 2:22⁴/5 for 1¹/2 miles on the turf in the Oak Tree Invitational. More recently, in 2001, McAnally sent out Affluent to win the Queen Elizabeth II Challenge Cup at Keeneland.

DONALD "GINGER" MCCAIN Trainer

◆ **Born: 1930**

Donald "Ginger" McCain, also referred to as "Mr. Aintree", commenced his training career in 1969. Three years later, he spent 6,000 guineas on a horse named Red Rum, a transaction that proved to be one of the outstanding bargains in the annals of steeplechase racing. Red Rum, affectionately known to jump fans as "Rummy", won the Grand National in consecutive years, 1973 and 1974, and he won the race again in 1977 – forever securing McCain a niche as one of the great trainers in the history of the sport. But McCain still had chapters to write at Aintree. In 2003, he sent out Amberleigh House to finish third in the Grand National. And in 2004, Amberleigh House provided McCain with his fourth Grand National triumph, tying him with Fred Rimell for the most victories any trainer is known to have achieved (the Grand National dates back to 1837, and its early record-keeping was patchy). McCain's base was Cholmondeley in Cheshire. In 2006, he turned over his stable to his son, who is also named Donald, and with whom he will continue as an assistant. McCain also intends to continue to visit the grave of his beloved Red Rum, located fittingly at the finish line at Aintree.

PAUL MELLON Owner/breeder

◆ **Born: 1907 Died: 1999**

Distinguished in various fields, wealthy from his family's banking interests, a philanthropist and connoisseur of art, Paul Mellon had few peers, within racing circles or elsewhere. Although his

Annus mirabilis: Joe Mercer became the oldest first-time jockeys' champion of the 20th century aged 45 in 1979.

best successes were on the flat – he is the only owner to win the Kentucky Derby, Epsom Derby, and Prix de l'Arc de Triomphe – his very first winner was a jumper, Drinmore Lad, who won at Far Hills, New Jersey, in 1934. His interest in jumping had been kindled by his days at Cambridge University. Mellon's best horse was Mill Reef, whose wins included the Derby and Prix de l'Arc de Triomphe in 1971. Other top Mellon horses trained in Britain included Silly Season, Secret Step and Irish 1,000 Guineas winner Forest Flower. His best jumpers were Drinny's Double, Red Tide and Early to Rise. Mellon's long-time wish was to win the Kentucky Derby, and in 1993 Sea Hero made it come true. It was his third U.S. classic victory, as Quadrangle (in 1964) and Arts And Letters (1969) had won the Belmont Stakes. Mellon is one of five men to be honoured by the U.S. National Museum of Racing as "Exemplar" of the sport.

JOE MERCER Jockey

◆ **Born: 1934**

Joe Mercer is regarded by many experts as the most stylish flat jockey of his era. He rode 2,810 winners in Britain, 12 European classic winners and was champion jockey in 1979. Mercer, whose elder brother Manny was killed at Ascot in 1959, was apprenticed to Fred Sneyd and had his first winner on Eldoret at Bath in 1950. Three years later, while still an apprentice, he gained his first classic success on Ambiguity in the Oaks of 1953. The best horse Mercer rode was Brigadier Gerard, with whose trainer Dick Hern he had a long and successful association. He rode for the West Ilsley stable, which was run by Hern after Jack Colling retired, from 1953 to 1976. Brigadier Gerard won all but one of his 18 races, headed by the King George VI And Queen Elizabeth Stakes and 2,000 Guineas. Mercer also rode the Queen's Highclere to win the 1,000 Guineas and Prix de Diane, Bustino to land the Coronation Cup and St. Leger and Light Cavalry to take the St. Leger for Henry Cecil. He rode for Cecil from 1977 to 1980 and for Peter Walwyn until he retired in 1985.

TIM MOLONY Jockey/trainer

◆ **Born: 1919 Died: 1989**

Tim Molony rode many top winners in the years after World War II. He was champion jockey five times in Britain, in consecutive seasons from 1948–49 through 1951–52 – when he had 99 winners, his best return – and again in 1954–55. Though he never won the Grand National, he was successful in the Cheltenham Gold Cup on Knock Hard and Champion Hurdle in four consecutive seasons, on Hatton's Grace (in 1951) and Sir Ken (1952–54). He also rode winners of just about all the other chases over the big fences at Liverpool, including the Grand Sefton Chase twice on Wot No Sun and Key Royal. He started training in 1960 and enjoyed his biggest winner just before he retired 20 years later when he won the William Hill Gold Cup with Carpet General. He also did well with the sprinter Geopelia, but the most successful horse he trained was the subsequent triple Grand National winner Red Rum, of whom he had charge at two and three. Tim Molony's younger brother Martin won the Cheltenham Gold Cup on Silver Fame and the Irish Grand National three times.

CHARLES MORTON Trainer

◆ **Born: 1855 Died: 1936**

Charles Morton trained for a motley selection of owners including the hard-riding and rough living amateur "Abington" Baird, the corrupt American politician "Boss" Croker and the adventurer Bob Sievier, for whom he trained the outstanding filly Sceptre as a two-year-old. At the end of that year, 1901, Morton became private trainer for Jack Joel and in their second season together they won the 1,000 Guineas with Our Lassie; Glass Doll won that classic for them 1906; Your Majesty won the St. Leger in 1908; and, in 1909, Sunstar won the

2,000 Guineas and, in spite of breaking down terminally, also took the Derby. Morton also trained the smart handicapper Dean Swift, who won the Coronation Cup and ran in the City and Suburban Handicap for eight years in a row, winning it twice and being placed four times. Morton retired in 1924.

BILL MOTT Trainer

◆ **Born: 1953**

The youngest trainer ever elected to the Hall of Fame, Bill Mott won Eclipse Awards as North America's outstanding conditioner in 1995–96. Originally from South Dakota, the son of a veterinarian, Mott saddled his first thoroughbred winner at Park Jefferson in his home state when he was just 15. Mott is a former assistant to fellow Hall of Famer Jack Van Berg. The list of prominent owners for whom he has trained includes Sheikh Mohammed al-Maktoum and Allen E. Paulson. Mott's trainees include Cigar, who won a record-tying 16 consecutive races for Paulson from 1994–96. During the latter two of those seasons, Cigar was Horse of the Year. Other champions trained by Mott include Theatrical, Paradise Creek, Ajina, and Encina. He has eight times been the leading trainer at Saratoga. Mott also has five career triumphs in Breeders' Cup events. He tends to avoid the Triple Crown races – a second-place finish by 54–1 shot Vision and Verse in the 1999 Belmont Stakes is the best Mott has managed to achieve in a North American classic.

SIR NOEL MURLESS Trainer

◆ **Born: 1910 Died: 1987**

Noel Murless, who retired in 1976 and was knighted the following year, was an outstanding trainer. He started training in Yorkshire in 1935 and moved to Beckhampton on Fred Darling's retirement. Queenpot gave him the first of 19 British classic wins in the 1948 1,000 Guineas, helping him to become champion trainer for the first of nine occasions. A year later, Ridge Wood won the St. Leger. In 1952 he moved to Warren Place Stables at Newmarket, from where he enjoyed outstanding success. Lester Piggott replaced the retired Sir Gordon Richards as Murless' stable jockey in 1954. Their first top-level wins came in 1957 with Crepello's 2,000 Guineas and Derby, and they provided the Queen with her first classic winner when Carrozza won the Oaks – a classic Murless later won with Lupe, Altesse Royale and Mysterious. The last two of that trio also won the 1,000 Guineas, as did Fleet and Caergwrle. In 1967 Murless put up George Moore to win the Derby and 2,000 Guineas with Royal Palace, who took the King George VI And Queen Elizabeth Stakes and Eclipse Stakes in 1968, ridden by Sandy Barclay.

JOHNNY MURTAGH Jockey

◆ **Born: 1970**

Johnny Murtagh came back from the brink of the abyss to establish himself among the world's top riders thanks to an exceptional 2000 season,

Determination: Johnny Murtagh gives Dilshaan a powerful ride to win the Racing Post Trophy at Doncaster in 2000.

during which he rode 11 Group 1 winners. The highlight was his partnership with Sinndar to win the Derby, the Irish Derby and the Prix de l'Arc de Triomphe. He was apprenticed to Sinndar's trainer John Oxx, and rode his first winner on Chicago Style at Limerick in 1987. Murtagh was Ireland's leading apprentice in 1989 and champion jockey in 1995, when he also won the Breeders' Cup Mile, Coronation Stakes and Prix du Moulin on Ridgewood Pearl. Between his junior and senior championships Murtagh had problems with his weight and started drinking too much. Eventually he realised the error of his ways, and Oxx took him back into the fold. His successes for Sinndar's owner, the Aga Khan – one of John Oxx's major patrons – led to His Highness putting up Murtagh on horses trained by Michael Stoute when Kieren Fallon was injured in 2000. Murtagh was therfore fortunate to come in for top rides on Kalanisi in the Breeders' Cup Turf and Champion Stakes. In 2001–02, Murtagh won back-to-back runnings of the Gold Cup. In 2002 he was also victorious in the Derby with High Chaparral, and he additionally claimed the 2003 Irish Derby with Alamshar.

N

FLORENCE NAGLE
Owner/breeder/trainer

◆ **Born: 1894 Died: 1988**

Florence Nagle was involved in racing as owner, breeder and trainer for more than 60 years. In terms of results over that long period of time, a notable lack of significant successes suggest that she played no great part in racing history. But this is simply misleading and false. For many years she engaged in a running battle with the Jockey Club who refused to grant her, and other women, licences to train – solely on account of gender. Mrs. Nagle refused to submit to the Jockey Club's antiquated thinking and pursued them through the courts. Eventually she triumphed, with the Law Lords delivering scathing criticism of the Jockey Club. One of the Noble Lords said denying Mrs. Nagle a licence simply because she was a woman was, "as capricious as refusing a man a licence simply because of the colour of his hair." The nearest Mrs. Nagle came to a top-level winner was when her Sandsprite was second in the 1937 Derby. She also trained a useful stayer in Elf-Arrow, whose eight wins included the Liverpool St. Leger, and her Gelert was beaten by only a head in the Royal Hunt Cup.

O

AIDAN O'BRIEN Trainer

◆ **Born: 1969**

Aidan O'Brien trains at Ballydoyle in Co. Tipperary from where Vincent O'Brien – no relation – sent out many famous winners under both codes. He began training in 1993 while still enjoying a successful career in the saddle – he was champion amateur in 1993–94 in Ireland – and has accumulated a hugely impressive list of big-race winners. At one time he had a number of jumpers and he has sent out Istabraq to win at four consecutive Cheltenham Festivals, including the last three Champion Hurdles, but from 1998 he has concentrated almost entirely on the flat. The most successful flat horse he has trained has been Giant's Causeway, who won the Juddmonte International Stakes, Sussex Stakes, St. James's Palace Stakes, Eclipse Stakes and Irish Champion Stakes in 2000 before being narrowly beaten in the Queen Elizabeth II Stakes and Breeders' Cup Classic. Since then, O'Brien has figuratively been on fire at posts near and far, winning back-to-back runnings of both the English and Irish Derbies with Galileo and High Chaparral in 2001–02, back-to-back runnings of the Breeders' Cup Turf with High Chaparral in 2002–03, the St. Leger with Brian Boru in 2003, the Middle Park Stakes with Ad Valorem in 2004 and the St. Leger with Scorpion in 2005 – and this is just a brief list of O'Brien's recent accomplishments.

Flat specialist: Aidan O'Brien won successive runnings of the English and Irish Derbies in 2001 and 2002.

VINCENT O'BRIEN Trainer

◆ **Born: 1917**

It is unlikely that anyone will emulate Vincent O'Brien's record. His achievements on the flat alone, or just with jumpers, would stand high enough, but for one man to have done what he did under both codes is amazing. He began his career on his father's death in 1943 with just a handful of horses, but by the time he retired, at the end of 1994, O'Brien had won just about every major race in Britain, as well as the Prix de l'Arc de Triomphe three times, the Washington DC International and the Breeders' Cup Mile. He won the Triple Crown with Nijinsky, who was also one of his six Irish Derby winners – others include Epsom Derby winners The Minstrel and Sir Ivor. He also won the King George VI And Queen Elizabeth Stakes, 2,000 Guineas (four times), Oaks (twice) and St. Leger. In Ireland, O'Brien recorded nine St. Leger wins and five in the 2,000 Guineas. His many jumping successes included three consecutive Grand Nationals, 23 Cheltenham Festival winners – including four Cheltenham Gold Cups and three Champion Hurdles – and the Irish Grand National.

P

DOROTHY PAGET Owner/breeder

◆ **Born: 1905 Died: 1960**

Dorothy Paget deserved her reputation as a very difficult woman to work with, but she was a strong supporter of racing under both codes and also achieved top level success at both. The success of Straight Deal in the wartime Derby of 1943 helped her to be leading owner that season and she was top of the list with her jumpers in 1951–52, the year of Mont Tremblant's Gold Cup victory. Miss Paget, who also owned the Ballymacoll Stud in Ireland, enjoyed other good wins with Nucleus, who took the King Edward VII Stakes and Jockey Club Stakes as well as being second in the St. Leger, and Aldborough, winner of the Doncaster Cup and the Queen Alexandra Stakes. She also owned the five-time Cheltenham Gold Cup winner Golden Miller who, in 1934, became the only horse to win that race and the Grand National in the same year.

ALLEN E. PAULSON
Owner/breeder

◆ **Born: 1922 Died: 2000**

Recipient of the 1996 Eclipse Award of Merit, twice honoured as North America's outstanding owner, and once as outstanding breeder, Allen E. Paulson was one of the most influential figures to ever embrace the sport. Paulson bred and raced Cigar, who registered a record 16 consecutive victories from 1994–96. From 1986–98, Paulson campaigned, wholly and in partnership, eight divisional champions. Cigar, not surprisingly, was Horse of the Year in both 1995 and 1996. Virtually on his own since the age of 13, Paulson rose from menial jobs to be founder of Gulfsteam Aerospace Corporation. He maintained a small string of claiming horses in the late 1960s, but subsequently left racing, only to return in 1982. He quickly became one of the most prominent domestic buyers at yearling and bloodstock sales. Paulson horses won six Breeders' Cup races and his career earnings of $7,570,000 in Breeders' Cup events remains tops for an owner. Estrapade, the 1986 Arlington Million winner, and Theatrical, who won six Grade 1 races in 1987, were among Paulson's colour-bearers.

ANGEL PENNA Trainer

◆ **Born: 1923 Died: 1992**

Angel Penna was born in Argentina and achieved top level success there and in Venezuela before moving to the United States, where his successes continued, and then to France, where he arrived in 1971. Penna had his first winner at Buenos Aires in 1946, and in the U.S. his best successes came with Bold Reason, who won the Hollywood Derby and Travers Stakes – as well as finishing third in the 1971 Kentucky Derby and Belmont Stakes – and Czar Alexander, who took the Man o' War Stakes. In France his first job was training for Countess Margit Batthyany, for whom his wins included the Prix de l'Arc de Triomphe and Prix Vermeille with San San in 1973. At the end of that season he started training for Daniel Wildenstein. Their many successes were headed by Allez France, in 1974's Prix de l'Arc de Triomphe and Lianga in the Prix Jacques le Marois and Prix de l'Abbaye. In England in 1976, Penna won the Oaks and King George VI And Queen Elizabeth Stakes (with Pawneese), 1,000 Guineas (Flying Water) and St. Leger (Crow). He died in 1992.

OLIVIER PESLIER Jockey

◆ **Born: 1973**

Following the retirements of both Yves Saint-Martin and Freddie Head, Olivier Peslier became the dominant jockey in French flat racing. He rode his 1,000th winner in France in July 1999, just over a decade after his first success, at Rouen on

Top of the world: Olivier Peslier celebrates aboard Peintre Célebre after winning the 1997 Prix de l'Arc de Triomphe.

Cavallo d'Oro, when he was apprenticed to Patrick Biancone. Peslier's first classic win was on board Winged Love in the 1995 Irish Derby and, the following season, he managed to achieve the first of three successive wins in the Prix de l'Arc de Triomphe with Grand Prix de Saint-Cloud victor Helissio – followed by Grand Prix de Paris winner Peintre Celebre and Sagamix. Outside of France, he won the Deutsches Derby on Borgia, the Irish 2,000 Guineas and Queen Elizabeth II Stakes on Desert Prince, and the Derby on High-Rise. At courses even further afield, Peslier was victorious in the 2001 Japan Cup with Jungle Pocket and in that year's Breeders' Cup Filly and Mare Turf with Banks Hill. He registered a second triumph in the 2004 Japan Cup with Zenno Rob Roy, and in 2005 was victorious in the Gold Cup with Westerner.

OGDEN PHIPPS Owner/Breeder

◆ **Born: 1908 Died: 2002**

Breeder and owner of North America's 1966 Horse of the Year, Buckpasser, Ogden Phipps inherited his love of racing from his mother, Mrs. Henry Carnegie Phipps. Homebreds who represented Ogden Phipps also included Queen Of The Stage, Impressive, Numbered Account, Easy Goer, Vitriolic, Heavenly Prize, Personal Ensign and Relaxing. Phipps received the Eclipse Award as North America's outstanding breeder in 1988. He also received Eclipse Awards as outstanding owner in 1988–89. The former chairman of the Bessemer Trust banking firm, Phipps, in the twilight of his life, was a trustee emeritus of the New York Racing Association. He was elected to the Jockey Club in 1938, and was four times the US National Court Tennis Champion. Phipps bred to race, and not for the commercial market, but

actually didn't have his own breeding farm. His mares were boarded at Claiborne Farm in Kentucky. Phipps twice won the Travers Stakes at Saratoga, with Buckpasser in 1966 and with Easy Goer in 1989. From 1986–89, his homebred, Personal Ensign, went undefeated in her 13 career starts. Today, Phipps' son, Ogden Mills "Dinny" Phipps, carries on the family's proud racing tradition.

MARTIN PIPE Trainer

◆ **Born: 1945**

Martin Pipe, the son of a Somerset bookmaker, rode only one winner as a jockey in a point-to-point but he has set record after record since he started training in 1975. Although many of his early winners were over hurdles and in the humblest of grades, he progressed to have trained more winners under National Hunt rules and over jumps than any other trainer. Pipe's first winner came when Hit Parade won a selling hurdle at Taunton in May 1975 and his first big success came when Baron Blakeney landed the Triumph Hurdle at Cheltenham six years later. He won the Grand National with Miinnehoma and two Champion Hurdles, with Make A Stand and Granville Again. He twice trained four winners at the Cheltenham Festival meeting, and was one of only two trainers to have won all four Grand Nationals in the British Isles (Jenny Pitman is the other). Pipe – based near Wellington in Somerset – was champion jumps trainer ten times in the last 12 seasons of the century; it took David Nicholson with a pair of championships to interrupt the remarkable winning streak. Pipe claimed 15 championships all told, before illness forced him to retire in the spring of 2006.

Record-breaker: Trainer Martin Pipe with two of his horses.

All-time record: Todd Pletcher, the 2004 Eclipse Award winner as best trainer of the year.

JENNY PITMAN Trainer

◆ Born: 1946

Jenny Pitman was the leading woman trainer over jumps when she retired at the end of the 1998–99 season – her Weathercock House stables being taken over by her son Mark, her former assistant. Her career was somewhat controversial; she publicly lambasted people who incurred her displeasure. Mrs. Pitman – who was married to former jockey and TV presenter Richard Pitman – twice won the Grand National, with Corbiere and Royal Athlete, and nearly had a third when the Cheltenham Gold Cup winner Garrison Savannah finished second to Seagram after leading over the final fence. She also won the Cheltenham Gold Cup with Burrough Hill Lad, whose other successes included the Hennessy Gold Cup and the Welsh Grand National. Mrs. Pitman had point-to-point winners in 1975 and her first success as a public trainer came when Bonidon won at Southwell in August 1975. Her many other top wins include the Scottish Grand National with Willsford, the Irish with Mudahim and the Welsh with Stearsby. Only she and Martin Pipe have won the Aintree, Welsh, Scottish and Irish Nationals.

TODD PLETCHER Trainer

◆ Born: 1967

A former assistant to Hall of Famer D. Wayne Lukas, Todd Pletcher started his own stable in 1996, and has now risen to take a leading role among North American thoroughbred conditioners, receiving Eclipse Awards as outstanding trainer for both 2004 and 2005. His first really good horse was Jersey Girl, who won a trio of Grade 1 events in 1998. Included on Pletcher's CV are a pair of Breeders' Cup triumphs in 2004 at Lone Star Park, with Ashado in the Breeders' Cup Distaff and with Speightstown in the Breeders' Cup Sprint. In 2003, Pletcher set all-time records for a trainer with 40 victories during the Belmont Park spring meeting and 35 victories at the Saratoga meeting. Pletcher's father, Jake, was a thoroughbred trainer in the Midwestern United States. Pletcher himself graduated with a degree in animal science from the University of Arizona before spending seven years with Lukas, for whom he helped condition the 1995 Kentucky Derby and Belmont Stakes winner, Thunder Gulch. In 2004, Pletcher's horses won 240 races and earned $17.51 million in purses. In 2005, they won 257 (for a strike rate of 24.7%) races and earned $20.87 million in purses.

ETIENNE POLLET Trainer

◆ Born: 1911 Died: 1999

Etienne Pollet was one of the outstanding trainers in France in the quarter-century after World War II, despite never having a string of much over 50 horses. He began training in the French provinces in 1941, moving to Chantilly in 1945. His first big-race winner came when Pan – later an Ascot Gold Cup winner – took the 1950 Prix Royal-Oak. The best horse he trained was the outstanding Sea-Bird II, winner of the Derby and Prix de l'Arc de Triomphe in breathtaking style in 1965. Pollet also won the Prix de l'Arc de Triomphe with La Sorellina in 1953 and Vaguely Noble in 1968. Another top horse was Right Royal V, who won the King George VI And Queen Elizabeth Stakes and the Prix du Jockey Club. Among his best fillies was Hula Dancer, who won the Grand Criterium, 1,000 Guineas, Champion Stakes, Prix Jacques le Marois and Prix du Moulin. Pollet had planned to retire at the end of 1969, but stayed on for one year more to train Gyr, winner of the Grand Prix de Saint-Cloud and runner-up in the Derby.

EDGAR PRADO Jockey

◆ Born: 1967

Winner of the 2006 Kentucky Derby aboard Barbaro, Edgar Prado has also registered two of the greatest upsets in Belmont Stakes history, with his triumphs aboard the 70-1 shot Sarava in 2002 and the 35-1 shot Birdstone in 2004. Sarava's $142.50 mutuel return for a two-dollar win ticket remains a Belmont record. Originally from Lima, Peru, Prado was a star in his home country before relocating to South Florida in 1986. During most of the 1990s Prado was based in Maryland. He led all North American jockeys with 536 victories in 1997, 474 in 1998 and 403 in 1999. At the 1999 Saratoga meet, Prado finished in second position among riders with 36 victories - a two-dollar bet on each of his mounts during the meet would have produced an astonishing profit of 41%. In 2005 at Belmont Park, Prado registered his first Breeders' Cup triumphs, booting the 12-1 shot Silver Train to a photo-finish score in the Breeders' Cup Sprint and winning the Breeders' Cup Juvenile Fillies with favoured Folklore. Up until the end of 2005, Prado had accumulated a career total of 5,523 victories, and his mounts had earned purse monies totalling $167.49 million.

PADDY PRENDERGAST Trainer

◆ Born: 1909 Died: 1980

Paddy Prendergast's first racing involvement was as a very moderate jump jockey. His training career was at a very different level and he won almost all the top races in Britain and Ireland. Though always based in his native Ireland, he was champion trainer in Britain for three years in a row in the 1960s. He first made his mark with very speedy two-year-olds, such as Windy City, who won the 1951 Gimcrack Stakes, and The Pie King, who took that race and the Coventry Stakes in 1953. British classic wins came with Martial in the 1960 2,000 Guineas, Noblesse in the 1963 Oaks, Ragusa in the 1963 St. Leger and Pourparler in the 1964 1,000 Guineas. Ragusa and Meadow Court took the King George VI And Queen Elizabeth Stakes. Irish classic wins included those of Ragusa and Meadow Court in the Irish Derby, the 2,000 Guineas with Kythnos and Linacre, and the 1,000 with Gazpacho.

RYAN PRICE Trainer

◆ Born: 1912 Died: 1986

Ryan Price, a World War II commando, was one of post-war racing's most colourful characters; a versatile and successful trainer, he enjoyed top-level success on the flat and over jumps. Price won the 1962 Grand National with Kilmore, Cheltenham Gold Cup with What A Myth and Champion Hurdle with Clair Soleil, Fare Time and Eborneezer. He was champion trainer under NH rules four times. On the flat his top wins came with Ginevra in the 1972 Oaks and Bruni in the 1975 St. Leger. By the time he retired – in November 1982 – Price had trained nearly 2,000 winners. Four of those wins came in the first five runnings of the Schweppes Gold Trophy Hurdle, of which two came in circumstances of huge controversy. After Rosyth won for the second time in 1964 Price's licence and that of his jockey Josh Gifford were temporarily withdrawn, while Hill House's wide-margin triumph in 1967 was greeted by a storm of booing. A prolonged Jockey Club inquiry later concluded that Hill House had in some way created a stimulant inside himself.

Q

HM QUEEN ELIZABETH THE QUEEN MOTHER Owner/breeder

◆ **Born: 1900 Died: 2002**

Her Majesty Queen Elizabeth The Queen Mother – to give her official title – was the most popular racehorse owner in Britain. As the years went on, her enthusiasm for the sport never waned. The Queen Mother's involvement as an owner began when she and her daughter, then Princess Elizabeth, now HM The Queen, were successful with Monaveen at Fontwell in 1949. Her first big success came when Manicou took the 1950 King George VI Chase at Kempton; her 400th winner was Nearco Bay, at Uttoxeter in May 1994. The most dramatic moment of the Queen Mother's career as an owner was in the 1956 Grand National when her horse Devon Loch looked certain to win until he sprawled to the ground within sight of the line, and the most valuable race she has won was the Whitbread Gold Cup with Special Cargo in 1984. She had a Royal Ascot winner when Bali Ha'i took the Queen Alexandra Stakes in 1959, and her only Cheltenham Festival winner was Antiar in the Spa Hurdle. She died peacefully in her sleep, aged 101.

HM THE QUEEN Owner/breeder

◆ **Born: 1926**

The Queen's enthusiasm for racing and breeding has been a feature of her life since she first saw Fred Darling preparing her father's – King George VI – horses, such as Big Game and Sun Chariot, for their classic races during World War II. She took over the royal horses when she succeeded her father in 1952 having had her first success as an owner when Monaveen, owned in partnership with her mother, won at Fontwell in 1949. The Queen, though, is very much more a flat racing enthusiast. She had her first winner when she was still Princess Elizabeth in 1950 and her first winner as Queen when Choir Boy, who later won the Royal Hunt Cup, was successful at Newmarket in 1952. The Queen's classic victories comprise: the Oaks with Carrozza in 1957; the 1958 2,000

Guineas with Pall Mall; 1974's 1,000 Guineas and Prix de Diane with Highclere; and the Oaks and St. Leger in 1977 – Silver Jubilee year – with Dumfermline. The most valuable race she has won came when Unknown Quantity took the Arlington Handicap in 1989.

FRED RIMELL Jockey/trainer

◆ **Born: 1913 Died: 1981**

Fred Rimell was champion jockey and trainer during more than 50 distinguished years in the jumping world. He began on the flat as an apprentice jockey to his father Tom, riding his first winner at the age of 12. After 34 successes weight problems forced him to go jumping. A lack of experience persuaded his father not to put Fred up on the stable's 1932 Grand National winner, Forbra, and he would never win the National or the Cheltenham Gold Cup as a jockey. However, the four-time champion jockey did partner Brains Trust to win the Champion Hurdle. As a trainer he won every major race, including four Grand Nationals (with E.S.B., Gay Trip, Rag Trade and Nicolaus Silver), two Cheltenham Gold Cups (Royal Frolic and Woodland Venture) and two Champion Hurdles (Comedy of Errors – the only horse to regain that title). He topped the trainers' list on five occasions. After his death his widow Mercy, who had always played a major role at the Kinnersley stable, took over the licence and she became the first woman to take the Champion Hurdle when Gaye Brief won in 1983.

R

DAVID ROBINSON Owner

◆ **Born: 1906 Died: 1987**

David Robinson, who made his fortune from television rentals, was at one time by far the biggest owner on the flat-racing scene in terms of numbers. He had three private trainers at Newmarket and as many as 120 horses in action with them. He enjoyed plenty of success, though his only classic winner was Our Babu in the 1955 2,000 Guineas in 1955. Nijinksy was Robinson's nemesis in 1970 as his Yellow God was second in the 2,000 Guineas and Meadowville was runner-up in the St. Leger. Many of his best horses were sprinters, such as Green God, Deep Diver, Tudor Music, So Blessed and Bitty Girl. Almost all of Robinson's horses were bought at yearling sales, where he was hard to outbid once he had set his

mind on a horse. This was not lost on him – he called one of his horses Breeders' Dream. David Robinson shunned publicity to the extent that the first time he won the Gimcrack Stakes, he declined to make the speech at the traditional dinner.

5th LORD ROSEBERY Owner/breeder

◆ **Born: 1847 Died: 1929**

The racing and political interests of the fifth Earl of Rosebery spanned the 19th and 20th centuries. He enjoyed his first classic victory when Bonny Jean won the 1885 Oaks and the last of them came when Plack took the 1924 1,000 Guineas. In between he held high political office and he is the only serving Prime Minister to have owned the Derby winner, when in 1894 his 2,000 Guineas winner Ladas became the shortest priced winner of the Epsom classic at 2–9. Lord Rosebery also landed the 1895 Derby and St. Leger with Sir Visto, and the 1905 Derby with Cicero. His other classic victories were the 2,000 Guineas with Neil Gow and Ellangowan and the 1,000 Guineas with Chelandry and Vaucluse.

6th LORD ROSEBERY Owner/breeder

◆ **Born: 1882 Died: 1974**

The sixth Earl of Rosebery had great success as an owner-breeder and filled many public offices within and outside racing. He was twice senior steward of the Jockey Club, President of cricket's MCC, master of the Whaddon Chase hunt and President of the Thoroughbred Breeders' Association. Like his father, Lord Rosebery had his horses with Jack Jarvis and the best horse they had together was Blue Peter, who won the 1939 2,000 Guineas and Derby. The outbreak of World War II denied Blue Peter the chance to win the Triple Crown, but he did sire his owner-breeder's second Derby winner Ocean Swell (1944). Lord Rosebery's first classic success was the 1931 St. Leger with Sandwich and the last was the grey Sleeping Partner in the 1969 Oaks. She was trained by Doug Smith, who took over Rosebery's horses when Jack Jarvis retired. Lord Rosebery was leading owner and breeder in Blue Peter's year, 1939, and also top breeder in 1944 and 1969.

JAMES ROWE Sr. Trainer/jockey

◆ **Born: 1852 Died: 1929**

Had he accomplished nothing else in his career, the eight training triumphs registered by James Rowe Sr. in the Belmont Stakes would place him above almost any other trainer who ever saddled a racehorse. Even before this phenomenal run, Rowe had enjoyed success in the Belmont winning the 1872 and 1873 editions as a jockey. No other figure in North American racing has ever been able to account for ten winnings of a single classic event. Rowe's racing career began at age 10, when the horseman, Colonel David McDaniel, plucked him off a Richmond, Virginia, street corner where Rowe was selling newspapers. Rowe later recalled that his rewards for his first victory as a jockey were a large piece of red and white candy and permission to stay up until nine o'clock that night. During the 1907–08 seasons, Rowe sent out James R. Keene's homebred colt, Colin, to a perfect 15-for-15 career record. At the time of his passing, Rowe was Harold Payne Whitney's chief trainer.

S

EARL SANDE Jockey/trainer

◆ **Born: 1898 Died: 1968**

Man o' War, Sir Barton, Grey Lag, Zev, Gallant Fox – great horses, indeed, and Earl Sande rode all of them. With Gallant Fox, Sande swept the 1930 Triple Crown. All told he was victorious three times in the Kentucky Derby, once in the Preakness Stakes, and five times in the Belmont Stakes. With 968 victories from 3,673 mounts, Sande's career win ratio of 26.4 percent is one of the highest in North American racing history. A native South Dakotan, Sande rode at local ovals as a boy, and registered his initial victory at a recognized track in 1918 at Fair Grounds in New Orleans. Within short order, Sande became the contract rider for the Canadian sportsman J.K.L. Ross. Sande booted home 158 winners in 1918. It was to be his highest total for a single season. Sande retired numerous times. He trained racehorses, became a radio entertainer and signed for movie roles. An alcoholic and a recluse in his later years, he passed away in a nursing home.

ROBERT SANGSTER
Owner/breeder

◆ **Born: 1936 Died: 2004**

Robert Sangster was a major worldwide player over many years and enjoyed the peak of his successes during his association with Vincent O'Brien. Their wins together included successes for The Minstrel in the King George VI And Queen Elizabeth Stakes, Derby and Irish Derby;

Golden Fleece in the Derby; Alleged twice in the Prix de l'Arc de Triomphe; Caerleon in the Prix du Jockey Club and York International Stakes; and Sadler's Wells in the Irish Champion Stakes. Other trainers to have won top races for Robert Sangster include Vincent O'Brien's son David, who took the Irish Derby and the Prix du Jockey Club with Assert; John Gosden, who sent out Royal Heroine to land the Breeders' Cup Mile; Olivier Douieb, who gave him another Prix de l'Arc de Triomphe with Detroit; and Barry Hills, whose many successes for Sangster are headed by two Gold Cups at Ascot for Gildoran. He was champion owner in Britain on five occasions, the last of which was in 1984. The turn of the new century did not see Sangster enjoying the firepower of the major players from the Middle East, either in Britain or worldwide.

SIR VICTOR SASSOON
Owner/breeder

◆ **Born: 1881 Died: 1961**

Sir Victor Sassoon came into racing in the 1920s when he bought about 100 horses in India and Britain from an acquaintance who was in financial difficulties. His colt Pinza gave Sir Gordon Richards his only Derby victory at the 28th and final attempt in 1953. Although his Hot Night was second to Call Boy in the 1927 Derby, Sir Victor had to wait until 1937 for his first classic success, when Exhibitionnist, trained by Joe Lawson, won the 1,000 Guineas and Oaks. Following Pinza's success Sir Victor had three more Derby winners in eight years. Noel Murless trained the injury-prone Crepello to success in the 2,000 Guineas and the Epsom classic in 1957, and also prepared St Paddy in 1960, who added the St. Leger for Sir Victor later that year. There been an earlier Epsom triumph, in 1958, with the Irish-trained – by Micky Rogers – Irish 2,000 Guineas winner Hard Ridden. Sir Victor's Honeylight was trained by Charlie Elsey to land the 1956 1,000 Guineas and there were other such wins in Ireland by Museum and Phideas, both of whom also took the Irish Derby.

PETER SCUDAMORE Jockey

◆ **Born: 1958**

Peter Scudamore's success in the saddle maintained a family tradition. His grandfather Geoffrey rode winners as an amateur and his father Michael won the Grand National on Oxo and the Cheltenham Gold Cup on Linwell, though in numerical terms neither came anywhere near Peter's achievements. He rode a

then record 1,678 winners in Great Britain and was champion jockey on eight occasions, setting another record with 221 in a season when he took the title in 1988–89 and setting records for the fastest 50, 100, 150 and 200 winners in a season. His two biggest wins came in the Champion Hurdle on Granville Again and Celtic Shot. His association with trainer Martin Pipe brought Scudamore 792 of his career wins and they were champions together on four occasions. Scudamore's other top wins came on Pearlyman in the Queen Mother Champion Chase, Granville Again in the Scottish Champion Hurdle and Carvills Hill in the Welsh Grand National. He retired in 1993, becoming a newpaper columnist for an English tabloid newspaper, a racing analyst on television, and assistant to trainer Nigel Twiston-Davies.

CHARLES SEMBLAT
Jockey/trainer

◆ **Born: 1897 Died: 1972**

Charles Semblat was champion jockey in France on six occasions. He won the Prix du Jockey Club four times and Prix de l'Arc de Triomphe three times. He made occasional visits to England and won the 1937 2,000 Guineas on Le Ksar. In 1940 he became first jockey to Marcel Boussac's very powerful stable and rode Djebel to win that year's Poule d'Essai des Poulains. A bad fall in 1941 led to Semblat's retirement from the saddle and he became Boussac's trainer in 1944. Boussac's horses carried almost all before them and Semblat trained four winners of the Prix de l'Arc de Triomphe, five in the Prix du Jockey Club and eight in the Poule d'Essai des Pouliches. A three-time champion trainer in France, Semblat won the British equivalent in 1950, thanks to classic wins by Galcador (Derby), Asmena (Oaks) and Scratch II (St. Leger). He won the St. Leger again in 1951 with Talma II as well as the Ascot Gold Cup with Arbar and Caracalla. Semblat's association with Boussac ended in 1954 and he had his last major success when Thymus won the Poule d'Essai des Poulains in 1959.

BOB SIEVIER Gambler/owner/trainer

◆ **Born: 1860 Died: 1939**

Bob Siever, who was born in the back of a hansom cab in London, was a chancer who made his way through life by gambling and at one time owned and trained the outstanding filly Sceptre, who won every classic bar the Derby in 1902. He paid the then staggering sum of 10,000gns to buy Sceptre as a yearling and she was trained by Charles Morton as a two-year-old when she won the July Stakes. Sievier took over her training the next season, which she began in the Lincoln Handicap before winning her four classics. Her wins enabled Sievier to be champion owner and trainer, but he had backed too many losers and sold her for 25,000 gns. During his up and down later years he trained Royal Bucks to win the Lincoln Handicap and Warlingham to take the Cesarewitch Handicap.

TOD SLOAN Jockey

◆ Born: 1874 Died: 1933

James Forman (Tod) Sloan came to Britain from America at the end of the 19th century and revolutionized the riding style of jockeys with the forward seat and short leathers. He was much derided when he first appeared but it did not take long for the benefits of his style to be appreciated. His only classic winner was Sibola in 1899's 1,000 Guineas, but he was placed in seven other classics, and won Ascot's Gold Cup on Merman in 1900 and some big handicaps. Sloan took scant notice of the rules of racing; jockeys were not by this time allowed to bet but this did not stop him wagering to win vast sums until, by the end of the 1900 season it was made clear to him that his licence would not be renewed. He had ridden 254 winners from 801 mounts during his short spell as a jockey in Britain. Sloan remained in England despite having no job until he was deported in 1915 for running an illegal gaming house. He died in the U.S. in impoverished circumstances.

CHARLIE SMIRKE Jockey

◆ Born: 1906 Died: 1993

Charlie Smirke was a tough, rugged character with a superb temperament for big races. During a roller-coaster career in the saddle he was warned off (suspended – in what later appeared debatable cirumstances) for five years in the late 1920s, but went on to win 20 classics in Britain and Ireland as well as the Prix de l'Arc de Triomphe, the King George VI And Queen Elizabeth Stakes and the Washington DC International. Smirke's 1934 Derby win on Windsor Lad came less than a year after he regained his jockey's licence. He also rode that colt to St. Leger victory and won the Derby thrice more on Mahmoud (in 1936) Tulyar (1952) and Hard Ridden (1958). Two other St. Leger victories were notable: he came in for the injured Freddy Fox to complete Bahram's 1935 Triple Crown and replaced the suspended Lester Piggott

Sitting pretty: Peter Scudamore, on Sabin Du Loir, set a new jump jockeys' record in 1988–89 with 221 winners.

on Never Say Die in 1954. Smirke won the Prix de l'Arc de Triomphe on Migoli, the Washington DC International on Worden II and the Irish Derby on Turkhan and Fraise du Bois. He retired in 1959.

DOUG SMITH Jockey/trainer

◆ Born: 1917 Died: 1989

Doug Smith was one of the leading jockeys in the middle third of the 20th century and became a trainer, without quite matching his successes in the saddle. The younger of two jockey brothers – Eph was two years his senior – Doug Smith was apprenticed to the hard taskmaster, Fred Sneyd, and gained his first big win on Doreen Jane in the 1935 Ascot Stakes. He excelled in longer-distance races, where his best wins came on Alycidon in the Ascot Gold Cup, Doncaster Cup and Goodwood Cup, and he enjoyed classic success on two royal winners, Hypericum in 1946's 1,000 Guineas and Pall Mall in 1958's 2,000 Guineas. He also won the 2,000 Guineas on Our Babu (in 1955) and the 1,000 Guineas on Petite Etoile (1959). Smith was champion jockey five times after Sir Gordon Richards retired. He started training in 1968 and gained his only classic success when Sleeping Partner took the 1969 Oaks, but the filly's owner Lord Rosebery parted company with him two years later. Smith retired in 1980.

TOMMY SMITH Trainer

◆ Born: 1918 Died: 1988

A failed jockey, Tommy Smith, or T.J. as he was known, secured his trainers' licence from the Australian Jockey Club in 1941. He began with one horse, named Bragger, who set Smith on the path to fame and fortune with a series of wins. Smith's first major success was in 1949 A.J.C. Derby at Randwick with Playboy – ridden by George Moore – and his career continued to blossom. He won the Sydney Trainers' Premiership with 54 winners in 1952–53 and remained the champion trainer for an unprecedented 33 consecutive seasons. After losing his crown in 1985–86 he recaptured it in 1988–89. Smith, who won Melbourne Cups with Toparoa in 1955 and Just A Dash in 1981, also won a record 35 Derbys and the prestigious Cox Plate at Moonee Valley on seven occasions. The best horse he trained was Tulloch, who had 36 wins and 16 placings from 53 starts, while other greats were Redcraze, Silver Sharpe, Toy Show, Gunsynd, Red Anchor and Bounding Away.

CHRISTOPHE SOUMILLON
Jockey

◆ Born: 1981

A native of Belgium and the son of a steeplechase jockey, Christophe Soumillon is

Change of heart: Early retirement didn't suit Gary Stevens.

an emerging star on the international racing scene. In 1996, he moved to Chantilly, France, to apprentice for trainer Cedric Boutin. The following year, Soumillon scored his initial career victory, aboard a 75–1 shot named Bruno at Maisons-Laffitte. In 2000 at Saint-Cloud, Soumillon equalled a French record by winning five races on a single card. After briefly riding in the United States, he returned to Europe and in 2001 was victorious in the Prix du Jockey Club at Chantilly with Anabaa Blue. The following year, Soumillon tied for second position in France jockey standings, and in 2003 he was France's champion. On 11 May, 2003, he won three Group 1 races on a single day at Longchamp, including a pair of classics - the Poule d'Essai des Pouliches with Musical Chimes and the Poule d'Essai des Poulains. Later that season, Soumillon accounted for the Prix de l'Arc de Triomphe with Dalakhani. In 2005, Soumillon was again France champion, and on the other side of the Atlantic won the Breeders' Cup Turf at Belmont Park with Shirocco.

ARTHUR STEPHENSON Trainer

◆ **Born: 1920 Died: 1992**

Until his records were beaten by Martin Pipe, Arthur Stephenson had trained more winners overall and more winners under National Hunt (jumping) rules than anyone else. However, he was never champion trainer and only a small proportion of his winners came in top-level races. The first of his 2,644 jumping winners came when he trained and rode

T.O.D., to success at a bona fide meeting at Rothbury in 1946. Stephenson's first major victory was when Kinmont Wullie took the 1961 Scottish Grand National. He also won that race with Killone Abbey and the Welsh version with Rainbow Battle. His biggest success came when The Thinker won the Cheltenham Gold Cup in 1987, while other big winners included Pawnbroker in the Mackeson Gold Cup, Blazing Walker (Melling Chase) and Rigton Prince and Villierstown (Topham/John Hughes Memorial Trophy). The Thinker was one of five who was placed for him in the Grand National – Durham Edition was twice runner-up. He also had some good wins on the flat, including Forlorn River in the July Cup and the Nunthorpe Stakes and Rapid River in the Gimcrack Stakes.

GARY STEVENS Jockey

◆ **Born: 1963**

Gary Stevens' career record includes victories in eight Triple Crown events. He won the Kentucky Derby with Winning Colors, Thunder Gulch and Silver Charm. He won the Preakness Stakes with Silver Charm and Point Given. And he was triumphant in the Belmont Stakes with Thunder Gulch, Victory Charm and Point Given. Stevens also won eight Breeders' Cup races. Venturing to other shores, he won the Japan Cup with Golden Pheasant in 1991 and Dubai World Cup with Silver Charm in 1998. Stevens initially worked for his father, Ron, a quarter horse trainer. Gary's first thoroughbred victory came aboard a filly named Lil Star at Les Bois Park in his native Idaho on 18 May, 1979. In early 1995, Stevens rode in Hong Kong, winning with 21 of 86 mounts. In 1998, he received the Eclipse Award as North America's outstanding jockey. In 1999, Stevens spent 14 weeks in England – riding first call for Michael Stoute, he registered 47 wins from 229 mounts. Stevens retired from riding in November, 2005, having accumulated 5,005 career victories and purse earnings of $237.64 million. He had a supporting actor's role in the movie "Seabiscuit," and now works as a racing commentator on television.

SIR MICHAEL STOUTE Trainer

◆ **Born: 1945**

Michael Stoute came to Britain from Barbados, where his father was police chief. Stoute worked for Pat Rohan, Doug Smith and Tom Jones before establishing his own yard in

1972, and registered his first career win in April of that year with Sandal at Newmarket. Since then, Stoute has been England's champion trainer eight times, most recently in 2005. He has also won the Derby four times, with Shergar in 1981, Shahrastani in 1986, Kris Kin in 2003 and with North Light in 2004. In North America, Stoute won the Breeders' Cup Turf with Pilsudski in 1996, repeating victory in that race with Kalanisi in 2000, and won the Breeders' Cup Filly and Mare Turf with Islington in 2003. In 1996–97, Stoute was victorious in consecutive runnings of the Japan Cup, with Singspiel and Pilsudski. In 1998, Stoute was knighted by the Queen, and he commenced training for her the following season. Appropriately, Stoute has thrice won the King George VI and Queen Elizabeth Diamond Stakes, with Shergar, Opera House and with Golan in 2002.

FRANK STRONACH

Owner/breeder/racetrack magnate

◆ **Born: 1932**

In his youth, Frank Stronach was a hotel dishwasher. He's since become founder and board chairman of Magna International Inc., a world leader in supplying electronic components and automobile parts. Magna's subsidiary, Magna Entertainment, owns racetracks throughout the United States, including Santa Anita in California and Florida's Gulfstream Park. Second position has never suited Stronach. He wants to be the

Natural winner: Frank Stronach wins the Preakness trophy for the Preakness Stakes in May 2000.

biggest player in every game he's in. Master of Adena Springs Farm, which has divisions in Kentucky, Florida and Canada, the Austrian-born Stronach was a part-owner of Touch Gold, winner of the 1997 Belmont Stakes. The following year, Stronach's homebred, Awesome Again, was undefeated in six starts, completing his race career with a victory in the Breeders' Cup Classic. Stronach received Eclipse Awards as North America's leading owner for three consecutive years, from 1998–2000, and as North America's leading breeder for 2000 and for 2004. He also won his second Breeders' Cup Classic in 2004 with Ghostzapper, who was honoured as North America's champion older male runner and Horse of the Year.

WALTER SWINBURN Jockey

◆ **Born: 1961**

Walter Swinburn, whose father Wally was a successful jockey, became one of the youngest men to ride a Derby winner when he won on Shergar at the age of 19 in 1981. He acquired a deserved reputation as an ideal big-race rider. Swinburn rode his first winner in 1978 and in 1980 he was appointed stable jockey to Michael Stoute's powerful yard at Newmarket. The next year he rode Shergar to his Derby and King George VI And Queen Elizabeth Stakes successes, and he and Stoute enjoyed other top level wins with Shahrastani in the 1986 Derby and the Irish Derby, Unite in the 1987 Oaks, Doyoun in 1988's 2,000 Guineas, Musical Bliss in the following year's 1,000 Guineas and Shareef Dancer in the 1983 Irish Derby. Swinburn also won the 1995 Derby on Lammtara for Godolphin and the 1983 Prix de l'Arc de Triomphe on All Along for Daniel Wildenstein. His battles with weight and other personal problems, as well as a horrendous fall in Hong Kong, made things increasingly difficult for him and he retired, after a final comeback winner, in 2000.

T

MICHAEL TABOR
Bookmaker/owner

◆ **Born: 1942**

Born in the East End of London, Michael Tabor began his professional career as a ladies' hairdresser, but abandoned that pursuit to establish the Arthur Prince chain of betting shops, which eventually numbered 113. In 1970 he was "warned off for life" by the British Jockey Club for allegedly paying jockeys for information, but the ban was subsequently reduced to three years. In 1975, Tabor was represented by his first winner, Tornado, who scored in a selling race at Haydock. As the years passed, Tabor's interest in the sport increased, and in 1995 he sold his chain of shops and has since concentrated on horse ownership – often in partnership with Susan Magnier. In 1995, Tabor campaigned the Kentucky Derby and Belmont Stakes winner, Thunder Gulch, who was North America's champion three-year-old that season. Tabor won the 1999 Prix de l'Arc de Triomphe with Montjeu, and he partnered Magnier in campaigning Johannesburg and High Chaparral, the latter of whom was a champion in England, and a multiple champion in both Ireland and North America.

JOHN TAIT Trainer/owner

◆ **Born: 1813 Died: 18**

Scottish-born John Tait settled in Tasmania after emigrating in 1837, but moved to New South Wales in 1843. In 1847 his first horse Whalebone won the St. Leger Stakes. As an owner in the early 1850s, he frequently won races run in the Sydney area, including two further St. Legers with Cossack and Surplice. As the 1860s began, Tait, who was known as "Honest" John, decided to train in his own right and bought Byron Lodge at Randwick. His greatest horse was The Barb, who won the 1866 Melbourne Cup and 16 other events – including the 1868 and 1869 Sydney Cups – from 24 starts. Tait also won the Melbourne Cup in 1868 with Glencoe, in 1871 with 100–1 chance The Pearl, and The Quack, in 1872. Among his other horses were Fireworks, who won 12 of his 16 races including three Derbies, Florence, who was also successful in three Derbies as well as the V.R.C. Oaks; and Goldsborough, who won the Epsom and Metropolitan Handicaps in 1875. He is said to have have won £30,000 in prize-money between 1865 and 1880.

ALEC TAYLOR Trainer

◆ **Born: 1862 Died: 1943**

Alec Taylor, whose father and grandfather were successful trainers – his father won the1878 Derby with Sefton – was the outstanding trainer of the first quarter of the 20th century when he won 22 classics and was champion 12 times, seven of them in succession, 1917–23. His first classic winner was Challacombe in the 1905 St. Leger. Taylor trained consecutive Triple Crown winners, 1917–18, in Gay Crusader and Gainsborough, respectively, after his first Derby success had come with Lemberg in 1910. He won two more 2,000 Guineas – Kennymore (1914) and Craig an Eran (1921) – and a further two St. Legers (Bayardo in 1909 and Book Law in 1927). He won the Oaks on eight occasions and the 1,000 Guineas twice as well as the Grand Prix de Paris with Lemonora, and when he retired at the end of 1927 he had won 1,003 races worth £839,000 in Great Britain.

GEORGE TODD Trainer

◆ **Born: 1894 Died: 1974**

Like Alec Taylor, George Todd trained with great success at Manton though his approach was somewhat different. Although he won the 1966 Irish Derby and the St. Leger with Sodium, many of his successes were in big handicaps. In further contrast to Taylor, he liked nothing better than a successful gamble and was never champion trainer. Todd learned much of his trade with Tom Coulthwaite, who sent out three Grand National winners in Eremon, Jenkinstown and Grakle (in 1907,

Dynamic duo: Walter Swinburn rode Shergar to Derby glory.

1910 and 1931, respectively) before setting up in 1928. He gained his first big win when Retsel took the 1946 Chester Cup and moved to Manton the following season. Apart from Sodium, he gained top level wins with Roan Rocket, Oncidium, River Chanter and Parthian Glance. Among Todd's major handicap successes before he retired in 1973 were the Cesarewitch Handicap with French Design, the Goodwood Cup with Trelawny, the Ascot Stakes with Shira and the Lincoln Handicap and Stewards' Cup with Dramatic.

JACK VAN BERG Trainer

◆ **Born: 1936**

The son of the late Marion H. Van Berg, a fellow Hall of Fame trainer, Jack C. Van Berg has long appreciated his father's advice: "Run your horses where they belong, and try to keep them as sound as possible." This philosophy has helped Van Berg accumulate over 5,000 career training victories. His triumphs include the 1984 Preakness Stakes with Gate Dancer (in track-record time), and the 1987 Kentucky Derby and Preakness with Alysheba. Between 1968–86, Van Berg led North American conditioners in wins nine times. He registered a record 496 triumphs in 1976 alone. Van Berg received an Eclipse Award as outstanding trainer in 1984. Three years later, he was presented with the Jockey Club Medal, one the most prestigious honours in the sport. The 1990s proved to be disappointingly quiet for Van Berg, and he was beset by financial problems – it is often said he was North America's best trainer and its worst businessman. Since the turn of the new century, his presence has all but vanished, although his former assistants, such as Hall of Famer Bill Mott, continue to praise the influence he has had on their careers. Van Berg's horsemanship remains a standard against which the skills of others are measured.

ALFRED VANDERBILT JR.

Owner/breeder/racetrack operator

◆ **Born: 1912 Died: 1999**

Master of Sagamore Farm in Maryland, where Native Dancer was bred, president of Pimlico Race Course and Belmont Park – these are just a few of the notations on the resume of Alfred Gwyne Vanderbilt Jr. Although born into wealth, Vanderbilt's early childhood saw great tragedy. He was not yet three years old when his father was lost as the *Luisitania* went down. In 1923, Vanderbilt's maternal grandfather, Isaac Emerson, took him to the Preakness Stakes. Thus began a devotion to the sport that Vanderbilt held for the remainder of his life. Discovery carried Vanderbilt's colours, as did homebred Native Dancer, "the Gray Ghost of Sagamore". Both are Hall of Famers. Vanderbilt led the earnings lists for all North American owners in 1935 and 1953. In 1937, he was elected to the Jockey Club. In 1994, Vanderbilt was honoured with the Eclipse Award of Merit. As Pimlico's president from 1938–42, Vanderbilt arranged the Seabiscuit vs. War Admiral match race in the 1938 Pimlico Special. At Belmont, he helped effect the switch from licensed bookmakers to pari-mutuel wagering.

JORGE VELASQUEZ Jockey

◆ **Born: 1946**

A native of Panama, Jorge Velasquez spent part of his youth working in a bakery, where his pay was loaves of bread for his family. He subsequently became a leading jockey in his home country, breaking a number of records that had been set by Braulio Baeza. In 1965, Velasquez was brought to the United States by the Florida-based owner and breeder, Fred Hooper. Velasquez went on to ride nine Eclipse Award-winning fillies and four champion turf horses. In 1967, he led all North American riders with 438 wins. Velasquez won the 1981 Kentucky Derby and Preakness Stakes aboard Pleasant Colony, who was also champion of his division that year. In 1985, Velasquez registered 57 stakes triumphs, an all-time North American record for a single season. In 1987, Velasquez spent most of the year in France and, a year later, became the fourth jockey in history to reach $100 million in career earnings. Since retiring, he has taken various jobs, including stints as jockeys' agent and racing official.

JOHN VELAZQUEZ Jockey

◆ **Born: 1971**

The recipient of the Eclipse Award as North America's outstanding jockey for both 2004 and 2005, John Velazquez is a native of Puerto Rico and has been based in the United States since 1990. His initial pair of Grade 1 triumphs came in 1995, with Turk Passer in the Turf Classic Invitational Stakes at Belmont Park and with Perfect Arc in the Queen Elizabeth II Challenge Cup at Keeneland. Velazquez has since scored six times in Breeders' Cup events: the 1998 Breeders' Cup Mile with Da Hoss; the 2000 Breeders' Cup Juvenile Fillies with Caressing; the 2002 Breeders' Cup Filly and Mare Turf with Starine; the 2002 Breeders' Cup Juvenile Fillies with Storm Flag Flying; the 2004 Breeders' Cup Distaff with Ashado; and the 2004 Breeders' Cup Sprint with Speightstown. On 3 September, 2001, Velazquez set a new standard as he became the first jockey in history to win six races on a Saratoga card. In 2004, he set a Saratoga single-meeting record with 65 victories, breaking his own standard of 61 wins that he had set the season before. At the end of the 2005 season, North American career totals for Velazquez included 3,399 victories and purse earnings of $162.77 million.

FULKE WALWYN Jockey/trainer

◆ **Born: 1910 Died: 1991**

Fulke Walwyn was one of the outstanding trainers of jumpers after World War II. He was one of the very few to have ridden and trained winners of the Grand National, partnering Reynoldstown to the horse's second success in 1936 and sending out Team Spirit 28 years later. He won the Cheltenham Gold Cup four times with Mont Tremblant, Mandarin, Mill House and The Dikler. Leading Walwyn's seven Whitbread Gold Cup victories was Diamond Edge, who won twice. He won the Champion Hurdle with Anzio and Kirriemuir, and the King George VI Chase five times, including the inaugural running in 1947 with Rowland Boy, and twice with Mandarin, who also won the Grand Steeplechase de Paris after a highly dramatic race. The horse's bridle broke right at the start of the race, forcing jockey Fred Winter to steer him with hands and heels; then he broke down three fences from home. Fulke Walwyn was five times champion trainer over jumps and also trained some good winners on the flat. On Peter Cazalet's death he took over Queen Elizabeth the Queen Mother's horses and had his best wins for her when Special Cargo won the Whitbread Gold Cup and Tammuz took the Schweppes Gold Trophy.

PETER WALWYN Trainer

◆ **Born: 1933**

Peter Walwyn retired in 1999 after more than 40 years with a training licence, though for the first four of those he was holding it on behalf of Mrs. Helen Johnson Houghton because women had not yet been permitted to hold licences as trainers. He enjoyed classic success with Humble Duty in 1970's 1,000 Guineas, Polygamy in the 1974 Oaks and English Prince in the 1974 Irish Derby. Humble Duty also contributed to Walwyn's big-race victories by taking the Sussex, Coronation and Cheveley Park Stakes. Walwyn, who was champion trainer in 1974 and 1975 and had a best total of 121 UK winners in the latter year, had other notable wins with Rock Roi (who was twice disqualified after finishing first in the Gold Cup) in the Prix du Cadran, which he also won with Buckskin, the Coronation Cup with Crow and the July Cup with Hamas. His best horse was Grundy, winner of the Derby, Irish Derby and King George VI And Queen Elizabeth Stakes in 1975.

TOMMY WESTON Jockey

◆ **Born: 1903 Died: 1981**

Tommy Weston was retained by the 17th Earl of Derby when the owner-breeder was enjoying his halcyon days of the 1920s and 1930s. Eight of the 11 British classics that Weston won were for his principal owner, and it was for Lord Derby that he gained his first classic, Tranquil winning the 1923 St. Leger. The following year he and Sansovino powered through the Epsom mud to win the Derby by six lengths; this was the first time since 1787 that the Earl of Derby had won the race named after his forbear. Weston regarded Sansovino as the best horse he rode, even though in 1933 he partnered Hyperion to victory in the Derby and the St. Leger and also won the St. Leger on Fairway. Though Lord Derby did not renew the retainer for 1935, Weston's career did not suffer to any extent. He won the 1936 Oaks on Lovely Rosa and, having served in the Royal Navy during the war, came back to win the 2,000 Guineas on Happy Knight in 1946. He retired in 1950.

JAMES WHITE
Breeder/administrator/owner

◆ **Born: 1828 Died: 1890**

Taking over the management of his father's estate at the age of 16, James White soon

Long life: Fulke Walwyn was still training 50 years after riding Reynoldstown to win the 1936 Grand National.

became a major property owner in the Upper Hunter Valley region of New South Wales. Beginning with Edinglassie and Kirkham Studs he subsequently developed the historic Segenhoe Stud, which became one of the nation's leading thoroughbred breeding grounds. Furthermore White was a member of the State's Legislative Assembly and later the Legislative Council as well as being Australian Jockey Club chairman in 1880 and from 1883 to 1888. White also raced horses most successfully, with his representatives Chester, in 1877, and Martini-Henri, in 1883, winning both the Victoria Derby and Melbourne Cup. He recorded additional victories in the Victoria Derby with Nordenfelt, Trident, Ensign And Dreadnought. Other wins included the V.R.C. St. Leger five times in succession from 1886 and the A.J.C. St. Leger five times in the six runnings, 1884–89. White bred Narellan and Kirkham – both sons of Chester – to Northern Hemisphere time to compete in the English classics. Narellan went wrong in training but Kirkham carried White's colours into sixth place behind Sainfoin in the 1890 Derby.

C.V. WHITNEY Owner/breeder

◆ **Born: 1899 Died: 1992**

The breeder of 176 stakes winners, C.V. Whitney was the most recent recipient of the Hall of Fame's highest designation, "Exemplar". Racing was in his family as his father, Harry Payne Whitney, was eight times North America's leading thoroughbred owner. C.V. inherited his father's estate, which included the crack two-year-old, Equipoise. "The Chocolate Soldier", as the colt was known, registered 24 career stakes triumphs. Equipoise was instrumental in C.V. Whitney

being North America's leading owner from 1930–33. He and his late father shared the title of leading breeder in 1933 and 1934, and C.V. captured it outright in 1938 and 1960. His homebred champions included the 1951 Horse of the Year, Counterpoint, along with First Flight and Silver Spoon. In 1947, Whitney won the Belmont Stakes with Phalanx. In 1956, his homebred grass champion, Career Boy, became the first American horse to win the Washington DC International. Multi-faceted in business, Whitney produced *Gone With the Wind* and *The Searchers*, two of the greatest American films ever made.

CHARLES WHITTINGHAM
Trainer

◆ **Born: 1913 Died: 1999**

"Get them sound and strong, then work them hard and long," was the motto of Charlie Whittingham. Known as "the Bald Eagle" on the backsides of Southern California racetracks, Whittingham thrice won Eclipse Awards as North America's outstanding conditioner. Ack Ack won the Horse of the Year title in 1971, as did Ferdinand in 1987, and Sunday Silence in 1989. All three were Whittingham trainees. An eighth-grade drop out, Whittingham received his initial trainer's licence in 1934. His horses won over 600 stakes races, including a record nine runnings of the Santa Anita Handicap. Disinclined to go to the Triple Crown events, Whittingham nevertheless won the 1986 Kentucky Derby with Ferdinand, and the 1989 Derby and Preakness Stakes with Sunday Silence. He further sent out those same colts to victories in the 1987 and 1989 editions of the Breeders' Cup Classic. Possessed of extraordinary energy, Whittingham continued to train almost until the time he died. He was known literally to engage in head-butting contests to settle disagreements .

GEORGE WIDENER
Administrator/owner/breeder

◆ **Born: 1889 Died: 1971**

Chairman of the Jockey Club, president of Belmont Park and the National Museum of Racing, George D. Widener exercised enormous influence on the sport during for almost 60 years. In 1971, Widener was honoured by the museum as its first of five "Exemplars". He bred 100 stakes winners, many of whom raced in his colours, including the champions Jamestown, High Fleet, Platter, Stefanita, Jaipur and What A

Treat. Widener horses won the Travers Stakes five times and the Flash Stakes at Belmont Park on nine occasions. In 1962, a long-time Widener dream was fulfilled when Jaipur won the Belmont Stakes. Major two-year-old events at Saratoga were a George D. Widener specialty; his horses won the Hopeful and Saratoga Special four times each, and the Sanford five times. Widener's father, George Widener Sr., was lost on the *Titanic*. The fortune Widener subsequently inherited allowed him to devote nearly all of his time to racing and breeding.

LORD WIGG Administrator

◆ **Born: 1900 Died: 1983**

George Wigg, a regular soldier from 1919 to 1937, and again 1940–46, reaching the rank of colonel, was later a socialist MP and Paymaster General in Harold Wilson's Labour Goverment elected to office in 1964. He was appointed chairman of the Levy Board in 1967, holding that post until 1972. Though he seemed to spend a lot of time instigating arguments with the Jockey Club, his concern for racing – and those professionally involved in it – was very genuine. He was an efficient racing administrator; during his tenure, the Levy Board became owners of Epsom and Sandown racecourses and his deal with Stanley Wootton ensured the preservation of Walton Downs for racing and training in perpetuity. He also

enforced the ruling that the Home Secretary had to approve how the Jockey Club spent the levy income. Having had constant battles with the bookmakers during his Levy Board days, Lord Wigg was a poacher turned gamekeeper in 1972, when he took on the role of chairman of the Betting Office Licensees' Association.

DANIEL WILDENSTEIN
Owner/breeder

◆ **Born: 1917**

Daniel Wildenstein is a millionaire art dealer and historian who has enjoyed major racing success worldwide. His reputation was for being difficult to get on with and he fell out with Peter Walwyn and Henry Cecil, both of whom trained big winners for him. Wildenstein's first classic was Don II's victory in 1969's Poule d'Essai des Poulains, to follow his victory in the 1968 Prix de la Fôret. In 1970 his filly Allez France began a career which included successes in the 1973 Prix de Diane and 1974 Prix de l'Arc de Triomphe, as well as the Washington DC International and Prix Vermeille. He had other Prix de l'Arc de Triomphe successes with Sagace in 1984 (he was disqualified after finishing first again 12 months later) and Peintre Celebre in 1997. Wildenstein's best winners in Britain include the King George VI And Queen Elizabeth Stakes with Oaks and Prix de Diane winner Pawneese in 1976. He won the 1,000 Guineas

and St. Leger that year with Flying Water and Crow, respectively, and ended the season as leading owner in Britain.

BILL WILLIAMSON Jockey

◆ **Born: 1922 Died: 1979**

Although his profile was never as high as those of some of his compatriots, Bill Williamson was among the very best Australian jockeys who came to ride in Europe in the 1960s. He was Victoria's champion jockey seven times and won the 1952 Mebourne Cup on Dalray, before moving to Ireland. Williamson rode Lynchris to win the 1960 Irish Oaks and St. Leger for John Oxx, with whom he maintained a successful link for many years, riding other Irish classic winners, Arctic Storm (1962 2,000 Guineas), Hibernia III (1963 Oaks) and Biscayne (St. Leger). His association with Seamus McGrath led to victories on Levmoss in 1969's Prix de l'Arc de Triomphe and Ascot's Gold Cup – he had also won the former race in 1968 on Vaguely Noble. In Britain, Williamson won 1,000 Guineas on Abermaid and Night Off, in 1962 and 1965, respectively, and rode Gyr into second place behind Nijinsky in the 1970 Derby. He retired in 1973 and was later racing manager to Ravi Tikkoo, on whose Steel Pulse he had won the 1972 Irish Derby.

FRED WINTER Jockey/Trainer

◆ **Born: 1926 Died: 2004**

The career record of Fred Winter is truly extraordinary – he's one of those rare men who has topped the tree at both riding and training. As a jump jockey, he rode 923 winners and was Britain's champion four times. As a trainer, he won eight championships, including five consecutively from 1971–1975. Twice he booted home Grand National winners, Sundew in 1957 and Kilmore in 1962; and twice he trained Grand National winners as well, sending out Jay Trump and Anglo to gain the top prizes in 1965 and 1966, respectively. Winter rode Saffron Tartan and Mandarin to back-to-back victories in the Cheltenham Gold Cup in 1961 and 1962; and he trained the 1978 Cheltenham Gold Cup winner, Midnight Court. Further, Winter won the Champion Hurdle four times as a jockey and three times as a trainer. He remains the only person to have triumphed in all three of these events as both rider and conditioner. His father, also Fred, had been a successful jockey on the flat, before turning his attention to training, and Fred junior was apprenticed first to him, then to Henri Jellis. He rode a few winners on

Bald eagle: Southern California's tracks, such as Hollywood Park, were long the domain of Charlie Whittingham (right).

the flat, but weight then told its tale and he did not resume racing seriously until 1947. He won on his second jumping ride when Carton was successful at Kempton, but he had had only three such winners when he broke his back in a fall at Wye, which kept him out of action for more than a year. However, soon after he resumed riding, he caught the eye of the brilliant trainer, Ryan Price, and their link continued with huge success until Winter retired from the saddle in 1964. Winter gained the first of his four riding championships in 1952–53, when he recorded 121 winners, becoming only the second jump jockey to reach a century of winners in a season. Winter rode Halloween to a pair of victories in the King George VI Chase, an event in which he was also successful aboard Saffron Tartan. After suffering a stroke and having a severe fall at his Lambourn home in 1988, Winter was rarely again seen in public. He spent the final 16 years of his life in a wheelchair, and died in 2004.

GEORGE WOOLF Jockey

◆ **Born: 1909 Died: 1946**

Known as "The Iceman", George Woolf was famous for his strong, calculated finishes. He most notably employed this technique when he claimed victory in the 1936 Preakness Stakes by a nose aboard Bold Venture. But Woolf could adapt his style as circumstances warranted. Taking the lead from the first stride out of the gate, he rode Seabiscuit to a wire-to-wire, four-length triumph over the Triple Crown winner, War Admiral, in the 1938 Pimlico Special. Alberta-born, Woolf began riding racehorses in Canada and Montana as a boy. His first major score came aboard Gallant Sir in the 1933 Agua Caliente Handicap. In 1935, Woolf won the inaugural Santa Anita Handicap aboard Azucar. From 1942–44, he triumphed in three consecutive runnings of Belmont Park's Futurity Stakes. In a departure from most other first-class jockeys, Woolf accepted limited engagements. A diabetic, he would sometimes go weeks without riding a race. Still, Woolf was North America's leading jockey in earnings in both 1942 and 1944. He died from injuries received in a riding accident at Santa Anita.

FRANK AND STANLEY WOOTTON
Jockey (Frank), Jockey/trainer (Stanley)

◆ **Born: 1893 (Frank) Died: 1940 (Frank)**
◆ **Born: 1897 (Stanley) Died: 1986 (Stanley)**

The sons of Richard Wootton, himself a succesful

trainer in Australia, South Africa and England, Frank and Stanley Wootton were immersed amongst racehorses from their earliest days. After arriving in England in 1906, Frank rode a winner that same year and was champion jockey from four times 1909–12, riding Perola to win the 1909 Oaks and Swynford to take the 1910 St. Leger. Weight difficulties meant that after World War I, Frank switched to jumpers, riding 61 winners over hurdles. He returned to Australia in 1933. Stanley rode a few winners before enlisting in the Army during World War I. Awarded a Military Cross for bravery in the Battle of the Somme, Stanley moved into Treadwell House at Epsom in the early 1920s and turned out winners for the next 30 years. In 1924 Stanley bought the Walton Downs on which Epsom racecourse is situated before assigning them to the Levy Board in 1969 to ensure their use in perpetuity for racing and training. After World War II Stanley focussed on breeding and, in 1950, sent the Gimcrack Stakes-winning Star King to Australia. As Star Kingdom, he reshaped Australia's breeding industry. Stanley visited Australia annually and raced numerous champions, while breeding influential sires, including Todman, the first Golden Slipper Stakes winner; Noholme, who claimed the honours in the W.S.Cox Plate; the triple Australian Champion Sire Bletchingly and the brilliant sire of sires Biscay.

HARRY WRAGG Jockey/trainer

◆ **Born: 1902 Died: 1985**

Harry Wragg, whose brothers Sam and Arthur were also successful jockeys, was champion jockey in 1941 and won every classic as a jockey and trainer – except for training an Oaks winner. Wragg was a great exponent of riding a waiting race and gained his first classic victory when Felstead won the 1928 Derby. He claimed victory in the Derby twice more, on Blenheim in 1930 and Watling Street 12 years later, won the Oaks four times, including on Sun Stream in 1945, who also triumphed in the 1,000 Guineas; and took the St. Leger in 1943, on Herringbone, who herself had also won the 1,000 Guineas. Wragg was an innovative trainer, one of the first people to weigh horses, time their gallops and regularly send them abroad for major races. Wragg took the 1961 Derby with Psidium, who at 66–1 was the longest-priced post-war winner of the race, the 1969 St. Leger with Intermezzo, and 1954's 2,000 Guineas with Darius, as well as achieving major overseas successes with Nagami, Espresso, Atilla and

Innovator: Harry Wragg weighed horses, timed their training gallops and sent them overseas for valuable races.

Salvo. He retired in 1982 and his son Geoffrey took over the stables.

Y

WILLIAM T. YOUNG
Owner/Breeder

◆ **Born: 1918 Died: 2004**

Master of the 2,100-acre Overbrook Farm in Central Kentucky's Bluegrass region, William T. Young was brilliant in his lifelong business dealings, and philanthropic beyond fault. He made fortunes in the food manufacturing, real estate, trucking and storage businesses, and endowed universities with library facilities and scholarship programmes. He also ranked within the top echelon of horsemen on the North American continent. Overbrook was (and remains) the home of Storm Cat, whose $500,000 annual stud fee is unmatched by any other stallion on the globe. Young campaigned the 1996 Kentucky Derby winner, Grindstone. He also partnered in the ownership of Tabasco Cat, who won the 1994 Preakness and Belmont Stakes, and in Timber Country, winner of the 1995 Preakness. Young further campaigned the 1996 Belmont with Editor's Note. And Young's horses were triumphant in four Breeders' Cup races, the most prominent being the 1999 Breeders' Cup Classic, which was won by Cat Thief. Almost all of the horses Young campaigned were homebreds, and in 1994, he received the Eclipse Award as North America's top trainer. Overbrook is now maintained by his son, William T. Young Jr.

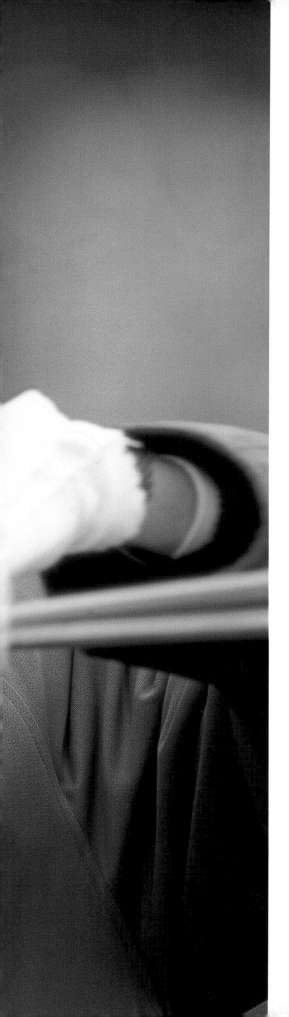

CHAPTER 8

GAMBLING

Although racing began as a test between owners to see whose horse was fastest, it undoubtedly was the result of a wager. Betting and horse racing are undeniably and irreversibly linked – when New York State's legislature outlawed gambling in 1910, the Belmont Stakes, a Triple Crown event, was scrapped for two years – and it will always be so. For all the excitement, colour, beauty and grace of horse racing, how many racegoers would go to a meeting if it was not for a bet?

GAMBLING IN BRITAIN

IN GREAT BRITAIN, racing is now primarily financed via the Horserace Betting Levy Board, which was introduced in 1961, and legalized betting shops. Previously it was possible to bet legally only in cash on the Tote (Horserace Totalisator Board), on-course with bookmakers, or via a credit account with a bookmaker. The ruling had been ignored for years and illegal bookmaking was rife; just about every factory used to have its runner, who would ferry bets (and winnings when relevant) between punter and illicit bookmaker and make regular appearances in court as a result.

The 1961 act which introduced the Levy and

betting shops was regarded by the advocates of a Tote monpoly as a missed opportunity. The Tote came into being in 1928 with the intention that its profits should be used, as are those of the Levy, for the general improvement of racing and breeding. If there was a Tote monopoly, its supporters claimed, prize money and facility levels at British racecourses would be vastly superior to what they are now.

It was simultaneously alleged that poor levels of prize money led inevitably to owners and trainers preventing their horses from doing their best so that their merits would be concealed from racing officials and racegoers. In

Tic tac: Mickey "Hokey" Stewart, a tic-tac man, uses hand signals to indicate the odds to bookmakers in the ring.

turn connections could then land a gamble when they felt the moment was opportune. In short, the very existence of bookmakers was a conduit to villainy, and that if they were abolished there would never be any misdeed in racing because prize money would be so good that such actions would be unnecessary.

This conveniently ignores a number of salient facts. In the first place gambling has never been the prerogative of only those without vast bank balances and some of the biggest gambling stables have belonged to owners and trainers who are far from the breadline. Nor does the existence of a Tote monopoly mean that sharp practice does not happen; in France, for example – where there has been a monopoly since 1872 – and the United States, there are plenty of examples of cheating. The temptation is always there when money is involved and it can be argued that the bigger the prize the greater the temptation.

There has been betting on racing ever since the idea of such competition first began. If, as is at least possible, there were races on the Knavesmire at York during the Roman occupation of Britain between its conquest in the first century AD and the legions' return to what is now Italy in 410, it seems almost inevitable that the spectators wagered denarii and sesterces on the outcome of the contests.

In later years, when many races were simply matches between one man's horse and another's, money would change hands on the outcome and gradually, as racing's popularity increased and those who watched it were no longer only the participants, the spectators would bet among themselves on which horse would beat which.

For many years betting took place in private clubs, like those later operated by the villainous William Crockford. His favourite trick was to lay a horse to lose vast sums and then make sure that it did not win, using whatever illegal means came most easily to hand. This was usually to bribe or otherwise persuade the jockey on the horse in question to make sure that victory was the last thing on his mind when he went out to ride a horse. You had to be careful whom you chose as, even in the darkest days of Victorian villainy, many jockeys could not be bribed in such a way.

The first bookmaker appeared on a racecourse around 1790 but there was already some sort of system to return what we know as starting prices before that. It is highly unlikely that the odds offered on the course were of any significance at this stage, and the SPs that appear in the records are an indication of what was on offer in the clubs where most of the business was transacted.

Odds were returned for only some of the runners; of the nine runners in the first Derby of

1780 only four qualified for a price; in 1794 the losing favourite Drone was returned at 4–5 and 4–6, and not until 1842, when for the first time the unfancied horses were put together as "others" and given a price, was there a full SP as we now know it.

And even when an official system was devised, and representatives of the sporting papers were charged with the duty of returning starting prices, there was no guarantee that those of the Sporting Chronicle and the Sporting Life would agree, although it was increasingly the tendency for them to do so. It took until 1926 for the trade papers agreed to return a common SP.

There have always been professional gamblers. Although the bookmakers usually won, some clever men have made punting pay. Alec Bird and Phil Bull both bet very successfully for many years, with Bird in particular developing a flair for betting on photo finishes which in their early days took quite some time to resolve, in contrast to the pre-camera days when the judge gave the result almost instantly.

Irishman John (J.P.) McManus, is probably the biggest and best-known gambler of the late 20th century, and he has also been very adroit in the money market as well as in the ring. He bets fearlessly and without visible emotion and apparently taking reverses and successes just the

Feeding frenzy: The betting ring at Cheltenham during the National Hunt Festival is a seething mass of humanity, everyone looking for the best price for their "can't miss" selection.

Shrewd investor: J.P. McManus is one of racing's biggest and most successful gamblers as well as owning top horses.

same. McManus also owns a considerable number of horses – most notably the multiple Champion Hurdle-winner Istabraq – but it was another one, Shannon Gale, which was the subject of a £100,000 bet at Cheltenham in March 1999, when he came fourth.

One of the changes that has taken place in the betting ring in the later years of the 20th century has been the difficulty of making big bets. Because the leading bookmaking firms are now largely part of vast multi-national conglomerates with interests in many other areas, the people who represent them are under strict control as to the size of the bets they are allowed to lay.

Although most wagering takes place in off-course betting offices rather than with on-course bookmakers, it is on the course that the starting prices are decided and via these SPs that most off-course bets are settled. Representatives – the number varies according to the status of the meeting and the money that is likely to be invested – of professional bodies have the responsibilty of noting the bets struck before the race and deciding the odds of each horse in every race. The system is designed to take note of all the activities of the major layers and it has stood the test of time in spite of periodical complaints.

The bookmakers whose odds are taken into account for deciding prices work either in Tattersalls' ring or on the rails which separate that enclosure from the Members'. The ring

bookmakers mark the odds they are offering on boards, and until very recently the rails firms operated solely by word of mouth; a bettor asks the bookie what price he is prepared to lay and then, if that suits him, he indicates how much he wants to invest.

For many years all the betting transactions with rails bookmakers were credit transactions, while those with those in Tattersalls were largely in cash. Considering that the rails bets were simply word of mouth affairs, with a clerk noting the wagers in a ledger and the punter receiving in due course a bill or a cheque it is amazing how seldom the details of wagers are disputed. In event of bookmaker and punter being unable to agree, the case can be taken to Tattersalls Committee which adjudicates in such matters. It also deals with cases when either party refuses to or cannot pay and has the power to warn off defaulters from either side, though its ambition is to reach a compromise between the two parties.

The Tote, which is a pool betting system introduced with the aspiration that its profits would be put directly back into racing, came into existence in 1929 with the 2pm race at Newmarket on that day being the first race for which a Tote dividend was declared.

The Totalisator literally adds up the totals laid against each horse in any given race and pays out proportionally, taking into account a built-in profit. This is why the Tote payouts reported in the press sometimes bear so little similarity to the SP returns from bookmakers. For example, in

1946, the Grand National winner was 25–1 Lovely Cottage; three years later it was 66–1 Russian Hero. The respective Tote returns were a skinny 11–1 for Lovely Cottage, but a juicy 202–1 for Russian Hero.

But the introduction of pools which gave the potential of a vast win for a small outlay, like the Jackpot (naming the winners of all six races at specific meetings) or the recently introduced Scoop6 – a similar venture though confined to Saturdays and not to one specific meeting – are indicative of the manner in which the Tote has made up ground. Its promoters, though, have to accept the fact that punters prefer to bet with bookmakers; if that was not the case they would all bet with the Tote and bookmakers would be a fading force.

In their heyday, there were about 14,000 betting shops in Great Britain, many of them belonging to small, independent companies, although, when shops were first operating, leading bookmaker William Hill set his face firmly against them. He was in due course persuaded of the error of his ways and, along with the other two members of the "Big Three", Coral and Ladbrokes, Hill's have a large presence in this sphere. Many of the independents have gone to the wall and/or been taken over, though some enterprisingly run small companies are still flourishing. Betting shops have changed dramatically since they first appeared in 1961. They had to have blacked-out fronts, so that passers-by would not be corrupted by looking through the window and seeing money change

Racing press: Newspapers give their ideas of what will win, then on the following day, explain why they did or didn't.

hands, and the insides were dank, dreary, smoke-filled cells with an appalling tannoy system relaying news from racecourses up and down the country. Punters hardly needed to be encouraged not to frequent such dingy premises.

In recent years, though, shops have been transformed out of all recognition. They are now allowed to have open fronts so that people can see what goes on inside them. They are bright, welcoming establishments which offer a great variety of events on which to bet, though whether the chance to bet on golf, cricket, the Irish lottery etc. is necessarily beneficial to racing (which is why the shops became legal in the first place) may be a matter of opinion.

The bane of betting in Britain has been the betting tax, introduced in 1966. It had first been imposed 40 years earlier, but the tax cost more to collect than it yielded, and it was abandoned three years later. The rate fluctuated over the years but on-course tax soon became lower than off-course

in a bid to encourage punters to bet on-course and for the big firms to send money back to the tracks, so strengthening the on-course market and making the SPs a more accurate reflection of business. In 1987, on-course tax was abolished entirely and subsequently there have been two decreases in the off-course rate.

Entering 2001, the tax was nine percent. Punters had the option of paying tax with their stake and receiving the actual starting price (i.e. a 10–1 winner returning £11 – £10+£1 – for a stake of £1.09) or paying tax on the pay-out (i.e. a 10–1 winner returning £10.01 – £11–9% – for a £1 stake). The actual profits on the examples seem to suggest paying tax in advance is beneficial – £9.91 (10.091743119%) against £9.01 (10.01%) – but the bettor is actually staking a larger sum. There were indications before the budget of 2001 that the system of tax collection might be changed. This proved to be the case as the abolition of betting tax, with effect from 1 January 2002, was

announced by the Chancellor. Instead bookmakers would be subject to a 15 percent tax on their profits.

In May 1999, Victor Chandler announced the establishment of a base in Gibraltar, to which punters could bet via the internet, and where the only form of deduction would be a 3% service charge. Chandler – one of the most fearless layers when betting at British tracks – had the advantage of being in charge of his own firm and could do precisely what he liked when it came to laying big bets. His example was followed by other major firms and there were fears that the revenue to the levy and thus to racing would be seriously diminished.

However, the vast majority of punters did not want to bet in this way, preferring the personal contact of a racecourse or a betting shop, and feeling the winnings in their hands. The decision to abolish tax was followed by at least some of the firms closing down their off-shore operations.

GAMBLING IN THE U.S.

HARD STATISTICS are not always easy to find, but indications are that the aggregate pari-mutuel handle on thoroughbred races now approaches $15billion annually in the U.S. The heaviest wagering takes place in New York, followed by California. Legal on-site bookmaking, once a staple of the industry, has been banned at tracks across the U.S. But wagering at off-premise simulcast sites expanded tremendously in the late 20th century as did betting by telephone.

In the early 1900s, a track's prominence was often gauged by the number of books operating on its grounds. Official charts in such publications as Daily Racing Form and The Morning Telegraph, Belmont Park would commence a meet with over a hundred books in operation. A less prestigious track might max out at 25.

As the decades passed, tracks throughout the U.S. adopted the pari-mutuel system, although this wasn't always an easy sell. Pari-mutuels were invented by a Frenchman, M. Joseph Oller, and were originally called "Paris Mutuals". Churchill Downs exhibited a machine for this form of

Gambling capital of the Western World: Las Vegas is where one goes to place a winter book wager on the Kentucky Derby.

wagering at its opening meet in 1875, formally adopted it in the early 1880s (referring to the mutuel machines as "French pool boxes"), then ditched them in 1889 when on-site bookmakers complained they were losing too much business.

Pari-mutuel machines returned to Churchill in 1908, and they have remained in operation there ever since. The bookmakers, or "Knights of the Chalk" as they were also called, were banished from Kentucky's tracks the following year, as stated in a report filed by Charles F. Granger to Kentucky's racing commission: "Bookmakers owned and raced large stables of horses, engaged by contract skilled jockeys, employed clockers, and paid for and secured stable information, gaining to them advantages not possessed or attainable by the public. Adverse comment followed and in some cases scandal."

As time went on, other states fell in line with Kentucky's philosophy, and legal bookmakers vanished from U.S. tracks altogether. Curiously, though, the jurisdiction that held out the longest in regards to instituting pari-mutuel machines was New York, which didn't adapt this form of wagering until 1940. There are still legal "winter books" operating in Las Vegas, offering ante-post odds on Kentucky Derby contenders.

Nevertheless, pari-mutuel wagers constitute the primary life support system for most U.S. race tracks, funding track operation costs, purses, promotion of the sport, capital improvement programmes, breeder incentive programmes, racing commission offices, and other ventures. A return to the days of the on-site bookmakers is something that most concede will never happen.

Measures allowing for off-track wagering were being put before state legislative bodies at least as far back as 1937, when an enabling bill was introduced in Texas. It died, and shortly thereafter so did Texas racing for half a century. Similar measures in New York date at least as far back as 1944. OTB parlours were ultimately approved in New York in the early 1970s, with the first ones starting on 8 April 1971. In retrospect, the acceptance of pari-mutuels and the advent of OTB constituted the two most revolutionary changes affecting New York racing in the 20th century.

Prior to OTB, Aqueduct averaged as many as 30,000 on-site patrons per day for live racing and no New York track raced during the winter months. Nowadays, Aqueduct's on-site crowds average closer to 5,500, and live racing is conducted in New York year-round. Total wagering handle on New York races, though, has never been higher. The New York Racing Association simulcast signal is sent to well over 200 sites throughout the state, and to hundreds of other locales throughout North America as well.

Commissions that the NYRA takes from simulcast dollars are not nearly as high as the ones it takes from on-site dollars, but income was substantial – in the period 1980–2005, OTB contributed far more to New York's purses than on-site betting.

Louisiana and Pennsylvania also have well-developed systems of OTB parlours (although neither even barely approaches the magnitude of the off-track wagering systems in New York). Others, such as Kentucky and Maryland, have OTB parlour networks that are small, but have opportunity for expansion. Simulcast signals, of course, are sent from track to track and other places where betting is legal.

Alternative forms of wagering affected OTB dramatically, so more and more U.S. tracks adopted the philosophy, "If you can't lick them, join them." In the 1980s, tracks in some U.S. jurisdictions began selling lottery tickets. In the 1990s, enabling legislation was passed in a number of states to allow tracks to operate dually as casinos. Many tracks were threatened with insolvency during the early 1990s, but after installing thousands of slot machines on their premises, they generated profits beyond anything most U.S. tracks had ever experienced. Tracks such as Delaware Park, Del., Charles Town and Mountaineer Park, W.V., and Prairie Meadows, Iowa, became dependent upon slot machine revenues for their survival. In every case, the slot machines, while generating many more customers, have not brought an appreciable rise in pari-mutuel wagering. If the slots were to go, the tracks would close down.

This contrasts with a track such as Saratoga, in upstate New York, which offers no casino gaming, but remains one of the most successful operations in the history of the sport. On-site daily attendance for Saratoga's 36-day meet in 2005 averaged 25,915. Daily on-site wagering averaged $3.25 million. Daily wagering from all sources averaged $14.95 million.

In 1982 Pennsylvania established telephone wagering on horse racing. Other states, New York among them, have also extended their offerings into that area. Such systems as the Television Games Network (TVG) now allow the bettor to watch and wager on races from around the U.S. in their homes. It raised a huge question: Were there enough customers to make the multi-millions of dollars needed annually to set up and operate systems such as TVG worthwhile? Organizations such as the National Thoroughbred Racing Association (NTRA) argued that there were.

Entering 2006, political problems within the industry continued to prevent TVG from achieving its full potential – it is not allowed, for example, to offer races from Frank Stronach's

Slot receiver: Revenues from on-site slot machines have become the salvation of a number of smaller U.S. tracks.

Magna Entertainment tracks, which include Gulfstream Park and Santa Anita. But TVG continues to expand and improve upon its programming from such major racing sites as Churchill Downs, Keeneland, Belmont Park, Saratoga and Arlington Park.

Some doomsayers believed that horse racing was a dying sport within the U.S., arguing that the lure of racing's romance and heritage had largely disappeared, and that the gamblers had come to pretty much dictate the show. As recently as 1970, most U.S. tracks offered only straight and daily double wagering. Now, there are exactas, quinellas, trifectas, superfectas, pick sixes, pick sevens, much of which bewilders the $2 bettor.

Many, however, contended that the pari-mutuel wager was still one of the most enjoyable of sporting endeavors. By putting down $2, $5, or $10, one became more than just a spectator, the bettor was a participant in the outcome of an event. They pointed to the rebirth of racing in such states as Texas, the excellence of Southern California racing, the growth of interest in the Triple Crown and Breeders' Cup and the continued popularity of Saratoga.

CHAPTER 9

SCANDALS AND CONTROVERSIES

Scandal and controversy is a part of all sports – in fact all walks of life – and horse racing has never been exempt. "Bung" allegations have blighted football (soccer); baseball had the Black Sox scandal; basketball has had points shaving; boxing holds an almost magnetic attraction to the seamy side of society. In horse racing, however, it is almost always either the gambler or the bookmaker who is duped or does the duping, but at the root of it all is money.

The Prince of Wales and Escape

The Prince of Wales, who later became King George IV, won the Derby as an owner in 1788. Three years later he was an apparently innocent participant in a major inquiry by the Stewards of the Jockey Club, who were beginning to become increasingly authoritative in matters of racing discipline – especially as far as racing at Newmarket was concerned.

In autumn 1791 the Prince's colt Escape – ridden by Sam Chifney, undoubtedly the best jockey of his era – ran in a four-horse race at Newmarket. He started favourite, but finished last. The following day, he came out again and won convincingly from a field which included two horses who had beaten him the day before. The starting price was 5–1.

Escape's dramatic turn-around in form caused such a brouhaha that the stewards started to investigate. Chifney said that Escape was first, inconsistent; second, needed the first race, making him sharper for the next outing; and third, more suited to the four-mile distance of the second race than the two miles of the first. These explanations were not accepted.

The stewards did not however, warn off Chifney, but instead passed the buck to the Prince, who was told that if he continued to put Chifney up on his horses, no gentleman would start against him. In other words, if Chifney, who had been not found guilty of anything, let alone been directly punished, maintained the Prince's patronage, the Prince would be ostracized. In short, the heir to the throne would, effectively, be disqualified from racing.

The Prince's attitude to Chifney was admirable. He could easily have continued with his much-loved racing and left his jockey to his fate, but he declined to do so and withdrew from racing for more than 15 years, giving the jockey an allowance of 200gns per year.

The Battle of Narragansett Park

What is still called "The Battle of Narragansett Park" took place in Pawtucket, Rhode Island, in 1937. The track's founder, president and managing director, Walter O'Hara, enjoyed making bets and having a drink or two, and sometimes four or five. One day during the course of racing, he stormed into the stewards' stand in the Narragansett infield, and profanely (and drunkenly) berated officials for a minor ruling they had made.

The stewards cited O'Hara for contempt of the State Racing Board. The case was referred to Rhode Island's Democratic governor, Robert

No escape: The Prince of Wales (later George IV) stood by his jockey Sam Chifney Sr. after the Escape affair at Newmarket.

Daniel Dawson The Poisoner

Whether they like it or not, bookmakers are invariably in the frame when any racing skulduggery takes place, and it is easy to understand why. If a bookmaker knows that, for whatever reason, a horse cannot win a race, then it is obviously in his interest to have as many people as possible bet on it with the confidence that you will not have to pay. Over the years plenty of horses have been nobbled to prevent them from winning, and there have undoubtedly been instances when bookmakers were at the bottom of the plot.

This was the case when Daniel Dawson died on the scaffold in Cambridge in August 1812. Dawson had previously worked in stables but became a tout – someone who watched horses working on the gallops – and sold what they learned to anyone who was interested. Bookmakers would certainly fall into that category. A brace of bookmaking brothers, the Blands, found themselves, in 1811, with heavy liabilities over some horses trained by Richard Prince.

Dawson's orders were to give Prince's horses something to make them too ill to run let alone win. In these days, trainers had troughs on Newmarket Heath for horses to drink from after exercise. Poisoning the water in the trough was an obvious way for Dawson to get at Prince's horses. The trainer, however, learned that something was amiss with his trough and did not send them to it. Having put the poison into the trough, Dawson made himself scarce from the Heath, unaware that Prince had made alternative arrangements. Having later seen the horses still in action, however, Dawson concluded that his dose was not strong enough and next time doubled it. This killed them.

Dawson tried to get away, but a reward of 500gns from the Jockey Club was more than enough for him to be shopped. He was arrested in Brighton and tried and sentenced in Cambridge, where he was hanged, but the Blands emerged unscathed.

Ryan Price and the Schweppes Gold Trophy

Ryan Price was one of the most colourful characters in racing, an exceedingly talented trainer who also very much liked to tilt at the betting ring. One of the races which particularly took his fancy was the Schweppes Gold Trophy which was first run at Aintree in 1963. Price won the race with the 20–1 shot Rosyth, ridden by Josh Gifford, and the trio repeated their success the following year, at odds of 10–1, by which time the race had been moved to Newbury, but

Quinn, who was one of O'Hara's political foes. Quinn demanded that Narragansett's board of directors remove O'Hara from his position. Writs, injunctions, counter writs and counter injunctions began to flow in both directions. O'Hara owned a local newspaper, the *Providence Star-Tribune*, and constantly wrote editorials attacking Quinn. O'Hara further put out a special edition of the paper that bore a headline suggesting that Quinn belonged in a mental hospital.

Governor Quinn responded by issuing warrants for O'Hara's arrest. The state police and state militia shut down racing at the track. Meanwhile, the Pawtucket police rallied to O'Hara's support, acting as his bodyguards while

he holed up in his private penthouse atop the Narragansett grandstand. In the end, though, Quinn won out. O'Hara surrendered to the state police, was arrested, released on bail, and issued a public apology. His directors deposed him, and bought out his financial interest in Narragansett. The following year, O'Hara, himself, ran for governor. He got trounced.

O'Hara died in an automobile accident 3½ years later. Narragansett continued to operate until 1978. Its facilities have since been replaced by a flea market and industrial park. Unfortunately, there is no historical marker to commemorate the battle that once took place upon the hallowed ground.

this time all was not so satisfactory.

The stewards took the view that Rosyth had not run entirely on his merits in his pre-Newbury races and disciplined trainer and jockey. Price was declared a disqualified person and Gifford's licence suspended. In those days warnings off were issued on a sine die basis, but Price did not have to wait long for his disqualification to be lifted and in 1966 he won the race for the third time with Le Vermontois. He had not been directly involved in 1965, but his shadow was very much on the race as John Sutcliffe, Jr., who trained the successful Elan, had at one time been pupil-assistant at Price's stable at Findon. Rosyth, who had been sent to Tom Masson's stables across Sussex at Lewes, when Price lost his licence, finished second.

But the big drama was still to come. By now, almost as soon as the season started, people started wondering what Price was going to run in the Schweppes and any horse connected with him was rigorously scrutinised, so that for the

1967 race Hill House was one of those who attracted this sort of attention.

Hill House was something of a character in his own right and Josh Gifford later recalled how he was one horse that the normally dominant Price allowed to get away with almost anything. Sometimes he declined to start at all, and this is what happened two runs before he went to Newbury in early 1967.

That was too much for the suspicious who declared that it was all part of a plot and when Hill House ran a respectable fourth a week later at Sandown they declared that the mistakes he made during the race were yet more of the skulduggery. Professionals, though, were not impressed by this argument.

Come Newbury a week later and some of the most amazing scenes ever seen on a racecourse: Hill House went to the front at the second last hurdle and simply came further and further away, winning what should have been a very competitive race by 12 lengths.

This was too much for the spectators, who let rip with their disapproval, booing and jeering Hill House all the way to the line and after it, having convinced themselves that the whole exercise was crooked. The stewards felt, understandably enough, that an investigation was imperative and sent the matter on to the Disciplinary Committee.

In the course of all this Hill House was tested after the race and his urine sample showed evidence of a banned substance, cortisol. So, as far as many punters were concerned, Hill House had not only been cheated with in order to improve his chances of winning the race, he had also been drugged to make extra sure.

The official inquiry dragged on and on and on and was not over until the beginning of August, some six months after the race, with the Committee accepting the possibility that Hill House's system produced its own cortisol and that no one had done anything wrong. Hill House was an odd horse – you need only to talk to Josh Gifford about him to appreciate that – but him winning what people at the time regarded as his trainer's favourite race in the manner that he did was all too much for some of them and probably always will be.

Breeders' Cup Ultra Pick Six

Chris Harn, Derrick Davis and Glen DaSilva are not familiar figures within international racing circles. But in 2002, they came close to pulling off a scam that would have gained them nearly $3.07 million from the Breeders' Cup Ultra Pick Six wagering pool.

Harn was a software engineer for Autotote Systems Inc., the totalizator company that handles roughly 65 per cent of the pari-mutuel wagering that occurs in North America. Davis and DaSilva operated computer business in Baltimore, Maryland, and New York City, respectively. The trio had been college fraternity brothers and after entering the professional world had devised a way to alter pick six wagers on given race cards after the races involved had actually commenced.

The key figure in the scheme was Harn, who had access to the computer system at Catskill Off-Track Betting in New York, which served as an Autotote hub. Data detailing pick six bets made through Catskill's system were stored there through the fourth of the six races involved. At that point, the "live" tickets were passed on to the host track, which in the case of the 2002 Breeders' Cup was Arlington Park.

What the conspirators had done is devise a way to alter a ticket after the first four races so

Beating the odds: Ryan Price won the Schweppes Gold Trophy four times 1963–67, courting controversy more than once.

Come on you beauty: Dancer's Image (9) leads Forward Pass (13) as they cross the finish at the end of the 1968 Kentucky Derby, but the winner failed a dope test and was disqualified.

that it would carry the numbers of all four winners. For the remaining two races in the pick six, the ticket would carry the numbers of all the horses in each field, thus guaranteeing a large payoff for the holders.

Prior to the Breeders' Cup, Harn, Davis and DaSilva had twice pulled off the scheme successfully in regards to pick six wagers at a standardbred track named Balmoral Park near Chicago and at Belmont Park in New York.

But in trying this a third time in the Breeders' Cup, the conspirators got caught. One circumstance that tripped them up was the victory in the Breeders' Cup Classic by Volponi, who at 43–1 odds was the longest shot on the board. Had the 5–2 favourite, Medaglia d'Oro been victorious, there would have been numerous holders of winning pick six tickets.

Because of Volponi's triumph, however, only a half-dozen tickets containing all six winning horses existed. And all of the tickets had been purchased through Davis's Catskill telephone wagering account.

The Ultra Pick Six wagering pool was frozen, state and federal investigations ensued and Harn, Davis and DaSilva eventually pleaded guilty to criminal charges. The pool payout was eventually divided amongst ticket holders who had legally selected five of six winners. Measures

have been installed that, in theory, should prevent the recurrence of similar chicanery.

Derby Dope

Dancer's Image was sent away as the 3.60–1 second choice in the 1968 Kentucky Derby. Owned by Peter Fuller, he defeated Calumet Farm's favoured colour bearer, Forward Pass, by 1 1/2 lengths. Three days later, the startling announcement was made that a post-race test of Dancer's Image revealed the presence of Butazolidin (Bute) in his system. At the time, the painkilling drug was illegal in Kentucky and Dancer's Image was disqualified, with first place (for all but wagering purposes), including the $122,600 winner's share of the purse, being awarded to Forward Pass.

But seven months later, the Kentucky Racing Commission declared that Dancer's Image should be recognized as the Derby winner, even though Forward Pass's owners would be allowed to keep the winner's purse. This satisfied no one. A legal case ensued, which dragged on for another 3 1/2 years. At one point the Commission's decision pertaining to the purse was overruled, with the money being awarded to Fuller. The Commission then took the case to the Kentucky Court of Appeals, which on 28 April

1972, overruled the overruling, giving the money to Calumet Farm.

To this day, the subject of which horse actually won the 1968 Derby can still generate a lively debate. Churchill Downs officially recognizes Forward Pass. His name appears in the track's media guide as the winner, and his name adorns a wall near the paddock, along with those of other Derby victors. But Dancer's Image still has his supporters. Their voices can be heard every year at Derby time. And no one has ever confessed to administering the Bute.

Non-Existent Trodmore

Even nowadays, when everything in racing is carefully regulated and rigidly controlled, some of the meetings held on Bank Holidays are at places which not everybody can immediately locate. Cartmel, Fontwell Park and Market Rasen are not locations which can be instantly pinpointed on the map.

Back in 1898 there was no such thing as an official fixture list and little jungly meetings took place all over the country, making it a nightmare for the newspapers to cover them. There was gratitude in the London office of *The Sportsman* newspaper when the clerk of the course at Trodmore in Cornwall sent details of the meeting he was running, and a racegoer promised to supply the results. *The Sportsman* showed the runners and riders, various people placed bets with street bookmakers and, on the day after the races, the paper published the results with starting prices.

The Sportsman's rival paper, *The Sporting Life*, was not told about Trodmore, but did not want to be left out, so they copied the results from *The Sportsman* 24 hours later. There was, though, one big difference between the two sets of details; one winner had been shown at 5–1 in *The Sportsman*, but at only 5–2 in the *Life*. Bookmakers and punters alike wanted this detail checked, so they, and the papers, got in touch with the Trodmore management ... or tried to.

None could be found. The police got nowhere and detailed investigation of the largest-scale map gave no sign of Trodmore. Light dawned – newspapers and bookmakers had been well and truly conned into believing in the existence of a totally fictitious meeting.

Many punters who had placed bets on the spurious races were paid before the ruse was rumbled, and if it had not been for the alteration of just one digit no one would have known that there was anything untoward.

Phar Lap

Phar Lap's death remains an unexplained American mystery. The New Zealand-bred is still regarded as the greatest horse in Australia's racing history, winning 13 races (including nine stakes) at age three, and 14 consecutive stakes, including the 1930 Melbourne Cup at age four.

He was subsequently shipped to North America, where it was expected that Phar Lap's stardom would continue. He had won 36 of 50 career starts, and his career earnings totalled US$282,200. Phar Lap's target was the $100,000-added Aqua Caliente Handicap in northern Mexico in March 1932. The winner's share would raise his earnings to a world-record level.

But the Aqua Caliente track had financial problems, and the purse was reduced to $50,000-added. Still, trainer Tom Woodcock continued to put Phar Lap through his unusual conditioning regimen in California, galloping up and down hills, avoiding the early morning breezes and blowouts that most American competitors go through in preparation for a big effort.

Race day came and Phar Lap, favoured at 3–2 in the field of 11, drew away under his regular Australian jockey, Billy Elliott, to win by two lengths. Woodcock then took Phar Lap back to Menlo Park, a stabling facility 30 miles from San Francisco. Tracks from around the nation began vying for Phar Lap's participation in their major stakes for older horses. Bowie, in Maryland, offered $10,000 just to have him make an appearance under silks.

On 4 April it all fell apart. Phar Lap was dead. An autopsy stated that his death was caused by "acute enteritus", effected by consumption of either a fungus or an insecticide. Was Phar Lap a victim of spoiled feed? Tainted forage? Deliberate poisoning? The answer remains uncertain. Woodcock was inconsolable. "He's dead," was all the trainer could say to reporters, as tears poured from his eyes.

A taxidermist stuffed and mounted Phar Lap's body. It was put on public display at New York's Belmont Park, then taken back to Australia. Nearly seven decades later, Australian horsemen still voice the question, "Hey, what do you think the Yanks really did to Phar Lap?"

The Day they Cut the Telephone Wires

In 1966, Gomer Charles, a former bookmaker, was murdered on the doorstep of his Cardiff home. He had once looked destined for high rank in his chosen profession, but Charles became involved with the Francasal ringer affair and ended up in prison.

Francasal was nominally a two-year-old of strictly limited ability who was due to run in a selling race at Bath in July 1953. The horse who actually ran was, in fact, the much better Santa Amaro. Unsurprisingly, he won easily, apparently landing hefty bets for some who had backed him away from the racecourse. Hardly anyone had done so at Bath, where his odds drifted from 7–1 to 10–1, to the delight of those who had laid out £6,000 to back him at starting price.

In such circumstances, office-based bookmakers usually contact their on-course representatives and tell them to back the horse in question. This reduces the odds and obviously, if the horse wins, their pay-outs too. However, another horse in the race, Eastern Magic, was the subject of a huge racecourse gamble so money for "Francasal" might not have made that much impression on the market.

But the plotters made one move too many. Somebody cut the local telephone wire, making communication between racecourse and offices impossible. This immediately gave rise to suspicion. The police caught the man who cut the

Paying their respects: Phar Lap's body, stuffed and mounted by a taxidermist, was displayed at the Belmont Park paddock before being shipped back to Australia.

Happier times: Tony Collins (left) went on trial over his involvement in the Gay Future coup at Cartmel in August 1974.

cable, and he was sent to jail before Christmas.

Early the following year, Charles was one of five men found guilty of conspiracy. He had become acquainted with the promoting villain, Maurice Williams – another bookmaker – and had invested £2,500 on the ringer. He would have picked up £22,500; instead he got two years in jail and, later, a bullet in his head.

The Gay Future Coup That Should Have Been

Some rules in bookmaking, give the impression that they were framed by bookmakers solely for their benefit. One such revolves around multiple bets. If a bettor gambles on a straight treble, i.e. three horses to win three races in one bet, then if one of them does not run, the stake becomes a double on the two horses that do race, and if two horses don't run, it becomes a single. (This is not the case if multiple bets involve all permutations of doubles and singles; then the bettor is refunded all stake-money which doesn't involve the remaining runner.)

However, on August Bank Holiday Monday 1974, the bookmakers' rules were nearly manipulated for the benefit of an enterprising team of punters. It all revolved round a horse called Gay Future, allegedly trained under permit in Scotland by Tony Collins. Gay Future was to run in a novice hurdle at the Cumbria track of Cartmel – one hour south of the Scottish border – while two of his stablemates, Opera Cloak and Ankerwyke, were declared for races at Southwell in Nottinghamshire – a further 170 miles to the south – and Plumpton in Sussex, 200 miles beyond that.

The team placed bets involving doubles and

trebles on the three horses, in small sums and in many different places, gambling that such small wagers would not be noticed during a busy Bank Holiday's trading. But the doubles and trebles were a blind; there was never any plan to run Opera Cloak and Ankerwyke, so all the bets would become singles on Gay Future.

Cartmel, though very successful, is one of Britain's smaller tracks and its racing rarely attracts national attention. Partly because of this – also as it was a holiday and there were many more meetings than usual – the blower service, by which big office bookmakers make contact with racecourse representatives, was not in operation there.

This was vital to the scheme. If there was no betting support for Gay Future at Cartmel – there was not – his odds would drift out – they did – so those who had backed at starting price would have received a healthy dividend. Gay Future won by 15 lengths at 10–1.

One bookmaker's representative smelled a rat, because of the number of bets involving the three Collins horses, and the fact that two of them were not running. He drove as fast as he could from Manchester to Cartmel – 80 miles – but arrived too late to affect the betting.

So the bookmakers had been caught out, but the plot came to light later in the day. A newspaper reporter rang the Collins yard and, during general conversation with a member of the staff there, inquired casually about the other two horses. The reply was, "They are here, I can see them through the window."

This put a different complexion on things. If the two horses were at the stables at that moment, had there ever been any intention of them running? Was the whole thing an exercise

to defraud, rather than outwit, the bookmakers?

The police decided that it was and some of the principals were charged and prosecuted. In spite of a summing up by the judge which virtually told the jury to acquit him, Tony Collins was found guilty.

Mare Reproductive Loss Syndrome

The outbreak of Mare Reproductive Loss Syndrome (MRLS) that blighted Central Kentucky's breeding industry in the spring of 2001 remains a mystery as to its cause, but not to its effects. More than 5,100 foals and foetuses were lost among horses of at least 17 breeds – standardbreds, quarter horses, Morgan horses and Tennessee walkers among them.

But the thoroughbred breeders suffered the greatest cumulative damages, as 516 late-term foals and 2,998 foetuses were lost during a period that extended from late April to early June. These figures represent 5.3% of the anticipated foal crop for 2001 and 30.5% of the anticipated foal crop for 2002. The estimated monetary loss to the thoroughbred industry was $300.5 million.

Major farms were heavily hit, including Lane's End, Three Chimneys, Taylor Made, Overbrook and Mill Ridge. Ironically, the syndrome appeared to reach its zenith on Saturday, May 5, the same day that Monarchos cruised to victory in the 127th running of the Kentucky Derby. What is annually recognized as America's greatest day of racing was, in this case, the most catastrophic day in history for its breeding industry, as 73 stillborn and aborted foals were brought to the University of Kentucky's Livestock Disease Diagnostic Center in Lexington.

Veterinarians throughout the region were dumbfounded. Thousands of mares, many of whom seemed healthily in foal only weeks and even days beforehand, were suddenly aborting their foetuses. Some of the foetuses simply seemed to vanish within the wombs. Late-term foals were being stillborn in unprecedented numbers. Other foals were being born sickly, with eye, heart and respiratory problems and other ailments. Cases of pericarditis (a condition in which the surface tissue of the heart becomes inflamed) were being diagnosed at ten times the normal rate.

An immense amount of pressure was immediately placed up the University of Kentucky's Maxwell H. Gluck Equine Research Centre to find the cause and cure for what was happening. Early hypotheses by Gluck scientists

Attacked at home: After winning the Lingfield Derby Trial in 1958, Alcide (left) became a much-fancied horse for the Epsom classic … until he was assaulted in his box and could not run.

included the possibility of naturally produced toxins in the pastures that were being grazed, perhaps brought on by a run of freakish weather (unusually warm temperatures, followed by sudden hard freezes and quick thaws) that had occurred in Central Kentucky in early spring.

It was also noted that the population of eastern tent caterpillars had exploded in Central Kentucky that spring. The caterpillars' favourite habitats are black cherry trees, which exist by the tens of thousands on Central Kentucky's horse farms. The caterpillars feed on cyanogens from the cherry trees. It was theorized that the caterpillars transported the cyanide to the paddocks and water troughs on the farms, where the mares consumed them via their normal eating and drinking habits.

The cyanide portion of the theory was subsequently abandoned, but it is still believed that the abundance of caterpillars somehow brought about the foal and foetus losses. A much smaller outbreak of MRLS occurred in the same region in 2002. By this time, the caterpillars' numbers were in rapid decline – scientists who have studied them say their population peaks and crashes in ten-year cycles. Meanwhile, many, if not most, of Central Kentucky's breeding farms have completely rid their landscapes of black cherry trees to prevent a recurrence.

Many questions remain regarding this immense riddle. The eastern tent caterpillar is indigenous all the way from the Canadian border southwards to Florida, and westwards to beyond the Mississippi River Valley. Many of Kentucky's neighbouring states – Virginia, West Virginia and Tennessee among them – were beset with explosions in their eastern tent caterpillar populations in 2001, and have substantial equine breeding industries, but were not hit by MRLS.

Kentucky's neighbour to the north, Ohio, did have a very limited number of what may have been MRLS cases in 2001, but nothing close to the magnitude of what took place in the Bluegrass region. Since then, isolated cases of what may have been MRLS have been reported in New York and, as recently as 2006, in Florida.

But eastern tent caterpillars have been indigenous to all these regions, Central Kentucky included, for tens of thousands of years, and horses have been bred in these regions for hundreds of years. Historical records indicate there may have been minor incidents of MRLS in the past, but nothing of the magnitude of what happened in 2001.

Scientific discovery almost always involves a long process of elimination. One possibility is investigated, and then another, followed by examination of numerous other possibilities. Many years, even decades, may ensue before conclusions begin to be reached. In the situation with MRLS, however, the eastern tent caterpillar was almost immediately identified as the culprit. The possibility of other causal agents has largely been ignored.

More Victims of the Villains

If Alcide had won the Derby in 1958 he would have cost the bookmakers a fortune. In the Derby Trial at Lingfield, his final pre-Epsom race, he had romped home and money poured on him for the Derby. He would have started a hot favourite but, to the relief of the bookies, he did not run. Eight days after Lingfield, Alcide was found in his stable with a large swelling on his side and a broken rib. Someone had attacked him with the firm intention of making sure that he did not run.

A couple of years later, Pinturischio was favourite for the Derby, but he was twice drugged and was unable to run again.

Nobody was ever caught for either offence. Even though security measures and detecting skills improved considerably over the years, catching the culprits, let alone successfully prosecuting them remained almost impossible.

Naughty 1990s

At the St. Leger meeting at Doncaster in 1990, Bravefoot started favourite to win the Champagne Stakes. He finished last. At the same meeting the three-year-old Norwich started joint-favourite for a Group 3 seven-furlong race, but ran below expectations in finishing fourth. It later emerged that both colts had been doped. Former jockey Dermot Browne, who at the time held a training licence, was arrested in connection with that action. The case, though, has never come to court.

In March 1997, Avanti Express started an uneasy second favourite for a novice hurdle at Exeter and ran very poorly, eventually being pulled up as Give And Take, for whom there had been strong market support, won easily. A few weeks later, a novice chaser called Lively Knight started at 1–7 in a three-horse race at Plumpton but was well beaten by Stormhill Pilgrim, who had been the subject of some market support despite the loser's odds.

It later emerged that both horses had been doped with a sedative to make them run more slowly and, once the Jockey Club had completed their investigations, they called in the police. The police's first move was – in a blaze of publicity – to arrest the two losing jockeys in dawn raids. No jockey would ever be so foolish as to consider doping a horse they were about to ride over fences – it is a perilous enough profession without riding a horse that is not sound – but they became the prime suspects.

In due course they, and other trainers and jockeys who were interviewed, were dismissed from the case. In autumn 2000, five professional punters were prosecuted. The case was lamentably presented and proper evidence against any of the five was almost non-existent. The judge told the jury to find all five not guilty.

Sponges

During a 6½-month period in 1996, nine horses competing on the Kentucky circuit were found to have had sponges shoved up their nostrils. Seven incidents were discovered at Churchill Downs – home of the Kentucky Derby – and two at Ellis Park, in western Kentucky.

The FBI, Thoroughbred Racing Protective

Looking lively: Lively Knight (9) was a 1–7 favourite when he was doped with a sedative before a race at Plumpton.

Bureau, Kentucky Racing Commission and Kentucky Attorney General's office all assigned personnel to investigate the cases. A reward of $25,000 was also offered for information leading to the arrest and conviction of whoever was responsible.

As the months went on, though, one dead lead followed another. The sponges measured either 2 x 2 inches, or 2 x 3 inches, and were of gauze, available to anyone who wished to purchase them. Sponges are porous, and don't hold fingerprints. All of the investigative agencies had long-standing, well-developed networks of informants, and the back-stretches of racetracks are notoriously poor places to hold

secrets. But nothing came to light.

Even a motive was difficult to discern. No evidence was uncovered indicating that someone had scored a betting coup. Post-time odds on the horses who had been "sponged" ranged from 8–5 to 34.30–1. One of the horses actually won its race after being sponged. The tip-off, in virtually every case, was not a dramatically altered performance, but a foul-smelling discharge from a horse's nostrils several days after he ran.

Some of the sponges had been shoved so far up the horses' nostrils they almost reached their eyes. In these cases, surgical instruments had to be used to remove them. The person (or persons) responsible for the spongings needed time and privacy to perform the acts. In 1996, there were 21,000 people who were licensed with access to the stable areas at Kentucky tracks. How was it that none of them saw anyone do anything at any time?

The sponging cases were never solved. It has been theorized that the incidents were carried out in order to embarrass racetrack security, and perhaps the racing commission as well. The races at Churchill, especially, are simulcast to sites throughout North America, and maybe the idea was, somehow and for some unknown reason, to make the track's management look irresponsible.

Dope trick: Bravefoot was the favourite for Doncaster's Champagne Stakes 1990, but he been got at by dopers.

CHAPTER 10

TRIVIA AND RECORDS

Horse racing does not lend itself to records in the way of most sports. Facts and figures vary from country to country and records are, in many cases, sparse or incomplete; in Britain, for example, the leading owner and trainer are not those who have the most winners, but whose horses earn the most prize money. And as no two racetracks are identical, timing records are kept as local. After all, time is of no concern to a horse!

TWO BRITISH HORSES won major races for four years in a row in the 1990s, with Further Flight doing so in the Jockey Club Cup at Newmarket and Morley Street in the Aintree Hurdle at Liverpool. In the 1930s, Golden Miller won the Cheltenham Gold Cup five consecutive seasons, 1932–36 (there was no race in either 1931 or 1937), and Brown Jack claimed the Queen Alexandra Stakes at Royal Ascot, 1929–34. The best such sequence in the previous century was that of Dr Syntax, who won the Preston Gold Cup every year, 1815–21. Franc Picard won the Grand Steeple-Chase de Dieppe seven times, but they were not consecutive successes.

● A father and son rode the winners of the first two races at Salisbury on 20 August 1959. First of all Thomas Michael (Buck) Jones won the apprentice race on Hasty Hook, and half an hour later his father Davy rode Lemlem to land the two-year-old maiden at closing race.

● A brother and sister rode winners on the same programme for what is thought to be the first time at Musselburgh, Scotland, on 12 January 2001. Amateur rider Lorna Bradburne, a

Horses for courses: Morley Street won the Aintree Hurdle at Liverpool in four consecutive years in the 1990s.

Golden monopoly: Dickinson horses, from left: Captain John (4th), Silver Buck (2nd), Bregawn (1st) and Wayward Lad (3rd).

student at Glasgow University, rode Miss Ellie to win a handicap hurdle, and half an hour later her brother Mark, who is a professional jockey, won a 2¹/2-mile chase on Chergan. Both horses were trained by the riders' mother, Sue.

● Two sisters trained winners on the same card at Newcastle on 21 February 1981. Waggoners Walk, trained by Caroline Mason, won the four-mile Eider Chase, and in the very next race Honourable Man, owned, trained and bred by Miss Mason's sister Patricia Russell, was successful in the hunter chase.

● For many years it was possible to have re-runs when horses dead-heated as long as all parties agreed, though this is no longer the case. The last race to have a run-off was at Newbury on 25 June 1930, when Ruby's Love beat Walloon.

● There have been three instances when the judge has been unable to separate four horses at the end of a race, the most recent being for a two-year-old race at Newmarket on 22 October 1855.

● The only known example where horses finished in a triple dead-heat for victory in a North American stakes took place in the Carter Handicap at Aqueduct on 10 June 1944, when Bossuet, Brownie, and Wait a Bit reached the wire simultaneously at the conclusion of the seven-furlong event.

● Fifty-nine racecourses closed in Great Britain, 1900–2000. The most famous included Gatwick, where the Grand National was staged during World War I and which is now the site of the airport. There was no racing there after 1940. The Manchester November Handicap, for many years the traditional last day big race of the flat season, took place at the Castle Irwell course until 1963. Manchester also staged the 1941 St. Leger.

● In the fifth race at Fairmount Park in East St. Louis, Illinois, on 9 September 1983, the horses Show The Way and J.C.'s Jackpot finished in a dead-heat for first, while Kahtzencup, Lemon Orchard and Our City finished in a triple dead-heat for third.

● Martin Pipe, champion jumping trainer in every season bar two since he first won the title in 1988–89, saddled nine of the 18 runners in the conditional jockeys' handicap hurdle at Taunton on 18 January 2001, and won the race with the 25–1 chance Big Wheel.

● It has always been supposed to be the bottom line of racing's credibility that every horse in every race was doing its best to win. But until 1927 an owner with more than one horse in a race was allowed to declare which one he preferred to win, so that riders of his other runners could let the other go past if the situation arose.

● In the Queen Anne Stakes, the first race at

Royal Ascot on 18 June 1974, was temporarily won by the appropriately named Confusion, who beat Gloss and Royal Prerogative by a head and ³/4 length. But at a subsequent stewards' inquiry those first three were all disqualified and the race was awarded to Brook, who had finished a well-beaten fourth.

● Michael Dickinson, who sent out the first five to finish in the Cheltenham Gold Cup of 1983 – Bregawn, Captain John, Wayward Lad, Silver Buck and Ashley House – trained the winners of 12 races on 27 December 1982.

● The first race in Great Britain to be started from stalls was the Chesterfield Stakes for two-year-olds at Newmarket in July 1965. It was won by the odds-on Track Spare, ridden by Lester Piggott. Stalls were used for the classics for the first time two seasons later.

● The first winner officially trained in Britain by a woman was Pat, trained by Miss Norah Wilmot and ridden by Scobie Breasley, at Brighton on 3 August 1966.

● It was a Jockey Club rule that the death of an owner voided any entries made for his horses, and it was not until 1927 that steps were taken to alter the situation, with the considerable involvement of the thriller writer Edgar Wallace. The relevant rule was amended in 1929, so that when Lord Dewar died in 1930 and his nephew John Dewar inherited his horses, the entries were still valid. One of the horses was Cameronian, who won the 1931 Derby; under the old rule he would not have been allowed to run.

● The photo finish camera was introduced in Britain in 1947, when it was first used at the Epsom spring meeting. The first classic for

Landing together: Gatwick hosted the replacement "Wartime National" from 1916–18, but is now London's second airport.

which it was needed was the 2,000 Guineas of 1949 in which Nimbus just got up to beat Abernant.

- The authorities were almost as reluctant to allow women to ride under rules as they were to let them train, but they finally saw sense at the end of 1971. The first race for women on the flat was won by Meriel Tufnell on the 50–1 chance Scorched Earth at Kempton on 6 May 1972. On 7 February 1976, Diana Thorne became the first woman to ride a winner under rules over jumps (they had been allowed to compete in some point-to-points) when she won on Ben Ruler, beating her father John on Air General.

- Bill O'Gorman was responsible for the British horses who have won the most races in a season in the 20th century. Provideo in 1984 and Timeless Times six years later both won 16 times. This equalled the two-year-old record set by The Bart in 1885, though the most wins in one season ever is the 23 achieved by Fisherman as a three-year-old in 1856.

- The record for the most stakes wins by an American horse in a single season is 16, set by Citation during his three-year-old campaign in 1948. They were accomplished at nine different tracks in seven different states – Florida, Maryland, Kentucky, New Jersey, New York, Illinois and California – and included a sweep of the Triple Crown along with a walkover triumph in the Pimlico Special.

- After Matt J. Winn formed a syndicate to take over control of Churchill Downs in 1902, one of the first events the track hosted was the Kentucky State Fair, which featured a staged collision of two railroad locomotives. The *Louisville Courier-Journal* reported that a crowd between 35,000 and 40,000 witnessed the event, "and they all came away pleased and satisfied."

- In the 1911 running of the Preakness Stakes, the third-place finisher was a gelding named The Nigger. This would be considered profoundly incorrect nowadays, but apparently the Jockey Club had no qualms about a racehorse being registered as such back then. The Nigger raced for Thomas R. Condran, and his colour was officially recorded as black.

- On 4 June 1923, a jockey whose name was recorded as F. Hayes booted a steeplechase mare named Sweet Kiss to victory in the second race at Belmont Park. It was Hayes' initial career win. He received congratulations in the winner's circle, then dropped dead.

First among equals: Britain's first all-women jockeys' race was won by Meriel Tufnell, on 50–1 shot Scorched Earth, in 1972.

- The 1932 renewal of the King's Plate at the Blue Bonnet track in Montreal, Canada, resulted in a triple disqualification. Tout Seu and Logwood, who were first and second under the wire, had their numbers taken down for fouling Step Off, who had finished third. But since he was coupled with Tout Seu, Step Off was disqualified as well. The winner, therefore, was declared to be Nipigon, even though he had been beaten by more than 13 lengths.

- Plucky Baby, a three-year-old filly, won the sixth race at Alamo Downs in San Antonio, Texas, on 30 January 1934. The race that immediately followed on the card was won by Plucky Baby's dam, Plucky Lady, who was then age seven. Both events were contested at one mile and 70 yards. Plucky Baby returned $8 for a two-dollar win wager. Plucky Lady returned $8.60.

- In the fourth race at the Tanforan track, near San Francisco, on 10 November 1936, five horses were entered, their odds ranging from 13–10 to 21–1. The favourite ran last, the second choice next to last, and so on in perfect reverse order, with the longest shot on the board winning.

- On 21 September 1938, one of the most powerful hurricanes in U.S. history struck New England. Officials at New Hampshire's Rockingham Park attempted to conduct racing anyway. Activities were finally suspended when winds exceeded 70 miles per hour, blowing apart the announcer's booth and lifting jockey Warren Yarberry off his horse as he swung into the stretch on the leader in the sixth race.

- Golden Gate Fields is a track in Albany, California, on the Oakland side of San Francisco Bay. It initially opened ten months prior to the

U.S.'s entrance into World War II, and sits on Point Fleming, which was formerly the site of Giant Powder Company, a manufacturer of dynamite, nitroglycerine and other blasting material. Records indicate that the Giant Powder factory blew up at least four times, hurtling debris into the bay and surrounding countryside, and 67 of its employees into the life beyond.

- Jim Berger, a 19-year-old jockey, won five consecutive races at Sportsman's Park near Chicago on 15 May 1941. None of Berger's mounts were favoured: they returned $15.20, $33.80, $12.80, $11.00, and $31.80 for two-dollar win wagers. A two-dollar win parlay on all five would have theoretically returned $143,770.

- A steeplechase horse named Never Mind II refused a jump in an event during the 1945 season. His disgusted jockey gave up and took Never Mind II to the paddock. The rider was subsequently informed, however, that all the other horses in the race had either fallen or been disqualified. The jockey then rode Never Mind II back on the course, and completed the race, registering a clocking of 11 minutes and 28 seconds for the two-mile distance. This is generally regarded as the slowest winning time in the history of U.S. racing.

- At the culmination of his four-year-old campaign in 1953, Tom Fool was considered so formidable that he was challenged by a grand total of only six other starters in his final four career efforts. He won the Wilson Stakes and Whitney Stakes at Saratoga by eight and 3$\frac{1}{2}$ lengths, respectively, the Sysonby Stakes at Belmont Park by three lengths, and the Pimlico Special by eight lengths. All were run as non-wagering events.

If at first: Quixall Crossett's losing streak stretches 99 races across 11 seasons, but he has won £8,000 in place prize money.

forced to vault the alligator, as was also the case for the second-place finisher, Swamp Rabbit.

• The 16-year-old steeplechaser Quixall Crosset, owned and trained by Ted Caine on his High Crosset Farm in North Yorkshire and named after the 1950s football star Albert Quixall, may be the horse to have lost more races than any other. As of February 2001 he had run 99 times, without winning a race, easily eclipsing the previous record run of losses that of 74 by another chaser, Amrullah. Occasionally he has earned some prize money by being placed, collecting about £8,000 during his 11 years' racing. His lack of success has even earned him a fan club and, although he is clearly very slow, he is usually a safe jumper of the fences and it is a tribute to his toughness that he has been able to run so many times.

• Victory Tour, a four-year-old gelding, holds the North American record for a race of 4 1/8 miles in length, completing the distance in 8:08 at the Finger Lakes track in Farmington, New York, on 2 November 1974. Victory Tour had to make four circuits of the track's one-mile oval. A quartet of Playboy bunnies stood on a platform at the finish line. One bunny climbed down every time a lap was completed. The race was carded as the first half of the daily double.

• As a multi-alarm fire was burning down the grandstand and clubhouse at Garden State Park in Cherry Hill, New Jersey, on 14 April 1977, numerous patrons attempted to cash mutuel tickets from the sixth race, won by Duty Booster, who returned $3.20 for a two-dollar straight wager. Most of the aforesaid bettors, though reluctant, ultimately abandoned their efforts and heeded warnings to flee for their lives.

• Celestial Ballet, second choice in the 1984 Seven Valley Stakes at the Keystone track in Philadelphia, Pennsylvania, ran over a goose on the first turn, but continued onward for a 4 1/4-length victory. The favourite, Springtime Sharon, ran over the same goose, then was forced to jump over another, and finished second.

• Early in his three-year-old season, Broad Brush's training regimen included running up hills on a Maryland Farm with 12 inches of snow on the ground. "It keeps him fit," said the colt's trainer, Richard W. Small. Broad Brush went on to win four Grade 1 stakes during his race career, including the 1987 Santa Anita Handicap, and earned over $2.6 million. He was North America's leading sire in 1994.

• Ricks Natural Star, a seven-year-old gelding

• In the sixth race at the Bowie track in Maryland on 9 February 1959, a field of nine distaff claimers were entered to contest the six-furlong event. One of them was a four-year-old, Dorothy's Best, who went postward at 8.60–1 odds. As the horses were being lined up, the starting gate malfunctioned, its doors slamming open without any triggering from the starter, so a false start was declared. The horses were immediately pulled up, except for Dorothy's Best, whose apprentice rider, Robert Corle, felt his saddle slip. He hung on in terror as his mount zoomed around the track, covering a full mile before an outrider caught her. Dorothy's Best was then put back in the gate. The race was run and Dorothy's Best was last throughout, defeated at the wire by 27 lengths.

• Shannon's Hope, a seven-year-old gelding, won five races in eight calendar days at tracks on the Massachusetts fair circuit in August 1963. When the Humane Society threatened action, Carlos Figueroa, the trainer of Shannon's Hope, said, "Why are they so upset? I run my horse short distances. This Paul Revere, he's such an American hero, but he ran his horse 26 miles in one night." Shannon's Hope campaigned soundly through the age of 12, making 296 career starts, winning 29 of them, and earning $39,535.

• A 1 1/2-mile hurdles event run at Delaware Park on 29 June 1964, resulted in the disqualifications of the horses who finished first, second, third, fifth, sixth, eighth, and last in the field of 11 competitors. All who had their numbers taken down had mistakenly left the course following the fifth hurdle. It is unclear what punishment was accorded the aforesaid last-placed finisher, Court-A-Buck, seeing that he finished to the rear of everyone anyway.

• The Michigan Mile and One-Eighth Handicap had a history that extended from 1949 through 1993. Never kind to chalk players, the race wasn't won by a favourite until its 14th running. The longest-priced horse to ever go postward in the race was Estreno II, who shocked nearly everyone by winning, returning $250.60 for a two-dollar straight wager (124.3–1) in 1967.

• During the fourth race at Tropical Park in South Florida on 8 January 1969, an alligator crawled out of an infield lake onto the track, forcing several horses to jump over him as they rounded the clubhouse turn. The favourite, Hans II, won anyway, even though he was one of those who had last started in cheap claiming company 14 months earlier, was entered by his owner/trainer, William Livingston, in the 1996 Breeders' Cup Turf at Woodbine. Ricks Natural Star was second through the first half-mile of the $2-million race, but thereafter found himself to the rear of the 14-horse field, and finished last by a margin that outdistanced the length of the stretch.

• The U.S. track situated on a parcel of land where thoroughbred racing dates back the longest is Fair Grounds, on Gentilly Boulevard in New Orleans, Louisiana. On 1 April 1853, it was the site of the first Union Course meeting, a five-day affair staged by the Metairie Jockey Club. The track officially became Fair Grounds in 1872. It now annually conducts live racing from Thanksgiving Day (the fourth Thursday in November) through late March, offering five Graded events, including the $750,000 Louisiana Derby. Thoroughbred racing at Fair Grounds predates Saratoga racing by ten years.

• Wishing Ring, a four-year-old filly, scored at odds of 941.75–1 in the final event on the six-race card at the Latonia track in Covington, Kentucky, on 17 June 1912. Her resulting payoff of $1,885.50 for a two-dollar win ticket is the largest ever recorded for a live event at a U.S. track. Wishing Ring further returned $644.40 to place and $172.60 to show. The event, itself, was a 1¹/₁₆-mile "selling" contest, which was the precursor of the modern-day claiming race. Wishing Ring was, not surprisingly, the longest shot in the 11-horse field.

• The longest-priced winner under rules in the British Isles was Equinoctial, who was returned at 250–1 when successful at Kelso on 21 November 1990. The longest odds at which a horse has been backed for a race under the Rules of Racing is the 5,000–1 at which Countess Crossett was supported at the same course on 6 April 1992. She was returned at 500–1.

• Alydar, a chestnut colt by Raise a Native out of the On-and-On mare, Sweet Tooth, is the only horse to finish second in all three of America's Triple Crown events. The year was 1978. Alydar's overall career record included 26 starts, 14 victories, 10 placings, and earnings of $957,195. He ran against Affirmed 10 times, but defeated him only thrice, in the Great American Stakes and Champagne Stakes at Belmont Park at age two, and the Travers Stakes at Saratoga (via disqualification) at age three.

• The smallest payoff on a two-dollar win wager is thought to be $2.02, which was thrice

returned by Man o' War, following his eight-length victory in the Stuyvesant Handicap at Jamaica on 22 June 1920, his 100-length victory in the Lawrence Realization Stakes on 4 September that year at Belmont Park, and his 15-length victory in Belmont's Jockey Club Stakes a week later. A two-dollar parlay on all three races would have returned either $2.02 or $2.03, depending upon how the individual bookmaker handled breakage.

• Rushaway, a three-year-old gelding, is thought to be the only 20th century horse to have achieved two victories in major U.S. stakes on consecutive days. On 22 May 1936, the Al G. Tarn colour bearer won the 1¹/₈-mile Illinois Derby at the Aurora track near Chicago by 1¹/₂ lengths. He was then with his jockey, John Longden, put on an overnight freight train for a 300-mile trip to northern Kentucky. The following afternoon, 23 May Longden rode Rushaway to a a six-length triumph in the 1¹/₂-mile Latonia Derby. Thereafter, Rushaway steadily declined as a runner.

• Marion H. Van Berg led all American owners in annual victories a record 13 times, in 1952, 1955, and 1960–70 inclusive. His career triumphs as an owner numbered a record 4,775. Van Berg trained most of the horses he owned.

• Swaps holds the record for establishing the most world standards in a single season, registering a quartet of them during his four-year-old campaign in 1956. Included (in chronological order) were a time of 1:39³/₅ for 1 mile, 70 yards in the Broward Handicap at Gulfstream Park; a time of 1:33¹/₅ for one mile in the Argonaut Handicap at Hollywood Park; a time

of 1:39 for 1¹/₁₆ miles in Hollywood's Inglewood Handicap; and a time of 2:38¹/₅ for 1⁵/₈ miles in Hollywood's Sunset Handicap. William Shoemaker was the jockey for all four efforts.

• Bold Ruler is the only 20th century American stallion to lead the general sire list eight times, doing so in consecutive years from 1963–69, and again in 1973. He is the first American sire whose progeny earnings exceeded $2million in a single season, which was 1966. However, Bold Ruler's dominance still could not compare with that of the great 19th century sire, Lexington, who led America's general sire standings 16 times.

• It is generally believed that the nine horses assembled for the Flamingo Stakes on 3 March 1966, at Hialeah Park constitute the largest field for a major U.S. race upon which wagering was cancelled. The reason was the presence of Buckpasser, who was considered so formidable by Hialeah management that they envisioned the track awash in minus pools if wagering was allowed. Inside the eighth pole the colt Abe's Hope opened up a clear lead, but Buckpasser accelerated suddenly in the final strides and won by a nose, thus leaving management happy and bettors disgruntled.

• The largest margin of victory in a 20th century U.S. match race was 50 lengths, when Chris Evert defeated her fellow three-year-old distaffer, Miss Musket, at Hollywood Park on 20 July 1974. The winner-take-all purse, $350,000, remains the richest for a match event on North America's shores. On 6 July 1975, a match race between Foolish Pleasure and Ruffian had a similar purse. Technically, Foolish Pleasure won by an even greater distance because the brilliant

Not this time: Alydar (left) got the better of Affirmed on a disqualification at Saratoga, but lost all three Triple Crown races.

filly Ruffian was injured in the race and did not finish.

- Richard DePass is the only American jockey credited with seven victories from seven mounts on a single race card, achieving the feat at Florida Downs (now Tampa Bay Downs) in Oldsmar, Florida, on 15 March 1980. Five of the horses were favourites. DePass also booted home a 2.20–1 second choice and a 10.50–1 longshot.

- Chris W. Antley is the only American jockey credited with nine victories on a single day. On 31 October 1987, Antley scored with four of his six mounts at Aqueduct in New York, then journeyed to The Meadowlands track in northern New Jersey where he won with five of eight mounts. Aqueduct races afternoons, and The Meadowlands at night, allowing Antley to register his feat.

- Two jockeys have ridden seven winners in a day in Britain. Pat Eddery rode three at Newmarket in the afternoon and four at Newcastle in the evening, but Frankie Dettori rode all seven winners on the same card at Ascot on 28 September 1996 at accumulative odds of 25,095–1. Dettori is one of only three jockeys to have gone through the card. Gordon Richards did so at Chepstow on 4 October 1933, part of a sequence of 12 consecutive winners for Richards as he won the final race at Nottingham on the previous day and the first five at Chepstow on the following afternoon. The other jockey to have gone through the card is Alec Russell, who rode all six winners at Bogside on 19 July 1957.

- The longest sequence of winning rides for a jump jockey is ten, achieved by Johnny Gilbert in September 1959 and equalled by Phil Tuck in August and September 1986.

- When Pat Eddery rode his 100th winner of the season, on Sirene at Southwell on 22 October 1999, it was the 26th century of his career. The previous best was 25 by Lester Piggott; Sir Gordon Richards and Willie Carson reached three figures on 23 occasions.

- The first jockey to ride 200 winners in a season was Fred Archer, who had 207 in 1876 and a best of 246 in 1885. Tommy Loates rode 222 winners in 1893, but then none did so until Gordon Richards in 1933. Richards' tally of 269 in 1947 remains a record, but in the closing years of the 20th century Pat Eddery, Michael Roberts, Frankie Dettori, Jason Weaver and Kieren Fallon have all reached double centuries.

- Over jumps the first centurion was Dick Rees, who achieved 108 in 1924 (when totals were assessed on an annual basis). Peter Scudamore was the first man to have a jumping double century with a score of 221 in 1988–89. Tony McCoy passed that mark with 253 winners in 1997–98 and 245 in 1999–2000.

- The highest price ever paid for a yearling at public auction is $13.1 million, fetched by Seattle Dancer at Keeneland on 23 July, 1985.

- The largest entry in an individual Breeders' Cup race involved the five horses sent postward by trainer D. Wayne Lukas in the 1988 Breeders' Cup Juvenile Fillies at Churchill Downs. The Lukas entry finished first, second, and third with Open Mind, Darby Shuffle and Lea Lucinda, respectively, sixth with Some Romance, and eleventh with One Of A Klein. All five were ridden by jockeys now in the Hall of Fame: Angel Cordero Jr., Julie A. Krone, Laffit Pincay Jr., Gary L. Stevens, and Chris J. McCarron (in their order of finish).

- The largest bonus ever bestowed upon an American horse for a series of race victories is $2 million. It was awarded to Spend A Buck in 1985 for winning the Cherry Hill Mile, Garden State Stakes, Kentucky Derby and Jersey Derby, in that order. The award was offered by New Jersey's Garden State Park, the site of the first, second and fourth events of the series.

- According to figures compiled by the Jockey Club, a total of 51,296 registered thoroughbred foals were born in North America in 1986. This figure remains the largest foal crop in history.

Run for the money: Churchill Downs at Louisville, Kentucky, home of the Derby, is the most famous race track in the U.S.

True Grit: Dick Saunders (in purple) was aged 48 when he and Grittar won the 1982 Grand National at Aintree; he was younger than the rider of second-placed Spartan Missile, John Thorne.

• The largest field for the Grand National was in 1929 when 66 took part and the race was won by the 100–1 chance Gregalach. The smallest was the very first running in 1837, when only six took part, and in 1899 when Manifesto gained the second of his two wins in the race against just eight rivals.

• There were a number of small fields in the early days of the Derby and only four took part in 1794 when Daedalus was successful, with odds-on Leon only third. The biggest turn-out was the 34 in Caractacus' year of 1862.

• Dick Saunders was 48 when he rode Grittar to win the Grand National in 1982. That was his only ride in the race and the last of his career, as he retired immediately afterwards.

• Lester Piggott, who was 18 when he won the Derby on Never Say Die in 1954, is the youngest man to ride the winner of the race in the modern era, but the youngest in the Derby's history is John Parsons, who was 16 years old when he won on Caractacus in 1862.

• The youngest man to ride the winner of the Grand National is Bruce Hobbs, who was 17 when he scored on the American-owned and bred Battleship, trained by his father Reg in 1938.

• The oldest man to triumph in the Derby is John Forth, who was 60 when he won on Frederick, whom he also trained, in 1829.

• In the jumping world the top price paid at auction was at Doncaster in May 2000 when the four-year-old Mister Banjo was bought for owner John Hales for 240,000 guineas.

• The oldest horse to win a race on the flat is Marksman, who was 19 when he triumphed at Ashford in 1826. The oldest winning jumper was Sonny Somers, aged 18, at Southwell and Lingfield. Creggmore Boy was 22 years old when he ran his final race at Cartmel in June 1962.

• Kent J. Desormeaux holds the American standard for the most victories by a jockey in a single calendar year, registering 598 in 1989. Desormeaux's mounts that season totalled 2,312; the majority of them on the Maryland circuit. His win ratio was 25.9 per cent. From 1987–89, the Louisiana native won 1,522 races, which is a record for a three-year span.

• Cigar, who raced from 1993–96, holds the record for the highest career earnings by an American-based racehorse, $9,999,815. He also holds the single season mark for earnings, $4,910,000, achieved in 1996.

• With a purse value of $4,689,920, the 1998 running of the Breeders' Cup Classic at Churchill Downs remains the richest race ever run in North America. The winner, Awesome Again, earned a $2,662,400 share for his owner, Frank H. Stronach.

• It is generally believed that the greatest single-day haul by any trainer was achieved on 27 December, 1982, by Michael Dickinson. He sent out 21 runners in 20 races at six different courses, gaining 12 victories, five second-place finishes, two third-place finishes and a fourth. Dickinson is also renowned for saddling the first five finishers in the 1983 Cheltenham Gold Cup. He further sent out Da Hoss to win the 1996 and 1998 renewals of the Breeders' Cup Mile.

• The Australian race horse Ajax, a foal of 1934, set a modern-day world record by winning his initial 18 races. His overall career record included 46 starts, 36 victories, nine placings and purse earnings of 40,250 (pounds). Ajax was triumphant 17 times in stakes events.

• The all-time record for victories by a trainer in a single calendar year is 555, set by Steve Asmussen (the younger brother of Cash Asmussen) in 2004. Asmussen sent 2,293 starters postward that season, and had a win ratio of 24.2 per cent. He eclipsed the old record of 496 victories, which was set by Hall of Famer Jack Van Berg (the son of Marion Van Berg) in 1976.

• Inconsistent record-keeping makes it impossible to identify an exact total, but it's known with certainty that as a thoroughbred trainer Dale Baird had accumulated at least 9,300 career victories through 2005. Baird continues to ply his trade at Mountaineer Race Track and Gaming Resort in Hanford County, West Virginia.

• During a four month period in 1949–50 at the Agua Caliente racetrack in Mexico, a female jockey named Wantha Davis competed eight times in match races against male jockeys, and won seven of them. Among the riders she defeated were Hall of Famers John Longden and Jack Westrope. So miffed was Longden following his defeat that he refused to shake Davis's hand.

CHRONOLOGY

1511 The first instance of racing being recorded in Britain when the Reverend Robert Rogers details sport on the Roodeye at **Chester**, which is the oldest racecourse in the country.

1689 The **Byerley Turk**, one of the three Arab stallions from whom the modern thoroughbred is descended, carries his owner Captain Robert Byerley, at the Battle of the Boyne. He is followed to these shores five years later by the **Darley Arabian**, the second of the three founding fathers. The last of the trio, the **Godolphin Arabian**, arrived around 1730.

1711 Queen Anne sets up the first meeting at **Ascot**, which is why the first race at the Royal meeting carries her name.

1715 Birth of **Flying Childers**, a son of the Darley Arabian and the first great racehorse.

c1750 The **Jockey Club** comes into existence at the Star and Garter Club at Pall Mall, London, though its immediate influence was only limited. Some 20 years elapse before it publishes its rules to cover racing at Newmarket.

1752 The first **steeplechase** race was literally a chase to a steeple when Mr. Edmund Blake and Mr. Callaghan raced across country between Buttevant Church and St. Leger Church in Co. Cork, Ireland. There is no record of who won.

1764 Eclipse, the best horse of the 18th century, is born. Bred by King George III's son, the Duke of Cumberland, he took his name because there was an eclipse in the year of his birth.

1765 The birth of **Robert Robson**, the first outstanding, trainer who sent out the winners of 34 classics. He died in 1828.

1776 What is to become the first of the five British classics, the **St. Leger**, is run at Doncaster. Six take part and the winner, though un-named at the time of the race, is in due course called **Allabaculia**.

1779 The Oaks is staged at Epsom. **Bridget** is the winner.

1780 The first running of the **Derby** over a mile at Epsom is won by **Diomed**, whose owner

Dying for the cause: Suffragette Emily Davison tried to disrupt the 1913 Derby at Epsom by bringing down a horse. The horse she grabbed (the King's Anmer) was unhurt, but she was killed.

Sir Charles Bunbury was the first leading turf administrator and lost the toss for the race to be named after him.

1791 The birth of **Admiral Henry Rous**, the man who invented the weight-for-age scale (still in use today with only minor modifications) and became arguably the most important race administrator of all time.

1809 The first running of the **2,000 Guineas** at Newmarket. The **1,000 Guineas**, the last of the five classics, is introduced five years later.

1839 The first running of the **Grand National** at Aintree is, very appropriately in view of the race's record, won by a horse called **Lottery**. There is a theory that the two previous such-named races were also at Aintree, though majority opinion favours Maghull as the venue.

1844 The first horse home in the Derby under the name of **Running Rein** is revealed as a four-year-old called Maccabeus. The race is awarded to **Orlando**, who finished second.

1848 Lord George Bentinck, the second of the leading turf administrators, dies at the age of 46. It was at his insistence that Orlando's owner sued for the Derby prize money four years earlier.

1853 West Australian becomes the first winner of what is now known as the Triple Crown, the 2,000 Guineas, the Derby and the St. Leger. He was trained by John Scott and ridden by Frank Butler.

1861 The first **Melbourne Cup** is run. The winner **Archer**, trained by Etienne de Mestre, is walked 500 miles to Flemington. Archer wins again a year later.

1865 Gladiateur is the second winner of the Triple Crown and the first winner of the Derby to have been bred outside the British Isles. He is nicknamed "Avenger of Waterloo" by the French.

1866 The **National Hunt Committee**, which is the counterpart of the Jockey Club for administering steeplechasing, is established.

1868 The filly **Formosa** wins all the classics apart from the Derby, though she has to settle for a dead heat in the 2,000 Guineas.

1870 The **Jockey Club** assumes overall control of flat racing in Great Britain; meetings which are staged other than under its rules will not be recognized.

1877 The **draw for starting positions** for flat racing is introduced. Until then it was a matter of first there, first served, though seniority among the riding ranks carried a lot of weight.

1881 The birth of **St. Simon**, a top class racehorse even though he never ran in a classic, and later an outstanding sire. He was champion for seven years in a row.

Iroquois is the first American-owned and bred winner of the Derby. He is ridden by Fred Archer and trained by the American Jacob Pincus, though at Newmarket.

1886 Fred Archer, the leading rider of his time, shoots himself at his Newmarket home in a fit of depression. Though he rode for only 17 seasons he was champion 13 times and rode 2,748 winners.

1897 The **starting gate** is used for the first time. Previously the official had to try to get all the horses to stand in a line before allowing them to go, and false starts were numerous.

1902 Sceptre, who begins her season by running in the Lincoln Handicap, wins four classics. The Derby is the only one to elude her.

1903 Doping horses is declared illegal by the Stewards of the Jockey Club in response to a campaign by trainer George Lambton against the practices of trainers who have come here from the U.S.

1905 A crowd of 40,000 attends the inaugural day of racing at New York's **Belmont Park**. Races are run clockwise for Belmont's initial 16 seasons.

1910 The **National Hunt Committee** follows its colleagues on the flat and bars doping.

1911 The **National Hunt Chase**, the four-mile race for amateur riders which is one of the most important events of the season, ends its itinerant existence by settling permanently at Cheltenham.

1913 All **horses aged three or more must have a name** before they are allowed to race.

In the most sensational of all Derbys a **suffragette is killed** when she brings down Anmer, the King's runner; the hot favourite Craganour is disqualified in favour of **Aboyeur**, a 100–1 chance.

1915 Regret becomes the first filly to win the Kentucky Derby. The 2.65–1 favourite faces 15 male competitors, but leads wire-to-wire to triumph by two lengths.

1919 Sir Barton becomes the first horse to sweep the American Triple Crown (Kentucky Derby, Preakness Stakes and Belmont Stakes).

1920 In his career finale, **Man o' War** defeats Sir Barton by seven lengths in the Kenilworth Park Gold Cup, across the river from Detroit.

1924 The **Cheltenham Gold Cup** is held for the

Rough ride: Aboyeur, at 100–1, was awarded the 1913 Derby at Epsom after favourite Craganour was disqualified.

first time and is won by **Red Splash**. It becomes compulsory for jump jockeys to wear skull caps for protective purposes.

1925 Gordon Richards is British champion jockey for the first of 26 occasions.

1926 Chancellor of the Exchequer Winston Churchill introduces a **tax on betting**, but because its collection costs prove greater than its yield it is abandoned three years later.

The trade newspapers agree on a joint system for returning **starting prices**, so that each will show the same odds for every runner.

1927 Blaris, ridden by top hurdles jockey George Duller, wins the first running of the Champion Hurdle at Cheltenham.

1929 The organisation which becomes known as the **Horserace Totalisator Board** comes into existence. Its pool betting system is first operated at Newmarket and Carlisle on 2 July.

1930 Jim Dandy, sent off at odds of 100–1, upsets the Triple Crown winner, Gallant Fox, in the Travers Stakes at Saratoga.

Phar Lap wins the Melbourne Cup at 8–11, the only odds-on winner of the race.

1932 The Derby is shown on **television** for the first time. It was first broadcast on radio five years earlier.

Phar Lap dies in America and Australia mourns.

1936 Oaklawn Park in Hot Springs, Arkansas, hosts the first running of the **Arkansas Derby**. The race now anchors the annual "Racing Festival of the South".

1939 Gulfstream Park opens, giving South Florida its second track. Gulfstream's advent culminates a decade of extraordinary racetrack growth in the U.S.

1940 Seabiscuit completes his six seasons of racing with a $1^1/2$-length triumph in the Santa Anita Handicap, in a track record time of $2:01^1/5$ for $1^1/4$ miles.

1942 In one of history's greatest match races, three-year-old **Alsab** defeats four-year-old Whirlaway by a nose at Rhode Island's Narragansett Park.

1943 Count Fleet, undefeated at age three, completes his Triple Crown sweep and closes out his race career with a 25-length victory in the Belmont Stakes.

1946 After a three-year hiatus brought by World War II travel restrictions, racing returns to **Saratoga**.

1947 The **photo-finish camera** is used on a British track for the first time at Epsom on 22 April. The first classic for which it is needed is the 1949 2,000 Guineas.
　　Evening racing is staged for the first time, at Hamilton Park near Glasgow.

1948 Calumet Farm, America's most fabled racing stable, finishes one-two in the Kentucky Derby with its homebred colts, **Citation** and Coaltown.
　　Lester Piggott rides his first winner, on The Chase, trained by his father Keith, at Haydock.

1951 Supreme Court wins the first **King George VI And Queen Elizabeth Stakes** at Ascot.
　　Citation becomes the first horse in history to accumulate $1million in earnings with a four-length victory in his career finale, the Hollywood Gold Cup.

1953 At the 28th and, as it turns out, final attempt, **Sir Gordon Richards** riding Pinza wins the Derby ahead of the Queen's colt Aureole. In the same week he is knighted.

Tom Fool's Pimlico Special triumph completes his four-year-old campaign, in which he was undefeated in ten starts. He is retired to stud.

1955 In a match race between America's best three-year-olds at Washington Park near Chicago, **Nashua** beats Swaps by $6^1/2$ lengths.

1960 The **camera patrol**, which enables stewards to see replays of races when they are adjudicating into disciplinary matters, comes into use.

1961 The establishment of the **Horserace Betting Levy Board** is accompanied by the introduction of legal off-course betting shops.

1964 For the fifth consecutive year, **Kelso** wins the two-mile Jockey Club Gold Cup Stakes at Aqueduct. No other horse has ever done this in any U.S. stakes.

1965 Starting stalls are used for the first time on a racecourse in Great Britain.

1966 The determined actions of **Florence Nagle** force the Jockey Club to grant training licences to women, though she needs to go to court to do so.
　　Chancellor of the Exchequer James Callaghan **re-introduces betting tax** for the first time since Winston Churchill was forced to abandon the idea. It is levied at 2.5 percent.

1967 Buckpasser's $1^1/4$-length triumph in Belmont Park's Metropolitan Handicap is his 15th victory in a row. All but one have come in stakes.

1968 The **National Hunt Committee** amalgamates with **the Jockey Club** 102 years after its formation.
　　Despite an impost of 134 pounds, **Dr. Fager** wins the Washington Park Handicap by ten lengths in a world-record time of $1:32^1/5$ for one mile on the dirt.

1970 Nijinsky wins the British Triple Crown and is the first horse to do since Bahram in 1935.

1971 New York officially becomes the first U.S. jurisdiction to have **off-track betting**. OTB parlours do a combined $66,098 handle on the nine-race Aqueduct card.

1972 Having recognised women as trainers six years ago, the Jockey Club now agrees that they can ride in races on the flat. The first such event is won by the 50–1 shot Scorched Earth at Kempton ridden by **Meriel Tufnell**.

1973 Handicapping is to be organised on a centralised basis with ratings listed on computer.
　　Red Rum wins a thrilling Grand National sweeping past an exhausted Crisp on the run from the Elbow. Both horses beat the previous course record by over a quarter of a minute.
　　Secretariat completes his Triple Crown sweep with a 31-length victory in the Belmont Stakes in the world-record time of 2:24 for $1^1/2$ miles on the dirt.

1974 A crowd of 163,628, the **largest on-site gathering in U.S. racing history**, is on hand for Cannonade's triumph in the 100th running of the Kentucky Derby.

1975 The great filly, **Ruffian**, breaks down in a match race against Kentucky Derby winner Foolish Pleasure at Belmont Park. Ruffian is put down the following day.

1977 Seattle Slew completes his Triple Crown sweep, giving him nine victories in his initial nine career starts. Three weeks later, he loses his next outing.
　　Red Rum becomes the first horse to win the Grand National for a third time.

1978 Affirmed completes his Triple Crown sweep, defeating Alydar by a head in the Belmont Stakes. Alydar finishes second in all three Triple Crown events. .

1980 Spectacular Bid culminates his undefeated four-year-old campaign and race career with a walkover win in Belmont Park's Woodward Stakes.

1981 John Henry defeats The Bart by a nose in the inaugural running of the Arlington Million at Arlington Park near Chicago.
　　Mairzy Doates wins the inaugural **Japan Cup**, run at Tokyo's Fuchu track.

1984 The inaugural running of the **Breeders' Cup** is held at Hollywood Park near Los Angeles. A crowd of 64,254 attends.

Blazing a trail: Scorched Earth, ridden by Meriel Tufnell, won the first all-women jockeys' race in Britain at Kempton Park.

1985 Fire razes the clubhouse and grandstand at **Arlington Park**. Twenty-four days later, tent facilities host the Arlington Million's "miracle renewal".

The filly **Pebbles**, trained by Clive Brittain and ridden by Pat Eddery, becomes the first British-trained winner of a Breeders' Cup race, takes the Breeders' Cup Turf at Aqueduct in New York.

1988 Churchill Downs hosts its first Breeders' Cup. Because of murky weather and a late post, **Alysheba** wins the $3million Breeders' Cup Classic in virtual darkness.

1989 Peter Scudamore becomes the first jumps jockey to ride 200 winners in a season. His final tally is 221.

All-weather racing is staged for the first time in Britain with 12 races on the equitrack surface at Lingfield Park on 31 October. Less than a month later, an all-weather card at Southwell is called off because of fog!

1990 Lester Piggott, who returned to the saddle in October after having retired from riding, turned to training and served a jail sentence for tax offences, completes an amazing comeback when riding Royal Academy to victory in the Breeders' Cup Mile at Belmont.

Pat Eddery becomes the first jockey since Sir Gordon Richards in 1952 to ride 200 winners in a flat season. He is champion with a final tally of 209.

1992 Longacres Park near Seattle, Washington, concludes its six decades of racing. Its all-time single-card wagering record is set on closing day.

1993 The **British Horseracing Board** takes over the administration of racing, though matters involving discipline and integrity will continue to be dealt with by the Jockey Club.

The **Grand National is abandoned** after disruption by animal rights campaigners and two false starts.

Fire destroys the grandstand and clubhouse of New Orleans' historic **Fair Grounds** track. Full-card racing resumes 18 days later.

1994 All-weather jump racing is discontinued. Its fatality rate has become unacceptable.

1996 The **Dubai World Cup** is staged for the first time. Cigar, ridden by Jerry Bailey, is the winner.

Cigar's extraordinary 16-race winning streak ends as he is defeated by Dare And Go in the Pacific Classic at Del Mar.

1997 After a 60-year hiatus, major-league **racing returns to Texas** with the opening of Lone Star Park near Dallas.

National glory: Red Rum (left) passes long-time leader Crisp in the last few strides of the 1973 Grand National at Aintree.

A bomb scare forces the **Grand National to be postponed**. It is run as the only event on the card on the Monday and is won by Lord Gyllene.

1998 Tony McCoy sets a record for a jump jockey of 253 winners in a season.

Victory Gallop, trailing by four lengths at the eighth pole, beats **Real Quiet** by a nose, thus denying him a Belmont Stakes victory and Triple Crown sweep.

1999 A broken leg, suffered on the stretch run of the Belmont Stakes, brings **Charismatic's** Triple Crown bid to an end. He finishes third but doesn't run again.

2000 John Oxx's first-ever Derby runner, **Sinndar**, wins the Epsom race. He goes on to claim the Irish Derby and the Prix de l'Arc de Triomphe making it a memorable season for jockey **Johnny Murtagh**.

2001 In his Budget, Chancellor Gordon Brown announces the **end of betting tax in Britain**.

2001 Trainer **Aidan O'Brien** sets a record for a single season with 23 Group1/Grade 1 victories.

2002 Rock of Gibraltar wins seven consecutive Group 1 races, breaking the record of six straight wins set by Mill Reef 30 years earlier.

Locally-based horses win three of the four major events on the **Hong Kong International Races** card, as All Thrills Too accounts for the Hong Kong Sprint, Olympic Express takes the Hong Kong Mile and Precision is victorious in the Hong Kong Cup.

2003 On the Breeders' Cup card at Santa Anita, 52-year-old trainer **Richard Mandella** wins four races – the Breeders' Cup Juvenile Fillies with Halfbridled, the Breeders' Cup Juvenile with Action This Day, the Breeders' Cup Turf with Johar (who dead-heated for first) and the Breeders' Cup Classic with Pleasantly Perfect.

2004 Joss Collins, one of the most respected bloodstock agents in the world, dies at the age of 56. In July, 1985, Collins signed the ticket at Keeneland for **Seattle Dancer**, who had been sold for $13.1 million, which is still the highest price ever paid for a yearling at public auction.

Fusao Sekiguchi pays a world record 490 million yen ($4.38 million) for a weanling at the Japan Racing Association Sale. The colt was by **Dance In The Dark** out of Japan's 1997 Horse of the Year, Air Groove.

2005 Extensive damage by Hurricane Katrina causes the **cancellation of the Fair Grounds race meeting** in New Orleans.

At Hong Kong's Sha Tin racecourse, the five-year-old gelding **Silent Witness** registers his 17th consecutive victory, which tops the North American standard of 16 straight wins shared by Citation, Cigar and Hallowed Dreams, as well as the European standard held by Ribot.

2006 A two-year-old colt, later named **The Green Monkey**, is sold for $16 million at the Fasig-Tipton Florida Sale at Calder Race Course. The price is a world record for a horse of any age, sex or breed at public auction.

The Breeders' Cup raises its **total purses to $20 million** for 2006.

Index

Picture Credits

Carlton Books Limited would like to thank the following sources for theirkind permission to reproduce the pictures in the book:

Barbados Turf Club 35

Adam Coglianese 32, 96

Corbis /Bettmann: 107, 112, 220, 229, /Jerry Cooke: 71, 72, 106, 116bl, 117, 179bc, 189, 219, /Hulton-Deutsch Collection: 12, 91, 92, 158, 169, 192, /Reuters New Media: 66

Empics AP/Kamran Jebreili: 85

Fair Grounds Racetrack 14

Getty Images 51tr, /AFP/Timothy A.Clary: 204, /Jeff Haynes: 74tr, 98, /Stan Honda: 147, /Rabih Moghrabi:

178tr, /Scott Olson: 119, /Peter Parks: 86, /John Zich: 131, /William West: 102, /ALLSPORT: 69, 90, 94, 104, 105, 108, 125, 128, 130, 134bl, 138bl, 140, 143, 148, 164, 167, 172, 183bl, 185, 194tl, 196l, 197, 199b, 205, 228, /Scott Barbour: 84, /Shaun Botterill: 40, 82, /Darrin Braybrook: 191, /MN Chan: 87, /Russell Cheyne: 56, /Chris Cole: 60br, /Phil Cole: 60tl, 81, 88-9, /Mark Dadswell: 3, 78, 183tr, /Stephen Dunn: 77, /Steve Grayson: 171, /John Gichigi: 4, /Julian Herbert: 38, 39tr, 57, 58, 62, 79, 97, 114-5, /Mike Hewitt: 6-7, /Hulton Deutsch: 80, /Trevor Jones: 170, /Koichi Kamoshida: 175, /Doug Pensinger: 73, /David Rogers: 120, /Matthew Stockman: 70, 74bl, 76, 154-5, 198, /Time Life Pictures/Art Shay: 110, /David Turnley: 200

Hipodromo San Isidro 36

Kit Houghton Photography 5bl, 26, 33, 45, 50, 100, 129, 168, 174, 179tl,187, 213br

Hulton Archive 11bc, 11tr, 13, 217, 222, 226br, 227, 232, 233, 234

Inpho Photography 22

Trevor Jones 224–5

Keeneland Museum 16, 95, 101, 103, 109, 111, 121, 129, 152, 139, 136c, 138, 156

Kentucky Derby Photo Archive 166

Ern McQuillan 47, 48, 113

Mirrorpix 99, 178bl

Grazia Neri/Stefano Casati 28, 29

Popperfoto 212, 218, 231, 235

Prairie Meadows Racetrack 215

George Selwyn endpapers, 5tr, 8-9, 18-9, 20, 21, 23, 24, 25, 27, 30, 31, 34, 41, 42, 43, 49tr, 49b, 52-3, 54, 63, 64, 68, 83, 116tr, 126, 127tl, 122tr, 134tr, 135, 136, 137bl, 137tr, 141, 144, 150, 157, 159, 160, 161, 162, 165, 173, 176-7, 180, 181, 182, 184, 188, 190, 194br, 196r, 199t, 203, 204tl, 207, 208, 209, 210-1, 213tl, 221, 223bl, 223tr, 226tl, 230

Thoroughbred Advertising 93, 163

World Features-Pix Colour Library Ltd 214

Every effort has been made to acknowledge correctly and contact the source and/or copyright holder of each picture, and Carlton Books Limited apologises for any unintentional errors or omissions which will be correctedin future editions of this book.

The Publishers wish to express their sincere gratitude to George Selwyn and Naresh Joshi for the time and assistance they have contributed to this project.